Writing Arguments

Why Do You Need This New Edition?

If you're wondering why you should buy this new edition of *Writing Arguments*, here are eleven great reasons!

1. A new full color design visually differentiates key ideas, making reading a user-friendly experience and ensuring it is easier for you to find important information.

2. A new Chapter 8, Analyzing Arguments Rhetorically, shows you how to read arguments critically so you will be able to identify and explain the strategies writers use to persuade their audiences.

3. New Writing Assignments in Parts 1, 2, and 3 on analysis, invention, planning, drafting, and revising include both instruction and samples to guide you as you build your argument skills.

4. New readings and visual arguments on current topics such as immigration, video games, sports, and the connection between gender and math ability model the different argument types your instructor may assign.

5. New student essays include several that are researched to help you see how to integrate researched material into your argument as well as how to cite and document it.

6. New Organization Plan diagrams for various types of arguments show you how to introduce, develop, and conclude your own arguments.

7. New Toulmin Analysis charts represent complicated concepts—such as the Toulmin system of argument—in a visual way, helping you see the underlying conceptual structure of an argument and make effective arguments in your course (Ch. 4, 11–15).

8. Thoroughly revised Chapters 11–15 (Part 4) on different types of arguments have been rewritten to improve clarity and ease of use, removing a language of mathematic variables ("x" and "y") and replacing it with simpler, clearer instruction.

9. New illustrations of research sources show you where to find author, title, and publication information so that you can cite and document your research correctly (Ch. 17).

10. Up-to-date MLA and APA citation examples, including examples of the most recent style changes, show you how to correctly cite and document sources in your research papers (Ch. 17).

11. A dynamic e-book version of *Writing Arguments* provides access to comprehensive writing, research, editing, and grammar resources within MyCompLab to give you extra practice with your writing skills.

Writing Arguments

A Rhetoric with Readings

Eighth Edition

John D. Ramage
Arizona State University

John C. Bean
Seattle University

June Johnson
Seattle University

Longman

New York   San Francisco   Boston
London   Toronto   Sydney   Tokyo   Singapore   Madrid
Mexico City   Munich   Paris   Cape Town   Hong Kong   Montreal

Acquisitions Editor: Lauren A. Finn
Senior Development Editor: Marion B. Castellucci
Senior Marketing Manager: Sandra McGuire
Senior Supplements Editor: Donna Campion
Senior Media Producer: Stefanie Liebman
Production Manager: Savoula Amanatidis
Project Coordination and Text Design: Elm Street
   Publishing Services

Electronic Page Makeup: Integra Software Services, Pvt. Ltd.
Cover Design Manager: John Callahan
Cover Designer: Marie Ilardi
Cover Images: Courtesy of Alamy
Photo Researcher: Rebecca Karamehmedovic
Senior Manufacturing Buyer: Alfred C. Dorsey
Printer and Binder: Courier Corporation—Kendallville
Cover Printer: Lehigh-Phoenix Color Corporation

For permission to use copyrighted material, grateful acknowledgment is made to the copyright holders on pp. 659–664, which are hereby made part of this copyright page.

Library of Congress Cataloging-in-Publication Data

Ramage, John D.
  Writing arguments: a rhetoric with readings/John D. Ramage, John C. Bean, June Johnson.—8th ed.
     p. cm.
  Includes bibliographical references and index.
  ISBN 978-0-205-64836-8
  1. English language—Rhetoric. 2. Persuasion (Rhetoric) 3. College readers. 4. Report writing.
  I. Bean, John C. II. Johnson, June, 1953— III. Title.
  PE1431.R33 2010
  808'.0427—dc21

                                                                    2008036898

3 4 5 6 7 8 9 10—CRK—12 11 10

Complete Edition
ISBN-13: 978-0-205-64836-8
ISBN-10: 0-205-64836-3

Brief Edition
ISBN-13: 978-0-205-66576-1
ISBN-10: 0-205-66576-4

Concise Edition
ISBN-13: 978-0-205-66577-8
ISBN-10: 0-205-66577-2

Longman
is an imprint of

www.pearsonhighered.com

Brief Contents

Detailed Contents

The News Media: Responsible Production, Responsible Consumption   467

Preface

Through its first seven editions, *Writing Arguments* has established itself as the leading college textbook in argumentation. By focusing on argument as dialogue in search of solutions to problems instead of as pro-con debate with winners and losers, *Writing Arguments* treats argument as a process of inquiry as well as a means of persuasion. Users and reviewers have consistently praised the book for teaching the critical thinking skills needed for *writing* arguments: how to analyze the occasion for an argument; how to ground an argument in the values and beliefs of the targeted audience; how to develop and elaborate an argument; and how to respond sensitively to objections and alternative views. The text is available in three versions—a regular edition, which includes an anthology of readings; a brief edition, which offers the complete rhetoric without the anthology; and a concise edition with fewer readings and examples—to support many instructional approaches and course designs. We are pleased that in this eighth edition we have made many improvements while retaining the text's signature strengths.

The Big Picture: What's New in the Eighth Edition?

Based on our continuing research into argumentation theory and pedagogy, as well as on the advice of users, we have made significant improvements in the eighth edition that increase the text's flexibility for teachers and its appeal to students. We have made the following major changes:

- **New full-color design and increased focus on visual arguments throughout the text.** The interest level and reader-friendliness of the text has been greatly increased by the new full-color design and by the many new photographs, ads, cartoons, drawings, and other visual arguments that deepen students' encounters with persuasive messages. Each claim-type chapter in Part Four opens with a **visual case** illustrating the claim type, and includes an **Examining Visual Arguments** feature that asks students to analyze advocacy ads, political cartoons, posters, and other visual arguments.

- **A new Chapter 8 on the rhetorical analysis of written arguments.** In response to user requests that we expand the text's treatment of rhetorical analysis of arguments, the new Chapter 8 provides detailed instruction on how to write a rhetorical analysis of a written text. This chapter teaches students to identify a writer's strategies for reaching a targeted audience, to analyze the writer's angle of vision, and to evaluate the argument's overall effectiveness for both insider and outsider audiences. New Writing Assignment options and a student example increase the text's flexibility for instructors in planning major assignments.

- **A thoroughly updated and revised anthology.** The anthology now contains six new units: "Immigration in the Twenty-First Century: Accommodation and Change," "Web 2.0 and Online Identity," "Video Games and Their Influence," "Women in Math and Science," "Energy and the Search for Sustainability," and "Argument

Classics." In addition, the units on Wal-Mart, soldiers and the draft, the news media, and food issues have been substantially updated.

- **Many concepts are now displayed graphically, particularly in the Toulmin Analysis** charts, which help students see the conceptual framework of an argument, and the **Organization Plans** for various types of arguments, which help students outline their own arguments.

- **Simpler, shorter, and more accessible claim-type chapters (Part Four)** through elimination of the XYZ templates, through new examples, and through substantive tightening. In the first seven editions of *Writing Arguments,* we used X and Y as place-holders in templates to explain a stasis: *Is this X a Y?* or *Does X cause Y?* Although this approach worked for some students, many complained that certain passages in these chapters seemed like a math text. In the eighth edition, we have eliminated this feature by adopting a simpler, more straightforward, and clearer approach for explaining each claim type. We have also made these chapters shorter and crisper and have used many new examples and new student essays.

- **An increased emphasis on rhetorical analysis within a new Part Three.** Our new Chapter 8 on analyzing written arguments is paired with an updated Chapter 9 on analyzing visual arguments to create a new Part Three explicitly devoted to rhetorical analysis. The background knowledge students need for rhetorical analysis is provided in Part Two, where students learn about *logos, ethos,* and *pathos,* about audience-based reasons, and about analysis of evidence, identification of assumptions, and methods of treating alternative views. In Part Three, students bring these analytical tools to bear on verbal and visual arguments.

- **A significantly revised Chapter 2, which places the reading of arguments within a context of inquiry and exploration.** Our newly revised Chapter 2, "Argument as Inquiry: Reading and Exploring," combines features of the seventh edition's Chapters 2 and 3. The chapter continues to focus on reading arguments (summary writing, reading to believe and to doubt), but places greater emphasis on argument as inquiry and truth seeking. A new Writing Assignment, an exploratory essay, is illustrated with a student example, increasing the instructor's options for course planning and providing students with a productive tool for reading arguments and generating ideas.

- **An improved emphasis on writing throughout Part Two with new Writing Assignments.** The new title of Part Two, "Writing an Argument," reflects the absorption of the seventh edition's Chapter 3 ("Writing Arguments") into Part Two, where a series of new examples illustrates a student writer's process in producing an argument on women and video games. Writing Assignments now appear in each chapter in Part Two, allowing teachers to coordinate students' reading of Part Two with the development and writing of their own arguments. In addition, Part Two introduces a new Writing Assignment—a "supporting-reasons" argument—that focuses on reasons in support of the writer's claim without requiring students to summarize and respond to opposing views.

- **Updated MLA documentation based on the new seventh edition of the** *MLA Handbook for Writers of Research Papers* **(2009), and updated APA** documentation based on the *Publication Manual of the American Psychological Association*, **Sixth Edition (2010).** In Chapter 17 we explain and show the far-ranging changes in the citing of both print and web sources according to the new MLA handbook, including the use of italics rather than underscoring and the inclusion of medium of publication in each citation. We also show examples of citations based on the APA's latest style guide. Three new source samples show students where to find information for their citations of web documents, online scholarly journals, and blogs.

- **77 new professional readings and 5 new student essays throughout the text, chosen for their illustrative power and student interest.** High-interest topics that recur throughout the text include immigration, women in math and science, video games, and alternative energy.

The Details: What Has Changed in the Eighth Edition?

Our part titles now signal a clear progression from argument as inquiry (Part One), to writing arguments (Part Two), to analyzing arguments (Part Three), to a deeper understanding of claim types (Part Four), to using research (Part Five). This revised arrangement provides an improved pedagogical framework for the teaching of argument while giving instructors the flexibility to use what they need. In the context of this framework, we have made many changes to the content of each chapter.

Part One, Overview of Argument Part One (Chapters 1 and 2) has been refocused to emphasize argument as truth seeking and inquiry and to encourage students to enter a disputed conversation with an open mind, searching for the best solution to a problem.

- Chapter 1, "Argument: An Introduction," has an improved and expanded explanation of implicit versus explicit arguments illustrated by the controversy over phthalates in toys. Two implicit visual arguments opposing phthalates (pictures of a baby with a "poison bib" and of a phthalates protest) are juxtaposed with an explicit argument supporting the chemical industry's position. In addition, Chapter 1 has a new class activity analyzing implicit visual arguments and a new role-playing exercise on regulating student self-presentations on Facebook.
- Chapter 2, "Argument as Inquiry: Reading and Exploring," combines elements of Chapter 2 and Chapter 3 from the seventh edition to better explain how to evaluate rhetorical context, read arguments, and explore issues. The chapter's focus on inquiry and exploration is supported by new readings, photos, and cartoons about undocumented workers and illegal immigration. The chapter offers two Writing Assignment options—an argument summary or a new exploratory essay, which is described in detail and illustrated with a new student essay.

Part Two, Writing an Argument   Part Two, which has absorbed the material on writing arguments from the seventh edition's Chapter 3, places increased attention on the writing process. Part Two introduces the classical argument and leads students through a series of brief writing assignments that help them plan and draft an argument. Each of the chapters in Part Two includes changes as follows:

- Chapter 3, "The Core of an Argument: A Claim with Reasons," introduces the structure of classical argument and the classical appeals of *logos, ethos,* and *pathos* at the outset to frame the discussion of the principles of argument. A new Writing Assignment option asks students to frame an issue question and produce a working thesis statement.
- In Chapter 4, "The Logical Structure of Arguments," the explanation of the Toulmin system is clarified with examples in graphic form. A new Writing Assignment option asks students to use the Toulmin schema to plan details for an argument in progress.
- Chapter 5, "Using Evidence Effectively," expands its treatment of visual evidence and includes new exercises on angle of vision and photographs. A new Writing Assignment option asks students to write a "supporting-reasons" argument, which is illustrated by student writer Carmen Tieu's "Why Violent Video Games Are Good for Girls."
- Chapter 6, "Moving Your Audience: *Ethos, Pathos,* and *Kairos,*" has an improved section on how audience-based reasons enhance *logos, ethos,* and *pathos* and includes a new chart of questions for analyzing an audience. It also contains a new Examining Visual Arguments feature that asks students to analyze the appeals of a Toyota Prius ad. Its new Writing Assignment option asks students to revise a draft for improved focus on *ethos, pathos,* and audience-based reasons.
- Chapter 7, "Responding to Objections and Alternative Views," has been tightened. The seventh edition's student example of a classical argument ("A Plea for Fair Treatment of Skateboarders") has been moved to this chapter, where the Writing Assignment options are to write either a classical argument or a dialogic argument aimed at conciliation.

Part Three, Analyzing Arguments   Part Three includes a new Chapter 8 on analyzing written arguments along with Chapter 9 on analyzing visual arguments.

- Chapter 8, "Analyzing Arguments Rhetorically," provides comprehensive instruction to students on how to write a rhetorical analysis of an argument using the theory and principles of argument explained in Part Two. As examples for analysis, it presents two arguments about ethical issues in reproductive technology: Kathryn Jean Lopez's "Egg Heads" and Ellen Goodman's "Womb for Rent—For a Price." The chapter provides our own analysis of Lopez's argument, a student analysis of Goodman's, and a new Writing Assignment, a rhetorical analysis of an argument.
- Chapter 9 has been updated with new visual argument examples and provides a new Writing Assignment option: to write a rhetorical analysis of a visual argument.

Part Four, Arguments in Depth: Five Types of Claims Part Four has been condensed, updated, and made simpler and more accessible by elimination of the XY templates. In each chapter, the Toulmin analysis of an argument has been clarified with a chart to help students pinpoint the elements of the argument. We have also added in each claim-type chapter an Examining Visual Arguments feature and a new section on identifying audience and determining what's at stake. Numerous other local changes include the following:

- In Chapter 10, "An Introduction to the Types of Claims," the example of a hybrid argument is now annotated to help students identify the various claim-types used in the essay.
- In Chapter 11, "Definitional Arguments," we have simplified the vocabulary and eliminated the distinction between definition arguments and what the seventh edition called "simple categorical arguments." The chapter opens with a visual argument case—a ConocoPhillips ad—and has an Examining Visual Arguments feature analyzing a poster defining fascism. The chapter has two new readings: Jenefer Domingo (student), "Protecting Our Homes Can Lead to Animal Cruelty" and David Andriesen, "What Defines a Sport?"
- Chapter 12, "Causal Arguments," opens with a new visual case using global warming graphs, has several new cause-and-effect diagrams, and has an Examining Visual Arguments feature analyzing an Adbusters ad. The chapter has also been shortened and reorganized to explain causal arguing more crisply. A new student example of a causal argument is Julee Christianson, "Why Lawrence Summers Was Wrong."
- Chapter 13, "Resemblance Arguments," opens with a new visual case and includes new examples of resemblance argument: An American Association of University Professors argument against the high salaries of football coaches and a pro-gay-marriage cartoon with a letter to the editor in response.
- Chapter 14, "Evaluation and Ethical Arguments," opens with a new visual case (the ad for *A Day without a Mexican*) and includes a new Examining Visual arguments feature on the Daily Show.
- Chapter 15, "Proposal Arguments," opens with a visual argument supporting T. Boone Pickens's wind farm proposal and includes two new readings: an MLA format research paper by student Juan Vazquez, "Why the United States Should Adopt Nuclear Power," and Donald Shoup, "Gone Parkin'."

Part Five, The Researched Argument Part Five has been updated to reflect new MLA and APA guidelines for citations. Other local changes include the following:

- In Chapter 16, "Finding and Evaluating Sources," political blogs have been added to Table 16.6, Angles of Vision in U.S. Media and Think Tanks. In addition, many of the search illustrations have been updated, as well as the evaluation of a Web site.

- Chapter 17, "Using, Citing, and Documenting Sources," includes new MLA citations based on the new seventh edition of the *MLA Handbook for Writers of Research Papers* (2009), and updated APA documentation based on the *Publication Manual of the American Psychological Association* (2010). It also includes three source samples—Web article, online database article, and blog posting.

Part Six, An Anthology of Arguments Part Six includes six new units on topics of interest to students: "Web 2.0 and Online Identity," "Immigration in the Twenty-First Century: Accommodation and Change," "Video Games and Their Influence," "Women in Math and Science," "Sustainability: The Search for Clean Energy," and "Classic Arguments." The latter unit has been included in response to numerous requests from users and reviewers for arguments that have stood the test of time. In addition, the units on Wal-Mart, soldiers and the draft, the news media, and food issues have been substantially updated. Wherever possible, we have included visual arguments and researched academic arguments in each unit, as well as arguments from newspapers, magazines, blogs, and other sources to provide a wide variety of genres. For details, see the genre table of contents on the inside back cover.

What Hasn't Changed? The Distinguishing Features of *Writing Arguments*

Building on earlier success, we have preserved the signature features of earlier editions praised by students, instructors, and reviewers:

- **Focus throughout on writing arguments.** Grounded in composition theory, this text combines explanations of argument with class-tested discussion tasks, exploratory writing tasks, and sequenced writing assignments aimed at developing skills of writing and critical thinking. This text builds students' confidence in their ability to enter the argumentative conversations of our culture, understand diverse points of view, synthesize ideas, and create their own persuasive texts.
- **Equal focus on argument as a rhetorical act, particularly on analyzing audience, on understanding the real-world occasions for argument, and on appreciating the rhetorical context and genre of arguments.** Focusing on both the reading and the writing of arguments, the text emphasizes the critical thinking that underlies effective arguments, particularly the skills of critical reading, of believing and doubting, of empathic listening, of active questioning, and of negotiating ambiguity and seeking synthesis.
- **Integration of four different approaches to argument:** The Toulmin system as a means of invention and analysis of arguments; the enthymeme as a logical structure rooted in the beliefs and values of the audience; the classical concepts of *logos, pathos,* and *ethos* as persuasive appeals; and stasis theory (called claim-types) as an aid to inventing and structuring arguments through understanding of generic argumentative moves associated with different categories of claims.

- **Copious treatment of the research process,** including two student examples of documented research papers—one using the MLA system and one using the APA system.
- **Numerous "For Class Discussion" exercises, "Examining Visual Argument" features, and sequenced Writing Assignments** designed to teach critical thinking and build argumentative skills. All "For Class Discussion" exercises can be used either for whole-class discussions or for collaborative group tasks.
- **Numerous student and professional arguments** to illustrate argumentative strategies and stimulate discussion, analysis, and debate. Altogether, the eighth edition contains 68 written arguments and 55 visual arguments drawn from the public and academic arenas and 16 student essays and 2 student visual arguments.

Our Approaches to Argumentation

Our interest in argumentation grows out of our interest in the relationship between writing and thinking. When writing arguments, writers are forced to lay bare their thinking processes in an unparalleled way, grappling with the complex interplay between inquiry and persuasion, between issue and audience. In an effort to engage students in the kinds of critical thinking that argument demands, we draw on four major approaches to argumentation:

1. **The enthymeme as a rhetorical and logical structure.** This concept, especially useful for beginning writers, helps students "nutshell" an argument as a claim with one or more supporting *because* clauses. It also helps them see how real-world arguments are rooted in assumptions granted by the audience rather than in universal and unchanging principles.
2. **The three classical types of appeal—*logos, ethos,* and *pathos.*** These concepts help students place their arguments in a rhetorical context focusing on audience-based appeals; they also help students create an effective voice and style.
3. **Toulmin's system of analyzing arguments.** Toulmin's system helps students see the complete, implicit structure that underlies an enthymeme and develop appropriate grounds and backing to support an argument's reasons and warrants. It also highlights the rhetorical, social, and dialectical nature of argument.
4. **Stasis theory concerning types of claims.** This approach stresses the heuristic value of learning different patterns of support for different types of claims and often leads students to make surprisingly rich and full arguments.

Throughout the text these approaches are integrated and synthesized into generative tools for both producing and analyzing arguments.

Structure of the Text

The text has six main parts plus two appendixes. Part One gives an overview of argumentation with an initial focus on argument as inquiry and truth seeking. These first two chapters present our philosophy of argument, showing how argument helps writers clarify their own thinking and connect with the values and beliefs of a questioning audience. By emphasizing argument as a community's search for the best solution to a problem, we invite students to enter arguments with an open-mind rather than with their minds already made up. Chapter Two teaches students to read arguments first by summarizing them fairly (listening) and then by systematically engaging with the writer's ideas through believing and doubting.

Part Two teaches students how to write arguments by applying key principles. Chapters 3 through 5 show that the core of an effective argument is a claim with reasons. These reasons are often stated as enthymemes, the unstated premise of which must sometimes be brought to the surface and supported. In effective arguments, the reasons are audience-based so that the argument proceeds from underlying beliefs, values, or assumptions held by the intended audience. Discussion of Toulmin logic shows students how to discover both the stated and unstated premises of their arguments and how to provide audience-based structures of reasons and evidence to support them. Chapter 6 focuses on *ethos, pathos,* and *kairos* as means of persuasion, while Chapter 7 focuses on strategies for summarizing and responding to opposing views in order to accommodate different kinds of audiences from sympathetic to neutral to hostile.

Part Three focuses on analyzing arguments. Chapter 8 teaches students to do a rhetorical analysis of a written argument. Chapter 9 focuses on the theory and practice of visual arguments—both images and quantitative data—giving students the tools for analyzing visual arguments and for creating their own.

Part Four discusses five different types of argument: definitional arguments, causal arguments, resemblance arguments, evaluation arguments including ethics, and proposal arguments. These chapters introduce students to recurring strategies of argument that cut across the different category types:

- Criteria-match arguing, in which the writer establishes criteria for making a judgment and argues whether a specific case does or does not meet those criteria
- Causal arguing, in which the writer shows that one event or phenomenon can be linked to others in a causal chain
- Resemblance arguing, in which the writer uses analogy or precedent to shape the writer's view of a phenomenon
- Proposal arguing, in which the writer identifies a problem, presents a proposed solution, and justifies that solution, often using a hybrid of criteria-match, causal, or resemblance strategies.

Part Five shows students how to incorporate research into their arguments, including the skills of formulating a research question; understanding differences in the kinds of sources; conducting effective searches of online catalogs, electronic databases, and the Web; reading sources rhetorically to understand context and bias; evaluating sources according to one's purpose, audience, and genre; understanding the rhetoric of Web sites; incorporating sources into the writer's own argument using summary, paraphrase, and judicious quotation; and documenting sources according to MLA or APA conventions. Unlike standard treatments of the research paper, our discussion explains to students how the writer's meaning and purpose control the selection and shaping of source materials.

The appendixes provide important supplemental information useful for courses in argument. Appendix 1 gives an overview of informal fallacies, while Appendix 2 shows students how to get the most out of collaborative groups in an argument class. Appendix 2 also provides a sequence of collaborative tasks that will help students learn to peer-critique their classmates' arguments in progress. The numerous For Class Discussion exercises within the text provide additional tasks for group collaboration.

Finally, Part Six, the anthology, provides a rich and varied selection of professional arguments arranged into ten high-interest units including military recruitment and the draft, Web 2.0 and online identity, the influence of video games, energy and the search for sustainability, and a collection of classic arguments. The anthology selections are grouped by topic rather than by issue question to encourage students to see that any conversation of alternative views gives rise to numerous embedded and intertwined issues. Formulating the issue question, targeting an audience, framing the issue as a claim, and determining the depth and complexity of the argument are all part of the writer's task. Many of the issues raised in the anthology are first raised in the rhetoric (Parts One through Five) so that students' interest in the anthology topics will already be piqued.

Writing Assignments

The text provides a variety of sequenced Writing Assignments.

- In Part One the Writing Assignment options are an argument summary or an exploratory essay.
- Part Two includes as options a "supporting-reasons" argument (with earlier scaffolding assignments), a classical argument, a delayed-thesis or Rogerian argument, and an advocacy ad. It also includes "microthemes" for practicing basic argumentative moves (for example, supporting a reason with evidence).
- In Part Three the Writing Assignment options are a rhetorical analysis of a written argument and a rhetorical analysis of a visual argument.
- Each chapter in Part Four on claim types includes a Writing Assignment option based on the claim type covered in the chapter. (Chapter 15 includes a practical proposal assignment, a researched policy proposal assignment, and an advocacy poster.)
- Finally, Part Six, the anthology, provides Writing Assignments focusing on problems related to each anthology unit. Instructors can also design anthology assignments requiring argument analysis.

The Instructor's Manual

The Instructor's Manual is written by Tim N. Taylor of Eastern Illinois University. New to the eighth edition are nine detailed sample writing assignments. In addition, the Instructor's Manual has the following features:

- Discussion of planning decisions an instructor must make in designing an argument course: for example, how to use readings; how much to emphasize Toulmin or claim-type theory; how much time to build into the course for invention, peer review of drafts, and other writing instruction; and how to select and sequence assignments.

- Three detailed syllabi showing how *Writing Arguments* can support a variety of course structures and emphases:

  Syllabus #1: This course emphasizes argumentative skills and strategies, uses readings for rhetorical analysis, and asks students to write on issues drawn from their own interests and experiences.

  Syllabus #2: This more rigorous course works intensely with the logical structure of argument, the classical appeals, the Toulmin schema, and claim-type theory. It uses readings for rhetorical analysis and for an introduction to the argumentative controversies that students will address in their papers.

  Syllabus #3: This course asks students to experiment with genres of argument (for example, op-ed pieces, visual arguments, white papers, and researched freelance or scholarly arguments) and focuses on students' choice of issues and claim types.
- For instructors who include Toulmin, an independent, highly teachable introductory lesson on the Toulmin schema, and an additional exercise giving students practice using Toulmin to generate argument frames.
- For new instructors, a helpful discussion of how to sequence writing assignments and how to use a variety of collaborative tasks in the classroom to promote active learning and critical thinking.
- Chapter-by-chapter responses to the For Class Discussion exercises.
- Numerous teaching tips and suggestions placed strategically throughout the chapter material, including several sample quizzes asking students to explain and apply argumentative concepts.
- For instructors who teach visual arguments, suggestions for encouraging students to explore how visual arguments have molded and continue to mold public thinking about issues and controversies.
- For instructors who like to use student essays in class exercises and discussions, a number of new student essays showing how students responded to assignments in the text. Several of these student pieces exemplify stages of revision.
- Helpful suggestions for using the exercises on critiquing readings in Part Four, "Arguments in Depth: Five Types of Claims." By focusing on rhetorical context as well as on the strengths and weaknesses of these arguments, our suggestions will help students connect their reading of arguments to their writing of arguments.
- At the end of each claim-type chapter in Part Four, a list of anthology readings that employ the same claim type, either as a major claim or as a substantial portion of the argument.
- An analysis of anthology readings that better connects the anthology to the rhetoric portion of the text. Using a bulleted, quick-reference format, each analysis briefly discusses (1) the core of the argument, (2) the major or dominant claims of the argument, (3) the argument's use of evidence and argumentative strategies, (4) the appeals to *ethos* and *pathos* in the argument, and (5) the argument's genre. This

easy-to-scan format helps instructors select readings and provides good starting points for class discussion. Our analyses also point out striking connections among readings, suggesting how the readings participate in larger societal argumentative conversations.

MyCompLab

 The new MyCompLab integrates the market-leading instruction, multimedia tutorials, and exercises for writing, grammar, and research that users have come to identify with the program with a new online composing space and new assessment tools. The result is a revolutionary application that offers a seamless and flexible teaching and learning environment built specifically for writers. Created after years of extensive research and in partnership with composition faculty and students across the country, the new MyCompLab provides help for writers in the context of their writing, with instructor and peer commenting functionality; proven tutorials and exercises for writing, grammar, and research; an e-portfolio; an assignment builder; a bibliography tool; tutoring services; and a gradebook and course management organization created specifically for writing classes. Visit www.mycomplab.com for more information.

Interactive E-Book

An e-book version of *Writing Arguments,* Eighth Edition, is also available in MyCompLab. The many resources of MyCompLab link into the text to create an enriched, interactive learning experience for writing students.

Acknowledgments

We are happy for this opportunity to give public thanks to the scholars, teachers, and students who have influenced our approach to composition and argument. For this edition, we owe special thanks to Tamara Fish of the University of Houston for her insightful and revitalizing work on the anthology. She brought her expertise as a composition instructor, her knowledge as a long-time user and reviewer of *Writing Arguments,* and her experience as a veteran mentor of graduate student instructors to her research, selection of readings, and presentation of the issues.

We want to thank our talented students who contributed their ideas, research, and time to this edition, especially, Michael Banks for his researching and writing about illegal immigration in Chapter 2; Mike Bowersox for dialoguing with us on rhetorical analysis and contributing ideas to Chapter 8; Carmen Tieu for her essay on women and violent video games; Julee Christianson for her MLA research paper on the nature/nurture controversy about women and mathematics; and Juan Vazquez for his researched white paper on nuclear power. Additionally, we are grateful to all our students whom we have been privileged to teach in our writing classes and to our other students who have enabled us to include their arguments in this text. Their insights and growth as writers have inspired our ongoing study of rhetoric and composition.

We thank too the many users of our texts who have given us encouragement about our successes and offered helpful suggestions for improvements. Particularly we thank the following scholars and teachers who reviewed this revision of *Writing Arguments* in its various stages: JoAnn Dadisman, West Virginia University; Christine Caver, The University of Texas at San Antonio; Josh Gehl, San Jose State University; Joseph Jones, University of Memphis; William B. Matta, McLennan Community College; Ann Spurlock, Mississippi State University; Elizabeth Metzger, University of South Florida; Pat Tyrer, West Texas A & M University; Sandy Jordan, University of Houston; Mary Anne Reiss, Elizabethtown Community & Technical College; Jeffrey Schneider, St. Louis Community College Meramec; Diane Abdo, The University of Texas at San Antonio; Gary S. Montano, Tarrant Country College; Shavawn M. Berry, Arizona State University; Carl Runyon, Owensboro Community and Technical College, Kentucky Community and Technical College System; Jordan Sanderson, Auburn University; Linda Gladden, University of South Florida; Laura Gray-Rosendale, Northern Arizona University; Amy Tomasi, Roger Williams University; and Brenda S. Martin, Kansas State University.

We are especially grateful to our editor, Lauren Finn, whose keen understanding of the needs of argument instructors and whose commitment to producing the most useful texts has guided us with her support and professional expertise. Finally, we owe our deepest thanks to Marion Castellucci, our development editor, without whom we could not maintain the pace and quality of our textbook revisions. Marion's invaluable mastery of both the big picture and specific dimensions of this work and her calmness, encouragement, and wit have shepherded this project at every point.

As always, we want to conclude by thanking our families. John Bean thanks his wife, Kit, also a professional composition teacher, and his children, Matthew, Andrew, Stephen, and Sarah, who have grown to adulthood since he first began writing textbooks. June Johnson thanks her husband, Kenneth Bube, a mathematics professor and researcher, and her daughter, Jane Ellen Bube, now completing her high school experience. Ken and Janie have played major roles in the ongoing family analysis of argumentation in the public sphere and of specific arguments on wide-ranging issues. They have also made it possible for her to meet the demands and challenges of continuing to infuse new ideas and material into this text in each revision.

John D. Ramage
John C. Bean
June Johnson

PART ONE
Overview of Argument

1 Argument: An Introduction
2 Argument as Inquiry: Reading and Exploring

These stills from the film *Under the Same Moon* (2007) depict the painful separation and longing for connection of an immigrant mother in the United States and her young son, Carlitos, left behind in Mexico. The telephone booth and the furtive, precious calls symbolize the plight of families divided by economics and immigration policy. The film's appeals to our emotions are discussed in Michael Banks' exploratory essay in Chapter 2, pages 52–57.

Argument: An Introduction

At the outset of a book on argument, we ought to explain what an argument is. Instead, we're going to explain why no universally accepted definition is possible. Over the centuries, philosophers and rhetoricians have disagreed about the meaning of the term and about the goals that arguers should set for themselves. This opening chapter introduces you to some of these controversies. Our goal is to show you various ways of thinking about argument as a way of helping you become a more powerful arguer yourself.

We begin by asking what we mean by argument, suggesting what argument isn't as well as what it is. We then proceed to three defining features of argument: it requires writers or speakers to justify their claims, it is both a product and a process, and it combines elements of truth seeking and persuasion. Next, we explore more deeply the relationship between truth seeking and persuasion by asking questions about the nature of "truth" that arguments seek. Finally, we give you an example of a successful arguing process.

What Do We Mean by Argument?

Let's begin by examining the inadequacies of two popular images of argument—fight and debate.

Argument Is Not a Fight or a Quarrel

To many, the word *argument* connotes anger and hostility, as when we say, "I just got in a huge argument with my roommate," or "My mother and I argue all the time." What we picture here is heated disagreement, rising pulse rates, and an urge to slam doors. Argument imagined as fight conjures images of shouting talk-show guests, flaming e-mailers, or fist-banging speakers.

But to our way of thinking, argument doesn't imply anger. In fact, arguing is often pleasurable. It is a creative and productive activity that engages us at high levels of inquiry and critical thinking, often in conversation with people we like and respect. For your primary image of argument, we invite you to think not of a shouting match on cable news but of a small group of reasonable people seeking the best solution to a problem. We will return to this image throughout the chapter.

Argument Is Not Pro-Con Debate

Another popular image of argument is debate—a presidential debate, perhaps, or a high school or college debate tournament. According to one popular dictionary, *debate* is "a formal contest of argumentation in which two opposing teams defend and attack a given proposition." Although formal debate can develop critical thinking, its weakness is that it can turn argument into a game of winners and losers rather than a process of cooperative inquiry.

For an illustration of this weakness, consider one of our former students, a champion high school debater who spent his senior year debating the issue of prison reform. Throughout the year he argued for and against propositions such as "The United States should build more prisons" and "Innovative alternatives to prison should replace prison sentences for most crimes." We asked him, "What do you personally think is the best way to reform prisons?" He replied, "I don't know. I haven't thought about what I would actually choose."

Here was a bright, articulate student who had studied prisons extensively for a year. Yet nothing in the atmosphere of pro-con debate had engaged him in truth-seeking inquiry. He could argue for and against a proposition, but he hadn't experienced the wrenching process of clarifying his own values and taking a personal stand. As we explain throughout this text, argument entails a desire for truth; it aims to find the best solutions to complex problems. We don't mean that arguers don't passionately support their own points of view or expose weaknesses in views they find faulty. Instead, we mean that their goal isn't to win a game but to find and promote the best belief or course of action.

Arguments Can Be Explicit or Implicit

Before proceeding to some defining features of argument, we should note also that arguments can be either explicit or implicit. An *explicit* argument directly states its controversial claim and supports it with reasons and evidence. An *implicit* argument, in contrast, may not look like an argument at all. It may be a bumper sticker, a billboard, a poster, a photograph, a cartoon, a vanity license plate, a slogan on a T-shirt, an advertisement, a poem, or a song lyric. But like an explicit argument, it persuades its audience toward a certain point of view.

Consider the striking photograph in Figure 1.1—a baby wearing a bib labeled "POISON." This photograph enters a conversation about the safety of toys and other baby products sold in the United States. In recent years, fears about toy safety have come mostly from two sources: the discovery that many toys imported from China used lead paint and the discovery that a substance used to make plastics pliable and soft—called *phthalates* (pronounced "thalates")—may be harmful. Phthalates have been shown to interfere with hormone production in rat fetuses and, based on other rodent studies, may produce some kinds of cancers and other ailments. Because many baby products contain phthalates—bibs, edges of cribs, rubber duckies, and

FIGURE 1.1 An implicit argument against phthalates

any number of other soft rubbery toys—parents worry that babies can ingest phthalates by chewing on these toys.

The photograph of the baby and bib makes the argumentative claim that baby products are poisonous; the photograph implicitly urges viewers to take action against phthalates. But this photograph is just one voice in a surprisingly complex conversation. Is the bib in fact poisonous? Such questions were debated during a recent campaign to ban the sale of toys containing phthalates in California. A legislative initiative (2007 California Assembly Bill 1108) sparked intense lobbying from both child-advocacy groups and representatives of the toy industry. At issue were a number of scientific questions about the risk posed by phthalates. To what extent do studies on rats apply to humans? How much exposure to phthalates should be considered dangerous? (Experiments on rats used large amounts of phthalates—amounts that, according to many scientists, far exceed anything a baby could absorb by chewing on a toy.) Also at issue is the level of health risks a free market society should be willing to tolerate. The European Union, operating on the "precautionary principle," and citing evidence that such toys *might* be dangerous, has banned toys containing phthalates. The U.S. government sets less strict standards than does the European Union. A federal agency generally doesn't ban a substance unless it has been *proven* harmful to humans, not merely suspected of being harmful. In defense of free markets, the toy and chemical industries accused opponents of phthalates of using "junk science" to produce scary but inaccurate data.

Our point in summarizing the toxic toy controversy is to demonstrate the persuasive roles of both implicit and explicit arguments. What follows—a photograph and a short letter—provide examples. Figure 1.2 shows a speaker at a public hearing surrounded by implicit arguments that many toys are unsafe—a poster labeled "Trouble in Toyland" and potentially unsafe toys, many of them soft, pliable plastics using phthalates.

In contrast, Dr. Louis W. Sullivan, who was secretary of health and human services under the Clinton administration, makes an explicit argument in a letter to the governor of California. Sullivan opposes the bill banning phthalates, claiming that scientific agencies charged with public safety haven't found phthalates harmful. Instead, he supports an alternative "green chemistry initiative" that would make public policy decisions based on "facts, not fear."

FIGURE 1.2 Implicit arguments (the toys and poster) against phthalates

Let the Facts Decide, Not Fear: Ban AB 1108

LOUIS W. SULLIVAN, M.D.

Dear Governor Schwarzenegger:

As a physician and public servant who has worked in the field of medicine and public health all my life, I am writing to urge your veto of AB 1108, a bill that would ban the use of compounds used to make vinyl toys and childcare products soft and flexible. AB 1108 widely misses the mark on the most fundamental underpinning of all good public health policy—sound science.

AB 1108 ignores a recent, comprehensive review of the safety of vinyl toys conducted by the U.S. Consumer Product Safety Commission. The CPSC took a long, hard look at the primary softener used in children's toys and concluded that vinyl toys containing this compound are safe as used. In fact, its experts warned that using substitutes could make toys more brittle and less safe.

The CPSC's conclusions are reinforced by the findings of many scientific bodies around the globe—including the European Union's European Chemicals Bureau, the U.S. National Toxicology Program, and the U.S. Centers for Disease Control and Prevention. At a time when public officials are trying to deal with the serious issue of lead paint in toys imported from China, California lawmakers should not confuse the safety of these softening compounds in vinyl toys with that issue. Signing AB 1108 will do nothing to resolve the lead paint in toys issue.

California needs public health policies based on science. That's why I resoundingly support your Green Chemistry Initiative. This is a coordinated, comprehensive strategy for addressing possible risk from products—in a holistic, science-based fashion—that would serve the interests of California families and their children.

5   I urge you to reject AB 1108 and allow your health and safety experts, not legislators, to make judgments about the chemicals in our environment—based on facts, not fear.

Sincerely,

Louis W. Sullivan, M.D.
U.S. Secretary of Health & Human Services 1989–1993
President Emeritus, Morehouse School of Medicine

■ ■ ■   **FOR CLASS DISCUSSION**   **Implicit and Explicit Arguments**

1. Any argument, whether implicit or explicit, tries to influence the audience's stance on an issue, moving the audience toward the arguer's claim. Arguments work on us psychologically as well as cognitively, triggering emotions as well as thoughts and ideas. How would you describe the differences in the way that the poster and toy display in Figure 1.2 and the letter from Sullivan "work on us"?

2. Assume that you are explaining implicit arguments to an international exchange student who is not yet familiar with U.S. politics and popular culture. Each of the implicit arguments in Figures 1.3–1.7 makes a claim on its audience, trying to get viewers to adopt the arguer's position, perspective, belief, or point of view on an issue. For each argument, answer the following questions for your new international friend:

   a. What conversation does this argument join? What is the issue or controversy? What is at stake?

   b. What is the argument's claim? That is, what value, perspective, belief, or position does the argument ask its viewers to adopt?

   c. What is an opposing or alternative view? What views is the argument pushing against?

   d. How does the argument try to do its work on the brains or hearts of the audience?

FIGURE 1.3 These colors don't run

FIGURE 1.4 These colors don't run the world

FIGURE 1.5 Assisted suicide isn't "natural"

FIGURE 1.6 Ethanol versus food

FIGURE 1.7 Airplane baggage dilemma

The Defining Features of Argument

We turn now to examine arguments in more detail. (Unless we say otherwise, by *argument* we mean explicit arguments that attempt to supply reasons and evidence to support their claims.) This section examines three defining features of such arguments.

Argument Requires Justification of Its Claims

To begin defining argument, let's turn to a humble but universal site of disagreement: the conflict between a parent and a teenager over rules. In what way and in what circumstances do such conflicts constitute arguments?

Consider the following dialogue:

YOUNG PERSON (*racing for the front door while putting coat on*): Bye. See you later.

PARENT: Whoa! What time are you planning on coming home?

YOUNG PERSON (*coolly, hand still on doorknob*): I'm sure we discussed this earlier. I'll be home around 2 A.M. (*The second sentence, spoken very rapidly, is barely audible.*)

PARENT (*mouth tightening*): We did *not* discuss this earlier and you're *not* staying out till two in the morning. You'll be home at twelve.

At this point in the exchange, we have a quarrel, not an argument. Quarrelers exchange antagonistic assertions without any attempt to support them rationally. If the dialogue never gets past the "Yes-you-will/No-I-won't" stage, it either remains a quarrel or degenerates into a fight.

Let us say, however, that the dialogue takes the following turn:

YOUNG PERSON (*tragically*): But I'm *sixteen years old!*

Now we're moving toward argument. Not, to be sure, a particularly well-developed or cogent one, but an argument all the same. It's now an argument because one of the quarrelers has offered a reason for her assertion. Her choice of curfew is satisfactory, she says, *because* she is sixteen years old, an argument that depends on the unstated assumption that sixteen-year-olds are old enough to make decisions about such matters.

The parent can now respond in one of several ways that will either advance the argument or turn it back into a quarrel. The parent can simply invoke parental authority ("I don't care—you're still coming home at twelve"), in which case argument ceases. Or the parent can provide a reason for his or her view ("You will be home at twelve because your dad and I pay the bills around here!"), in which case the argument takes a new turn.

So far we've established two necessary conditions that must be met before we're willing to call something an argument: (1) a set of two or more conflicting assertions and (2) the attempt to resolve the conflict through an appeal to reason.

But good argument demands more than meeting these two formal requirements. For the argument to be effective, an arguer is obligated to clarify and support the reasons presented. For example, "But I'm sixteen years old!" is not yet a clear support for the assertion "I should be allowed to set my own curfew." On the surface, Young Person's argument seems absurd. Her parent, of all people, knows precisely how old she is. What makes it an argument is that behind her claim lies an unstated assumption—all sixteen-year-olds are old enough to set their own curfews. What Young Person needs to do now is to support that assumption.* In doing so, she must anticipate the sorts of questions the assumption will raise in the minds of her parent: What is the legal status of sixteen-year-olds? How psychologically mature, as opposed to chronologically mature, is Young Person? What is the actual track record of Young Person in being responsible? and so forth. Each of these questions will force Young Person to reexamine and clarify her assumptions about the proper degree of autonomy for sixteen-year-olds. And her response to those questions should in turn force the parents to reexamine their assumptions about the dependence of sixteen-year-olds on parental guidance and wisdom. (Likewise, the parents will need to show why "paying the bills around here" automatically gives them the right to set Young Person's curfew.)

As the argument continues, Young Person and Parent may shift to a different line of reasoning. For example, Young Person might say: "I should be allowed to stay out until 2 A.M. because all my friends get to stay out that late." (Here the unstated assumption is that the rules in this family ought to be based on the rules in other families.) The parent might in turn respond, "But I certainly never stayed out that late when I was your age"—an argument assuming that the rules in this family should follow the rules of an earlier generation.

As Young Person and Parent listen to each other's points of view (and begin realizing why their initial arguments have not persuaded their intended audience), both parties find themselves in the uncomfortable position of having to examine their own beliefs and to justify assumptions that they have taken for granted. Here we encounter one of the earliest senses of the term *to argue,* which is "to clarify." As an arguer begins to clarify her own position on an issue, she also begins to clarify her audience's position. Such clarification helps the arguer see how she might accommodate her audience's views, perhaps by adjusting her own position or by developing reasons that appeal to her audience's values. Thus Young Person might suggest an argument like this:

> I should be allowed to stay out until two on a trial basis because I need enough space to demonstrate my maturity and show you I won't get into trouble.

---

*Later in this text we will call the assumption underlying a line of reasoning its *warrant* (see Chapter 4).

The assumption underlying this argument is that it is good to give teenagers freedom to demonstrate their maturity. Because this reason is likely to appeal to her parent's own values (the parent wants to see his or her daughter grow in maturity) and because it is tempered by the qualifier "on a trial basis" (which reduces some of the threat of Young Person's initial demands), it may prompt productive discussion.

Whether or not Young Person and Parent can work out a best solution, the preceding scenario illustrates how argument leads people to clarify their reasons and provide justifications that can be examined rationally. The scenario also illustrates two specific aspects of argument that we will explore in detail in the next sections: (1) Argument is both a process and a product. (2) Argument combines truth seeking and persuasion.

Argument Is Both a Process and a Product

As the preceding scenario revealed, argument can be viewed as a *process* in which two or more parties seek the best solution to a question or problem. Argument can also be viewed as a *product,* each product being any person's contribution to the conversation at a given moment. In an informal discussion, the products are usually short, whatever time a person uses during his or her turns in the conversation. Under more formal settings, an orally delivered product might be a short impromptu speech (say, during an open-mike discussion of a campus issue) or a longer, carefully prepared formal speech (as in a PowerPoint presentation at a business meeting or an argument at a public hearing for or against a proposed city project).

Similar conversations occur in writing. Roughly analogous to a small-group discussion is an exchange of the kind that occurs regularly through informal chat groups or professional e-mail discussion lists. In an online discussion, participants have more thinking time to shape their messages than they do in a real-time oral discussion. Nevertheless, messages are usually short and informal, making it possible over the course of several days to see participants' ideas shift and evolve as conversants modify their initial views in response to others' views.

Roughly equivalent to a formal speech would be a formal written argument, which may take the form of an academic argument for a college course; a grant proposal; a guest column for the op-ed* section of a newspaper; a legal brief; a letter to a member of Congress; or an article for an organizational newsletter, popular magazine, or professional journal. In each of these instances, the written argument

---

Op-ed stands for "opposite-editorial." It is the generic name in journalism for a signed argument that voices the writer's opinion on an issue, as opposed to a news story that is supposed to report events objectively, uncolored by the writer's personal views. Op-ed pieces appear in the editorial-opinion section of newspapers, which generally features editorials by the resident staff, opinion pieces by syndicated columnists, and letters to the editor from readers. The term *op-ed* is often extended to syndicated columns appearing in newsmagazines, advocacy Web sites, and online news services.

(a product) enters a conversation (a process)—in this case, a conversation of readers, many of whom will carry on the conversation by writing their own responses or by discussing the writer's views with others. The goal of the community of writers and readers is to find the best solution to the problem or issue under discussion.

Argument Combines Truth Seeking and Persuasion

In thinking about argument as a product, the writer will find herself continually moving back and forth between truth seeking and persuasion—that is, between questions about the subject matter (What is the best solution to this problem?) and about audience (What do my readers already believe or value? What reasons and evidence will most persuade them?). Back and forth she'll weave, alternately absorbed in the subject of her argument and in the audience for that argument.

Neither of the two focuses is ever completely out of mind, but their relative importance shifts during different phases of the development of a paper. Moreover, different rhetorical situations place different emphases on truth seeking versus persuasion. We could thus place arguments on a kind of continuum that measures the degree of attention a writer gives to subject matter versus audience. (See Figure 1.8.) At the far truth-seeking end of the continuum might be an exploratory piece that lays out several alternative approaches to a problem and weighs the strengths and weaknesses of each with no concern for persuasion. At the other end of the continuum would be outright propaganda, such as a political campaign advertisement that reduces a complex issue to sound bites and distorts an opponent's position through out-of-context quotations or misleading use of data. (At its most blatant, propaganda obliterates truth seeking; it will do anything, including the knowing use of bogus evidence, distorted assertions, and outright lies, to win over an audience.) In the middle ranges of the continuum, writers shift their focuses back and forth between truth seeking and persuasion but with varying degrees of emphasis.

As an example of a writer focusing primarily on truth seeking, consider the case of Kathleen, who, in her college argument course, addressed the definitional question "Is American Sign Language (ASL) a 'foreign language' for purposes of meeting the

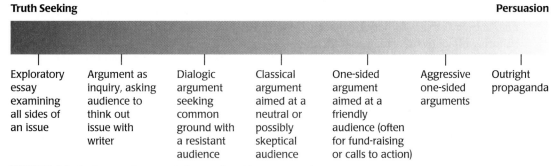

Truth Seeking   **Persuasion**

| Exploratory essay examining all sides of an issue | Argument as inquiry, asking audience to think out issue with writer | Dialogic argument seeking common ground with a resistant audience | Classical argument aimed at a neutral or possibly skeptical audience | One-sided argument aimed at a friendly audience (often for fund-raising or calls to action) | Aggressive one-sided arguments | Outright propaganda |

FIGURE 1.8 Continuum of arguments from truth seeking to persuasion

university's foreign language requirement?" Kathleen had taken two years of ASL at a community college. When she transferred to a four-year college, the chair of the foreign languages department at her new college would not allow her ASL proficiency to count for the foreign language requirement. ASL isn't a "language," the chair said summarily. "It's not equivalent to learning French, German, or Japanese."

Kathleen disagreed, so she immersed herself in developing her argument. While doing research, she focused almost entirely on subject matter, searching for what linguists, neurologists, cognitive psychologists, and sociologists had said about the language of deaf people. Immersed in her subject matter, she was only tacitly concerned with her audience, whom she thought of primarily as her classmates and the professor of her argument class—people who were friendly to her views and interested in her experiences with the deaf community. She wrote a well-documented paper, citing several scholarly articles, that made a good case to her classmates (and the professor) that ASL is indeed a distinct language.

Proud of the big red A the professor had placed on her paper, Kathleen decided for a subsequent assignment to write a second paper on ASL—but this time aiming it directly at the chair of foreign languages and petitioning him to accept her ASL proficiency for the foreign language requirement. Now her writing task falls closer to the persuasive end of our continuum. Kathleen once again immersed herself in research, but this time focused not on subject matter (whether ASL is a distinct language) but on audience. She researched the history of the foreign language requirement at her college and discovered some of the politics behind it (an old foreign language requirement had been dropped in the 1970s and reinstituted in the 1990s, partly—a math professor told her—to boost enrollments in foreign language courses). She also interviewed foreign language teachers to find out what they knew and didn't know about ASL. She discovered that many teachers thought ASL was "easy to learn," so that accepting ASL would allow students a Mickey Mouse way to avoid the rigors of a "real" foreign language class. Additionally, she learned that foreign language teachers valued immersing students in a foreign culture; in fact, the foreign language requirement was part of her college's effort to create a multicultural curriculum.

This new understanding of her target audience helped Kathleen reconceptualize her argument. Her claim that ASL was a real language (the subject of her first paper) became only one section of her second paper, much condensed and abridged. She added sections showing the difficulty of learning ASL (to counter her audience's belief that learning ASL was easy), showing how the deaf community formed a distinct culture with its own customs and literature (to show how ASL met the goals of multiculturalism), and showing that the number of transfer students with ASL credits would be negligibly small (to allay fears that accepting ASL would threaten enrollments in language classes). She ended her argument with an appeal to her college's public emphasis (declared boldly in its mission statement) on eradicating social injustice and reaching out to the oppressed. She described the isolation of deaf people in a world where almost no hearing people learn ASL, and she argued that the deaf community on her campus could be integrated more fully into campus life if more students could "talk" with them. Thus the ideas included in her new argument—the reasons selected, the evidence used, the arrangement and tone—all were determined by her primary focus on persuasion.

Our point, then, is that all along the continuum writers attempt both to seek truth and to persuade, but not necessarily with equal balance. Kathleen could not have written her second paper, aimed specifically at persuading the chair of foreign languages, if she hadn't first immersed herself in truth-seeking research that convinced her that ASL is indeed a distinct language. Nor are we saying that her second argument was better than her first. Both fulfilled their purposes and met the needs of their intended audiences. Both involved truth seeking and persuasion, but the first focused primarily on subject matter whereas the second focused primarily on audience.

Argument and the Problem of Truth

The tension that we have just examined between truth seeking and persuasion raises an ancient issue in the field of argument: Is the arguer's first obligation to truth or to winning the argument? And just what is the nature of the truth to which arguers are supposed to be obligated?

In Plato's famous dialogues from ancient Greek philosophy, these questions were at the heart of Socrates' disagreement with the Sophists. The Sophists were professional rhetoricians who specialized in training orators to win arguments. Socrates, who valued truth seeking over persuasion and believed that truth could be discovered through philosophic inquiry, opposed the Sophists. For Socrates, Truth resided in the ideal world of forms, and through philosophic rigor humans could transcend the changing, shadowlike world of everyday reality to perceive the world of universals where Truth, Beauty, and Goodness resided. Through his method of questioning his interlocutors, Socrates would gradually peel away layer after layer of false views until Truth was revealed. The good person's duty, Socrates believed, was not to win an argument but to pursue this higher Truth. Socrates distrusted rhetoricians because they were interested only in the temporal power and wealth that came from persuading audiences to the orator's views.

Let's apply Socrates' disagreement with the Sophists to a modern instance. Suppose your community is divided over the issue of raising environmental standards versus keeping open a job-producing factory that doesn't meet new guidelines for waste discharge. The Sophists would train you to argue any side of this issue on behalf of any lobbying group willing to pay for your services. If, however, you followed the spirit of Socrates, you would be inspired to listen to all sides of the dispute, peel away false arguments, discover the Truth through reasonable inquiry, and commit yourself to a Right Course of Action.

But what is the nature of Truth or Right Action in a dispute between jobs and the environment? The Sophists believed that truth was determined by those in power; thus they could enter an argument unconstrained by any transcendent beliefs or assumptions. When Socrates talked about justice and virtue, the Sophists could reply contemptuously that these were fictitious concepts invented by the weak to protect themselves from the strong. Over the years, the Sophists' relativist beliefs became so repugnant to people that the term *sophistry* became synonymous with trickery in argument.

However, in recent years the Sophists' critique of a transcendent Universal Truth has been taken seriously by many philosophers, sociologists, and other thinkers who doubt Socrates' confident belief that arguments, properly conducted, necessarily arrive at a single Truth. For these thinkers, as for the Sophists, there are often different degrees of truth and different kinds of truths for different situations or cultures. From this perspective, when we consider questions of interpretation or value, we can never demonstrate that a belief or assumption is true—not through scientific observation, not through reason, and not through religious revelation. We get our beliefs, according to these contemporary thinkers, from the shared assumptions of our particular cultures. We are condemned (or liberated) to live in a pluralistic, multicultural world with competing visions of truth.

If we accept this pluralistic view of the world, do we then endorse the Sophists' radical relativism, freeing us to argue any side of any issue? Or do we doggedly pursue some modern equivalent of Socrates' truth?

Our own sympathies are with Socrates, but we admit to a view of truth that is more tentative, cautious, and conflicted than his. For us, truth seeking does not mean finding the "Right Answer" to a disputed question, but neither does it mean a valueless relativism in which all answers are equally good. For us, truth seeking means taking responsibility for determining the "best answer" or "best solution" to the question for the good of the whole community when taking into consideration the interests of all stakeholders. It means making hard decisions in the face of uncertainty. This more tentative view of truth means that you cannot use argument to "prove" your claim, but only to make a reasonable case for your claim. One contemporary philosopher says that argument can hope only to "increase adherence" to ideas, not absolutely convince an audience of the necessary truth of ideas. Even though you can't be certain, in a Socratic sense, that your solution to the problem is the best one available, you must ethically take responsibility for the consequences of your claim and you must seek justice for stakeholders beyond yourself. You must, in other words, forge a personal stance based on your examination of all the evidence and your articulation of values that you can make public and defend.

To seek truth, then, means to seek the best or most just solution to a problem while observing all available evidence, listening with an open mind to the views of all stakeholders, clarifying and attempting to justify your own values and assumptions, and taking responsibility for your argument. It follows that truth seeking often means delaying closure on an issue, acknowledging the pressure of alternative views, and being willing to change one's mind. Seen in this way, learning to argue effectively has the deepest sort of social value: It helps communities settle conflicts in a rational and humane way by finding, through the dialectic exchange of ideas, the best solutions to problems without resorting to violence or to other assertions of raw power.

■ ■ ■ **FOR CLASS DISCUSSION** Role-Playing Arguments

On any given day, newspapers provide evidence of the complexity of living in a pluralistic culture. Issues that could be readily decided in a completely homogeneous culture raise questions in a society that has fewer shared assumptions. Choose one of the following cases as the subject for a "simulation game" in which class members present the points of view of the people involved.

Case 1: College Athletes Caught in Tangled Web

As the following newspaper excerpt shows, social networking Web sites such as MySpace and Facebook create conflicts between free speech and the reputations of people and institutions in the public domain.

> College students across the country have been cited or disciplined for content they posted on social networking Web sites such as MySpace and Facebook, including such things as criticism of a student government candidate (at the University of Central Florida), complaints about the theater department (Cowley College in Kansas) or vulgar comments about a teaching assistant (Syracuse).
>
> "College administrators are very nervous about this huge new forum," said Greg Lukianoff, president of the Foundation for Individual Rights in Education.
>
> The most nervous of those might be coaches and athletic directors, whose student-athletes are under a more intense public spotlight than the general student body and who usually are required to adhere to more stringent policies and rules of conduct. One distasteful picture of a prominent football player on the Internet could be seen by anybody and might end up on the front page of a newspaper. It's why some athletic departments have stricter policies about such sites and restrict usage as part of individual team rules.

Your task: Imagine an open meeting on your campus on the issue of students' free speech rights versus the rights of your college or university and its athletic departments to establish rules and monitor students' online social network pages. Hold a meeting in which classmates play the following roles: (a) a student athlete who has been warned to remove from his Facebook profile a photograph of himself chugging beer at fraternity party; (b) students who are not on athletic teams but are concerned about institutionally imposed restrictions on students' freedom; (c) a faculty member who feels he has been libeled on a former student's MySpace page; (d) a women's basketball coach who forbids student athletes on her teams from having personal online social networking accounts; (e) a tennis coach who establishes clear team policies for postings on students' sites; (f) the athletic director, who is considering buying tracking technology to monitor athletes' online social networking pages; (g) a representative of the American Civil Liberties Union, who supports student rights and free speech; and (h) the dean of students, who is concerned for the reputation of the institution and for the future well-being of students who might be embarrassed by current postings or endangered by disclosing too much personal information.

Case 2: Homeless Hit the Streets to Protest Proposed Ban

The homeless stood up for themselves by sitting down in a peaceful but vocal protest yesterday in [name of city].

About 50 people met at noon to criticize a proposed set of city ordinances that would ban panhandlers from sitting on sidewalks, put them in jail for repeatedly urinating in public, and crack down on "intimidating" street behavior.

"Sitting is not a crime," read poster boards that feature mug shots of [the city attorney] who is pushing for the new laws. [. . .] "This is city property; the police want to tell us we can't sit here," yelled one man named R. C. as he sat cross-legged outside a pizza establishment.

Your task: Imagine a public hearing seeking reactions to the proposed city ordinance. Hold a mock hearing in which classmates play the following roles: (a) a homeless person; (b) an annoyed merchant; (c) a shopper who avoids places with homeless people; (d) a citizen advocate for the homeless; (e) the city attorney.

A Successful Process of Argumentation:
The Well-Functioning Committee

We have said that neither the fist-banging speaker nor the college debate team represents our ideal image of argument. The best image for us, as we have implied, is a well-functioning small group seeking a solution to a problem. In professional life such small groups usually take the form of committees.

We use the word *committee* in its broadest sense to indicate all sorts of important work that grows out of group conversation and debate. The Declaration of Independence is essentially a committee document with Thomas Jefferson as the chair. Similarly, the U.S. Supreme Court is in effect a committee of nine judges who rely heavily, as numerous books and articles have demonstrated, on small-group decision-making processes to reach their judgments and formulate their legal briefs.

To illustrate our committee or small-group model for argument, let's briefly consider the workings of a university committee on which coauthor John Ramage once served, the University Standards Committee. The Arizona State University (ASU) Standards Committee plays a role in university life analogous to that of the Supreme Court in civic life. It's the final court of appeal for ASU students seeking exceptions to various rules that govern their academic lives (such as registering under a different catalog, waiving a required course, or being allowed to retake a course for the third time).

The issues that regularly come before the committee draw forth all the argument types and strategies discussed throughout this text. For example, the different argument claim types discussed in Part Four regularly surface during committee deliberations, as shown in the following list:

- Definition issues: Is math anxiety a "learning disability" for purposes of exempting a student from a math requirement?
- Cause/consequence issues: What were the causes of this student's sudden poor performance during spring semester? What will be the consequences of approving or denying her appeal?
- Resemblance issues: How is this case similar to a case from the same department that we considered last semester?

- Evaluation issues: What criteria need to be met before we allow a student to graduate under a previous catalog?
- Proposal issues: Should we make it a policy to allow course X to substitute for course Y in the General Studies requirements?

On any given day, the committee's deliberations show how dialogue can lead to clarification of thinking. On many occasions, committee members' initial views shift as they study the specifics of individual cases and listen to opposing arguments from their colleagues. What allows this committee to function as well as it does is the fundamental civility of its members and their collective concern that their decisions be just. Because of the importance of these decisions to students' lives, committee members are willing to concede a point to another member in the name of reaching a better decision and to view the deliberations as an ongoing process of negotiation rather than a series of win-lose debates.

To give you firsthand experience at using argument as a process of clarification, we conclude this chapter with an actual case that came before the University Standards Committee in the early 1990s when Ramage was a member of the committee. We invite you to read the following letter, pretending that you are a member of the University Standards Committee, and then proceed to the exercises that follow.

Petition to Waive the University Mathematics Requirement

Standards Committee Members,

I am a 43-year-old member of the Pawnee Tribe of Oklahoma and a very nontraditional student currently pursuing Justice Studies at the Arizona State University (ASU) College of Public Programs. I entered college as the first step toward completion of my goal— becoming legal counsel for my tribe, and statesman.

I come before this committee in good faith to request that ASU suspend, in my special case, its mathematics requirement for undergraduate degree completion so I may enter the ASU college of Law during Fall 1993. The point I wish to make to this committee is this: I do not need algebraic skills; I will never use algebra in my intended profession; and, if forced to comply with ASU's algebra requirement, I will be needlessly prevented from graduating in time to enter law school next fall and face an idle academic year before my next opportunity in 1994. I will address each of these points in turn, but a few words concerning my academic credentials are in order first.

Two years ago, I made a vow of moral commitment to seek out and confront injustice. In September of 1990, I enrolled in college. Although I had only the benefit of a ninth grade education, I took the General Equivalency Diploma (GED) examination and placed in the top ten percent of those, nationwide, who took the test. On the basis of this score

I was accepted into Scottsdale Community College (SCC). This step made me the first in my entire family, and practically in my tribe, to enter college. During my first year at SCC I maintained a 4.0 GPA, I was placed on the President's list twice, was active in the Honors Program, received the Honors Award of Merit in English Humanities, and was conferred an Honors Scholarship (see attached) for the Academic year of 1991–1992 which I declined, opting to enroll in ASU instead.

At the beginning of the 1991 summer semester, I transferred to ASU. I chose to graduate from ASU because of the courses offered in American Indian studies, an important field ignored by most other Universities but necessary to my commitment. At ASU I currently maintain a 3.6 GPA, although my cumulative GPA is closer to 3.9, I am a member of the Honors and Justice Colleges, was appointed to the Dean's List, and awarded ASU's prestigious Maroon and Gold Scholarship twice. My academic standing is impeccable. I will enter the ASU College of Law to study Indian and criminal law during the Fall of 1993—if this petition is approved. Upon successful completion of my juris doctorate I will return to Oklahoma to become active in the administration of Pawnee tribal affairs as tribal attorney and advisor, and vigorously prosecute our right to sovereignty before the Congress of the United States.

5   When I began my "college experience," I set a rigid time schedule for the completion of my goal. By the terms of that self-imposed schedule, founded in my belief that I have already wasted many productive years, I allowed myself thirty-five months in which to achieve my Bachelor of Science degree in Justice Studies, for indeed justice is my concern, and another thirty-six months in which to earn my juris doctorate—summa cum laude. Consistent with my approach to all endeavors, I fell upon this task with zeal. I have willingly assumed the burden of carrying substantial academic loads during fall, spring and summer semesters. My problem now lies in the fact that in order to satisfy the University's math requirement to graduate I must still take MAT-106 and MAT-117. I submit that these mathematics courses are irrelevant to my goals, and present a barrier to my fall matriculation into law school.

Upon consideration of my dilemma, the questions emerged: Why do I need college algebra (MAT-117)? Is college algebra necessary for studying American Indian law? Will I use college algebra in my chosen field? What will the University gain or lose, from my taking college algebra—or not? I decided I should resolve these questions.

I began my inquiry with the question: "Why do I need college algebra (MAT-117)?" I consulted Mr. Jim _____ of the Justice College and presented this question to him. He referred to the current ASU catalog and delineated the following answer: I need college algebra (1) for a minimum level of math competency in my chosen field, and (2) to satisfy the university math requirement in order to graduate. My reply to the first answer is this: I already possess ample math skills, both practical and academic; and, I have no need for algebra in my chosen field. How do I know this? During the spring 1992 semester at ASU I successfully completed introductory algebra (MAT-077), scoring the highest class grade on one test (see attached transcript and test). More noteworthy is the fact that I was a machine and welding contractor for fifteen years. I used geometry and algebra commonly in the design of many welded structures. I am proficient in the use of Computer Assisted Design (CAD) programs, designing and drawing all my own blueprints for jobs. My blueprints and designs are always approved by city planning departments. For example, my most recent job consisted of the manufacture, transportation and installation of one linear mile of anodized, aluminum handrailing at a luxury resort condo on Maui, Hawaii. I applied extensive use of math to calculate the amount of raw materials to order, the logistics of mass production and transportation for both men and materials from Mesa to Maui, the job site installation itself, and cash flow. I have successfully completed many jobs of this nature—all without a mathematical hitch. As to the application of math competency in my chosen field, I can guarantee this committee that there will not be a time in my practice of Indian law that I will need algebra. If an occasion ever occurs that I need algebra, I will hire a mathematician, just as I would an engineer if I need engineering, or a surgeon if I need an operation.

I then contacted Dr. _____ of the ASU Mathematics Department and presented him with the same question: "Why do I need college algebra?" He replied: (1) for a well rounded education; (2) to develop creative thinking; and (3) to satisfy the university math requirement in order to graduate. Responding to the first answer, I have a "well rounded education." My need is for a specific education in justice and American Indian law. In fact, I do not really need the degree to practice Indian law as representative of my tribe, just the knowledge. Regarding the second, I do not need to develop my creative thinking. It has been honed to a keen edge for many years. For example, as a steel contractor, I commonly create huge, beautiful and intricate structures from raw materials. Contracting is not my only experience in creative thinking. For twenty-five years I have also enjoyed the status of being one of this country's foremost designers and builders of racebikes. Machines I have designed and brought into existence from my imagination have topped some of Japan and Europe's best engineering efforts. To illustrate this point, in 1984 I rode a bike of my own design to an international victory over Honda, Suzuki, Laverda, BMW and Yamaha. I have excelled at creative thinking my entire life—I called it survival.

Expanding on the question of why I need college algebra, I contacted a few friends who are practicing attorneys. All responded to my question in similar manner. One, Mr. Billy _____, Esq., whose law firm is in Tempe, answered my two questions as follows: "When you attended law school, were there any courses you took which required algebra?" His response was "no." "Have you ever needed algebra during the many years of your practice?" Again, his response was "no." All agreed there was not a single occasion when they had need for algebra in their professional careers.

10   Just to make sure of my position, I contacted the ASU College of Law, and among others, spoke to Ms. Sierra _____. I submitted the question "What law school courses will I encounter in which I will need algebra?" The unanimous reply was, they knew of none.

I am not proposing that the number of credit hours I need for graduation be lowered. In fact, I am more than willing to substitute another course or two in its place. I am not trying to get out of anything hard or distasteful, for that is certainly not my style. I am seeking only to dispose of an unnecessary item in my studies, one which will prevent me from entering law school this fall—breaking my stride. So little holds up so much.

I agree that a young adult directly out of high school may not know that he needs algebraic skills. Understandably, he does not know what his future holds—but I am not that young adult. I claim the advantage. I know precisely what my future holds and that future holds no possibility of my needing college algebra.

Physically confronting injustice is my end. On reservations where government apathy allows rapacious pedophiles to pose as teachers; in a country where a million and a half American Indians are held hostage as second rate human beings whose despair results in a suicide, alcohol and drug abuse rate second to no other people; in prisons where helpless inmates are beaten like dogs by sadistic guards who should be the inmates—this is the realm of my chosen field—the disenfranchised. In this netherworld, algebra and justice exist independently of one another.

In summary, I am convinced that I do not need college algebra for a minimum level of math competency in my chosen field. I do not need college algebra for a well rounded education, nor to develop my creative thinking. I do not need algebra to take the LSAT. I do not need algebra for any courses in law school, nor will I for any purpose in the practice of American Indian law. It remains only that I need college algebra in order to graduate.

15   I promise this committee that ASU's integrity will not be compromised in any way by approving this waiver. Moreover, I assure this committee that despite not having a formal accreditation in algebra, I will prove to be nothing less than an asset to this University and its Indian community, both to which I belong, and I will continue to set a standard for integrity, excellence and perseverance for all who follow. Therefore, I ask this committee, for all the reasons described above, to approve and initiate the waiver of my University mathematics requirement.

[Signed] Gordon Adams

■ ■ ■ **FOR CLASS DISCUSSION**   **Responding to Adam's Argument**

1. Before class discussion, decide how you would vote on this issue. Should this student be exempted from the math requirement? Write out the reasons for your decision.
2. Working in small groups or as a whole class, pretend that you are the University Standards Committee, and arrive at a group decision on whether to exempt this student from the math requirement.
3. After the discussion, write for five to ten minutes in a journal or notebook describing how your thinking evolved during the discussion. Did any of your classmates' views cause you to rethink your own? Class members should share with each other their descriptions of how the process of argument led to clarification of their own thinking.

We designed this exercise to help you experience argument as a clarifying process. But we had another purpose. We also designed the exercise to stimulate thinking about a problem we introduced at the beginning of this chapter: the difference between argument as clarification and argument as persuasion. Is a good argument necessarily a persuasive argument? In our opinion, this student's letter to the committee is a *good* argument. The student writes well, takes a clear stand, offers good reasons for his position, and supports his reasons with effective evidence. To what extent, however, is the letter a *persuasive* argument? Did it win its case? You know how you and your classmates stand on this issue. But what do you think the University Standards Committee at ASU actually decided during its deliberations?

We will return to this case again in Chapter 4.

Conclusion

In this chapter we have explored some of the complexities of argument, showing you why we believe that argument is a matter not of fist banging or of win-lose debate but of finding, through a process of rational inquiry, the best solution to a problem or issue. What is our advice for you at the close of this introductory chapter? Briefly, to see the purpose of argument as truth seeking as well as persuasion. We suggest that throughout the process of argument you seek out a wide range of views, that you especially welcome views different from your own, that you treat these views respectfully, and that you see them as intelligent and rationally defensible. (Hence you must look carefully at the reasons and evidence on which they are based.)

Our goal in this text is to help you learn skills of argument. If you choose, you can use these skills, like the Sophists, to argue any side of any issue. Yet we hope you won't. We hope that, like Socrates, you will use argument for truth seeking and that you will consequently find yourselves, on at least some occasions, changing your position on an issue while writing a rough draft (a sure sign that the process of arguing has complicated your views). We believe that the skills of reason and inquiry developed through the writing of arguments can help you get a clearer sense of who you are. If our culture sets you adrift in pluralism, argument can help you take a stand, to say, "These things I believe." In this text we will not pretend to tell you what position to take on any given issue. But as a responsible being, you will often need to take a stand, to define yourself, to say, "Here are the reasons that choice A is better than choice B, not just for me but for you also." If this text helps you base your commitments and actions on reasonable grounds, then it will have been successful.

For additional writing, reading, and research resources, go to www.mycomplab.com

2 Argument as Inquiry
Reading and Exploring

In the previous chapter we explained that argument is both a process and a product, both inquiry and persuasion. In this chapter, we focus on inquiry as the entry point into argumentative conversations. Although our social environment is rich with these conversations—think of the oral, visual, print, and hypertext arguments that surround us—argument in the early twenty-first century is often degraded into talk-show shouting matches or antagonistic sound bites and "talking points." This reductive trend has elicited the concern of many cultural critics, journalists, rhetoricians, scholars, and citizens. Journalist Matt Miller recently posed the questions, "Is it possible in America today to convince anyone of anything he doesn't already believe?...[A]re there enough places where this mingling of minds occurs to sustain a democracy?"* How can argument's role as a community's search for the best answers to disputed questions be emphasized? How can arguers participate in a "mingling of minds" and use argument productively to seek answers to problems?

We believe that the best way to reinvigorate argument is to approach the reading and writing of arguments as an exploratory process. To do so means to position ourselves as inquirers as well as persuaders, engaging thoughtfully with alternative points of view, truly listening to other perspectives, examining our own values and assumptions, and perhaps even changing our views. Rhetorician Wayne Booth proposes that when we enter an argumentative conversation we should first ask, "When should I change my mind?" rather than, "How can I change your mind?"†

In this chapter, we present some practical strategies for reading and exploring arguments in an open-minded and sophisticated way. You will learn to play what rhetorician Peter Elbow calls the believing and doubting game, in which a thinker systematically stretches her thinking by willing herself to believe positions that she finds threatening and to doubt positions that she instinctively

---

*Matt Miller, "Is Persuasion Dead?" *New York Times* 4 June 2005, A29.
†Wayne Booth raised these questions in a featured session with Peter Elbow titled "Blind Skepticism vs. the Rhetoric of Assent: Implications for Rhetoric, Argument, and Teaching" presented at the CCCC annual convention, Chicago, Illinois, March 2002.

accepts.* The thinker's goal is to live with questions, to acknowledge uncertainty and complexity, and to resist settling for simple or quick answers. In this chapter, we propose the following main exploratory strategies:

- Using a variety of means to find complex, puzzling issues to explore
- Placing a text in its rhetorical context
- Reading to believe an argument's claims
- Reading to doubt an argument's claims
- Thinking dialectically

Although we present these strategies separately here, as you become familiar with them you will use them automatically and often implement several at once. In this chapter, we show how one student, Michael Banks, jumped into the puzzling, complex problem of illegal immigration and used these strategies to guide his thoughtful exploration of various viewpoints and texts.

Finding Issues to Explore

The mechanisms by which you enter a controversy will vary, but most likely they will include reflecting on your experiences or reading. Typically, the process goes like this: Through reading or talking with friends, you encounter a contested issue on which you are undecided or a viewpoint with which you disagree. Your curiosity, confusion, or concern then prompts you to learn more about the issue and to determine your own stance. In this section we examine some strategies you can use to find issues worth exploring.

Do Some Initial Brainstorming

As a first step, make an inventory of issues that interest you. Many of the ideas you develop may become subject matter for arguments that you will write later in this course. The chart on page 26 will help you generate a productive list.

Once you've made a list, add to it as new ideas strike you and return to it each time you are given a new argumentative assignment.

Be Open to the Issues All around You

We are surrounded by argumentative issues. You'll start noticing them everywhere once you get attuned to them. You will be invited into argumentative conversations by posters, bumper stickers, blog sites, newspaper editorial pages, magazine articles, the sports section, movie reviews, song lyrics, and so forth. When you read or listen, watch for "hot spots"—passages or moments that evoke strong agreement, disagreement, or confusion. As an illustration of how arguments are all around us, try the following exercise on the issue of illegal immigration.

---

*Peter Elbow, *Writing without Teachers* (New York: Oxford University Press, 1973), 147–90.

Brainstorming Issues to Explore

What You Can Do	How It Works
Make an inventory of the communities to which you belong. Consider classroom communities; clubs and organizations; residence hall, apartment, neighborhood, or family communities; church/synagogue or work communities; communities related to your hobbies or avocations; your city, state, region, nation, and world communities.	Because arguments arise out of disagreements within communities, you can often think of issues for argument by beginning with a list of the communities to which you belong.
Identify controversies within those communities. Think both big and small: ■ Big issue in world community: What is the best way to prevent destruction of rain forests? ■ Small issue in residence hall community: Should quiet hours be enforced?	To stimulate thinking, use prompts such as these: ■ People in this community frequently disagree about _____ . ■ Within my work community, Person X believes _____ ; however, this view troubles me because _____ . ■ In a recent residence hall meeting, I didn't know where I stood on _____ . ■ The situation at _____ could be improved if _____ .
Narrow your list to a handful of problematic issues for which you don't have a position; share it with classmates. Identify a few issues that you would like to explore more deeply. When you share with classmates, add their issues to yours.	Sharing your list with classmates stimulates more thinking and encourages conversations. The more you explore your views with others, the more ideas you will develop. Good writing grows out of good talking.
Brainstorm a network of related issues. Any given issue is always embedded in a network of other issues. To see how open-ended and fluid an argumentative conversation can be, try connecting one of your issues to a network of other issues including subissues and side issues.	Brainstorm questions that compel you to look at an issue in a variety of ways. For example, if you explored the controversy over whether toys with phthalates should be banned (see Chapter 1), you might generate questions such as these about related issues: ■ How dangerous are phthalates? ■ Is the testing that has been done on rats adequate or accurate for determining the effects on humans? ■ Is the European "precautionary principle" a good principle for the United States to follow? ■ To what extent are controversies over phthalates similar to controversies over steroids, genetically modified foods, nitrites in cured meat, or mercury in dental fillings?

■ ■ ■ **FOR CLASS DISCUSSION** Responding to Visual Arguments about Immigration

Suppose, in your casual reading, you encounter some photos and political cartoons on the U.S. problems with illegal immigration (see Figures 2.1–2.4). Working individually or in small groups, generate exploratory responses to these questions:

1. What claim is each cartoon or photo making?
2. What background information about the problems of illegal immigration do these cartoons and photos assume?
3. What network of issues do these visual texts suggest?
4. What puzzling questions do these visual texts raise for you?

FIGURE 2.1 Protest photo

FIGURE 2.2 Protest photo

FIGURE 2.3 Political cartoon on immigration and labor

FIGURE 2.4 Political cartoon on immigrant labor

Explore Ideas by Freewriting

Freewriting is useful at any stage of the writing process. When you freewrite, you put fingers to keyboard (or pen to paper) and write rapidly *nonstop,* usually five to ten minutes at a stretch, without worrying about structure, grammar, or correctness. Your goal is to generate as many ideas as possible without stopping to edit your work. If you can't think of anything to say, write "relax" or "I'm stuck" over and over until new ideas emerge. Here is how Michael Banks did a freewrite in response to the cartoon in Figure 2.3.

Michael's Freewrite

At first when I looked at this cartoon I didn't quite see what it meant. I understood the wall keeping immigrants out, but I didn't connect the $20 minimum wage to the wall. OK. Now I see. The argument is that if the United States raised the minimum wage to $20/hour, then Americans would be willing to do the job that Mexicans now do much cheaper. But that seems to really sidestep the entire issue surrounding immigrant labor—sure, there'd be a lot more Americans willing to work harder if they were earning $20 an hour and getting benefits, but it isn't as if there are a bunch of contractors out there who'd rather pay that than hire an immigrant worker, under the table, for much cheaper. The problem isn't finding someone to work, it's finding someone to work for substandard wages who's still motivated to work hard and for long hours. Hmmm. Relax relax relax relax. I'm really puzzled by the immigration question. I can remember growing up in Southern California that a lot of the low pay work was done by Mexicans. I was in a high school service group that took free lunches to immigrants waiting for work in front of a Home Depot. They would take any kind of job at really low pay, and they seemed like really nice people. Why won't our homeless people or unemployed people in the United States take these low pay jobs? Relax relax. I don't really know whether I agree with the cartoon that it would be best to force immigrants out of the country, but I'm fairly certain that raising the minimum wage for legal workers to $20.00 isn't the way to go about it because that would drive up the price of goods so much nobody could afford to buy anything and the economy would come to a halt. Immigrants are willing to work, hard, for much less than the proposal in the cartoon. They benefit by making more money than they could make in Mexico and Americans benefit by lower prices. Also, the image of the wall raises concerns of mine—I'm aware of organizations like the Border Fence Project that are all about walling off the entire southern border of the country, but it seems like a really ineffective way to enforce the border. I wonder whose "crazy fantasy" this cartoon really depicts.

Explore Ideas by Idea Mapping

Another good technique for exploring ideas is *idea mapping.* When you make an idea map, draw a circle in the center of the page and write some trigger idea (a broad topic, a question, or working thesis statement) in the center of the circle. Then record your ideas on branches and subbranches extending from the center circle. As long as you pursue one train of thought, keep recording your ideas on the branch. But when that line of thinking gives out, start a new branch. Often your thoughts jump back and forth between branches. That's a major advantage of "picturing" your thoughts; you can see them as part of an emerging design rather than as strings of unrelated ideas.

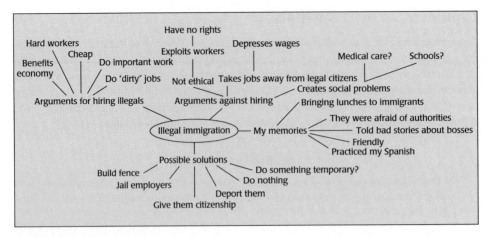

FIGURE 2.5 Michael's idea map

Idea maps usually generate more ideas, though less well-developed ones, than freewrites. Figure 2.5 shows an idea map that student Michael Banks created on the issue of illegal immigration after class discussion of the photographs and cartoons in Figures 2.1–2.4.

Explore Ideas by Playing the Believing and Doubting Game

The believing and doubting game, a term coined by rhetorician Peter Elbow, is an excellent way to imagine views different from your own and to anticipate responses to those views.

- **As a believer, your role is to be wholly sympathetic to an idea.** You must listen carefully to the idea and suspend all disbelief. You must identify all the ways in which the idea may appeal to different audiences and all the reasons for believing the idea. The believing game can be difficult, even frightening, if you are asked to believe an idea that strikes you as false or threatening.
- **As a doubter, your role is to be judgmental and critical, finding fault with an idea.** The doubting game is the opposite of the believing game. You do your best to find counterexamples and inconsistencies that undermine the idea you are examining Again, it is can be threatening to doubt ideas that you instinctively want to believe.

When you play the believing and doubting game with an assertion, simply write two different chunks, one chunk arguing for the assertion (the believing game) and one chunk opposing it (the doubting game). Freewrite both chunks, letting your ideas flow without censoring. Or, alternatively, make an idea map with believing and doubting branches. Here is how student writer Michael Banks played the believing and doubting game with an assertion about stopping illegal immigration. "Employers of illegal immigrants should be jailed."

Michael's Believing and Doubting Game

Believe: If we really want to stop illegal immigration, then we should jail employers who hire illegals. What draws illegal immigrants to this country is the money they can make, so if the government eliminated these jobs by jailing the employers then illegal immigration would stop. This would be just because employers of illegal immigrants benefit by not having to pay a fair wage and what's more they often do this hiring under the table so that they don't pay taxes. They are breaking laws and deserve to go to jail. By avoiding taxes and not providing medical insurance etc., they cost every American taxpayer more, and it is not fair to law abiding citizens. Employers also often exploit immigrant laborers, because they have nobody to be held accountable to. They also lower the wages of American workers. Their actions can cause rifts in communities already troubled by an influx of immigration. Like anybody else who supports illegal activity, employers of illegal immigration should be jailed. If employers faced charges for hiring illegal immigrants, it seems likely that there would be much less of a market for the services of immigrant workers. I could see this being a more effective way to combat illegal immigration than building fences or trying to deport them all.

 Doubt: Jailing employers of illegal immigration probably would stop some people from hiring undocumented immigrants, but I doubt it would be a reliable long-term solution. Especially for people who only hire a few immigrants at a time, it would likely be hard to prosecute them. Besides, I'm not convinced there is anything necessarily wrong with the employer's actions in hiring undocumented immigrants. If the government cannot enforce its own immigration laws, employers shouldn't be forced to do so for them. Many businesses, especially in agriculture, absolutely depend on good workers who will work long hours in hot fields to pick fruit and vegetables. Employers can't possibly be expected to do background checks on every employee. Moreover, if undocumented workers weren't available, the fruit wouldn't get picked. To send the employers to jail would mean to cause horrible disruption to much of our food supply. We are lucky to have these workers. The United States has a long history of people capitalizing on good business opportunities when the opportunity presents itself, and that's just what illegal immigrants are. It does not make sense to jail people for taking advantage of cheap and motivated labor.

Although Michael sees the injustice of paying workers substandard wages, he sees that much of our economy depends on this cheap labor. Playing the believing and doubting game has helped him articulate his dilemma and see the issue in more complex terms.

■ ■ ■ **FOR CLASS DISCUSSION** Playing the Believing and Doubting Game
Individual task: Choose one or more of the following controversial claims and play the believing and doubting game with it, through either freewriting or idea mapping.
Group task: Working in pairs, in small groups, or as a whole class, share your results with classmates.

1. A student should report a fellow student who is cheating on an exam or plagiarizing an essay.
2. Women should be assigned to combat duty equally with men.
3. Athletes should be allowed to take steroids and human growth hormone under a doctor's supervision.
4. Illegal immigrants already living in the United States should be granted amnesty and placed on a fast track to U.S. citizenship.

Placing Texts in a Rhetorical Context

In the previous section, we suggested strategies for finding issues and entering argumentative conversations. Once you join a conversation, you will typically read a number of different arguments addressing your selected issue. The texts you read may be supplied for you in a textbook, anthology, or course pack, or you may find them yourself through library or Internet research. In this section and the ones that follow, we turn to productive strategies for reading arguments. We begin by explaining the importance of analyzing a text's rhetorical context as a preliminary step prior to reading. In subsequent sections, we explain powerful strategies for reading an argument—reading to believe, reading to doubt, and placing texts in conversation with each other through dialectic thinking.

As you read arguments on a controversy, try to place each text within its rhetorical context. It is important to know, for example, whether a blog that you are reading appears on Daily Kos (a liberal blog site) or on Little Green Footballs (a conservative blog site). In researching an issue, you may find that one article is a formal policy proposal archived on the Web site of an economics research institute, whereas another is an op-ed piece by a nationally syndicated columnist or a letter to the editor written by someone living in your community. To help you reconstruct a reading's rhetorical context, you need to understand the genres of argument as well as the cultural and professional contexts that cause people to write arguments. We'll begin with the genres of argument.

Genres of Argument

To situate an argument rhetorically, you should know something about its genre. A *genre* is a recurring type or pattern of argument such as a letter to the editor, a political cartoon, or the home page of an advocacy Web site. Genres are often categorized by recurring features, formats, and style. The genre of any given argument helps determine its length, tone, sentence complexity, level of informality or formality, use of visuals, kinds of evidence, depth of research, and the presence or absence of documentation.

When you read arguments reprinted in a textbook such as this one, you lose clues about the argument's original genre. (You should therefore note the information about genre provided in our introductions to readings.) Likewise, you can lose clues about genre when you download articles from the Internet or from licensed databases such as LexisNexis or ProQuest. (See Chapter 16 for explanations of these research tools.) When you do your own research, you therefore need to be aware of the original genre of the text you are reading: was this piece originally a newspaper editorial, a blog, an organizational white paper, a scholarly article, a student paper posted to a Web site, or something else?

In the chart on pages 33–35, we identify most of the genres of argument through which readers and writers carry on the conversations of a democracy.

Cultural Contexts: Who Writes Arguments and Why?

A democratic society depends on the lively exchange of ideas—people with different points of view creating arguments for their positions. Now that you know something about the genre of arguments, we ask you to consider who writes arguments and why.

Genres of Argument

Genre	Explanation and Examples	Stylistic Features
Personal correspondence	▪ Letters or e-mail messages ▪ Often sent to specific decision makers (complaint letter, request for an action)	▪ Style can range from a formal business letter to an informal note
Letters to the editor	▪ Published in newspapers and some magazines ▪ Provide a forum for citizens to voice views on public issues	▪ Very short (fewer than three hundred words) and time sensitive ▪ Can be summaries of longer arguments, but often focus in "sound bite" style on one point
Newspaper editorials and op-ed pieces	▪ Published on the editorial or op-ed ("opposite-editorial") pages ▪ Editorials promote views of the newspaper owners/editors ▪ Op-ed pieces, usually written by professional columnists or guest writers, range in bias from ultraconservative to socialist (see page 362 in Chapter 16) ▪ Often written in response to political events or social problems in the news	▪ Usually short (500–1,000 words) ▪ Vary from explicit thesis-driven arguments to implicit arguments with stylistic flair ▪ Have a journalistic style (short paragraphs) without detailed evidence ▪ Sources usually not documented
Articles in public affairs or niche magazines	▪ Usually written by staff writers or freelancers ▪ Appear in public affairs magazines such as *National Review* or *The Progressive* or in niche magazines for special-interest groups such as *Rolling Stone* (popular culture), *Minority Business Entrepreneur* (business), or *The Advocate* (gay and lesbian issues) ▪ Often reflect the political point of view of the magazine	▪ Often have a journalistic style with informal documentation ▪ Frequently include narrative elements rather than explicit thesis-and-reasons organization ▪ Often provide well-researched coverage of various perspectives on a public issue
Articles in scholarly journals	▪ Peer-reviewed articles published by nonprofit academic journals subsidized by universities or scholarly societies ▪ Characterized by scrupulous attention to completeness and accuracy in treatment of data	▪ Usually employ a formal academic style ▪ Include academic documentation and bibliographies ▪ May reflect the biases, methods, and strategies associated with a specific school of thought or theory within a discipline.

(Continued)

Genre	Explanation and Examples	Stylistic Features
Legal briefs and court decisions	▪ Written by attorneys or judges ▪ "Friend-of-the-court" briefs are often published by stakeholders to influence appeals courts ▪ Court decisions explain the reasoning of justices on civic cases (and often include minority opinions)	▪ Usually written in legalese, but use a logical reasons-and-evidence structure ▪ Friend-of-the-court briefs are sometimes aimed at popular audiences
Organizational white papers	▪ In-house documents or PowerPoint presentations aimed at influencing organizational policy or decisions or to give informed advice to clients ▪ Sometimes written for external audiences to influence public opinion favorable to the organization ▪ External white papers are often posted on Web sites or sent to legislators	▪ Usually desktop or Web published ▪ Often include graphics and other visuals ▪ Vary in style from the dully bureaucratic (satirized in *Dilbert* cartoons) to the cogent and persuasive
Blogs and postings to chat rooms and electronic bulletin boards	▪ Web-published commentaries, usually on specific topics and often intended to influence public opinion ▪ Blogs (web logs) are gaining influence as alternative commentaries to the established media ▪ Reflect a wide range of perspectives	▪ Often blend styles of journalism, personal narrative, and formal argument ▪ Often difficult to determine identity and credentials of blogger ▪ Often provide hyperlinks to related sites on the Web
Public affairs advocacy advertisements	▪ Published as posters, fliers, Web pages, or paid advertisements ▪ Condensed verbal/visual arguments aimed at influencing public opinion ▪ Often have explicit bias and ignore alternative views	▪ Use succinct "sound bite" style ▪ Employ document design, bulleted lists, and visual elements (graphics, photographs, or drawings) for rhetorical effect
Advocacy Web sites	▪ Usually identified by the extension ".org" in the Web site address ▪ Often created by well-financed advocacy groups such as the NRA (National Rifle Association) or PETA (People for the Ethical Treatment of Animals) ▪ Reflect the bias of the site owner ▪ For further discussion of reading and evaluating Web sites, see Chapter 16, pages 363–367	▪ Often contain many layers with hyperlinks to other sites ▪ Use visuals and verbal text to create an immediate visceral response favorable to the site owner's views ▪ Ethically responsible sites announce their bias and purpose in an "About Us" or "Mission Statement" link on the home page

Genre	Explanation and Examples	Stylistic Features
Visual arguments	■ Political cartoons, usually drawn by syndicated cartoonists ■ Other visual arguments (photographs, drawings, graphics, ads), usually accompanied by verbal text	■ Make strong emotional appeals, often reducing complex issues to one powerful perspective (see Chapter 9).
Speeches and PowerPoint presentations	■ Political speeches, keynote speeches at professional meetings, informal speeches at hearings, interviews, business presentations ■ Often made available via transcription in newspapers or on Web sites ■ In business or government settings, often accompanied by PowerPoint slides	■ Usually organized clearly with highlighted claim, supporting reasons, and transitions ■ Accompanying PowerPoint slides designed to highlight structure, display evidence in graphics, mark key points, and sometimes provide humor
Documentary films	■ Formerly nonfiction reporting, documentary films now range widely from efforts to document reality objectively to efforts to persuade viewers to adopt the filmmaker's perspective or take action ■ Usually cost less to produce than commercial films and lack special effects ■ Cover topics such as art, science, and economic, political, and military crises	■ Often use extended visual arguments, combined with interviews and voice-overs, to influence as well as inform viewers ■ The filmmaker's angle of vision may dominate, or his or her perspective and values may be more subtle.

In reconstructing the rhetorical context of an argument, consider how any given writer is spurred to write by a motivating occasion and by the desire to change the views of a particular audience. In this section, we'll return to our example of illegal immigration. The following list identifies the wide range of writers, cartoonists, filmmakers, and others who are motivated to enter the conversation about immigration.

Who Writes Arguments about Immigration and Why?

■ *Lobbyists and advocacy groups.* Lobbyists and advocacy groups commit themselves to a cause, often with passion, and produce avidly partisan arguments aimed at persuading voters, legislators, government agencies, and other decision makers. They often maintain advocacy Web sites, buy advertising space in newspapers and magazines, and lobby legislators face to face. For example, the immigrant advocacy group La Raza defends immigrant rights, whereas the Federation for American Immigration Reform (FAIR) fights to end illegal immigration and rallies people to pressure businesses not to hire undocumented workers.

- *Legislators, political candidates, and government officials.* Whenever new laws, regulations, or government policies are proposed, staffers do research and write white papers recommending positions on an issue. Often these are available on the Web. On the perplexing problem of illegal immigration, numerous staff researchers for legislators, political candidates, and government officials have produced white papers on the practicality of extending a wall along the U.S.- Mexican border, of beefing up border patrol to increase national security, and of offering temporary guest worker visas to immigrant laborers.

- *Business professionals, labor union leaders, and bankers.* Business spokespeople often try to influence public opinion in ways that support corporate or business interests, whereas labor union officials support wage structures favorable to union members. Typically businesspeople produce "corporate image" advertisements, send white papers to legislators, or write op-ed pieces that frame issues from a business perspective, whereas labor unions produce arguments favorable to workers. Professionals that could profit from undocumented labor (fruit growers, winemakers, landscapers, construction companies, and so forth) or could be harmed by it (labor unions) are active participants in the public controversy.

- *Lawyers and judges.* Immigration issues are frequently entangled in legal matters. Lawyers write briefs supporting their clients' cases. Sometimes lawyers or legal experts not directly connected to a case, particularly law professors, file "friend-of-the-court" briefs aimed at influencing the decision of judges. Finally, judges write court opinions explaining their decisions on a case. As more illegal immigrants are deported and others die trying to cross the border, more legal professionals are writing about these cases.

- *Media commentators.* Whenever immigration issues are in the news, media commentators (journalists, editorial writers, syndicated columnists, bloggers, political cartoonists) write articles and blogs or op-ed pieces on the issue or produce editorial cartoons, filtering their arguments through the perspective of their own political views. For example, conservative commentator Lou Dobbs is known for his strong stand on keeping illegal immigrants out of the country.

- *Professional freelance or staff writers.* Some of the most thoughtful analyses of public issues are composed by freelance or staff writers for public forum magazines such as *Atlantic Monthly, The Nation, Ms., The National Review, The New Yorker,* and many others. Arguments about immigration policy reform and immigrants' integration into American society surface whenever the the topic seems timely to magazine editors.

- *Think tanks.* Because today many political, economic, and social issues are very complex, policy makers and commentators often rely on research institutions or think tanks to supply statistical studies and in-depth investigation of problems. These think tanks range across the political spectrum, from conservative (the Hoover Institute, the Heritage Foundation) or libertarian (the Cato Institute) to the centrist or liberal (the Brookings Institution, the Pew Foundation, the Economic Policy Institute). They usually maintain many-layered Web sites that include background on research writers, recent publications, and archives of past publications, including policy statements and white papers. Recently the conservative Center for

Immigration Studies published articles on the cost of legal and illegal immigration to Americans; the Center for American Progress, a liberal think tank, outlined the important features for a reform of the U.S. immigration system.

■ *Scholars and academics.* College professors play a public role through their scholarly research, contributing data, studies, and analyses to public debates. Scholarly research differs substantially from advocacy argument in its systematic attempt to arrive at the best answers to questions based on the full examination of relevant data. Much scholarship investigates the patterns of immigrant participation in American political life, the relationship between crime and immigration, possibilities of worker solidarity, and the cost of products and services if the United States were to raise the minimum wage substantially. Scholarly research is usually published in refereed academic journals rather than popular magazines.

■ *Independent and commercial filmmakers.* Testifying to the growing popularity of film and its power to involve people in issues, documentary filmmakers often reflect on issues of the day, and commercial filmmakers often embed arguments within their dramatic storytelling. The global film industry is adding international perspectives as well. Many recent documentary and dramatic films present the experiences of immigrants and undocumented workers and their struggle to fit into American society while preserving their cultural roots. For instance, the documentary film *Farmingville*, shown on PBS, follows the antagonism among immigrant day laborers, homeowners, and other residents of the town of Farmingville on Long Island, New York, and depicts the town debating the practicality of establishing a hiring site to remove day laborers from the streets.

■ *Citizens and students.* Engaged citizens influence social policy through letters, contributions to advocacy Web sites, guest editorials for newspapers, blogs, and speeches in public forums. Students also write for university communities, present their work at undergraduate research conferences, and influence public opinion by writing to political leaders and decision makers. For example, students involved in a service learning project tutoring children of immigrant laborers might write to spread their knowledge of immigrants' educational needs.

Analyzing Rhetorical Context and Genre

The background we have just provided about the writers and genres of argument will help you situate arguments in their rhetorical context. When you encounter any argumentative text, whether reprinted in a textbook or retrieved through your own library and Web research, use the following guide questions to analyze its rhetorical context:

Questions about Rhetorical Context and Genre

1. What genre of argument is this? How do the conventions of that genre help determine the depth, complexity, and even appearance of the argument?
2. Who is the author? What are the author's credentials and what is his or her investment in the issue?
3. What audience is he or she writing for?

4. What motivating occasion prompted the writing? The motivating occasion could be a current event, a crisis, pending legislation, a recently published alternative view, or another ongoing problem.

5. What is the author's purpose? The purpose could range from strong advocacy to inquiring truth seeker (analogous to the continuum from persuasion to truth seeking discussed in Chapter 1, pages 13–15).

6. What information about the publication or source (magazine, newspaper, advocacy Web site) helps explain the writer's perspective or the structure and style of the argument?

7. What is the writer's angle of vision? By angle of vision, we mean the filter, lens, or selective seeing through which the writer is approaching the issue. What is left out in this argument? What does this author not see? (Chapter 5, pages 94–96, discusses how angle of vision operates in the selection and framing of evidence.)

This rhetorical knowledge becomes important in helping you select a diversity of voices and genres of argument when you are exploring an issue. Note how Michael Banks makes use of his awareness of rhetorical context in his exploratory paper on pages 52–57.

■ ■ ■ **FOR CLASS DISCUSSION** Placing Readings in Their Rhetorical Context

Find two recent arguments on the illegal immigration issue.* Your arguments should (1) represent different genres and (2) represent different kinds of arguers (syndicated newspaper columnists, bloggers, freelance magazine writers, scholars, and so forth). You can find your arguments in any of these places:

- In magazines: news commentary/public affairs magazines or niche magazines
- On the Web: on Web sites for think tanks, advocacy organizations, or blogs
- In newspapers: local, regional, or national

For each argument, answer the "Questions about Rhetorical Context and Genre" on pages 37–38. Then share your findings with classmates. ■ ■ ■

Reading to Believe an Argument's Claims

Once you have established the rhetorical context of an argument, you are ready to begin reading. We suggest that you read arguments in the spirit of the believing and doubting game, beginning with "believing," in which you practice what psychologist Carl Rogers calls *empathic listening*. Empathic listening requires that you see the world through the author's eyes, temporarily adopt the author's beliefs and values, and suspend your skepticism and biases long enough to hear what the author is saying.

To illustrate what we mean by reading to believe, we will continue with our example of illegal immigration. As you may have discovered through prior experience, reading, and examining the cartoons and photos at the beginning of this chapter, this issue

---

*For help on how to find articles through Web or licensed database searches, see Chapter 16.

includes many related issues: Why do millions of foreigners risk their lives to come illegally to the United States? How can the United States reduce the number of illegal immigrants? What should the United States do about the people currently living in the United States illegally? Does the U.S. economy need the workforce represented by these undocumented workers? The following article, "Amnesty?" by Roman Catholic priest and professor of philosophy John F. Kavanaugh, appeared in the March 10, 2008, issue of *America*, a Jesuit publication that describes itself as "the only national Catholic weekly magazine in the United States." Please read this article carefully in preparation for the exercises and examples that follow.

Amnesty?
Let Us Be Vigilant and Charitable
JOHN F. KAVANAUGH

Let's call her María. She was illegally brought into the United States at the age of 2. Now 27, she is a vital member of her parish and has three young children. María was recently deported to Ciudad Juárez, where, in the last 15 years, 600 young women have been kidnapped, raped, murdered and buried in the desert. Luckily, she was able to find a way into the United States, again illegally, to be with her children. If she is discovered again, she will spend five years in a U.S. federal prison.

My Jesuit friend and neighbor, Dick Vogt, has told me of people like María and many others of the 12 to 14 million "undocumented aliens." She is not necessarily typical of the masses who have illegally entered this country. Some, no doubt, are drunks and dealers; many are incarcerated for other crimes than their immigrant status. But most have come at great risk to their lives, because their lives were already at risk from poverty and displacement. They want to make a living, form a family, and help their families back home.

The Catholic bishops of Mexico pointed out in January that the recent surge of immigration is a direct effect of the North American Free Trade Agreement. Open trade, while benefiting the most powerful and technologically advanced, has threatened poor farmers and their small rural communities. They cannot compete with heavily subsidized U.S. and Canadian producers. It is this phenomenon that drives so many to leave their homeland for a livelihood in the United States, despite, as the bishops put it, "its anti-humane immigration program."

The U.S. bishops, witnessing everything from evictions in California to employment raids in Massachusetts, have stirred the consciences of their dioceses and taken stands in conscience of their own. The bishop of Oklahoma City and 10 of his pastors have publicly professed defiance of a punitive state law that makes felons of all who "aid, assist, or transport any undocumented person." The bishops of Missouri have expressed their alarm over politicians "who vie to see who can be tougher on illegal immigrants." Cognizant of the economic pressures on many families in rural Mexico, they call for a more compassionate, fair, and realistic reform of our immigration system, including education and humanitarian assistance to all children, "without regard to legal status."

5   There has been some resistance to the bishops' proposals and some resentment. It is reminiscent of the outrage directed by anti-immigrant groups toward last year's immigration reform bill, a very harsh measure that they nonetheless condemned for proposing what they called amnesty.

Some of the resentment is understandable. There are householders, especially on the border, who have had their land and yards trashed. Residents of some towns feel flooded with immigrants they cannot engage or manage. A few businesspersons who have refused to hire undocumented or cheaper labor have lost sales and customers.

But this does not explain the seething hostility that can be read in some nativist opinion columns and popular books or heard on radio talk shows: "They are criminals, felons; and that's that."

"They have broken the law." This is an interesting standard of ethics, justice or charity for a nation that sees itself as Judeo-Christian and humane. It is puzzling that we do not think of the Good Samaritan or of the "least of our brothers and sisters" in Matthew 25, or of the passage from Leviticus that the Missouri bishops quote: "The stranger who sojourns with you shall be to you as the native among you, and you shall love him as yourself."

As for making the law our bottom line, do Christians know how many times Jesus was in trouble with the law? Do they know that the natural law tradition, articulated in the work of Thomas Aquinas, holds an unjust law to be no law at all? Do they forget that our nation was founded upon an appeal to a higher law than positive law, an appeal shared by the labor movement, by Martin Luther King Jr., and by Elizabeth Cady Stanton and Susan B. Anthony?

10   A nation has every right to secure its borders. Unrestrained immigration will hurt our country, the immigrants, and their homeland. So let us indeed protect our borders (even though that will not solve the problem of those who enter legally and overstay their visa). Let us also honestly face the multiple cause of illegal immigration. As an excellent position paper from the Center for Concern notes, illegal immigration involves many factors: trade negotiation, the governments involved, the immigrants who break the law by entering our country, employers who take advantage of them, corporate leaders who profit from them, and consumers who benefit from lower food and service costs.

We must devise ways to offer legal status to anyone who contributes to our common good, whether as a future citizen or a temporary guest worker. If that means using the dirty word "amnesty," so be it.

As to those who sojourn in our midst, let us be vigilant if they are threats and charitable if they are friends. It would be a good, if unusual, move if our legislators had the imagination to call for citizen panels before which an illegal immigrant could request amnesty, leniency, and a path to citizenship based on his or her contribution to the community, solid employment record, faithful payment of taxes, family need, and crime-free record.

Instead of fearing some abstract horde of millions, we might see the faces of people like María and hear their stories. If we turn them away, we will have to face the fact that we are not so much a nation of Judeo-Christian values as a punitive and self-interested people hiding under the protection of lesser, human-made laws.

Summary Writing as a Way of Reading to Believe

One way to show that you have listened well to an article is to summarize its argument in your own words. A summary (also called an *abstract,* a *précis,* or a *synopsis)* presents only a text's major points and eliminates supporting details. Writers often incorporate summaries of other writer's views into their own arguments, either to support their own views or to represent alternative views that they intend to oppose. (When opposing someone else's argument, writers often follow the template "Although X contends that [summary of X's argument], I argue that _____."), Summaries can be any length, depending on the writer's purpose, but usually they range from several sentences to one or two paragraphs. To maintain your own credibility, your summary should be as neutral and fair to that piece as possible.

To help you write an effective summary, we recommend the following steps:

Step 1: *Read the argument for general meaning.* Don't judge it. Put your objections aside; just follow the writer's meaning, trying to see the issue from the writer's perspective. Try to adopt the writer's values and belief system. Walk in the writer's shoes.

Step 2: *Reread the article slowly, writing brief* does *and* says *statements for each paragraph (or group of closely connected paragraphs).* A *does* statement identifies a paragraph's function, such as "summarizes an opposing view," "introduces a supporting reason," "gives an example," or "uses statistics to support the previous point." A *says* statement summarizes a paragraph's content. Your challenge in writing *says* statements is to identify the main idea in each paragraph and translate that idea into your own words, most likely condensing it at the same time. This process may be easier with an academic article that uses long developed paragraphs headed by clear topic sentences than it is for more informal journalistic articles such as Kavanaugh's that use shorter, less developed paragraphs. What follows are *does* and *says* statements for the first six paragraphs of Kavanaugh's article:

Does/Says Analysis of Kavanaugh's Article

Paragraph 1: *Does:* Uses a vivid example to introduce the injustice of the current treatment of illegal immigrants. *Says:* The U.S. government is separating productive, long-term illegal immigrants from their families, deporting them, exposing them to dangerous conditions, and threatening them with felony charges.

Paragraph 2: *Does:* Puts the problem of illegal immigrants in a larger international context. *Says:* Although some illegal immigrants are involved in criminal activities, most have been pushed here by poverty and loss of opportunity in their own countries and have come to the United States seeking a better life for themselves and their families.

Paragraph 3: *Does:* Further explores the reasons behind the increase in immigration rates. *Says:* Catholic bishops have spoken out against the North American Free Trade Agreement and corporate interests, which have sought their own trade benefits at the expense of poor farmers and rural communities.

Paragraph 4: *Does:* Presents a sketch of Catholic leaders protesting the recent crackdowns on illegal immigrants. *Says:* U.S. bishops are protesting recent punitive laws against illegal immigrants and advocating for "a more compassionate, fair, and realistic reform of our immigration system."

Paragraph 5: *Does:* Sketches some opposing views. *Says:* Anti-immigration groups and others object to humane treatment of illegal immigrants, seeing it as akin to amnesty.

Paragraph 6: *Does:* Recognizes the validity of some opposing views. *Says:* The problems of some groups of Americans, including homeowners living on the border and businesses trying not to hire illegally, need to be heard.

■ ■ ▨ **FOR CLASS DISCUSSION**   Writing *Does/Says* Statements

Working individually or in small groups, write *does* and *says* statements for the remaining paragraphs of Kavanaugh's article.   ▨ ■ ■

Step 3: *Examine your* does *and* says *statements to determine the major sections of the argument.* Create a list of the major points (and subpoints) that must appear in a summary in order to represent that argument accurately. If you are visually oriented, you may prefer to make a diagram, flowchart, or scratch outline of the sections of Kavanaugh's argument.

Step 4: *Turn your list, outline, flowchart, or diagram into a prose summary.* Typically, writers do this in one of two ways. Some start by joining all their *says* statements into a lengthy paragraph-by-paragraph summary and then prune it and streamline it. They combine ideas into sentences and then revise those sentences to make them clearer and more tightly structured. Others start with a one-sentence summary of the argument's thesis and major supporting reasons and then flesh it out with more supporting ideas. Your goal is to be as neutral and objective as possible by keeping your own response to the writer's ideas out of your summary. To be fair to the writer, you also need to cover all the writer's main points and give them the same emphasis as in the original article.

Step 5: *Revise your summary until it is the desired length and is sufficiently clear, concise, and complete.* Your goal is to spend your words wisely, making every word count. In a summary of several hundred words, you will often need transitions to indicate structure and create a coherent flow of ideas: "Kavanaugh's second point is that…," or "Kavanaugh concludes by…." However, don't waste words with meaningless transitions such as "Kavanaugh goes on to say…." When you incorporate a summary into your own essay, you must distinguish that author's views from your own by using *attributive tags* (expressions such as "Kavanaugh asserts" or "according to Kavanaugh"). You must also put any directly borrowed wording in quotation marks. Finally, you must cite the original author using appropriate conventions for documenting sources.

What follows are two summaries of Kavanaugh's article—a one-paragraph version and a one-sentence version—by student writer Michael Banks. Michael's one-paragraph version illustrates the MLA documentation system in which page numbers for direct quotations are placed in parentheses after the quotation and complete bibliographic information is placed in a Works Cited list at the end of the paper. See Chapter 17 for a complete explanation of the MLA and APA documentation systems.

Michael's One-Paragraph Summary of Kavanaugh's Argument

In his article "Amnesty?" from *America* magazine John F. Kavanaugh, a Jesuit priest and professor of philosophy at St. Louis University, questions the morality of the current U.S. treatment of undocumented immigrants and advocates for a frank dealing with "the multiple causes of illegal immigration" (40). He points out that most immigrants are not criminals but rather hard-working, family-oriented people. He attributes recent increases in immigration to the North American Free Trade Agreement and the poverty it causes among rural Mexican farmers. Kavanaugh reports that recently U.S. bishops have protested the "anti-humane" treatment of immigrants and called for "compassionate, fair, and realistic reform" (39). He also mentions the anti-immigration groups, residents on the border, and business owners who have resisted the bishops and any treatment that resembles "amnesty." Kavanaugh's piece culminates with his argument that a nation that identifies itself as "Judeo-Christian and humane" should follow biblical teaching, "higher law," and the courageous example of leaders such as Martin Luther King, Jr., in challenging unjust laws (40). Admitting that unrestrained immigration would help nobody, Kavanaugh exhorts the country to move constructively toward "legal status for anyone who contributes to our common good" (40) and suggests a radically new solution to the problem: a citizen panel for the review of an immigrant's legal status. He concludes by stating that turning away undocumented immigrants is an immoral act motivated by self-interest.

Work Cited

Kavanaugh, John F. "Amnesty?" *America* 10 Mar. 2008: 8. Rpt. in *Writing Arguments: A Rhetoric with Readings*. John D. Ramage, John C. Bean, and June Johnson. 8th ed. New York: Pearson Longman, 2010. 39–40. Print.

Michael's One-Sentence Summary of Kavanaugh's Argument

In his article in *America*, Jesuit professor of philosophy John F. Kavanaugh questions the morality of the current treatment of undocumented immigrants in the United States, arguing that in a Judeo-Christian nation anyone who contributes positively to their community should be afforded some level of legal status.

Practicing Believing: Willing Your Own Belief in the Writer's Views

Although writing an accurate summary of an argument shows that you have listened to it effectively and understood it, summary writing by itself doesn't mean that you have actively tried to enter the writer's worldview. Before we turn in the next section to doubting an argument, we want to stress the importance of believing it. Rhetorician Peter Elbow reminds us that before we critique a text, we should try to "dwell with" and "dwell in" the writer's ideas—play the believing game—in order to "earn" our right to criticize.* He asserts, and we agree, that this use of the believing game to engage with strange, threatening, or unfamiliar views can lead to a deeper understanding and may provide a new vantage point on our own knowledge, assumptions, and values. To believe a writer and dwell with his or her ideas, find places in the text that resonate positively for you, look for values and beliefs you hold in common (however few), and search for personal experiences and values that affirm his or her argument.

Reading to Doubt

After willing yourself to believe an argument, will yourself to doubt it. Turn your mental energies toward raising objections, asking questions, expressing skepticism, and withholding your assent. When you read as a doubter, you question the writer's logic, the writer's evidence and assumptions, and the writer's strategies for developing the argument. You also think about what is *not* in the argument by noting what the author has glossed over, unexplained, or left out. You add a new layer of marginal notes, articulating what is bothering you, demanding proof, doubting evidence, challenging the author's assumptions and values, and so forth. Writing your own notes helps you read a text actively, bringing your own voice into conversation with the author.

■ ■ ■   **FOR CLASS DISCUSSION**   **Raising Doubts about Kavanaugh's Argument**
Return now to Kavanaugh's article and read it skeptically. Raise questions, offer objections, and express doubts. Then, working as a class or in small groups, list all the doubts you have about Kavanaugh's argument.   ■ ■ ■

Now that you have doubted Kavanaugh's article, compare your questions and doubts to some raised by student writer Michael Banks.

Michael's Doubts about Kavanaugh's Article

■ Kavanaugh's introductory paragraph seems sensational. María's situation is disturbing, but I doubt that every deported immigrant is likely to be "kidnapped, raped, murdered, and buried in the desert" as he seems to be insinuating.

■ His argument often seems to be based too much upon vague statements about the opposition. He talks about "some resentment," "some towns," "a few people," and "some hateful columns," but he doesn't provide specifics. He also doesn't provide any specific data about the effects of NAFTA, which seems like something he really should have provided.

■ In his second paragraph, he says that María's story "is not necessarily typical of the masses who have illegally entered" the U.S and that "many are incarcerated for other crimes than their immigrant status." However, he never considers the rate of criminal behavior of illegal immigrants in further detail. Are illegal immigrants more likely to commit crimes? This might be the start of an argument against him.

---

*Peter Elbow, "Bringing the Rhetoric of Assent and the Believing Game Together—Into the Classroom." In *College English* 67.4 (March 2005), p. 389.

■ His references to opinion columns and popular books and radio talk shows seem to suggest that the majority of opposition to immigration reform is simplistic and ignorant. He only pays lip service to a few "understandable" objections. There must be more to the opposition than this. It would be particularly interesting to find an ethical justification for an anti-immigration stance.

■ Perhaps because he's a member of the Society of Jesus, he draws hardly any line at all between church and state. However, most U.S. citizens I know believe that government should be secular. This contrasts harshly with his notion that the U.S. self-identifies as "Judeo-Christian" and limits his audience to people who would probably already agree with him. If we remove religion from the equation, the capitalistic values behind NAFTA and immigration policy seem much more understandable. I would need to investigate the economic impact of illegal immigration. Who really benefits the most from it? Who's really harmed?

These are only some of the objections that might be raised against Kavanaugh's argument. The point here is that doubting as well as believing is a key part of the exploratory process and purpose. *Believing* takes you into the views of others so that you can expand your views and perhaps see them differently and modify or even change them. *Doubting* helps protect you from becoming overpowered by others' arguments and teaches you to stand back, consider, and weigh points carefully. It also leads you to new questions and points you might want to explore further.

Thinking Dialectically

This chapter's final strategy—thinking dialectically to bring texts into conversation with each other—encompasses all the previous strategies and can have a powerful effect on your growth as a thinker and arguer. The term *dialectic* is associated with the German philosopher Georg Wilhelm Friedrich Hegel, who postulated that each thesis prompts an opposing thesis (which he calls an "antithesis") and that the conflict between these views can lead thinkers to a new claim (a "synthesis") that incorporates aspects of both views. Dialectic thinking is the philosophical underpinning of the believing and doubting game, pushing us toward new and better ideas. As Peter Elbow puts it, "Because it's so hard to let go of an idea we are holding (or more to the point, an idea that's holding us), our best hope for leverage in learning to doubt such ideas is *to take on different ideas.*"*

This is why expert thinkers actively seek out alternative views—not to shout them down but to listen to them. If you were an arbitrator, you wouldn't settle a dispute between A and B on the basis of A's testimony only. You would also insist on hearing B's side of the story (and perhaps also C's and D's if they are stakeholders in the dispute). Dialectic thinking means playing ideas against each other, creating a tension that forces you to keep expanding your perspective. It helps you achieve the "mingling of minds" that we discussed in the introduction to this chapter.

---

*Peter Elbow, "Bringing the Rhetoric of Assent and the Believing Game Together—Into the Classroom." In *College English.* 67.4 (March 2005), p. 390.

As you listen to differing views, try to identify sources of disagreement among arguers, which often fall into two categories: (1) disagreement about the facts of the case and (2) disagreement about underlying values, beliefs, or assumptions. We saw these disagreements in Chapter 1 in the conversation about phthalates in children's toys. At the level of facts, disputants disagreed about the amount of phthalates a baby might ingest when chewing a rubber toy or about the quantity of ingested phthalates needed to be harmful. At the level of values, disputants disagreed on the amount of risk that must be present in a free market economy before a government agency should ban a substance. As you try to determine your own position on an issue, consider what research you might have to do to resolve questions of fact; also try to articulate your own underlying values, beliefs, and assumptions.

Questions to Stimulate Dialectic Thinking

As you consider multiple points of view on an issue, try using the following questions to promote dialectic thinking:

Questions to Promote Dialectic Thinking

1. What would writer A say to writer B?
2. After I read writer A, I thought _____; however, after I read writer B, my thinking on this issue had changed in these ways: _____.
3. To what extent do writer A and writer B disagree about facts and interpretations of facts?
4. To what extent do writer A and writer B disagree about underlying beliefs, assumptions, and values?
5. Can I find any areas of agreement, including shared values and beliefs, between writer A and writer B?
6. What new, significant questions do these texts raise for me?
7. After I have wrestled with the ideas in these two texts, what are my current views on this issue?

Responding to questions like these—either through class discussion or through exploratory writing—can help you work your way into a public controversy. Earlier in this chapter you read John Kavanaugh's article expressing a Catholic, pro-immigrant, anti-corporate view of immigrants. Now consider an article expressing a quite different point of view, "Why Blame Mexico?" by freelance journalist Fred Reed, published in *The American Conservative* on March 10, 2008. We ask you to read the article and then use the preceding questions to stimulate dialectic thinking about Kavanaugh versus Reed.

■ ■ ■   **FOR CLASS DISCUSSION   Practicing Dialectic Thinking with Two Articles**
Individual task: Freewrite your responses to the preceding questions, in which Kavanaugh is writer A and Reed is writer B. **Group task:** Working as a whole class or in small groups, share your responses to the two articles, guided by the dialectic questions.   ■ ■ ■

Why Blame Mexico?

FRED REED

To grasp American immigration policy, one needs only remember that the United States frowns on smoking while subsidizing tobacco growers.

We say to impoverished Mexicans, "See this river? Don't cross it. If you do, we'll give you good jobs, drivers licenses, citizenship for your kids born here, school for said kids, public assistance, governmental documents in Spanish for your convenience, and a much better future. There is no penalty for getting caught. Now, don't cross this river, hear?"

How smart is that? We're baiting them. It's like putting out a salt lick and then complaining when deer come. Immigrant parents would be irresponsible not to cross.

The problem of immigration, note, is entirely self-inflicted. The U.S. chose to let them in. It didn't have to. They came to work. If Americans hadn't hired them, they would have gone back.

5   We have immigration because we want immigration. Liberals favor immigration because it makes them feel warm and fuzzy and from a genuine streak of decency. Conservative Republican businessmen favor immigration, frequently *sotto voce*, because they want cheap labor that actually shows up and works.

It's a story I've heard many times—from a landscaper, a construction firm, a junkyard owner, a group of plant nurserymen. "We need Mexicans." You could yell "Migra!" in a lot of restaurants in Washington, and the entire staff would disappear out the back door. Do we expect businessmen to vote themselves out of business? That's why we don't take the obvious steps to control immigration. (A $1,000 a day fine for hiring illegals, half to go anonymously to whoever informed on the employer would do the trick.)

In Jalisco, Mexico, where I live, crossing illegally is regarded as casually as pirating music or smoking a joint and the coyotes who smuggle people across as a public utility, like light rail. The smuggling is frequently done by bribing the border guards, who are notoriously corrupt.

Why corrupt? Money. In the book *De Los Maras a Los Zetas*, by a Mexican journalist, I find an account of a tunnel he knew of that could put 150 illegals a day across the border. (I can't confirm this.) The price of passage is about $2,000 a person. That's $300,000 a day, tax-free. What does a border guard make? (And where can I find a shovel?) The author estimated that perhaps 40 tunnels were active at any given time. Certainly some are. A woman I know says she came up in a restaurant and just walked out the door. Let's hear it for Homeland Security.

There is much noise about whether to grant amnesty. The question strikes me as cosmetic. We are not going to round up millions of people and physically throw them across the border. Whether we should doesn't matter. It's fantasy. Too many people want them here or don't care that they are here or don't want to uproot families who have established new lives here. Ethnic cleansing is ugly. Further, the legal Latino population is just starting to vote. A bumper crop of Mexican-American kids, possessed of citizenship, are growing headlong toward voting age. These people cannot be thrown out, even in principle.

10   People complain that Mexico doesn't seal the borders. Huh? Mexico is a country, not a prison. It has no obligation to enforce American laws that America declines to enforce. Then there was the uproar when some fast-food restaurant in the U.S. began accepting pesos. Why? Mexican border towns accept dollars. Next came outrage

against Mexico because its consulates were issuing ID cards to illegals, which they then used to get drivers licenses. Why outrage? A country has every right to issue IDs to its citizens. America doesn't have to accept them. If it does, whose problem is that?

If you want to see a reasonable immigration policy, look to Mexico. You automatically get a 90-day tourist visa when you land. To get residency papers, you need two things apart from photographs, passport, etc. First, a valid tourist visa to show that you entered the country legally. Mexico doesn't do illegal aliens. Second,

a demonstrable income of $1,000 a month. You are welcome to live in Mexico, but you are going to pay your own way. Sounds reasonable to me.

You want a Mexican passport? Mexico allows dual citizenship. You (usually) have to be a resident for five years before applying. You also have to speak Spanish. It's the national language. What sense does it make to have citizens who can't talk to anybody?

It looks to me as though America thoughtlessly adopted an unwise policy, continued it until reversal became approximately impossible, and now doesn't like the results. It must be Mexico's fault.

Three Ways to Foster Dialectic Thinking

In this concluding section, we suggest three ways to stimulate and sustain the process of dialectic thinking: Effective discussions in class, over coffee, or online; a reading log in which you make texts speak to each other; or a formal exploratory essay. We'll look briefly at each in turn.

Effective Discussions   Good rich talk is one of the most powerful ways to stimulate dialectic thinking and foster a "mingling of minds." The key is to keep these discussions from being shouting matches or bully pulpits for those who like to dominate the airtime. Discussions are most productive if people are willing to express different points of view or to role-play those views for the purpose of advancing the conversation. Try Rogerian listening, in which you summarize someone else's position before you offer your own different position. (See Chapter 7 for more explanation of Rogerian listening.) Probe deeply to discover whether disagreements are primarily about facts and evidence or about underlying values and beliefs. Be respectful of other's views, but don't hesitate to point out where you see problems or weaknesses. Good discussions can occur in class, in late-night coffee shops, or in online chat rooms or on discussion boards.

Reading Logs   In our classes, we require students to keep reading logs or journals in which they use freewriting and idea mapping to explore their ideas as they encounter multiple perspectives on an issue. One part of a journal or reading log should include summaries of each article you read. Another part should focus on your own dialectic thinking as you interact with your sources while you are reading them. Adapt the questions for promoting dialectic thinking on page 46.

A Formal Exploratory Essay   A formal exploratory essay tells the story of an intellectual journey. It is both a way of promoting dialectical thinking and a way of narrating one's struggle to negotiate multiple views. The keys to writing successful exploratory essays are (1) choosing an issue to explore on which you don't have an answer or position (or on which you are open to changing your mind); (2) wrestling with an issue or problem by resisting quick, simple answers and by exploring diverse perspectives; and (3) letting your thinking evolve and your own stance on the issue grow out of this exploration.

Exploratory essays can be powerful thinking and writing experiences in their own right, but they can also be a valuable precursor to a formal argument. Many instructors assign a formal exploratory paper as the first stage of a course research project——what we might call a "thesis-seeking" stage. (The second stage is a formal argument that converts your exploratory thinking into a hierarchically organized argument using reasons and evidence to support your claim.) Although often used as part of a research project, exploratory essays can also be low-stakes reflective pieces narrating the evolution of a writer's thinking during a class discussion.

An exploratory essay includes these thinking moves and parts:

- The essay is opened and driven by the writer's issue question or research problem—not a thesis.
- The introduction to the essay presents the question and shows why it interests the writer, why it is significant, and why it is problematic rather than clear-cut or easy to resolve.
- The body of the essay shows the writer's inquiry process. It demonstrates how the writer has kept the question open, sincerely wrestled with different views on the question, accepted uncertainty and ambiguity, and possibly redefined the question in the midst of his or her reading and reflection on multiple perspectives.
- The body of the essay includes summaries of the different views or sources that the writer explored and often includes believing and doubting responses to them.
- In the essay's conclusion, the writer may clarify his or her thinking and discover a thesis to be developed and supported in a subsequent argument. But the conclusion can also remain open because the writer may not have discovered his or her own position on the issue and may acknowledge the need or desire for more exploration.

One of the writing assignment options for this chapter is a formal exploratory paper. Michael Banks's exploratory essay on pages 52–57 shows how he explored different voices in the controversy over illegal immigration.

Conclusion

This chapter has focused on inquiry as a way to enrich your reading and writing of arguments. This chapter has offered five main strategies for deep reading: (1) Use a variety of questions and prompts to find an issue to explore; (2) place readings in their rhetorical context; (3) read as a believer; (4) read as a doubter; and (5) think dialectically. This chapter has also shown you how to summarize an article and incorporate summaries into your own writing, using attributive tags to distinguish the ideas you are summarizing from your own. It has explained why a reading's rhetorical context (purpose, audience, and genre) must be considered in any thoughtful response to an argument. Finally, it has emphasized the importance of dialectic thinking and has offered the exploratory essay as a way to encourage wrestling with multiple perspectives rather than seeking early closure.

WRITING ASSIGNMENT An Argument Summary or a Formal Exploratory Essay

Option 1: An Argument Summary Write a 250-word summary of an argument selected by your instructor. Then write a one-sentence summary of the same argument. Use as models Michael Banks' summaries of John Kavanaugh's argument on immigration (page 43).

Option 2: A Formal Exploratory Essay Write an exploratory essay in which you narrate in first-person, chronological order the evolution through time of your thinking about an issue or problem. Rather than state a thesis or claim, begin with a question or problem. Then describe your inquiry process as you worked your way through sources or different views. Follow the guidelines for an exploratory paper shown on page 48–49. When you cite the sources you have considered, be sure to use attributive tags so that the reader can distinguish between your own ideas and those of the sources you have summarized. If you use research sources, use MLA documentation for citing ideas and quotations and for creating a Works Cited at the end (see Chapter 17).

Explanation and Organization

An exploratory essay could grow out of class discussion, course readings, field work and interviews, or simply the writer's role-playing of alternative views. In all cases, the purpose of an exploratory paper is not to state and defend a thesis. Its purpose is to think dialectically about multiple perspectives, narrating the evolution through time of the writer's thought process. Many students are inspired by the open, "behind-the-scenes" feel of an exploratory essay. They enjoy taking readers on the same intellectual and emotional journey they have just traveled. A typical organization plan for an exploratory essay is shown on the next page. ∎

Organization Plan for an Exploratory Essay

Introduction (one to several paragraphs)	• Establish that your question is complex, problematic, and significant. • Show why you are interested in it. • Present relevant background on your issue. Begin with your question or build up to it, using it to end your introductory section.
Body section 1: First view or source	• Introduce your first source and show why you started with it. • Provide rhetorical context and information about it. • Summarize the source's content and argument. • Offer your response to this source, including both believing and doubting points. • Talk about what this source contributes to your understanding of your question: What did you learn? What value does this source have for you? What is missing from this source that you want to consider? Where do you want to go from here?
Body section 2: Second view or source	• Repeat the process with a new source selected to advance the inquiry. • Explain why you selected this source (to find an alternative view, pursue a sub-question, find more data, and so forth). • Summarize the source's argument. • Respond to the source's ideas. Look for points of agreement and disagreement with other sources. • Show how your cumulative reading of sources is shaping your thinking or leading to more questions.
Body sections 3, 4, 5, etc.	• Continue exploring views or sources.
Conclusion	• Wrap up your intellectual journey and explain where you are now in your thinking and how your understanding of your problem has changed. • Present your current answer to your question based on all that you have learned so far, or explain why you still can't answer your question, or explain what research you might pursue further.

Reading

What follows is Michael Banks's exploratory essay on the subject of illegal immigration. His research begins with the articles by Kavanaugh and Reed that you have already read and discussed. He then moves off in his own direction.

Should the United States Grant Legal Status to Undocumented Immigrant Workers?

MICHAEL BANKS (STUDENT)

Introduction shows the writer's interest and investment in the issue, which, in this case, began with personal experience.

Having grown up in the California Bay Area, I have long been aware of illegal immigration. In high school, I volunteered through a school program to deliver free lunches to Mexican workers waiting for day jobs at popular hiring sites such as local hardware stores. One time we even went out to one of the farm fields to deliver lunches, and some of the workers scattered when they saw us coming. Apparently they thought we were police or immigration officials. Although the relationships were not deep or lasting, I had the opportunity to talk with some of the workers in my stumbling high-school Spanish, and they would tell me about some of their bad experiences such as employers who wouldn't pay them what was promised. They had no recourse to file a complaint because they lacked legal status. Our program supervisor often stressed the importance of recognizing the workers as friends or equals rather than as charity cases. I often wondered how they could work with such low wages and still live a dignified life. However, my experiences did not push me to consider deeply the reality of being an illegal immigrant.

Writer presents the problem he is going to investigate. He shows why the problem is complex, significant, and difficult to resolve. The introduction shows his genuine perplexity.

With this background, I entered our class discussions sympathetic towards the immigrants. However, I also recognized that the cheap labor they provided allowed Americans to keep food prices affordable or to find workers for any kind of hard day-labor job such as landscaping or digging up a backyard septic system. I am still not sure whether illegal immigrants are taking away jobs that Americans want, but I do know that I and most of my college friends would not be willing to work low-paying summer jobs picking tomatoes or weeding lettuce. For this exploratory essay, I wanted to look more deeply into this complicated ethical and economic dilemma. I set for myself this question:

Writer states his research question.

What is the best way for the United States to handle the problem of illegal immigration?

Writer explains his
starting point,
introduces his first
source, and gives
some rhetorical
context for it.

Writer summarizes
the article.

Writer includes
believing and
doubting points as
he discusses what he
learned from this
article and how it
influenced his
thinking on his
research question.

Here the writer
doubts the article
and challenges some
of its ideas.

Writer moves to his
next source and
provides some
rhetorical context,
including information
about the author.

My exploration began with an article that our instructor assigned to the whole class: "Amnesty?" from *America* magazine by John F. Kavanaugh, a Jesuit priest and professor of philosophy at St. Louis University. In this article, Kavanaugh questions the morality of the current U.S. treatment of undocumented immigrants. He points out that most immigrants are not criminals but rather hard-working, family-oriented people. He attributes recent increases in immigration to the North American Free Trade Agreement and the poverty it causes among rural Mexican farmers. He also notes that anti-immigration groups have a "seething hostility" (40) for these persons and strongly resist any granting of amnesty or legal status. Kavanaugh disagrees with these groups, arguing that a nation that identifies itself as "Judeo-Christian and humane" should follow biblical teaching, "higher law," and the courageous example of leaders such as Martin Luther King, Jr., in challenging unjust laws (40). Although admitting that unrestrained immigration would help nobody, Kavanaugh exhorts the country to give "legal status to anyone who contributes to our common good" (40). He recommends that a citizen panel be used to review an immigrant's status and make recommendations for amnesty.

I found Kavanaugh's article to be quite persuasive. This article could particularly inspire its Catholic readers, and I too had an easy time agreeing with much of what Kavanaugh says. In fact, he reminded me of the director of my high school outreach program. I like the argument that people who contribute to the community should not be labeled as "illegal" as if they are in the same category as thieves or welfare cheaters. But I wasn't yet convinced that the laws governing immigration were "unjust" in the same way that segregation laws were unjust. It seems to me that a country has the right to control who enters the country, but doesn't have the right to make certain people sit in the back of the bus. So the references to Martin Luther King's fighting unjust laws didn't quite connect with me. So I was still caught in the dilemma. Also, I saw some other major problems with Kavanaugh's argument. First, it may not be fair to apply Judeo-Christian ethics to everyone in the country, especially considering our Constitutional separation of church and state. His appeal to religious beliefs may be appropriate to persuade Christians to volunteer for a cause but not to change a secular nation's laws. Also, his solution of having a citizen panel seemed impractical, especially for handling the number of illegal immigrants. Finally, Kavanaugh doesn't address the economic side of this argument. He didn't help me see what the disadvantages would be to granting amnesty to millions of undocumented workers.

5 My next article, which the class also read together, was from *The American Conservative* titled "Why Blame Mexico?" by Fred Reed. According to Reed's biographical sketch on the Web ("Fred on Everything: Biography"), Reed is an ex-marine, former scientist, wanderer and world traveler, former law-enforcement columnist for the *Washington Times*, and a freelance journalist currently living in Mexico. He is known for his

provocative columns. Reed's article was hard to summarize because it jumps around and is very sarcastic. His overall view is best exemplified by his very first statement: "To grasp American immigration policy, one needs only remember that the United States frowns on smoking while subsidizing tobacco growers" (47). Reed argues that illegal immigration occurs not mainly because there are millions of impoverished Mexicans in need of work, but because liberals feel good about tolerating them and because "[c]onservative Republican businessmen favor immigration...because they want cheap labor that actually shows up and works" (47). Reed points out that Mexico itself is clear and consistent in its own immigration policies: Immigrants into Mexico must possess clear residency papers, must have regular monthly earnings, and must be fluent in Spanish. In contrast to Kavanaugh, who focuses on immigrants, Reed focuses on the Americans who hire them; without Americans wanting cheap labor, immigrants would have no reason to cross the border. He takes it for granted that illegal immigrants should not be given legal status. Reed offers no solutions for the tangled mess of U.S. treatment of illegal immigrants, but underscores the fact that it is this country's self-created problem.

Reed's article pulled me back away from Kavanaugh's call for amnesty. It made me see more clearly the entangled economic issues. Many American citizens *want* a source of cheap labor. Reed, in contrast, wants to eliminate cheap labor. If we followed the logical path that Reed seems to propose, we'd start jailing employers in order to cut off the job supply. At this point in my research, the status quo seemed to be a better situation. If cheap labor is so important to America's economy and if a low paying job in the United States is better than no job, perhaps some kind of legal status other than amnesty and citizenship would help resolve the situation. My head was spinning because I could picture all my classmates who would disagree with my last sentence! At this point, I felt I needed to explore other approaches to this controversy.

The day after I read the Reed article, I was talking with a friend, who suggested I watch a recent movie about immigration called *Under the Same Moon.* I figured it would be a fun diversion, if nothing else, and rented it. The movie tells the tale of a nine-year-old boy, Carlitos, who lives with his grandmother until she dies and then sets out to cross the border illegally to find his mother, who has been working several jobs at once as an undocumented immigrant for four years in Los Angeles. The dramatic story—shown from the dual perspective of mother and son—highlights many of the dangers faced by the immigrants themselves: separation from family members and support networks, exploitation by border-crossing agencies, INS raids on job sites, and dangerous jobs such as picking pesticide-coated tomatoes, just to name a few. The main characters' immigrant laborer status also draws attention to the undeniable humanity of immigrants.

Writer discusses and analyzes the ideas in the film by presenting believing and doubting points.

Writer mentions problems the source raises for him.

Writer explains his choice of another film.

A brief summary prepares for his discussion.

Writer presents some information about the rhetorical context of this film, including statements from the directors and details about how it was first received.

Writer demonstrates how he is grappling with the issue of illegal immigration and how this film complicates his views.

This film works powerfully to create sympathy for illegal immigrants but without the explicit religious coating provided by Kavanaugh. I cannot help but admire the sacrifices made by immigrant workers who leave behind children and family in order to try to provide a brighter future for their loved ones. In cases where immigrants are separated from their young children, granting these parents legal status could help unite families more quickly and could ease the great pain that comes with being separated while allowing them the opportunity to forge a better life. On the other hand, families would also be reunited if the parents were sent back to Mexico. The great sympathy I feel for illegal immigrants doesn't necessarily mean that granting amnesty and citizenship is the best solution. While the film evokes compassion for individual immigrants, it does not address the magnitude of the problem.

I had heard about a number of films about illegal immigration and immigrants' experiences and wanted to continue with another film, so I headed back to Blockbuster and asked one of the workers if he could point me towards a recent documentary on illegal immigration. What I came up with was *A Day Without a Mexican*, a mock documentary, or "mockumentary." The movie's plot imagines the complete disappearance of the entire Latino population in California, both legal and illegal. The state grinds to a complete halt, widespread panic occurs, and homes, restaurants, supermarkets, orchards, farms, schools, and construction services are completely dysfunctional. The story and structure of the film viciously satirize anti-immigrant organizations, the news media, the border patrol, and waffling politicians. I visited the movie's Web site to search for further information, as I was curious about its reception. The Latino audience saw this film as a hit; it took in the second best per screen average the weekend it was released in Southern California. According to the general sales manager of Televisa Cine, *A Day Without a Mexican*'s success "underscores that there is not only a broad Hispanic audience who wants to see this film, but also a significant crossover audience," while the director, Sergio Arau, and lead actress/screenwriter, Yareli Arizmendi, add "we still believe we can change the world one screen at a time" ("Missing Jose Found").

10   The film's success at the box office suggests to me that Arau and Arizmendi have revealed the important truth that Latino immigration makes California a better place. The comic film works by exaggeration, but its image of a helpless California without immigrants is easy to believe. Since California, and presumably the rest of the country, relies so heavily upon its immigrants, it would make very little sense to create new immigration policies that made the status quo worse. Perhaps a solution might lie in somehow recognizing the worth of immigrants, as *A Day Without a Mexican* suggests is important, while maintaining the status quo of paying them wages lower than American standards. A moral dilemma remains, however, because this approach places economics above justice.

At this stage, I decided to review some of the possible "solutions" that I had encountered so far to the illegal immigration problem. One solution, based on our valuing the humanity of immigrants, is to offer them amnesty, legal status, and eventual citizenship. Another, based on our valuing the economic benefits of cheap labor, is to keep the status quo. Still another solution is to get rid of illegal aliens altogether either by deporting them or by jailing their employers and thus eliminating their source of income. None of these options appealed to me. In search of another approach, I decided to head for the library to do more research. A friendly reference librarian suggested that I start with a couple of overview articles from *CQ Researcher*. These articles, which I just skimmed, provided some background information, statistical data on immigration, and summaries of different bills before Congress. I found my head swimming with so many little details that I began losing the big picture about an actual direction I wanted to go. However, one idea that kept emerging from the *CQ Researcher* was the possibility of guest worker programs. I decided I wanted to find out more about what these programs were. With the reference librarian's guidance, I used *Academic Search Complete* to find a number of articles on guest worker programs. I also entered "guest worker program" into Google and found a number of bloggers supporting or attacking guest worker programs.

I focused first on an editorial "That's Hospitality" from *The New Republic*, a news commentary magazine that is in the political center, neither dominantly liberal nor conservative. The editorial opposes a congressional bill that would establish a guest worker program wherein businesses could hire foreigners as "guest workers" for up to six years. These workers would be granted temporary legal status, but they would have to return to their home country when the six years were up. Although supporters of the bill called it "humane" and "compassionate," the editorial writer opposes it because it is "un-American." No other group of immigrants, the editorial states, has been treated this way—as second class transients who had no opportunity to make a full life in America. The article compares this proposed guest worker program to similar programs in Europe after WWII, where workers from Eastern Europe or Turkey came to countries like Germany or Netherlands and stayed but never assimilated. What the article supports instead is an alternative bill that grants "temporary worker" status but allows workers to apply for a green card after six years and for citizenship after five more years.

This article excited me because it seemed to promote a compromise that turned undocumented workers who were afraid of getting caught and deported into persons with legal status and with the hope of eventually becoming citizens. It shared the pro-immigrant spirit of Kavanaugh and *Under the Same Moon* but didn't directly undermine the economic benefits provided by cheap labor. Rather than offering direct amnesty, it specified a waiting period of at least eleven years before a person could apply for citizenship. Although this article did not specify how the United States might manage the volume and rate of people seeking guest worker and then citizen status, I thought that this proposal would be the position I would like to argue for in a later persuasive paper.

But I decided next to look at the negative side of a guest worker program and was amazed at how many anti-immigration groups hated this bill. One provocative blog "Guest Worker Program Illusion" is by a freelance writer Frosty Wooldridge, who maintains his own Web site aimed at combating "overpopulation and immigration." According to his blog site he has written hundreds of articles for seventeen national and two international magazines and has been an invited speaker on environmental issues at many universities. Wooldridge favors strict border enforcement and deportation of anyone who has illegally entered the country. He sees all forms of guest worker programs as amnesty that will lead to overpopulation and an increasing welfare burden on middle-class Americans who try to provide services for the guest workers. He also argues that the guest workers will suppress wages for American workers. His strategy is to point out all the problems that the guest worker program will open up: Can the guest worker bring his or her family? Will children born to guest workers automatically be U.S. citizens? Must the states provide tax-payer supported schools and hospital services for the guest workers? If so, must the schools be bilingual? Will guest workers pay social security taxes and thus become eligible for social security? Will they be eligible for Workers Compensation if they get hurt on the job? Will their older children get in-state rates at public universities? Will their younger children be covered by child labor laws? Will they actually leave after six years or simply revert back to undocumented illegal status?

15   All these problems raised by Woolridge were never mentioned in the *New Republic* editorial, and they severely dampened my spirits. As I end this exploratory paper, I still have a number of articles left to read and much left to learn, but I think I have a pretty good grasp of what the issues and disagreements are. I definitely think that the plan supporting a guest worker program with the chance of eventual citizenship is the best approach. But it has to be linked with other approaches also, including ways to improve the economies of Mexico and other Latin American countries so that poor people wouldn't have to come to the United States to find work. My hope is that many of the objections raised by Woolridge are solvable. I have realized from my inquiry that my heart is with the immigrants and that I don't share Woolridge's desire to close America off from future immigration.

Works Cited

A Day Without a Mexican. Dir. Sergio Arau. Xenon Pictures, 2004. DVD.

Kavanaugh, John F. "Amnesty?" *America* 10 March 2008: 8. Print.

"Missing Jose Found: Walks His Way to Box Office Success Throughout Southern California." *ADWAM News.* A Day Without a Mexican, n.d. Web. 12 July 2008.

Reed, Fred. "Why Blame Mexico?" *The American Conservative* 10 March
    2008: 35. Print.

"That's Hospitality." *New Republic* 17 April 2006: 7. *Academic Search
    Complete*. Web. 30 August 2008.

Under the Same Moon. Dir. Patricia Riggen. Perf. Adrián Alonso, Kate del
    Castillo, Eugenio Derbez. Twentieth Century Fox, 2008. DVD.

Woolridge, Frosty. "Guest Worker Program Illusion." *Newswithviews.com*.
    2 Dec. 2005. Web. 22 May 2008.

PART TWO
Writing an Argument

This still from the *Tomb Raider* video game series features main character Lara Croft engaged in one of her typical combats with humans, beasts, or supernatural creatures. Lara, an adventurer and archeologist, represents both a sexualized and an empowered woman. Women and violent video games are the focus of student Carmen Tieu's argument developed in Chapters 3–5; however, Carmen explores gender roles from the perspective of a woman playing a "male" video game, *Halo.*

3 The Core of an Argument
A Claim with Reasons

In Part One we explained that argument combines truth seeking with persuasion. Part One, by highlighting the importance of exploration and inquiry, emphasizes the truth-seeking dimension of argument. The suggested writing assignments in Part One included a variety of exploratory tasks: freewriting, playing the believing and doubting game, and writing a formal exploratory essay. In Part Two we show you how to convert your exploratory ideas into a thesis-governed classical argument that uses effective reasons and evidence to support its claims. Each chapter in Part Two focuses on a key skill or idea needed for responsible and effective persuasion.

The Classical Structure of Argument

Classical argument is patterned after the persuasive speeches of ancient Greek and Roman orators. In traditional Latin terminology, the main parts of a persuasive speech are the *exordium,* in which the speaker gets the audience's attention; the *narratio,* which provides needed background; the *propositio,* which is the speaker's claim or thesis; the *partitio,* which forecasts the main parts of the speech; the *confirmatio,* which presents the speaker's arguments supporting the claim; the *confutatio,* which summarizes and rebuts opposing views; and the *peroratio,* which concludes the speech by summing up the argument, calling for action, and leaving a strong, lasting impression. (Of course, you don't need to remember these tongue-twisting Latin terms. We cite them only to assure you that in writing a classical argument you are joining a time-honored tradition that links back to the origins of democracy.)

Let's go over the same territory again using more contemporary terms. We provide an organization plan showing the structure of a classical argument on page 61, which shows these typical sections:

- **The introduction**. Writers of classical argument typically begin with an attention grabber such as a memorable scene, illustrative story, or startling statistic. They continue the introduction by focusing the issue—often by stating it directly as a question or by briefly summarizing opposing views—and providing needed background and context. They conclude the introduction by presenting their claim (thesis statement) and forecasting the argument's structure.

Organization Plan for an Argument with a Classical Structure

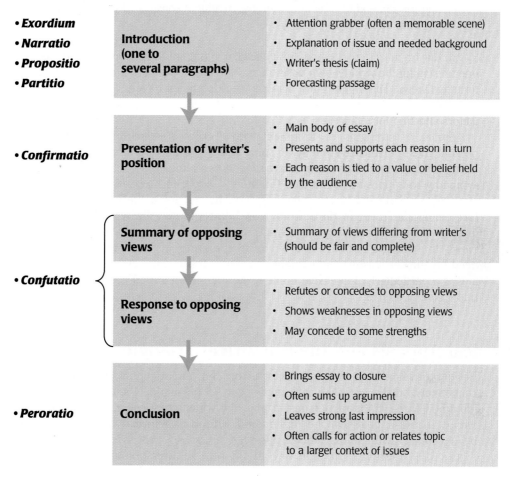

- *Exordium*
- *Narratio*
- *Propositio*
- *Partitio*

Introduction (one to several paragraphs)

- Attention grabber (often a memorable scene)
- Explanation of issue and needed background
- Writer's thesis (claim)
- Forecasting passage

- *Confirmatio*

Presentation of writer's position

- Main body of essay
- Presents and supports each reason in turn
- Each reason is tied to a value or belief held by the audience

- *Confutatio*

Summary of opposing views

- Summary of views differing from writer's (should be fair and complete)

Response to opposing views

- Refutes or concedes to opposing views
- Shows weaknesses in opposing views
- May concede to some strengths

- *Peroratio*

Conclusion

- Brings essay to closure
- Often sums up argument
- Leaves strong last impression
- Often calls for action or relates topic to a larger context of issues

- **The presentation of the writer's position.** The presentation of the writer's own position is usually the longest part of a classical argument. Here writers present the reasons and evidence supporting their claims, typically choosing reasons that tie into their audience's values, beliefs, and assumptions. Usually each reason is developed in its own paragraph or sequence of paragraphs. When a paragraph introduces a new reason, writers state the reason directly and then support it with evidence or a chain of ideas. Along the way, writers guide their readers with appropriate transitions.
- **The summary and critique of alternative views.** When summarizing and responding to opposing views, writers have several options. If there are several opposing arguments, writers may summarize all of them together and then compose a single response, or they may summarize and respond to each argument in turn. As we will explain in Chapter 7, writers may respond to opposing views either by refuting them or by conceding to their strengths and shifting to a different field of values.

- **The conclusion.** Finally, in their conclusion, writers sum up their argument, often calling for some kind of action, thereby creating a sense of closure and leaving a strong final impression.

In this organization, the body of a classical argument has two major sections—the one presenting the writer's own position and the other summarizing and critiquing alternative views. The organization plan and our discussion have the writer's own position coming first, but it is possible to reverse that order. (In Chapter 7 we consider the factors affecting this choice.)

For all its strengths, an argument with a classical structure may not always be your most persuasive strategy. In some cases, you may be more effective by delaying your thesis, by ignoring alternative views altogether, or by showing great sympathy for opposing views (see Chapter 7). Even in these cases, however, the classical structure is a useful planning tool. Its call for a thesis statement and a forecasting statement in the introduction helps you see the whole of your argument in miniature. And by requiring you to summarize and consider opposing views, the classical structure alerts you to the limits of your position and to the need for further reasons and evidence. As we will show, the classical structure creates is a particularly persuasive mode of argument when you address a neutral or undecided audience.

Classical Appeals and the Rhetorical Triangle

Besides developing a template or structure for an argument, classical rhetoricians analyzed the ways that effective speeches persuaded their audiences. They identified three kinds of persuasive appeals, which they called *logos, ethos,* and *pathos.* These appeals can be understood within a rhetorical context illustrated by a triangle with points labeled *message, writer or speaker,* and *audience* (see Figure 3.1). Effective arguments pay attention to all three points on this *rhetorical triangle.*

As Figure 3.1 shows, each point on the triangle corresponds to one of the three persuasive appeals:

- *Logos* (Greek for "word") focuses attention on the quality of the message—that is, on the internal consistency and clarity of the argument itself and on the logic of its reasons and support. The impact of *logos* on an audience is referred to as its *logical appeal.*
- *Ethos* (Greek for "character") focuses attention on the writer's (or speaker's) character as it is projected in the message. It refers to the credibility of the writer. *Ethos* is often conveyed through the tone and style of the message, through the care with which the writer considers alternative views, and through the writer's investment in his or her claim. In some cases, it's also a function of the writer's reputation for honesty and expertise independent of the message. The impact of *ethos* on an audience is referred to as its *ethical appeal* or *appeal from credibility.*

Message
LOGOS: *How can I make the argument internally consistent and logical? How can I find the best reasons and support them with the best evidence?*

Audience
PATHOS: *How can I make the reader open to my message? How can I best appeal to my reader's values and interests? How can I engage my reader emotionally and imaginatively?*

Writer or Speaker
ETHOS: *How can I present myself effectively? How can I enhance my credibility and trustworthiness?*

FIGURE 3.1 The rhetorical triangle

▪ *Pathos* (Greek for "suffering" or "experience") focuses attention on the values and beliefs of the intended audience. It is often associated with emotional appeal. But *pathos* appeals more specifically to an audience's imaginative sympathies—their capacity to feel and see what the writer feels and sees. Thus, when we turn the abstractions of logical discourse into a tangible and immediate story, we are making a pathetic appeal. Whereas appeals to *logos* and *ethos* can further an audience's intellectual assent to our claim, appeals to *pathos* engage the imagination and feelings, moving the audience to a deeper appreciation of the argument's significance.

A related rhetorical concept, connected to the appeals of *logos, ethos,* and *pathos,* is that of *kairos,* from the Greek word for "right time," "season," or "opportunity." This concept suggests that for an argument to be persuasive, its timing must be effectively chosen and its tone and structure in right proportion or measure. You may have had the experience of composing an argumentative e-mail and then hesitating before clicking the "send" button. Is this the right moment to send this message? Is my audience ready to hear what I'm saying? Would my argument be more effective if I waited for a couple of days? If I send this message now, should I change its tone and content? This attentiveness to the unfolding of time is what is meant by *kairos.* We will return to this concept in Chapter 6, when we consider *ethos* and *pathos* in more depth.

Given this background on the classical appeals, let's turn now to *logos*—the logic and structure of arguments.

Issue Questions as the Origins of Argument

At the heart of any argument is an issue, which we can define as a controversial topic area such as "the labeling of biotech foods" or "racial profiling," that gives rise to differing points of view and conflicting claims. A writer can usually focus an issue by asking an issue question that invites at least two alternative answers. Within any complex issue—for example, the issue of abortion—there are usually a number of separate issue questions: Should abortions be legal? Should the federal government authorize Medicaid payments for abortions? When does a fetus become a human being (at conception? at three months? at quickening? at birth?)? What are the effects of legalizing abortion? (One person might stress that legalized abortion leads to greater freedom for women. Another person might respond that it lessens a society's respect for human life.)

Difference between an Issue Question and an Information Question

Of course, not all questions are issue questions that can be answered reasonably in two or more differing ways; thus not all questions can lead to effective arguments. Rhetoricians have traditionally distinguished between *explication,* which is writing that sets out to inform or explain, and *argumentation,* which sets out to change a reader's mind. On the surface, at least, this seems like a useful distinction. If a reader is interested in a writer's question mainly to gain new knowledge about a subject, then the writer's essay could be considered explication rather than argument. According to this view, the following questions about teenage pregnancy might be called information questions rather than issue questions:

> How does the teenage pregnancy rate in the United States compare with the rate in Sweden? If the rates are different, why?

Although both questions seem to call for information rather than for argument, we believe that the second one would be an issue question if reasonable people disagreed on the answer. Thus, different writers might agree that the teenage pregnancy rate in the United States is seven times higher than the rate in Sweden. But they might disagree about why. One writer might emphasize Sweden's practical, secular sex-education courses, leading to more consistent use of contraceptives among Swedish teenagers. Another writer might point to the higher use of oral contraceptives among teenage girls in Sweden (partly a result of Sweden's generous national health program) and to less reliance on condoms for preventing pregnancy. Another might argue that moral decay in the United States or a breakdown of the traditional family is at fault. Thus, underneath the surface of what looks like a simple explication of the "truth" is really a controversy.

How to Identify an Issue Question

You can generally tell whether a question is an issue question or an information question by examining your purpose in relationship to your audience. If your relationship to your audience is that of teacher to learner, so that your audience hopes to gain new information, knowledge, or understanding that you possess, then your question is probably an information question. But if your relationship to your audience is that of advocate to decision maker or jury, so that your audience needs to make up its mind on something and is weighing different points of view, then the question you address is an issue question.

Often the same question can be an information question in one context and an issue question in another. Let's look at the following examples:

- How does a diesel engine work? (This is probably an information question, because reasonable people who know about diesel engines will probably agree on how they work. This question would be posed by an audience of new learners.)
- Why is a diesel engine more fuel efficient than a gasoline engine? (This also seems to be an information question, because all experts will probably agree on the answer. Once again, the audience seems to be new learners, perhaps students in an automotive class.)
- What is the most cost-effective way to produce diesel fuel from crude oil? (This could be an information question if experts agree and you are addressing new learners. But if you are addressing engineers and one engineer says process X is the most cost-effective and another argues for process Y, then the question is an issue question.)
- Should the present highway tax on diesel fuel be increased? (This is certainly an issue question. One person says yes; another says no; another offers a compromise.)

■ ■ ■ **FOR CLASS DISCUSSION** Information Questions versus Issue Questions
Working as a class or in small groups, try to decide which of the following questions are information questions and which are issue questions. Many of them could be either, depending on the rhetorical context. For such questions, create hypothetical contexts to show your reasoning.

1. What percentage of public schools in the United States are failing?
2. What is the cause of failing public schools in the United States?
3. What is the effect of violent TV shows on children?
4. Is genetically modified corn safe for human consumption?
5. Should a woman with newly detected breast cancer opt for a radical mastectomy (complete removal of the breast and surrounding lymph tissue) or a lumpectomy (removal of the malignant lump without removal of the whole breast)? ■ ■ ■

Difference between a Genuine Argument and a Pseudo-Argument

Although every argument features an issue question with alternative answers, not every dispute over answers is a rational argument. Rational arguments require two additional factors: (1) reasonable participants who operate within the conventions of reasonable behavior and (2) potentially sharable assumptions that can serve as a starting place or foundation for the argument. Lacking one or both of these conditions, disagreements remain stalled at the level of pseudo-arguments.

Pseudo-Arguments: Fanatical Believers and Fanatical Skeptics   A reasonable argument assumes the possibility of growth and change; disputants may modify their views as they acknowledge strengths in an alternative view or weaknesses in their own. Such growth becomes impossible—and argument degenerates to pseudo-argument—when disputants are fanatically committed to their positions. Consider the case of the fanatical believer or the fanatical skeptic.

Fanatical believers believe that their claims are true because they say so, period. Often fanatical believers follow some party line with knee-jerk predictability, their ideological convictions often shaped by their favorite, not-to-be-disputed texts, Web sites, blogs, or radio shows. Once you've pushed their buttons on global warming, welfare, abortion, gun control, gay marriage, or some other issue, you can expect only a barrage of never-changing pronouncements. Disagreeing with a fanatical believer is like ordering the surf to quiet down. The only response is another crashing wave.

The fanatical skeptic, in contrast, dismisses the possibility of proving anything. So what if the sun has risen every day of recorded history? That's no proof that it will rise tomorrow. Short of absolute proof, which never exists, fanatical skeptics accept nothing. In a world where the most we can hope for is increased audience adherence to our ideas, the fanatical skeptic demands an ironclad, logical demonstration of our claim's rightness. In the presence of fanatical believers or skeptics, then, genuine argument is impossible.

Another Source of Pseudo-Arguments: Lack of Shared Assumptions   A reasonable argument is difficult to conduct unless the participants share common assumptions on which the argument can be grounded. Like axioms in geometry, these shared assumptions serve as the starting point for the argument. Consider the following conversation, in which Randall refuses to accept Rhonda's assumptions:

RHONDA: Smoking should be banned because it causes cancer.

RANDALL: So it causes cancer. What's so bad about that?

RHONDA: Don't be perverse, Randy. Cancer causes suffering and death.

RANDALL: Rhonda, my dear girl, don't be such a twinkie. Suffering and death are just part of the human condition.

RHONDA: But that doesn't make them desirable, especially when they can be avoided.

RANDALL: Perhaps in particular cases they're avoidable for a while, but in the long run, we all suffer and we all die, so who cares if smoking causes what's inevitable anyway?

This, we would suggest, is a doomed argument. Without any shared assumptions (for example, that cancer is bad, that suffering should be minimized and death delayed), there's no "bottom" to this argument, just an endless regress of reasons based on more reasons. Although calling assumptions into question is a legitimate way to deepen and complicate our understanding of an issue, unwillingness to accept any assumption makes argument impossible.

Lack of shared assumptions often dooms arguments about purely personal opinions—for example, someone's claim that opera is boring or that pizza is better than nachos. Of course, a pizza-versus-nachos argument might be possible if the disputants agreed on a criterion such as the value of balanced nutrition. For example, a nutritionist could argue that pizza is better than nachos because it provides more balanced nutrients per calorie. But if one of the disputants responds, "Nah, nachos are better than pizza because nachos taste better," then he makes a different assumption—"My sense of taste is better than your sense of taste." This is a wholly personal standard, an assumption that others are unable to share.

■ ■ ■   **FOR CLASS DISCUSSION**   Reasonable Arguments versus Pseudo-Arguments
The following questions can all be answered in alternative ways. However, not all of them will lead to reasonable arguments. Try to decide which questions will lead to reasonable arguments and which will lead only to pseudo-arguments.

1. Are the *Star Wars* films good science fiction?
2. Is postmodern architecture beautiful?
3. Should cities subsidize professional sports venues?
4. Is this abstract oil painting by a monkey smearing paint on a canvas a true work of art?
5. Are nose rings and tongue studs attractive?

■ ■ ■

Frame of an Argument: A Claim Supported by Reasons

We said earlier that an argument originates in an *issue question,* which by definition is any question that provokes disagreement about the best answer. When you write an argument, your task is to take a position on the issue and to support it with reasons and evidence. The *claim* of your essay is the position you want your audience to accept. To put it another way, your claim is your essay's thesis statement, a one-sentence summary answer to your issue question. Your task, then, is to make a claim and support it with reasons.

What Is a Reason?

A *reason* (also called a *premise*) is a claim used to support another claim. In speaking or writing, a reason is usually linked to the claim with connecting words such as *because, since, for, so, thus, consequently,* and *therefore,* indicating that the claim follows logically from the reason.

Let's take an example. In one of our recent classes a female naval ROTC student argued that women should be allowed to serve on submarines. A heated discussion quickly followed, expanding into the more general issue of whether women should be allowed to join military combat units. Here are frameworks the class developed for two alternative positions on that issue:

One View

CLAIM: Women should be barred from joining military combat units.

REASON 1:   Women for the most part don't have the strength or endurance for combat roles.

REASON 2:   Women in close-knit combat units would hurt unit morale by introducing sexual jealousies.

REASON 3:   Women haven't been socialized into fighters and wouldn't have the "Kill them with a bayonet" spirit that men can get.

REASON 4: Women would be less reliable to a combat unit if they became pregnant or had to care for infants or small children.

Alternative View

CLAIM: Women should be allowed to join combat units in the military.

REASON 1:   Millions of women are stronger and more physically fit than most men; women selected for combat duty would have the strength and endurance for the job.

REASON 2:   The image of women as combat soldiers would help society overcome harmful gender stereotyping.

REASON 3:   Women have already proven combat effectiveness in the Iraq war, where there are no front lines.

REASON 4:   Women would have more opportunities for career advancement in the military if they could serve in combat units.

REASON 5:   Allowing women to serve in combat units promotes equal rights.

Formulating a list of reasons in this way breaks your argumentative task into a series of subtasks. It gives you a frame for building your argument in parts. In the previous example, the frame for the argument supporting women in combat suggests five different lines of reasoning a writer might pursue. A writer might use all five reasons or select only two or three, depending on which reasons would most persuade the intended audience. Each line of reasoning would be developed in its own separate section of the argument.

For example, you might begin one section of your argument with the following sentence: "Women should be allowed to join combat units because they have already proven their combat effectiveness in the Iraq war, where there are no front lines." You would then provide examples of women engaged in heavy fighting in Iraq (even though they are assigned to support units) and show their combat effectiveness. You might also need to support the underlying assumption that women's combat effectiveness, demonstrated in support units, would be transferred to combat units. (How one articulates and supports the underlying assumptions of an argument will be developed in Chapter 4 when we discuss warrants and backing.) You would then proceed in the same way for each separate section of your argument.

To summarize our point in this section, the frame of an argument consists of a claim (the thesis statement of the essay), which is supported by one or more reasons, which are in turn supported by evidence or sequences of further reasons.

Expressing Reasons in Because Clauses

Chances are that when you were a child the word *because* contained magical explanatory powers:

DOROTHY: I want to go home now.

TOMMY: Why?

DOROTHY: Because.

TOMMY: Because why?

DOROTHY: Just because.

Somehow *because* seemed decisive. It persuaded people to accept your view of the world; it changed people's minds. Later, as you got older, you discovered that *because* only introduced your arguments and that it was the reasons following *because* that made the difference. Still, *because* introduced you to the powers potentially residing in the adult world of logic.

Of course, there are many other ways to express the logical connection between a reason and a claim. Our language is rich in ways of stating *because* relationships:

- Women shouldn't be allowed to join combat units because they don't have the strength or endurance for combat roles.
- Women don't have the strength or endurance for combat roles. Therefore women should not be allowed to join combat units.
- Women don't have the strength or endurance for combat roles, so they should not be allowed to join combat units.
- One reason why women should not be allowed to join combat units is that they don't have the strength or endurance for combat roles.
- My argument that women should not be allowed to join combat units is based mainly on evidence that women don't have the strength or endurance for combat roles.

Even though logical relationships can be stated in various ways, writing out one or more *because* clauses seems to be the most succinct and manageable way to clarify an argument for oneself. We therefore suggest that sometime in the writing process you create a *working thesis statement* that summarizes your main reasons as *because* clauses attached to your claim.* Just when you compose your own working thesis statement depends largely on your writing process. Some writers like to plan out their whole argument from the start and often compose their working thesis statements with *because* clauses before they write their rough drafts. Others discover their arguments as they write. And sometimes it is a combination of both. For these writers, an extended working thesis statement is something they might write halfway through the composing process as a way of ordering their argument when various branches seem to be growing out of control. Or they might compose a working thesis statement at the very end as a way of checking the unity of the final product.

Whenever you write your extended thesis statement, the act of doing so can be simultaneously frustrating and thought provoking. Composing *because* clauses can be a powerful discovery tool, causing you to think of many different kinds of arguments to support your claim. But it is often difficult to wrestle your ideas into the *because* clause shape, which sometimes seems to be overly tidy for the complex network of ideas you are trying to work with. Nevertheless, trying to summarize your argument as a single claim with reasons should help you see more clearly what you have to do.

■ ■ ■   **FOR CLASS DISCUSSION**   **Developing Claims and Reasons**

Try this group exercise to help you see how writing *because* clauses can be a discovery procedure. Divide into small groups. Each group member should contribute an issue that he or she would like to explore. Discussing one person's issue at a time, help each member develop a claim supported by several reasons. Express each reason as a *because* clause. Then write out the working thesis statement for each person's argument by attaching the *because* clauses to the claim. Finally, try to create *because* clauses in support of an alternative claim for each issue. Recorders should select two or three working thesis statements from the group to present to the class as a whole.   ■ ■ ■

Conclusion

This chapter has introduced you to the structure of classical argument, to the rhetorical triangle (message, writer or speaker, and audience) and to the classical appeals of *logos, ethos,* and *pathos.* It has also shown how arguments originate in issue questions, how issue questions differ from information questions, and how arguments differ from pseudo-arguments. At the heart of this chapter we explained that the frame of an argument is a claim supported by reasons. As you generate reasons to support your own arguments, it is often helpful to articulate them as *because* clauses attached to the claim.

---

*A working thesis statement for an argument opposing women in combat units might look like this: *Women should not be allowed to join combat units because they lack the strength, endurance, and "fighting spirit" needed in combat; because being pregnant or having small children would make them unreliable for combat at a moment's notice; and because women's presence would hurt morale of tight-knit combat units.* You might not put a bulky thesis statement like this into your essay itself; rather, a working thesis statement is a behind-the-scenes way of summarizing your argument for yourself so that you can see it whole and clear.

In the next chapter we will see how to support a reason by examining its logical structure, uncovering its unstated assumptions, and planning a strategy of development.

WRITING ASSIGNMENT An Issue Question and Working Thesis Statements

Decide on an issue and a claim for a classical argument that you would like to write. Write a one-sentence question that summarizes the controversial issue that your claim addresses. Then draft a working thesis statement for your proposed argument. Organize the thesis as a claim with bulleted *because* clauses for reasons. You should have at least two reasons, but it is okay to have three or four. Also include an *opposing thesis statement*—that is, a claim with *because* clauses for an alternative position on your issue.

Recall that in Part One we emphasized exploratory writing as a way of resisting closure and helping you wrestle with multiple perspectives. Now we ask you to begin a process of closure by developing a thesis statement that condenses your argument into a claim with supporting reasons. However, as we emphasize throughout this text, drafting itself is an *exploratory process*. Writers almost always discover new ideas when they write a first draft; as they take their writing project through multiple drafts, their views may change substantially. Often, in fact, honest writers can change positions on an issue by discovering that a counterargument is stronger than their own. So the working thesis statement that you submit for this assignment may evolve substantially once you begin to draft.

In this chapter, as well as in Chapters 4 and 5, we will follow the process of student writer Carmen Tieu as she constructed an argument on violent video games. During earlier exploratory writing, she wrote about a classroom incident in which her professor had described video game playing as gendered behavior (overwhelmingly male). The professor indicated his dislike for such games, pointing to their antisocial, dehumanizing values. In her freewrite, Carmen described her own enjoyment of violent video games—particularly first-person-shooter games—and explored the pleasure that she derived from beating boys at Halo 2. She knew that she wanted to write an argument on this issue. What follows is Carmen's submission for this assignment.

Carmen's Issue Question and Working Thesis Statements

Issue Question: Should girls be encouraged to play first-person-shooter video games?

My claim: First-person-shooter (FPS) video games are great activities for girls

- because beating guys at their own game is empowering for girls
- because being skilled at FPS games frees girls from feminine stereotypes
- because they give girls a different way of bonding with males
- because they give girls new insights into a male subculture

Opposing claim: First-person shooter games are a bad activity for anyone, especially girls,

- because they promote antisocial values such as indiscriminate killing
- because they amplify the bad macho side of male stereotypes
- because they waste valuable time that could have been spent on something constructive
- because FPS games could encourage women to see themselves as objects ■

For additional writing, reading, and research resources, go to
www.mycomplab.com

The Logical Structure of Arguments

4

In Chapter 3 you learned that the core of an argument is a claim supported by reasons and that these reasons can often be stated as *because* clauses attached to a claim. In the present chapter we examine the logical structure of arguments in more depth.

An Overview of *Logos:* What Do We Mean by the "Logical Structure" of an Argument?

As you will recall from our discussion of the rhetorical triangle, *logos* refers to the strength of an argument's support and its internal consistency. *Logos* is the argument's logical structure. But what do we mean by "logical structure"?

Formal Logic versus Real-World Logic

First of all, what we *don't* mean by logical structure is the kind of precise certainty you get in a philosophy class in formal logic. Logic classes deal with symbolic assertions that are universal and unchanging, such as "If all ps are qs and if r is a p, then r is a q." This statement is logically certain so long as p, q, and r are pure abstractions. But in the real world, p, q, and r turn into actual things, and the relationships among them suddenly become fuzzy. For example, p might be a class of actions called "Sexual Harassment," while q could be the class called "Actions That Justify Dismissal from a Job." If r is the class "Telling Off-Color Stories," then the logic of our p–q–r statement suggests that telling off-color stories (r) is an instance of sexual harassment (p), which in turn is an action justifying dismissal from one's job (q).

Now, most of us would agree that sexual harassment is a serious offense that might well justify dismissal from a job. In turn, we might agree that telling off-color stories, if the jokes are sufficiently raunchy and are inflicted on an unwilling audience, constitutes sexual harassment. But few of us would want to say categorically that all people who tell off-color stories are harassing their listeners and ought to be fired. Most of us would want to know the particulars of the case before making a final judgment.

In the real world, then, it is difficult to say that rs are always ps or that every instance of a p results in q. That is why we discourage students from using the word *prove* in claims they write for arguments (as in "This paper will prove that euthanasia is wrong"). Real-world arguments seldom *prove* anything. They can only make a good case for something, a case that is more or less strong, more or less probable. Often the best you can hope for is to strengthen the resolve of those who agree with you or weaken the resistance of those who oppose you.

The Role of Assumptions

A key difference, then, between formal logic and real-world argument is that real-world arguments are not grounded in abstract, universal statements. Rather, as we shall see, they must be grounded in beliefs, assumptions, or values granted by the audience. A second important difference is that in real-world arguments these beliefs, assumptions, or values are often unstated. So long as writer and audience share the same assumptions, it's fine to leave them unstated. But if these underlying assumptions aren't shared, the writer has a problem.

To illustrate the nature of this problem, consider one of the arguments we introduced in the last chapter.

> Women should be allowed to join combat units because the image of women in combat would help eliminate gender stereotypes.

On the face of it, this is a plausible argument. But the argument is persuasive only if the audience agrees with the writer's assumption that it is a good thing to eliminate gender stereotyping. The writer assumes that gender stereotyping (for example, seeing men as the fighters who are protecting the women and children back home) is harmful and that society would be better off without such fixed gender roles. But what if you believed that some gender roles are biologically based, divinely intended, or otherwise culturally essential and that society should strive to maintain these gender roles rather than dismiss them as "stereotypes"? If such were the case, you might believe as a consequence that our culture should socialize women to be nurturers, not fighters, and that some essential trait of "womanhood" would be at risk if women served in combat. If these were your beliefs, the argument wouldn't work for you because you would reject its underlying assumption. To persuade you with this line of reasoning, the writer would have to show not only how women in combat would help eliminate gender stereotypes but also why these stereotypes are harmful and why society would be better off without them.

The Core of an Argument: The Enthymeme

The previous core argument ("Women should be allowed to join combat units because the image of women in combat would help eliminate gender stereotypes") is an incomplete logical structure called an *enthymeme*. Its persuasiveness depends on an underlying assumption or belief that the audience must accept. To complete the enthymeme and make it effective, the audience must willingly supply a missing premise—in this case, that gender stereotypes are harmful and should be eliminated.

The Greek philosopher Aristotle showed how successful enthymemes root the speaker's argument in assumptions, beliefs, or values held by the audience. The word *enthymeme* comes from the Greek *en* (meaning "in") and *thumos* (meaning "mind"). Listeners or readers must have "in mind" an assumption, belief, or value that lets them willingly supply the missing premise. If the audience is unwilling to supply the missing premise, then the argument fails. Our point is that successful arguments depend both on what the arguer says and on what the audience already has "in mind."

To clarify the concept of "enthymeme," let's go over this same territory again more slowly, examining what we mean by "incomplete logical structure." The sentence "Women should be allowed to join combat units because the image of women in combat would help eliminate gender stereotypes" is an enthymeme. It combines a claim (women should be allowed to join combat units) with a reason expressed as a *because* clause (because the image of women in combat would help eliminate gender stereotypes). To render this enthymeme logically complete, the audience must willingly supply a missing assumption—that gender stereotypes are harmful and should be eliminated. If your audience accepts this assumption, then you have a starting place on which to build an effective argument. If your audience doesn't accept this assumption, then you must supply another argument to support it, and so on until you find common ground with your audience.

To sum up:

1. Claims are supported with reasons. You can usually state a reason as a *because* clause attached to a claim (see Chapter 3).
2. A *because* clause attached to a claim is an incomplete logical structure called an enthymeme. To create a complete logical structure from an enthymeme, the underlying assumption (or assumptions) must be articulated.
3. To serve as an effective starting point for the argument, this underlying assumption should be a belief, value, or principle that the audience grants.

Let's illustrate this structure by putting the previous example into schematic form.

ENTHYMEME

CLAIM Women should be allowed to join combat units

REASON because the image of women in combat would help eliminate gender stereotypes.

Audience must supply this assumption ⟶

UNDERLYING ASSUMPTION
Gender stereotypes are harmful and should be eliminated.

■ ■ ■   **FOR CLASS DISCUSSION**   Identifying Underlying Assumptions

Working individually or in small groups, identify the unstated assumption that the audience must supply in order to make the following enthymemes persuasive.

Example

Enthymeme: Rabbits make good pets because they are gentle.

Underlying assumption: Gentle animals make good pets.

1. We shouldn't elect Joe as committee chair because he is too bossy.
2. Drugs should not be legalized because legalization would greatly increase the number of drug addicts.
3. Airport screeners should use racial profiling because doing so will increase the odds of stopping terrorists.
4. Racial profiling should not be used by airport screeners because it violates a person's civil rights.
5. We should strengthen the Endangered Species Act because doing so will preserve genetic diversity on the planet.
6. The Endangered Species Act is too stringent because it severely damages the economy.   ■ ■ ■

Adopting a Language for Describing Arguments: The Toulmin System

Understanding a new field usually requires us to learn a new vocabulary. For example, if you were taking biology for the first time, you'd have to memorize dozens and dozens of new terms. Luckily, the field of argument requires us to learn a mere handful of new terms. A particularly useful set of argument terms, one we'll be using occasionally throughout the rest of this text, comes from philosopher Stephen Toulmin. In the 1950s, Toulmin rejected the prevailing models of argument based on formal logic in favor of a very audience-based courtroom model.

Toulmin's courtroom model differs from formal logic in that it assumes that (1) all assertions and assumptions are contestable by "opposing counsel" and that (2) all final "verdicts" about the persuasiveness of the opposing arguments will be rendered by a neutral third party, a judge or jury. As writers, keeping in mind the "opposing counsel" forces us to anticipate counterarguments and to question our assumptions. Keeping in mind the judge and jury reminds us to answer opposing arguments fully, without rancor, and to present positive reasons for supporting our case as well as negative reasons for disbelieving the opposing case. Above all else, Toulmin's model reminds us not to construct an argument that appeals only to those who already agree with us. In short, it helps arguers tailor arguments to their audiences.

The system we use for analyzing arguments combines Toulmin's language with Aristotle's concept of the enthymeme. It builds on the system you have already been practicing. We simply need to add a few key terms from Toulmin. The first term is Toulmin's *warrant,* the name we will now use for the underlying assumption that turns an enthymeme into a complete logical structure as shown at the top of page 77.

Toulmin derives his term *warrant* from the concept of "warranty" or "guarantee." The warrant is the value, belief, or principle that the audience has to hold if the soundness of

> **ENTHYMEME**
>
> CLAIM Women should be allowed to join combat units
>
> REASON because the image of women in combat would help eliminate gender stereotypes.

Audience must accept this warrant

> **WARRANT**
> Gender stereotypes are harmful and should be eliminated.

the argument is to be guaranteed or warranted. We sometimes make similar use of this word in ordinary language when we say, "That is an unwarranted conclusion," meaning one has leaped from information about a situation to a conclusion about that situation without any sort of general principle to justify or "warrant" that move. Thus the warrant—once accepted by the audience—"guarantees" the soundness of the argument.

But arguments need more than claims, reasons, and warrants. These are simply one-sentence statements—the frame of an argument, not a developed argument. To give body and weight to our arguments and make them convincing, we need what Toulmin calls *grounds* and *backing*. Let's start with grounds. Grounds are the supporting evidence that cause an audience to accept your reason. Grounds are facts, data, statistics, causal links, testimony, examples, anecdotes—the blood and muscle that flesh out the skeletal frame of your enthymeme. Toulmin suggests that grounds are "what you have to go on" in an argument—the stuff you can point to and present before a jury. Here is how grounds fit into our emerging argument schema.

> **ENTHYMEME**
>
> CLAIM Women should be allowed to join combat units
>
> REASON because the image of women in combat would help eliminate gender stereotypes.

Grounds support the reason

> **GROUNDS**
>
> • Examples showing how the image of women in combat gear packing a rifle, driving a tank, firing a machine gun from a foxhole, or radioing in artillery would counter the prevailing stereotypes of woman as soft and nuturing.
>
> • Arguments showing how the shock impact of these combat images would help eliminate gender stereotypes.

In many cases, successful arguments require just these three components: a claim, a reason, and grounds. If the audience already accepts the unstated assumption behind the reason (the warrant), then the warrant can safely remain in the background unstated and unexamined. But if there is a chance that the audience will question or doubt the warrant, then the writer needs to back it up by providing an argument in its support. *Backing* is the argument that supports the warrant. It may require no more than one or two sentences or as much as a major section in your argument. Its goal is to persuade the audience to accept the warrant. Here is how *backing* is added to our schema:

Backing supports the warrant

WARRANT
Gender stereotypes are harmful and should be eliminated.

BACKING
• Arguments showing why gender stereotypes are harmful.
  • Macho male stereotypes keep men from developing their nurturing side.
  • Girly-girl stereotypes hinder women from developing power and autonomy.
• Examples of benefits that would come from eliminating gender stereotypes such as promoting equality between genders

Toulmin's system next asks us to imagine how a resistant audience would try to refute our argument. Specifically, the adversarial audience might challenge our reason and grounds by showing how letting women become combat soldiers wouldn't do much to end gender stereotyping. Or the adversary might attack our warrant and backing by showing how some gender stereotypes are worth keeping.

In the case of the argument supporting women in combat, an adversary might offer one or more of the following rebuttals:

ENTHYMEME

CLAIM Women should be allowed to join combat units

REASON because the image of women in combat would eliminate gender stereotypes.

GROUNDS
• Examples showing how the image of women in combat gear packing a rifle, driving a tank, firing a machine gun from a foxhole, or radioing in artillery would counter the prevailing stereotypes of women as soft and nurturing.
• Arguments showing how the shock impact of these combat images would help eliminate gender stereotypes.

Writer must anticipate these attacks from skeptics

CONDITIONS OF REBUTTAL
A skeptic can attack the reason and grounds

Arguments that letting women serve in combat wouldn't eliminate gender stereotypes
• Few women would join combat units.
• Those who did would be considered freaks.
• Most girls would still identify with Barbie dolls, not women as combat soldiers.

WARRANT
Gender stereotypes are harmful and should be eliminated.

BACKING
• Arguments showing why gender stereotypes are harmful
  • Macho male stereotypes keep men from developing their nurturing side
  • Girly-girl stereotypes hinder women from developing power and autonomy
• Examples of benefits that would come from eliminating gender stereotypes such as promoting equality between genders

POSSIBLE CONDITIONS OF REBUTTAL
A skeptic can attack the warrant and backing

Arguments showing that it is important to maintain traditional distinctions between men and women
• These role differences are biologically determined, divinely inspired, or otherwise important culturally.
• Women's strength is in nurturing, not fighting.
• Nature of womanhood would be sullied by putting women in combat.

78

As this example shows, adversarial readers can question an argument's reasons and grounds or its warrant and backing or sometimes both. Conditions of rebuttal remind writers to look at their arguments from the perspective of skeptics. The same principle can be illustrated in the following analysis of an argument that cocaine and heroin should be legalized.

ENTHYMEME

CLAIM Cocaine and heroin should be legalized

REASON because legalization would eliminate the black market in drugs.

GROUNDS

Statistical evidence and arguments showing how legalization would end black market:

- Statistics and data showing the size of the current black market

- Examples, anecdotes, facts showing how the black market works

- Causal explanation showing that selling cocaine and heroin legally in state-controlled stores would lower price and eliminate drug dealers

WARRANT

Eliminating the black market in drugs is good

BACKING

Statistics and examples about the ill effects of the black market

- The high cost of the black market to crime victims

- The high cost to taxpayers of waging the war against drugs

- The high cost of prisons to house incarcerated drug dealers

- Evidence that huge profits make drug dealing more attractive than ordinary jobs

CONDITIONS OF REBUTTAL
Attacking the reason and grounds

- Arguments showing that legalizing cocaine and heroin would not eliminate the black market in drugs

- Perhaps taxes on the drugs would keep the costs above black market prices

- Perhaps new kinds of illegal designer drugs would be developed and sold on the black market

CONDITIONS OF REBUTTAL
Attacking the warrant and backing

Arguments showing that the benefits of eliminating the black market are outweighed by the costs

- The number of new drug users and addicts would be unacceptably high.

- The health and economic cost of treating addiction would be too high.

- The social costs of selling drugs legally in liquor stores would bring harmful change to our cultural values.

Toulmin's final term, used to limit the force of a claim and indicate the degree of its probable truth, is *qualifier*. The qualifier reminds us that real-world arguments almost never prove a claim. We may say things such as *very likely, probably,* or *maybe* to indicate the strength of the claim we are willing to draw from our grounds and warrant. Thus if there are exceptions to your warrant or if your grounds are not very strong, you will have to qualify your claim. For example, you might say, "Except in rare cases, women should not be allowed in combat units," or "With full awareness of the potential dangers, I suggest we consider the option of legalizing drugs as a way of ending the ill effects of the black market." In our future displays of the Toulmin scheme we will omit the qualifiers, but you should always remember that no argument is 100 percent persuasive.

■ ■ ■   **FOR CLASS DISCUSSION**   Developing Enthymemes with the Toulmin Schema

Working individually or in small groups, imagine that you have to write arguments developing the six enthymemes listed in the For Class Discussion exercise on page 76. Use the Toulmin schema to help you determine what you need to consider when developing each enthymeme. We suggest that you try a four-box diagram structure as a way of visualizing the schema. We have applied the Toulmin schema to the first enthymeme: "We shouldn't elect Joe as committee chair because he is too bossy."

ENTHYMEME

CLAIM We shouldn't elect Joe as committee chair
REASON because he is too bossy.

GROUNDS

Evidence of Joe's bossiness

• Examples of the way he dominates meetings—doesn't call on people, talks too much

• Testimony about his bossiness from people who have served with him on committees

• Anecdotes about his abrasive style

WARRANT
Bossy people make bad committee chairs.

BACKING
Problems caused by bossy committee chairs

• Bossy people don't inspire cooperation and enthusiam.

• Bossy people make others angry.

• Bossy people tend to make bad decisions because they don't incorporate advice from others

CONDITIONS OF REBUTTAL
Attacking the reason and grounds

Evidence that Joe is not bossy or is only occasionally bossy

• Counterevidence showing his collaborative style

• Testimony from people who have liked Joe as a leader and claim he isn't bossy; testimony about his cooperativeness and kindness

• Testimony that anecdotes about Joe's bossiness aren't typical

CONDITIONS OF REBUTTAL
Attacking the warrant and backing

• Arguments that bossiness can be a good trait

  • Sometimes bossy people make good chairpersons.

  • Argument that this committee needs a bossy person who can make decisions and get things done.

• Argument that Joe has other traits of good leadership that outweigh his bossiness

■ ■ ■

Using Toulmin's Schema to Determine a Strategy of Support

So far we have seen that a claim, a reason, and a warrant form the frame for a line of reasoning in an argument. Most of the words in an argument, however, are devoted to grounds and backing.

For an illustration of how a writer can use the Toulmin schema to generate ideas for an argument, consider the following case. In April 2005, the Texas house of representatives passed a bill banning "sexually suggestive" cheerleading. Across the nation, evening television show comics poked fun at the bill, while newspaper editorialists debated its wisdom and constitutionality. In one of our classes, however, several students, including one who had earned a high school varsity letter in competitive cheerleading, defended the bill by contending that provocative dance moves hurt the athletic image of cheerleading. In the following example, which draws on ideas developed in class discussion, we create a hypothetical student writer (we'll call her Chandale) who argues in defense of the Texas bill. Chandale's argument is based on the following enthymeme:

> The cheerleading bill to ban suggestive dancing is good because it promotes a view of female cheerleaders as athletes rather than exotic dancers.

Chandale used the Toulmin schema to brainstorm ideas for developing her argument. Here are her notes:

Chandale's Planning Notes Using the Toulmin Schema

Enthymeme: The cheerleading bill to ban suggestive dancing is good because it promotes a view of female cheerleaders as athletes rather than exotic dancers.

Grounds: First, I've got to use evidence to show that that cheerleaders are athletes.

- Cheerleaders at my high school are carefully chosen for their stamina and skill after exhausting two-week tryouts.
- We begin all practices with a mile run and an hour of warm-up exercises—also expected to work out on our own for at least an hour on weekends and on days without practice.
- We learned competitive routines and stunts consisting of lifts, tosses, flips, catches, and gymnastic moves. This requires athletic ability! We'd practice these stunts for hours each week.
- Throughout the year cheerleaders have to attend practices, camps, and workshops to learn new routines and stunts.
- Our squad competed in competitions around the state.
- Competitive cheerleading is a growing movement across the country—University of Maryland has made it a varsity sport for women.
- Skimpy uniforms and suggestive dance moves destroy this image by making women eye candy like the Dallas Cowboys cheerleaders.

Warrant: It is a good thing to view female cheerleaders as athletes.

Backing: Now I need to make the case that it is good to see cheerleaders as athletes rather than as eye candy.

- Athletic competition builds self-esteem, independence, a powerful sense of achievement— contributes to health, strength, conditioning.
- Competitive cheerleading is one of the few sports where teams are made up of both men and women. (Why is this good? Should I use this?)

■ The suggestive dance moves turn women into sex objects whose function is to be gazed at by men—suggests that women's value is based on their beauty and sex appeal.

■ We are talking about HIGH SCHOOL cheerleading—very bad early influence on girls to model themselves on Dallas Cowboys cheerleaders or sexy MTV videos of rock stars.

■ Junior high girls want to do what senior high girls do—suggestive dance moves promote sexuality way too early.

Conditions of Rebuttal: Would anybody try to rebut my reasons and grounds that cheerleading is an athletic activity?

■ No. I think it is obvious that cheerleading is an athletic activity once they see my evidence.

■ However, they might not think of cheerleading as a sport. They might say that the University of Maryland just declared it a sport as a cheap way to meet Title IX federal rules to have more women's sports. I'll have to make sure that I show this is really a sport.

■ They also might say that competitive cheerleading shouldn't be encouraged because it is too dangerous—lots of serious injuries including paralysis have been caused by mistakes in doing flips, lifts, and tosses. If I include this, maybe I could say that other sports are dangerous also—and it is in fact danger that makes this sport so exciting.

Would anyone doubt my warrant and backing that it is good to see female cheerleaders as athletes?

■ Yes, all those people who laughed at the Texas legislature think that people are being too prudish and that banning suggestive dance moves violates free expression. I'll need to make my case that it is bad for young girls to see themselves as sex objects too early.

The information that Chandale lists under "grounds" is what she sees as the facts of the case—the hard data she will use as evidence to support her contention that cheerleading is an athletic activity. The paragraph that follows shows how this argument might look when placed into written form.

First Part of Chandale's Argument

Although evening television show comedians have made fun of the Texas legislature's desire to ban "suggestive" dance moves from cheerleading routines, I applaud this bill because it promotes a healthy view of female cheerleaders as athletes rather than show-girls. I was lucky enough to attend a high school where cheerleading is a sport, and I earned a varsity letter as a cheerleader. To get on my high school's cheerleading squad, students have to go through an exhausting two-week tryout of workouts and instruction in the basic routines; then they are chosen based on their stamina and skill. Once on the squad, cheerleaders begin all practices with a mile run and an hour of grueling warm-up exercises and are expected to exercise on their own on weekends. As a result of this regimen, cheerleaders achieve and maintain a top level of physical fitness. In addition, to get on the squad, students must be able to do handstands, cartwheels, handsprings, high jumps, and the splits. Each year the squad builds up to its complex routines and stunts consisting of lifts, tosses, flips, catches, and gymnastic moves that only trained athletes can do. In tough competitions at the regional and state levels, the cheerleading squad demonstrates its athletic talent. This view of cheerleading as a competitive sport is also spreading to colleges. As reported recently in a number of newspapers, the University of Maryland has made cheerleading a varsity sport, and many other universities are following suit. Athletic performance of this caliber is a far cry from the sexy dancing that many high school girls often associate with cheerleading. By banning suggestive dancing in cheerleading routines, the Texas legislature creates an opportunity for schools to emphasize the athleticism of cheerleading.

As you can see, Chandale has plenty of evidence for arguing that competitive cheerleading is an athletic activity quite different from sexy dancing. But how effective is this argument as it stands? Is this all she needs? The Toulmin schema encourages writers to include—if needed for the intended audience—explicit support for their warrants as well as attention to conditions for rebuttal. Because the overwhelming national response to the Texas law was ridicule at the perceived prudishness of the legislators, Chandale decides to expand her argument as follows:

Continuation of Chandale's Argument

Whether we see cheerleading as a sport or as sexy dancing is an important issue for women. The erotic dance moves that many high school cheerleaders now incorporate into their routines show that they are emulating the Dallas Cowboys cheerleaders or pop stars on MTV. Our already sexually saturated culture (think of the suggestive clothing marketed to little girls) pushes girls and women to measure their value by their beauty and sex appeal. It would be far healthier, both physically and psychologically, if high school cheerleaders were identified as athletes. For women and men both, competitive cheerleading can build self-esteem, pride in teamwork, and a powerful sense of achievement, as well as promote health, strength, and fitness.

Some people might object to competitive cheerleading by saying that cheerleading isn't really a sport. Some have accused the University of Maryland of making cheerleading a varsity sport only as a cheap way of meeting Title IX requirements. But anyone who has watched competitive cheerleading, and imagined what it would be like to be thrown high into the air, knows instinctively that this is a sport indeed. In fact, other persons might object to competitive cheerleading because it is too dangerous with potential for very severe injuries including paralysis. Obviously the sport is dangerous—but so are many sports, including football, gymnastics, diving, or trampoline. The danger and difficulty of the sport is part of its appeal. Part of what can make cheerleaders as athletes better role models for girls than cheerleaders as erotic dancers is the courage and training needed for success. Of course, the Texas legislators might not have had athleticism in mind when they banned suggestive dancing. They might only have been promoting their vision of morality. But at stake are the role models we set for young girls. I'll pick an athlete over a Dallas Cowboys cheerleader every time.

Our example suggests how a writer can use the Toulmin schema to generate ideas for an argument. For evidence, Chandale draws primarily on her personal experiences as a cheerleader/athlete and on her knowledge of popular culture. She also draws on her reading of several newspapers articles about the University of Maryland's making cheerleading a varsity sport. (In an academic paper rather than a newspaper editorial, she would need to document these sources through formal citations.) Although many arguments depend on research, many can be supported wholly or in part from your own personal experiences, so don't neglect the wealth of evidence from your own life when searching for data. A more detailed discussion of evidence in arguments occurs in Chapter 5.

■ ■ ■ **FOR CLASS DISCUSSION**   Reasons, Warrants, and Conditions of Rebuttal

1. Working individually or in small groups, consider ways you could use evidence to support the stated reason in each of these following partial arguments.

   a. Another reason to oppose a state sales tax is that it is so annoying.

   b. Rap music has a bad influence on teenagers because it promotes disrespect for women.

   c. Professor X is an outstanding teacher because he (she) generously spends so much time outside of class counseling students with personal problems.

2. Now create arguments to support the warrants in each of the partial arguments in exercise 1. The warrants for each of the arguments are stated below.

   a. Support this warrant: We should oppose taxes that are annoying.

   b. Support this warrant: It is bad to promote disrespect for women.

   c. Support this warrant: Time spent counseling students with personal problems is an important criterion for identifying outstanding teachers.

3. Using Toulmin's conditions of rebuttal, work out a strategy for refuting either the stated reasons or the warrants or both in each of the preceding arguments.   ■ ■ ■

The Power of Audience-Based Reasons

As we have seen, both Aristotle's concept of the enthymeme and Toulmin's concept of the warrant focus on the arguer's need to create what we will now call "audience-based reasons." Whenever you ask whether a given piece of writing is persuasive, the immediate rejoinder should always be, "Persuasive to whom?" What seems like a good reason to you may not be a good reason to others. Finding audience-based reasons means finding arguments whose warrants the audience will accept—that is, arguments effectively rooted in your audience's beliefs and values.

Difference between Writer-Based and Audience-Based Reasons

To illustrate the difference between writer-based and audience-based reasons, consider the following hypothetical case. Suppose you believed that the government should build a dam on the nearby Rapid River—a project bitterly opposed by several environmental groups. Which of the following two arguments might you use to address environmentalists?

1. The government should build a dam on the Rapid River because the only alternative power sources are coal-fired or nuclear plants, both of which pose greater risk to the environment than a hydroelectric dam.

2. The government should build a hydroelectric dam on the Rapid River because this area needs cheap power to attract heavy industry.

Clearly, the warrant of argument 1 ("Choose the source of power that poses least risk to the environment") is rooted in the values and beliefs of environmentalists, whereas the warrant of argument 2 ("Growth of industry is good") is likely to make them wince. To environmentalists, new industry means more congestion, more smokestacks, and more pollution. However, argument 2 may appeal to out-of-work laborers or to the business community, to whom new industry means more jobs and a booming economy.

From the perspective of logic alone, arguments 1 and 2 are both sound. They are internally consistent and proceed from reasonable premises. But they will affect different audiences very differently. Neither argument proves that the government should build the dam; both are open to objection. Passionate environmentalists, for example, might counter argument 1 by asking why the government needs to build any power plant at all. They could argue that energy conservation would obviate the need for a new power plant. Or they might argue that building a dam hurts the environment in ways unforeseen by dam supporters. Our point, then, isn't that argument 1 will persuade environmentalists. Rather, our point is that argument 1 will be more persuasive than argument 2 because it is rooted in beliefs and values that the intended audience shares.

Let's consider a second example by returning to Chapter 1 and student Gordon Adams's petition to waive his math requirement. Gordon's central argument, as you will recall, was that as a lawyer he would have no need for algebra. In Toulmin's terms, Gordon's argument looks like this:

ENTHYMEME

CLAIM: I should be exempted from the algebra requirement

REASON: because in my chosen field of law I will have no need for algebra

Stated explicitly in Gordon's argument

GROUNDS

• Testimony from lawyers and others that lawyers never use algebra

Fully developed in Gordon's argument

WARRANT

General education requirements should be based on career utility (that is, if a course is not needed for a particular student's career, it shouldn't be required).

Left unstated in Gordon's argument

BACKING

• Arguments that career utility should be the chief criterion for requiring general education courses

Missing from Gordon's argument

In our discussions of this case with students and faculty, students generally vote to support Gordon's request, whereas faculty generally vote against it. And in fact, the University Standards Committee rejected Gordon's petition, thus delaying his entry into law school.

Why do faculty and students differ on this issue? Mainly they differ because faculty reject Gordon's warrant that general education requirements should serve students' individual career interests. Most faculty believe that general education courses, including math, provide a base of common learning that links us to the past and teaches us modes of understanding useful throughout life.

Gordon's argument thus challenges one of college professors' most cherished beliefs—that the liberal arts and sciences are innately valuable. Further, it threatens his immediate audience, the committee, with a possible flood of student requests to waive other general education requirements on the grounds of their irrelevance to a particular career choice.

How might Gordon have created a more persuasive argument? In our view, Gordon might have prevailed had he accepted the faculty's belief in the value of the math requirement and argued that he had fulfilled the "spirit" of that requirement through alternative means. He could have based his argument on an enthymeme like this:

> I should be exempted from the algebra requirement because my experience as a contractor and inventor has already provided me with equivalent mathematical knowledge.

Following this audience-based approach, he would drop all references to algebra's uselessness for lawyers and expand his discussion of the mathematical savvy he acquired on the job. This argument would honor faculty values and reduce the faculty's fear of setting a bad precedent. Few students are likely to have Gordon's background, and those who do could apply for a similar exemption without threatening the system. Again, this argument might not have won, but it would have gotten a more sympathetic hearing.

■ ■ ■ **FOR CLASS DISCUSSION**   **Audience-Based Reasons**
Working in groups, decide which of the two reasons offered in each instance would be more persuasive to the specified audience. Be prepared to explain your reasoning to the class. Write out the implied warrant for each *because* clause and decide whether the specific audience would likely grant it.

1. Audience: people who advocate a pass/fail grading system on the grounds that the present grading system is too competitive

   a. We should keep the present grading system because it prepares people for the dog-eat-dog pressures of the business world.

   b. We should keep the present grading system because it tells students that certain standards of excellence must be met if individuals are to reach their full potential.

2. Audience: young people ages fifteen to twenty-five

   a. You should become a vegetarian because an all-vegetable diet will help you lower your cholesterol.

   b. You should become a vegetarian because doing so will help eliminate the suffering of animals raised in factory farms.

3. Audience: conservative proponents of "family values"

   a. Same-sex marriages should be legalized because doing so will promote public acceptance of homosexuality.

   b. Same-sex marriages should be legalized because doing so will make it easier for gay people to establish and sustain long-term, stable relationships.

Conclusion

Chapters 3 and 4 have provided an anatomy of argument. They have shown that the core of an argument is a claim with reasons that usually can be summarized in one or more *because* clauses attached to the claim. Often, it is as important to articulate and support the underlying assumptions in your argument (warrants) as it is to support the stated reasons because a successful argument should be rooted in your audience's beliefs and values. In order to plan an audience-based argument strategy, arguers can use the Toulmin schema, which helps writers discover grounds, warrants, and backing for their arguments and to test them through conditions of rebuttal. Finally, we showed how the use of audience-based reasons helps you keep your audience in mind from the start whenever you design a plan for an argument.

WRITING ASSIGNMENT Plan of an Argument's Details

This assignment asks you to return to the working thesis statement that you created for the brief writing assignment in Chapter 3. From that thesis statement extract one of your enthymemes (your claim with one of your *because* clauses). Write out the warrant for your enthymeme. Then use the Toulmin schema to brainstorm the details you might use (grounds, backing, conditions of rebuttal) to convert your enthymeme into a fleshed-out argument. Use as your model Chandale's planning notes on pages 81–82.

Like the brief assignment for Chapter 3, this is a process-oriented brainstorming task aimed at helping you generate ideas for one part of your classical argument. You may end up changing your ideas substantially as you compose the actual argument. What follows is Carmen's submission for this assignment. ■

Carmen's Plan for Part of an Argument

Enthymeme: First-person-shooter (FPS) video games are great activities for girls because playing these games gives girls new insights into male subculture.

Grounds: I've got to show the insights I learned into male subculture.

- The guys who play these video games are intensely competitive.
  - They can play for hours without stopping—intense concentration.
  - They don't multitask—no small talk during the games; total focus on playing.
  - They take delight in winning at all costs—they boast with every kill; they call each other losers.
- They often seem homophobic or misogynist.
  - They put each other down by calling opponents "faggot" and "wussy," or other similar names that are totally obscene.
  - They associate victory with being macho.

Warrant: It is beneficial for a girl to get these insights into male subculture.

Backing: How can I show these benefits?

- Although I enjoy winning at FPS games, as a girl I feel alienated from this male subculture.
- I'm glad that I don't feel the need to put everyone else down.
- It was a good learning experience to see how girls' way of bonding is very different from that of boys; girls tend to be nicer to each other rather than insulting each other.
- The game atmosphere tends to bring out these traits; guys don't talk this way so much when they are doing other things.
- This experience helped me see why men may progress faster than women in a competitive business environment—they seem programmed to crush each other and they devote enormous energy to the process.
- What else can I say? I need to think about this further.

Conditions of Rebuttal: Would anybody try to rebut my reasons and grounds?

- I think my evidence is pretty convincing that males put each other down, concentrate intensely, use homophobic or misogynist insults, etc.
- However, some guys may say "Hey, I don't talk that way," etc.
- Maybe people would say that my sample is biased.

Would anyone try to rebut my warrant and backing?

- Skeptics may say that girls are just as mean to each other as guys are, but they display their meanness in a different way.

For additional writing, reading, and research resources, go to www.mycomplab.com

Using Evidence Effectively 5

In Chapters 3 and 4 we introduced you to the concept of *logos*—the logical structure of reasons and evidence in an argument—and showed you how an effective argument advances the writer's claim by linking its supporting reasons to one or more assumptions, beliefs, or values held by the intended audience. In this chapter, we turn to the uses of evidence in argument. By "evidence," we mean all the verifiable information a writer might use as support for an argument, such as facts, observations, examples, cases, testimony, experimental findings, survey data, statistics, and so forth. In Toulmin's terms, evidence is part of the "grounds" or "backing" of an argument in support of reasons or warrants.

In this chapter, we show you how to use evidence effectively. We begin by explaining some general principles for the persuasive use of evidence. Next we describe and illustrate various kinds of evidence and then present a rhetorical way to think about evidence, particularly the way writers select and frame evidence to support the writer's reasons while simultaneously guiding and limiting what the reader sees. By understanding the rhetorical use of evidence, you will better understand how to use evidence ethically, responsibly, and persuasively in your own arguments. We conclude the chapter by suggesting strategies to help you gather evidence for your arguments, including advice on conducting interviews and using questionnaires.

The Persuasive Use of Evidence

Consider a target audience of educated, reasonable, and careful readers who approach an issue with healthy skepticism, open-minded but cautious. What demands would such readers make on a writer's use of evidence? To begin to answer that question, let's look at some general principles for using evidence persuasively.

Apply the STAR Criteria to Evidence

Our open-minded but skeptical audience would first of all expect the evidence to meet what rhetorician Richard Fulkerson calls the STAR criteria:*

---

*Richard Fulkerson, *Teaching the Argument in Writing* (Urbana, IL: National Council of Teachers of English, 1996), 44–53. In this section, we are indebted to Fulkerson's discussion.

Sufficiency: Is there enough evidence?

Typicality: Is the chosen evidence representative and typical?

Accuracy: Is the evidence accurate and up-to-date?

Relevance: Is the evidence relevant to the claim?

Let's examine each in turn.

Sufficiency of Evidence How much evidence you need is a function of your rhetorical context. In a court trial, opposing attorneys often agree to waive evidence for points that aren't in doubt in order to concentrate on contested points. The more a claim is contested or the more your audience is skeptical, the more evidence you may need to present. If you provide too little evidence, you may be accused of *hasty generalization* (see Appendix 1), a reasoning fallacy in which a person makes a sweeping conclusion based on only one or two instances. On the other hand, if you provide too much evidence your argument may become overly long and tedious. You can guard against having too little or too much evidence by appropriately qualifying the claim your evidence supports.

> **Strong claim:** Working full time seriously harms a student's grade point average. (much data needed—probably a combination of examples and statistical studies)
>
> **Qualified claim:** Working full time often harms a student's grade point average. (a few representative examples may be enough)

Typicality of Evidence Whenever you select evidence, readers need to believe the evidence is typical and representative rather than extreme instances. Suppose that you want to argue that students can combine full-time work with full-time college and cite the case of your friend Pam who pulled a straight-A grade average while working forty hours per week as a night receptionist in a small hotel. Your audience might doubt the typicality of Pam's case since a night receptionist can often use work hours for studying. What about more typical jobs, they'll ask, where you can't study while you work?

Accuracy of Evidence Evidence can't be used ethically unless it is accurate and up-to-date, and it can't be persuasive unless the audience believes in the writer's credibility. As a writer, you must be scrupulous in using the most recent and accurate evidence you can find. Faith in the accuracy of a writer's data is one function of *ethos*—the audience's confidence in the writer's credibility and trustworthiness (see Chapter 6, page 111).

Relevance of Evidence Finally, evidence will be persuasive only if the reader considers it relevant to the contested issue. Consider the following student argument: "I deserve an A in this course because I worked exceptionally hard." The student then cites substantial evidence of how hard he worked—a log of study hours, copies of multiple drafts of papers, testimony from friends, and so forth. Such evidence is ample support for the claim "I worked very hard" but is irrelevant to the claim "I deserve an A." Although some instructors may give partial credit for effort, the criteria for grades usually focus on the quality of the student's performance, not the student's time spent studying.

Use Sources That Your Reader Trusts

Another way to enhance the persuasiveness of your evidence is to choose data, whenever possible, from sources you think your readers will trust. Because questions of fact are often at issue in arguments, readers may be skeptical of certain sources. When you research an issue, you soon get a sense of who the participants in the conversation are and what their reputations tend to be. Knowing the political biases of sources and the extent to which a source has financial or personal investment in the outcome of a controversy will also help you locate data sources that both you and your readers can trust. Citing a peer-reviewed scholarly journal is often more persuasive than citing an advocacy Web site. Similarly, citing a conservative magazine such as the *National Review* may be unpersuasive to liberal audiences, just as citing a Sierra Club publication may be unpersuasive to conservatives. (See Chapter 16 for further discussion of how to evaluate research sources from a rhetorical perspective.)

Rhetorical Understanding of Evidence

In the previous section we presented some general principles for effective use of evidence. We now want to deepen your understanding of how evidence persuades by asking you to consider more closely the rhetorical context in which evidence operates. We'll look first at the kinds of evidence used in arguments and then show you how writers select and frame evidence for persuasive effect.

Kinds of Evidence

Writers have numerous options for the kinds of evidence they can use in an argument, including personal experience data, research findings, and hypothetical examples. To explain these options, we present a series of charts that categorize different kinds of evidence, illustrate how each kind might be worked into an argument, and comment on the strengths and limitations of each.

Data from Personal Experience   One powerful kind of evidence comes from personal experience:

Example	Strengths and Limitations
Despite recent criticism that Ritalin is overprescribed for hyperactivity and attention deficit disorder, it can often seem like a miracle drug. My little brother is a perfect example. Before he was given Ritalin he was a terror in school.…[Tell the "before" and "after" story of your little brother.]	▪ Personal-experience examples help readers identify with writer; they show writer's personal connection to the issue. ▪ Vivid stories capture the imagination. ▪ Skeptics may sometimes argue that personal-experience examples are insufficient (writer is guilty of hasty generalization), not typical, or not adequately scientific or verifiable.

Data from Observation or Field Research   You can also develop evidence by personally observing a phenomenon or by doing your own field research:

Example	Strengths and Limitations
The intersection at Fifth and Montgomery is particularly dangerous because pedestrians almost never find a comfortable break in the heavy flow of cars. On April 29, I watched fifty-seven pedestrians cross the street. Not once did cars stop in both directions before the pedestrian stepped off the sidewalk onto the street. [Continue with observed data about danger.]	■ Field research gives the feeling of scientific credibility. ■ It increases typicality by expanding database beyond example of one person. ■ It enhances *ethos* of the writer as personally invested and reasonable. ■ Skeptics may point to flaws in how observations were conducted, showing how data are insufficient, inaccurate, or nontypical.

Data from Interviews, Questionnaires, Surveys   You can also gather data by interviewing stakeholders in a controversy, creating questionnaires, or doing surveys. (See pages 101–103 for advice on how to conduct this kind of field research.)

Example	Strengths and Limitations
Another reason to ban laptops from classrooms is the extent to which laptop users disturb other students. In a questionnaire that I distributed to fifty students in my residence hall, a surprising 60 percent said that they were annoyed by fellow students' sending e-mail, paying their bills, or surfing the Web while pretending to take notes in class. Additionally, I interviewed five students, who gave me specific examples of how these distractions interfere with learning. [Report the examples.]	■ Interviews, questionnaires, and surveys enhance the sufficiency and typicality of evidence by expanding the database beyond the experiences of one person. ■ Quantitative data from questionnaires and surveys often increase the scientific feel of the argument. ■ Surveys and questionnaires often uncover local or recent data not available in published research. ■ Interviews can provide engaging personal stories enhancing *pathos*. ■ Skeptics can raise doubts about research methodology, questionnaire design, or typicality of interview subjects.

Data from Library or Internet Research   For many arguments, evidence is derived from reading, particularly from library or Internet research. Part Five of this text helps you conduct effective research and incorporate research sources into your arguments:

Example	Strengths and Limitations
The belief that a high-carbohydrate–low-fat diet is the best way to lose weight has been challenged by research conducted by Walter Willett and his colleagues in the department of nutrition in the Harvard School of Public Health. Willett's research suggests that complex carbohydrates such as pasta and potatoes spike glucose levels, increasing the risk of diabetes. Additionally, some fats—especially monounsaturated and polyunsaturated fats found in nuts, fish, and most vegetable oils—help lower "bad" cholesterol levels (45).*	▥ Researched evidence is often powerful, especially when sources are respected by your audience; writers can spotlight source's credentials through attributive tags (see Chapter 17, pages 370–371). ▥ Researched data may take the form of facts, examples, quotations, summaries of research studies, and so forth (see Chapters 16 and 17). ▥ Skeptics might doubt the accuracy of facts, the credentials of a source, or the research design of a study. They might also cite studies with different results. ▥ Skeptics might raise doubts about sufficiency, typicality, or relevance of your research data.

Testimony   Writers frequently use testimony when direct data are either unavailable or highly technical or complex. Testimonial evidence can come from research or from interviews:

Example	Strengths and Limitations
Although the Swedish economist Bjorn Lomborg claims that acid rain is not a significant problem, many environmentalists disagree. According to David Bellamany, president of the Conservation Foundation, "Acid rain does kill forests and people around the world, and it's still doing so in the most polluted places, such as Russia" (qtd. in *BBC News*).	▥ By itself, testimony is generally less persuasive than direct data. ▥ Persuasiveness can be increased if source has impressive credentials, which the writer can state through attributive tags introducing the testimony (see Chapter 17, pages 370–371). ▥ Skeptics might undermine testimonial evidence by questioning credentials of source, showing source's bias, or quoting a countersource.

Statistical Data   Many contemporary arguments rely heavily on statistical data, often supplemented by graphics such as tables, pie charts, and graphs. (See Chapter 9 for a discussion of the use of graphics in argument.)

Example	Strengths and Limitations
Americans are delaying marriage at a surprising rate. In 1970, 85 percent of Americans between ages fifteen and twenty-nine were married. In 2000, however, only 54 percent were married (U.S. Census Bureau).	▥ Statistics can give powerful snapshots of aggregate data from a wide database. ▥ They are often used in conjunction with graphics (see pages 191–197). ▥ They can be calculated and displayed in different ways to achieve different rhetorical effects, so the reader must be wary (see pages 99–100). ▥ Skeptics might question statistical methods, research design, and interpretation of data.

*Parenthetical citations in this example and the next follow the MLA documentation system. See Chapter 17 for a full discussion of how to cite and document sources.

Hypothetical Examples, Cases, and Scenarios Arguments occasionally use hypothetical examples, cases, or scenarios, particularly to illustrate conjectured consequences of an event or to test philosophical hypotheses.

Example	Strengths and Limitations
Consider what might happen if we continue to use biotech soybeans that are resistant to herbicides. The resistant gene, through cross-pollination, might be transferred to an ordinary weed, creating an out-of-control superweed that herbicides couldn't kill. Such a superweed could be an ecological disaster.	■ Scenarios have strong imaginative appeal. ■ They are persuasive only if they seem plausible. ■ A scenario narrative often conveys a sense of "inevitability," even if the actual scenario is unlikely; hence rhetorical effect may be illogical. ■ Skeptics might show the implausibility of the scenario or offer an alternative scenario.

Reasoned Sequence of Ideas Sometimes arguments are supported with a reasoned sequence of ideas rather than with concrete facts or other forms of empirical evidence. The writer's concern is to support a point through a logical progression of ideas. Such arguments are conceptual, supported by linked ideas, rather than evidential. This kind of support occurs frequently in arguments and is often intermingled with evidentiary support.

Example	Strengths and Limitations
Embryonic stem cell research, despite its promise in fighting diseases, may have negative social consequences. This research encourages us to place embryos in the category of mere cellular matter that can be manipulated at will. Currently we reduce animals to this category when we genetically alter them for human purposes, such as engineering pigs to grow more human-like heart valves for use in transplants. Using human embryos in the same way—as material that can be altered and destroyed at will—may benefit society materially, but this quest for greater knowledge and control involves a reclassifying of embryos that could potentially lead to a devaluing of human life.	■ These sequences are often used in causal arguments to show how causes are linked to effects or in definitional or values arguments to show links among ideas. ■ They have great power to clarify values and show the belief structure on which a claim is founded. ■ They can sketch out ideas and connections that would otherwise remain latent. ■ Their effectiveness depends on the audience's acceptance of each link in the sequence of ideas. ■ Skeptics might raise objections at any link in the sequence, often by pointing to different values or outlining different consequences.

Angle of Vision and the Selection and Framing of Evidence

You can increase your ability to use evidence effectively—and to analyze how other arguers use evidence—by becoming more aware of a writer's rhetorical choices when using evidence to support a claim. Where each of us stands on an issue is partly a function of our own critical thinking, inquiry, and research—our search for the best solution to a problem. But it is also partly a function of who we are as people—our values and beliefs as formed by the particulars of our existence such as our family history, education, gender and sexual orientation, age, class, and ethnicity. In other words, we don't enter the argumentative arena like disembodied computers arriving at our claims through a value-free calculus. We enter with our own ideologies, beliefs, values, and guiding assumptions.

These guiding assumptions, beliefs, and values work together to create a writer's "angle of vision." (Instead of "angle of vision," we could also use other words or metaphors such as *perspective, bias, lens,* or *filter*—all terms that suggest that our way of seeing the world is shaped by our values and beliefs.) A writer's angle of vision,

EXAMINING VISUAL ARGUMENTS

Angle of Vision

Because of nationally reported injuries and near-death experiences resulting from stage diving and crowd surfing at rock concerts, many cities have tried to ban mosh pits. Critics of mosh pits have pointed to the injuries caused by crowd surfing and to the ensuing lawsuits against concert venues. Meanwhile, supporters cite the almost ecstatic enjoyment of crowd-surfing rock fans who seek out concerts with "festival seating."

These photos display different angles of vision toward crowd surfing. Suppose you were writing a blog in support of crowd surfing. Which image would you include in your posting? Why? Suppose alternatively that you were blogging against mosh pits, perhaps urging local officials to outlaw them. Which image would you choose? Why?

Analyze the visual features of these photographs in order to explain how they are constructed to create alternative angles of vision on mosh pits.

Crowd surfing in a mosh pit

An alternative view of a mosh pit

like a lens or filter, helps determine what stands out for that writer in a field of data—that is, what data are important or trivial, significant or irrelevant, worth focusing on or worth ignoring.

To illustrate the concept of selective seeing, we ask you to consider how two hypothetical speakers might select different data about homeless people when presenting speeches to their city council. The first speaker argues that the city should increase its services to the homeless. The second asks the city to promote tourism more aggressively. Their differing angles of vision will cause the two speakers to select different data about homeless people and to frame these data in different ways. (Our use of the word *frame* derives metaphorically from a window frame or the frame of a camera's viewfinder. When you look through a frame, some part of your field of vision is blocked off, while the material appearing in the frame is emphasized. Through framing, a writer maximizes the reader's focus on some data, minimizes the reader's focus on other data, and otherwise guides the reader's vision and response.)

Because the first speaker wants to increase the council's sympathy for the homeless, she frames homeless people positively by telling the story of one homeless man's struggle to find shelter and nutritious food. Her speech focuses primarily on the low number of tax dollars devoted to helping the homeless. In contrast, the second speaker, using data about lost tourist income, might frame the homeless as "panhandlers" by telling the story of obnoxious, urine-soaked winos who pester shoppers for handouts. As arguers, both speakers want their audience to see the homeless from their own angles of vision. Consequently, lost tourist dollars don't show up at all in the first speaker's argument, whereas the story of a homeless man's night in the cold doesn't show up in the second speaker's argument. As this example shows, one goal writers have in selecting and framing evidence is to bring the reader's view of the subject into alignment with the writer's angle of vision. The writer selects and frames evidence to limit and control what the reader sees.

To help you better understand the concepts of selection and framing, we offer the following class discussion exercise to give you practice in a kind of controlled laboratory setting. As you do this exercise, we invite you to observe your own processes for selecting and framing evidence.

■ ■ ■ **FOR CLASS DISCUSSION** **Creating an Angle of Vision by Selecting Evidence**

Suppose that your city has scheduled a public hearing on a proposed ordinance to ban mosh pits at rock concerts. (See the Examining Visual Arguments feature on page 95, where we introduced this issue.) Among the possible data available to various speakers for evidence are the following:

- Some bands, such as Nine Inch Nails, specify festival seating that allows a mosh pit area.
- A female mosher writing on the Internet says: "I experience a shared energy that is like no other when I am in the pit with the crowd. It is like we are all a bunch of atoms bouncing off of each other. It's great. Hey, some people get that feeling from basketball games. I get mine from the mosh pit."

- A student conducted a survey of fifty students on her campus who had attended rock concerts in the last six months. Of the respondents, 80 percent thought that mosh pits should be allowed at concerts.
- Narrative comments on these questionnaires included the following:
  - Mosh pits are a passion for me. I get an amazing rush when crowd surfing.
  - I don't like to be in a mosh pit or do crowd surfing. But I love festival seating and like to watch the mosh pits. For me, mosh pits are part of the ambience of a concert.
  - I know a girl who was groped in a mosh pit, and she'll never do one again. But I have never had any problems.
  - Mosh pits are dangerous and stupid. I think they should be outlawed.
  - If you are afraid of mosh pits just stay away. Nobody forces you to go into a mosh pit! It is ridiculous to ban them because they are totally voluntary. They should just post big signs saying "City assumes no responsibility for accidents occurring in mosh pit area."
- A teenage girl suffered brain damage and memory loss at a 1998 Pearl Jam concert in Rapid City, South Dakota. According to her attorney, she hadn't intended to body surf or enter the mosh pit but "got sucked in while she was standing at its fringe."
- Twenty-four concert deaths were recorded in 2001, most of them in the area closest to the stage where people are packed in.
- A twenty one-year-old man suffered cardiac arrest at a Metallica concert in Indiana and is now in a permanent vegetative state. Because he was jammed into the mosh pit area, nobody noticed he was in distress.
- In 2005, a blogger reported breaking his nose on an elbow; another described having his lip ring pulled out. Another blogger on the same site described having his lip nearly sliced off by the neck of a bass guitar. The injury required 78 stitches. In May 2008, fifty people were treated at emergency rooms for mosh pit injuries acquired at a Bamboozle concert in New Jersey.

Tasks: Working individually or in small groups, complete the following tasks:

1. Compose two short speeches, one supporting the proposed city ordinance to ban mosh pits and one opposing it. How you use these data is up to you, but be able to explain your reasoning in the way you select and frame them. Share your speeches with classmates.
2. After you have shared examples of different speeches, explain the approaches that different classmates employed. What principle of selection was used? If arguers included evidence contrary to their positions, how did they handle it, respond to it, minimize its importance, or otherwise channel its rhetorical effect?
3. In the first task, we assigned you two different angles of vision—one supporting the ordinance and one opposing it. If you had to create your own argument on a proposal to ban mosh pits and if you set for yourself a truth-seeking goal—that is, finding the best solution for the problem of mosh pit danger, one for which you would take ethical responsibility—what would you argue? How would your argument use the list of data we provided? What else might you add?

Rhetorical Strategies for Framing Evidence

What we hope you learned from the preceding exercise is that an arguer consciously selects evidence from a wide field of data and then frames these data through rhetorical strategies that emphasize some data, minimize others, and guide the reader's response. Now that you have a basic idea of what we mean by framing of evidence, here are some strategies writers can use to guide what the reader sees and feels.

Strategies for Framing Evidence

- *Controlling the space given to supporting versus contrary evidence:* Depending on their audience and purpose, writers can devote most of their space to supporting evidence and minimal space to contrary evidence (or omit it entirely). Thus people arguing in favor of mosh pits may have used lots of evidence supporting mosh pits, including enthusiastic quotations from concertgoers, while omitting (or summarizing very rapidly) the data about the dangers of mosh pits.

- *Emphasizing a detailed story versus presenting lots of facts and statistics:* Often, writers can choose to support a point with a memorable individual case or with aggregate data such as statistics or lists of facts. A memorable story can have a strongly persuasive effect. For example, to create a negative view of mosh pits, a writer might tell the heartrending story of a teenager suffering permanent brain damage from being dropped on a mosh pit floor. In contrast, a supporter of mosh pits might tell the story of a happy music lover turned on to the concert scene by the rush of crowd surfing. A different strategy is to use facts and statistics rather than case narratives—for example, data about the frequency of mosh pit accidents, financial consequences of lawsuits, and so forth. The single-narrative case often has a more powerful rhetorical effect, but it is always open to the charge that it is an insufficient or nonrepresentative example. Vivid anecdotes make for interesting reading, but by themselves they may not be compelling logically. In contrast, aggregate data, often used in scholarly studies, can provide more compelling, logical evidence but sometimes make the prose wonkish and dense.

- *Providing contextual and interpretive comments when presenting data:* When citing data, writers can add brief contextual or interpretive comments that act as lenses over the readers' eyes to help them see the data from the writer's perspective. Suppose you want to support mosh pits, but want to admit that mosh pits are dangerous. You could make that danger seem irrelevant or inconsequential by saying: "It is true that occasional mosh pit accidents happen, just as accidents happen in any kind of recreational activity such as swimming or weekend softball games." The concluding phrase frames the danger of mosh pits by comparing them to other recreational accidents that don't require special laws or regulations. The implied argument is this: banning mosh pits because of an occasional accident would be as silly as banning recreational swimming because of occasional accidents.

- *Putting contrary evidence in subordinate positions:* Just as a photographer can place a flower at the center of a photograph or in the background, a writer can place a piece of data in a subordinate or main clause of a sentence. Note how the structure of the following sentence minimizes emphasis on the rarity of mosh pit accidents:

"Although mosh pit accidents are rare, the danger to the city of multimillion-dollar liability lawsuits means that the city should nevertheless ban them for reasons of fiscal prudence." The factual data that mosh pit accidents are rare is summarized briefly and tucked away in a subordinate *although* clause, while the writer's own position is elaborated in the main clause where it receives grammatical emphasis. A writer with a different angle of vision might say, "Although some cities may occasionally be threatened with a lawsuit, serious accidents resulting from mosh pits are so rare that cities shouldn't interfere with the desires of music fans to conduct concerts as they please."

- *Choosing labels and names that guide the reader's response to data:* One of the most subtle ways to control your readers' response to data is to choose labels and names that prompt them to see the issue as you do. If you like mosh pits, you might refer to the seating arrangements in a concert venue as "festival seating, where concertgoers have the opportunity to create a free-flowing mosh pit." If you don't like mosh pits, you might refer to the seating arrangements as "an accident-inviting use of empty space where rowdies can crowd together, slam into each other, and occasionally punch and kick." The labels you choose, along with the connotations of the words you select, urge your reader to share your angle of vision.

- *Using images (photographs, drawings) to guide the reader's response to data:* Another strategy for moving your audience toward your angle of vision is to include a photograph or drawing that portrays a contested issue from your perspective. You've already tried your hand at selecting mosh pit photographs that make arguments through their angle of vision. (See page 95.) Most people agree that the first photo supports a positive view of mosh pits. The crowd looks happy and relaxed (rather than rowdy or out of control), and the young woman lifted above the crowd smiles broadly, her body relaxed, her arms extended. In contrast, the second photo emphasizes muscular men (rather than a smiling and relaxed woman) and threatens danger rather than harmony. The crowd seems on the verge of turning ugly. (See Chapter 9 for a complete discussion of the use of visuals in argument.)

- *Revealing the value system that determines the writer's selection and framing of data:* Ultimately, how a writer selects and frames evidence is linked to the system of values that organize his or her argument. If you favor mosh pits, you probably favor maximizing the pleasure of concertgoers, promoting individual choice, and letting moshers assume the risk of their own behavior. If you want to forbid mosh pits, you probably favor minimizing risks, protecting the city from lawsuits, and protecting individuals from the danger of their own out-of-control actions. Sometimes you can foster connections with your audience by openly addressing the underlying values that you hope your audience shares with you. You can often frame your selected data by stating explicitly the values that guide your argument.

Special Strategies for Framing Statistical Evidence

Numbers and statistical data can be framed in so many ways that this category of evidence deserves its own separate treatment. By recognizing how writers frame numbers to support the story they want to tell, you will always be aware that other stories are also possible. Ethical use of numbers means that you use reputable sources for your basic data, that you don't invent or intentionally distort numbers for your own purposes, and that you don't ignore alternative points of view. Here are some of the choices writers make when framing statistical data:

- *Raw numbers versus percentages.* You can alter the rhetorical effect of a statistic by choosing between raw numbers or percentages. In the summer of 2002, many American parents panicked over what seemed like an epidemic of child abductions. If you cited the raw number of these abductions reported in the national news, this number, although small, could seem scary. But if you computed the actual percentage of American children who were abducted, that percentage was so infinitesimally small as to seem insignificant. You can apply this framing option directly to the mosh pit case. To emphasize the danger of mosh pits, you can say that twenty-four deaths occurred at rock concerts in a given year. To minimize this statistic, you could compute the percentage of deaths by dividing this number by the total number of people who attended rock concerts during the year, certainly a number in the several millions. From the perspective of percentages, the death rate at concerts is extremely low.
- *Median versus mean.* Another way to alter the rhetorical effect of numbers is to choose between the median and the mean. The mean is the average of all numbers on a list. The median is the middle number when all the numbers are arranged sequentially from high to low. In 2006 the mean annual income for retired families in the United States was $41,928—not a wealthy amount but enough to live on comfortably if you owned your own home. However, the median income was only $27,798, a figure that gives a much more striking picture of income distribution among older Americans. This median figure means that half of all retired families in the United States had annual incomes of $27,798 or less. The much higher mean income indicates that many retired Americans are quite wealthy. This wealth raises the average of all incomes (the mean) but doesn't affect the median.
- *Unadjusted versus adjusted numbers.* Suppose your boss told you that you were getting a 5 percent raise. You might be happy—unless inflation rates were running at 6 percent. Economic data can be hard to interpret across time unless the dollar amounts are adjusted for inflation. This same problem occurs in other areas. For example, comparing grade point averages of college graduates in 1970 versus 2008 means little unless one can somehow compensate for grade inflation.
- *Base point for statistical comparisons.* In 2008, the stock market was in precipitous decline if one compared 2008 prices with 2007 prices. However, the market still seemed vigorous and healthy if one compared 2008 with 2002. One's choice of the base point for a comparison often makes a significant rhetorical difference.

■ ■ ■   **FOR CLASS DISCUSSION**   **Using Strategies to Frame Statistical Evidence**
A proposal to build a new ballpark in Seattle, Washington, yielded a wide range of statistical arguments. All of the following statements are reasonably faithful to the same facts:

- The ballpark would be paid for by raising the sales tax from 8.2 percent to 8.3 percent during a twenty-year period.
- The sales tax increase is one-tenth of 1 percent.
- This increase represents an average of $7.50 per person per year—about the price of a movie ticket.
- This increase represents $750 per five-person family over the twenty-year period of the tax.
- For a family building a new home in the Seattle area, this tax will increase building costs by $200.
- This is a $250 million tax increase for the residents of the Seattle area.

How would you describe the costs of the proposed ballpark if you opposed the proposal? How would you describe the costs if you supported the proposal?   ■ ■ ■

Gathering Evidence

We conclude this chapter with some brief advice on ways to gather evidence for your arguments. We begin with a list of brainstorming questions that may help you think of possible sources for evidence. We then provide suggestions for conducting interviews and creating surveys and questionnaires, since these powerful sources are often overlooked by students. For help in conducting library and Internet research—the most common sources of evidence in arguments—see Part Five: "The Researched Argument."

Creating a Plan for Gathering Evidence

As you begin contemplating an argument, you can use the following checklist to help you think of possible sources for evidence.

A Checklist for Brainstorming Sources of Evidence

- What personal experiences have you had with this issue? What details from your life or the lives of your friends, acquaintances, or relatives might serve as examples or other kinds of evidence?
- What observational studies would be relevant to this issue?
- What people could you interview to provide insights or expert knowledge on this issue?
- What questions about your issue could be addressed in a survey or questionnaire?

- What useful information on this issue might encyclopedias, specialized reference books, or the regular book collection in your university library provide? (See Chapter 16.)
- What evidence might you seek on this issue using licensed database indexing sources in magazines, newspapers, and scholarly journals? (See Chapter 16.)
- How might an Internet search engine help you research this issue? (See Chapter 16.)
- What evidence might you find on this issue from reliable statistical resources such as U.S. Census Bureau data, the Centers for Disease Control, or *Statistical Abstract of the United States*? (See Chapter 16.)

Gathering Data from Interviews

Conducting interviews is a useful way not only to gather expert testimony and important data but also to learn about alternative views. To make interviews as productive as possible, we offer these suggestions.

- *Determine your purpose.* Think out why you are interviewing the person and what information he or she is uniquely able to provide.
- *Do background reading.* Find out as much as possible about the interviewee before the interview. Your knowledge of his or her background will help establish your credibility and build a bridge between you and your source. Also, equip yourself with a good foundational understanding of the issue so that you will sound informed and truly interested in the issue.
- *Formulate well-thought-out questions but also be flexible.* Write out beforehand the questions you intend to ask, making sure that every question is related to the purpose of your interview. However, be prepared to move in unexpected directions if the interview opens up new territory. Sometimes unplanned topics can end up being the most illuminating and useful.
- *Come well prepared for the interview.* As part of your professional demeanor, be sure to have all the necessary supplies (notepaper, pens, pencils, perhaps a tape recorder, if your interviewee is willing) with you.
- *Be prompt and courteous.* It is important to be punctual and respectful of your interviewee's time. In most cases, it is best to present yourself as a listener seeking clarity on an issue rather than an advocate of a particular position or an opponent. During the interview, play the believing role. Save the doubting role for later, when you are looking over your notes.
- *Take brief but clear notes.* Try to record the main ideas and be accurate with quotations. Ask for clarification of any points you don't understand.
- *Transcribe your notes soon after the interview.* Immediately after the interview, while your memory is still fresh, rewrite your notes more fully and completely.

When you use interview data in your writing, put quotation marks around any direct quotations. In most cases, you should also identify your source by name and indicate his or her title or credentials—whatever will convince the reader that this person's remarks are to be taken seriously.

Gathering Data from Surveys or Questionnaires

A well-constructed survey or questionnaire can provide lively, current data that give your audience a sense of the popularity and importance of your views. To be effective and responsible, however, a survey or questionnaire needs to be carefully prepared and administered, as we suggest in the following guidelines.

- *Include both closed-response questions and open-response questions.* To give you useful information and avoid charges of bias, you will want to include a range of questions. Closed-response questions ask participants to check a box or number on a scale and yield quantitative data that you can report statistically, perhaps in tables or graphs. Open-response questions elicit varied responses and often short narratives that allow participants to offer their own input. These may contribute new insights to your perspective on the issue.
- *Make your survey or questionnaire clear and easy to complete.* Think out the number, order, wording, and layout of the questions in your questionnaire. Your questions should be clear and easy to answer. The neatness and overall formal appearance of the questionnaire will also invite serious responses from your participants.
- *Explain the purpose of the questionnaire.* Respondents are usually more willing to participate if they know how the information gained from the questionnaire will benefit others. Therefore, it is a good idea to state at the beginning of the questionnaire how it will be used.
- *Seek a random sample of respondents in your distribution of the questionnaire.* Think out where and how you will distribute and collect your questionnaire to ensure a random sampling of respondents. For example, if a questionnaire about the university library went only to dorm residents, then you wouldn't learn how commuting students felt.
- *Convert questionnaires into usable data by tallying and summarizing responses.* Tallying the results and formulating summary statements of the information you gathered will yield material that might be used as evidence.

Conclusion

Effective use of evidence is an essential skill for arguers. In this chapter we introduced you to the STAR criteria and other strategies for making your data persuasive. We showed you various kinds of evidence and then examined how a writer's angle of vision influences the selection and framing of evidence. We also described framing strategies for emphasizing evidence, de-emphasizing it, and guiding your reader's response to it. Finally we concluded with advice on how to gather evidence, including the use of interviews, surveys, and questionnaires.

WRITING ASSIGNMENT   A Microtheme or a Supporting-Reasons Argument

Option 1: A Microtheme   Write a one- or two-paragraph argument in which you support one of the following enthymemes, using evidence from personal experience, field observation, interviews, or data from a brief questionnaire or survey. Most of your microtheme should support the stated reason with evidence. However, also include a brief passage supporting the implied warrant. The opening sentence of your microtheme should be the enthymeme itself, which serves as the thesis statement for your argument. (Note: If you disagree with the enthymeme's argument, recast the claim or the reason to assert what you want to argue.)

1. Reading fashion magazines can be detrimental to teenage girls because such magazines can produce an unhealthy focus on beauty.
2. Surfing the Web might harm your studying because it causes you to waste time.
3. Service-learning courses are valuable because they allow you to test course concepts within real-world contexts.
4. Summer internships in your field of interest, even without pay, are the best use of your summer time because they speed up your education and training for a career.
5. Any enthymeme (a claim with a *because* clause) of your choice that can be supported without library or Internet research. (The goal of this microtheme is to give you practice using data from personal experience or from brief field research.) You may want to have your instructor approve your enthymeme in advance.

Option 2: A Supporting-Reasons Argument   Write an argument that uses at least two reasons to support your claim. Your argument should include all the features of a classical argument except the section on summarizing and responding to opposing views, which we will cover in Chapter 7. This assignment builds on the brief writing assignments in Chapter 3 (create a thesis statement for an argument) and Chapter 4 (brainstorm support for one of your enthymemes using the Toulmin schema). We now ask you to expand your argument frame into a complete essay.

A *supporting-reasons argument* is our term for a classical argument without a section that summarizes and responds to opposing views. Even though alternative views aren't dealt with in detail, the writer usually summarizes an opposing view briefly in the introduction to provide background on the issue being addressed. Follow the explanations and organization chart for a classical argument as shown on page 61, but omit the section called "summary and critique of opposing views."

Like a complete classical argument, a supporting-reasons argument has a thesis-governed structure in which you state your claim at the end of the introduction, begin body paragraphs with clearly stated reasons, and use effective transitions throughout to keep your reader on track. In developing your own argument, place your most important, persuasive, or interesting reason last, where it will have the greatest impact on your readers. This kind of tightly organized structure is sometimes called a *self-announcing* or *closed-form* structure because the writer states his or her claim before beginning the body of the argument and forecasts the structure that is to follow. In contrast, an *unfolding* or *open-form* structure doesn't give away the writer's position until late in the essay. (We discuss delayed-thesis arguments in Chapter 7.)

In writing a self-announcing argument, students often ask how much of the argument to summarize in the thesis statement. Consider your options:

- You might announce only your claim:

   Women should be allowed to join combat units.

- You might forecast a series of parallel reasons:

   Women should be allowed to join combat units for several reasons.

- You might forecast the actual number of reasons:

   Women should be allowed to join combat units for five reasons.

- Or you might forecast the whole argument by including your *because* clauses with your claim:

   Women should be allowed to join combat units because they are physically capable of doing the job; because the presence of women in combat units would weaken gender stereotypes; because they are already seeing combat in Iraq; because opening combat units to women would expand their military career opportunities; and because it would advance the cause of civil rights.

This last thesis statement forecasts not only the claim, but also the supporting reasons that will serve as topic sentences for key paragraphs throughout the body of the paper.

No formula can tell you precisely how much of your argument to forecast in the introduction. However these suggestions can guide you. In writing a self-announcing argument, forecast only what is needed for clarity. In short arguments readers often need only your claim. In longer arguments, however, or in especially complex ones, readers appreciate your forecasting the complete structure of the argument (claim with reasons). ■

Reading

What follows is Carmen Tieu's supporting-reasons argument. Carmen's earlier explorations for this assignment are shown at the end of Chapters 3 and 4 (page 71 and page 87).

Why Violent Video Games Are Good for Girls

CARMEN TIEU (STUDENT)

It is ten o'clock P.M., game time. My entire family knows by now that when I am home on Saturday nights, ten P.M. is my gaming night when I play my favorite first-person shooter games, usually *Halo 3,* on Xbox Live. Seated in my mobile chair in front of my family's 42-inch flat screen HDTV, I log onto Xbox Live. A small message in the bottom of the screen appears with the words "Kr1pL3r is online," alerting me that one of my male friends is online and already playing. As the game loads, I send Kr1pL3r a game invite, and he joins me in the pre-game room lobby.

In the game room lobby, all the players who will be participating in the match are chatting aggressively with each other: "Oh man, we're gonna own you guys so bad." When a member of the opposing team notices my gamer tag, "embracingapathy," he begins to insult me by calling me various degrading, gay-associated names: "Embracing apa-what? Man, it sounds so emo. Are you some fag? I bet you want me so bad. You're gonna get owned!" Players always assume from my gamer tag that I am a gay male, never a female. The possibility that I am a girl is the last thing on their minds. Of course, they are right that girls seldom play first-person shooter games. Girls are socialized into activities that promote togetherness and talk, not high intensity competition involving fantasized shooting and killing. The violent nature of the games tends to repulse girls. Opponents of violent video games typically hold that these games are so graphically violent that they will influence players to become amoral and sadistic. Feminists also argue that violent video games often objectify women by portraying them as sexualized toys for men's gratification. Although I understand these objections, I argue that playing first-person shooter games can actually be good for girls.

First, playing FPS games is surprisingly empowering because it gives girls the chance to beat guys at their own game. When I first began playing *Halo 2,* I was horrible. My male friends constantly put me down for my lack of skills, constantly telling me that I was awful, "but for a girl, you're good." But it didn't take much practice until I learned to operate the two joy sticks with precision and with quick instinctual reactions. While guys and girls can play many physical games together, such as basketball or touch football, guys will always have the advantage because on average they are taller, faster, and stronger than females. However, when it comes to video games, girls can compete equally because physical strength isn't required, just quick reaction time and manual dexterity—skills that women possess in abundance. The adrenaline rush that I receive from beating a bunch of testosterone-driven guys at something they supposedly excel at is exciting; I especially savor the look of horror on their faces when I completely destroy them.

Since female video gamers are so rare, playing shooter games allows girls to be freed from feminine stereotypes and increases their confidence. Culture generally portrays females as caring, nonviolent, and motherly beings who are not supposed to enjoy FPS games with their war themes and violent killings. I am in no way rejecting these traditional female values since I myself am a compassionate, tree-hugging vegan. But I also like to break these stereotypes. Playing video games offers a great way for females to break the social mold of only doing "girly" things and introduces them to something that males commonly enjoy. Playing video games with sexist males has also helped me become more outspoken. Psychologically, I can stand up to aggressive males because I know that I can beat them at their own game. The confidence I've gotten from excelling at shooter games may have even carried over into the academic arena because I am majoring in chemical engineering and have no fear whatsoever of intruding into the male-dominated territory of math and science. Knowing that I can beat all the guys in my engineering classes at *Halo* gives me that little extra confidence boost during exams and labs.

5   Another reason for girls to play FPS games is that it gives us a different way of bonding with guys. Once when I was discussing my latest *Halo 3* matches with one of my regular male friends, a guy whom I didn't know turned around and said, "You play *Halo*? Wow, you just earned my respect." Although I was annoyed that this guy apparently didn't respect women in general, it is apparent that guys will talk to me differently now that I can play video games. From a guy's perspective I can also appreciate why males find video games so addicting. You get joy from perfecting your skills so that your high-angle grenade kills become a thing of beauty. While all of these skills may seem trivial to some, the acknowledgment of my skills from other players leaves me with a perverse sense of pride in knowing that I played the game better than everyone else. Since I have started playing, I have also noticed that it is much easier to talk to males about lots of different subjects. Talking video games with guys is a great ice-breaker that leads to different kinds of friendships outside the realm of romance and dating.

Finally, playing violent video games can be valuable for girls because it gives them insights into a disturbing part of male subculture. When the testosterone starts kicking in, guys become blatantly homophobic and misogynistic. Any player, regardless of gender, who cannot play well (as measured by having a high number of kills and a low number of deaths) is made fun of by being called gay, a girl, or worse. Even when some guys finally meet a female player, they will also insult her by calling her a lesbian or an ugly fat chick that has no life. Their insults towards the girl will dramatically increase if she beats them because they feel so humiliated. In their eyes, playing worse than a girl is embarrassing because girls are supposed to be inept at FPS games. Whenever I play *Halo* better than my male friends, they often comment on how "it makes no sense that we're getting owned by Carmen."

When males act like such sexist jerks it causes one to question if they are always like this. My answer is no because I know, first hand, that when guys like that are having one-on-one conversations with a female, they show a softer side, and the macho side goes away. They don't talk about how girls should stay in the kitchen and make them dinner, but rather how they think it is cool that they share a fun, common interest with a girl. But when they are in a group of males their fake, offensive macho side comes out. I find this phenomenon troubling because it shows a real problem in the way boys are socialized. To be real "man" around other guys, they have to put down women and gays in activities involving aggressive behavior where men are supposed to excel. But they don't become macho and aggressive in activities like reading and writing, which they think of as feminine. I've always known that guys are more physically aggressive than women, but until playing violent video games I had never realized how this aggression is related to misogyny and homophobia. Perhaps these traits aren't deeply ingrained in men but come out primarily in a competitive male environment. Whatever the cause, it is an ugly phenomenon, and I'm glad that I learned more about it. Beating guys at FPS games has made me a more confident woman while being more aware of gender differences in the way men and women are socialized. I joined the guys in playing *Halo*, but I didn't join their subculture of ridiculing women and gays.

For additional writing, reading, and research resources, go to www.mycomplab.com

Moving Your Audience
Ethos, Pathos, and *Kairos*

6

In Chapters 4 and 5 we focused on *logos*—the logical structure of reasons and evidence in argument. Even though we have treated *logos* in its own chapters, an effective arguer's concern for *logos* is always connected to *ethos* and *pathos* (see the rhetorical triangle introduced in Chapter 3, p. 63). By seeking audience-based reasons—so that an arguer connects her message to the assumptions, values, and beliefs of her audience—she appeals also to *ethos* and *pathos* by enhancing the reader's trust and by triggering the reader's sympathies and imagination. In this chapter, we turn specifically to *ethos* and *pathos*. We also introduce you to a related rhetorical concept, *kairos,* which concerns the timeliness, fitness, and appropriateness of an argument for its occasion.

Ethos and *Pathos* as Persuasive Appeals: An Overview

At first, one may be tempted to think of *logos, ethos,* and *pathos* as "ingredients" in an essay, like spices you add to a casserole. But a more appropriate metaphor might be that of different lamps and filters used on theater spotlights to vary lighting effects on a stage. Thus if you switch on a *pathos* lamp (possibly through using more concrete language or vivid examples), the resulting image will engage the audience's sympathy and emotions more deeply. If you overlay an *ethos* filter (perhaps by adopting a different tone toward your audience), the projected image of the writer as a person will be subtly altered. If you switch on a *logos* lamp (by adding, say, more data for evidence), you will draw the reader's attention to the logical appeal of the argument. Depending on how you modulate the lamps and filters, you shape and color your readers' perception of you and your argument.

Our metaphor is imperfect, of course, but our point is that *logos, ethos,* and *pathos* work together to create an impact on the reader. Consider, for example, the different impacts of the following arguments, all having roughly the same logical appeal.

1. People should adopt a vegetarian diet because doing so will help prevent the cruelty to animals caused by factory farming.
2. If you are planning to eat chicken tonight, please consider how much that chicken suffered so that you could have a tender and juicy meal. Commercial growers cram the chickens so tightly together into cages that

they never walk on their own legs, see sunshine, or flap their wings. In fact, their beaks must be cut off to keep them from pecking each other's eyes out. One way to prevent such suffering is for more and more people to become vegetarians.

3. People who eat meat are no better than sadists who torture other sentient creatures to enhance their own pleasure. Unless you enjoy sadistic tyranny over others, you have only one choice: become a vegetarian.

4. People committed to justice might consider the extent to which our love of eating meat requires the agony of animals. A visit to a modern chicken factory—where chickens live their entire lives in tiny, darkened coops without room to spread their wings—might raise doubts about our right to inflict such suffering on sentient creatures. Indeed, such a visit might persuade us that vegetarianism is a more just alternative.

Each argument has roughly the same logical core:

ENTHYMEME

CLAIM People should adopt a vegetarian diet

REASON because doing so will help prevent the cruelty to animals caused by factory farming.

GROUNDS

• Evidence of suffering in commercial chicken farms, where chickens are crammed together and lash out at one another

• Evidence that only widespread adoption of vegetarianism will end factory farming

WARRANT

If we have an alternative to making animals suffer, we should use it.

But the impact of each argument varies. The difference between arguments 1 and 2, most of our students report, is the greater emotional power of argument 2. Whereas argument 1 refers only to the abstraction "cruelty to animals," argument 2 paints a vivid picture of chickens with their beaks cut off to prevent their pecking each other blind. Argument 2 makes a stronger appeal to *pathos* (not necessarily a stronger argument), stirring feelings by appealing simultaneously to the heart and to the head.

The difference between arguments 1 and 3 concerns both *ethos* and *pathos*. Argument 3 appeals to the emotions through highly charged words such as *torture, sadist,* and *tyranny.* But argument 3 also draws attention to its writer, and most of our students report not liking that writer very much. His stance is self-righteous and insulting. In contrast, argument 4's author establishes a more positive *ethos*. He establishes rapport by assuming his audience is committed to justice and by qualifying his argument with conditional terms such as *might* and *perhaps*. He also invites sympathy for his problem—an appeal to *pathos*—by offering a specific description of chickens crammed into tiny coops.

Which of these arguments is best? They all have appropriate uses. Arguments 1 and 4 seem aimed at receptive audiences reasonably open to exploration of the issue, whereas arguments 2 and 3 seem designed to shock complacent audiences or to rally a group of True Believers. Even argument 3, which is too abusive to be effective in most instances, might work as a rallying speech at a convention of animal liberation activists.

Our point thus far is that *logos, ethos,* and *pathos* are different aspects of the same whole, different lenses for intensifying or softening the light beam you project onto the screen. Every choice you make as a writer affects in some way each of the three appeals. The rest of this chapter examines these choices in more detail.

How to Create an Effective *Ethos:* The Appeal to Credibility

The ancient Greek and Roman rhetoricians recognized that an argument would be more persuasive if the audience trusted the speaker. Aristotle argued that such trust resides within the speech itself, not in the prior reputation of the speaker. In the speaker's manner and delivery, tone, word choice, and arrangement of reasons, in the sympathy with which he or she treats alternative views, the speaker creates a trustworthy persona. Aristotle called the impact of the speaker's credibility the appeal from *ethos*. How does a writer create credibility? We suggest three ways:

- **Be Knowledgeable about Your Issue.** The first way to gain credibility is to *be* credible—that is, to argue from a strong base of knowledge, to have at hand the examples, personal experiences, statistics, and other empirical data needed to make a sound case. If you have done your homework, you will command the attention of most audiences.

- **Be Fair.** Besides being knowledgeable about your issue, you need to demonstrate fairness and courtesy to alternative views. Because true argument can occur only where people may reasonably disagree with one another, your *ethos* will be strengthened if you demonstrate that you understand and empathize with other points of view. There are times, of course, when you may appropriately scorn an opposing view. But these times are rare, and they mostly occur when you address audiences predisposed to your view. Demonstrating empathy to alternative views is generally the best strategy.

- **Build a Bridge to Your Audience.** A third means of establishing credibility—building a bridge to your audience—has been treated at length in our earlier discussions of audience-based reasons. By grounding your argument in shared values and assumptions, you demonstrate your goodwill and enhance your image as a trustworthy person respectful of your audience's views. We mention audience-based reasons here to show how this aspect of *logos*—finding the reasons that are most rooted in the audience's values—also affects your *ethos* as a person respectful of your readers' views.

How to Create *Pathos:* The Appeal to Beliefs and Emotions

Before the federal government outlawed unsolicited telephone marketing, newspapers published flurries of articles complaining about annoying telemarketers. Within this context, a United Parcel Service worker, Bobbi Buchanan, wanted to create sympathy for telemarketers. She wrote a *New York Times* op-ed piece entitled "Don't Hang Up, That's My Mom Calling," which begins as follows:

> The next time an annoying sales call interrupts your dinner, think of my 71-year-old mother, LaVerne, who works as a part-time telemarketer to supplement her social security income. To those Americans who have signed up for the new national do-not-call list, my mother is a pest, a nuisance, an invader of privacy. To others, she's just another anonymous voice on the other end of the line. But to those who know her, she's someone struggling to make a buck, to feed herself and pay her utilities—someone who personifies the great American way.

The editorial continues with a heartwarming description of LaVerne. Buchanan's rhetorical aim is to transform the reader's anonymous, depersonalized image of telemarketers into the concrete image of her mother: a "hardworking, first generation American; the daughter of a Pittsburgh steelworker; survivor of the Great Depression; the widow of a World War II veteran; a mother of seven, grandmother of eight, great-grandmother of three...." The intended effect is to alter our view of telemarketers through the positive emotions triggered by our identification with LaVerne.

By urging readers to think of "my mother, LaVerne" instead of an anonymous telemarketer, Buchanan illustrates the power of *pathos,* an appeal to the reader's emotions. Arguers create pathetic appeals whenever they connect their claims to readers' values, thus triggering positive or negative emotions depending on whether these values are affirmed or transgressed. Pro-life proponents appeal to *pathos* when they graphically describe the dismemberment of a fetus during an abortion. Proponents of improved women's health and status in Africa do so when they describe the helplessness of wives forced to have unprotected sex with husbands likely infected with HIV. Opponents of oil exploration in the Arctic National Wildlife Refuge (ANWR) do so when they lovingly describe the calving grounds of caribou.

Are such appeals legitimate? Our answer is yes, if they intensify and deepen our response to an issue rather than divert our attention from it. Because understanding is a matter of feeling as well as perceiving, *pathos* can give access to nonlogical, but not necessarily nonrational, ways of knowing. *Pathos* helps us see what is deeply at stake in an issue, what matters to the whole person. Appeals to *pathos* help readers walk in the writer's shoes. That is why arguments are often improved through the use of stories that make issues come alive or sensory details that allow us to see, feel, and taste the reality of a problem.

Appeals to *pathos* become illegitimate, we believe, when they confuse an issue rather than clarify it. Consider the case of a student who argues that Professor Jones ought to raise his grade from a D to a C, lest he lose his scholarship and leave college, shattering the dreams of his dear old grandmother. To the extent that students' grades should be based on performance or effort, the student's image of the dear old grandmother is an illegitimate appeal to *pathos* because it diverts the reader from rational to irrational criteria. The weeping grandmother may provide a legitimate motive for the student to study harder but not for the professor to change a grade.

Although it is difficult to classify all the ways that writers can create appeals from *pathos,* we will focus on four strategies: concrete language; specific examples and illustrations; narratives; and connotations of words, metaphors, and analogies. Each of these strategies lends "presence" to an argument by creating immediacy and emotional impact.

Use Concrete Language

Concrete language—one of the chief ways that writers achieve voice—can increase the liveliness, interest level, and personality of a writer's prose. When used in argument, concrete language typically heightens *pathos.* For example, consider the differences between the first and second drafts of the following student argument:

First Draft

> People who prefer driving a car to taking a bus think that taking the bus will increase the stress of the daily commute. Just the opposite is true. Not being able to find a parking spot when in a hurry to be at work or school can cause a person stress. Taking the bus gives a person time to read or sleep, etc. It could be used as a mental break.

Second Draft (Concrete Language Added)

> Taking the bus can be more relaxing than driving a car. Having someone else behind the wheel gives people time to chat with friends or cram for an exam. They can balance their checkbooks, do homework, doze off, read the daily newspaper, or get lost in a novel rather than foam at the mouth looking for a parking space.

In this revision, specific details enliven the prose by creating images that trigger positive feelings. Who wouldn't want some free time to doze off or to get lost in a novel?

Use Specific Examples and Illustrations

Specific examples and illustrations serve two purposes in an argument. They provide evidence that supports your reasons; simultaneously, they give your argument presence and emotional resonance. Note the flatness of the following draft arguing for the value of multicultural studies in a university core curriculum:

First Draft

> Another advantage of a multicultural education is that it will help us see our own culture in a broader perspective. If all we know is our own heritage, we might not be inclined to see anything bad about this heritage because we won't know anything else. But if we study other heritages, we can see the costs and benefits of our own heritage.

Now note the increase in "presence" when the writer adds a specific example:

Second Draft (Example Added)

Another advantage of multicultural education is that it raises questions about traditional Western values. For example, owning private property (such as buying your own home) is part of the American dream. However, in studying the beliefs of American Indians, students are confronted with a very different view of private property. When the U.S. government sought to buy land in the Pacific Northwest from Chief Sealth, he is alleged to have replied:

> The president in Washington sends words that he wishes to buy our land. But how can you buy or sell the sky? The land? The idea is strange to us. If we do not own the freshness of the air and the sparkle of the water, how can you buy them?[…]We are part of the earth and it is part of us.[…]This we know: The earth does not belong to man, man belongs to the earth.

> Our class was shocked by the contrast between traditional Western views of property and Chief Sealth's views. One of our best class discussions was initiated by this quotation from Chief Sealth. Had we not been exposed to a view from another culture, we would have never been led to question the "rightness" of Western values.

The writer begins his revision by evoking a traditional Western view of private property, which he then questions by shifting to Chief Sealth's vision of land as open, endless, and unobtainable as the sky. Through the use of a specific example, the writer brings to life his previously abstract point about the benefit of multicultural education.

Use Narratives

A particularly powerful way to evoke *pathos* is to tell a story that either leads into your claim or embodies it implicitly and that appeals to your readers' feelings and imagination. Brief narratives—whether true or hypothetical—are particularly effective as opening attention grabbers for an argument. To illustrate how an introductory narrative (either a story or a brief scene) can create pathetic appeals, consider the following first paragraph to an argument opposing jet skis:

> I dove off the dock into the lake, and as I approached the surface I could see the sun shining through the water. As my head popped out, I located my cousin a few feet away in a rowboat waiting to escort me as I, a twelve-year-old girl, attempted to swim across the mile-wide, pristine lake and back to our dock. I made it, and that glorious summer day is one of my most precious memories. Today, however, no one would dare attempt that swim. Jet skis have taken over this small lake where I spent many summers with my grandparents. Dozens of whining jet skis crisscross the lake, ruining it for swimming, fishing, canoeing, rowboating, and even waterskiing. More stringent state laws are needed to control jet skiing because it interferes with other uses of lakes and is currently very dangerous.

This narrative makes a case for a particular point of view toward jet skis by winning our identification with the writer's experience. She invites us to relive that experience with her while she also taps into our own treasured memories of summer experiences that have been destroyed by change.

Opening narratives to evoke *pathos* can be powerfully effective, but they are also risky. If they are too private, too self-indulgent, too sentimental, or even too dramatic and forceful, they can backfire on you. If you have doubts about an opening narrative, read it to a sample audience before using it in your final draft.

Use Words, Metaphors, and Analogies with Appropriate Connotations

Another way of appealing to *pathos* is to select words, metaphors, or analogies with connotations that match your aim. We have already described this strategy in our discussion of the "framing" of evidence (Chapter 5, pages 94–96). By using words with particular connotations, a writer guides readers to see the issue through the writer's angle of vision. Thus if you want to create positive feelings about a recent city council decision, you can call it "bold and decisive"; if you want to create negative feelings, you can call it "haughty and autocratic." Similarly, writers can use favorable or unfavorable metaphors and analogies to evoke different imaginative or emotional responses. A tax bill might be viewed as a "potentially fatal poison pill" or as "unpleasant but necessary economic medicine." In each of these cases, the words create an emotional as well as intellectual response.

■ ■ ■ **FOR CLASS DISCUSSION** Incorporating Appeals to Pathos

Outside class, rewrite the introduction to one of your previous papers (or a current draft) to include more appeals to *pathos*. Use any of the strategies for giving your argument presence: concrete language, specific examples, narratives, metaphors, analogies, and connotative words. Bring both your original and your rewritten introductions to class. In pairs or in groups, discuss the comparative effectiveness of these introductions in trying to reach your intended audience. ■ ■ ■

Using Images for Emotional Appeal

One of the most powerful ways to engage an audience emotionally is to use photos or other images. (Chapter 9 focuses exclusively on visual rhetoric—the persuasive power of images.) Although many written arguments do not lend themselves to visual illustrations, we suggest that when you construct arguments you consider the potential of visual support. Imagine that your argument were to appear in a newspaper, in a magazine, or on a Web site where space would be provided for one or two visuals. What photographs or drawings might help persuade your audience toward your perspective?

When images work well, they are analogous to the verbal strategies of concrete language, specific illustrations, narratives, and connotative words. The challenge in using visuals is to find material that is straightforward enough to be understood without elaborate explanations, that is timely and relevant, and that clearly adds impact to a specific part of your argument. As an example, suppose you are writing an argument supporting fund-raising efforts to help third-world countries. To add a powerful appeal to *pathos,* you might consider incorporating into your argument the photograph shown in Figure 6.1, a Haitian woman walking on a rickety bridge over a vast garbage heap in a Haitian slum. A photograph such as this one can create an almost immediate emotional and imaginative response.

■ ■ ■ **FOR CLASS DISCUSSION** Analyzing Images as Appeals to Pathos

Working in small groups or as a whole class, share your responses to the following questions:

1. How would you describe the emotional/imaginative impact of Figure 6.1?
2. Many appeals for helping third-world countries show pictures of big-bellied, starving children during a famine, often in Africa. How is your response to Figure 6.1 similar to or different from the commonly encountered pictures of starving children? How is Figure 6.1's story about the ravages of poverty different from the stories of starving children?

FIGURE 6.1 La Saline, a slum in Port-au-Prince, Haiti ■ ■ ■

Kairos: **The Timeliness and Fitness of Arguments**

To increase your argument's effectiveness, you need to consider not only its appeals to *logos, ethos,* and *pathos,* but also its *kairos*—that is, its timing, its appropriateness for the occasion. *Kairos* is one of those wonderful words, adopted from another language (in this case ancient Greek), that is impossible to define, yet powerful in what it represents. In Greek, *kairos* means "right time," "season," or "opportunity." It differs subtly from the ordinary Greek word for time, *chronos,* the root of our words "chronology" and "chronometer." You can measure *chronos* by looking at your watch, but you measure *kairos* by sensing the opportune time through psychological attentiveness to situation

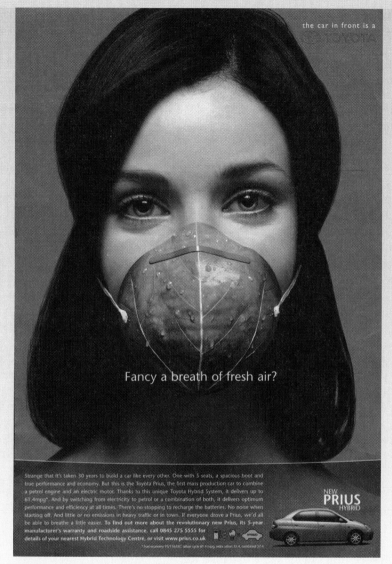

Logos, Ethos, Pathos, and Kairos

Increasing sales of Toyota's Prius, a hybrid car that runs on both electricity and gasoline, confirm that American consumers are willing to switch from SUVs to more energy-efficient cars. As this advertisement for the Prius shows, energy efficient cars are connected to a constellation of issues, including the need to decrease carbon emissions because of pollution-caused health problems and environmental concern for cleaner energy.

How does this ad attempt to move its audience? Analyze the ad's visual and verbal appeals to *logos, ethos, pathos* and *kairos*.

and meaning. To think *kairotically* is to be attuned to the total context of a situation in order to act in the right way at the right moment. By analogy, consider a skilled base runner who senses the right moment to steal second, a wise teacher who senses the right moment to praise or critique a student's performance, or a successful psychotherapist who senses the right moment to talk rather than listen in a counseling session. *Kairos* reminds us that a rhetorical situation is not stable and fixed, but evolves as events unfold or as audiences experience the psychological ebbs and flows of attention and care. Here are some examples that illustrate the range of insights contained by the term *kairos:*

- If you write a letter to the editor of a newspaper, you usually have a one- or two-day window before a current event becomes "old news" and is no longer interesting. An out-of-date letter will be rejected, not because it is poorly written or argued but because it misses its *kairotic* moment. (Similar instances of lost timeliness occur in class discussions: On how many occasions have you wanted to contribute an idea to class discussion, but the professor doesn't acknowledge your raised hand? When you finally are called on, the *kairotic* moment has passed.)
- Bobbi Buchanan's "Don't Hang Up, That's My Mom Calling," which we used to illustrate *pathos* (page 112), could have been written only during a brief historical period when telemarketing was being publicly debated. Moreover, it could have been written only late in that period after numerous writers had attacked telemarketers. The piece was published in the *New York Times* because the editor received it at the right *kairotic* moment.
- A sociology major is writing a senior capstone paper for graduation. The due date for the paper is fixed, so the timing of the paper isn't at issue. But *kairos* is still relevant. It urges the student to consider what is appropriate for such a paper. What is the "right way" to produce a sociology paper at this moment in the history of the discipline? Currently, what are leading-edge versus trailing-edge questions in sociology? What theorists are now in vogue? What research methods would most impress a judging committee? How would a good capstone paper written in 2010 differ from one written a decade earlier?

As you can see from these examples, *kairos* concerns a whole range of questions connected to the timing, fitness, appropriateness, and proportions of a message within an evolving rhetorical context. There are no rules to help you determine the *kairotic* moment for your argument, but being attuned to *kairos* will help you "read" your audience and rhetorical situation in a dynamic way.

■ ■ ■ **FOR CLASS DISCUSSION** Analyzing An Argument from the Perspective
of *Kairos, Logos, Ethos,* and *Pathos*

Your instructor will select an argument for analysis. Working in small groups or as a whole class, analyze the assigned argument first from the perspective of *kairos* and then from the perspectives of *logos, ethos,* and *pathos.*

1. As you analyze the argument from the perspective of *kairos,* consider the following questions:
    a. What is the motivating occasion for this argument? That is, what causes this writer to put pen to paper or fingers to keyboard?

b. What conversation is the writer joining? Who are the other voices in this conversation? What are these voices saying that compels the writer to add his or her own voice? How was the stage set to create the *kairotic* moment for this argument?

c. Who is the writer's intended audience and why?

d. What is the writer's purpose? Toward what view or action is the writer trying to persuade his or her audience?

e. To what extent can various features of the argument be explained by your understanding of its *kairotic* moment?

2. Now analyze the same argument for its appeals to *logos, ethos,* and *pathos.* How successful is this argument in achieving its writer's purpose?

How Audience-Based Reasons Enhance *Logos, Ethos,* and *Pathos*

We conclude this chapter by returning to the concept of audience-based reasons that we introduced in Chapter 4. Audience-based reasons enhance *logos* because they are built on underlying assumptions (warrants) that the audience is likely to accept. But they also enhance *ethos* and *pathos* by helping the writer identify with the audience, entering into their beliefs and values. To consider the needs of your audience, you can ask yourself the following questions:

Questions for Analyzing Your Audience

What to Ask	Why to Ask It
1. Who is your audience?	Your answer will help you think about audience-based reasons.
	▪ Are you writing to a single person, a committee, or the general readership of a newspaper, magazine, blog site, and so forth?
	▪ Are your readers academics, professionals, fellow students, general citizens, or people with specialized background and interests?
	▪ Can you expect your audience to be politically and culturally liberal, middle of the road, conservative, or all over the map? What about their religious views?
	▪ How do you picture your audience in terms of social class, ethnicity, gender, sexual orientation, age, and cultural identity?
	▪ To what extent does your audience share your own interests and cultural position? Are you writing to insiders or outsiders with regard to your own values and beliefs?

(Continued)

What to Ask	Why to Ask It
2. How much does your audience know or care about your issue?	Your answer can especially affect your introduction and conclusion: ▓ Do your readers need background on your issue or are they already in the conversation? ▓ If you are writing to specific decision makers, are they currently aware of the problem you are addressing? If not, how can you get their attention? ▓ Does your audience care about your issue? If not, how can you get them to care?
3. What is your audience's current attitude toward your issue?	Your answer will help you decide the structure and tone of your argument. ▓ Are your readers already supportive of your position? Undecided? Skeptical? Strongly opposed? ▓ What other points of view besides your own will your audience be weighing?
4. What will be your audience's likely objections to your argument?	Your answer will help determine the content of your argument and will alert you to extra research you may need. ▓ What weaknesses will audience members find? ▓ What aspects of your position will be most threatening to them and why? ▓ How are your basic assumptions, values, or beliefs different from your audience's?
5. What values, beliefs, or assumptions about the world do you and your audience share?	Your answer will help you find common ground with your audience. ▓ Despite different points of view on this issue, where can you find common links with your audience? ▓ How might you use these links to build bridges to your audience?

To see how a concern for audience-based reasons can enhance *ethos* and *pathos,* suppose that you support racial profiling (rather than random selection) for determining which people receive intensive screening at airports. Suppose further that you are writing a guest op-ed column for a liberal campus newspaper and imagine readers repulsed by the notion of racial profiling (as indeed you are repulsed too in most cases). It's important from the start that you understand and acknowledge the interests of those opposed to your position. Middle Eastern men, the most likely candidates for racial profiling, will object to your racial stereotyping, which lumps all people of Arabic or Semitic appearance into the category "potential terrorists." African Americans and Hispanics, frequent victims of racial profiling by police in U.S. cities, may object to further extension of this hated practice. Also, most political liberals, as well as many moderates and conservatives, may object to the racism inherent in selecting people for airport screening on the basis of ethnicity.

What shared values might you use to build bridges to those opposed to racial profiling at airports? You need to develop a strategy to reduce your audience's fears and to link your reasons to their values. Your thinking might go something like this:

Problem: How can I create an argument rooted in shared values? How can I reduce fear that racial profiling in this situation endorses racism or will lead to further erosion of civil liberties?

Bridge-building goals: I must try to show that my argument's goal is to increase airline safety by preventing terrorism like that of 9/11/01. My argument must show my respect for Islam and for Arabic and Semitic peoples. I must also show my rejection of racial profiling as normal police practice.

Possible strategies:
- Stress the shared value of protecting innocent people from terrorism.
- Show how racial profiling significantly increases the efficiency of secondary searches. (If searches are performed at random, then we waste time and resources searching people who are statistically unlikely to be terrorists.)
- Argue that airport screeners must also use indicators other than race to select people for searches (for example, traits that might indicate a domestic terrorist).
- Show my respect for Islam.
- Show sympathy for people selected for searching via racial profiling and acknowledge that this practice would normally be despicable except for the extreme importance of airline security, which overrides personal liberties in this case.
- Show my rejection of racial profiling in situations other than airport screening—for example, stopping African Americans for traffic violations more often than whites and then searching their cars for drugs or stolen goods.
- Perhaps show my support of affirmative action, which is a kind of racial profiling in reverse.

These thinking notes allow you to develop the following plan for your argument.
- Airport screeners should use racial profiling rather than random selection to determine which people undergo intensive screening
  - because doing so will make more efficient use of airport screeners' time, increase the odds of finding terrorists, and thus lead to greater airline safety (*WARRANT: increased airline safety is good;* or, at a deeper level, *The positive consequences of increasing airline safety through racial profiling outweigh the negative consequences*)
  - because racial profiling in this specific case does not mean allowing it in everyday police activities nor does it imply disrespect for Islam or for Middle Eastern males (WARRANT: *Racial profiling is unacceptable in everyday police practices. It is wrong to show disrespect for Islam or Middle Eastern males.*)

As this plan shows, your strategy is to seek reasons whose warrants your audience will accept. First, you will argue that racial profiling will lead to greater airline safety, allowing you to stress that safe airlines benefit all passengers. Your concern is the lives of hundreds of passengers as well as others who might be killed in a terrorist attack. Second, you plan to reduce adversaries' resistance to your proposal by showing that the consequences aren't as severe as they might fear. Using racial profiling in airports would not justify using it in urban police work (a practice you find despicable) and it would not imply disrespect for Islam or Middle Eastern males. As this example shows, your focus on audience—on the search for audience-based reasons—shapes the actual invention of your argument from the start.

■ ■ ■ **FOR CLASS DISCUSSION** **Planning an Audience-Based Argumentative Strategy**

1. How does the preceding plan for an argument supporting racial profiling make appeal to *ethos* and *pathos* as well as to *logos*?

2. Working individually or in small groups, plan an audience-based argumentative strategy for one or more of the following cases. Follow the thinking process used by the writer of the racial-profiling argument: (1) state several problems that the writer must solve to reach the audience, and (2) develop possible solutions to those problems.

    a. An argument for the right of software companies to continue making and selling violent video games: aim the argument at parents who oppose their children's playing these games.

    b. An argument to reverse grade inflation by limiting the number of As and Bs a professor can give in a course: aim the argument at students who fear getting lower grades.

    c. An argument supporting the legalization of cocaine: aim the argument at readers of *Reader's Digest,* a conservative magazine that supports the current war on drugs.

■ ■ ■

Conclusion

In this chapter, we have explored ways that writers can strengthen the persuasiveness of their arguments by creating appeals to *ethos* and *pathos,* by being attentive to *kairos,* and by building bridges to their readers through audience-based reasons. Arguments are more persuasive if readers trust the credibility of the writer and if the argument appeals to readers' hearts and imaginations as well as to their intellects. Sometimes images such as drawings or photographs may reinforce the argument by evoking strong emotional responses, thus enhancing *pathos.* Additionally, attentiveness to *kairos* keeps the writer attuned to the dynamics of a rhetorical situation in order to create the right message at the right time. Finally, all these appeals come together when the writer explicitly focuses on finding audience-based reasons.

WRITING ASSIGNMENT   Revising a Draft for *Ethos, Pathos,* and Audience-Based Reasons

Part 1: Choose an argument that you have previously written or that you are currently drafting. Revise the argument with explicit focus on increasing its appeals to *ethos, pathos,* and *logos* via audience-based reasons and other strategies. Consider especially how you might improve *ethos* by building bridges to the audience or improve *pathos* through concrete language, specific examples, metaphors, or connotations of words. Imagine also how you might include an effective photograph or image. Finally, consider the extent to which your reasons are audience-based.

Part 2: Attach to your revision a reflective letter explaining the choices you made in your revision. Describe for your instructor the changes you made and explain how or why these changes are intended to enhance your argument's effectiveness at moving its audience. ■

PEARSON
mycomplab

For additional writing, reading, and research resources, go to
www.mycomplab.com

7 Responding to Objections and Alternative Views

In the previous chapter we discussed strategies for moving your audience through appeals to *ethos, pathos,* and *kairos.* In this chapter we examine strategies for addressing opposing or alternative views—whether to omit them, refute them, concede to them, or incorporate them through compromise and conciliation. We show you how your choices about structure, content, and tone may differ depending on whether your audience is sympathetic, neutral, or resistant to your views. The strategies explained in this chapter will increase your flexibility as an arguer and enhance your chance of persuading a wide variety of audiences.

One-Sided, Multisided, and Dialogic Arguments

Arguments are said to be one-sided, multisided, or dialogic:

- *A one-sided argument* presents only the writer's position on the issue without summarizing and responding to alternative viewpoints.
- *A multisided argument* presents the writer's position, but also summarizes and responds to possible objections and alternative views.
- *A dialogic argument* has a much stronger component of inquiry, in which the writer presents himself as uncertain or searching, the audience is considered a partner in the dialogue, and the writer's purpose is to seek common ground perhaps leading to a consensual solution to a problem. (See our discussion in Chapter 1 of argument as truth seeking versus persuasion, pages 13–15.)

One-sided and *multisided* arguments often take an adversarial stance in that the writer regards alternative views as flawed or wrong and supports his own claim with a strongly persuasive intent. Although multisided arguments can be adversarial, they can also be made to feel dialogic, depending on the way the writer introduces and responds to alternative views.

At issue, then, is the writer's treatment of alternative views. Does the writer omit them (a one-sided argument), summarize them in order to rebut them (an adversarial kind of multisided argument), or summarize them in order to acknowledge their validity, value, and force (a more dialogic kind of multisided argument)? Each of these approaches can be appropriate for certain occasions, depending on your purpose, your confidence in your own stance, and your audience's resistance to your views.

How can one determine the kind of argument that would be most effective in a given case? As a general rule, one-sided arguments occur commonly when an issue is not highly contested. If the issue is highly contested, then one-sided arguments tend to strengthen the convictions of those who are already in the writer's camp, but alienate those who aren't. In contrast, for those initially opposed to a writer's claim, a multisided argument shows that the writer has considered other views and thus reduces some initial hostility. An especially interesting effect can occur with neutral or undecided audiences. In the short run, one-sided arguments are often persuasive to a neutral audience, but in the long run multisided arguments have more staying power. Neutral audiences who have heard only one side of an issue tend to change their minds when they hear alternative arguments. By anticipating and rebutting opposing views, a multisided argument diminishes the surprise and force of subsequent counterarguments. If we move from neutral to highly resistant audiences, adversarial approaches—even multisided ones—are seldom effective because they increase hostility and harden the differences between writer and reader. In such cases, more dialogic approaches have the best chance of establishing common ground for inquiry and consensus.

In the rest of this chapter we will show you how your choice of writing one-sided, multisided, or dialogic arguments is a function of how you perceive your audience's resistance to your views as well as your level of confidence in your own views.

Determining Your Audience's Resistance to Your Views

When you write an argument, you must always consider your audience's point of view. One way to imagine your relationship to your audience is to place it on a scale of resistance ranging from strong support of your position to strong opposition (see Figure 7.1). At the "Accord" end of this scale are like-minded people who basically agree with your position on the issue. At the "Resistance" end are those who strongly disagree with you, perhaps unconditionally, because their values, beliefs, or assumptions sharply differ from your own. Between "Accord" and "Resistance" lies a range of opinions. Close to your position will be those leaning in your direction but with less conviction than you have. Close to the resistance position will be those basically opposed to your view but willing to listen to your argument and perhaps willing to acknowledge some of its strengths. In the middle are those undecided people who are still sorting out their feelings, seeking additional information, and weighing the strengths and weaknesses of alternative views.

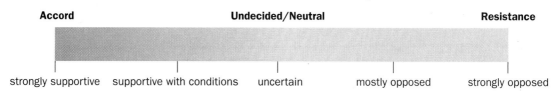

FIGURE 7.1 Scale of resistance

Seldom, however, will you encounter an issue in which the range of disagreement follows a simple line from accord to resistance. Often resistant views fall into different categories so that no single line of argument appeals to all those whose views are different from your own. You have to identify not only your audience's resistance to your ideas but also the causes of that resistance.

Consider, for example, the issues surrounding publicly financed sports stadiums. In one city, a ballot initiative asked citizens to raise sales taxes to build a new retractable-roof stadium for its baseball team. Supporters of the initiative faced a complex array of resisting views (see Figure 7.2). Opponents of the initiative could be placed into four categories. Some simply had no interest in sports, cared nothing about baseball, and saw no benefit in building a huge publicly financed sports facility. Another group loved baseball and followed the home team passionately, but was philosophically opposed to subsidizing rich players and owners with taxpayer money. This group argued that the whole sports industry needed to be restructured so that stadiums were paid for out of sports revenues. Still another group was opposed to tax hikes in general. It focused on the principle of reducing the size of government and of using tax revenues only for essential services. Finally, another powerful group supported baseball and supported the notion of public funding of a new stadium but opposed the kind of retractable-roof stadium specified in the initiative. This group wanted an old-fashioned, open-air stadium like Baltimore's Camden Yards or Cleveland's Jacobs Field.

Writers supporting the initiative found it impossible to address all of these resisting audiences at once. If a supporter of the initiative wanted to aim an argument at sports haters, he or she could stress the spinoff benefits of a new ballpark (for example, the new ballpark would attract tourist revenue, renovate a deteriorating downtown neighborhood, create jobs, make sports lovers more likely to vote for public subsidies of the arts, and so forth). But these arguments were irrelevant to those who wanted an open-air stadium, who opposed tax hikes categorically, or who objected to public subsidy of millionaires.

Another kind of complexity occurs when a writer is positioned between two kinds of resisting views. Consider the position of student writer Sam, a gay man who wished to argue that gay and lesbian people should actively support legislation to legalize same-sex marriage (see Figure 7.3). Most arguments that support same-sex marriage hope to persuade conservative heterosexual audiences who tend to disapprove of homosexuality and stress traditional family values. But Sam imagined writing

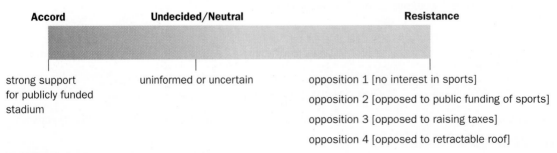

FIGURE 7.2 Scale of resistance, baseball stadium issue

HETEROSEXUAL AUDIENCE   GAY AUDIENCE

Resistance   **Neutral**   **Sam's position**   **Neutral**   **Resistance**

Opposition from proponents of "family values" unconditionally opposed to homosexuality

Same-sex marriage should be legalized

Opposition from gays and lesbians skeptical of traditional marriage as a model for gay relationships

FIGURE 7.3 Scale of resistance for same-sex marriage issue

for a gay magazine such as the *Harvard Gay and Lesbian Review* or *The Advocate,* and he wished to aim his argument at liberal gay and lesbian activists who opposed traditional marriage on different grounds. These thinkers, critiquing traditional marriage for the way it stereotypes gender roles and limits the freedom of partners, argued that heterosexual marriage is not a good model for relationships in the gay community. These people constituted an audience 180 degrees removed from the conservative proponents of family values who oppose same-sex marriage on moral and religious grounds.

In writing his early drafts, Sam was stymied by his attempt to address both audiences at once. Only after he blocked out the conservative "family values" audience and imagined an audience of what he called "liberationist" gays and lesbians was he able to develop a consistent argument. (You can read Sam's essay on pages 301–303.)

The baseball stadium example and the same-sex marriage example illustrate the difficulty of adapting your argument to your audience's position on the scale of resistance. Yet doing so is important because you need a stable vision of your audience before you can determine an effective content, structure, and tone for your argument. As we showed in Chapter 4, an effective content derives from choosing audience-based reasons that appeal to your audience's values, assumptions, and beliefs. As we show in the rest of this chapter, an effective structure and tone are often a function of where your audience falls on the scale of resistance. The next sections show how you can adjust your arguing strategy depending on whether your audience is supportive, neutral, or hostile.

Appealing to a Supportive Audience: One-Sided Argument

One-sided arguments commonly occur when an issue isn't highly contested and the writer's aim is merely to put forth a new or different point of view. When an issue is contested, however, one-sided arguments are used mainly to stir the passions of supporters—to convert belief into action by inspiring a party member to contribute to a senator's campaign or a bored office worker to sign up for a change-your-life weekend seminar.

Typically, appeals to a supportive audience are structured as one-sided arguments that either ignore opposing views or reduce them to "enemy" stereotypes. Filled with motivational language, these arguments list the benefits that will ensue from your donations to the cause and the horrors just around the corner if the other side wins. One of the authors of this text recently received a fund-raising letter from an environmental lobbying group declaring, "It's crunch time for the polluters and their pals on Capitol Hill." The "corporate polluters" and "anti-environment politicians," the letter continues, have "stepped up efforts to roll back our environmental protections—relying on large campaign contributions, slick PR firms and well-heeled lobbyists to get the job done before November's election." This letter makes the reader feel part of an in-group of good guys fighting the big business "polluters." Nothing in the letter examines environmental issues from business's perspective or attempts to examine alternative views fairly. Because the intended audience already believes in the cause, nothing in the letter invites readers to consider the issues more thoroughly. Rather, the goal is to solidify support, increase the fervor of belief, and inspire action. Most appeal arguments make it easy to act, ending with an 800 phone number to call, a Web site to visit, a tear-out postcard to send in, or a congressperson's address to write to.

Appealing to a Neutral or Undecided Audience: Classical Argument

The in-group appeals that motivate an already supportive audience can repel a neutral or undecided audience. Because undecided audiences are like jurors weighing all sides of an issue, they distrust one-sided arguments that caricature other views. Generally the best strategy for appealing to undecided audiences is the classically structured argument described in Chapter 3 (pages 60–62).

What characterizes the classical argument is the writer's willingness to summarize opposing views fairly and to respond to them openly—either by trying to refute them or by conceding to their strengths and then shifting to a different field of values. Let's look at these strategies in more depth.

Summarizing Opposing Views

The first step toward responding to opposing views in a classical argument is to summarize them fairly. Follow the *principle of charity,* which obliges you to avoid loaded, biased, or "straw man" summaries that oversimplify or distort opposing arguments, making them easy to knock over.

Consider the difference between an unfair and a fair summary of an argument. In the following example, a hypothetical supporter of genetically engineered foods intends to refute the argument of organic-food advocate Lisa Turner, who opposes all forms of biotechnology.

Unfair Summary of Turner's Argument

In a biased article lacking scientific understanding of biotechnology, natural-foods huckster Lisa Turner parrots the health food industry's party line that genetically altered crops are Frankenstein's monsters run amok. She ignorantly claims that consumption of biotech foods will lead to worldwide destruction, disease, and death, ignoring the wealth of scientific literature showing that genetically modified foods are safe. Her misinformed attacks are scare tactics aimed at selling consumers on overpriced "health food" products to be purchased at boutique organic-food stores.

Fair Summary of Turner's Argument

In an article appearing in a nutrition magazine, health food advocate Lisa Turner warns readers that much of our food today is genetically modified using gene-level techniques that differ completely from ordinary crossbreeding. She argues that the potential, unforeseen, harmful consequences of genetic engineering offset the possible benefits of increasing the food supply, reducing the use of pesticides, and boosting the nutritional value of foods. Turner asserts that genetic engineering is imprecise, untested, unpredictable, irreversible, and also uncontrollable because of animals, insects, and winds.

In the unfair summary, the writer distorts and oversimplifies Turner's argument, creating a straw man argument that is easy to knock over because it doesn't make the opponent's best case. In contrast, a fair summary follows the "principle of charity," allowing the strength of the opposing view to come through clearly.

■ ■ ■ **FOR CLASS DISCUSSION**   **Distinguishing Fair from Unfair Summaries**
Working in small groups or as a whole class, analyze the differences between the two summaries.

1. What makes the first summary unfair? How can you tell?
2. In the unfair summary, what strategies does the writer use to make the opposing view seem weak and flawed? In the fair summary, how is the opposing view made strong and clear?
3. In the unfair summary, how does the writer attack Turner's motives and credentials? This attack is sometimes called an *ad hominem* argument ("against the person"—see Appendix 1 for a definition of this reasoning fallacy) in that it attacks the arguer rather than the argument. How does the writer treat Turner differently in the fair summary?
4. Do you agree with our view that arguments are more persuasive if the writer summarizes opposing views fairly rather than unfairly? Why?   ■ ■ ■

Refuting Opposing Views

Once you have summarized opposing views, you can either refute them or concede to their strengths. In refuting an opposing view, you attempt to convince readers that its argument is logically flawed, inadequately supported, or based on erroneous assumptions. In refuting an argument, you can rebut (1) the writer's stated reason and grounds, (2) the writer's warrant and backing, or (3) both. Put in less specialized language, you can rebut a writer's reasons and evidence or the writer's underlying assumptions. Suppose, for example, that you wanted to refute this argument:

We shouldn't elect Joe as committee chair because he is too bossy.

We can clarify the structure of this argument by showing it in Toulmin terms:

ENTHYMEME

CLAIM We shouldn't elect Joe as committee chair.

REASON because he is too bossy.

WARRANT

Bossy people make bad committee chairs.

One way to refute this argument is to rebut the stated reason that Joe is too bossy. Your rebuttal might go something like this:

> I disagree that Joe is bossy. In fact, Joe is very unbossy. He's a good listener who's willing to compromise, and he involves others in decisions. The example you cite for his being bossy wasn't typical. It was a one-time circumstance that doesn't reflect his normal behavior. [The writer could then provide examples of Joe's cooperative nature.]

Or you could concede that Joe is bossy but rebut the argument's warrant that bossiness is a bad trait for committee chairs:

> I agree that Joe is bossy, but in this circumstance bossiness is just the trait we need. This committee hasn't gotten anything done for six months and time is running out. We need a decisive person who can come in, get the committee organized, assign tasks, and get the job done.

Let's now illustrate these strategies in a more complex situation. Consider the controversy inspired by a *New York Times Magazine* article titled "Recycling Is Garbage." Its author, John Tierney, argued that recycling is not environmentally sound and that it is cheaper to bury garbage in a landfill than to recycle it. In criticizing recycling, Tierney argued that recycling wastes money; he provided evidence that "every time a sanitation department crew picks up a load of bottles and cans from the curb, New York City loses money." In Toulmin's terms, one of Tierney's arguments is structured as follows:

ENTHYMEME

CLAIM Recycling is bad policy

REASON because it costs more to recycle material than to bury it in a landfill.

GROUNDS

• Evidence of the high cost of recycling [Tierney says it costs New York City $200 more per ton for recyclables than trash]

> **WARRANT**
> We should dispose of garbage in the least
> expensive way.

A number of environmentalists responded angrily to Tierney's argument, challenging either his reason, his warrant, or both. Those refuting the reason offered counterevidence showing that recycling isn't as expensive as Tierney claimed. Those refuting the warrant said that even if the costs of recycling are higher than burying wastes in a landfill, recycling still benefits the environment by reducing the amount of virgin materials taken from nature. These critics, in effect, offered a new warrant: We should dispose of garbage in the way that most saves the world's resources.

Strategies for Rebutting Evidence

Whether you are rebutting an argument's reasons or its warrant, you will frequently need to question a writer's use of evidence. Here are some strategies you can use:

- *Deny the truth of the data.* Arguers can disagree about the facts of a case. If you have reasons to doubt a writer's facts, call them into question.
- *Cite counterexamples and countertestimony.* You can often rebut an argument based on examples or testimony by citing counterexamples or countertestimony that denies the conclusiveness of the original data.
- *Cast doubt on the representativeness or sufficiency of examples.* Examples are powerful only if the audience feels them to be representative and sufficient. Many environmentalists complained that John Tierney's attack on recycling was based too largely on data from New York City and that it didn't accurately take into account the more positive experiences of other cities and states. When data from outside New York City were examined, the cost-effectiveness and positive environmental impact of recycling seemed more apparent.
- *Cast doubt on the relevance or recency of the examples, statistics, or testimony.* The best evidence is up-to-date. In a rapidly changing universe, data that are even a few years out-of-date are often ineffective. For example, as the demand for recycled goods increases, the cost of recycling will be reduced. Out-of-date statistics will skew any argument about the cost of recycling.
- *Call into question the credibility of an authority.* If an opposing argument is based on testimony, you can undermine its persuasiveness if you show that a person being cited lacks up-to-date or relevant expertise in the field. (This procedure is different from the *ad hominem* fallacy discussed in Appendix 1 because it doesn't attack the personal character of the authority but only the authority's expertise on a specific matter.)
- *Question the accuracy or context of quotations.* Evidence based on testimony is frequently distorted by being either misquoted or taken out of context. Often scientists qualify their findings heavily, but these qualifications are omitted by the popular media. You can thus attack the use of a quotation by putting it in its original context or by restoring the qualifications accompanying the quotation in its original source.

■ *Question the way statistical data were produced or interpreted.* Chapter 5 provides fuller treatment of how to question statistics. In general, you can rebut statistical evidence by calling into account how the data were gathered, treated mathematically, or interpreted. It can make a big difference, for example, whether you cite raw numbers or percentages or whether you choose large or small increments for the axes of graphs.

Conceding to Opposing Views

In writing a classical argument, a writer must sometimes concede to an opposing argument rather than refute it. Sometimes you encounter portions of an argument that you simply can't refute. For example, suppose you support the legalization of hard drugs such as cocaine and heroin. Adversaries argue that legalizing hard drugs will increase the number of drug users and addicts. You might dispute the size of their numbers, but you reluctantly agree that they are right. Your strategy in this case is not to refute the opposing argument but to concede to it by admitting that legalization of hard drugs will promote heroin and cocaine addiction. Having made that concession, your task is then to show that the benefits of drug legalization still outweigh the costs you've just conceded.

As this example shows, the strategy of a concession argument is to switch from the field of values employed by the writer you disagree with to a different field of values more favorable to your position. You don't try to refute the writer's stated reason and grounds (by arguing that legalization will *not* lead to increased drug usage and addiction) or the writer's warrant (by arguing that increased drug use and addiction is not a problem). Rather, you shift the argument to a new field of values by introducing a new warrant, one that you think your audience can share (that the benefits of legalization—eliminating the black market and ending the crime, violence, and prison costs associated with procurement of drugs—outweigh the costs of increased addiction). To the extent that opponents of legalization share your desire to stop drug-related crime, shifting to this new field of values is a good strategy. Although it may seem that you weaken your own position by conceding to an opposing argument, you may actually strengthen it by increasing your credibility and gaining your audience's goodwill. Moreover, conceding to one part of an opposing argument doesn't mean that you won't refute other parts of that argument.

Example of a Student Essay Using Refutation Strategy

The following extract from a student essay is the refutation section of a classical argument appealing to a neutral or undecided audience. In this essay, student writer Marybeth Hamilton argues for continued taxpayer support of First Place, an alternative public school for homeless children that also provides job counseling and mental health services for families. Because running First Place is costly and because it can accommodate only 4 percent of her city's homeless children, Marybeth recognizes that her audience may object to continued public funding. Consequently, to reach the neutral or skeptical members of her audience, she devotes the following portion of her argument to summarizing and refuting opposing views.

From "First Place: A Healing School for Homeless Children"

MARYBETH HAMILTON (STUDENT)

…As stated earlier, the goal of First Place is to prepare students for returning to mainstream public schools. Although there are many reasons to continue operating an agency like First Place, there are some who would argue against it. One argument is that the school is too expensive, costing many more taxpayer dollars per child than a mainstream school. I can understand this objection to cost, but one way to look at First Place is as a preventative action by the city to reduce the future costs of crime and welfare. Because all the students at First Place are at risk for educational failure, drug and alcohol abuse, or numerous other long-term problems, a program like First Place attempts to stop the problems before they start. In the long run, the city could be saving money in areas such as drug rehabilitation, welfare payments, or jail costs.

Others might criticize First Place for spending some of its funding on social services for the students and their families instead of spending it all on educational needs. When the city is already making welfare payments and providing a shelter for the families, why do they deserve anything more? Basically, the job of any school is to help a child become educated and have social skills. At First Place, students' needs run deep, and their entire families are in crisis. What good is it to help just the child when the rest of the family is still suffering? The education of only the child will not help the family out of poverty. Therefore, First Place helps parents look for jobs by providing job search help including assistance with résumés. They even supply clothes to wear to an interview. First Place also provides a parent support group for expressing anxieties and learning coping skills. This therapy helps parents deal with their struggles in a productive way, reducing the chance that they will take out their frustration on their child. All these "extras" are an attempt to help the family get back on its feet and become self-supporting.

Another objection to an agency like First Place is that the short-term stay at First Place does no long-term good for the student. However, in talking with Michael Siptroth, a teacher at First Place, I learned that the individual attention the students receive helps many of them catch up in school quite quickly. He reported that some students actually made a three-grade-level improvement in one year. This improvement definitely contributes to the long-term good of the student, especially in the area of self-esteem. Also, the students at First Place are in desperate situations. For most, any help is better than no help. Thus First Place provides extended day care for the children so they won't have to be unsupervised at home while their parents are working or looking for work. For example, some homeless children live in motels on Aurora Avenue, a major highway that is overrun with fast cars, prostitutes, and drugs. Aurora Avenue is not a safe place for children to play, so the extended day care is important for many of First Place's students.

Finally, opponents might question the value of removing students from mainstream classrooms. Some might argue that separating children from regular classrooms is not good because it further highlights their differences from the mainstream children. Also, the separation period might cause additional alienation when the First Place child does return to a mainstream school. In reality, though, the effects are quite different. Children at

First Place are sympathetic to each other. Perhaps for the first time in their lives, they do not have to be on the defensive because no one is going to make fun of them for being homeless; they are all homeless. The time spent at First Place is usually a time for catching up to the students in mainstream schools. When students catch up, they have one fewer reason to be seen as different from mainstream students. If the students stayed in the mainstream school and continued to fall behind, they would only get teased more.

5   First Place is a program that merits the community's ongoing moral and financial support. With more funding, First Place could help many more homeless children and their families along the path toward self-sufficiency. While this school is not the ultimate answer to the problem of homelessness, it is a beginning. These children deserve a chance to build their own lives, free from the stigma of homelessness, and I, as a responsible citizen, feel a civic and moral duty to do all I can to help them.

■ ■ ■   **FOR CLASS DISCUSSION**   Refutation Strategies

1. Individually or in groups, analyze the refutation strategies that Marybeth employs in her argument.

   a. Summarize each of the opposing reasons that Marybeth anticipates from her audience.

   b. How does she attempt to refute each line of reasoning in the opposing argument? Where does she refute her audience's stated reason? Where does she refute a warrant? Where does she concede to an opposing argument but then shift to a different field of values?

   c. How effective is Marybeth's refutation? Would you as a city resident vote for allotting more public money for this school? Why or why not?

2. Examine each of the following arguments, imagining how the enthymeme could be fleshed out with grounds and backing. Then attempt to refute each argument. Suggest ways to rebut the reason or the warrant or both, or to concede to the argument and then switch to a different field of values.

   a. Signing the Kyoto treaty (pledging that the United States will substantially lower its emission of greenhouse gases) is a bad idea because reducing greenhouse emissions will seriously harm the American economy.

   b. Majoring in engineering is better than majoring in music because engineers make more money than musicians.

   c. The United States should reinstitute the draft because doing so is the only way to maintain a large enough military to defend American interests in several different trouble spots in the world.

   d. The United States should build more nuclear reactors because nuclear reactors will provide substantial electrical energy without emitting greenhouse gases.

   e. People should be allowed to own handguns because owning handguns helps them protect their homes against potentially violent intruders.

■ ■ ■

Appealing to a Resistant Audience: Dialogic Argument

Whereas classical argument is effective for neutral or undecided audiences, it is often less effective for audiences strongly opposed to the writer's views. Because resistant audiences hold values, assumptions, or beliefs widely different from the writer's, they are often unswayed by classical argument, which attacks their worldview too directly. On many values-laden issues such as abortion, gun control, gay rights, or the role of religion in the public sphere, the distance between a writer and a resistant audience can be so great that dialogue seems impossible. In these cases the writer's goal may be simply to open dialogue by seeking common ground—that is, by finding places where the writer and audience agree. For example, pro-choice and pro-life advocates may never agree on a woman's right to an abortion, but they might share common ground in wanting to reduce teenage pregnancy. There is room, in other words, for conversation, if not for agreement.

Because of these differences in basic beliefs and values, the goal of dialogic argument is seldom to convert resistant readers to the writer's position. The best a writer can hope for is to reduce somewhat the level of resistance, perhaps by increasing the reader's willingness to listen as preparation for future dialogue. In fact, once dialogue is initiated, parties who genuinely listen to each other and have learned to respect each other's views might begin finding solutions to shared problems. A recent example of this process can be seen in former Louisiana senator John Breaux's call for a common-ground strategy for solving the U.S. health care crisis characterized by soaring medical costs and rising numbers of Americans without medical insurance. Breaux objects to cable news talk shows in which political opponents shout at each other. "Why not," he asked in an interview, "try a program where the moderator would invite people of opposing philosophies to seek common ground?"* Breaux hopes to address the health care crisis by bringing together liberals and conservatives, patients and insurance companies, doctors and pharmaceutical executives, hospital managers and nurses to find common ground on which they can begin a dialogic search for solutions.

The dialogic strategies we explain in this section—the delayed-thesis strategy and Rogerian strategy—are aimed at promoting understanding between a writer and a resistant audience. They work to disarm hostility by showing the writer's respect for alternative views and by lessening the force with which the writer presents his or her own views.

Delayed-Thesis Argument

In many cases you can reach a resistant audience by using a *delayed-thesis* structure in which you wait until the end of your argument to reveal your thesis. Classical argument asks you to state your thesis in the introduction, support it with reasons and evidence, and then summarize and refute opposing views. Rhetorically, however, it is not always advantageous to tell your readers where you stand at the start of your argument or to separate yourself so definitively from alternative views. For resistant audiences, it may be better to keep the issue open, delaying the revelation of your own position until the end of the essay.

---

*David S. Broder, "Building Bipartisan Consensus on Health-Care Solutions," *Seattle Times* 14 July 2005, B8.

To illustrate the different effects of classical versus delayed-thesis arguments, we invite you to read a delayed-thesis argument by nationally syndicated columnist Ellen Goodman. The article appeared in 1985 at the height of feminist arguments about pornography. The *kairotic* moment for Goodman's article was the nation's shock at a brutal gang rape in New Bedford, Massachusetts, in which a woman was raped on a pool table by patrons of a local bar.*

Minneapolis Pornography Ordinance

ELLEN GOODMAN

Just a couple of months before the pool-table gang rape in New Bedford, Mass., *Hustler* magazine printed a photo feature that reads like a blueprint for the actual crime. There were just two differences between *Hustler* and real life. In *Hustler,* the woman enjoyed it. In real life, the woman charged rape.

There is no evidence that the four men charged with this crime had actually read the magazine. Nor is there evidence that the spectators who yelled encouragement for two hours had held previous ringside seats at pornographic events. But there is a growing sense that the violent pornography being peddled in this country helps to create an atmosphere in which such events occur.

As recently as last month, a study done by two University of Wisconsin researchers suggested that even "normal" men, prescreened college students, were changed by their exposure to violent pornography. After just ten hours of viewing, reported researcher Edward Donnerstein, "the men were less likely to convict in a rape trial, less likely to see injury to a victim, more likely to see the victim as responsible." Pornography may not cause rape directly, he said, "but it maintains a lot of very callous attitudes. It justifies aggression. It even says you are doing a favor to the victim."

If we can prove that pornography is harmful, then shouldn't the victims have legal rights? This, in any case, is the theory behind a city ordinance that recently passed the Minneapolis City Council. Vetoed by the mayor last week, it is likely to be back before the Council for an overriding vote, likely to appear in other cities, other towns. What is unique about the Minneapolis approach is that for the first time it attacks pornography, not because of nudity or sexual explicitness, but because it degrades and harms women. It opposes pornography on the basis of sex discrimination.

5   University of Minnesota Law Professor Catherine MacKinnon, who co-authored the ordinance with feminist writer Andrea Dworkin, says that they chose this tactic because they believe that pornography is central to "creating and maintaining the inequality of the sexes. . . . Just being a woman means you are injured by pornography."

---

*The rape was later the subject of an Academy Award–winning movie, *The Accused,* starring Jodie Foster.

They defined pornography carefully as, "the sexually explicit subordination of women, graphically depicted, whether in pictures or in words." To fit their legal definition it must also include one of nine conditions that show this subordination, like presenting women who "experience sexual pleasure in being raped or…mutilated…." Under this law, it would be possible for a pool-table rape victim to sue *Hustler.* It would be possible for a woman to sue if she were forced to act in a pornographic movie. Indeed, since the law describes pornography as oppressive to all women, it would be possible for any woman to sue those who traffic in the stuff for violating her civil rights.

In many ways, the Minneapolis ordinance is an appealing attack on an appalling problem. The authors have tried to resolve a long and bubbling conflict among those who have both a deep aversion to pornography and a deep loyalty to the value of free speech. "To date," says Professor MacKinnon, "people have identified the pornographer's freedom with everybody's freedom. But we're saying that the freedom of the pornographer is the subordination of women. It means one has to take a side."

But the sides are not quite as clear as Professor MacKinnon describes them. Nor is the ordinance.

Even if we accept the argument that pornography is harmful to women—and I do—then we must also recognize that anti-Semitic literature is harmful to Jews and racist literature is harmful to blacks. For that matter, Marxist literature may be harmful to government policy. It isn't just women versus pornographers. If women win the right to sue publishers and producers, then so could Jews, blacks, and a long list of people who may be able to prove they have been harmed by books, movies, speeches or even records. The Manson murders, you may recall, were reportedly inspired by the Beatles.

10   We might prefer a library or book store or lecture hall without *Mein Kampf* or the Grand Whoever of the Ku Klux Klan. But a growing list of harmful expressions would inevitably strangle freedom of speech.

This ordinance was carefully written to avoid problems of banning and prior restraint, but the right of any woman to claim damages from pornography is just too broad. It seems destined to lead to censorship.

What the Minneapolis City Council has before it is a very attractive theory. What MacKinnon and Dworkin have written is a very persuasive and useful definition of pornography. But they haven't yet resolved the conflict between the harm of pornography and the value of free speech. In its present form, this is still a shaky piece of law.

Consider now how this argument's rhetorical effect would be different if Ellen Goodman had revealed her thesis in the introduction using the classical argument form. Here is how this introduction might have looked:

Goodman's Introduction Rewritten in Classical Form

Just a couple of months before the pool-table gang rape in New Bedford, Mass., *Hustler* magazine printed a photo feature that reads like a blueprint for the actual crime. There were just two differences between *Hustler* and real life. In *Hustler,* the woman enjoyed it. In real life, the woman charged rape. Of course, there is no evidence that the four men charged with this crime had actually read the magazine. Nor is there evidence that the spectators who yelled encouragement for two hours had held previous ringside seats at pornographic events.

But there is a growing sense that the violent pornography being peddled in this country helps to create an atmosphere in which such events occur. One city is taking a unique approach to attack this problem. An ordinance recently passed by the Minneapolis City Council outlaws pornography not because it contains nudity or sexually explicit acts, but because it degrades and harms women. Unfortunately, despite the proponents' good intentions, the Minneapolis ordinance is a bad law because it has potentially dangerous consequences.

Even though Goodman's position can be grasped more quickly in this classical form, our students generally find the original delayed-thesis version more effective. Why is this?

Most people point to the greater sense of complexity and surprise in the delayed-thesis version, a sense that comes largely from the delayed discovery of the writer's position. Whereas the classical version immediately labels the ordinance a "bad law," the original version withholds judgment, inviting the reader to examine the law more sympathetically and to identify with the position of those who drafted it. Rather than distancing herself from those who see pornography as a violation of women's rights, Goodman shares with her readers her own struggles to think through these issues, thereby persuading us of her genuine sympathy for the ordinance and for its feminist proponents. In the end, her delayed thesis renders her final rejection of the ordinance not only more surprising but more convincing.

Clearly, then, a writer's decision about when to reveal her thesis is critical. Revealing the thesis early makes the writer seem more hardnosed, more sure of her position, more confident about how to divide the ground into friendly and hostile camps, more in control. Delaying the thesis, in contrast, complicates the issues, increases reader sympathy for more than one view, and heightens interest in the tension among alternative views and in the writer's struggle for clarity.

Rogerian Argument

An even more powerful strategy for addressing resistant audiences is a conciliatory strategy often called *Rogerian argument,* named after psychologist Carl Rogers, who used this strategy to help people resolve differences.* Rogerian argument emphasizes "empathic listening," which Rogers defined as the ability to see an issue sympathetically from another person's perspective. He trained people to withhold judgment of another person's ideas until after they listened attentively to the other person, understood that person's reasoning, appreciated that person's values, respected that person's humanity—in short, walked in that person's shoes. What Carl Rogers understood is

---

*See Carl Rogers's essay "Communication: Its Blocking and Its Facilitation" in his book *On Becoming a Person* (Boston: Houghton Mifflin, 1961), 329–37. For a fuller discussion of Rogerian argument, see Richard Young, Alton Becker, and Kenneth Pike, *Rhetoric: Discovery and Change* (New York: Harcourt Brace, 1972).

that traditional methods of argumentation are threatening. Because Rogerian argument stresses the psychological as well as logical dimensions of argument, and because it emphasizes reducing threat and building bridges rather than winning an argument, it is particularly effective when dealing with emotionally laden issues.

Under Rogerian strategy, the writer reduces the sense of threat in her argument by showing that *both writer and resistant audience share many basic values.* Instead of attacking the audience as wrongheaded, the Rogerian writer respects the audience's views and demonstrates an understanding of the audience's position before presenting her own position. Finally, the Rogerian writer seldom asks the audience to capitulate entirely to the writer's side—just to shift somewhat toward the writer's views. By acknowledging that she has already shifted toward the audience's views, the writer makes it easier for the audience to accept compromise. All of this negotiation ideally leads to a compromise between—or better, a synthesis of—the opposing positions.

The key to successful Rogerian argument, besides the art of listening, is the ability to point out areas of agreement between the writer's and reader's positions. For example, if you support a woman's right to choose abortion and you are arguing with someone completely opposed to abortion, you're unlikely to convert your reader, but you might reduce the level of resistance. You begin this process by summarizing your reader's position sympathetically, stressing your shared values. You might say, for example, that you also value babies; that you also are appalled by people who treat abortion as a form of birth control; that you also worry that the easy acceptance of abortion diminishes the value society places on human life; and that you also agree that accepting abortion lightly can lead to lack of sexual responsibility. Building bridges like these between you and your readers makes it more likely that they will listen to you when you present your own position.

In its emphasis on establishing common ground, Rogerian argument has much in common with recent feminist theories of argument. Many feminists criticize classical argument as rooted in a male value system and tainted by metaphors of war and combat. Thus, classical arguments, with their emphasis on assertion and refutation, are typically praised for being "powerful" or "forceful." The writer "defends" his position and "attacks" his "opponent's" position using facts and data as "ammunition" and reasons as "big guns" to "blow away" his opponent's claim. According to some theorists, viewing argument as war can lead to inauthenticity, posturing, and game playing.

Writers who share this distrust of classical argumentation often find Rogerian argument appealing because it stresses self-examination, clarification, and accommodation rather than refutation. Rogerian argument is more in tune with win-win negotiation than with win-lose debate.

An example of a student's Rogerian argument is shown on pages 143–144.

Conclusion

This chapter has explained strategies for addressing alternative views. When intending to engage supportive audiences in a cause, writers often compose one-sided arguments. Neutral or undecided audiences generally respond most favorably to classical arguments that set out strong reasons in support of the writer's position yet openly address alternative views, which are first summarized fairly and then either rebutted or conceded to. Strongly resistant audiences typically respond most favorably to dialogic strategies, such as delayed-thesis or Rogerian argument, which seek common ground with an audience, aim at reducing hostility, and take a more inquiring or conciliatory stance.

WRITING ASSIGNMENT A Classical Argument or a Dialogic Argument Aimed at Conciliation

Option 1: A Classical Argument   Write a classical argument following the explanations in Chapter 3, pages 60–62, and using the guidelines for developing such an argument throughout Chapters 3–7. Depending on your instructor's preferences, this argument could be on a new issue, or it could be a final stage of an argument in progress throughout Part 2. This assignment expands the supporting-reasons assignment from Chapter 5 by adding sections that summarize opposing views and respond to them through refutation or concession. For an example of a classical argument, see "'Half-Criminals' or Urban Athletes? A Plea for Fair Treatment of Skateboarders," by David Langley (page 141).

Option 2: A Dialogic Argument Aimed at Conciliation   Write a dialogic argument aimed at a highly resistant audience. A good approach is to argue against a popular cultural practice or belief that you think is wrong, or argue for an action or belief that you think is right even though it will be highly unpopular. Your claim, in other words, must be controversial—going against the grain of popular actions, values, and beliefs—so that you can anticipate considerable resistance to your views. This assignment invites you to stand up for something you believe in even though your view will be highly contested. Your goal is to persuade your audience toward your position or toward a conciliatory compromise. In writing and revising your argument, draw upon appropriate strategies from Chapters 6 and 7. From Chapter 6, consider strategies for increasing your appeals to *ethos* and *pathos*. From Chapter 7, consider strategies for appealing to highly resistant audiences through delayed-thesis or Rogerian approaches. Your instructor may ask you to attach to your argument a reflective letter explaining and justifying the choices you made for appealing to your audience and accommodating their views. For an example of a Rogerian argument written in response to this assignment, see Rebekah Taylor's "Letter to Jim" on page 143. ■

Readings

Our first student essay illustrates a classical argument. This essay grew out of a class discussion about alternative sports, conflicts between traditional sports and newer sports (downhill skiing versus snowboarding), and middle-age prejudices against groups of young people.

"Half-Criminals" or Urban Athletes? A Plea for Fair Treatment of Skateboarders

(A Classical Argument)

DAVID LANGLEY (STUDENT)

For skateboarders, the campus of the University of California at San Diego is a wide-open, huge, geometric, obstacle-filled, stair-scattered cement paradise. The signs posted all over campus read, "No skateboarding, biking, or rollerblading on campus except on Saturday, Sunday, and holidays." I have always respected these signs at my local skateboarding spot. On the first day of 1999, I was skateboarding here with my hometown skate buddies and had just landed a trick when a police officer rushed out from behind a pillar, grabbed me, and yanked me off my board. Because I didn't have my I.D. (I had emptied my pockets so I wouldn't bruise my legs if I fell—a little trick of the trade), the officer started treating me like a criminal. She told me to spread my legs and put my hands on my head. She frisked me and then called in my name to police headquarters.

"What's the deal?" I asked. "The sign said skateboarding was legal on holidays."

"The sign means that you can only *roll* on campus," she said.

But that's *not* what the sign said. The police officer gave one friend and me a warning. Our third friend received a fifty-dollar ticket because it was his second citation in the last twelve months.

5   Like other skateboarders throughout cities, we have been bombarded with unfair treatment. We have been forced out of known skate spots in the city by storeowners and police, kicked out of every parking garage in downtown, compelled to skate at strange times of day and night, and herded into crowded skateboard parks. However, after I was searched by the police and detained for over twenty minutes in my own skating sanctuary, the unreasonableness of the treatment of skateboarders struck me. Where are skateboarders supposed to go? Cities need to change their unfair treatment of skateboarders because skateboarders are not antisocial misfits as popularly believed, because the laws regulating skateboarding are ambiguous, and because skateboarders are not given enough legitimate space to practice their sport.

Possibly because to the average eye most skateboarders look like misfits or delinquents, adults think of us as criminal types and associate our skateboards with antisocial behavior. But this view is unfair. City dwellers should recognize that skateboards are a natural reaction to the urban environment. If people are surrounded by cement, they are going to figure out a way to ride it. People's different environments have always produced transportation and sports to suit the conditions: bikes, cars, skis, ice skates, boats, canoes, surfboards. If we live on snow, we are going to develop skis or snowshoes to move around. If we live in an environment that has flat panels of cement for ground with lots of curbs and stairs, we are going to invent an ingeniously designed flat board with wheels. Skateboards are as natural to cement as surfboards are to water or skis to snow. Moreover, the resulting sport is as healthful, graceful, and athletic. A fair assessment of skateboarders should respect our elegant, nonpolluting means of transportation and sport, and not consider us hoodlums.

A second way that skateboarders are treated unfairly is that the laws that regulate skateboarding in public places are highly restrictive, ambiguous, and open to abusive application by police officers. My being frisked on the UCSD campus is just one example. When I moved to Seattle to go to college, I found the laws in Washington to be equally unclear. When a sign says "No Skateboarding," that generally means you will get ticketed if you are caught skateboarding in the area. But most areas aren't posted. The general rule then is that you can skateboard so long as you do so safely without being reckless. But the definition of "reckless" is up to the whim of the police officer. I visited the front desk of the Seattle East Precinct and asked them exactly what the laws against reckless skateboarding meant. They said that skaters are allowed on the sidewalk as long as they travel at reasonable speed and the sidewalks aren't crowded. One of the officers explained that if he saw a skater sliding down a handrail with people all around, he would definitely arrest the skater. What if there were no people around, I asked? The officer admitted that he might arrest the lone skater anyway and not be questioned by his superiors. No wonder skateboarders feel unfairly treated.

One way that cities have tried to treat skateboarders fairly is to build skateboard parks. Unfortunately, for the most part these parks are no solution at all. Most parks were designed by nonskaters who don't understand the momentum or gravity pull associated with the movement of skateboards. For example, City Skate, a park below the Space Needle in Seattle, is very appealing to the eye, but once you start to ride it you realize that the transitions and the verticals are all off, making it unpleasant and even dangerous to skate there. The Skate Park in Issaquah, Washington, hosts about thirty to fifty skaters at a time. Collisions are frequent and close calls, many. There are simply too many people in a small area. The people who built the park in Redmond, Washington, decided to make a huge wall in it for graffiti artists "to tag on" legally. They apparently thought they ought to throw all us teenage "half-criminals" in together. At this park, young teens are nervous about skating near a gangster "throwing up his piece," and skaters become dizzy as they take deep breaths from their workouts right next to four or five cans of spray paint expelling toxins in the air.

Of course, many adults probably don't think skateboarders deserve to be treated fairly. I have heard the arguments against skateboarders for years from parents, storeowners, friends, police officers, and security guards. For one thing, skateboarding tears up public and private property, people say. I can't deny that skating leaves marks on handrails and benches, and it does chip cement and granite. But in general skateboarders help the environment more than they hurt it. Skateboarding places are not littered or tagged up by skaters. Because skaters need smooth surfaces and because any small object of litter can lead to painful accidents, skaters actually keep the environment cleaner than the average citizen does. As for the population as a whole, skateboarders are keeping the air a lot cleaner than many other commuters and athletes such as boat drivers, car drivers, and skiers on ski lifts. In the bigger picture, infrequent repair of curbs and benches is cheaper than attempts to heal the ozone.

10   We skateboarders aren't going away, so cities are going to have to make room for us somewhere. Here is how cities can treat us fairly. We should be allowed to skate when

others are present as long as we skate safely on the sidewalks. The rules and laws should be clearer so that skaters don't get put into vulnerable positions that make them easy targets for tickets. I do support the opening of skate parks, but cities need to build more of them, need to situate them closer to where skateboarders live, and need to make them relatively wholesome environments. They should also be designed by skateboarders so that they are skater-friendly and safe to ride. Instead of being treated as "half-criminals," skaters should be accepted as urban citizens and admired as athletes; we are a clean population, and we are executing a challenging and graceful sport. As human beings grow, we go from crawling to walking; some of us grow from strollers to skateboards.

To illustrate a conciliatory or Rogerian approach to an issue, we show you student writer Rebekah Taylor's argument written in response to this assignment. Rebekah chose to write a Rogerian argument in the form of a letter. An outspoken advocate for animal rights on her campus, Rebekah addressed her letter to an actual friend, Jim, with whom she had had many long philosophical conversations when she attended a different college. Note how Rebekah "listens" empathically to her friend's position on eating meat and proposes a compromise action.

A Letter to Jim
(A Rogerian Argument)
REBEKAH TAYLOR (STUDENT)

Dear Jim,

I decided to write you a letter today because I miss our long talks. Now that I have transferred colleges, we haven't had nearly enough heated discussions to satisfy either of us. I am writing now to again take up one of the issues we vehemently disagreed on in the past—meat-based diets.

Jim, I do understand how your view that eating meat is normal differs from mine. In your family, you learned that humans eat animals, and this view was reinforced in school where the idea of the food pyramid based on meat protein was taught and where most children had not even heard of vegetarian options. Also, your religious beliefs taught that God intended humans to have ultimate dominion over all animals. For humans, eating meat is part of a planned cycle of nature. In short, you were raised in a family and community that accepted meat-based diets as normal, healthy, and ethically justifiable whereas I was raised in a family that cared very deeply for animals and attended a church that frequently entertained a vegan as a guest speaker.

Let me now briefly reiterate for you my own basic beliefs about eating animals. As I have shared with you, my personal health is important to me, and I, along with other vegetarians and vegans, believe that a vegetarian diet is much more healthy than a meat diet. But my primary motivation is my deep respect for animals. I have always felt an overpowering sense of compassion for animals and forceful sorrow and regret for the injuries that humans inflict upon them. I detest suffering, especially when it is forced upon creatures that cannot speak out against it. These deep feelings led me to become a vegetarian at the age of 5. While lying in bed one night, I looked up at the poster of a silky-white harbor seal that had always hung on my wall. As I looked at the face of that seal, I made a connection between that precious animal on my wall and the animals that had been killed for the food I ate every day. In the dim glow of my Strawberry Shortcake night light, I promised those large, dark seal eyes that I would never eat animals again. Seventeen years have passed now and that promise still holds true. Every day I feel more dedicated to the cause of animal rights around the world.

I know very well that my personal convictions are not the same as yours. However, I believe that we might possibly agree on more aspects of this issue than we realize. Although we would not be considered by others as allies on the issue of eating meat, we do share a common enemy—factory farms. Although you eat animal products and I do not, we both share a basic common value that is threatened by today's factory farms. We both disapprove of the unnecessary suffering of animals.

5   Though we might disagree on the morality of using animals for food at all, we do agree that such animals should not be made to suffer. Yet at factory farms, billions of animals across the world are born, live, and die in horribly cramped, dark, and foul-smelling barns. None of these animals knows the feeling of fresh air, or of warm, blessed sunlight on their backs. Most do not move out of their tight, uncomfortable pens until the day that they are to be slaughtered. At these factory farms, animals are processed as if they were inanimate objects, with no regard for the fact that they do feel fear and pain.

It is because of our shared opposition to animal suffering that I ask you to consider making an effort to buy meat from small, independent local farmers. I am told by friends that all supermarkets offer such meat options. This would be an easy and effective way to fight factory farms. I know that I could never convince you to stop eating meat, and I will never try to force my beliefs on you. As your friend, I am grateful simply to be able to write to you so candidly about my beliefs. I trust that regardless of what your ultimate reaction is to this letter, you will thoughtfully consider what I have written, as I will thoughtfully consider what you write in return.

Sincerely,

Rebekah

PART THREE
Analyzing Arguments

This advocacy poster fuses three big contemporary public controversies over environmentalism, sustainability, and vegetarianism. What tactics does this poster use to appeal to viewers' emotions and dramatize its claim that meat-eating is destroying the world? Chapters 8 and 9 provide guidance for conducting rhetorical analyses of verbal and visual texts that work in a complex way, as this one does.

8 Analyzing Arguments Rhetorically

In Part Two of this book, we explained thinking and writing strategies for composing your own arguments. Now in Part Three we show you how to use your new rhetorical knowledge to conduct in-depth analyses of other people's arguments. To analyze an argument rhetorically means to examine closely how it is composed and what makes it an effective or ineffective piece of persuasion. A rhetorical analysis identifies the text under scrutiny, summarizes its main ideas, presents some key points about the text's rhetorical strategies for persuading its audience, and elaborates on these points.

Becoming skilled at analyzing arguments rhetorically will have multiple payoffs for you. Rhetorical analysis will help you develop your ability to read complex texts critically; speak back to texts from your own insights; apply the strategies of effective argumentation to your own arguments; and prepare you as a citizen to distinguish sound, ethical arguments from manipulative, unreasonable ones. By themselves, rhetorical analyses are common assignments in courses in critical thinking and argument. Rhetorical analysis also plays a major role in constructing arguments. Writers often work into their own arguments summaries and rhetorical analyses of other people's arguments—particularly in sections dealing with opposing views. This chapter focuses on the rhetorical analysis of written arguments, and the next one (Chapter 9) equips you to analyze visual arguments.

Thinking Rhetorically about a Text

The suggested writing assignment for this chapter is to write your own rhetorical analysis of an argument selected by your instructor (see p. 158). This section will help you get started by showing you what it means to think rhetorically about a text.

Before we turn directly to rhetorical analysis, we should reconsider the key word *rhetoric*. In popular usage, *rhetoric* often means empty or deceptive language, as in, "Well, that's just rhetoric." Another related meaning of *rhetoric* is decorative or artificial language. The Greek Stoic philosopher Epictetus likened rhetoric to hairdressers fixing hair*—a view that sees

---

*Chaim Perelman, "The New Rhetoric: A Theory of Practical Reasoning." In *Professing the New Rhetorics: A Sourcebook,* eds. Theresa Enos and Stuart C. Brown (Englewood Cliffs, NJ: Prentice Hall, 1994), 149.

rhetoric as superficial decoration. Most contemporary rhetoricians, however, adopt the larger view of rhetoric articulated by Greek philosopher Aristotle: the art of determining what will be persuasive in every situation. Contemporary rhetorician Donald C. Bryant has described rhetoric in action as "the function of adjusting ideas to people and of people to ideas."* Focusing on this foundational meaning of rhetoric, this chapter will show you how to analyze a writer's motivation, purpose, and rhetorical choices for persuading a targeted audience.

Most of the knowledge and skills you will need to write an effective rhetorical analysis have already been provided in Parts One and Two of the text. You have already learned how to place a text in its rhetorical context (Chapter 2), and from Chapters 3–7 you are already familiar with such key rhetorical concepts as audience-based reasons, the STAR criteria for evidence, and the classical appeals of *logos, ethos,* and *pathos.* This chapter prepares you to apply these argument concepts to the arguments you encounter.

■ ■ ■   **FOR CLASS DISCUSSION**   **An Initial Exercise in Rhetorical Analysis**
In the following exercise, consider the strategies used by two different writers to persuade their audiences to act against climate change. The first is from the opening paragraphs of an editorial in the magazine *Creation Care: A Christian Environmental Quarterly.* The second is from the Web site of the Sierra Club, an environmental action group. Please study each passage and then proceed to the questions that follow.

Passage 1

As I sit down to write this column, one thing keeps coming to me over and over: "Now is the time; now is the time."

In the New Testament the word used for this type of time is *kairos.* It means "right or opportune moment." It is contrasted with *chronos,* or chronological time as measured in seconds, days, months, or years. In the New Testament *kairos* is usually associated with decisive action that brings about deliverance or salvation.

The reason the phrase, "Now is the time" kept coming to me over and over is that I was thinking of how to describe our current climate change moment.

The world has been plodding along in chronological time on the problem of climate change since around 1988. No more.

Simply put: the problem of climate change has entered *kairos* time; its *kairos* moment has arrived. How long will it endure? Until the time of decisive action to bring about deliverance comes—or, more ominously, until the time when the opportunity for decisive action has passed us by. Which will we choose? Because we do have a choice.

—Rev. Jim Ball, Ph.D., "It's *Kairos* Time for Climate Change: Time to Act," *Creation Care: A Christian Environmental Quarterly* (Summer 2008), 28.

---

*Donald C. Bryant, "Rhetoric: Its Functions and Its Scope." In *Professing the New Rhetorics: A Sourcebook,* eds. Theresa Enos and Stuart C. Brown (Englewood Cliffs, NJ: Prentice Hall, 1994), 282.

Passage 2

[Another action that Americans must take to combat global warming is to transition] to a clean energy economy in a just and equitable way. Global warming is among the greatest challenges of our time, but also presents extraordinary opportunities to harness home-grown clean energy sources and encourage technological innovation. These bold shifts toward a clean energy future can create hundreds of thousands of new jobs and generate billions of dollars in capital investment. But in order to maximize these benefits across all sectors of our society, comprehensive global warming legislation must auction emission allowances to polluters and use these public assets for public benefit programs.

Such programs include financial assistance to help low and moderate-income consumers and workers offset higher energy costs as well as programs that assist with adaptation efforts in communities vulnerable to the effects of climate change. Revenue generated from emissions allowances should also aid the expansion of renewable and efficient energy technologies that quickly, cleanly, cheaply, and safely reduce our dependence on fossil fuels and curb global warming. Lastly, it is absolutely vital that comprehensive global warming legislation not preempt state authority to cut greenhouse gas emissions more aggressively than mandated by federal legislation.

—Sierra Club, "Global Warming Policy Solutions," 2008, http://www.sierraclub.org/energy/energypolicy/.

Group task: Working in small groups or as a whole class, try to reach consensus answers to the following questions:

1. How do the strategies of persuasion differ in these two passages?
2. How can you explain these differences in terms of targeted audience and original genre?
3. How effective is each argument for its intended audience?
4. Would either argument be effective for readers outside the intended audience? Why or why not?

Questions for Rhetorical Analysis

Conducting a rhetorical analysis asks you to bring to bear on an argument your knowledge of argument and your repertoire of reading strategies. The chart of questions for analysis on pages 149–150 can help you examine an argument in depth. Although a rhetorical analysis will not include answers to all of these questions, using some of these questions in your thinking stages can give you a thorough understanding of the argument while helping you generate insights for your own rhetorical analysis essay.

An Illustration of Rhetorical Analysis

To illustrate rhetorical analysis in this section and in the student example at the end of the chapter, we will use two articles on reproductive technology, a subject that continues to generate arguments in the public sphere. By *reproductive technology* we mean scientific advances in the treatment of infertility such as egg and sperm donation, artificial insemination, in vitro fertilization, and surrogate motherhood. Our first article, from a

Questions for Rhetorical Analysis

What to Focus On	Questions to Ask	Applying These Questions
The *kairotic* moment and writer's motivating occasion	▪ What motivated the writer to produce this piece? ▪ What social, cultural, political, legal, or economic conversations does this argument join?	▪ Is the writer responding to a bill pending in Congress, a speech by a political leader, or a local event that provoked controversy? ▪ Is the writer addressing cultural trends such as the impact of science or technology on values?
Rhetorical context: Writer's purpose and audience	▪ What is the writer's purpose? ▪ Who is the intended audience? ▪ What assumptions, values, and beliefs would readers have to hold to find this argument persuasive? ▪ How well does the text suit its particular audience and purpose?	▪ Is the writer trying to change readers' views by offering a new interpretation of a phenomenon, calling readers to action, or trying to muster votes or inspire further investigations? ▪ Does the audience share a political or religious orientation with the writer?
Rhetorical context: Writer's identity and angle of vision	▪ Who is the writer and what is his or her profession, background, and expertise? ▪ How does the writer's personal history, education, gender, ethnicity, age, class, sexual orientation, and political leaning influence the angle of vision? ▪ What is emphasized and what is omitted in this text? ▪ How much does the writer's angle of vision dominate the text?	▪ Is the writer a scholar, researcher, scientist, policy maker, politician, professional journalist, or citizen blogger? ▪ Is the writer affiliated with conservative or liberal, religious or lay publications? ▪ Is the writer advocating a stance or adopting a more inquiry-based mode? ▪ What points of view and pieces of evidence are "not seen" by this writer?
Rhetorical context: Genre	▪ What is the argument's original genre? ▪ What is the original medium of publication? How does the genre and its place of publication influence its content, structure, and style?	▪ How popular or scholarly, informal or formal is this genre? ▪ Does the genre allow for in-depth or only sketchy coverage of an issue? (See Chapter 2, pp. 32–37, for detailed explanations of genre.)
***Logos* of the argument**	▪ What is the argument's claim, either explicitly stated or implied? ▪ What are the main reasons in support of the claim? Are the reasons audience-based? ▪ How effective is the writer's use of evidence? How is the argument supported and developed? ▪ How well has the argument recognized and responded to alternative views?	▪ Is the core of the argument clear and soundly developed? Or do readers have to unearth or reconstruct the argument? ▪ Is the argument one-sided, multisided, or dialogic? ▪ Does the argument depend on assumptions the audience may not share? ▪ What evidence does the writer employ? Does this evidence meet the STAR criteria? (See pp. 89–90.)

(Continued)

What to Focus On	Questions to Ask	Applying These Questions
***Ethos* of the argument**	■ What *ethos* does the writer project? ■ How does the writer try to seem credible and trustworthy to the intended audience? ■ How knowledgeable does the writer seem in recognizing opposing or alternative views and how fairly does the writer respond to them?	■ If you are impressed or won over by this writer, what has earned your respect? ■ If you are filled with doubts or skepticism, what has caused you to question this writer? ■ How important is the character of the writer in this argument?
***Pathos* of the argument**	■ How effective is the writer in using audience-based reasons? ■ How does the writer use concrete language, word choice, narrative, examples, and analogies to tap readers' emotions, values, and imaginations?	■ What examples, connotative language, and uses of narrative or analogy stand out for you in this argument? ■ Does this argument rely heavily on appeals to *pathos*? Or is it more brainy and logical?
Writer's style	■ How do the writer's language choices and sentence length and complexity contribute to the impact of the argument? ■ How well does the writer's tone (attitude toward the subject) suit the argument?	■ How readable is this argument? ■ Is the argument formal, scholarly, journalistic, informal, or casual? ■ Is the tone serious, mocking, humorous, exhortational, confessional, urgent, or something else?
Design and visual elements	■ How do design elements—layout, font sizes and styles, and use of color—influence the effect of the argument? (See Chapter 9 for a detailed discussion of these elements.) ■ How do graphics and images contribute to the persuasiveness of the argument?	■ Do design features contribute to the logical or the emotional/imaginative appeals of the argument? ■ How would this argument benefit from visuals and graphics or some different document design?
Overall persuasiveness of the argument	■ What features of this argument contribute most to making it persuasive or not persuasive for its target audience and for you yourself? ■ How would this argument be received by different audiences? ■ What features contribute to the rhetorical complexity of this argument? ■ What is particularly memorable, disturbing, or problematic about this argument? ■ What does this argument contribute to its *kairotic* moment and the argumentative controversy of which it is a part?	■ For example, are appeals to *pathos* legitimate and suitable? Does the quality and quantity of the evidence help build a strong case or fall short? ■ What specifically would count as a strength for the target audience? ■ If you differ from the target audience, how do you differ and where does the argument derail for you? ■ What gaps, contradictions, or unanswered questions are you left with? ■ How does this argument indicate that it is engaged in a public conversation? How does it "talk" to other arguments you have read on this issue?

decade ago, springs from the early and increasing popularity of these technological options. Our second article—to be used in our later student example—responds to the recent globalization of this technology.

At this point, please read the following article, "Egg Heads" by Kathryn Jean Lopez, and then proceed to the discussion questions that follow. Lopez's article was originally published in the September 1, 1998, issue of the biweekly conservative news commentary magazine *National Review.*

Egg Heads

KATHRYN JEAN LOPEZ

Filling the waiting room to capacity and spilling over into a nearby conference room, a group of young women listen closely and follow the instructions: Complete the forms and return them, with the clipboard, to the receptionist. It's all just as in any medical office. Then they move downstairs, where the doctor briefs them. "Everything will be pretty much normal," she explains. "Women complain of skin irritation in the local area of injection and bloating. You also might be a little emotional. But, basically, it's really bad PMS."

This is not just another medical office. On a steamy night in July, these girls in their twenties are attending an orientation session for potential egg donors at a New Jersey fertility clinic specializing in in-vitro fertilization. Within the walls of IVF New Jersey and at least two hundred other clinics throughout the United States, young women answer the call to give "the gift of life" to infertile couples. Egg donation is a quietly expanding industry, changing the way we look at the family, young women's bodies, and human life itself.

It is not a pleasant way to make money. Unlike sperm donation, which is over in less than an hour, egg donation takes the donor some 56 hours and includes a battery of tests, ultrasound, self-administered injections, and retrieval. Once a donor is accepted into a program, she is given hormones to stimulate the ovaries, changing the number of eggs matured from the usual one per month up to as many as fifty.

A doctor then surgically removes the eggs from the donor's ovary and fertilizes them with the designated sperm.

Although most programs require potential donors to undergo a series of medical tests and counseling, there is little indication that most of the young women know what they are getting themselves into. They risk bleeding, infection, and scarring. When too many eggs are matured in one cycle, it can damage the ovaries and leave the donor with weeks of abdominal pain. (At worst, complications may leave her dead.) Longer term, the possibility of early menopause raises the prospect of future regret. There is also some evidence of a connection between the fertility drugs used in the process and ovarian cancer.

5   But it's good money—and getting better. New York's Brooklyn IVF raised its "donor compensation" from $2,500 to $5,000 per cycle earlier this year in order to keep pace with St. Barnabas Medical Center in nearby Livingston, New Jersey. It's a bidding war. "It's obvious why we had to do it," says Susan Lobel, Brooklyn IVF's assistant director. Most New York–area IVF programs have followed suit.

Some infertile couples and independent brokers are offering even more for "reproductive material." The International Fertility Center in Indianapolis, Indiana, for instance, places ads in the *Daily Princetonian* offering Princeton girls as much as

$35,000 per cycle. The National Fertility Registry, which, like many egg brokerages, features an online catalogue for couples to browse in, advertises $35,000 to $50,000 for Ivy League eggs. While donors are normally paid a flat fee per cycle, there have been reports of higher payments to donors who produce more eggs.

College girls are the perfect donors. Younger eggs are likelier to be healthy, and the girls themselves frequently need money—college girls have long been susceptible to classified ads offering to pay them for acting as guinea pigs in medical research. One 1998 graduate of the University of Colorado set up her own website to market her eggs. She had watched a television show on egg donation and figured it "seemed like a good thing to do"—especially since she had spent her money during the past year to help secure a country-music record deal. "Egg donation would help me with my school and music expenses while helping an infertile couple with a family." Classified ads scattered throughout cyberspace feature similar offers.

The market for "reproductive material" has been developing for a long time. It was twenty years ago this summer that the first test-tube baby, Louise Brown, was born. By 1995, when the latest tally was taken by the Centers for Disease Control, 15 percent of mothers in this country had made use of some form of assisted-reproduction technology in conceiving their children. (More recently, women past menopause have begun to make use of this technology.) In 1991 the American Society for Reproductive Medicine was aware of 63 IVF programs offering egg donation. That number had jumped to 189 by 1995 (the latest year for which numbers are available).

Defenders argue that it's only right that women are "compensated" for the inconvenience of egg donation. Brooklyn IVF's Dr. Lobel argues, "If it is unethical to accept payment for loving your neighbor, then we'll have to stop paying babysitters." As long as donors know the risks, says Glenn McGee of the University of Pennsylvania's Center for Bioethics, this transaction is only "a slightly macabre version of adoption."

10 Not everyone is enthusiastic about the "progress." Egg donation "represents another rather large step into turning procreation into manufacturing," says the University of Chicago's Leon Kass. "It's the dehumanization of procreation." And as in manufacturing, there is quality control. "People don't want to say the word any more, but there is a strong eugenics issue inherent in the notion that you can have the best eggs your money can buy," observes sociology professor Barbara Katz Rothman of the City University of New York.

The demand side of the market comes mostly from career-minded baby-boomers, the frontiers-women of feminism, who thought they could "have it all." Indeed they *can* have it all—with a little help from some younger eggs. (Ironically, feminists are also among its strongest critics; *The Nation*'s Katha Pollitt has pointed out that in egg donation and surrogacy, once you remove the "delusion that they are making babies for other women," all you have left is "reproductive prostitution.")

Unfortunately, the future looks bright for the egg market. Earlier this year, a woman in Atlanta gave birth to twins after she was implanted with frozen donor eggs. The same technology has also been successful in Italy. This is just what the egg market needed, since it avoids the necessity of co-ordinating donors' cycles with recipients' cycles. Soon, not only will infertile couples be able to choose from a wider variety of donor offerings, but in some cases donors won't even be needed. Young women will be able to freeze their own eggs and have them thawed and fertilized once they are ready for the intrusion of children in their lives.

There are human ovaries sitting in a freezer in Fairfax, Virginia. The Genetics and IVF Institute offers to cut out and remove young women's ovaries and cryopreserve the egg-containing tissue for future implantation. Although the technology was originally designed to give the hope of fertility to young women undergoing treatment for cancer, it is now starting to attract the healthy. "Women can wait to have children until they are well established in their careers and getting a little bored, sometime in their forties or fifties," explains Professor Rothman. "Basically, motherhood is being reduced to a good leisure-time activity."

Early this summer, headlines were made in Britain, where the payment of egg donors is forbidden, when an infertile couple traveled to a California clinic where the woman could be inseminated with an experimental hybrid egg. The egg was a combination of the recipient's and a donor's eggs. The clinic in question gets its eggs from a Beverly Hills brokerage, the Center for Surrogate Parenting and Egg Donation, run by Karen Synesiou and Bill Handel, a radio shock-jock in Los Angeles. Miss Synesiou recently told the London *Sunday Times* that she is "interested in redefining the family. That's why I came to work here."

15   The redefinition is already well under way. Consider the case of Jaycee Buzzanca. After John and Luanne Buzzanca had tried for years to have a child, an embryo was created for them, using sperm and an egg from anonymous donors, and implanted in a surrogate mother. In March 1995, one month before the baby was born, John filed for divorce. Luanne wanted child support from John, but he refused—after all, he's not the father. Luanne argued that John is Jaycee's father legally. At this point the surrogate mother, who had agreed to carry a baby for a stable two-parent household, decided to sue for custody.

Jaycee was dubbed "Nobody's Child" by the media when a California judge ruled that John was not the legal father nor Luanne the legal mother (neither one was genetically related to Jaycee, and Luanne had not even borne her). Enter Erin Davidson, the egg donor, who claims the egg was used without her permission. Not to be left out, the sperm donor jumped into the ring, saying that his sperm was used without his permission, a claim he later dropped. In March of this year, an appeals court gave Luanne custody

and decided that John is the legal father, making him responsible for child support. By contracting for a medical procedure resulting in the birth of a child, the court ruled, a couple incurs "the legal status of parenthood." (John lost an appeal in May.) For Jaycee's first three years on earth, these people have been wrangling over who her parents are.

In another case, William Kane left his girlfriend, Deborah Hect, 15 vials of sperm before he killed himself in a Las Vegas hotel in 1991. His two adult children (represented by their mother, his ex-wife) contested Miss Hect's claim of ownership. A settlement agreement on Kane's will was eventually reached, giving his children 80 percent of his estate and Miss Hect 20 percent. Hence she was allowed three vials of his sperm. When she did not succeed in conceiving on the first two tries, she filed a petition for the other 12 vials. She won, and the judge who ruled in her favor wrote, "Neither this court nor the decedent's adult children possess reason or right to prevent Hect from implementing decedent's pre-eminent interest in realizing his 'fundamental right' to procreate with the woman of his choice." One day, donors may not even have to have lived. Researchers are experimenting with using aborted female fetuses as a source of donor eggs.

And the market continues to zip along. For overseas couples looking for donor eggs, Bill Handel has the scenario worked out. The couple would mail him frozen sperm of their choice (presumably from the recipient husband); his clinic would use it to fertilize donor eggs, chosen from its catalogue of offerings, and reply back within a month with a frozen embryo ready for implantation. (Although the sperm does not yet arrive by mail, Handel has sent out embryos to at least one hundred international customers.) As for the young women at the New Jersey clinic, they are visibly upset by one aspect of the egg-donation process: they can't have sexual intercourse for several weeks after the retrieval. For making babies, of course, it's already obsolete.

■ ■ ■ **FOR CLASS DISCUSSION**   **Identifying Rhetorical Features**
Working in groups, develop responses to the following questions:

1. How does Lopez appeal to *logos*? What is her main claim and what are her reasons? What does she use for evidence? What ideas would you have to include in a short summary?
2. What appeals to *pathos* does Lopez make in this argument? How well are these suited to the conservative readers of the *National Review*?
3. How would you characterize Lopez's *ethos*? Does she seem knowledgeable and credible? Does she seem fair to stakeholders in this controversy?
4. Choose an additional focus from the "Questions for Rhetorical Analysis" on pages 149–150 to apply to "Egg Heads." How does this question expand your understanding of Lopez's argument?
5. What strikes you as problematic, memorable, or disturbing in this argument?   ■ ■ ■

A Rhetorical Analysis of "Egg Heads"

Now that you have identified some of the rhetorical features of "Egg Heads," we offer our own notes for a rhetorical analysis of this argument.

Rhetorical Context   As we began our analysis, we reconstructed the rhetorical context in which "Egg Heads" was published. In the late 1990s, a furious debate about egg donation rippled through college and public newspapers, popular journalism, Web sites, and scholarly commentary. This debate had been kicked off by several couples placing ads in the newspapers of the country's most prestigious colleges offering up to $50,000 for the eggs of brilliant, attractive, athletic college women. Coinciding with these consumer demands, advances in reproductive technology provided an increasing number of complex techniques to surmount the problem of infertility, including fertilizing eggs in petri dishes and implanting them into women through surgical procedures. These procedures could use either a couple's own eggs and sperm or donated eggs and sperm. All these social and medical factors created the *kairotic* moment for Lopez's article and motivated her to protest the increasing use of these procedures. (Egg donation, surrogate motherhood, and the potential dehumanizing of commercial reproduction continue to be troubling and unresolved controversies across many genres, as you will see when you read Ellen Goodman's op-ed piece at the end of this chapter and student Zachary Stumps's rhetorical analysis of it.)

Genre and Writer   When we considered the genre and writer of this article and its site of publication, we noted that this article appeared in the *National Review*, which describes itself as "America's most widely read and influential magazine and Web site for Republican/conservative news, commentary, and opinion." It reaches "an affluent, educated, and highly responsive audience of corporate, financial elite, educators, journalists, community and association leaders, as well as engaged activists all across America" (http://www.nationalreview.com). According to our Internet search, Kathryn Jean Lopez is known nationally for her conservative journalistic writing on social and political issues. Currently the editor of *National Review Online*, she has also published in the *Wall Street Journal*, the *New York Post*, and the *Washington Times*. This information told us that in her article "Egg Heads," Lopez is definitely on home territory, aiming her article at a conservative audience.

Logos   Turning to the *logos* of Lopez's argument, we decided that the logical structure of Lopez's argument is clear throughout the article. Her claim is that egg donation and its associated reproductive advances have harmful, long-reaching consequences for society. Basically, she argues that egg donation and reproductive technology represent bad scientific developments for society because they are potentially harmful to the long-range health of egg donors and because they lead to an unnatural dehumanizing of human sexuality. She states a version of this last point at the end of the second paragraph: "Egg donation is a quickly expanding industry, changing the way we look at the family, young women's bodies, and human life itself" (page 151).

The body of her article elaborates on each of these reasons. In developing her reason that egg donation endangers egg donors, Lopez lists the risks but doesn't supply supporting evidence about the frequency of these problems: damage to the ovaries, persistent pain, early menopause, possible ovarian cancer, and even death. She supports her claim about "the expanding industry" by showing how the procedures have become commercialized. To show the popularity of these procedures as well as their commercial value, she quotes a variety of experts such as directors of in vitro clinics, fertility centers, bioethicists, and the American Society for Reproductive Medicine. She also cleverly bolsters her own case by showing that even liberal cultural critics agree with her views about the big ethical questions raised by the reproductive-technology business. In addition to quoting experts, Lopez has sprinkled impressive numbers and vivid examples throughout the body of her argument, which give her argument momentum as it progresses from the potential harm to young egg donors to a number of case studies that depict increasingly disturbing ethical problems.

Pathos   Much of the impact of this argument, we noted, comes from Lopez's appeals to *pathos*. By describing in detail the waiting rooms for egg donors at fertility clinics, Lopez relies heavily on pathetic appeals to move her audience to see the physical and social dangers of egg donation. She conveys the growing commercialism of reproductive technology by giving readers an inside look at the egg donation process as these young college women embark on the multi-step process of donating their eggs. These young women, she suggests in her title, "Egg Heads," are largely unaware of the potential physical dangers to themselves and of the ethical implications and consequences of their acts. She asserts that they are driven largely by the desire for money. Lopez also appeals to *pathos* in her choice of emotionally loaded and often cynical language that creates an angle of vision opposing reproductive technology: "turning procreation into manufacturing"; "reproductive prostitution"; "the intrusion of children in their lives"; "motherhood...reduced to a leisure-time activity"; "aborted female fetuses as a source of donor eggs"; and intercourse as an "obsolete" way to make babies (pages 152, 153).

Audience Despite Lopez's success at spotlighting serious medical and ethical questions, her lack of attention to alternative views and the alarmism of her language caused us to wonder: Who might find this argument persuasive and who would challenge it? What is noticeably missing from her argument—and apparently from her worldview—is the perspective of infertile couples hoping for a baby. Pursuing our question, we decided that a provocative feature of this argument—one worthy of deeper analysis—is the disparity between how well this argument is suited to its target audience and yet how unpersuasive it is for readers who do not share the assumptions, values, and beliefs of this primary audience.

To Lopez's credit, she has attuned her reasons to the values and concerns of her conservative readers of the *National Review* who believe in traditional families, gender differences, and gender roles. Opposed to feminism as they understand it, this audience sanctions careers for women only if women put their families first. Lopez's choice of evidence and her orchestrating of it are intended to play to her audience's fears that science has uncontrollably fallen into the hands of those who have little regard for the sanctity of the family or traditional motherhood. For example, in playing strongly to the values of her conservative readers, Lopez belabors the physical, social, and ethical dangers of egg donation, mentioning worst-case scenarios; however, these appeals to *pathos* will most likely strike other readers who do some investigation into reproductive technology as overblown. She emphasizes the commercialism of the process as her argument moves from college girls as egg donors to a number of sensationalist case studies that depict intensifying ethical ambiguity. In other words, both the *logos* and *pathos* of her argument skillfully focus on details that tap her target audience's values and beliefs and feed that audience's fears and revulsion.

Use of Evidence For a broader or skeptical audience, the alarmism of Lopez's appeals to *pathos*, her use of atypical evidence, and her distortion of the facts weaken the *logos* and *ethos* of her argument. First, Lopez's use of evidence fails to measure up to the STAR criteria (that evidence should be sufficient, typical, accurate, and relevant). She characterizes all egg donors as young women seeking money. But she provides little evidence that egg donors are only out to make a buck. She also paints these young women as shortsighted, uninformed, and foolish. Lopez weakens her ethos by not considering the young women who have researched the process and who may be motivated, at least in part, by compassion for couples who can't conceive on their own. Lopez also misrepresents the people who are using egg donation, placing them all into two groups: (1) wealthy couples eugenically seeking designer babies with preordered special traits and (2) feminist career women. She directs much of her criticism toward this latter group: "The demand side of the market comes mostly from career-minded baby-boomers, the frontierswomen of feminism, who thought they could 'have it all'" (page 152). However, readers who do a little research on their own, as we did, will learn that infertility affects one in seven couples; that it is often a male and female problem, sometimes caused by an incompatibility between the husband's and wife's reproductive material; and that most couples who take the big step of investing in these expensive efforts to have a baby have been trying to get pregnant for a number of years. Rather than being casual about having children, they are often deeply desirous of children and depressed about their inability to conceive. In addition, far from being the sure thing and quick fix that Lopez suggests, reproductive technology has a success rate of only 50 percent overall and involves a huge investment of time, money, and physical discomfort for women receiving donor eggs.

Another way that Lopez violates the STAR criteria is her choice of extreme cases. For readers outside her target audience, her argument appears riddled with straw man and slippery-slope fallacies. (See Appendix 1, "Informal Fallacies," pages 401–408.) Her examples become more bizarre as her tone becomes more hysterical. Here are some specific instance of extreme, atypical cases:

- her focus on career women casually and selfishly using the service of young egg donors
- the notorious case of Jaycee Buzzanca, dubbed "Nobody's Child" because her adoptive parents who commissioned her creation divorced before she was born
- the legal contest between a dead man's teen girlfriend and his ex-wife and adult children over his vials of sperm
- the idea of taking eggs from aborted female fetuses

By keeping invisible the vast majority of ordinary couples who come to fertility clinics out of last-hope desperation, Lopez uses extreme cases to create a "brave new world" intended to evoke a vehement rejection of these reproductive advances. These skeptical readers would offer the alternative view of the sad, ordinary couples of all ages sitting week after week in fertility clinics, hoping to conceive a child through the "miracle" of these reproductive advances and grateful to the young women who have contributed their eggs.

Concluding Points   In short, we concluded that Lopez's angle of vision, although effectively in sync with her conservative readers of the *National Review*, exaggerates and distorts her case against these reproductive advances. Lopez's traditional values and slanting of the evidence undermine her *ethos*, limit the value of this argument for a wider audience, and compel that audience to seek out alternative views for a more complete view of egg donation.

Conclusion

To analyze a text rhetorically means to determine how it works: what effect it has on readers and how it achieves or fails to achieve its persuasiveness. Assignments involving rhetorical analysis are present in courses across the curriculum, and analyzing texts rhetorically is a major step in constructing your own arguments. In this chapter, we showed you how to apply your understanding of argument concepts, such as the influence of genre and appeals to *logos, ethos,* and *pathos,* to examining the strength of verbal texts. We conclude with a student's rhetorical analysis written for the assignment in this chapter.

WRITING ASSIGNMENT   A Rhetorical Analysis

Write a thesis-driven rhetorical analysis essay in which you examine the rhetorical effectiveness of an argument specified by your instructor. Unless otherwise stated direct your analysis to an audience of your classmates. In your introduction, establish the argumentative conversation to which this argument is contributing. Briefly summarize the argument and present your thesis highlighting two or more rhetorical features of the argument that you find central to the effectiveness or ineffectiveness of this argument. To develop and support your own points, you will need to include textual evidence, in the form of examples or short quotations from the argument. Use attributive tags to distinguish your ideas from those of the writer of the article. Use MLA documentation to cite points and quotations in your essay and in a Works Cited list at the end. Think of your rhetorical analysis as a way to shine a spotlight on important aspects of this argument and make the argument understandable and interesting for your readers. A student paper written for this assignment is shown at the end of this chapter—Zachary Stumps's analysis of Ellen Goodman's "Womb for Rent."

Generating Ideas for Your Rhetorical Analysis

To develop ideas for your essay, you might follow these suggested steps:

Step1	How to Do It
Familiarize yourself with the article you are analyzing.	Read your article several times. Divide it into sections to understand its structure.
Place the article in its rhetorical context.	Follow the strategies in Chapter 2 and use the "Questions for Rhetorical Analysis" on pages 149–150.
Summarize the article.	Follow the steps in Chapter 2 on pages 41–42. You may want to produce a longer summary of 150–200 words as well as a short one-sentence summary.
Reread the article identifying "hot spots."	Note hot spots in the article—points that impress you, disturb you, confuse you, or puzzle you.
Use the "Questions for Rhetorical Analysis" on page 149.	Choose several of these questions and freewrite responses to them.
From your notes and freewriting, identify the focus for your analysis.	Choose several features of the article that you find particularly important and that you want to discuss in depth in your essay. Identify points that will bring something new to your readers and that will help them see this article with new understanding. You may want to list your ideas and then look for ways to group them together around main points.
Write a thesis statement for your essay.	Articulate your important points in one or two sentences, setting up these points clearly for your audience.

In finding a meaningful focus for your rhetorical analysis essay, you will need to create a focusing thesis statement that avoids wishy-washy formulas such as, "This argument has some strengths and some weaknesses." To avoid a vapid thesis statement, focus on the complexity of the argument, the writer's strategies for persuading the target audience, and the features that might impede its persuasiveness for skeptics. These thesis statements articulate how their writers see the inner workings of these arguments as well as the arguments' contribution to their public conversations.

> Lopez's angle of vision, although effectively in sync with her conservative readers of the *National Review*, exaggerates and distorts her case against these reproductive advances, weakening her ethos and the value of her argument for a wider audience. [This is the thesis we would use if we were writing a stand-alone essay on Lopez.]

> In his editorial, "Why Blame Mexico?" published in *The American Conservative*, Fred Reed's irony and hard-hitting evidence undercut his desire to contrast the United States' hypocritical and flawed immigration policies with Mexico's successful ones.

> In his editorial, "Amnesty?" in the Jesuit news commentary *America*, John F. Kavanaugh makes a powerful argument for his Catholic and religious readers; however, his proposal based on ethical reasoning may fail to reach other readers.

To make your rhetorical analysis of your article persuasive, you will need to develop each of the points stated or implied in your thesis statement using textual evidence, including short quotations. Your essay should show how you have listened carefully to the argument you are analyzing, summarized it fairly, and probed it deeply.

Organizing Your Rhetorical Analysis

A stand-alone rhetorical analysis can be organized as shown below. ■

Organization Plan for a Rhetorical Analysis of an Argument

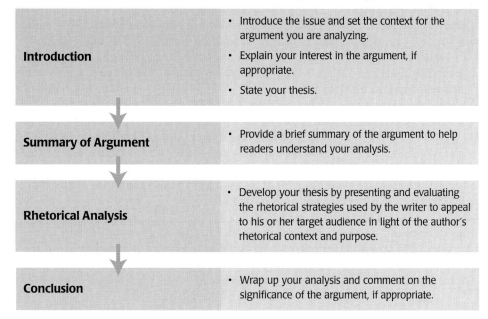

Introduction	• Introduce the issue and set the context for the argument you are analyzing. • Explain your interest in the argument, if appropriate. • State your thesis.
Summary of Argument	• Provide a brief summary of the argument to help readers understand your analysis.
Rhetorical Analysis	• Develop your thesis by presenting and evaluating the rhetorical strategies used by the writer to appeal to his or her target audience in light of the author's rhetorical context and purpose.
Conclusion	• Wrap up your analysis and comment on the significance of the argument, if appropriate.

Readings

Our first reading is by journalist Ellen Goodman, whose columns are syndicated in U.S. newspapers by the Washington Post Writers Group. This column, which appeared in 2008, is analyzed rhetorically by student Zachary Stumps in our second reading.

Womb for Rent—For a Price

ELLEN GOODMAN

BOSTON—By now we all have a story about a job outsourced beyond our reach in the global economy. My own favorite is about the California publisher who hired two reporters in India to cover the Pasadena city government. Really.

There are times as well when the offshoring of jobs takes on a quite literal meaning. When the labor we are talking about is, well, labor.

In the last few months we've had a full nursery of international stories about surrogate mothers. Hundreds of couples are crossing borders in search of lower-cost ways to fill the family business. In turn, there's a new coterie of international workers who are gestating for a living.

Many of the stories about the globalization of baby production begin in India, where the government seems to regard this as, literally, a growth industry. In the little town of Anand, dubbed "The Cradle of the World," 45 women were recently on the books of a local clinic. For the production and

delivery of a child, they will earn $5,000 to $7,000, a decade's worth of women's wages in rural India.

5   But even in America, some women, including Army wives, are supplementing their income by contracting out their wombs. They have become surrogate mothers for wealthy couples from European countries that ban the practice.

This globalization of baby-making comes at the peculiar intersection of a high reproductive technology and a low-tech work force. The biotech business was created in the same petri dish as Baby Louise, the first IVF baby. But since then, we've seen conception outsourced to egg donors and sperm donors. We've had motherhood divided into its parts from genetic mother to gestational mother to birth mother and now contract mother.

We've also seen the growth of an international economy. Frozen sperm is flown from one continent to another. And patients have be-

come medical tourists, searching for cheaper health care whether it's a new hip in Thailand or an IVF treatment in South Africa that comes with a photo safari thrown in for the same price. Why not then rent a foreign womb?

I don't make light of infertility. The primal desire to have a child underlies this multinational Creation, Inc. On one side, couples who choose surrogacy want a baby with at least half their own genes. On the other side, surrogate mothers, who are rarely implanted with their own eggs, can believe that the child they bear and deliver is not really theirs.

As one woman put it, "We give them a baby and they give us much-needed money. It's good for them and for us." A surrogate in Anand used the money to buy a heart operation for her son. Another raised a dowry for her daughter. And before we talk about the "exploitation" of the pregnant woman, consider her alternative in

Anand: a job crushing glass in a factory for $25 a month.

10   Nevertheless, there is—and there should be—something uncomfortable about a free market approach to baby-making. It's easier to accept surrogacy when it's a gift from one woman to another. But we rarely see a rich woman become a surrogate for a poor family. Indeed, in Third World countries, some women sign these contracts with a fingerprint because they are illiterate.

For that matter, we have not yet had stories about the contract workers for whom pregnancy was a dangerous occupation, but we will. What obligation does a family that simply contracted for a child have to its birth mother? What control do—should—contractors have over their "employees" lives while incubating "their" children? What will we tell the offspring of this international trade?

"National boundaries are coming down," says bioethicist Lori Andrews, "but we can't stop human emotions. We are expanding families and don't even have terms to deal with it."

It's the commercialism that is troubling. Some things we cannot sell no matter how good "the deal." We cannot, for example, sell ourselves into slavery. We can-not sell our children. But the surrogacy business comes perilously close to both of these deals. And international surrogacy tips the scales.

So, these borders we are crossing are not just geographic ones. They are ethical ones. Today the global economy sends everyone in search of the cheaper deal as if that were the single common good. But in the biological search, humanity is sacrificed to the economy and the person becomes the product. And, step by step, we come to a stunning place in our ancient creation story. It's called the marketplace.

Critiquing "Womb for Rent—For a Price"

1. What is Goodman's main claim and what are her reasons? In other words, what ideas would you have to include in a short summary?
2. What appeals to *pathos* does Goodman make in this argument? How do these appeals function in the argument?
3. Choose an additional focus from the "Questions for Rhetorical Analysis" to apply to "Womb to Rent—For a Price." How does this question affect your perspective of Goodman's argument?
4. What strikes you as problematic, memorable, or disturbing in this argument?

Our second reading shows how student writer Zachary Stumps analyzed the Ellen Goodman article.

A Rhetorical Analysis of Ellen Goodman's "Womb for Rent—For a Price"

ZACHARY STUMPS (STUDENT)

With her op-ed piece "Womb for Rent—For a Price," published in the *Seattle Times* on April 11, 2008 (and earlier in the *Boston Globe*), syndicated columnist Ellen Goodman enters the murky debate about reproductive technology gone global. Since Americans are outsourcing everything else, "Why not then rent a foreign womb?" (161) she asks. Goodman, a

Pulitzer Prize–winning columnist for the Washington Post Writers Group, is known for helping readers understand the "tumult of social change and its impact on families," and for shattering "the mold of men writing exclusively about politics" ("Ellen Goodman"). This op-ed piece continues her tradition of examining social change from the perspective of family issues.

Goodman launches her short piece by asserting that one of the most recent and consequential "jobs" to be outsourced is having babies. She explains how the "globalization of baby production" is thriving because it brings together the reproductive desires of people in developed countries and the bodily resources of women in developing countries like India. Briefly tracing how both reproductive technology and medical tourism have taken advantage of global possibilities, Goodman acknowledges that the thousands of dollars Indian women earn by carrying the babies of foreign couples represent a much larger income than these women could earn in any other available jobs. After appearing to legitimize this global exchange, however, Goodman shifts to her ethical concerns by raising some moral questions that she says are not being addressed in this trade. She concludes with a full statement of her claim that this global surrogacy is encroaching on human respect and dignity, exploiting business-based science, and turning babies into products.

In this piece, Goodman's delay of her thesis has several rhetorical benefits: it gives Goodman space to present the perspective of poor women, enhanced by her appeals to *pathos*, and it invites readers to join her journey into the complex contexts of this issue; however, this strategy is also risky because it limits the development of her own argument.

Instead of presenting her thesis up front, Goodman devotes much of the first part of her argument to looking at this issue from the perspective of foreign surrogate mothers. Using the strategies of *pathos* to evoke sympathy for these women, she creates a compassionate and progressively minded argument that highlights the benefits to foreign surrogate mothers. She cites factual evidence showing that the average job for a woman in Anand, India, yields a tiny "$25 a month" gotten through the hard work of "crushing glass in a factory," compared to the "$5,000 to $7,000" made carrying a baby to term (160). To carry a baby to term for a foreign couple represents "a decade's worth of women's wages in rural India" (160). Deepening readers' understanding of these women, Goodman cites one woman who used her earnings to finance her son's heart operation and another who paid for her daughter's dowry. In her fair presentation of these women, Goodman both builds her own positive *ethos* and adds a dialogic dimension to her argument by helping readers walk in the shoes of otherwise impoverished surrogate mothers.

Develops second point in thesis: the complex contexts of this issue—outsourcing and medical tourism

The second rhetorical benefit of Goodman's delayed thesis is that she ₅ invites readers to explore this complex issue of global surrogacy with her before she declares her own view. To help readers understand and think through this issue, she relates it to two other familiar global topics: outsourcing and medical tourism. First, she introduces foreign surrogacy as one of the latest forms of outsourcing: "This globalization of baby-making comes at the peculiar intersection of a high reproductive technology and a low-tech work force" (160). Presenting these women as workers, she explains that women in India are getting paid for "the production and delivery of a child" (160) that is analogous to the production and delivery of sneakers or bicycle parts. Goodman also sets this phenomenon in the context of global medical tourism. If people can pursue lower-cost treatment for illnesses and health conditions in other countries, why shouldn't an infertile couple seeking to start a family not also have such access to these more affordable and newly available means? This reasoning provides a foundation for readers to begin understanding the many layers of the issue.

Shows how the delayed-thesis structure creates two perspectives in conflict

The result of Goodman's delayed-thesis strategy is that the first two-thirds of this piece seem to justify outsourcing surrogate motherhood. Only after reading the whole op-ed piece can readers see clearly that Goodman has been dropping hints about her view all along through her choice of words. Although she clearly sees how outsourcing surrogacy can help poor women economically, her use of market language such as "production," "delivery," and "labor" carry a double meaning. On first reading of this op-ed piece, readers don't know if Goodman's punning is meant to be catchy and entertaining or serves another purpose. This other purpose becomes clear in the last third of the article when Goodman forthrightly asserts her criticism of the commercialism of the global marketplace that promotes worldwide searching for a "cheaper deal": "humanity is sacrificed to the economy and the person becomes the product" (161). This is a bold and big claim, but does the final third of her article support it?

Restates the third point in his thesis: lack of space limits development of Goodman's argument

In the final five paragraphs of this op-ed piece, Goodman begins to develop the rational basis of her argument; however, the brevity of the op-ed genre and her choice not to state her view openly initially have left Goodman with little space to develop her own claim. The result is that she presents some profound ideas very quickly. Some of the ethically complex ideas she introduces but doesn't explore much are these:

- The idea that there are ethical limits on what can be "sold"
- The idea that surrogate motherhood might be "dangerous work"
- The idea that children born from this "international trade" may be confused about their identities.

Discusses examples of ideas raised by Goodman but not developed

Goodman simply has not left herself enough space to develop these issues and perhaps leaves readers with questions rather than with changed views. I am particularly struck by several questions. Why have European countries banned surrogacy in developing countries and why has the United States not banned this practice? Does Goodman intend to argue that the United States should follow Europe's lead? She could explore more how this business of finding illiterate women to bear children for the wealthy continues to exploit third-world citizens much as sex tourism exploits women in the very same countries. It seems to perpetuate a tendency for the developed world to regard developing countries as a poor place of lawlessness where practices outlawed in the rest of the world (e.g. child prostitution, slave-like working conditions) are somehow tolerable. Goodman could have developed her argument more to state explicitly that a woman who accepts payment for bearing a baby becomes an indentured servant to the family. Yet another way to think of this issue is to see that the old saying of "a bun in the oven" is more literal than metaphoric when a woman uses her womb as a factory to produce children, a body business not too dissimilar to the commercialism of prostitution. Goodman only teases readers by mentioning these complex problems without producing an argument.

Conclusion

Still, although Goodman does not expand her criticism of outsourced surrogate motherhood or explore the issues of human dignity and rights, this argument does introduce the debate on surrogacy in the global marketplace, raise awareness, and begin to direct the conversation toward a productive end of seeking a responsible, healthy, and ethical future. Her op-ed piece lures readers into contemplating deep, perplexing ethical and economic problems and lays a foundation for readers to create an informed view of this issue.

Works Cited

Uses MLA format to list sources cited in the essay

"Ellen Goodman." *Postwritersgroup.com.* Washington Post Writer's Group, 2008. Web. May 19, 2008.

Goodman, Ellen. "Womb for Rent—For a Price." *Seattle Times* 11 April 2008: B6. Rpt. in *Writing Arguments.* John D. Ramage, John C. Bean, and June Johnson. 8th ed. New York: Pearson Longman, 2010. Print.

For additional writing, reading, and research resources, go to www.mycomplab.com

Analyzing Visual Arguments

To see how images can make powerful arguments, consider the rhetorical persuasiveness of the "polar bear" marching in a small town parade (Figure 9.1). Sponsored by local environmentalists advocating action against global warming, the polar bear uses arguments from *logos* (drawing on audience knowledge that climate change threatens polar bears), *pathos* (evoking the bears' vulnerability), and *ethos* (conveying the commitment of the citizens group). Delighting children and adults alike, the bear created a memorable environmental argument.

This chapter is aimed at increasing your ability to analyze visual arguments and use them rhetorically in your own work. We begin with some basic components of document and visual design. We then examine genres of visual argument ranging from posters to Web pages, explain how you can use visuals in your own arguments, and conclude by explaining how to display numeric data graphically.

Figure 9.1 A visual argument about climate change

Understanding Design Elements in Visual Argument

To understand how visual images can produce an argument, you need to understand the design elements that work together to create a visual text. In this section we'll explain and illustrate the four basic components of visual design: use of type, use of space and layout, use of color, and use of images and graphics.

Use of Type

Type is an important visual element of written arguments. Variations in type, such as size, boldface, italics, or all caps, can direct a reader's attention to an argument's structure and highlight main points. In arguments designed specifically for visual impact, such as posters or advocacy advertisements, type is often used in eye-catching and meaningful ways. In choosing type, you need to consider the typeface or font style, the size of the type, and formatting options. The main typefaces or fonts are classified as serif, sans serif, and specialty type. Serif type has little extensions on the letters. (This text is set in serif type.) Sans serif type lacks these extensions. Specialty type includes script fonts and special symbols. In addition to font style, type comes in different sizes. It is measured in points, with 1 point equal to $\frac{1}{72}$ of an inch. Most text-based arguments consisting mainly of body text are written in 10- to 12-point type, whereas more image-based arguments may use a mixture of type sizes that interact with the images for persuasive effect. Type can also be formatted using bold, italics, underlining, or shading for emphasis. Table 9.1 shows examples of type styles, as well as their typical uses.

The following basic principles for choosing type for visual arguments can help you achieve your overall goals of readability, visual appeal, and suitability.

Table 9.1   Examples and Uses of Type Fonts

Font Style	Font Name	Example	Use
Serif fonts	Times New Roman Courier New Bookman Old Style	Use type wisely. Use type wisely. Use type wisely.	Easy to read; good for long documents, good for *body type*, or the main verbal parts of a document
Sans serif fonts	Arial Century Gothic	Use type wisely. Use type wisely.	Tiring to read for long stretches; good for *display type* such as headings, titles, slogans
Specialty fonts	*Zapf Chancery* Onyx MT	*Use type wisely.* Use type wisely.	Difficult to read for long stretches; effective when used sparingly for playful or decorative effect

Principles for Choosing Type for Visual Arguments

1. If you are creating a poster or advocacy advertisement, you will need to decide how much of your argument will be displayed in words and how much in images. For the text portions, choose *display type* (sans serif) or specialty fonts for titles, headings, and slogans, and *body or text type* (serif) for longer passages of text.
2. Make type functional and appealing by using only two or three font styles per document.
3. Use consistent patterns of type (similar type styles, sizes, and formats) to indicate relationships among similar items or different levels of importance.
4. Choose type to project a specific impression (a structured combination of serif and sans serif type to create a formal, serious, or businesslike impression; sans serif and specialty type to create a casual, informal, or playful impression, and so forth).

Besides these general principles, rhetorical considerations of genre and audience expectations should govern decisions about type. Text-based arguments in scholarly publications generally use plain, conservative fonts with little variation, whereas text-based arguments in popular magazines may use more variations in font style and size, especially in headings and opening leads. Visual arguments such as posters, fliers, and advocacy ads exploit the aesthetic potential of type.

Use of Space or Layout

A second component of visual design is layout, which is critical for creating the visual appeal of an argument and for conveying meaning. Even visual arguments that are mainly textual should use space very purposefully. By spacing and layout we mean all of the following points:

- Page size and type of paper
- Proportion of text to white space
- Proportion of text to image(s) and graphics
- Arrangement of text on page (space, margins, columns, size of paragraphs, spaces between paragraphs, justification of margins)
- Use of highlighting elements such as bulleted lists, tables, sidebars, boxes
- Use of headings and other means of breaking text into visual elements

In arguments that don't use visuals directly, the writer's primary visual concern is document design, in which the writer tries to meet the conventions of a genre and the expectations of the intended audience. For example, Megan Matthews's researched argument on pages 394–400 is designed to meet the document conventions of the American Psychological Association (APA). Note the use of a plain, conventional typeface (for easy reading); double spacing and 1-inch margins (to leave room for editorial marking and notations); and special title page, headers, and page number locations (to meet expectations of readers familiar with APA documents—which all look exactly the same).

But in moving from verbal-only arguments to visual arguments that use visual elements for direct persuasive effect—for example, posters, fliers, or advocacy ads— creative use of layout is vital. Here are some ideas to help you think about the layout of a visual argument.

Principles for Laying Out Parts of a Visual Text

1. Choose a layout that avoids clutter and confusion by limiting how much text and how many visual items you put on a page.
2. Focus on creating coherence and meaning with layout.
3. Develop an ordering or structuring principle that clarifies the relationships among the parts.
4. Use layout and spacing to indicate the importance of items and to emphasize key ideas. Because Western readers read from left to right and top to bottom, top and center are positions that readily draw readers' eyes.

An Analysis of a Visual Argument Using Type and Spatial Elements

To illustrate the persuasive power of type and layout, we ask you to consider Figure 9.1, which shows an advocacy ad sponsored by a coalition of organizations aimed at fighting illegal drugs.

This ad, warning about the dangers of the drug Ecstasy, uses different sizes of type and layout to present its argument. The huge word "Ecstasy" first catches the reader's attention. The first few words at the top of the ad, exuding pleasure, lull the reader with the congruence between the pleasurable message and the playful type. Soon, however, the reader encounters a dissonance between the playful type and the meaning of the words: *dehydrate, hallucinate, paranoid,* and *dead* name unpleasant ideas. By the end of the ad, readers realize they have been led through a downward progression of ideas beginning with the youth culture's belief that Ecstasy creates wonderfully positive feelings and ending with the ad's thesis that Ecstasy leads to paranoia, depression, and death. The playful informality of the font styles and the unevenly scattered layout of the type convey the seductiveness and unpredictability of the drug. The ad concedes that the first effects are "falling in love with the world" but implies that what comes next is increasingly dark and dangerous. At the end of the ad, in the lines of type near the bottom, the message and typestyle are congruent again. The question "Does that sound harmless to you?" marks a shift in type design and layout. The designer composed this section of the ad in conventional fonts centered on the page in a rational, businesslike fashion. This type design signals a metaphoric move from the euphoria of Ecstasy to the ordered structure of everyday reality, where the reader can now consider rationally the drug's harm. The information at the bottom of the ad identifies the ad's sponsors and gives both a Web address and a telephone number to call for more information about Ecstasy and other illegal drugs.

■ ■ ■   **FOR CLASS DISCUSSION**   Comparing the Rhetorical Appeal of Two Advocacy Ads

This exercise asks you to examine Figure 9.2, an advocacy ad sponsored by Common Sense for Drug Policy, and to compare it to the ad in Figure 9.1. Figure 9.2 also

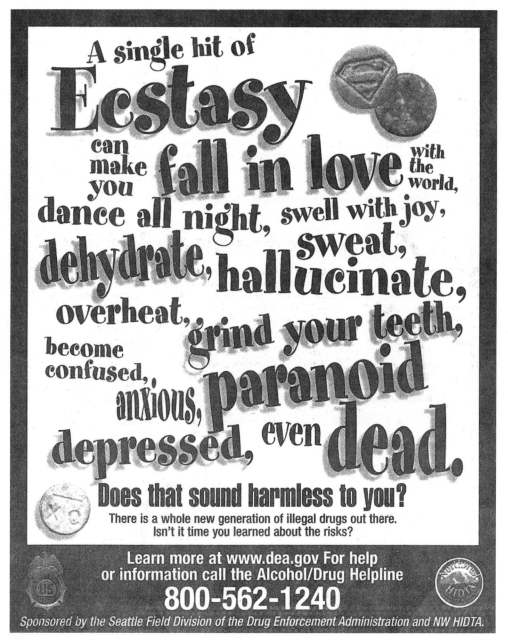

FIGURE 9.2 Advocacy advertisement warning against Ecstasy

What We Know About Ecstasy

What is Ecstasy?

Ecstasy, MDMA,[1] is a semi-synthetic drug patented by Merck Pharmaceutical Company in 1914 and abandoned for 60 years. In the late 1970s and early 1980s psychiatrists and psychotherapists in the US used it to facilitate psychotherapy.[2] In 1985 its growing recreational use caused the DEA to criminalize it.

Ecstasy's effects last 3 to 6 hours. It is a mood elevator that produces feelings of empathy, openness and well-being. People who take it at all night "rave" dances say they enjoy dancing and feeling close to others. It does not produce violence or physical addiction.[3]

What are the greatest risks from Ecstasy?

Death is a possibility when using MDMA. According to coroner reports, there were nine Ecstasy-related deaths (three of these involved Ecstasy alone) in 1998.[4] Some of these deaths are related to overheating. MDMA slightly raises body temperature. This is potentially lethal in hot environments where there is vigorous dancing and the lack of adequate fluid replacement.[5] Many of these tragic deaths were preventable with simple harm reduction techniques such as having free water available and rooms where people can rest and relax.

One of the recent risks associated with Ecstasy is the possibility of obtaining adulterated drugs that may be more toxic than MDMA. Some of the reported deaths attributed to Ecstasy are likely caused by other, more dangerous drugs.[6] Deaths from adulterated drugs are another consequence of a zero tolerance approach. While we do not encourage Ecstasy use, we recommend that the drug be tested for purity to minimize the risk from adulterated drugs by those who consume it.[7] However, MDMA itself has risks. For example, it raises blood pressure and heart rate. Persons with known cardiovascular or heart disease should not take MDMA.

Recent studies have indicated that individuals who have used MDMA may have decreased performance in memory tests compared to nonusers. These studies are presently controversial because they involved people who used a variety of other drugs. Furthermore, it is difficult to rule out possible pre-existing differences between research subjects and controls.[8]

What is a rave?

Raves are all-night dance parties popular with young people that feature electronic music. A variety of drug use, from alcohol to nicotine, and including ecstasy, occurs at raves. Hysteria is leading to criminalization of raves, thus pushing them underground and into less safe and responsible settings.

Let's deal with legal and illegal drugs knowledgeably, understand their relative dangers, act prudently and avoid hysteria.

Kevin B. Zeese, President, Common Sense for Drug Policy, 3220 N Street, NW #141, Washington, DC 20007
www.csdp.org * www.DrugWarFacts.org * www.AddictintheFamily.org * info@csdp.org
202-299-9780 * 202-518-4028 (fax)

1, 3 & 4 - methylenedioxymethamphetamine. 2 - Greer G. and Tolbert R., A Method of Conducting Therapeutic Sessions with MDMA. In Journal of Psychoactive Drugs 30 (1998) 4:371.379. For research on the therapeutic use of MDMA see: www.maps.org. 3 - Beck J. and Rosenbaum M., Pursuit of Ecstasy: The MDMA Experience. Albany: State University of New York Press, 1994. 4 - Drug Abuse Warning Network, Office of Applied Studies, Substance Abuse and Mental Health Services Administration, Report of March 21, 2000. (This was a special report because the published report only includes drugs where there were over 10 deaths.) 5 - C.M. Milroy; J.C. Clark; A.R.W. Forrest, Pathology of deaths associated with "ecstasy" and "eve" misuse, Journal of Clinical Pathology Vol 49 (1996) 149-153. 6 - Laboratory Pill Analysis Program, DanceSafe. For results visit www.DanceSafe.org. See also, Byard RW et al., Amphetamine derivative fatalities in South Australia—is "Ecstasy" the culprit?, American Journal of Forensic Medical Pathology, 998 (Sep) 19(3): 261-5. 7 - DanceSafe provides testing equipment and a testing service which can be used to determine what a substance is. See www.DanceSafe.org. 8 - E. Gouzoulis-Mayfrank; J. Daumann; F. Tuchtenhagen; S. Pelz; S. Becker; H.J. Kunert; B. Fimm; H. Sass; Impaired cognitive performance in drug-free users of recreational ecstasy (MDMA), by Journal Neurol Neurosurg Psychiatry Vol 68, June 2000, 719-725; K.I.Bolla; U.D.; McCann; G.A. Ricaurte; Memory impairment in abstinent MDMA ('Ecstasy') users, by Neurology Vol 51, Dec 1998, 1532-1537.

FIGURE 9.3 Common Sense for Drug Policy advocacy ad

focuses on the drug Ecstasy and also uses type and layout to convey its points. (This ad appeared in the liberal magazine *The Progressive.*) Individually or in groups, study this advocacy ad and then answer the following questions.

1. What is the core argument of this ad? What view of drug use and what course of action is this ad promoting? What similarities and differences do you see between the argument about Ecstasy in this ad and the ad in Figure 9.1?
2. What are the main differences in the type and layout of the two ads in Figures 9.1 and 9.3? To what extent do the ad makers' choices about type and layout match the arguments made in each ad?
3. How would you analyze the use of type and layout in Figure 9.3? How does this ad use typestyles to convey its argument? How does it use layout and spacing?
4. The ad in Figure 9.2 appeared in the weekly entertainment section of the *Seattle Times,* a newspaper with a large general readership, whereas the ad in Figure 9.3 appeared in a liberal news commentary magazine. In what ways is each ad designed to reach its audience?

Use of Color

A third important element of visual design is use of color, which can contribute significantly to the visual appeal of an argument and move readers emotionally and imaginatively. In considering color in visual arguments, writers are especially controlled by genre conventions. For example, academic arguments use color minimally, whereas popular magazines often use color lavishly. The appeal of colors to an audience and the associations that colors have for an audience are also important. For instance, the psychedelic colors of 1960s rock concert posters would probably not be effective in poster arguments directed toward conservative voters. Color choices in visual arguments often have crucial importance, including the choice of making an image black-and-white when color is possible. As you will see in our discussions of color throughout this chapter, makers of visual arguments need to decide whether color will be primarily decorative (using colors to create visual appeal), functional (for example, using colors to indicate relationships), realistic (using colors like a documentary photo), aesthetic (for example, using colors that are soothing, exciting, or disturbing), or some intentional combination of these.

Use of Images and Graphics

The fourth design element includes images and graphics, which can powerfully condense information into striking and memorable visuals; clarify ideas; and add depth, liveliness, and emotion to your arguments. A major point to keep in mind when using images is that a few simple images may be more powerful than complicated and numerous images. Other key considerations are (1) how you intend an image to work in your argument (for example, to convey an idea, illustrate a point, or evoke an emotional response) and (2) how you will establish the relationship between the image or graphic and the verbal text. Because using images and graphics effectively is especially challenging, we devote the rest of this chapter to explaining how images and graphics can be incorporated into visual arguments. We treat the use of photographs and drawings in the next main section and the use of quantitative graphics in the final section.

An Analysis of a Visual Argument Using All the Design Components

Before we discuss the use of images and graphics in detail, we would like to illustrate how all four of the design components—use of type, layout, color, and images—can reinforce and support each other to achieve a rhetorical effect. Consider the "Save the Children" advocacy ad appearing as Figure 9.4. This advocacy ad combines type, layout, color, and image skillfully and harmoniously through its dominant image complemented by verbal text that interprets and applies the ideas conveyed by the image. The layout of the ad divides the page into three main parts, giving central focus to the image of the mother standing and looking into the eyes of the child she is holding in her arms. The blank top panel leads readers to look at the image. Two color panels, mauve behind the child and rose behind the mother, also highlight the two figures, isolate them in time and space, and concentrate the readers' attention on them. The large type in the black borders ("SHE'S THE BEST QUALIFIED TEACHER FOR HER CHILDREN" and "IMAGINE IF SHE HAD AN EDUCATION") frames the image, attracts readers' eyes, and plants the main idea in readers' minds: mothers should be equipped to teach their children.

This advocacy ad, which appeared in *Newsweek,* skillfully blends familiar, universal ideas—a mother's love for her child and the tenderness and strength of this bond—with unfamiliar, foreign associations: a mother and child from a third-world country, wearing the traditional clothing of their country depicted by the head scarf the mother is wearing and the elaborate design on her sleeve. In addition to the familiar-unfamiliar dynamic, a universal-particular dynamic also operates in this ad. This woman and baby are *every* mother and child (after all, we don't know exactly where she is from), but they are also from some specific third-world country. The two figures have been posed to conjure up Western paintings and statues of the Madonna and Christ child. With this pose, the ad intends that readers will connect with this image of motherly love and devotion and respond by supporting the "Every Mother/Every Child" campaign. Color in this ad also accents the warm, cozy, hopeful impression of the image; pink in Western culture is a feminine color often associated with women and babies. In analyzing the photographic image, you should note what is *not* shown: any surroundings, any indication of housing or scenery, any concrete sense of place or culture. The text of the ad interprets the image, provides background information, and seeks to apply the ideas and feelings evoked by the image to urging readers to action. The image, without either the large type or the smaller type, does convey an idea as well as elicit sympathy from readers, but the text adds meaning to the image and builds on those impressions and applies them.

The ad designer could have focused on poverty, illiteracy, hunger, disease, and high mortality rates but instead has chosen to evoke positive feelings of identification and to convey hopeful ideas. While acknowledging their cultural difference from this mother and child, readers recognize their common humanity and are moved to "give mothers and children the best chance to survive and thrive." The large amounts of blank space in this ad help convey that the main points here are important, serious, elemental, but also simple—as if the ad has gotten to the heart of the matter. The bottom panel of the ad gives readers the logo and name of the organization "Save the Children" and a phone number and Web address to use to show their support.

In a world where almost one-third of women are illiterate, improving access to education is urgent. Studies show that an educated mother is more likely to provide her children with adequate nutrition, seek needed health care, and send her girls, as well as boys, to school. Support the Every Mother / Every Child campaign, and give mothers and children the best chance to survive and thrive.

SHE'S THE BEST QUALIFIED TEACHER FOR HER CHILDREN.

IMAGINE IF SHE HAD AN EDUCATION.

1-800-728-3843 • savethechildren.org

Save the Children®

FIGURE 9.4 Save the Children advocacy ad

The Compositional Features of Photographs and Drawings

Now that we have introduced you to the four major elements of visual design—type, layout, color, and images—we turn to an in-depth discussion of photographic images and drawings. Used with great shrewdness in product advertisements, photos and drawings can be used with equal shrewdness in posters, fliers, advocacy ads, and Web sites. When an image is created specifically for an argument, almost nothing is left to chance. Although such images are often made to seem spontaneous and "natural," they are almost always composed: designers consciously select the details of staging and composition as well as manipulate camera techniques (filters, camera angle, lighting) and digital or chemical development techniques (airbrushing, merging of images). Even news photography can have a composed feel. For example, public officials often try to control the effect of photographs by creating "photo ops" (photographing opportunities), wherein reporters are allowed to photograph an event only during certain times and from certain angles. Political photographs appearing in newspapers are often press releases officially approved by the politician's staff. (See the campaign photographs later in this chapter on page 180.) To analyze a photograph or drawing, or to create visual images for your own arguments, you need to think both about the composition of the image and about the camera's relationship to the subject. Because drawings produce a perspective on a scene analogous to that of a camera, design considerations for photographs can be applied to drawings as well. The following list of questions can guide your analysis of any persuasive image.

- *Type of photograph or drawing:* Is the image documentary-like (representing a real event), fictionlike (intended to tell a story or dramatize a scene), or conceptual (illustrating or symbolizing an idea or theme)? The two photos of mosh pits—a girl shown crowd surfing and an unruly, almost menacing mosh pit crowd (Chapter 5, page 95)—are documentary photos capturing real events in action. In contrast, the drawing of the lizards in the Earthjustice ad in Figure 9.5 is both a fictional narrative telling a story and a conceptual drawing illustrating a theme.
- *Distance from the subject:* Is the image a close-up, medium shot, or long shot? Close-ups tend to increase the intensity of the image and suggest the importance of the subject; long shots tend to blend the subject into the background. In the baby photograph opposing phthalates in children's toys (Chapter 1, page 4), the effect of the baby's wearing a "poison" bib is intensified by the close-up shot without background. In contrast, the photograph of the young woman crossing the bridge in Haiti (Chapter 6, page 117) is a long-range shot showing her blending into the poverty-stricken background, suggesting the devastating effect of poverty.
- *Orientation of the image and camera angle:* Is the camera (or artist) positioned in front of or behind the subject? Is it positioned below the subject, looking up (a low-angle shot)? Or is it above the subject, looking down (a high-angle shot)? Front-view shots, such as those of Carlitos and his mother in the stills from *Under the Same Moon* (page 1), tend to emphasize the persons being photographed. In contrast, rear-view shots often emphasize the scene

Just then, the three lizards came home and found Goldilocks eating their porridge...

IT'S JUST NOT THE SAME WITHOUT BEARS.

Once upon a time there were over 100,000 grizzly bears in the lower 48 states. Now, there are less than a thousand grizzly bears left. The health of the grizzly is dependent on vast, undisturbed, wild lands. When bears disappear, other species will follow. Bears are such an important part of our wilderness, history, and culture that it's hard to imagine a world without them in the picture.

Grizzly bears are a threatened species, protected by the Endangered Species Act. But some special interests are pushing the U.S. Fish and Wildlife Service to remove Yellowstone grizzlies from the endangered species list. Why? They want to open up wild lands around Yellowstone

National Park to destructive logging, mining, off-road vehicle use, and development.

You can help protect our wilderness and grizzly bears. Please take a moment to contact Secretary Bruce Babbitt, Department of Interior, 1849 C St. NW, Washington DC 20240, or email Bruce_Babbitt@os.doi.gov – Tell him to keep grizzly bears on the Endangered Species List and that grizzly bears need more protection, not less.

Earthjustice Legal Defense Fund is working tirelessly to protect the grizzly bears and the wilderness they stand for. If we all work together, the grizzly bears will live happily ever after.

HELP KEEP BEARS IN THE PICTURE

www.earthjustice.org

 EARTHJUSTICE
LEGAL DEFENSE FUND
1-800-584-6460

designed by Sustain

FIGURE 9.5 Earthjustice advocacy ad

or setting. A low-angle perspective tends to make the subject look superior and powerful, whereas a high-angle perspective can reduce the size—and by implication, the importance—of the subject. A level angle tends to imply equality. The high-angle shot of the girl in the mosh pit (page 95) emphasizes the superiority of the camera and harmlessness of the mosh pit. In contrast, the low-angle perspective of the lizards in the Earthjustice advocacy ad in Figure 9.5 emphasizes the power of the lizards and the inferiority of the viewer.

- *Point of view:* Does the camera or artist stand outside the scene and create an objective effect as in the Haiti photograph on page 116? Or is the camera or artist inside the scene as if the photographer or artist is an actor in the scene, creating a subjective effect as in the drawing of the lizards in Figure 9.4?
- *Use of color:* Is the image in color or in black and white? Is this choice determined by the restrictions of the medium, (such as images designed to run in black-and-white in newspapers) or is it the conscious choice of the photographer or artist? Are the colors realistic or muted? Have special filters been used (a photo made to look old through the use of brown tints)? The bright colors in the lizard and Goldilocks drawing in Figure 9.5 and in the forest scene in the Saturn VUE ad later in this chapter on page 178 resemble illustrations in books for children.
- *Compositional special effects:* Is the entire image clear and realistic? Is any portion of it blurred? Is it blended with other realistic or nonrealistic images (a car ad that blends a city and a desert; a body lotion ad that merges a woman and a cactus)? Is the image an imitation of some other famous image such as a classic painting (as in parodies)? Both the Earthjustice ad in Figure 9.5 and the Saturn VUE ad later in this chapter on page 178 are conscious imitations of children's picture books.
- *Juxtaposition of images:* Are several different images juxtaposed, suggesting relationships between them? Juxtaposition can suggest sequential or causal relationships or can metaphorically transfer the identity of a nearby image or background to the subject (as when a bath soap is associated with a meadow). This technique is frequently used in public relations to shape viewers' perceptions of political figures as when Barack Obama was photographed beneath a huge American flag at a campaign appearance (page 180) to counter Republican Party charges that he was not "American enough."
- *Manipulation of images:* Are staged images made to appear real, natural, documentary-like? Are images altered with airbrushing? Are images actually composites of a number of images (for instance, using images of different women's bodies to create one perfect model in an ad or film)? Are images cropped for emphasis? What is left out? Are images downsized or enlarged? For an example of a staged photo that is intended to look natural, see the "Save the Children" advocacy ad on page 173. Note too how the figures in the "Save the Children" ad are silhouetted to remove all background.
- *Settings, furnishings, props:* Is the photo or drawing an outdoor or indoor scene? What is in the background and foreground? What furnishings and props, such as furniture, objects in a room, pets, and landscape features, help create the scene? What social associations of class, race, and gender are attached to these settings and props? Note, for example, how the designers of America's Army, the army

video game, used a few simple props to create a gritty urban street fighting scene (Figure 9.12). The burned-out vehicle hull suggests the aftermath of days of street fighting, whereas the telephone or power poles in the middle of a narrow, deserted street suggest a poor city in a third-world country.

- *Characters, roles, actions:* Does the photo or drawing tell a story? Are the people in the scene models? Are the models instrumental (acting out real-life roles) or are they decorative (extra and included for visual or sex appeal)? What are the facial expressions, gestures, and poses of the people? What are the spatial relationships of the figures? (Who is in the foreground, center, and background? Who is large and prominent?) What social relationships are implied by these poses and positions? In the "Save the Children" advocacy ad shown in Figure 9.4, the pose of the mother and child—each completely absorbed in adoration of the other—tells the story of the bonds of love between mothers and babies.

- *Presentation of images:* Are images separated from each other in a larger composition or connected to each other? Are the images large in proportion to verbal text? How are images labeled? How does the text relate to the image(s)? Does the image illustrate the text? Does the text explain or comment on the image? For example, the poster advocating vegetarianism (page 145) effectively juxtaposes words and images. The top is dominated by a question "Think you can be a meat-eating environmentalist?" The "answer" is the image of a world with a big bite taken out of it. The text beneath the image "Think again . . ." makes sense only after the viewer has interpreted the image. In contrast, the coat hanger hook dominates the advocacy ad on page 321.

An Analysis of a Visual Argument Using Images

To show you how images can be analyzed, let's examine the advertisement for a Saturn VUE sport-utility vehicle in Figure 9.6. At one level, the persuasive intent of this ad is to urge viewers to buy a Saturn VUE. But at a more subtle level, this advertisement participates in an international debate about SUVs and the environment. Whereas Europeans and now many Americans also are buying smaller, more fuel-efficient cars, some Americans are still buying SUVs that guzzle gas like trucks. Among their opponents, SUVs—whether fairly or unfairly—have become a worldwide symbol of Americans' greed for oil and their disdain for the environment.

How do car manufacturers fight back? Clearly, they can't make a logical argument that owning an SUV is good for the environment (although some car companies are coming out with hybrid SUVs that claim to be "green"). But they can use psychological strategies that urge consumers to associate SUVs with pro-environment sentiments. So in this ad Saturn turns to visual argument. Using a carefully designed drawing, the advertisement shows the Saturn VUE blending into an "evergreen forest" scene. Surrounded by a moose, a porcupine, a bear, a squirrel, and other forest birds and animals, the SUV seems to belong in its forest home. The brilliance of the ad is the insert legend at the bottom left, where the forest creatures are identified by name. The ad teaches city dwellers who buy SUVs the names of the forest animals—not just "bird" but "Black-Capped Chickadee," not just "rabbit" but "Snowshoe Hare." (Because the ad was designed as a two-page magazine spread, we had to reduce its size in Figure 9.5,

FIGURE 9.6 General Motors consumer ad for the Saturn VUE

making the animal names tiny. They are easily readable in the original.) The ad becomes a mini-lesson in identifying and naming the "creatures of the evergreen forest"—creature number one, of course, being the Saturn VUE.

To make the Saturn VUE blend harmoniously with the forest, this ad cleverly de-emphasizes the size of the vehicle, even though the dominant size of SUVs is part of their appeal to urban consumers. To compensate for this choice, the typical appeals of SUVs are rendered symbolically. For example, the VUE's power and agility, hinted at in the brief copy at the bottom right of the ad, are conveyed metaphorically in the image of the puma, "poised" like the Saturn, crouching and oriented in the same direction, like the car's guiding spirit. It enters the scene from the outside, the predator, silent and powerful—the main animal to be identified with the car itself. Other animals close to the car and facing the same direction as the car each stand for one of the car's attributes so that the VUE also possesses the speed of the hare, the brute size and strength of the bear, and the soaring freedom of the goshawk.

The whole ad works by association. The slogan "At home in almost any environment" means literally that the car can go from city to country, from desert to mountains, from snow to tropic heat. But so can any car. The slogan's purpose is to associate the car with the words *home* and *environment*—words that connote all the warm, fuzzy feelings that make you feel good about owning a Saturn VUE. In addition, the use of drawings and the identification of animals by numbers conjure up the delightful, instructive innocence of children's books: this car must be a good thing. And in its own special way, this ad has skillfully shifted consumers' attention away from global warming and environmental degradation.

■ ■ ■ **FOR CLASS DISCUSSION** Analyzing Photos Rhetorically

1. The techniques for constructing photos come into play prominently in news photography. In this exercise, we ask you to examine four photographs of American presidential campaigns. Working individually or in groups, study the four photos in Figures 9.7 through 9.10 , and then answer the following questions:

   a. What do you think is the dominant impression of each photo? In other words, what is each photo's implicit argument?

   b. What camera techniques and compositional features do you see in each photo?

   c. What image of the candidates do these photographs attempt to create for citizens and voters?

2. Three of these photographs (of Reagan, Clinton, and Obama) are mostly successful in promoting the image intended by their campaigns. But one of the photographs (of Democratic candidate John Kerry in 1994, running against George W. Bush) is an example of a photograph that "backfired." Republicans reversed the intended impact of the photograph and used it to ridicule Kerry.

   a. What is the intended effect of the Kerry photograph, which is from a windsurfing video showing Kerry zigzagging across the water?

FIGURE 9.7 Ronald Reagan at his California
ranch home

FIGURE 9.8 Presidential candidate John Kerry
windsurfing

FIGURE 9.9 Incumbent President Bill Clinton in a
campaign ad

FIGURE 9.10 Presidential candidate Barack
Obama making a speech

   b. How might the Kerry photograph (and the windsurfing video) produce an
      unintended effect that opens the candidate to ridicule from the opposing party?
      (Suggestion: Enter "Kerry windsurfing photo" into your Web search engine. For
      another example of a campaign photograph that backfired, search for "Michael
      Dukakis tank photo.")
3. The poster shown in Figure 9.10 is for the documentary film "Wal-Mart: The High
   Cost of Low Prices," produced in 2005 by filmmaker and political activist Robert

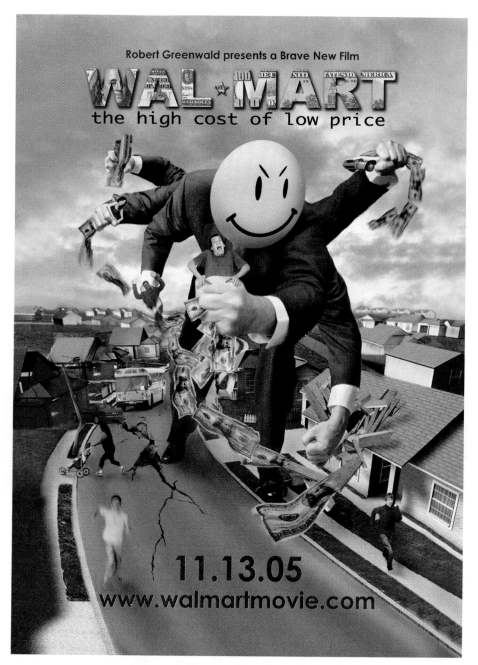

FIGURE 9.11 Poster for "Wal-Mart: The High Cost of Low Prices"

FIGURE 9.12 Urban assault scene, America's Army video game

FIGURE 9.13 Village scene, America's Army video game

Greenwald. According to its Web site, the movie features "the deeply personal stories and everyday lives of families and communities struggling to survive in a Wal-Mart world."

Working individually or in groups, answer the following questions:

   a. What compositional features and drawing techniques do you see in this image? What is striking or memorable about the visual features?

   b. How would you state the argument made by this image?

   c. This effect of this image derives partly from what cultural analysts call "intertextuality." By this term, analysts mean the way that a viewer's reading of an image depends on familiarity with a network of "connected" images—in this case, familiarity with posters for Godzilla films from the 1950s as well as with Wal-Mart's conventional use of the smiley face. How does this drawing use viewers' cultural knowledge of Godzilla and of smiley-faces to create an image of Wal-Mart? Why is this monster wearing a suit? Why does it have five or more arms? Why is this monster destroying a suburb or housing area rather than a city of skyscrapers? In short, what does it retain of conventional Godzilla images, what does it change, and why? Similarly, how is the monster's smiley face similar to and different from the traditional Wal-Mart smiley face?

4. The images in Figures 9.12 and 9.13 are screen captures from the very popular and controversial PC action game America's Army, created by the U.S. Army. This "virtual soldiering" game, free to download from the Web site http://www.americasarmy.com, claims to "provide players with the most authentic military experience available."

   a. In these screen captures from the game, what is the effect of the camera's distance from the subject and the camera's point of view on the viewer/player?

   b. How do color and composition affect the visual appeal of these images?

   c. What impressions do settings, characters, and roles convey?

   d. Based on these two scenes from the game, why do you think this game has provoked heated public discussion? How effective do you think this game is as a recruitment device?

The Genres of Visual Argument

We have already mentioned that verbal arguments today are frequently accompanied by photographs or drawings that contribute to the text's persuasive appeal. For example, a verbal argument promoting U.N. action to help AIDS victims in Africa might be accompanied by a photograph of a dying mother and child. However, some genres of argument are dominated by visual elements. In these genres, the visual design carries most of the argumentative weight; verbal text is used primarily for labeling, for focusing the argument's claim, or for commenting on the images. In this section we describe specifically these highly visual genres of argument.

Posters and Fliers

To persuade audiences, an arguer might create a poster designed for placement on walls or kiosks or a flier to be passed out on street corners. Posters dramatically attract and direct viewers' attention toward one subject or issue. They often seek to rally supporters, promote a strong stance on an issue, and call people to action. For example, during World War II, posters asked Americans to invest in war bonds and urged women to join the workforce to free men for active combat. During the Vietnam War, famous posters used slogans such as "Make Love, Not War" or "Girls say yes to boys who say no" to increase national resistance to the war.

The hallmark of an effective poster is the way it focuses and encodes a complex meaning in a verbal-visual text, often with one or more striking images. These images are often symbolic—for example, using children to symbolize family and home, a soaring bird to symbolize freedom, or three firefighters raising the American flag over the World Trade Center rubble on September 11, 2001, to symbolize American heroism, patriotism, and resistance to terrorism. These symbols derive potency from the values they share with their target audience. Posters tend to use words sparingly, either as slogans or as short, memorable directives. This terse verbal text augments the message encoded in an eye-catching, dominant image.

As an example of a contemporary poster, consider the poster on page 145, which is a call to stop eating red meat in order to protect the Earth. This poster uses compositional special effects, depicting the Earth from outer space against the backdrop of the Milky Way. The grain, color, and texture of pieces of red meat are superimposed over the continents of North and South America where viewers expect to see the familiar greens and browns of Earth's surface. The impact of the poster is intensified by the big bite that has been taken out of Alaska, western Canada, and the West Coast of the United States. The substitution of meat for land and the presence of the bitten-out piece of the Earth convey the message of immediate destruction. Framing this image of the Earth on the top and bottom are a question and an imperative phrased in casual but confrontational language: "Think you can be a meat-eating environmentalist? Think again." The summary caption of the poster urges readers to become vegetarians. As you can see, this poster tries to shock and push readers toward a more radical environmentalism—one without meat.

Fliers and brochures often use visual elements similar to those in posters. An image might be the top and center attraction of a flier or the main focus of the front cover of a brochure. However, unlike posters, fliers and brochures offer additional space for verbal arguments, which often present the writer's claim supported with bulleted lists of reasons. Sometimes pertinent data and statistics, along with testimony from supporters, are placed in boxes or sidebars.

Public Affairs Advocacy Advertisements

Public affairs advocacy advertisements share with posters an emphasis on visual elements, but they are designed specifically for publication in newspapers and magazines and, in their persuasive strategies, are directly analogous to product advertisements. Public affairs advocacy ads are usually sponsored by a corporation or an advocacy organization and often have a more time-sensitive message than do posters and a more immediate and defined target audience. Designed as condensed arguments aimed at influencing public opinion on civic issues, these ads are characterized by their brevity, audience-based appeals, and succinct "sound bite" style. Often, in order to sketch out their claim and reasons clearly and concisely, they employ headings and subheadings, bulleted lists, different sizes and styles of type, and a clever, pleasing layout on the page. They usually have some attention-getting slogan or headline like "MORE KIDS ARE GETTING BRAIN CANCER. WHY?" or "STOP THE TAX RE-VOLT JUGGERNAUT!" And they usually include a call to action, whether it be a donation, a letter of protest to legislators, or an invitation to join the advocacy group.

The balance between verbal and visual elements in an advocacy advertisement varies. Some advocacy ads are verbal only, with visual concerns focused on document design (for example, an "open letter" from the president of a corporation appearing as a full-page newspaper ad). Other advocacy ads are primarily visual, using images and other design elements with the same shrewdness as advertisements. We have looked closely at advocacy ads in this chapter when we examined the Ecstasy ads (Figures 9.2 and 9.3) and the Save the Children ad (Figure 9.4), These use text and images in different ways to present their messages.

As another example of a public affairs advocacy ad, consider the ad in Chapter 15, page 321, that attempts to counter the influence of the pro-life movement's growing campaign against abortion. As you can see, this ad is dominated by one stark image: a question mark formed by the hook of a coat hanger. The shape of the hook draws the reader's eye to the concentrated type centered below it. The hook carries most of the weight of the argument. Simple, bold, and harsh, the image of the hanger, tapping readers' cultural knowledge, evokes the dangerous experience of illegal abortions performed crudely by nonmedical people in the dark back streets of cities. The ad wants viewers to think of the dangerous last resorts that desperate women would have to turn to if they could not obtain abortions legally. The hanger itself creates a visual pun: As a question mark, it conveys the ad's dilemma about what will happen if abortions are made illegal. As a coat hanger, it provides the ad's frightening answer to the printed question—desperate women will return to back-street abortionists who use coat hangers as tools.

■ ■ ■ **FOR CLASS DISCUSSION** Analyzing an Advocacy Ad Rhetorically

Reexamine the Earthjustice public affairs advocacy ad shown in Figure 9.5 on page175. This ad defends the presence of grizzly bears in Yellowstone National Park as well as other wilderness areas in the Rocky Mountains. In our classes, this ad has yielded rich discussion of its ingenuity and complexity.

Working individually or in groups, conduct your own examination of this ad using the following questions:

1. What visual features of this ad immediately attract your eyes? What principles for effective use of type, layout, color, and image does this ad exemplify?
2. What is the core argument of this ad?
3. Why did Earthjustice use the theme of Goldilocks? How do the lizards function in this ad? Why does the ad *not* have any pictures of grizzlies or bears of any kind?
4. How would you design an advocacy ad for the preservation of grizzly bears? What visuals would you use? After discussing the Earthjustice advocacy ad, explore the

rhetorical appeals of a product advertisement such as the one that appears in Chapter 6 on page 117. The designers of this Toyota ad have made key choices in the use of the main image, the woman with the face mask. How does this product ad work to convey its argument? Consider questions about its use of type, layout, and image, about the core of its argument, and about its appeals to *ethos, pathos,* and *kairos.*

Cartoons

An especially charged kind of visual argument is the political cartoon. Although you are perhaps not likely to create your own political cartoons, it is useful to understand how cartoonists use visual and verbal elements to convey their message. British cartoonist Martin Rowson calls himself "a visual journalist" who employs "humor to make a journalistic point." Political cartoons are often mini-narratives, portraying an issue dramatically, compactly, and humorously. They employ images and a few well-chosen words to dramatize conflicts and problems. Using caricature, exaggeration, and distortion, cartoonists distill an issue down to an image that boldly reveals the creator's perspective and subsequent claim on a civic issue. The purpose of political cartoons is usually satirical, or, as cartoonist Rowson says, "about afflicting the comfortable and comforting the afflicted." Because they are so condensed and often connected to current affairs, political cartoons are particularly dependent on the audience's background knowledge of cultural and political events. When

FIGURE 9.14 Political cartoon protesting baseball players' use of steroids

Source: By permission of Steve Benson and Creators Syndicate, Inc.

political cartoons work well, through their perceptive combination of image and words, they flash a brilliant, clarifying light on a perspective or open a new lens on an issue, often giving readers a shock of insight.

As an illustration, note the Benson cartoon in Figure 9.14, which first appeared in the *Arizona Republic.* The *kairotic* moment for this piece is the national debate about baseball players' using steroids to blast more home runs or add velocity to their fastballs. Some athletes and sports commentators have accepted the use of steroids, seeing them as logical outcomes of other performance enhancers such as Ritalin for concentration or Botox for beauty. Others challenge the use of performance-enhancing drugs, citing health dangers to users, unfairness to nonusers, and loss of integrity to sports. In this wordless cartoon, Benson conjures up this controversy; the hefty batter and hypodermic needle substituting for a bat imply that this tampering with drugs and the great American tradition of baseball is abnormal, dangerous, and scary.

■ ■ ■   **FOR CLASS DISCUSSION**   **Analyzing a Cartoon Rhetorically**

1. Cartoons can often sum up a worldview in a single image. The political cartoons in Chapter 2 on page 28 show different perspectives on the United States' problems with illegal immigration. The cartoon in Chapter 1 on page 9 responds to the problem of limited resources. What mini-narrative does each convey? What is the cartoon arguing? How does the cartoon use caricature, exaggeration, or distortion to convey its perspective?

2. Cartoons can provide insight into how the public is lining up on issues. Choose a current issue such as the global economy, homeland security, dependence on foreign oil, reforming Social Security, U.S. Army recruitment, or stem cell research. Then, using a cartoon index on the Internet such as Daryl Cagle's Professional Cartoonists Index (http://www.cagle.com) or a Web search of your own, find several cartoons that capture different perspectives on your issue. What is the mini-narrative, the main claim, and the use of caricature, exaggeration, or distortion in each? How is *kairos,* or timeliness, important to each cartoon?

■ ■ ■

Web Pages

So far we have only hinted at the influence of the World Wide Web in accelerating the use of visual images in argument. The hypertext design of Web pages, along with its complex mix of text and image, has changed the way many writers think of argument. The home page of an advocacy site, for example, often has many features of a poster argument with hypertext links to galleries of images on the one hand, and to verbal arguments on the other. These verbal arguments themselves often contain photographs, drawings, and graphics. The strategies discussed in this chapter for analyzing and interpreting visual texts also apply to Web pages. Consider, for example, the "AAS Goals" page for Athletes Against Steroids (Figure 9.15; http://www.athletesagainststeroids.org/pgs/aboutaas.shtml). This advocacy site announces its purpose in the black-and-red type in the center of the

FIGURE 9.15 "About Us" page from Athletes Against Steroids Web site

Web page. The bottom half of the page briefly summarizes the problem with steroids and then outlines the organization's objectives. The links on the left-hand side of the page announce the range, depth, and relevance of material on steroid use posted on this site. Under the masthead for the organization, the quotation from President Bush's 2004 State of the Union address conveys that steroid use is a national problem needing immediate attention. Each page on this Web site follows the same basic design with subtle variations. For example, the "Steroid Side Effects" page features a tombstone with a skull and crossbones in place of the organizational shield; the "Are You Hooked on Steroids?" page has an ominous close-up of scattered pills and a steroid needle. As you examine this whole page, how do the layout and use of color support the *ethos* of this site and its appeal to *pathos*? AAS could have made the page much more dramatic with scary pictures, but they chose this more understated design. Do you agree with their choice?

Because the Web is such an important tool in research, we have placed our main discussion of Web sites in Chapter 16, pages 344–367. On these pages you will find our explanations for reading, analyzing, and evaluating Web sites.

Constructing Your Own Visual Argument

The most common visual arguments you are likely to create are posters and fliers, public affairs advocacy ads, and possibly Web pages. You may also decide that in longer verbal arguments, the use of visuals or graphics could clarify your points while adding visual variety to your paper. The following guidelines will help you apply your understanding of visual elements to the construction of your own visual arguments.

Guidelines for Creating Visual Arguments

1. *Genre:* Determine where this visual argument is going to appear (bulletin board, passed out as a flier, imagined as a one-page magazine or newspaper spread, or as a Web page).
2. *Audience-based appeals:* Determine who your target audience is.
   - What values and background knowledge of your issue can you assume that your audience has?
   - What specifically do you want your audience to think or do after reading your visual argument?
   - If you are promoting a specific course of action (sign a petition, send money, vote for or against a bill, attend a meeting), how can you make that request clear and direct?
3. *Core of your argument:* Determine what clear claim and reasons will form the core of your argument; decide whether this claim and these reasons will be explicitly stated or implicit in your visuals and slogans.
   - How much verbal text will you use?
   - If the core of your argument will be largely implicit, how can you still make it readily apparent and clear for your audience?
4. *Visual design:* What visual design and layout will grab your audience's attention and be persuasive?
   - How can font sizes and styles, layout, and color be used in this argument to create a strong impression?
   - What balance and harmony can you create between the visual and verbal elements of your argument? Will your verbal elements be a slogan, express the core of the argument, or summarize and comment on the image(s)?

Drink and Then Drive?
Jeopardize My Future?

- Arrest
- Financial Problems (fines up to $8,125)
- Increased Insurance Rates
- License Suspension
- Criminal Conviction
- Incarceration
- Serious Injury or Death

or
Designate a Driver?

It's a no-brainer.
Join your Senior Class at Thirsty Thursday, but
designate a driver.

FIGURE 9.16 Student poster argument promoting the use of designated drivers

5. *Use of images:* If your argument lends itself to images, what photo or drawing would support your claim or have emotional appeal? (If you want to use more than one image, be careful that you don't clutter your page and confuse your message. Simplicity and clarity are important.)
  - What image would be memorable and meaningful to your audience? Would a photo image or a drawing be more effective?

■ Will your image(s) be used to provide evidence for your claim or illustrate a main idea, evoke emotions, or enhance your credibility and authority?

As an example of a poster argument created by a student, consider Leah Johnson's poster in Figure 9.16. Intended for bulletin boards and kiosks around her college campus, Johnson's work illustrates how a writer can use minimal but well-chosen verbal text, layout, and images to convey a rhetorically effective argument. (That is Leah herself in the photograph.) In this ad, Leah is joining a national conversation about alcohol abuse on college campuses and is proposing a safe way of handling her university's weekly social get-together for older students, "Thirsty Thursdays." Notice how Leah in this visual argument has focused on her claim and reasons without seeing the need to supply evidence.

■ ■ ■   **FOR CLASS DISCUSSION**   Developing Ideas for a Poster Argument

This exercise asks you to do the thinking and planning for a poster argument to be displayed on your college or university campus. Working individually, in small groups, or as a whole class, choose an issue that is controversial on your campus (or in your town or city), and follow the Guidelines for Creating Visual Arguments on pages 189–190 to envision the view you want to advocate on that issue. What might the core of your argument be? Who is your target audience? Are you representing a group, club, or other organization? What image(s) might be effective in attracting and moving this audience? Possible topics for issues might be commuter parking; poor conditions in the computer lab; student reluctance to use the counseling center; problems with dorm life, financial aid programs, or intramural sports; ways to improve orientation programs for new students, work-study programs, or travel abroad opportunities; or new initiatives such as study groups for the big lecture courses or new service-learning opportunities.   ■ ■ ■

Using Information Graphics in Arguments

Besides images in the form of photographs and drawings, writers often use quantitative graphics to support arguments using numbers. In Chapter 5 we introduced you to the use of quantitative data in arguments. We discussed the persuasiveness of numbers and showed you ways to use them responsibly in your arguments. With the advent of spreadsheet and presentation programs, today's writers often create and import quantitative graphics into their documents. These visuals—such as tables, pie charts, and line or bar graphs—can have great rhetorical power by making numbers tell a story at a glance. In this section, we'll show you how quantitative graphics can make numbers speak. We'll also show you how to analyze graphics, incorporate them into your text, and reference them effectively.

How Tables Contain a Variety of Stories

Data used in arguments usually have their origins in raw numbers collected from surveys, questionnaires, observational studies, scientific experiments, and so forth.

Through a series of calculations, the numbers are combined, sorted, and arranged in a meaningful fashion, often in detailed tables. Some of the tables published by the U.S. Census Bureau, for example, contain dozens of pages. The more dense the table, the more their use is restricted to statistical experts who pore over them to analyze their meanings. More useful to the general public are midlevel tables contained on one or two pages that report data at a higher level of abstraction.

Consider, for example, Table 9.2, published by the U.S. Census Bureau in its document "America's Families and Living Arrangements: Population Characteristics," based on the 2000 census. This table shows the marital status of people age 15 and older, broken into gender and age groupings, in March 2000. It also provides comparative data on the "never married" percentage of the population in March 2000 and March 1970.

Take a few moments to peruse the table and be certain you know how to read it. You read tables in two directions: from top to bottom and from left to right. Always begin with the title, which tells you what the table contains and includes elements from both the vertical and horizontal dimensions of the table. In this case the vertical dimension presents demographic categories for people "15 years and over": for both sexes, for males, and for females. Each of these gender categories is subdivided into age categories. The horizontal dimension provides information about "marital status." Seven of the columns give total numbers (reported in thousands) for March 2000. The eighth column gives the "percent never married" for March 2000, while the last column gives the "percent never married" for March 1970. To make sure you know how to read the table, pick a couple of rows at random and say to yourself what each number means. For example, the first row under "Both sexes" gives total figures for the entire population of the United States age 15 and older. In March 2000 there were 213,773,000 people age 15 and older (remember that the numbers are presented in thousands). Of these, 113,002,000 were married and living with their spouses. As you continue across the columns, you'll see that 2,730,000 people were married but not living with their spouses (a spouse may be stationed overseas or in prison; or a married couple may be maintaining a "commuter marriage" with separate households in different cities). Continuing across the columns, you'll see that 4,479,000 people were separated from their spouses, 19,881,000 were divorced, and 13,665,000 were widowed, and an additional 60,016,000 were never married. In the next-to-last column, the number of never-married people is converted to a percentage: 28.1 percent. Finally, the last column shows the percentage of never-married people in 1970: 24.9%. These last two columns show us that the number of unmarried people in the United States rose 3.2 percentage points since 1970.

Now that you know how to read the table, examine it carefully to see the kinds of stories it tells. What does the table show you, for example, about the percentage of married people age 25–29 in 1970 versus 2000? What does it show about different age-related patterns of marriage in males and females? By showing you that Americans are waiting much later in life to get married, a table like this initiates many causal questions for analysis and argument. What has happened in American culture between 1970 and 2000 to explain the startling difference in the percentage of married people within, say, the 20–24 age bracket? In 2000 only 22 percent of people in this age bracket were married (we converted "unmarried" to "married" by subtracting 78.3 from 100). However, in 1970, 55 percent of people in this age bracket were married.

TABLE 9.2 Marital Status of People 15 Years and Over: March 1970 and March 2000 (in Thousands)

Characteristic	Total	March 2000 Number						Percent never married	March 1970 percent never married[a]
		Married spouse present	Married spouse absent	Separated	Divorced	Widowed	Never married		
Both sexes									
Total 15 years old and over.	213,773	113,002	2,730	4,479	19,881	13,665	60,016	28.1	24.9
15 to 19 years old.	20,102	345	36	103	64	13	19,541	97.2	93.9
20 to 24 years old.	18,440	3,362	134	234	269	11	14,430	78.3	44.5
25 to 29 years old.	18,269	8,334	280	459	917	27	8,252	45.2	14.7
30 to 34 years old.	19,519	11,930	278	546	1,616	78	5,071	26.0	7.8
35 to 44 years old.	44,804	29,353	717	1,436	5,967	399	6,932	15.5	5.9
45 to 54 years old.	36,633	25,460	492	899	5,597	882	3,303	9.0	6.1
55 to 64 years old.	23,388	16,393	308	441	3,258	1,770	1,218	5.2	7.2
65 years old and over.	32,620	17,827	485	361	2,193	10,484	1,270	3.9	7.6
Males									
Total 15 years old and over.	103,113	56,501	1,365	1,818	8,572	2,604	32,253	31.3	28.1
15 to 19 years old.	10,295	69	3	51	29	3	10,140	98.5	97.4
20 to 24 years old.	9,208	1,252	75	70	101	-	7,710	83.7	54.7
25 to 29 years old.	8,943	3,658	139	170	342	9	4,625	51.7	19.1
30 to 34 years old.	9,622	5,640	151	205	712	15	2,899	30.1	9.4
35 to 44 years old.	22,134	14,310	387	585	2,775	96	3,981	18.0	6.7
45 to 54 years old.	17,891	13,027	255	378	2,377	157	1,697	9.5	7.5
55 to 64 years old.	11,137	8,463	158	188	1,387	329	612	5.5	7.8
65 years old and over.	13,885	10,084	197	171	849	1,994	590	4.2	7.5
Females									
Total 15 years old and over.	110,660	56,501	1,365	2,661	11,309	11,061	27,763	25.1	22.1
15 to 19 years old.	9,807	276	33	52	35	10	9,401	95.9	90.3
20 to 24 years old.	9,232	2,110	59	164	168	11	6,720	72.8	35.8
25 to 29 years old.	9,326	4,676	141	289	575	18	3,627	38.9	10.5
30 to 34 years old.	9,897	6,290	127	341	904	63	2,172	21.9	6.2
35 to 44 years old.	22,670	15,043	330	851	3,192	303	2,951	13.0	5.2
45 to 54 years old.	18,742	12,433	237	521	3,220	725	1,606	8.6	4.9
55 to 64 years old.	12,251	7,930	150	253	1,871	1,441	606	4.9	6.8
65 years old and over.	18,735	7,743	288	190	1,344	8,490	680	3.6	7.7

[a] The 1970 percentages include 14-year-olds, and thus are for 14+ and 14–19.

Source: U.S. Census Bureau, Current Population Survey, March 2000.

Using a Graph to Tell a Story

Table 9.2, as we have seen, tells the story of how Americans are postponing marriage. However, one has to tease out the story from the dense columns of numbers. To focus on a key story and make it powerfully immediate, you can create a graph.

Bar Graphs   Suppose you are writing an argument in which you want to show that the percentage of married women in the 20–29 age bracket has dropped significantly since 1970. You could tell this story through a bar graph (Figure 9.17).

Bar graphs use bars of varying length, extending either horizontally or vertically, to contrast two or more quantities. As with any graphic presentation, you must create a comprehensive title. In the case of bar graphs, titles tell readers what is being compared to what. Most bar graphs also have "legends," which explain what the different features on the graph represent. Bars are typically distinguished from each other by use of different colors, shades, or patterns of crosshatching. The special power of bar graphs is that they can help readers make quick comparisons.

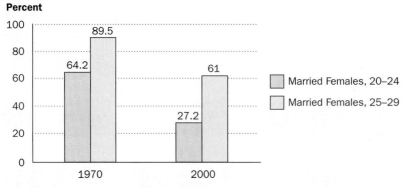

FIGURE 9.17   Percentage of married females ages 20–29, 1970 and 2000
Source: U.S. Census Bureau, *Current Population Survey,* March 2000.

Pie Charts   Another vivid kind of graph is a pie chart or circle graph, which depicts different percentages of a total (the pie) in the form of slices. Pie charts are a favorite way of depicting the way parts of a whole are divided up. Suppose, for example, that you wanted your readers to notice the high percentage of widows among women age 65 and older. To do so, you could create a pie chart (Figure 9.18) based on the data in the last row of Table 9.2. As you can see, a pie chart shows at a glance how the whole of something is divided into segments. The effectiveness of pie charts diminishes as you add more slices. In most cases, you'll begin to confuse readers if you include more than five or six slices.

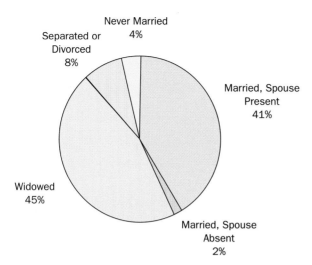

FIGURE 9.18 Marital status of females age 65 and older, 2000

Source: U.S. Census Bureau, *Current Population Survey,* March 2000.

Line Graphs   Another powerful quantitative graphic is a line graph, which converts numerical data into a series of points on a grid and connects them to create flat, rising, or falling lines. The result gives us a picture of the relationship between the variables represented on the horizontal and vertical axes.

Suppose you wanted to tell the story of the rising number of separated/divorced women in the U.S. population. Using Table 9.2, you can calculate the percentage of separated/divorced females in 2000 by adding the number of separated females (2,661,000) and the number of divorced females (11,309,000) and dividing that sum by the total number of females (110,660,000). The result is 12.6 percent. You can make the same calculations for 1990, 1980, and 1970 by looking at U.S. census data from those years (available on the Web or in your library). The resulting line graph is shown in Figure 9.19.

To determine what this graph is telling you, you need to clarify what's represented on the two axes. By convention, the horizontal axis of a graph contains the predictable, known variable that has no surprises—what researchers call the "independent variable." In this case the horizontal axis represents the years 1970–2000 arranged predictably in chronological order. The vertical axis contains the unpredictable variable that forms the graph's story—what researchers call the "dependent variable"—in this case, the percentage of divorced females. The ascending curve tells the story at a glance.

Note that with line graphs the steepness of a slope (and hence the rhetorical effect) can be manipulated by the intervals chosen for the vertical axis. Figure 9.19 shows vertical intervals of 2 percent. The slope could be made less dramatic by choosing intervals of, say, 10 percent and more dramatic by choosing intervals of 1 percent.

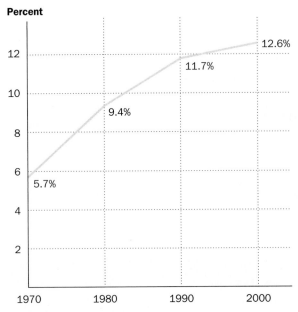

Percent

FIGURE 9.19 Percentage of females age 15 and older who are separated or divorced, 1970–2000
Source: U.S. Census Bureau, *Current Population Survey,* March 2000.

Incorporating Graphics into Your Argument

Today writers working with quantitative data usually use graphing software that automatically creates tables, graphs, or charts from data entered into the cells of a spreadsheet. For college papers, some instructors may allow you to make your graphs with pencil and ruler and paste them into your document.

Designing the Graphic When you design your graphic, your goal is to have a specific rhetorical effect on your readers, not to demonstrate all the bells and whistles available on your software. Adding extraneous data in the graph or chart or using such features as a three-dimensional effect can often distract from the story you are trying to tell. Keep the graphic as uncluttered and simple as possible and design it so that it reinforces the point you are making.

Numbering, Labeling, and Titling the Graphic In newspapers and popular magazines, writers often include graphics in boxes or sidebars without specifically referring to them in the text itself. However, in academic or professional workplace writing, graphics are always labeled, numbered, titled, and referred to directly in the text. By convention, tables are listed as "Tables," whereas line graphs, bar graphs, pie charts, or any other kinds of drawings or photographs are labeled as "Figures." Suppose you create a document that includes four graphics—a table, a bar graph, a pie chart, and a photograph. The table would be labeled as Table 1. The rest would be labeled as Figure 1, Figure 2, and Figure 3.

In addition to numbering and labeling, every graphic needs a comprehensive title that explains fully what information is being displayed. Look back over the tables and figures in this chapter and compare their titles to the information in the graphics. In a line graph showing changes over time, for example, a typical title will identify the information on both the horizontal and vertical axes and the years covered. Bar graphs also have a "legend" explaining how the bars are coded if necessary. When you import the graphic into your own text, be consistent in where you place the title—either above the graphic or below it.

Referencing the Graphic in Your Text   Academic and professional writers follow a referencing convention called *independent redundancy.* The general rule is this: the graphic should be understandable without the text; the text should be understandable without the graphic; the text should repeat the most important information in the graphic. An example is shown in Figure 9.20.

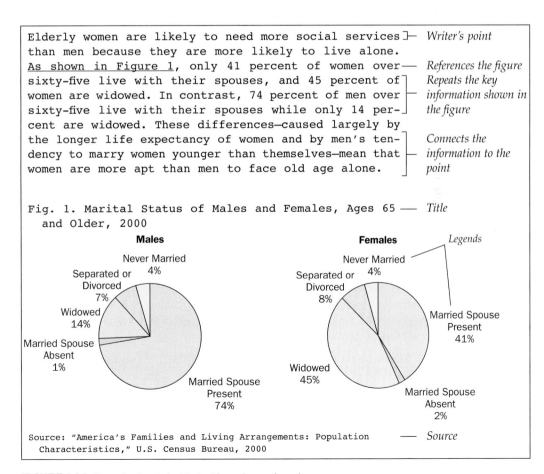

FIGURE 9.20 Example of a student text with a referenced graph

Conclusion

In this chapter we have explained the challenge and power of using visuals in arguments. We have examined the components of visual design—use of type, layout, color, and images—and shown how these components can be used for persuasive effect in arguments. We have also described the argumentative genres that depend on effective use of visuals—posters and fliers, advocacy advertisements, cartoons, and Web pages—and invited you to produce your own visual argument. Finally, we showed you that graphics can tell a numeric story in a highly focused and dramatic way. Particularly we explained the functions of tables, bar graphs, pie charts, and line graphs, and showed you how to incorporate into and reference graphics in your own prose.

WRITING ASSIGNMENT A Visual Argument Rhetorical Analysis, a Poster Argument, or a Microtheme Using Quantitative Data

Option 1: Writing a Rhetorical Analysis of a Visual Argument   Write a thesis-driven rhetorical analysis essay in which you examine the rhetorical effectiveness of a visual argument, either one of the visual arguments in this text or one specified by your instructor. Unless otherwise stated, direct your analysis to an audience of your classmates. In your introduction, establish the argumentative conversation to which this argument is contributing. Briefly summarize the argument and describe the visual text. Present your thesis, highlighting two or more rhetorical features of the argument that you find central to the effectiveness or ineffectiveness of this argument. To develop and support your own points, you will need to include visual features and details (such as color, design, camera angle, framing, and special effects) as well as short quotations from any verbal parts of the argument.

Option 2: A Poster Argument   Working with the idea for a poster argument that you explored in For Class Discussion on pages 191, use the visual design concepts and principles presented on pages 189–190, your understanding of visual argument and the genre of poster arguments, and your own creativity to produce a poster argument that can be displayed on your campus or in your town or city. Try out the draft of your poster argument on people who are part of your target audience. Based on these individuals' suggestions for improving the clarity and impact of this visual argument, prepare a final version of your poster argument.

Option 3: A Microtheme Using a Quantitative Graphic   Write a microtheme that tells a story based on data you select from Table 9.2 or from some other table provided by your instructor or located by you. Include in your microtheme at least one quantitative graphic (table, line graph, bar graph, pie chart), which should be labeled and referenced according to standard conventions. Use as a model the short piece shown in Figure 9.20 on page 197. ■

PEARSON
mycomplab   For additional writing, reading, and research resources, go to
                         www.mycomplab.com

PART FOUR

Arguments in Depth

Five Types of Claims

A shortage of body organs and long waiting lists have motivated some people to make personal appeals to the public on billboards like this one. In Chapter 14, a reading and the "Critiquing" exercise on pages 308–309 ask you to think about the evaluation and ethical issues involved in advertising for organs and in the selling and trading of body organs.

10 An Introduction to the Types of Claims

In Parts One, Two, and Three of this text, we showed how argument entails both inquiry and persuasion. We explained strategies for creating a compelling structure of reasons and evidence for your arguments (*logos*), for linking your arguments to the beliefs and values of your audience (*pathos*), and for establishing your credibility and trustfulness (*ethos*). We also explained how to do a rhetorical analysis of both verbal and visual texts.

Now in Part Four we examine arguments in depth by explaining five types of claims, each type having its own characteristic patterns of development and support. Because almost all arguments use one or more of these types of claims as "moves" or building blocks, knowing how to develop each claim type will advance your skills in argument. The claims we examine in Part Four are related to an ancient rhetorical concept called *stasis*, from a Greek term meaning "stand," as in "to take a stand on something." There are many competing theories of stasis, so no two rhetoricians discuss stasis in exactly the same way. But all the theories have valuable components in common.

In Part Four we present our own version of stasis theory, or, to use more ordinary language, our own approach to argument based on the types of claims. Understanding types of claims will pay off for you in two ways:

- It will help you focus an argument, generate ideas for it, and structure it persuasively.
- It will increase your flexibility as an arguer by showing you how most arguments are hybrids of different claim types working together.

An Overview of the Types of Claims

To appreciate what a study of claim types can do, imagine one of those heated but frustrating arguments in which the question at issue keeps shifting. Everyone talks at cross-purposes, each speaker's point unconnected to the previous speaker's. Suppose your heated discussion is about use of steroids. You might get such a discussion back on track if one person says: "Hold it for a moment. What are we actually arguing about here? Are we arguing about whether steroids are a health risk or whether steroids should be banned from sports? These are two different issues. We can't debate both at once." Whether she recognizes it or not, this person is applying the concept of claim types to get the argument focused.

To understand how claim types work, let's return to the concept of stasis. A stasis is an issue or question that focuses a point of disagreement. You and your audience may agree on the answer to question A and so have nothing to argue about. Likewise you may agree on the answer to question B. But on question C you disagree. Question C constitutes a stasis where you and your audience diverge. It is the place where disagreement begins, where as an arguer you take a stand against another view. Thus you and your audience may agree that steroids, if used carefully under a physician's supervision, pose few long-term health risks but still disagree on whether steroids should be banned from sports. This last issue constitutes a stasis, the point where you and your audience part company.

Rhetoricians have discovered that the kinds of questions that divide people have classifiable patterns. In this text we identify five broad types of claims—each type originating in a different kind of question. The following chart gives you a quick overview of these five types of claims, each of which is developed in more detail in subsequent chapters in Part Four. It also shows you a typical structure for each type of argument. Note that the first three claim types concern questions of truth or reality, whereas the last two concern questions of value. You'll appreciate the significance of this distinction as this chapter progresses.

Claims about Reality, Truth, or the Way Things Are

Claim Type and Generic Question	Examples of Issue Questions	Typical Methods for Structuring an Argument
Definitional arguments: *In what category does this thing belong?* (Chapter 11)	▪ Is sleep deprivation torture? ▪ Is an expert video game player an athlete?	▪ Create a definition that establishes criteria for the category. ▪ Use examples to show how the contested case meets the criteria.
Causal arguments: *What are the causes or consequences of this phenomenon?* (Chapter 12)	▪ What are the causes of autism? ▪ What might be the consequences of requiring a national ID card?	▪ Explain the links in a causal chain going from cause to effect. [or] ▪ Speculate about causes (consequences) or propose a surprising cause (consequence).
Resemblance arguments: *To what is this thing similar?* (Chapter 13)	▪ Is opposition to gay marriage like opposition to interracial marriage? ▪ Is steroid use to improve strength similar to LASIK surgery to improve vision?	▪ Let the analogy or precedent itself create the desired rhetorical-effect. [or] ▪ Elaborate on the relevant similarities between the given case and the analogy or precedent.

202 PART 4 Arguments in Depth

Claims about Values

Claim Type and Generic Question	Examples of Issue Questioins	Typical Methods for Structuring an Arguement
Evaluation and ethical arguments: *What is the worth or value of this thing?* (Chapter 14)	▪ Is behavior modification a good therapy for anxiety? ▪ Is it ethical to use steroids in sports?	▪ Establish the criteria for a "good" or "ethical" member of this class or category. ▪ Use examples to show how the contested case meets the criteria.
Proposal arguments *What action should we take?* (Chapter 15)	▪ Should the United State enact a single-payer health care system? ▪ To solve the problem of prison overcrowding, should we legalize possession of drugs?	▪ Make the problem vivid. ▪ Explain your solution. ▪ Justify your solution by showing how it is motivated by principle, by good consequences, or by resemblance to a previous action the audience approves.

▪ ▪ ▪ **FOR CLASS DISCUSSION** Identifying Types of Claims

Working as a class or in small groups, read the following questions and decide which claim type is represented by each. Sometimes the claim types overlap or blend together, so if the question fits two categories, explain your reasoning.

1. Should overnight camping be permitted in this state park?
2. Is taking Adderall to increase concentration for an exam a form of cheating?
3. Will an increase in gas taxes lead to a reduction in road congestion?
4. Is depression a learned behavior?
5. Were the terrorist attacks of September 11, 2001, more like Pearl Harbor (an act of war) or more like an earthquake (a natural disaster)?
6. How effective is acupuncture in reducing morning sickness?
7. Is acupuncture quackery or real medicine?
8. Should cities use tax dollars to fund professional sports arenas?
9. Are Mattel toy factories sweatshops?
10. Why are couples who live together before marriage more likely to divorce than couples who don't live together?

▪ ▪ ▪

Using Claim Types to Focus an Argument and Generate Ideas: An Example

Having provided an overview of the types of claims, we now show you some of the benefits of this knowledge. First of all, understanding claim types will help you focus an argument by asking you to determine what's at stake between you and your audience. Where do you and your audience agree and disagree? What are the questions at issue? Second, it will help you generate ideas for your argument by suggesting the kinds of reasons, examples, and evidence you'll need.

To illustrate, let's take a hypothetical case—one Isaac Charles Little (affectionately known as I. C. Little), who desires to chuck his contact lenses and undergo the new LASIK procedure to cure his nearsightedness. LASIK, or laser in-situ keratomileusis, is a surgical treatment for myopia. Sometimes known as "flap and zap" surgery, it involves using a laser to cut a thin layer of the cornea and then flattening it. It's usually not covered by insurance and is quite expensive.

I. C. Little has two different arguments he'd like to make: (1) he'd like to talk his parents into helping him pay for the procedure, and (2) he'd like to join with others who are trying to convince insurance companies that the LASIK procedure should be covered under standard medical insurance policies. In the discussions that follow, note how the five types of claims can help I. C. identify points of disagreement for each audience and simultaneously suggest lines of argument for persuading each one. Note, too, how the questions at issue vary for each audience.

Making the LASIK Argument to Parents

First imagine what might be at stake in I. C.'s discussions with his parents. Here is how thinking about claim types will help him generate ideas:

- *Definition argument:* Because I. C.'s parents will be concerned about the safety of LASIK surgery, the first stasis for I. C.'s argument is a question about categories: Is LASIK a safe procedure? I. C.'s mom has read about serious complications from LASIK and has also heard that ophthalmologists prefer patients to be at least in their midtwenties or older, so I. C. knows he will have to persuade her that the procedure is safe for twenty-year-olds.
- *Causal argument:* Both parents will question I. C.'s underlying motivation for seeking this surgery. "Why do you want this LASIK procedure?" they will ask. (I. C.'s dad, who has worn eyeglasses all his life, will not be swayed by cosmetic desires. "If you don't like contacts," he will say, "just wear glasses.") Here I. C. needs to argue the good consequences of LASIK. Permanently correcting his nearsightedness will improve his quality of life and even his academic and professional options. I. C. decides to emphasize his desire for an active, outdoor life, and especially his passion for water sports, where his need for contacts is a serious handicap. He is even thinking of majoring in marine biology, so LASIK surgery would help him professionally. He says that wearing scuba equipment is easier without worrying about contact lenses or corrective goggles.
- *Resemblance argument:* I. C. can't think of any resemblance questions at issue.
- *Evaluation argument:* When the pluses and minuses are weighed, is LASIK a good way to treat nearsightedness? Is it also a good way for the parents to spend family money? Would the results of the surgery be beneficial enough to justify the cost and the risks? In terms of costs, I. C. might argue that even though the

procedure is initially expensive (from $1,000 to $4,000), over the years he will save money by not needing glasses or contacts. The convenience of seeing well in the water and not being bothered by glasses or contacts while hiking and camping constitutes a major benefit. (Even though he thinks he'll look cooler without glasses, he decides not to mention the cosmetic benefits because his dad thinks wearing glasses is fine.)

■ *Proposal argument:* Should I. C.'s parents pay for a LASIK procedure to treat their son's nearsightedness? (All the previous points of disagreement are subissues related to this overarching proposal issue.)

This example shows that writers often need to argue issues of reality and truth in order to make claims about values. In this particular case, I. C. would need to convince his parents (1) that the procedure is safe (definition argument), (2) that the consequences of the procedure would be beneficial recreationally and professionally (causal argument), and (3) that the benefits outweigh the costs (evaluation argument). Only then would I. C. be able to persuade his parents (4) that he should have LASIK surgery with their financial help (proposal claim). Almost all arguments combine subarguments in this way so that lower-order claims provide supporting materials for addressing higher-order claims.

Making the LASIK Argument to Insurance Companies

The previous illustration focused on parents as audience. If we now switch audiences, we can use our claim types to identify different questions at issue. Let's suppose I. C. wants to persuade insurance companies to cover the LASIK procedure. He imagines his primary audience as insurance company executives, along with the general public and state legislators, who may be able to influence them. Again, I. C. generates ideas by considering the claim types.

■ *Definition argument:* For this audience the issue of safety is no longer relevant. (They share I. C.'s belief that LASIK is a safe procedure.) What's at stake is another definition issue: Should LASIK be considered "cosmetic surgery" (as insurance companies contend) or "medically justifiable surgery" (as I. C. contends)? This definitional question constitutes a major stasis. I. C. wants to convince his audience that LASIK belongs in the category of "medically justifiable surgery" rather than "cosmetic surgery." He will need to define "medically justifiable surgery" in such a way that LASIK can be included.

■ *Causal argument:* What will be the consequences to insurance companies and to the general public of making insurance companies pay for LASIK? Will there be an overwhelming crush of claims for LASIK surgery? Will there be a corresponding decrease in claims for eye exams, contacts, and glasses? What will happen to the cost of insurance?

■ *Resemblance argument:* Does LASIK more resemble a face-lift (not covered by insurance) or plastic surgery to repair a cleft palate (covered by insurance)?

- *Evaluation argument:* Would it be good for society as a whole if insurance companies had to pay for LASIK?
- *Proposal argument:* Should insurance companies be required to cover LASIK?

As this analysis shows, the questions at issue change when you consider a different audience. Now the chief question at issue is definition: Is LASIK cosmetic surgery or medically justifiable surgery? I. C. does not need to argue that the surgery is safe (a major concern for his parents); instead he must establish criteria for "medically justifiable surgery" and then argue that LASIK meets these criteria. Again note how the higher-order issues of value depend on resolving one or more lower-order issues of reality and truth.

Note also that any of the claim type examples just described could be used as the major focus of an argument. If I. C. were not concerned about a values issue (his proposal claims), he might tackle only a reality/truth issue. He could, for example, focus an entire argument on a definition question about categories: "Is LASIK safe?" (an argument requiring him to research the medical literature). Likewise he could write a causal argument focusing on what might happen to optometrists and eyeglass manufacturers if the insurance industry decided to cover LASIK.

The key insight here is that when you develop an argument, you may have to work through issues of reality and truth before you can tackle a values issue and argue for change or action. Before you embark on writing an evaluation or proposal argument, you must first consider whether you need to resolve a lower-order claim based on reality and truth.

Hybrid Arguments: How Claim Types Work Together in Arguments

As the LASIK example shows, hybrid arguments can be built from different claim types. A writer might develop a proposal argument with a causal subargument in one section, a resemblance subargument in another section, and an evaluation subargument in still another section. Although the overarching proposal argument follows the typical structure of a proposal, each of the subsections follows a typical structure for its own claim type.

Some Examples of Hybrid Arguments

The examples on page 206 show how these combinations of claim types can play out in actual arguments. (For more examples of these kinds of hybrid arguments, see Chapter 15, pages 318–320, where we explain how lower-order claims about reality and truth can support higher-order claims about values.)

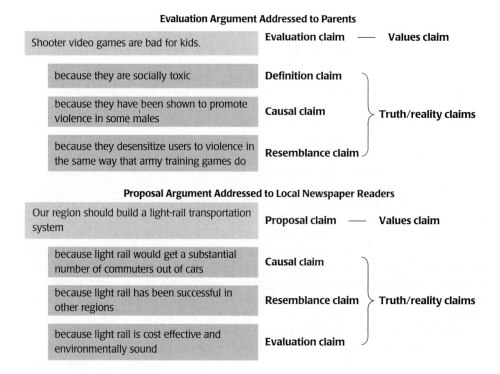

Evaluation Argument Addressed to Parents

Shooter video games are bad for kids.	Evaluation claim —— Values claim
because they are socially toxic	Definition claim
because they have been shown to promote violence in some males	Causal claim — Truth/reality claims
because they desensitize users to violence in the same way that army training games do	Resemblance claim

Proposal Argument Addressed to Local Newspaper Readers

Our region should build a light-rail transportation system	Proposal claim —— Values claim
because light rail would get a substantial number of commuters out of cars	Causal claim
because light rail has been successful in other regions	Resemblance claim — Truth/reality claims
because light rail is cost effective and environmentally sound	Evaluation claim

■ ■ ■ **FOR CLASS DISCUSSION** Exploring Different Claim Types and Audiences

1. Select an issue familiar to most members of the class—perhaps a current campus issue or an issue prominent in the local or national news—and generate possible issue questions and arguments using the claim types. Take as your models our discussion of I. C. Little's arguments about LASIK surgery. Consider how a writer or speaker might address two different audiences on this issue with a different purpose for each audience.

2. The following is the table of contents for a "friend of the court" legal brief opposing a contested Missouri law outlawing sale of violent video games to minors. How would you classify the claims put forward in this brief?

   ■ What is the overarching claim of this legal brief? What claim type is it?

   ■ What are the claim types for major sections I, II, and III? (Note: Section III develops two different claims: (a) violent video games are a form of fantasy violence and (b) fantasy violence can be good.

   ■ How does the "friend of the court" brief try to rebut the argument against violent video games shown in the example above?

No. 02-3010
In the
United States Court of Appeals for the Eighth Circuit
INTERACTIVE DIGITAL SOFTWARE ASS'N, et al.
Plaintiffs - Appellants,
v.
ST. LOUIS COUNTY, et al.

Defendants - Appellees

BRIEF *AMICI CURIAE* OF THIRTY-THREE MEDIA SCHOLARS
IN SUPPORT OF APPELLANTS, AND SUPPORTING REVERSAL

CONTENTS

An Extended Example of a Hybrid Argument

As the previous examples illustrate, different claim types often serve as building blocks for larger arguments. We ask you now to consider a more extended example. Read the following op-ed piece arguing the proposal claim that "New York City should ban car alarms." Note how the reasons are different claim-type subarguments that develop the overall proposal claim.

    As you can see, the thesis of Friedman's op-ed piece is a proposal claim, and the article follows the typical problem-solution structure of proposal arguments. Although the whole argument follows a proposal shape, the individual pieces—the various subarguments that support the main argument—comprise different kinds of claim types with their own characteristic structures.

All That Noise for Nothing

AARON FRIEDMAN

Main proposal claim:
City Council should
ban car alarms

Early next year, the New York City Council is supposed to hold a final hearing on legislation that would silence the most hated of urban noises: the car alarm. With similar measures having failed in the past, and with Mayor Michael R. Bloomberg withholding his support for the latest bill, let's hope the Council does right by the citizens it represents.

Reason 1: A
definitional claim
supported with
examples: Car
alarms belong in the
category of things
that harass

Every day, car alarms harass thousands of New Yorkers—rousing sleepers, disturbing readers, interrupting conversations and contributing to quality-of-life concerns that propel many weary residents to abandon the city for the suburbs. According to the Census Bureau, more New Yorkers are now bothered by traffic noise, including car alarms, than by any other aspect of city life, including crime or the condition of schools.

Reason 2: An
evaluation claim

So there must be a compelling reason for us to endure all this aggravation, right? Amazingly, no. Many car manufacturers, criminologists and insurers agree that car alarms are ineffective. When the nonprofit Highway Loss Data Institute surveyed insurance-claims data from 73 million vehicles nationwide in 1997, they concluded that cars with alarms "show no overall reduction in theft losses" compared with cars without alarms.

Criteria and evidence
supporting the
evaluation claim

There are two reasons they don't prevent theft. First, the vast majority of blaring sirens are false alarms, set off by passing traffic, the jostling of urban life or nothing at all. City dwellers quickly learn to disregard these cars crying wolf; a recent national survey by the Progressive Insurance Company found that fewer than 1 percent of respondents would call the police upon hearing an alarm.

5   In 1992, a car alarm industry spokesman, Darrell Issa (if you know his name that's because he would later spearhead the recall of Gov. Gray Davis in California), told the New York City Council that an alarm is effective "only in areas where the sound causes the dispatch of the police or attracts the owner's attention." In New York, this just doesn't happen.

Car alarms also fail for a second reason: they are easy to disable. Most stolen cars are taken by professional car thieves, and they know how to deactivate an alarm in just a few seconds.

Reason 3: A causal
claim developed
with causal links

Perversely, alarms can encourage more crime than they prevent. The New York Police Department, in its 1994 booklet "Police Strategy No. 5," explains how alarms (which "frequently go off for no apparent reason") can shatter the sense of civility that makes a community safe. As one of the "signs that no one cares," the department wrote, car alarms "invite both further disorder and serious crime."

I've seen some of my neighbors in Washington Heights illustrate this by taking revenge on alarmed cars: puncturing tires, even throwing a toaster oven through a windshield. False alarms enrage otherwise lawful citizens, and alienate the very people car owners depend on to call the police. In other words, car alarms work about as well as fuzzy dice at deterring theft while irritating entire neighborhoods.

Humorous resemblance claim sums up problem

The best solution is to ban them, as proposed by the sponsors of the City Council legislation, John Liu and Eva Moskowitz. The police could simply ticket or tow offending cars. This would be a great improvement over the current laws, which include limiting audible alarms to three minutes—something that has proved to be nearly impossible to enforce.

Main proposal claim, restated as evalution claim and supported by three criteria

10   Car owners could easily comply: more than 50 car alarm installation shops throughout the city have already pledged to disable alarms at no cost, according to a survey by the Center for Automotive Security Innovation.

And there is a viable alternative. People worried about protecting their cars can buy what are called silent engine immobilizers. Many European cars and virtually every new General Motors and Ford vehicle use the technology, in which a computer chip in the ignition key communicates with the engine. Without the key, the only way to steal the car is to tow it away, something most thieves don't have the time for. In the meantime, the rest of us could finally get some sleep.

Thus writers enlist other claim-type subarguments in building main arguments. This knowledge can help you increase your flexibility and effectiveness as an arguer. It encourages you to become skilled at four different kinds of arguers' "moves": (1) providing examples and evidence to support a simple categorical claim; (2) using a criteria-match strategy to support a definition or evaluation claim; (3) showing links in a causal chain to support a cause/consequence claim; or (4) using analogies and precedents to support a resemblance claim.

In the following chapters in Part Four, we discuss each of the claim types in more detail, showing you how they work and how you can develop skills and strategies for supporting each type of claim.

For additional writing, reading, and research resources, go to www.mycomplab.com

11 Definitional Arguments

CASE 1   Is ConocoPhillips a "Green" Company?

Today, many corporations not ordinarily considered environmentally friendly try to define themselves as "green." In this corporate advertisement, ConocoPhillips uses strategies of visual and verbal rhetoric to position itself as a "green company" rather than an "oil company." How does the ad work to create a "green" definition for ConocoPhillips? What's at stake in this argument?

Tomorrow begins today.

We're defined by what we pass on to the next generation. That's why ConocoPhillips is funding college and university programs, like biofuels research at Iowa State University, to develop new energy sources. And we're stepping up our own research to create new, cleaner fuels and improve environmental performance. So we can pass on what matters . . . to the ones who matter most.

ConocoPhillips
Energy for tomorrow

www.conocophillips.com

CASE 2   Is a Frozen Embryo a Person or Property?

An infertile couple conceived several embryos in a test tube and then froze the fertilized embryos for future use. During the couple's divorce, they disagreed about the disposition of the embryos. The woman wanted to use the frozen embryos to try to get pregnant, and the man wanted to destroy them. When the courts were asked to decide what should be done with the embryos, several questions of definition arose. Should the frozen embryos be categorized as "persons," thus becoming analogous to children in custody disputes? Or should they be divided up as "property," with the man getting half and the woman getting the other half? Or should a new legal category be created for them that regards them as more than property but less than actual persons? The judge decided that frozen embryos "are not, strictly speaking, either 'persons' or 'property,' but occupy an interim category that entitles them to special respect because of their potential for human life."*

An Overview of Arguments About Definition

Definition arguments are arguments about what category something belongs to. They are among the most common argument types you will encounter. They occur whenever you claim that a particular person, thing, act, or phenomenon belongs (or does not belong) within a certain category. Here are some examples of claims involving categories and definitions:

Claim	Specific Phenomenon	Category
Piping loud rap music into a prison cell twenty-four hours a day constitutes torture.	Constant loud rap music	Torture
Graffiti is often art, rather than vandalism.	Graffiti	Art
My swerving off the road while trying to slap a bee on my windshield does not constitute "reckless driving."	Swerving off the road while killing a bee	Not "reckless driving"

Much is at stake when we place things into categories, because the category that something belongs to can have real consequences. For example, if you favor growing biotech corn, you want to place it in the broad category "corn" and keep the term "genetically engineered" off food labels. If you oppose it, you might classify it as "Frankenfood." Thus the categories we choose are really implicit mini-arguments with subtle but powerful consequences.

Consider the competing categories proposed for whales in an international controversy occasioned by the desire of traditional whaling nations to resume commercial whaling. What category does a whale belong to? Some arguers place whales in the category "sacred animals" that should never be killed because of their intelligence, beauty, grace, and power. Others categorize whales as a "renewable food resource" like tuna, crabs, cattle, and chickens. Others worry whether the kinds of whales being hunted are an "endangered species"—a category that argues for the preservation of whale stocks but not necessarily for a ban on controlled hunting of individual whales. Each of these whaling arguments places whales in a different category that implicitly urges the reader to adopt that category's perspective on whaling.

---

*See Vincent F. Stempel, "Procreative Rights in Assisted Reproductive Technology: Why the Angst?" *Albany Law Review* 62 (1999), 1187.

The Rule of Justice: Things in the Same Category Should Be Treated the Same Way

As you can see, how we define a given word can have significant implications for people who must either use the word or have the word used on them. To ensure fairness, philosophers refer to the *rule of justice,* which states that "beings in the same essential category should be treated in the same way." For example, it makes a huge difference to detainees in Guantanamo Bay, Cuba, whether they are classified as "prisoners of war" or as "unlawful combatants." In the first case, they have considerable rights under the Geneva Conventions, including the right to be released and returned to their native country when the war is over. In the latter case, they seem to have few if any rights (although the issue is being debated in the courts) and may be held indefinitely without charges. Or, to take a more homely example, if a professor says that absence from an exam can be excused for emergencies only, is attending your best friend's wedding an "emergency"? How about missing an exam because your car wouldn't start? Although your interests may be best served by a broad definition of emergency, your professor, in the desire to be just to all students, may benefit from a narrow definition.

The rule of justice becomes even harder to apply when we consider contested cases marked by growth or slow change through time. At what point does a child become an adult? When does a binge drinker become an alcoholic, an Internet poker player a compulsive gambler, or a fetus a human person? Although we may be able arbitrarily to choose a particular point and declare that "adult" means eighteen years old or that "human person" means a fetus at conception, or at three months, or at birth, in the everyday world the distinction between child and adult, between fetus and person, between Friday night poker playing and compulsive gambling seems an evolution, not a sudden and definitive step. Nevertheless, our language requires an abrupt shift between categories. In short, applying the rule of justice often requires us to adopt a digital approach to reality (switches are either on or off, either a fetus is a human person or it is not), whereas our sense of life is more analogical (there are numerous gradations between on and off, there are countless shades of gray between black and white).

As we can see by the preceding examples, the promise of language to fix what psychologist William James called "the buzz and confusion of the world" into an orderly set of categories turns out to be elusive. In most definitional debates, an argument, not a quick trip to the dictionary, is required to settle the matter.

■ ■ ■   **FOR CLASS DISCUSSION**   Applying the Rule of Justice

Suppose your landlord decides to institute a "no pets" rule. The rule of justice requires that all pets have to go—not just your neighbor's barking dog, but also Mrs. Brown's cat, the kids' hamster downstairs, and your own pet tarantula. That is, all these animals have to go unless you can argue that some of them are not "pets" for purposes of a landlord's "no pets" rule.

1. Working in small groups or as a whole class, define *pets* by establishing the criteria an animal would have to meet to be included in the category "pets." Consider your landlord's "no pets" rule as the cultural context for your definition.

2. Based on your criteria, which of the following animals is definitely a pet that would have to be removed from the apartment? Based on your criteria, which animals could you exclude from the "no pets" rule? How would you make your argument to your landlord?
   - a German shepherd
   - a small housecat
   - a tiny, well-trained lapdog
   - a gerbil in a cage
   - a canary
   - a tank of tropical fish
   - a tarantula

Types of Definitional Arguments

Categorical claims shift from implied mini-arguments to explicit extended arguments whenever the arguer supplies reasons and evidence that a given phenomenon does (or does not) belong in a certain category. Such arguments can be divided into two kinds:

1. *simple categorical arguments,* in which the writer and an audience agree on the meaning of the category, and
2. *definitional arguments,* in which there is a dispute about the boundaries of the category and hence of its definition.

Simple Categorical Arguments   A categorical argument can be said to be "simple" if there is no disagreement about the definition of the category. For example, suppose you oppose electing David as committee chair "because he is too bossy." Your supporting reason ("David is too bossy") is a simple categorical claim. You assume that everyone agrees what *bossy* means; the point of contention is whether David is or is not bossy. To support your claim, you would supply examples of David's bossiness. To refute it, someone else might supply counterexamples of David's cooperative and kind nature.

As shown in the following chart, the basic procedure for supporting (or rebutting) a simple categorical claim is to supply examples and other data that show how the contested phenomenon fits or doesn't fit into the category:

Strategies for Supporting or Rebutting Simple Categorical Claims

Categorical Claim	Strategies for Supporting Claim	Strategies for Rebutting Claim
Joe is too bossy.	Show examples of his bossy behavior (for example, his poor listening skills, his shouting at people, or his making decisions without asking the committee).	Show counterexamples revealing his ability to listen and create community; reinterpret bossiness as leadership behavior, putting Joe in better light.
Low-carb diets are dangerous.	Cite studies showing the dangers; explain how low-carb diets produce dangerous substances in the body; explain their harmful effects.	Show design problems in the scientific studies; cite studies with different findings; cite counter examples of people who lost weight on low-carb diets with no bad health effects.
Little Green Footballs is a conservative blog.	Give examples of the conservative views it promotes; show the conservative leanings of pundits often cited on the blog.	Give examples from the blog that don't fit neatly into a conservative perspective.

■ ■ ■ **FOR CLASS DISCUSSION** Supporting and Rebutting Categorical Claims

Working individually or in small groups, consider how you would support the following categorical claims. What examples or other data would convince readers that the specified case fits within the named category? Then discuss ways you might rebut each claim.

1. Sport-utility vehicles are environmentally unfriendly.
2. Nelly is a gangsta rapper.
3. Americans today are obsessed with their appearance.
4. College football coaches are overpaid.
5. Competitive cheerleading is physically risky.

■ ■ ■

Definitional Arguments   Simple categorical arguments morph into definitional arguments whenever stakeholders disagree about the boundaries of a category. Suppose in the previous exercise that you had said, "Well, that depends on how you define 'gangsta rapper' or 'overpaid.'" The need to define these terms adds a new layer of complexity to arguments about categories. To understand definitional arguments, one must distinguish between cases where definitions are *needed* and cases where definitions are *disputed*. Many arguments require a definition of key terms. If you are arguing, for example, that therapeutic cloning might lead to cures for various diseases, you would probably need to define *therapeutic cloning* and distinguish it from *reproductive cloning*. Writers regularly define key words for their readers by providing synonyms, by citing a dictionary definition, by offering their own definition, or by some other means.

In the rest of this chapter, we focus on arguments in which the meaning of a key term is disputed. Consider, for example, the environmental controversy over the

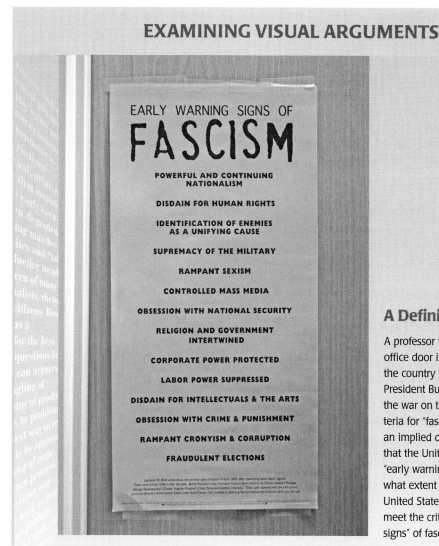

A Definitional Claim

A professor taped this poster to her office door in the mid-2000s when the country was divided over President Bush's policies, especially the war on terrorism. By stating criteria for "fascism," this poster makes an implied definitional argument that the United States is exhibiting "early warning signs" of fascism. To what extent do you think that the United States meets or does not meet the criteria for "early warning signs" of fascism?

definition of *wetland*. Section 404 of the federal Clean Water Act provides for federal protection of wetlands, but it leaves the task of defining *wetland* to administrative agencies and the courts. Currently about 5 percent of the land surface of the contiguous forty-eight states is potentially affected by the wetlands provision, and 75 percent of this land is privately owned. Efforts to define *wetland* have created a battleground between pro-environment and pro-development (or pro–private property rights) groups. Farmers, homeowners, and developers often want a narrow definition of wetlands so that more property is available for commercial or private use. Environmentalists favor a broad definition in order to protect different habitat types and maintain the environmental safeguards that wetland provide (control of water pollution, spawning grounds for aquatic species, floodwater containment, and so forth).

The problem is that defining *wetland* is tricky. For example, one federal regulation defines a wetland as any area that has a saturated ground surface for twenty-one consecutive days during the year. But how would you apply this law to a pine flatwood ecosystem that was wet for ten days this year but thirty days last year? And how should the courts react to lawsuits claiming that the regulation itself is either too broad or too narrow? One can see why the wetlands controversy provides hefty incomes for lawyers and congressional lobbyists.

The Criteria–Match Structure of Definitional Arguments

As the wetlands example suggests, definitional arguments usually have a two-part structure—(1) a definition part that tries to establish the boundaries of the category (What do we mean by *wetland*?) and (2) a match part that argues whether a given case meets that definition (Does this thirty-acre parcel of land near Swan Lake meet the criteria for a wetland?). To describe this structure, we use the term *criteria-match*. Here is an example:

> *Definitional issue:* In a divorce proceeding, is a frozen embryo a "person" rather than "property"?
>
> *Criteria part:* What criteria must be met for something to be a "person"?
>
> *Match part:* Does a frozen embryo meet these criteria?

Developing the Criteria-Match Structure for a Definitional Argument

To show how a definitional issue can be developed into a claim with supporting reasons, let's look more closely at this example:

> *Definitional issue:* For purposes of my feeling good about buying my next pair of running shoes, is the Hercules Shoe Company a socially responsible company?
>
> *Criteria part:* What criteria must be met for a company to be deemed "socially responsible"?
>
> *Match part:* Does the Hercules Shoe Company meet these criteria?

Let's suppose you work for a consumer information group that wishes to encourage patronage of socially responsible companies while boycotting irresponsible ones. Your group's first task is to define *socially responsible company*. After much discussion and research, your group establishes three criteria that a company must meet to be considered socially responsible:

> *Your definition:* A company is socially responsible if it (1) avoids polluting the environment, (2) sells goods or services that contribute to the well-being of the community, and (3) treats its workers justly.

The criteria section of your argument would explain and illustrate these criteria.

The match part of the argument would then try to persuade readers that a specific company does or does not meet the criteria. A typical thesis statement might be as follows:

> *Your thesis statement:* Although the Hercules Shoe Company is nonpolluting and provides a socially useful product, it is not a socially responsible company because it treats workers unjustly.

Toulmin Framework for a Definitional Argument

Here is how the core of the preceding Hercules definitional argument could be displayed in Toulmin terms. Note how the reason and grounds constitute the match argument while the warrant and backing constitute the criterion argument.

Toulmin Analysis of the Hercules Shoe Company Argument

ENTHYMEME

CLAIM The Hercules Shoe Company is not a socially responsible company

REASON because it treats workers unjustly.

CONDITIONS OF REBUTTAL
Attacking reasons and grounds

• Possible counter-evidence that the shops maintain humane working conditions

• Possible questioning of statistical data about hardships on displaced workers

GROUNDS

Evidence of unjust treatment:

• Evidence that the company manufactures its shoes in East Asian sweatshops

• Evidence of the inhumane conditions in these shops

• Evidence of hardships imposed on displaced American workers

WARRANT

Socially responsible companies treat workers justly.

BACKING

• Arguments showing that just treatment of workers is right in principle and also benefits society

• Arguments that capitalism helps society as a whole only if workers achieve a reasonable standard of living, have time for leisure, and are not exploited

CONDITIONS OF REBUTTAL
Attacking warrant and backing

Justice needs to be considered from an emerging nation's standpoint:

• The wages paid workers are low by American standards but are above average by East Asian standards.

• Displacement of American workers is part of the necessary adjustment of adapting to a global economy and does not mean that a company is unjust.

As this Toulmin schema illustrates, the writer's argument needs to contain a criteria section (warrant and backing) showing that just treatment of workers is a criterion for social responsibility and a match section (stated reason and grounds) showing that the Hercules Shoe Company does not treat its workers justly. Your audience's initial beliefs determine how much emphasis you need to place on justifying each criterion and supporting each match. The conditions of rebuttal help the writer imagine alternative views and see places where opposing views need to be acknowledged and rebutted.

■ ■ ■ **FOR CLASS DISCUSSION** Identifying Criteria and Match Issues
Consider the following definitional claims. Working individually or in small groups, identify the criteria issue and the match issue for each of the following claims.

> *Definitional issue:* A Honda assembled in Ohio is (is not) an American-made car.
>
> *Criteria part:* What criteria have to be met before a car can be called "American made"?
>
> *Match part:* Does a Honda assembled in Ohio meet these criteria?

1. American Sign Language is (is not) a "foreign language" for purposes of a college graduation requirement.
2. Burning an American flag is (is not) constitutionally protected free speech.
3. Bungee jumping from a crane is (is not) a "carnival amusement ride" subject to state safety inspections.
4. A Mazda Miata is (is not) a true sports car.
5. A race car driver is (is not) a true athlete.

■ ■ ■

Kinds of Definitions

In this section we discuss two methods of definition: Aristotelian and operational.

Aristotelian Definitions

Aristotelian definitions, regularly used in dictionaries, define a term by placing it within the next larger class or category and then showing the specific attributes that distinguish the term from other terms within the same category. For example, according to a legal dictionary, *robbery* is "the felonious taking of property" (next larger category) that differs from other acts of theft because it seizes property "through violence or intimidation." Legal dictionaries often provide specific examples to show the boundaries of the term. Here is one example:

> There is no robbery unless force or fear is used to overcome resistance. Thus, surreptitiously picking a man's pocket or snatching something from him without resistance on his part is *larceny,* but not robbery.

Many states specify degrees of robbery with increasingly heavy penalties. For example, *armed robbery* involves use of a weapon to threaten the victim. In all cases, *robbery* is distinguished from the lesser crime of *larceny,* in which no force or intimidation is involved.

As you can see, an Aristotelian definition of a term identifies specific attributes or criteria that enable you to distinguish it from other members of the next larger class. We created an Aristotelian definition in our example about socially responsible companies. A socially responsible company, we said, is any company (next larger class) that meets three criteria: (1) it doesn't pollute the environment; (2) it creates goods or services that promote the well-being of the community; and (3) it treats its workers justly.

In constructing Aristotelian definitions, you may find it useful to employ the concept of accidental, necessary, and sufficient criteria.

- An *accidental criterion* is a usual but not essential feature of a concept. For example, armed robbers frequently wear masks, but wearing a mask is an accidental criterion because it has no bearing on the definition of *robbery.* In our example about socially responsible companies, "makes regular contributions to charities" might be an accidental criterion; most socially responsible companies contribute to charities, but some do not. And many socially irresponsible companies also contribute to charities—often as a public relations ploy.
- A *necessary criterion* is an attribute that *must* be present for something to belong to the category being defined. To be guilty of robbery rather than larceny, a thief must have used direct force or intimidation. The use of force is thus a necessary criterion for robbery. However, for a robbery to occur another criterion must also be met: the robber must also take property from the victim.
- *Sufficient criteria* are all the criteria that must be present for something to belong to the category being defined. Together the use of force plus the taking of property are *sufficient criteria* for an act to be classified as robbery.

Consider again our defining criteria for a "socially responsible" company: (1) the company must avoid polluting the environment; (2) the company must create goods or services that contribute to the well-being of the community; **and** (3) the company must treat its workers justly. In this definition, each criterion is necessary, but none of the criteria alone is sufficient. In other words, to be defined as socially responsible, a company must meet all three criteria at once, as the word *and* signals. It is not enough for a company to be nonpolluting (a necessary but not sufficient criterion); if that company makes a shoddy product or treats its workers unjustly, it fails to meet the other necessary criteria and can't be deemed socially responsible. Because no one criterion by itself is sufficient, all three criteria together must be met before a company can be deemed socially responsible.

In contrast, consider the following definition of *sexual harassment* as established by the U.S. Equal Employment Opportunity Commission in its 1980 guidelines:

Unwelcome sexual advances, requests for sexual favors, and other verbal or physical conduct of a sexual nature constitute sexual harassment when (1) submission to such conduct is made either explicitly or implicitly a term or condition of an individual's employment, (2) submission to or rejection of such conduct by an individual is used as the basis for employment decisions affecting such individual, **or** (3) such conduct has the purpose or effect of unreasonably interfering with an individual's work performance or creating an intimidating, hostile, or offensive working environment.*

Here each of these criteria is sufficient, but none is necessary. In other words, an act constitutes sexual harassment if any one of the three criteria is satisfied, as the word *or* indicates.

■ ■ ■   **FOR CLASS DISCUSSION**   **Working with Criteria**
Working individually or in small groups, try to determine whether each of the following is a necessary criterion, a sufficient criterion, an accidental criterion, or no criterion for defining the indicated concept. Be prepared to explain your reasoning and to account for differences in points of view.

Criterion	**Concept to Be Defined**
Presence of gills	Fish
Profane and obscene language	R-rated movie
Line endings that form a rhyming pattern	Poem
Disciplining a child by spanking	Child abuse
Diet that excludes meat	Vegetarian
Killing another human being	Murder
Good sex life	Happy marriage

Operational Definitions

In some rhetorical situations, particularly those arising in the physical and social sciences, writers need precise *operational definitions* that can be measured empirically and are not subject to problems of context and disputed criteria. A social scientist studying the effects of television on aggression in children needs a precise, measurable definition of *aggression*. Typically, the scientist might measure "aggression" by counting the number of blows a child gives to an inflatable bobo doll over a fifteen-minute period when other play options are available. In our wetlands example, a federal authority created an operational definition of *wetland:* a wetland is a parcel of land that has a saturated ground surface for twenty-one consecutive days during the year.

---

*Quoted in Stephanie Riger, "Gender Dilemmas in Sexual Harassment Policies and Procedures," *American Psychologist* 46 (May 1991), 497–505.

Such operational definitions are useful because they are precisely measurable, but they are also limited because they omit criteria that may be unmeasurable but important. Thus, we might ask whether it is adequate to define a *superior student* as someone with a 3.5 GPA or higher or a *successful sex-education program* as one that results in a 25 percent reduction in teenage pregnancies. What important aspects of a superior student or a successful sex-education program are not considered in these operational definitions?

Conducting the Criteria Part of a Definitional Argument

In constructing criteria to define your contested term, either you can research how others have defined your term or you can make your own definitions. If you take the first approach, you turn to standard or specialized dictionaries, judicial opinions, or expert testimony to establish a definition based on the authority of others. A lawyer defining a wetland based on twenty-one consecutive days of saturated ground surface would be taking the first approach using federal regulation as his or her source. The other approach is to use your own critical thinking to make your own definition, thereby defining the contested term yourself. Our definition of a socially responsible company, specifying three criteria, is an example of an individual's own definition created through critical thinking. This section explains these approaches in more detail.

Approach 1: Research How Others Have Defined the Term

When you take this approach, you search for authoritative definitions acceptable to your audience yet favorable to your case. Student writer Kathy Sullivan uses this approach in her argument that photographs displayed at the Oncore Bar are not obscene (see pages 231–233). To define *obscenity,* she turns to *Black's Law Dictionary* and Pember's *Mass Media Laws.* (Specialized dictionaries are a standard part of the reference section of any library. See your reference librarian for assistance.) Other sources of specialized definitions are state and federal appellate court decisions, legislative and administrative statutes, and scholarly articles examining a given definitional conflict. Lawyers use this research strategy exhaustively in preparing court briefs. They begin by looking at the actual text of laws as passed by legislatures or written by administrative authorities. Then they look at all the court cases in which the laws have been tested and examine the ways courts have refined legal definitions and applied them to specific cases. Using these refined definitions, lawyers then apply them to their own case at hand.

If your research uncovers definitions that seem ambiguous or otherwise unfavorable to your case, you can sometimes appeal to the "original intentions" of those who defined the term. For example, if a scientist is dissatisfied with definitions of *wetland* based on consecutive days of saturated ground surface, she might proceed as follows:

"The original intention of Congress in passing the Clean Water Act was to preserve the environment." What Congress intended, she could then claim, was to prevent development of those wetland areas that provide crucial habitat for wildlife or that inhibit water pollution. She could then propose an alternative definition based on criteria other than consecutive days of ground saturation.

Approach 2: Create Your Own Extended Definition*

Often, however, you need to create your own definition of the contested term. An effective strategy is to establish initial criteria for your contested term by thinking of hypothetical cases that obviously fit the category you are trying to define and then by altering one or more variables until the hypothetical case obviously doesn't fit the category. You can then test and refine your criteria by applying them to borderline cases. For example, suppose you work at a homeless agency where you overhear street people discuss an incident that strikes you as potential "police brutality." You wonder whether you should write to your local paper to bring attention to the incident.

A Possible Case of Police Brutality

Two police officers confront an inebriated homeless man who is shouting obscenities on a street corner. The officers tell the man to quiet down and move on, but he keeps shouting obscenities. When the officers attempt to put the man into the police car, he resists and takes a wild swing at one of the officers. As eyewitnesses later testified, this officer shouted obscenities back at the drunk man, pinned his arms behind his back in order to handcuff him, and lifted him forcefully by the arms. The man screamed in pain and was later discovered to have a dislocated shoulder. Is this officer guilty of police brutality?

To your way of thinking, this officer seems guilty: An inebriated man is too uncoordinated to be a threat in a fight, and two police officers ought to be able to arrest him without dislocating his shoulder. But a friend argues that because the man took a swing at the officer the police were justified in using force. The dislocated shoulder was simply an accidental result of using justified force.

To make your case, you need to develop a definition of "police brutality." You can begin by creating a hypothetical case that is obviously an instance of "police brutality":

---

*The defining strategies and collaborative exercises in this section are based on the work of George Hillocks and his research associates at the University of Chicago. See George Hillocks Jr., Elizabeth A. Kahn, and Larry R. Johannessen, "Teaching Defining Strategies as a Mode of Inquiry: Some Effects on Student Writing," *Research in the Teaching of English* 17 (October 1983), 275–84. See also Larry R. Johannessen, Elizabeth A. Kahn, and Carolyn Calhoun Walter, *Designing and Sequencing Prewriting Activities* (Urbana, IL: NCTE, 1982).

A Clear Case of Police Brutality

A police officer confronts a drunk man shouting obscenities and begins hitting him in the face with his police baton. *[This is an obvious incidence of police brutality because the officer intentionally tries to hurt the drunk man without justification; hitting him with the baton is not necessary for making an arrest or getting the man into a police car.]*

You could then vary the hypothetical case until it is clearly *not* an instance of police brutality.

Cases that Are Clearly Not Police Brutality

Case 1: The police officer handcuffs the drunk man, who, in being helped into the police car, accidentally slips on the curb and dislocates his arm while falling. *[Here the injury occurs accidentally; the police officer does not act intentionally and is not negligent.]*

Case 2: The police officer confronts an armed robber fleeing from a scene and tackles him from behind, wrestling the gun away from him. In this struggle, the officer pins the robber's arm behind his back with such force that the robber's shoulder is dislocated. *[Here aggressive use of force is justified because the robber was armed, dangerous, and resisting arrest.]*

Using these hypothetical cases, you decide that the defining criteria for police brutality are (1) *intention* and (2) use of *excessive force*—that is, force beyond what was required by the immediate situation. After more contemplation, you are convinced that the officer was guilty of police brutality and have a clearer idea of how to make your argument. Here is how you might write the "match" part of your argument.

Match Argument Using Your Definition

If we define police brutality as the *intentional* use of *excessive* force, then the police officer is guilty. His action was intentional because he was purposefully responding to the homeless man's drunken swing and was angry enough to be shouting obscenities back at the drunk (according to an eyewitness). Second, he used excessive force in applying the handcuffs. A drunk man taking a wild swing hardly poses a serious danger to two police officers. Putting handcuffs on the drunk may have been justified, but lifting the man's arm violently enough to dislocate a shoulder indicates excessive force. The officer lifted the man's arms violently not because he needed to but because he was angry, and acting out of anger is no justification for that violence. In fact, we can charge police officers with "police brutality" precisely to protect us from being victims of police anger. It is the job of the court system to punish us, not the police's job. Because this officer acted intentionally and applied excessive force out of anger, he should be charged with police brutality.

The strategy we have demonstrated—developing criteria by imagining hypothetical cases that clearly do and do not belong to the contested category—gives you a systematic procedure for developing your own definition for your argument.

■ ■ ■   **FOR CLASS DISCUSSION**   **Developing a Definition**

1. Suppose you wanted to define the concept of *courage*. Working in groups, try to decide whether each of the following cases is an example of courage:
    a. A neighbor rushes into a burning house to rescue a child from certain death and emerges, coughing and choking, with the child in his arms. Is the neighbor courageous?
    b. A firefighter rushes into a burning house to rescue a child from certain death and emerges with the child in her arms. The firefighter is wearing protective clothing and a gas mask. When a newspaper reporter calls her courageous, she says, "Hey, this is my job." Is the firefighter courageous?
    c. A teenager rushes into a burning house to recover a memento given to him by his girlfriend, the first love of his life. Is the teenager courageous?
    d. A parent rushes into a burning house to save a trapped child. The fire marshal tells the parent to wait because there is no chance that the child can be reached from the first floor. The fire marshal wants to try cutting a hole in the roof to reach the child. The parent rushes into the house anyway and is burned to death. Was the parent courageous?
2. As you make your decisions on each of these cases, create and refine the criteria you use.
3. Make up your own series of controversial cases, like those given previously for "courage," for one or more of the following concepts:
    a. cruelty to animals
    b. child abuse
    c. true athlete
    d. sexual harassment
    e. free speech protected by the First Amendment

Then, using the strategy of making up hypothetical cases that do and do not belong to each category, construct a definition of your chosen concept.   ■ ■ ■

Conducting the Match Part of a Definitional Argument

In conducting a match argument, you need to supply examples and other evidence showing that your contested case does (does not) meet the criteria you established in your definition. In essence, you support the match part of your argument in much the same way you would support a simple categorical claim.

For example, if you were developing the argument that the Hercules Shoe Company is not socially responsible because it treats its workers unjustly, your match section would provide evidence of this injustice. You might supply data about the percentage of shoes produced in East Asia, about the low wages paid these workers, and about the working conditions in these factories. You might also describe the suffering of displaced American workers when Hercules closed its American factories and moved operations to Asia, where the labor was nonunion and cheap. The match section should also summarize and respond to opposing views.

WRITING ASSIGNMENT A Definitional Argument

Write an essay in which you argue that a borderline or contested case fits (or does not fit) within a given category. In the opening of your essay, introduce the borderline case you will examine and pose your definitional question. In the first part of your argument, define the boundaries of your category (criteria) by reporting a definition used by others or by developing your own extended definition. In the second part of your argument (the match), show how your borderline case meets (or doesn't meet) your definitional criteria.

Exploring Ideas

Ideally, in writing this argument you will join an ongoing conversation about a definitional issue that interests you. What cultural and social issues that concern you involve disputed definitions? In the public arena, you are likely to find numerous examples simply by looking through news stories—the strategy used by student writer Kathy Sullivan, who became interested in the controversy over allegedly obscene photographs in a gay bar (see pages 231–233). Other students have addressed definitional issues such as these: Is using TiVo to avoid TV commercials a form of theft? Is spanking a form of child abuse? Are cheerleaders athletes? Is flag burning protected free speech? Is a person who downloads instructions for making a bomb a terrorist? Are today's maximum-security prisons "cruel and unusual punishment"? Is Wal-Mart a socially responsible company? Can a man be a feminist?

If you have trouble discovering a local or national issue that interests you, you can create fascinating definitional controversies among your classmates by asking whether certain borderline cases are "true" or "real" examples of some category: Are highly skilled video game players (race car drivers, synchronized swimmers, marbles players) true athletes? Is a gourmet chef (skilled furniture maker, tagger) a true artist? Is a chiropractor (acupuncturist, naturopathic physician) a "real doctor"? Working as a whole class or in small groups inside or outside class, create an argumentative discussion on one or more of these issues. Listen to the various voices in the controversy, and then write out your own argument.

You can also stimulate definitional controversies by brainstorming borderline cases for such terms as *courage* (Is mountain climbing an act of courage?), *cruelty to animals* (Are rodeos [zoos, catch-and-release trout fishing, use of animals for medical research] cruelty to animals?), or *war crime* (Was the American firebombing of Tokyo in World War II a war crime?).

As you explore your definitional issue, try to determine how others have defined your category. If no stable definition emerges from your search, create your own definition by deciding what criteria must be met for a contested case to fit within your category. Try using the strategy for creating criteria that we discussed on pages 222–223 with reference to police brutality. Once you have determined your criteria, freewrite for five or ten minutes, exploring whether your contested case meets each of the criteria.

Identifying Your Audience and Determining What's at Stake

Before drafting your argument, identify your targeted audience and determine what's at stake. Consider your responses to the following questions:

- What audience are you targeting? What background do they need to understand your issue? How much do they already care about it?
- Before they read your argument, what stance on your issue do you imagine them holding? What change do you want to bring about in their view?

Organization Plan 1: Definitional Argument with Criteria and Match in Separate Sections

Introduce the issue and state your claim.	• Engage reader's interest in your definitional issue and show why it is controversial or problematic. • Show what's at stake. • Provide background information needed by your audience. • State your claim.
Present your criteria.	• State and develop criterion 1. • State and develop criterion 2. • Continue with the rest of your criteria. • Anticipate and respond to possible objections to the criteria.
Present your match argument.	• Consider restating your claim for clarity. • Argue that your case meets (does not meet) criterion 1. • Argue that your case meets (does not meet) criterion 2. • Continue with the rest of your match argument. • Anticipate and respond to possible objections to the match argument.
Conclude.	• Perhaps sum up your argument. • Help reader return to the "big picture" of what's at stake. • End with something memorable.

- What will they find new or surprising about your argument?
- What objections might they raise? What counterarguments or alternative points of view will you need to address?
- Why does your argument matter? Who might be threatened or made uncomfortable by your views? What is at stake?

Organizing a Definitional Argument

As you compose a first draft of your essay, you may find it helpful to know typical structures for definitional arguments. There are two basic approaches, as shown in Organization Plans 1 and 2. You can either discuss the criteria and the match separately or interweave the discussion.

Questioning and Critiquing a Definitional Argument

A powerful way to stimulate global revision of a draft is to role-play a skeptical audience. The following questions will help you strengthen your own argument or

Organization Plan 2: Definitional Argument with Criteria and Match Interwoven

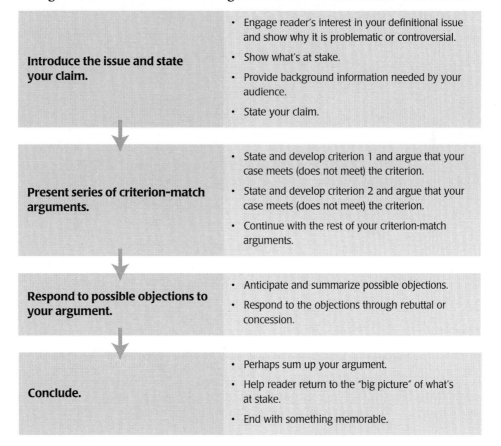

Introduce the issue and state your claim.	• Engage reader's interest in your definitional issue and show why it is problematic or controversial. • Show what's at stake. • Provide background information needed by your audience. • State your claim.
Present series of criterion-match arguments.	• State and develop criterion 1 and argue that your case meets (does not meet) the criterion. • State and develop criterion 2 and argue that your case meets (does not meet) the criterion. • Continue with the rest of your criterion-match arguments.
Respond to possible objections to your argument.	• Anticipate and summarize possible objections. • Respond to the objections through rebuttal or concession.
Conclude.	• Perhaps sum up your argument. • Help reader return to the "big picture" of what's at stake. • End with something memorable.

rebut the definitional arguments of others. In critiquing a definitional argument, you need to appreciate its criteria-match structure because you can question your criteria argument, your match argument, or both.

Questioning Your Criteria

- Could a skeptic claim that your criteria are not the right ones? Could he or she offer different criteria or point out missing criteria?
- Could a skeptic point out possible bad consequences of accepting your criteria?
- Could a skeptic cite unusual circumstances that weaken your criteria?
- Could a skeptic point out bias or slant in your definition?

Questioning Your Match

- Could a skeptic argue that your examples or data don't meet the STAR criteria (see Chapter 5, p. 89) for evidence?
- Could a skeptic point out counterexamples or alternative data that cast doubt on your argument?
- Could a skeptic reframe the way you have viewed your borderline case? ■

Our first reading, by student writer Jenefer Domingo, grew out of class- **READINGS**
room debate on cruelty to animals as part of the "For Class Discussion"
exercise on page 224. Students were given "borderline cases" regarding humans' interaction with animals and asked to determine whether the humans' actions constituted cruelty to animals. In the following essay, Jenefer offers her definition of the
term and applies it to the starling case.

Protecting Our Homes Can Lead to Animal Cruelty

JENEFER DOMINGO (STUDENT)

If you've ever squished a spider on your kitchen floor rather than captured it and taken it
outside, you'll know that questions about animal cruelty can involve shades of gray rather
than black and white. The problem of gray areas became clear to me in a recent classroom
discussion about the case of the starlings in the attic: A family was awakened every morning
by the sound of starlings chirping and flapping in their attic. A pair of starlings had entered
the attic through a torn vent screen, built a nest, and now flew in and out of the attic feeding
the nestlings. After being repeatedly awakened at dawn by the noisy birds, the family repaired the vent screen, making it impossible for the parent birds to feed the nestlings. In a
couple of days the starlings died, and the attic was quiet. Was the family's action an instance
of cruelty to animals? I was torn by this question. Although I believe that the family was
guilty of cruelty to animals, my reasoning put me at odds with many of my classmates.

First, I need to explain my definition of cruelty to animals. In my view humans are
guilty of animal cruelty if they intentionally inflict unnecessary pain for an unjust reason
or unworthy purpose. In this definition the most important criterion for cruelty to animals
is lacking a worthy purpose. An example of a worthy purpose would be butchering an animal for food. In contrast, an unworthy purpose would be harming an animal for entertainment as in dog fighting. Another criterion is inflicting pain beyond what is necessary to
accomplish one's purpose. If one kills an animal for food, it would be cruel to make the
animal suffer rather than killing it cleanly and quickly. Finally, the act must be intentional
rather than accidental. You wouldn't be guilty of cruelty to animals if you accidentally
backed your car over a sleeping cat. Based on my definition, the family in the starling case
had a worthy purpose for killing the starlings. But they are nevertheless guilty of cruelty to
animals because the way they killed them caused unnecessary pain.

The main controversy debated by our class was whether the family had a worthy purpose
in killing the starlings. I believe their purpose was worthy because the starlings were invasive pests that were damaging the family's attic and causing them psychological harm
through loss of sleep. The starlings would tear up insulation and make a mess on anything
stored in the attic. Moreover, starlings are a nonindigenous nuisance bird often hated by
farmers and gardeners. They drive out native birds, quickly overpopulate a region, and
cause considerable damage to crops. I did a Google search that revealed hundreds of Web
sites explaining strategies for killing starlings. I thus classify starlings as pests in the same

category as rats and mice. The family had the right, in my view, to get rid of the starlings just as they would have a right to get rid of rodents. Although it may make us sad to set traps for rats and mice, most people do not consider it ethically wrong to kill rats.

Some people might argue, as several of my classmates did, that starlings are not the same as rats because rats get everywhere in your home while starlings do not. Rats and mice crawl along pipes and air ducts and through walls. They get into your food supply, and their droppings can contaminate surfaces that people touch, making it easy to spread disease. These classmates claimed that because the starlings are confined to that attic and won't get into the family's food supply, they are less harmful than rats and don't belong in the category of dangerous pests that you are justified in killing. Therefore the family should have waited until the baby birds grew up and flew away before they fixed the vent screen.

5   This view, which illustrates how gray the area of animal cruelty is, has merit. I agree that the starlings in the attic do not pose the same health risks as mice and rats do. I also agree that the family could have waited until the baby birds grew up and left the attic. However, these arguments neglect the damage that starlings can do the attic and everything stored in it as well as the psychological damage caused by the noise. Starlings are much noisier than rats, and loss of sleep caused by loud and obnoxious birds is a serious problem. If you are awakened a couple of hours early every morning and can't go back to sleep, you become less efficient at work, grumbling around in a bad mood. So the family was justified in getting rid of the starlings, but they were obligated to do so in a humane way.

It is the family's failure to kill the starlings in the most painless way that makes me label them as cruel to animals. Some of my classmates argued that the family didn't need to kill the birds at all. They could have called a bird expert who would have moved the nest with the baby birds and relocated them out of the attic safely without any bad repercussions. But I believe it was impossible to move the nest based on my experience with blue jays. One summer a baby blue jay fell out of its nest on my roof. The baby seemed fine, so my brothers and I climbed up and put the baby back into the nest. However, we had heard that touching baby birds puts a human smell on them that parent birds will reject. We waited to watch what would happen when the parent birds came back. The rumor was right; the parent birds seemed to know that the baby bird we touched was tainted. The parent birds rejected that baby bird and shoved it out of the nest, killing it. Therefore, the family's only solution, if they were to get rid of the starlings, was to kill the starlings quickly rather than let them starve to death in the attic. The family members should have waited until the parent birds were outside the attic searching for food and then repaired the screen quickly. They should have then climbed into the attic and killed the baby birds quickly and painlessly by snapping their necks or drowning them in a bucket of water.

It is in the manner of which the birds were killed that makes fixing the attic screen an act of animal cruelty. This problem would not even have a chance to arise if the family had taken better care of their house. Just as people patch cracks, secure their trash cans, and seal their leftover foods to prevent infestation of insects, so should they have secured their attic against the starlings. In our dealings with nature, we have to be careful to avoid unnecessary conflicts leading to gray areas. Because we have the mental capacity to anticipate the consequences of our actions, we should avoid problems like starlings nesting in our homes. We have enough knowledge and smarts to outwit these birds, and we should use it to protect both ourselves and nature.

Critiquing "Protecting Our Homes Can Lead to Animal Cruelty"

1. Identify the following features of Jenefer's essay: (1) her definition of cruelty to animals, (2) her application of each criterion within her definition to the starling case, (3) her summary of opposing views, and (4) her responses to these opposing views.
2. To what extent do you accept Jenefer's definition of cruelty to animals? To what extent do you agree with her application of the criteria to the starling case? Particularly, do you agree with Jenefer's argument that the starlings were "pests" and that they caused enough physical or psychological damage to justify killing them?
3. Develop your own definition of cruelty to animals and apply it to one or more of the following borderline cases: (1) keeping animals in zoos, (2) catch-and-release fishing, (3) bullfighting, (4) factory farming of cattle or chickens, and (5) using animals for medical research.

The second reading, by student Kathy Sullivan, was written for the definition assignment on page 225. The definitional issue that she addresses—"Are the Menasee photographs obscene?"—was a local controversy in the state of Washington when the state liquor control board threatened to revoke the liquor license of a Seattle gay bar, the Oncore, unless it removed a series of photographs that the board deemed obscene.

Oncore, Obscenity, and the Liquor Control Board

KATHY SULLIVAN (STUDENT)

In early May, Geoff Menasee, a Seattle artist, exhibited a series of photographs with the theme of "safe sex" on the walls of an inner city, predominantly homosexual restaurant and lounge called the Oncore. Before hanging the photographs, Menasee had to consult with the Washington State Liquor Control Board because, under the current state law, art work containing material that may be considered indecent has to be approved by the board before it can be exhibited. Of the almost thirty photographs, six were rejected by the board because they partially exposed "private parts" of the male anatomy. Menasee went ahead and displayed the entire series of photographs, placing Band-Aids over the "indecent" areas, but the customers continually removed the Band-Aids.

The liquor control board's ruling on this issue has caused controversy in the Seattle community. The *Seattle Times* has provided news coverage, and a "Town Meeting" segment was filmed at the restaurant. The central question is this: Should an establishment that caters to a predominantly homosexual clientele be enjoined from displaying pictures promoting "safe sex" on the grounds that the photographs are obscene?

Before I can answer this question, I must first determine whether the art work should truly be classified as obscene. To make that determination, I will use the definition of obscenity in *Black's Law Dictionary:*

Material is "obscene" if to the average person, applying contemporary community standards, the dominant theme of material taken as a whole appeals to prurient interest, if it is utterly without redeeming social importance, if it goes substantially beyond customary limits of candor in description or representation, if it is characterized by patent offensiveness, and if it is hard core pornography.

An additional criterion is provided by Pember's *Mass Media Laws:* "A work is obscene if it has a tendency to deprave and corrupt those whose minds are open to such immoral influences (children for example) and into whose hands it might happen to fall" (394). The art work in question should not be prohibited from display at predominantly homosexual establishments like the Oncore because it does not meet the above criteria for obscenity.

First of all, to the average person applying contemporary community standards, the predominant theme of Menasee's photographs is not an appeal to prurient interests. The first element in this criterion is "average person." According to Rocky Breckner, manager of the Oncore, 90 percent of the clientele at the Oncore is made up of young white homosexual males. This group therefore constitutes the "average person" viewing the exhibit. "Contemporary community standards" would ordinarily be the standards of the Seattle community. However, this art work is aimed at a particular group of people—the homosexual community. Therefore, the "community standards" involved here are those of the gay community rather than the city at large. Since the Oncore is not an art museum or gallery, which attracts a broad spectrum of people, it is appropriate to restrict the scope of "community standards" to that group who voluntarily patronize the Oncore.

5   Second, the predominant theme of the photographs is not "prurient interest" nor do the photographs go "substantially beyond customary limits of candor." There are no explicit sexual acts found in the photographs; instead, their theme is the prevention of AIDS through the practice of safe sex. Homosexual displays of affection could be viewed as "prurient interest" by the larger community, but same-sex relationships are the norm for the group at whom the exhibit is aimed. If the exhibit were displayed at McDonald's or even the Red Robin it might go "substantially beyond customary limits of candor," but it is unlikely that the clientele of the Oncore would find the art work offensive. The manager stated that he received very few complaints about the exhibit and its contents.

Nor is the material pornographic. The liquor control board prohibited the six photographs based on their visible display of body parts such as pubic hair and naked buttocks, not on the basis of sexual acts or homosexual orientation. The board admitted that the photographs depicted no explicit sexual acts. Hence, it can be concluded that they did not consider the suggestion of same-sex affection to be hard-core pornography. Their sole objection was that body parts were visible. But visible genitalia in art work are not necessarily pornographic. Since other art work, such as Michelangelo's sculptures, explicitly depict both male and female genitalia, it is arguable that pubic hair and buttocks are not patently offensive.

It must be conceded that the art work has the potential of being viewed by children, which would violate Pember's criterion. But once again the incidence of minors frequenting this establishment is very small.

But the most important reason for saying these photographs are not obscene is that they serve an important social purpose. One of Black's criteria is that obscene material is "utterly without redeeming social importance." But these photographs have the explicit purpose of promoting safe sex as a defense against AIDS. Recent statistics reported in the *Seattle Times* show that AIDS is now the leading cause of death of men under forty in the Seattle area. Any methods that can promote the message of safe sex in today's society have strong redeeming social significance.

Those who believe that all art containing "indecent" material should be banned or covered from public view would most likely believe that Menasee's work is obscene. They would disagree that the environment and the clientele should be the major determining factor when using criteria to evaluate art. However, in the case of this exhibit I feel that the audience and the environment of the display are factors of overriding importance. Therefore, the exhibit should have been allowed to be displayed because it is not obscene.

Critiquing "Oncore, Obscenity, and the Liquor Control Board"

1. Kathy Sullivan here uses an authoritative definition for *obscenity*. Based on the definitions of *obscenity* in *Black's Law Dictionary* and Pember's *Mass Media Laws*, what criteria for obscenity does Kathy use?
2. How does she argue that the Menasee photographs do *not* meet the criteria?
3. Working as a whole class or in small groups, share your responses to the following questions: (a) If you find Kathy's argument persuasive, which parts were particularly influential or effective? (b) If you are not persuaded, which parts of her argument do you find weak or ineffective? (c) How does Kathy shape her argument to meet the concerns and objections of her audience? (d) How might a lawyer for the liquor control board rebut Kathy's argument?

Our third reading, by sports reporter David Andriesen, takes up the issue of whether "cup stacking" and other similar activities are really sports. In trying to decide this, Andriesen attempts to define just what a sport is. This article appeared in the *Seattle Post-Intelligencer* on January 17, 2008.

What Defines a Sport?

DAVID ANDRIESEN

Search for "cup stacking" on YouTube, and you can watch more than 1,000 videos of people taking nested stacks of plastic cups and arranging them into pyramids and back again so quickly the whole thing is almost a blur.

It's impressive. It takes skill and agility. But is it a sport?

Stacking supporters think so. In 2005, the governing body changed the name officially to "sport stacking."

"When people challenge me on whether it's a sport, I usually turn it around on them," said Matt Reed, executive director of the

World Sport Stacking Association. "I ask them, 'What's your definition of sport?' Invariably many of the things they mention are involved in our sport."

5   ESPN shows poker, cheerleading, arm wrestling, and, yes, sport stacking.

Bass fishing events offer million-dollar purses.

Mainstream newspaper sports sections report on hot dog–eating world records.

The Olympics offer medals for kayaking and bobsled, but not for golf or football (at least not the American kind).

Some school districts classify chess as a sport.

10   So how, in this age of media saturation and fringe activities clamoring for legitimacy, can we define "sport"?

It's one of the great barroom debates, usually triggered by the sight of billiards or the X Games on TV at a watering hole. But while fans have argued over it for decades, there hasn't really been any official effort to define sport.

Rodney Fort, a professor of sport management at the University of Michigan who taught for more than two decades at Washington State University, uses a discussion about the definition of sport as an exercise to get students thinking about the field.

Takeru Kobayashi won Nathan's Famous Hot Dog Eating Competition six years in a row. But is the event an actual sport?

Fort has narrowed his definition to three parameters:

- It must use a "large motor skill."
- It must have an objective scoring system.
- It must use nothing more complicated than a "simple machine," such as a baseball bat or vaulting pole.

"That's just me talking, my personal opinion," Fort said. "You'll never find a group of people who will reach total agreement."

15   There are many factors to consider, but most arguments end up centering on a few common factors.

Who's Got the Ball?

A ball helps a lot. Most things with a ball (or ball-like object, such as a puck) are generally considered to be sports. Heck, America's three top pro sports have "ball" right in the name.

If there are two people or teams on a playing surface at the same time competing with a ball, particularly the same ball, it's almost certainly a sport. Dozens of sports fit under this umbrella.

Who's Racing?

A footrace is the simplest form of sport, and most racing under human power is inarguably a sport. Whether people are racing over hurdles, through the woods, or in a pool, they're engaged in sport.

The question becomes what level of human power you require, and what other implements you accept.

20   For instance, horse racing might be "the sport of kings," but is it a sport?

"It's a sport for the horse," Fort said. "They're the ones doing the racing. Certainly the jockey has something to do with it, but it's hard to conclude that that's a sport in the same way, say, the 100-meter dash is."

And in horse racing, at least it's the horse that gets the glory. Most people can name horses that have won the Triple Crown, but not jockeys who have done it.

But what about auto racing? NASCAR is one of the most popular sports in America, but it's the cars that are providing the power, and the fastest car usually wins, even if it's not driven by the most skilled driver on a particular day. Purists would reject all motorized racing, though they'd get a powerful argument south of the Mason-Dixon line.

What about human-powered racing in disciplines where differences in the equipment can affect the outcome, such as cycling and crew? Fort rejects these under his "simple machines" provision, but if you set the standard at the conveyance being primarily human powered, pedaling and rowing qualify.

Whose Turn Is It?

25 Then there is the question of whether participants must compete head-to-head. In a footrace, first one to the finish wins. But what about races like downhill skiing, in which competitors are theoretically racing each other but really just racing a clock?

Golf and bowling also are turn-based. In the case of bowling, it's to assure two competitors have the same lane conditions, but in golf a field of 144 can experience vastly different conditions on the same course—some might play a hole early or late, with or without wind or rain. People often complete the same round on different days.

Are the golfers truly competing against each other? And if you could get the same results by having golfers drop by and play four rounds at a certain course at their leisure, and then comparing scores to determine a winner, can a golf tournament be said to be a sporting event?

What's the Score?

When the results of a competition are a matter of opinion, it's tough for many to accept it as a sport.

If a judge scores an athlete higher or lower based on politics, or loving or hating a certain move, or, heaven forbid, whether he likes his outfit, the notion of competition goes down the drain quickly.

30 We like to know for certain whether someone won a contest. The ball went in the net or it didn't. The runner beat the throw to the plate or he didn't. Our most popular sports have this in common, even though human error is sometimes a factor.

"We have to all know what constitutes you getting a point," Fort said. "This causes a problem for some people, because they confuse the existence of an objective scoring definition with the human fallibility of recognizing it when they see it.

"They say, 'Well, what about when a ref blows a call in the end zone?' But that's not the point.

40 We all know what constitutes a touchdown. We're just arguing about whether the ref saw it correctly or not."

Women often argue against the insistence on objective scoring, because it eliminates several sports most closely identified with women, or most popular when women are competing: figure skating, gymnastics, cheer.

But its sweep is much wider than that. Diving, out. Most extreme sports, out. Many rodeo events, out.

35 Even boxing, considered one of the most basic and pure sports, goes by the wayside if we insist on objective scoring. Are you ready to throw out boxing?

If you want boxing, you pretty much have to accept figure skating.

Getting Physical?

Even if you insist on humans doing the competing, head-to-head competition and objective scoring, you're still left with a lot of things that don't pass muster. Pinball. Poker. Darts. Which of your frat brothers can eat the most jalapeno poppers.

There has to be some level of physical effort. But where do you draw the line?

Golf looks pretty easy, but the average person might change his mind on that after playing 18 holes on foot carrying his own bag.

You could argue that throwing a 15-pound bowling ball for a

few hours requires more physical strength than swinging a golf club, but a trip to the local bowling alley doesn't exactly turn up a lot of world-class athletes.

Tennis is a sport, but how about table tennis? It's pretty much the same thing, only on a smaller scale—and if you watch an international match you see that there's some physical effort involved.

Curling is an Olympic medal sport, but requires about the same level of effort as sweeping the back porch.

The question of what is or is not a sport will continue to be argued, and the only point of agreement likely to be reached is that we'll never agree.

What combination of factors must exist to make something a sport is up to you. Or maybe it's like the famous definition of art: You know it when you see it.

"Are we going to be in the Olympics? I don't know about that," cup stacking, er, *sport stacking* chief Reed said. "We're never going to be one of the major sports, but we feel like we're legit."

For Reed, whether sport stacking is classified as a sport is less important than people having fun doing it.

After all, that's the point, isn't it?

Critiquing "What Defines a Sport?"

1. Andriesen explores some of the criteria that have been posited for an activity to be a sport. What position does he take on the issue of defining sport?
2. Under what circumstances might it be important to have accepted criteria for what constitutes a sport?
3. Develop your own definition of sport and apply it to one or more of the following cases: (1) synchronized swimming, (2) poker, (3) video game playing, (4) NASCAR racing.

Causal Arguments

12

Case 1   What Causes Global Warming?

One of the early clues linking global warming to atmospheric carbon dioxide (CO_2) came from side-by-side comparisons of graphs plotting atmospheric carbon dioxide and global temperatures over time. These graphs show that increases in global temperature parallel increases in the percentage of carbon dioxide in the atmosphere. These graphs, however, show only a correlation, or link, between increased carbon dioxide and higher average temperature. It's possible that the increase in carbon dioxide has caused global temperatures to rise. But it's also possible that the causal direction is the other way around—an increase in global temperature has caused the earth to release more carbon dioxide. Furthermore, it's possible that some third phenomenon causes an increase in both atmospheric carbon dioxide and global temperature. To show that atmospheric carbon dioxide contributes to global warming, scientists needed to create a model showing how increased carbon dioxide causes an increase in global temperature. Their model compares the earth to a greenhouse with carbon dioxide acting as glass windows. Carbon dioxide, like glass in a greenhouse, lets some of the earth's heat radiate into space but also reflects some of it back to the earth. The higher the concentration of carbon dioxide, the more heat is reflected back to the earth.

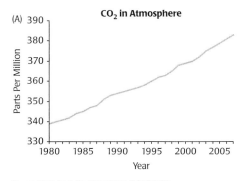

Source: Data from Dr. Pieter Tans, NOAA/ESRL

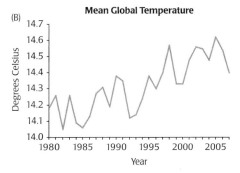

Source: Data from NASA Goddard Institute for Space Studies Surface Temperature Analysis

| Case 2 What Has Caused the Crime Rate to Decline Since the Early 1990s? |

Beginning in the 1990s, the crime rate in the United States dropped precipitously. For example, the number of murders in New York City decreased from 2,245 in 1990 to 494 in 2007. Similar reductions for all kinds of crime, ranging from murders to assaults to auto thefts, were reported across the nation. What caused this sudden and unexpected decline? Many causal theories were debated in social science journals and the popular media. Among the proposed causes were innovative policing strategies, increased incarceration of criminals, an aging population, tougher gun control laws, a strong economy, and more police officers. However, economist Steven Levitt proposed that the primary cause was *Roe v. Wade*, the 1973 Supreme Court decision that legalized abortion.* According to Levitt's controversial theory, the crime rate began dropping because the greatest source of criminals—unwanted children entering their teens and twenties—were largely absent from the cohort of young people coming of age in the 1990s and 2000s; they had been aborted rather than brought up in the crime-producing conditions of unstable families, poverty, and neglect.

An Overview of Causal Arguments

We encounter causal issues all the time. What caused the sudden decline in the U.S. crime rate beginning in the 1990s? What are the causes of global warming? Why did rap music become popular? Why are white teenage girls seven times as likely to smoke as African American teenage girls? Why do couples who live together before marriage have a higher divorce rate than those who don't? In addition to asking causal questions like these, we pose consequence questions as well: What might be the consequences of legalizing heroin and other hard drugs, of closing our borders to immigrants, or of overturning *Roe v. Wade*? What have been the consequences—expected or unexpected—of the invasion of Iraq or the emerging popularity of YouTube? What might be the consequences—expected or unexpected—of aggressively combating global warming as opposed to adapting to it? Often, arguments about causes and consequences have important stakes because they shape our view of reality and influence government policies and individual decisions.

Typically, causal arguments try to show how one event brings about another. When causal investigation focuses on material objects—for example, one billiard ball striking another—the notion of causality appears fairly straightforward. But when humans become the focus of a causal argument, the nature of causality becomes more vexing. If we say that something happened that "caused" a person to act in a certain way, what do we mean? Do we mean that she was "forced" to act in a certain way, thereby negating her free will (as in, an undiagnosed brain tumor caused her to act erratically), or do we mean more simply that she was "motivated" to act in a certain way (as in, her anger at her parents caused her to act erratically)?

---

*Steven D. Levitt and Stephen J. Dubner, "Where Have All the Criminals Gone?," in *Freakonomics: A Rogue Economist Explores the Hidden Side of Everything* (New York: HarperCollins, 2005), 117–44.

When we argue about causality in human beings, we must guard against confusing these two senses of "cause" or assuming that human behavior can be predicted or controlled in the same way that nonhuman behavior can. A rock dropped from a roof will always fall at thirty-two feet per second squared, and a rat zapped for turning left in a maze will always quit turning left. But if we raise interest rates, will consumers save more money? If so, how much? This is the sort of question we debate endlessly.

Kinds of Causal Arguments

Arguments about causality can take a variety of forms. Here are three typical kinds.

- *Speculations about possible causes.* Sometimes arguers speculate about possible causes of a phenomenon. For example, in 1999 at Columbine High School in Littleton, Colorado, two male students opened fire on their classmates, killing thirteen people, wounding twenty-three others, and then shooting themselves. Afterward, social scientists and media commentators spent months analyzing the massacre, trying to determine what caused it. Figure 12.1 illustrates some of the proposed theories. What was at stake was not only our desire to understand the sociocultural sources of school violence but also our desire to institute policies to prevent future school shootings. If a primary cause is the availability of guns, then we might push for more stringent gun control laws. But if the primary cause is the disintegration of the traditional family, inadequate funding for school counselors, or the dangerous side effects of Prozac, then we might seek different solutions.
- *Arguments for an unexpected or surprising cause.* Besides sorting out possible causes of a phenomenon, sometimes arguers try to persuade readers to see the plausibility of an unexpected or surprising cause. This was the strategy used by

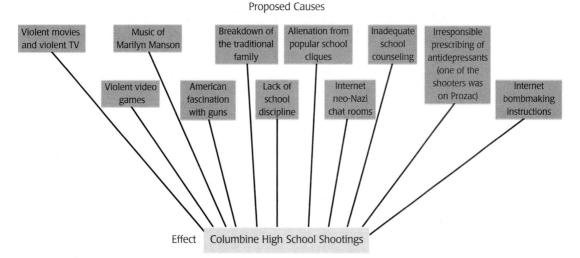

FIGURE 12.1 Speculation about possible causes: Columbine High School massacre

Many youngsters are left alone for long periods of time (because both parents are working).

They play violent video games obsessively.

Their feelings of resentment and powerlessness "pour into the killing games."

The video games break down a natural aversion to killing, analogous to psychological techniques employed by the military.

Realistic touches in modern video games blur the "boundary between fantasy and reality."

Youngsters begin identifying not with conventional heroes but with sociopaths who get their kicks from blowing away ordinary people ("pedestrians, marching bands, an elderly woman with a walker").

Having enjoyed random violence in the video games, vulnerable youngsters act out the same adrenaline rush in real life.

FIGURE 12.2 Argument for a surprising cause: Role of violent video games in the Columbine massacre

syndicated columnist John Leo, who wanted readers to consider the role of violent video games as a contributing cause to the Columbine massacre.* After suggesting that the Littleton killings were partly choreographed on video game models, Leo suggested the causal chain shown in Figure 12.2.

■ *Predictions of consequences.* Still another frequently encountered kind of causal argument predicts the consequences of current, planned, or proposed actions or events. Consequence arguments have high stakes because we often judge actions on whether their benefits outweigh their costs. As we will see in Chapter 15, proposal arguments usually require writers to predict the consequences of a proposed

---

*John Leo, "Kill-for-Kicks Video Games Desensitizing Our Children," *Seattle Times* 27 April 1999, B4.

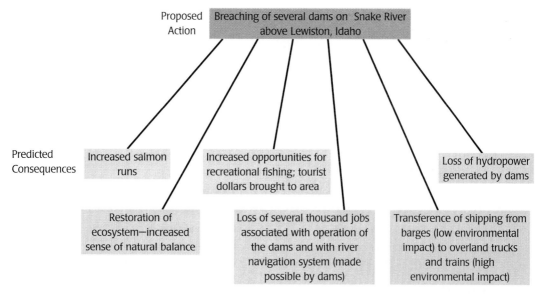

FIGURE 12.3   Predictions of consequences: Breaching dams on the Snake River

action, do a cost/benefit analysis, and persuade readers that no unforeseen negative consequences will result. Just as a phenomenon can have multiple causes, it can also have multiple consequences. Figure 12.3 shows the consequence arguments considered by environmentalists who propose eliminating several dams on the Snake River in order to save salmon runs.

Toulmin Framework for a Causal Argument

Because causal arguments can involve lengthy or complex causal chains, they are often harder to summarize in *because* clauses than are other kinds of arguments. Likewise, they are not as likely to yield quick analysis through the Toulmin schema. Nevertheless, a causal argument can usually be stated as a claim with *because* clauses. Typically, a *because* clause pinpoints one or two key elements in the causal chain rather than summarizes every link. John Leo's argument linking the Columbine massacre to violent videogames could be summarized in the following claim with a *because* clause:

> Violent video games may have been a contributing cause to the Littleton massacre because playing these games can make random, sociopathic violence seem pleasurable.

Once stated as an enthymeme, the argument can be analyzed using Toulmin's schema. It is easiest to apply Toulmin's schema to causal arguments if you think of the grounds as the observable phenomena at any point in the causal chain and the warrants as the shareable assumptions about causality that join links together.

Toulmin Analysis of the Violent Video Games Argument

ENTHYMEME

CLAIM Violent video games may have been a contributing cause to the Columbine school shooting

REASON because playing these games can make random, sociopathic violence seem pleasurable

Qualifiers

GROUNDS

• Evidence that the killers, like many young people, played violent video games

• Evidence that the games are violent

• Evidence that the games involve random, sociopathic violence (not good guys versus bad guys) such as killing ordinary people—marching bands, little old ladies, etc.

• Evidence that young people derive pleasure from these games

CONDITIONS OF REBUTTAL
Attacking the reason and grounds

• Perhaps the killers didn't play violent video games.

• Perhaps the video games are no more violent than traditional kids' games such as cops and robbers.

• Perhaps the video games do not feature sociopathic killing.

WARRANT

If young people derive pleasure from random, sociopathic killing in video games, they can transfer this pleasure to real life, thus leading to the Columbine shooting.

BACKING

• Testimony from psychologists

• Evidence that violent video games desensitize people to violence

• Analogy to military training in which video games are used to "make killing a reflex action"

• Evidence that the distinction between fantasy and reality becomes especially blurred for unstable young people

CONDITIONS OF REBUTTAL
Attacking the warrant and backing

• Perhaps kids are fully capable of distinguishing fantasy from reality.

• Perhaps the games are just fun with no transference to real life.

• Perhaps the games are substantially different from military training games.

■ ■ ■ **FOR CLASS DISCUSSION** Developing Causal Chains

1. Working individually or in small groups, create a causal chain to show how the item on the left could help lead to the item on the right.

   a. High price of oil   Redesign of cities

   b. Invention of the automobile   Changes in sexual mores

    c. Invention of the telephone   Loss of sense of community
                                      in neighborhoods

    d. Origin of rap in the black urban   The popularity of rap spreads from
          music scene   urban black audiences to white
                                                  middle-class youth culture

    e. Development of way to prevent   Liberalization of euthanasia laws
          rejections in transplant operations

2. For each of your causal chains, compose a claim with an attached *because* clause summarizing one or two key links in the causal chain—for example, "The high price of oil is causing homeowners to move from the suburbs into new high-density urban communities because the expense of gasoline is making people value easy access to their work."

Two Methods for Arguing That One Event Causes Another

One of the first things you need to do when preparing a causal argument is to note exactly what sort of causal relationship you are dealing with—a onetime phenomenon, a recurring phenomenon, or a puzzling trend. Here are some examples.

Kind of Phenomenon	Examples
Onetime phenomenon	▪ 2007 collapse of a freeway bridge in Minneapolis, Minnesota ▪ Firing of a popular teacher at your university ▪ Your friend's sudden decision to join the army
Recurring phenomenon	▪ Eating disorders ▪ Road rage ▪ Someone's tendency to procrastinate
Puzzling trend	▪ Rising popularity of extreme sports ▪ Declining audience for TV news ▪ Increases in diagnosis of autism

With recurring phenomena or with trends, one has the luxury of being able to study multiple cases, often over time. You can interview people, make repeated observations, or study the conditions in which the puzzling phenomenon occurs. But with a onetime occurrence, one's approach is more like that of a detective than a scientist. Because one can't repeat the event with different variables, one must rely only on the immediate evidence at hand, which can quickly disappear.

Having briefly stated these words of caution, let's turn now to two main ways that you can argue that one event causes another.

First Method: Explain the Causal Mechanism Directly

The most convincing kind of causal argument identifies every link in the causal chain, showing how an initiating cause leads step by step to an observed effect. A causes B, which

EXAMINING VISUAL ARGUMENTS

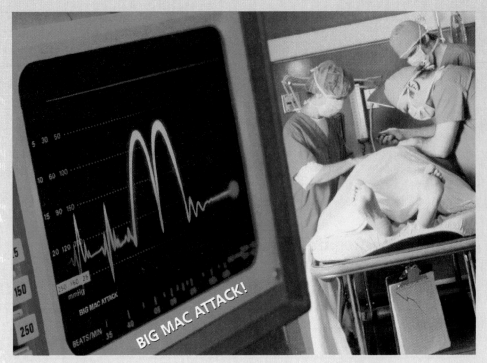

A Causal Claim

This spoof ad by Adbusters makes a causal argument against fast-food restaurants. How does the ad work visually to suggest the links in a causal chain? Place into your own words the argument implied by this ad. According to its Web site, Adbusters is "a global network of artists, activists, writers, pranksters, educators and entrepreneurs who want to advance the new social activist movement of the information age."

causes C, which causes D. In some cases, all you have to do is fill in the missing links. In other cases—when your assumptions about how one step leads to the next may seem questionable to your audience—you have to argue for the causal connection with more vigor.

A careful spelling out of each step in the causal chain is the technique used by science writer Robert S. Devine in the following passage from his article "The Trouble with Dams." Although the benefits of dams are widely understood (they produce pollution-free electricity while providing flood control, irrigation, barge transportation, and recreational boating), the negative effects are less commonly known and understood. In this article, Devine tries to persuade readers that dams have serious negative consequences. In the following passage, he explains how dams reduce salmon flows by slowing the migration of smolts (newly hatched young salmon) to the sea.

Causal Argument Describing a Causal Chain

Such transformations lie at the heart of the ongoing environmental harm done by dams. Rivers are rivers because they flow, and the nature of their flows defines much of their character. When dams alter flows, they alter the essence of rivers.

Consider the erstwhile river behind Lower Granite [a dam on Idaho's Snake River]. Although I was there in the springtime, when I looked at the water it was moving too slowly to merit the word "flow"—and Lower Granite Lake isn't even one of the region's enormous storage reservoirs, which bring currents to a virtual halt. In the past, spring snowmelt sent powerful currents down the Snake during April and May. Nowadays hydropower operators of the Columbia and Snake systems store the runoff behind the dams and release it during the winter, when demand—and the price—for electricity rises. Over the ages, however, many populations of salmon have adapted to the spring surge. The smolts used the strong flows to migrate, drifting downstream with the current. During the journey smolts' bodies undergo physiological changes that require them to reach salt water quickly. Before dams backed up the Snake, smolts coming down from Idaho got to the sea in six to twenty days; now it takes from sixty to ninety days, and few of the young salmon reach salt water in time. The emasculated current is the single largest reason that the number of wild adult salmon migrating up the Snake each year has crashed from predevelopment runs of 100,000–200,000 to what was projected to be 150–75 this year.*

This tightly constructed passage connects various causal chains to explain the decline of salmon runs:

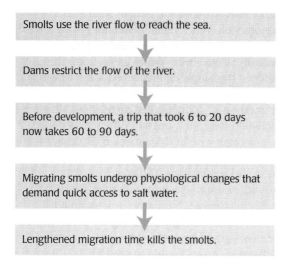

Smolts use the river flow to reach the sea.

Dams restrict the flow of the river.

Before development, a trip that took 6 to 20 days now takes 60 to 90 days.

Migrating smolts undergo physiological changes that demand quick access to salt water.

Lengthened migration time kills the smolts.

---

*Robert S. Devine, "The Trouble with Dams," *Atlantic* (August 1995), 64–75. The example quotation is from page 70.

Describing each link in the causal chain—and making each link seem as plausible as possible—is the most persuasive means of convincing readers that a specific cause leads to a specific effect.

Second Method: Infer Causal Links Using Inductive Reasoning

If we can't explain a causal link directly, we often employ a reasoning strategy called *induction.* Through induction we infer a general conclusion based on a limited number of specific cases. For example, if on several occasions you got a headache after drinking red wine but not after drinking white wine, you would be likely to conclude inductively that red wine causes you to get headaches, although you can't explain directly how it does so. However, because there are almost always numerous variables involved, inductive reasoning gives only probable truths, not certain ones.

Three Ways of Thinking Inductively   When your brain thinks inductively, it sorts through data looking for patterns of similarity and difference. In this section we explain three ways of thinking inductively: looking for a common element, looking for a single difference, and looking for correlations.

1. *Look for a common element.* One kind of inductive thinking places you on a search for a common element that can explain recurrences of the same phenomenon. For example, psychologists attempting to understand the causes of anorexia have discovered that many anorexics (but not all) come from perfectionist, highly work-oriented homes that emphasize duty and responsibility. This common element is thus a suspected causal factor leading to anorexia.
2. *Look for a single difference.* Another approach is to look for a single difference that may explain the appearance of a new phenomenon. When infant death rates in the state of Washington shot up in July and August 1986, one event stood out making these two months different: increased radioactive fallout over Washington from the April Chernobyl nuclear meltdown in Ukraine. This single difference led some researchers to suspect radiation as a possible cause of the increase in infant deaths.
3. *Look for correlations.* Still another method of induction is *correlation,* which expresses a statistical relationship between two phenomena: When A occurs, B is likely to occur also, although it is not clear whether A causes B, B causes A, or some third factor C causes both A and B. For example, there is a fairly strong correlation between nearsightedness and intelligence. (That is, in a given sample of nearsighted people and people with normal eyesight, a higher percentage of the nearsighted people will be highly intelligent. Similarly, in a sample of high-intelligence people and people with normal intelligence, a higher percentage of the high-intelligence group will be nearsighted.) But the direction of causality isn't clear. It could be that high intelligence causes people to read more, thus ruining their eyes (high intelligence causes nearsightedness). Or it could be that nearsightedness causes people to read more, thus raising their intelligence (nearsightedness causes high intelligence). Or it could be that some unknown phenomenon causes both nearsightedness and high intelligence. So keep in mind that correlation is not causation—it simply suggests possible causation.

Beware of Common Inductive Fallacies That Can Lead to Wrong Conclusions
Largely because of its power, informal induction can often lead to wrong conclusions.
You should be aware of two common fallacies of inductive reasoning that can tempt you
into erroneous assumptions about causality. (Both fallacies are treated more fully in
Appendix One.)

- *Post hoc fallacy:* The *post hoc, ergo propter hoc* fallacy ("after this, therefore because of this") mistakes sequence for cause. Just because event A regularly precedes event B doesn't mean that event A causes event B. The same reasoning
  that tells us that flipping a switch causes the light to go on can make us believe
  that low levels of radioactive fallout from the Chernobyl nuclear disaster caused
  a sudden rise in infant death rates in the state of Washington. The nuclear disaster clearly preceded the rise in death rates. But did it clearly *cause* it? Our point is
  that precedence alone is no proof of causality and that we are guilty of this fallacy whenever we are swayed to believe that one thing causes another just
  because it comes first.
- *Hasty generalization:* The *hasty generalization* fallacy occurs when you make a generalization based on too few cases or too little consideration of alternative explanations:
  You flip the switch, but the lightbulb doesn't go on. You conclude—too hastily—that the
  lightbulb has burned out. (Perhaps the power has gone off or the switch is broken.)
  How many trials does it take before you can make a justified generalization rather
  than a hasty generalization? It is difficult to say for sure.

Both the *post hoc* fallacy and the hasty generalization fallacy remind us that induction
requires a leap from individual cases to a general principle and that it is always possible
to leap too soon.

■ ■ ■   **FOR CLASS DISCUSSION   Developing Plausible Causal Chains Based on Correlations**
Working individually or in small groups, develop plausible causal chains that may
explain the relationship between the following pairs of phenomena:

a. A person who registers a low stress level on an   does daily meditation
electrochemical stress meter

b. A white female teenager   is seven times as likely to smoke as a black
female teenager

c. A person who grew up in a house with two   is likely to have higher SAT scores than a person
bathrooms   who grew up in a one-bathroom home

d. A person who buys lots of ashtrays   is more likely to develop lung cancer

e. A member of the National Rifle Association   supports the death penalty   ■ ■ ■

Glossary of Terms Encountered in Causal Arguments

Because causal arguments are often easier to conduct if writer and reader share a few
specialized terms, we offer the following glossary for your convenience.

- *Fallacy of oversimplified cause.* One of the great temptations when establishing causal relationships is to look for *the* cause of something. Most phenomena, especially the ones we argue about, have multiple causes. When you make a causal argument, be especially careful how you use words such as *all* or *some.* For example, to say that *all* the blame for recent school shootings comes from the shooters' playing violent video games is to claim that violent video games are *the* cause of school shootings—a universal statement. An argument will be stronger and more accurate if the arguer makes a less sweeping statement: *Some* of the blame for school shootings can be attributed to violent video games. Arguers sometimes deliberately mix up these quantifiers to misrepresent and dismiss opposing views. For example, someone may argue that because violent video games aren't the sole cause of students' violent behavior, they are not an influential factor at all. Something that is not a total cause can still be a partial cause.

- *Immediate and remote causes.* Every causal chain extends backward indefinitely into the past. An immediate cause is the closest in time to the event being examined. Consider the factors leading to the fatal plane crash of John F. Kennedy Jr. in July 1999. When Kennedy's plane crashed at night into the Atlantic Ocean south of Martha's Vineyard, experts speculated that the *immediate* cause was Kennedy's becoming disoriented in the night haze, losing visual control of the plane, and sending the plane into a fatal dive. A slightly less immediate cause was his decision to make an over-water flight at night without being licensed for instrument flying. (He and his wife and sister-in-law needed to get to Hyannis Port quickly to attend a wedding.) Further back in time were all the factors that made Kennedy the kind of risk taker who took chances with his own life. For example, several months earlier he had broken his ankle in a hang-gliding accident. Many commentators said that the numerous tragedies that befell the Kennedy family helped shape his risk-taking personality. Such causes going back into the past are considered *remote causes.*

- *Precipitating and contributing causes.* These terms are similar to *immediate* and *remote* causes but don't designate a temporal link going into the past. Rather, they refer to a main cause emerging out of a background of subsidiary causes. If, for example, a husband and wife decide to separate, the *precipitating cause* may be a stormy fight over money, after which one of the partners (or both) says, "I've had enough." In contrast, *contributing causes* would be all the background factors that are dooming the marriage—preoccupation with their careers, disagreement about priorities, in-law problems, and so forth. Note that contributing causes and the precipitating cause all coexist at the same time.

- *Constraints.* Sometimes an effect occurs because some stabilizing factor—a *constraint*—is removed. In other words, the presence of a constraint may keep a certain effect from occurring. For example, in the marriage we have been discussing, the presence of children in the home may be a constraint against divorce; as soon as the children graduate from high school and leave home, the marriage may well dissolve.

- *Necessary and sufficient causes.* A *necessary cause* is one that has to be present for a given effect to occur. For example, fertility drugs are necessary to cause the conception of septuplets. Every couple who has septuplets must have used fertility drugs. In contrast, a *sufficient cause* is one that always produces or guarantees a given effect. Smoking more than a pack of cigarettes per day is sufficient to raise the cost of one's life insurance policy. This statement means that if you are a smoker, no matter how healthy you appear to be, life insurance companies will always place you in a higher risk bracket and charge you a higher premium. In some cases, a single cause can be both necessary and sufficient. For example, lack of ascorbic acid is both a necessary and a sufficient cause of scurvy. (Think of those old-time sailors who didn't eat fruit for months.) It is a necessary cause because you can't get scurvy any other way except through absence of ascorbic acid; it is a sufficient cause because the absence of ascorbic acid always causes scurvy.

■ ■ ■   **FOR CLASS DISCUSSION**   **Brainstorming Causes and Constraints**

The terms in the preceding glossary can be effective brainstorming tools for thinking of possible causes of an event. For the following events, try to think of as many causes as possible by brainstorming possible *immediate causes, remote causes, precipitating causes, contributing causes,* and *constraints:*

1. Working individually, make a list of different kinds of causes/constraints for one of the following:
   a. Your decision to attend your present college
   b. An important event in your life or your family (a job change, a major move, etc.)
   c. A personal opinion you hold that is not widely shared
2. Working as a group, make a list of different kinds of causes/constraints for one of the following:
   a. Why women's fashion and beauty magazines are the most frequently purchased magazines in college bookstores
   b. Why American students consistently score below Asian and European students in academic achievement
   c. Why the number of babies born out of wedlock has increased dramatically in the last thirty years

WRITING ASSIGNMENT   A Causal Argument

Choose an issue about the causes or consequences of a trend, event, or other phenomenon. Write an argument that persuades an audience to accept your explanation of the causes or consequences of your chosen phenomenon. Within your essay you should examine alternative hypotheses or opposing views and explain your reasons for rejecting them. You can imagine your issue either as a puzzle or as a disagreement. If a puzzle, your task will be to create a convincing case for an audience that doesn't have an answer to your causal question already in mind. If a disagreement, your task will be more overtly persuasive because your goal will be to change your audience's views.

Exploring Ideas

Arguments about causes and consequences abound in public, professional, or personal life, so you shouldn't have difficulty finding a causal issue worth investigating and arguing.

In response to a public controversy over why women are underrepresented on science and math faculties, student writer Julee Christianson contributed her own argument to the conversation by claiming that culture, not biology, is the reason (see pages 254–257). Student writer Carlos Macias, puzzled by the ease with which college students are issued credit cards, wrote a researched argument disentangling the factors leading young people to bury themselves in debt (see pages 260–263). Other students have focused on causal issues such as these: Why do kids join gangs? What causes anorexia? What are the consequences of violent video games on children? What are the consequences of mandatory drug testing (written by a student who has to take amphetamines for narcolepsy)? What are the causes of different sexual orientations? What has happened since 1970 to cause young people to delay getting married? (This question was initiated by the student's interest in the statistical table in Chapter 9, page 193.) What effect will the Navy's low-frequency sonar system for finding enemy submarines have on whales and other marine mammals? (The student who posed this question eventually wrote the researched proposal argument on pages 394–400.)

If you have trouble finding a causal issue to write about, you can often create provocative controversies among your classmates through the following strategies:

- *Make a list of unusual likes and dislikes.* Think about unusual things that people like or dislike. We find it really strange, for example, that so many people like professional wrestling or dislike writing notes in margins while they read. You could summarize the conventional explanations that people give for an unusual pleasure or aversion and then argue for a surprising or unexpected cause. What attracts people to extreme sports? How do you explain the popularity of the Hummer or the tricked-out Cadillac Escalade as dream cars for urban youth?

- *Make a list of puzzling events or trends.* Another strategy is to make a list of puzzling phenomena and try to explain their causes. Start with onetime events (a cheating scandal at your school; the public's puzzling first reaction to a film, book, or new TV show). Then list puzzling recurring events (failure of knowledgeable teenagers to practice safe sex; use of steroids among athletes). Finally, list some recent trends (growth of naturopathic medicine; teen interest in the gothic; hatred of women in much gangsta rap). Engage classmates in discussions of one or more of the items on your list. Look for places of disagreement as entry points into the conversation.

- *Brainstorm consequences of a recent or proposed action.* Arguments about consequences are among the most interesting and important of causal disputes. If you can argue for an unanticipated consequence of a real, hypothetical, or proposed action—for example, a bad consequence of an apparently positive event or a good consequence of an apparently negative event—you can make an important contribution to the conversation. What might be the consequences, for example, of some of the following: requiring a passing grade on a high-stakes test for graduation from high school; depleting the world's oil supply; legalizing marijuana; overturning *Roe v. Wade;* greatly increasing public searches on subways, buses, trains, and ferries as a means of fighting terrorism; any similar recent, hypothetical, or proposed event?

Identifying Your Audience and Determining What's at Stake

Before drafting your argument, identify your targeted audience and determine what's at stake. Consider your responses to the following questions:

- What audience are you targeting? What background do they need to understand your issue? How much do they already care about it?
- Before they read your argument, what stance on your issue do you imagine them holding? What change do you want to bring about in their view?
- What will they find new or surprising about your argument?
- What objections might they raise? What counterarguments or alternative points of view will you need to address?
- Why does your argument matter? Who might be threatened or made uncomfortable by your views? What is at stake?

Organizing a Causal Argument

At the outset, it is useful to know some of the standard ways that a causal argument can be organized. Later, you may decide on a different organizational pattern, but the standard ways shown in Organization Plans 1, 2, and 3 on pages 252–253 will help you get started.

Plans 2 and 3 are similar in that they examine numerous possible causes or consequences. Plan 2, however, tries to establish the relative importance of each cause or consequence, whereas plan 3 aims at rejecting the causes or consequences normally assumed by the audience and argues for an unexpected surprising cause or consequence. Plan 3 can also be used when your purpose is to change your audience's mind about a cause or consequence.

Questioning and Critiquing a Causal Argument

Knowing how to question and critique a causal argument will help you anticipate opposing views in order to strengthen your own. It will also help you rebut another person's causal argument. Here are some useful questions to ask:

- When you explain the links in a causal chain, can a skeptic point out weaknesses in any of the links?
- If you speculate about the causes of a phenomenon, could a skeptic argue for different causes or arrange your causes in a different order of importance?
- If you argue for a surprising cause or a surprising consequence of a phenomenon, could a skeptic point out alternative explanations that would undercut your argument?
- If your argument depends on inferences from data, could a skeptic question the way the data were gathered or interpreted? Could a skeptic claim that the data weren't relevant (for example, research done with lab animals might not apply to humans)?
- If your causal argument depends on a correlation between one phenomenon and another, could a skeptic argue that the direction of causality should be reversed or that an unidentified third phenomenon is the real cause? ■

Organization Plan 1: Argument Explaining Links in a Causal Chain

Introduce the issue and state your claim.	• Engage reader's interest in your causal issue and show why it is controversial or problematic. • Show what's at stake. • State your claim.
Explain the links in the chain going from cause to effect.	• Explain the links and their connections in order. • Anticipate and respond to possible objections if needed.
Conclude.	• Perhaps sum up your argument. • Return to the "big picture" of what's at stake. • End with something memorable.

Organization Plan 2: Argument Proposing Multiple Causes or Consequences of a Phenomenon

Introduce the issue and state your claim.	• Engage reader's interest in your causal issue and show why it is problematic or controversial. • Show what's at stake. • State your claim.
Propose relative contributions of different causes of a phenomenon or relative importance of different consequences.	• Describe the first possible cause or consequence and explain your reasoning. • Continue with the rest of your causes or consequences. • Arrange causes or consequences in increasing order of importance, significance, or surprise.
Respond to possible objections to your argument (if needed).	• Anticipate and summarize possible objections. • Respond through rebuttal or concession.
Conclude.	• Perhaps sum up your argument. • Return to the "big picture" of what's at stake. • End with something memorable.

Organization Plan 3: Argument Proposing a Surprising Causes or Consequence

Introduce the issue and state your claim.	• Engage reader's interest in your causal issue and show why it is problematic or controversial. • Show what's at stake. • State your claim.
Reject commonly assumed causes or consequences.	• Describe the first commonly assumed cause or consequence and show why you don't think the explanation is adequate. • Continue with the rest of your commonly assumed causes or consequences.
Argue for your surprising cause or consequence.	• Describe your surprising cause or consequence. • Explain your causal reasoning. • Anticipate and respond to possible objections if needed.
Conclude.	• Perhaps sum up your argument. • Return to the "big picture" of what's at stake. • End with something memorable.

Our first reading, by student Julee Christianson, was written in response **READINGS**
to the assignment in this chapter. Julee was entering an intense public
debate about the underrepresentation of women in science, a controversy initiated by Lawrence Summers, then president of Harvard, who suggested that
there may be fewer women than men on prestigious science faculties because women
have less innate talent for science and math. A furious reaction ensued. The Web site of
the Women in Science and Engineering Leadership Institute has extensive coverage of
the controversy, including Summers's original speech (http://wiseli.engr.wisc.edu/
news/Summers.htm).

Why Lawrence Summers Was Wrong: Culture Rather Than Biology Explains the Underrepresentation of Women in Science and Mathematics

JULEE CHRISTIANSON (STUDENT)

In 2005, Harvard University's president, Lawrence H. Summers, gave a controversial
speech that suggested that the underrepresentation of women in tenured positions in math
and science departments was partly caused by biological differences. In his address,
Summers proposed three hypotheses explaining why women shy away from math and
science careers. First, he gave a "high-powered job hypothesis," which stated that women
naturally want to start a family and therefore will not have the time or desire to commit to
the high-stress workload required for research in math and science. His second hypothesis
was that genetic differences between the sexes cause more males than females to have high
aptitude for math and science. Lastly, he mentioned the hypothesis that women are under-
represented because of discrimination, but he dismissed discrimination as a significant factor. It was Summers's second hypothesis about biological differences that started a heated
national debate. The academic world seems split over this nature/nurture issue. Although
there is some evidence that biology plays a role in determining math ability, I argue that
culture plays a much larger role, both in the way that women are socialized and in the
continued existence of male discrimination against women in male-dominated fields.

Evidence supporting the role of biology in determining math ability is effectively
presented by Steven Pinker, a Harvard psychologist who agrees with Summers. In his
article "The Science of Difference: Sex Ed," Pinker focuses extensively on Summers's
"variability" argument. According to Pinker, "in many traits, men show greater variance
than women, and are disproportionately found at both the low and high ends of the distribution." He explains that males and females have similar average scores on math tests but that
there are more males than females in the top and the bottom percentiles. This greater
variance means that there are disproportionately more male than female math geniuses
(and math dunces) and thus more male than female candidates for top math and science

positions at major research universities. Pinker explains this greater variance through evolutionary biology: men can pass on their genes to dozens of offspring, whereas women can pass on their genes to only a few. Pinker also argues that men and women have different brain structures that result in different kinds of thinking. For example, Pinker cites research that shows that on average men are better at mental rotation of figures and mathematical word problems, while women are better at remembering locations, doing mathematical calculations, reading faces, spelling, and using language. Not only do males and females think differently, but they release different hormones. These hormones help shape gender because males release more testosterone and females more estrogen, meaning that men are more aggressive and apt to take risks, while women "are more solicitous to their children." One example Pinker uses to support his biological hypothesis is the case of males born with abnormal genitals and raised as females. These children have more testosterone than normal female children, and many times they show characteristically male interests and behavior. Pinker uses these cases as evidence that no matter how a child is raised, the child's biology determines the child's interests.

Although Pinker demonstrates that biology plays some role in determining math aptitude, he almost completely ignores the much larger role of discrimination and socialization in shaping the career paths of women. According to an editorial from *Nature Neuroscience* titled "Separating Science from Stereotype," "[t]he evidence to support [Summers's] hypothesis of 'innate difference' turns out to be quite slim" (253). The editorial reports that intercultural studies of the variance between boys' and girls' scores on math tests show significant differences between countries. For example, in Iceland girls outscore boys on math tests. The editorial also says that aptitude tests are not very good at predicting the future success of students and that the "SATs tend to underpredict female and over-predict male academic performance" (253). The editorial doesn't deny that men and women's brains work differently, but states that the differences are too small to be blamed for the underrepresentation of women in math and science careers.

If biology doesn't explain the low number of women choosing math and science careers, then what is the cause? Many believe the cause is culture, especially the gender roles children are taught at a very young age. One such believer is Deborah L. Rhode, an attorney and social scientist who specializes in ethics and gender, law, and public policy. In her book *Speaking of Sex: The Denial of Gender Inequality*, Rhode describes the different gender roles females and males are expected to follow from a very young age. Gender roles are portrayed in children's books and television shows. These gender roles are represented by male characters as heroes and problem solvers, while the female characters are the "damsels in distress." Another example of gender roles is that only a very small number of these shows and books portray working mothers or stay-at-home fathers. Rhodes also discussed how movies and popular music, especially rap and heavy metal, encourage violence and objectify women. As girls grow up, they face more and more gender stereotypes from toys to magazines. Parents give their boys interactive, problem-solving toys such as chemistry sets and telescopes, while girls are left with dolls. Although more organizations such as the Girl Scouts of America, who sponsor the Web site *girlsgotech.org*, are trying to interest girls in science and math and advertise careers in those fields to girls, the societal forces working against this encouragement are also still pervasive. For example, magazines for teenage girls encourage attracting male attention and the importance of looks, while being smart and successful is considered unattractive. Because adolescents face so many gender stereotypes, it is no wonder that they shape the career paths they chose later in life. The gender roles engraved in our adolescents' minds cause discrimination against women later in life. Once women are socialized to see themselves as dependent and not as smart as males, it becomes very difficult to break away from these gender stereotypes. With gender bias so apparent in our society, it is hard for females to have high enough self-confidence to continue to compete with males in many fields.

5   The effect of socialization begins at a very early age. One study by Melissa W. Clearfield and Naree M. Nelson shows how parents unconsciously send gendered messages to their infants and toddlers. This study examined differences in mothers' speech patterns and play behaviors based on the gender of infants ranging from six months to fourteen months. Although there was no difference in the actual play behavior of male and female infants, the researchers discovered interesting differences in the way mothers interacted with daughters versus sons. Mothers of daughters tended to ask their daughters more questions, encouraging social interaction, whereas mothers of sons were less verbal, encouraging their sons to be more independent. The researchers concluded that "the mothers in our study may have been teaching their infants about gender roles through modeling and reinforcement. . . . Thus girls may acquire the knowledge that they are 'supposed' to engage in higher levels of interaction with other people and display more verbal behavior than boys. . . . In contrast, the boys were reinforced for exploring on their own" (136).

One of the strongest arguments against the biological hypothesis comes from a transgendered Stanford neurobiologist, Ben A. Barres, who has been a scientist first as a woman and then as a man. In his article "Does Gender Matter?" Barres states that "there is little evidence that gender differences in [mathematical] abilities exist, are innate or are even relevant to the lack of advancement of women in science" (134). Barres provides much anecdotal evidence of the way women are discriminated against in this male-dominated field. Barres notes that simply putting a male name rather than a female name on an article or résumé increases its perceived value. He also describes research showing that men and women do equally well in gender-blind academic competitions but that men win disproportionately in contests where gender is revealed. As Barres says, "the bar is unconsciously raised so high for women and minority candidates that few emerge as winners" (134). In one study reported by Barres, women applying for a research grant needed more than twice the productivity of men in order to be considered equally competent. As a female-to-male transgendered person, Barres has personally experienced discrimination when trying to succeed in the science and math fields. When in college, Barres was told that her boyfriend must have done her homework, and she later lost a prestigious fellowship competition to a male even though she was told her application was stronger and she had published "six high-impact papers," while the man that won only published one. Barres even notices subtle differences, such as the fact that he can now finish a sentence without being interrupted by a male.

Barres urges women to stand up publicly against discrimination. One woman he particularly admires as a strong female role model is MIT biologist Nancy Hopkins, who sued the MIT administration for discrimination based on the lesser amount of lab space allocated to female scientists. The evidence from this study was so strong that even the president of MIT publicly admitted that discrimination was a problem (134). Barres wants more women to follow

Hopkins's lead. He believes that women often don't realize they are being discriminated against because they have faith that the world is equal. Barres explains this tendency as a "denial of personal disadvantage" (134). Very few women will admit to seeing or experiencing discrimination. Until discrimination and sexism are addressed, women will continue to be oppressed.

As a society, we should not accept Lawrence Summers's hypothesis that biological differences are the reason women are not found in high-prestige tenured job in math and science. In fact, in another generation the gap between men and women in math and science might completely disappear. In 2003–2004, women received close to one-third of all doctorates in mathematics, up from fifteen percent of doctorates in the early 1980s ("Women in Mathematics"). Although more recent data are not yet available, the signs point to a steadily increasing number of women entering the fields of math, science, and engineering. Blaming biology for the lack of women in these fields and refusing to fault our culture is taking the easy way out. Our culture can change.

Works Cited

Barres, Ben A. "Does Gender Matter?" *Nature* 44.7 (2006): 133–36. Print.

Clearfield, Melissa W., and Naree M. Nelson. "Sex Differences in Mothers' Speech and Play Behavior with 6-, 9-, and 14-Month-Old Infants." *Sex Roles* 54.1–2 (2006): 127–37. Print.

Girlsgotech. Girl Scouts of the United States of America, 2004. Web. 9 Feb. 2008.

Pinker, Steven. "The Science of Difference: Sex Ed." *New Republic.* The New Republic, 7 Feb. 2005. Web. 12 Feb. 2008.

Rhode, Deborah L. *Speaking of Sex: The Denial of Gender Inequality.* Cambridge, MA: Harvard UP, 1997. Print.

"Separating Science from Stereotype." Editorial. *Nature Neuroscience* 8.3 (2005): 253. Print.

Summers. Lawrence H. "Remarks at NBER Conference on Diversifying the Science and Engineering Workforce." *The Office of the President.* Harvard University, Jan. 2005. Web. 8 Feb. 2008.

"Women in Mathematics: Study Shows Gains." *American Mathematical Society.* American Mathematical Society, 6 July 2005. Web. 14 Feb. 2008.

Critiquing "Why Lawrence Summers Was Wrong"

1. The controversy sparked by Harvard President Lawrence Summers' remarks was a highly politicized version of the classic nature/nurture problem. Liberal commentators claimed that women were underrepresented in science because of cultural practices that discouraged young girls from becoming interested in math and science and that blocked women Ph.D.s from advancing in their scientific careers. In contrast, conservative commentators—praising Summers' courage for raising a politically incorrect subject—took the "nature" side of this argument by citing studies pointing to innate cognitive differences between human males and females. How would you characterize Christianson's position in this controversy?

2. How does Christianson handle opposing views in her essay?

3. Do you regard Christianson's essay as a valuable contribution to the controversy over the reasons for the low numbers of women in math and science? Why or why not?

4. How would you characterize Christianson's *ethos* as a student writer in this piece? Does her *ethos* help convince you that her argument is sound? Explain.

Our second reading, by evolutionary biologist Olivia Judson of Imperial College in London, was published as an op-ed piece in the *New York Times.* In this causal argument, a distinguished scientist looks at the scientific evidence bearing on Summers's remarks.

Different but (Probably) Equal

OLIVIA JUDSON

Hypothesis: males and females are typically indistinguishable on the basis of their behaviors and intellectual abilities.

This is not true for elephants. Females have big vocabularies and hang out in herds; males tend to live in solitary splendor, and insofar as they speak at all, their conversation appears mostly to consist of elephant for "I'm in the mood, I'm in the mood..."

The hypothesis is not true for zebra finches. Males sing elaborate songs. Females can't sing at all. A zebra finch opera would have to have males in all the singing roles.

And it's not true for green spoon worms. This animal, which lives on the sea floor, has one of the largest known size differences between male and female: the male is 200,000 times smaller. He spends his whole life in her reproductive tract, fertilizing eggs by regurgitating sperm through his mouth. He's so different from his mate that when he was first discovered by science, he was not recognized as being a green spoon

worm; instead, he was thought to be a parasite.

5   Is it ridiculous to suppose that the hypothesis might not be true for humans either?

No. But it is not fashionable—as Lawrence Summers, president of Harvard University, discovered when he suggested this month that greater intrinsic ability might be one reason that men are overrepresented at the top levels of fields involving math, science, and engineering.

There are—as the maladroit Mr. Summers should have known—good reasons it's not fashionable. Beliefs that men are intrinsically better at this or that have repeatedly led to discrimination and prejudice, and then they've been proved to be nonsense. Women were thought not to be world-class musicians. But when American symphony orchestras introduced blind auditions in the 1970s—the musician plays behind a screen so that his or her gender is invisible to those listening—the number of women

offered jobs in professional orchestras increased.

Similarly, in science, studies of the ways that grant applications are evaluated have shown that women are more likely to get financing when those reading the applications do not know the sex of the applicant. In other words, there's still plenty of work to do to level the playing field; there's no reason to suppose there's something inevitable about the status quo.

All the same, it seems a shame if we can't even voice the question. Sex differences are fascinating—and entirely unlike the other biological differences that distinguish other groups of living things (like populations and species). Sex differences never arise in isolation, with females evolving on a mountaintop, say, and males evolving in a cave. Instead, most genes—and in some species, all genes—spend equal time in each sex. Many sex differences are not, therefore, the result of *his* having one gene while *she* has another. Rather, they are attributable to the way particular genes behave when they find themselves in *him* instead of *her*.

10   The magnificent difference between male and female green spoon worms, for example, has nothing to do with their having different genes: each green spoon worm larva could go either way. Which sex it becomes depends on whether it meets a female during its first three weeks of life. If it meets a female, it becomes male and prepares to regurgitate; if it doesn't, it becomes female and settles into a crack on the sea floor.

What's more, the fact that most genes occur in both males and females can generate interesting sexual tensions. In male fruit flies, for instance, variants of genes that confer particular success—which on Mother Nature's abacus is the number of descendants you have—tend to be detrimental when they occur in females, and vice versa. Worse: the bigger the advantage in one sex, the more detrimental those genes are in the other. This means that, at least for fruit flies, the same genes that make a male a Don Juan would also turn a female into a wallflower; conversely, the genes that make a female a knockout babe would produce a clumsy fellow with the sex appeal of a cake tin.

But why do sex differences appear at all? They appear when the secret of success differs for males and females: the more divergent the paths to success, the more extreme the physiological differences. Peacocks have huge tails and strut about because peahens prefer males with big tails. Bull elephant seals grow to five times the mass of females because big males are better at monopolizing the beaches where the females haul out to have sex and give birth.

Meanwhile, the crow-like jackdaw has (as far as we can tell) no obvious sex differences and appears to lead a life of devoted monogamy. Here, what works for him also seems to work for her, though the female is more likely to sit on the eggs. So by studying the differences—and similarities—among men and women, we can potentially learn about the forces that have shaped us in the past.

And I think the news is good. We're not like green spoon worms or elephant seals, with males and females so different that aspiring to an egalitarian society would be ludicrous. And though we may not be jackdaws either—men and women tend to look different, though even here there's overlap—it's obvious that where there are intellectual differences, they are so slight they cannot be prejudged.

15   The interesting questions are, is there an average intrinsic difference? And how extensive is the variation? I would love to know if the averages are the same but the underlying variation is different—with members of one sex tending to be either superb or dreadful at particular sorts of thinking while members of the other are pretty good but rarely exceptional.

Curiously, such a result could arise even if the forces shaping men and women have been identical. In some animals—humans and fruit flies come to mind—males have an X chromosome and a Y chromosome while females have two Xs. In females, then, extreme effects of genes on one X chromosome can be offset by the genes on the other. But in males, there's no hiding your X. In birds and butterflies, though, it's the other way around: females have a Z chromosome and a W chromosome, and males snooze along with two Zs.

The science of sex differences, even in fruit flies and toads, is a ferociously complex subject. It's also famously fraught, given its malignant history. In fact, there was a time not so long ago when I would have balked at the whole enterprise: the idea there might be intrinsic cognitive differences between men and women was one I found insulting. But science is a great persuader. The jackdaws and spoon worms have forced me to change my mind. Now I'm keen to know what sets men and women apart—and no longer afraid of what we may find.

Critiquing "Different but (Probably) Equal"

1. What parts of Judson's article tend to support the "nurture" view that cultural practices account for women's underrepresentation in math and science? What parts tend to support the "nature" view?

2. Judson's argument relies heavily on analogies between humans and the animal world. In your own words, explain why the green spoon worm and the jackdaw (crow) are important to Judson's argument. Why does she say that the interesting questions involve "average intrinsic difference" and the extensiveness of "variation"?

3. How would you characterize Judson's *ethos* in this article? Pay particular attention to the narrative embedded in the last paragraph—her claim that she is no longer afraid of what we might find. How important is it that we know the author is a woman?

Our final causal argument, by student writer Carlos Macias, examines the phenomenon of credit card debt among college students. Note how Macias intermixes personal experiences and research data in order to make his case.

"The Credit Card Company Made Me Do It!"—The Credit Card Industry's Role in Causing Student Debt

CARLOS MACIAS (STUDENT)

One day on spring break this year, I strolled into a Gap store. I found several items that I decided to buy. As I was checking out, the cute female clerk around my age, with perfect hair and makeup, asked if I wanted to open a GapCard to save 10 percent on all purchases I made at Gap, Banana Republic, and Old Navy that day. She said I would also earn points toward Gap gift certificates in the future. Since I shop at the Gap often enough, I decided to take her up on her offer. I filled out the form she handed me, and within seconds I—a jobless, indebted-from-student-loans, full-time college student with no substantial assets or income whatsoever—was offered a card with a $1000 credit line. Surprised by the speed in which I was approved and the amount that I was approved for, I decided to proceed to both Banana Republic and Old Navy that day to see if there was anything else I might be interested in getting (there was). By the end of the day, I had rung up nearly $200 in purchases.

I know my $200 shopping spree on credit is nothing compared to some of the horror stories I have heard from friends. One of my friends, a college sophomore, is carrying $2000 on a couple of different cards, a situation that is not unusual at all. According to a May 2005 study, students with credit cards carry average balances of just under $3000 by the time they are seniors (Nellie Mae 2). The problem is that most students don't have the income to pay off their balances, so they become hooked into paying high interest rates and fees that enrich banks while exploiting students who have not yet learned how to exercise control on their spending habits.

Who is to blame for this situation? Many people might blame the students themselves, citing the importance of individual responsibility and proclaiming that no one forces students to use credit cards. But I put most of the blame directly on the credit card companies. Credit cards are enormously profitable; according to a *New York Times* article, the industry made $30 billion in pretax profits in 2003 alone (McGeehan). Hooking college students on credit cards is essential for this profit, not only because companies make a lot of money off the students themselves, but because hooking students on cards creates a habit that lasts a lifetime. Credit card companies' predatory lending practices—such as using exploitive advertising, using credit scoring to determine creditworthiness, disguising the real cost of credit, and taking advantage of U.S. government deregulation—are causing many unwitting college students to accumulate high levels of credit card debt.

First of all, credit card companies bombard students with highly sophisticated advertising. College students, typically, are in an odd "in-between" stage where they are not necessarily teens anymore, provided for by their parents, but neither are they fully adults, able to provide entirely for themselves. Many students feel the pressures from family, peers and themselves to assume adult roles in terms of their dress and jobs, not relying on Mom or Dad for help. Card companies know about these pressures. Moreover, college students are easy to target because they are concentrated on campuses and generally consume the same media. I probably get several mailings a month offering me a preapproved credit card. These advertisements are filled with happy campus scenes featuring students wearing just the right clothes, carrying their books in just the right backpack, playing music on their iPods or opening their laptop computers. They also appeal to students' desire to feel like responsible adults by emphasizing little emergencies that college students can relate to such as car breakdowns on a road trip. These advertisements illustrate a point made by a team of researchers in an article entitled "Credit Cards as Lifestyle Facilitators": The authors explain how credit card companies want consumers to view credit cards as "lifestyle facilitators" that enable "lifestyle building" and "lifestyle signaling" (Bernthal, Crockett, and Rose). Credit cards make it easy for students to live the lifestyle pictured in the credit card ads.

5   Another contributing cause of high credit card debt for college students is the method that credit card companies use to grant credit—through credit scoring that does not consider income. It was credit scoring that allowed me to get that quadruple-digit credit line at the Gap while already living in the red. The application I filled out never asked my income. Instead, the personal information I listed was used to pull up my credit score, which is based on records of outstanding debts and payment history. Credit scoring allows banks to grant credit cards based on a person's record of responsibility in paying bills rather than on income. According to finance guru Suze Orman, "Your FICO (credit) score is a great tool to size up how good you will be handling a new loan or credit card" (21). Admittedly, credit scoring has made the lending process as a whole much fairer, giving individuals such as minorities and women the chance to qualify for credit even if they have minimal incomes. But when credit card companies use credit scoring to determine college students' creditworthiness, many students are unprepared to handle a credit line that greatly exceeds their ability to pay

based on income. In fact, the Center for Responsible Lending, a consumer advocacy organization in North Carolina, lobbied Congress in September 2003 to require credit card companies to secure proof of adequate income for college-age customers before approving credit card applications ("Credit Card Policy Recommendations"). If Congress passed such legislation, credit card companies would not be able to as easily take advantage of college students who have not yet learned how to exercise control on their spending habits. They would have to offer students credit lines commensurate to their incomes. No wonder these companies vehemently opposed this legislation.

Yet another contributing cause of high levels of credit card debt is the high cost of having this debt, which credit card companies are especially talented at disguising. As credit card debt increases, card companies compound unpaid interest, adding it to the balance that must be repaid. If this balance is not repaid, they charge interest on unpaid interest. They add exorbitant fees for small slip-ups like making a late payment or exceeding the credit limit. While these costs are listed on statements when first added to the balance, they quickly vanish into the "New Balance" number on all subsequent statements, as if these fees were simply past purchases that have yet to be repaid. As the balance continues to grow, banks spike interest rates even higher. In his 2004 article "Soaring Interest Is Compounding Credit Card Pain for Millions," Patrick McGeehan describes a "new era of consumer credit, in which thousands of Americans are paying millions of dollars each month in fees that they did not expect…lenders are doubling or tripling interest rates with little warning or explanation." These rate hikes are usually tucked into the pages of fine print that come with credit cards, which many consumers are unable to fully read, let alone understand. Usually, a credit card company will offer a very low "teaser rate" that expires after several months. While this industry practice is commonly understood by consumers, many do not understand that credit card companies usually reserve the right to raise the rate at any time for almost any reason, causing debt levels to rise further.

Admittedly, while individual consumers must be held accountable for any debt they accumulate and should understand compound and variable interest and fees, students' ignorance is welcomed by the credit card industry. In order to completely understand how the credit card industry has caused college students to amass high amounts of credit card debt, it is necessary to explain how this vicious monster was let loose during banking deregulation over the past 30 years. In 1978, the Supreme Court opened the floodgates by ruling that the federal government could not set a cap on interest rates that banks charged for credit cards; that was to be left to the states. With Uncle Sam no longer protecting consumers, Delaware and South Dakota passed laws that removed caps on interest rates, in order to woo credit card companies to conduct nationwide business there (McGeehan). Since then, the credit card industry has become one of the most profitable industries ever. Credit card companies were given another sweet deal from the U.S. Supreme Court in 1996, when the Court deregulated fees. Since then, the average late fee has risen from $10 or less, to $39 (McGeehan). While a lot of these fees and finance charges are avoidable if the student pays the balance in full, on time, every month, for college students who carry balances for whatever reason, these charges are tacked on, further adding to the principal on which they pay a high rate of compounded interest. (79% of the students surveyed in the Nellie Mae study said that they regularly carried a balance on their cards [8].) Moreover, the U.S. government has refused to step in to regulate the practice of universal default, where a credit card company can raise the rate they charge if a consumer is late on an unrelated bill, like a utility payment. Even for someone who pays his or her bills in full, on time, 99% of the time, one bill-paying slip-up can cause an avalanche of fees and frustration, thanks to the credit card industry.

Credit card companies exploit college students' lack of financial savvy and security. It is no secret that most full-time college students are not independently wealthy; many have limited means. So why are these companies so willing to issue cards to poor college students? Profits, of course! If they made credit cards less available to struggling consumers such as college students, consumers would have a more difficult time racking up huge balances, plain and simple. It's funny that Citibank, one of the largest, most profitable credit card companies in the world, proudly exclaims "Live richly" in its advertisements. At the rate that it and other card companies collect interest and fees from their customers, a more appropriate slogan would be "Live poorly."

Works Cited

Bernthal, Matthew J., David Crockett, and Randall L. Rose. "Credit Cards as Lifestyle Facilitators." *Journal of Consumer Research* 32.1 (2005): 130–45. *Research Library Complete.* Web. 18 June 2005.

"Credit Card Policy Recommendations." *Center for Responsible Lending.* Center for Responsible Lending, Sept. 2003. Web. 18 June 2005.

McGeehan, Patrick. "Soaring Interest Is Compounding Credit Card Pain for Millions." *New York Times.* New York Times, 21 Nov. 2004. Web. 3 July 2005.

Nellie Mae. "Undergraduate Students and Credit Cards in 2004: An Analysis of Usage Rates and Trends." *Nellie Mae.* SLM Corporation, May 2005. Web. 3 July 2005.

Orman, Suze. *The Money Book for the Young, Fabulous and Broke.* New York: Riverhead, 2005. Print.

Critiquing "The Credit Card Company Made Me Do It!"

1. How effective is Macias's argument that the predatory practices of banks and credit card companies are the primary cause of credit card debt among college students?
2. Suppose that you wanted to join this conversation by offering a counterview with a thesis something like this: "Although Macias is partially correct that banks and credit card companies play a role in producing credit card debt among college students, he underestimates other important factors." What would you emphasize as the causes of credit card debt? How would you make your case?

For additional writing, reading, and research resources, go to www.mycomplab.com

13 Resemblance Arguments

Case 1   How Serious Is College Debt?

In this graduation day cartoon by political cartoonist Matt Davies, the burden of college debt is likened to the plight of an oarless rower pumping madly to stay afloat in a sinking boat. Sharpened by a pun on "pomp and circumstance," the cartoon's argument depends on a visual analogy between paying off loans and pumping water from a boat. Humorously we fill in the unstated assumptions: without the debt, this happy grad would be rowing swiftly toward his destination of, say, a new car, a satisfying job, a house, and a bunch of money bags at his feet. Cartoonists frequently use visual analogies to make their argumentative claims.

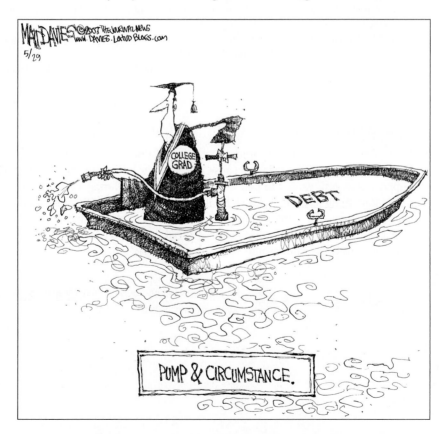

> **Case 2   Was the September 11, 2001, Terrorist Attack More Like a Criminal Act, an Act of War, or a Natural Disaster or Disease?**
>
> Following the September 11, 2001, terrorist attack on the World Trade Center and the Pentagon, media analysts tried to make sense of the horror by comparing it to different kinds of previous events. Some commentators likened it to Timothy McVeigh's bombing of the Alfred P. Murrah Federal Building in Oklahoma City in 1995—an argument that framed the terrorists as criminals who must be brought to justice. Others compared it to the 1941 Japanese attack on Pearl Harbor, an argument suggesting that the United States should declare war on some as-yet-to-be-defined enemy. Still others likened the event to an earthquake or an epidemic, arguing that terrorists will exist as long as the right conditions breed them and that it is useless to fight them using the strategies of conventional war. Under this analogy, the "war on terror" is a metaphorical war like the "war on poverty" or the "war against cancer." Clearly each of these resemblance arguments had high-stakes consequences. The Bush administration chose the Pearl Harbor argument and went to war. Critics of the war continued to say that war was an inappropriate strategy for fighting the "disease of terrorism."

An Overview of Resemblance Arguments

Resemblance arguments support a claim by comparing one thing to another with the intention of transferring the audience's understanding of (or feelings about) the second thing back to the first. Thus our dismay at seeing a graduate slowly sinking in his swamped rowboat is transferred to the issue of the burden of high education debts. The persuasive power of resemblance arguments comes from their ability to clarify an audience's conception of contested issues while conveying powerful emotions. The risk of resemblance arguments is that the differences between the two things being compared are often so significant that the argument may collapse under close examination. Thus the cartoon may misrepresent the relationship between college debt and a graduate's future success by not showing the higher earnings that college graduates can expect to receive over a lifetime.

Toulmin Framework for a Resemblance Argument

Like most other argument types, resemblance arguments can be analyzed using the Toulmin schema. Suppose you want to find a startling way to warn teenage girls away from excessive dieting. Simultaneously, you want to argue that excessive dieting is partially caused by a patriarchal construction of beauty that keeps women submissive and powerless. You decide to create a resemblance argument claiming that women's obsessive dieting is like foot binding in ancient China. This argument can be displayed in Toulmin terms as follows:

Toulmin Analysis of the Dieting Argument

ENTHYMEME

CLAIM Women's obsessive dieting in America serves the same harmful function as foot binding in ancient China

REASON because both practices keep women childlike, docile, dependent, and unthreatening to men.

GROUNDS

- Evidence that women, in attempting to imitate society's image of the "perfect woman," damage themselves (Chinese women were physically maimed; American women are psychologically maimed and often weakened by inadequate diet or constant worry about being fat.)

- Evidence that both practices make women childlike rather than grown-up (men call beautiful women "babes" or "dolls"; anorexia stops menstruation.)

- Evidence that women obsessed with beauty end up satisfied with less pay and subordinate positions in society as long as they are regarded as feminine and pretty.

POSSIBLE CONDITIONS OF REBUTTAL
Attacking the reason and grounds:

- Women who diet are concerned with health, not pursuit of beauty.

- Concern for healthy weight is "rational," not "obsessive."

- Thin women are often powerful athletes, not at all like Chinese victims of foot binding who can hardly walk.

- Dieting does not cause crippling deformity; a concern for beauty does not make a woman subordinate or satisfied with less pay.

- Dieting is a woman's choice—not something forced on her as a child.

WARRANT

Practices that are like ancient Chinese foot binding are bad.

BACKING

- Arguments that the subordinate position of women evidenced in both foot binding and obsession with weight is related to patriarchal construction of women's roles

- Arguments for why women should free themselves from patriarchal views

CONDITIONS OF REBUTTAL
Attacking the warrant and backing

- Perhaps arguments could be made that Chinese foot binding was not as repressive and patriarchal as the analogy implies (?). [We can't imagine a contemporary argument supporting footbinding.]

- Arguments supporting patriarchy and women's subordination

QUALIFIER: Perhaps the writer should say *"Under certain conditions* obsessive dieting can even seem like Chinese foot binding.

For many audiences, the comparison of women's dieting to Chinese foot binding will have an immediate and powerful emotional effect, perhaps causing them to see attitudes toward weight and food from a new, unsettling perspective. The analogy invites them to transfer their understanding of Chinese foot binding—which seems instantly repulsive and oppressive of women—to their understanding of obsessive concern for losing weight. Whereas social controls in ancient China were overt, the modern practice uses more subtle kinds of social controls, such as the influence of the fashion and beauty industry and peer pressure. But in both cases women feel forced to mold their bodies to a patriarchal standard of beauty—one that emphasizes soft curves, tiny waists, and daintiness rather than strength and power.

But this example also illustrates the dangers of resemblance arguments, which often ignore important differences or *disanalogies* between the terms of comparison. As the "conditions of rebuttal" show, there are many differences between dieting and foot binding. For example, the practice of foot binding was not a conscious choice of young Chinese girls, who were forced to have their feet wrapped at an early age. Dieting, on the other hand, is something one chooses, and it may reveal a healthy and rational choice rather than an obsession with appearance. When the practice degenerates to anorexia or bulimia, it becomes a mental disease, not a physical deformity forced on a girl in childhood. Thus a resemblance argument is usually open to refutation if a skeptic points out important disanalogies.

We now turn to the two types of resemblance arguments: analogy and precedent.

Arguments by Analogy

The use of *analogies* can constitute the most imaginative form of argument. If you don't like your new boss, you can say that she's like a Marine drill sergeant, the cowardly captain of a sinking ship, or a mother hen. Each of these analogies suggests a different management style, clarifying the nature of your dislike while conveying an emotional charge. The ubiquity of analogies undoubtedly stems from their power to clarify the writer's understanding of an issue through comparisons that grip the audience.

Analogies have the power to get an audience's attention like virtually no other persuasive strategy. But seldom are they sufficient in themselves to provide full understanding. At some point with every analogy you need to ask yourself, "How far can I legitimately go with this? At what point are the similarities between the two things I am comparing going to be overwhelmed by their dissimilarities?" They are useful attention-getting devices, but they can conceal and distort as well as clarify.

With this caveat, let's look at the uses of both undeveloped and extended analogies.

Using Undeveloped Analogies

Typically, writers use short, *undeveloped analogies* to drive home a point (and evoke an accompanying emotion) and then quickly abandon the analogy before the reader's awareness of disanalogies begins to set in. Suppose, for example, that you oppose taxpayer subsidies for the fine arts such as ballet or opera on the grounds that these are simply entertainments preferred by rich people. You might say: "Don't give my tax dollars to opera unless you also fund monster truck rallies. Opera is simply a monster truck rally for the rich." Your goal is to point out the hidden class bias in taxpayer support of opera and therefore to win your audience to your side: just as they would oppose a "National Endowment for Monster Truck Rallies," they ought to oppose a National Endowment for the Arts. But you don't want to linger too long on the analogy lest your audience begin pointing out important differences between taxpayer subsidies for the arts and subsidies for monster truck rallies.

Using Extended Analogies

Sometimes writers elaborate an analogy so that it takes on a major role in the argument. As an example of a claim based on an extended analogy, consider the following excerpt from a professor's argument opposing a proposal to require a writing proficiency exam for graduation. In the following portion of his argument, the professor compares development of writing skills to the development of physical fitness.

> A writing proficiency exam gives the wrong symbolic messages about writing. It suggests that writing is simply a skill, rather than an active way of thinking and learning. It suggests that once a student demonstrates proficiency then he or she doesn't need to do any more writing.
>
> Imagine two universities concerned with the physical fitness of their students. One university requires a junior-level physical fitness exam in which students must run a mile in less than 10 minutes, a fitness level it considers minimally competent. Students at this university see the physical fitness exam as a one-time hurdle. As many as 70 percent of them can pass the exam with no practice; another 10–20 percent need a few months' training; and a few hopeless couch potatoes must go through exhaustive remediation. After passing the exam, any student can settle back into a routine of TV and potato chips having been certified as "physically fit."
>
> The second university, however, believing in true physical fitness for its students, is not interested in minimal competency. Consequently, it creates programs in which its students exercise 30 minutes every day for the entire four years of the undergraduate curriculum. There is little doubt which university will have the most physically fit students. At the second university, fitness becomes a way of life with everyone developing his or her full potential. Similarly, if we want to improve our students' writing abilities, we should require writing in every course throughout the curriculum.

If you choose to write an extended analogy such as this, you will focus on the points of comparison that serve your purposes. The writer's purpose in the preceding case is to support the achievement of mastery rather than minimalist standards as the goal of the university's writing program. Whatever other disanalogous elements are involved (for example, writing requires the use of intellect, which may or may not be strengthened by daily exercise), the comparison reveals vividly that a commitment to mastery involves more than a minimalist test. Typically, then, in developing your analogy, you are not developing all possible points of comparison so much as you are bringing out those similarities consistent with the point you are trying to make.

■ ■ ■   **FOR CLASS DISCUSSION**   Developing Analogies
The following is a two-part exercise to help you clarify for yourself how analogies function in the context of arguments. Part 1 is to be done outside class; part 2 is to be done in class.

PART 1   Think of an analogy that expresses your point of view toward each of the following topics. Your analogy can urge your readers toward either a positive view of the topic or a negative view, depending on the rhetorical effect you seek. Write your analogy in the following one-sentence format:

_____ is like _____ : A, B, C…(in which the first term is the contested topic being discussed; the second term is the analogy; and A, B, and C are the points of comparison).

Example

Topic: Cramming for an exam

Negative analogy: Cramming for an exam is like pumping iron for ten hours straight to prepare for a weight-lifting contest: exhausting and counterproductive

Positive analogy: Cramming for an exam is like carbohydrate loading before a big race: it gives you the mental food you need for the exam, such as a full supply of concepts and details all fresh in your mind.

1. Using spanking to discipline children
2. Using racial profiling for airport security
3. Using steroids to increase athletic performance
4. Paying college athletes
5. Eating at fast-food restaurants

An effective analogy should influence both your audience's feelings toward the issue and your audience's understanding of the issue. For example, the writer of the negative analogy in the "cramming for an exam" illustration obviously believes that pumping iron for ten hours before a weight-lifting match is stupid. This feeling of stupidity is then transferred to the original topic—cramming for an exam. But the analogy also clarifies understanding. The writer imagines the mind as a muscle (which gets exhausted after too much exercise and which is better developed through some exercise every day rather than a lot all at once) rather than as a large container (into which lots of stuff can be "crammed").

PART 2   Bring your analogies to class and compare them to those of your classmates. Select the best analogies for each of the topics and be ready to say why you think they are good.

Arguments by Precedent

Precedent arguments are like analogy arguments in that they compare two phenomena. In precedent arguments, however, the second part of the comparison is usually a past event in which some sort of decision was reached, often a moral, legal, or political decision. An argument by precedent tries to show that a similar decision should (or should not) be reached for the present case because the situation for the present case is similar (or not similar) to that of the previous case.

A classic example of a precedent argument is the following excerpt from a speech by President Lyndon Johnson in the early years of the Vietnam War:

> Nor would surrender in Vietnam bring peace because we learned from Hitler at Munich that success only feeds the appetite of aggression. The battle would be renewed in one country and then another country, bringing with it perhaps even larger and crueler conflict, as we have learned from the lessons of history.

EXAMINING VISUAL ARGUMENTS

"AS A MATTER OF FACT, WE JUST BOUGHT ANOTHER SUV...."   www.IBDeditorials.com/cartoons

A Resemblance Claim

This political cartoon by Pulitzer Prize–winning cartoonist Michael Ramirez uses an analogy to link our desire for petroleum to Adam and Eve's desire for the apple, leading to a fall from Paradise. Explore how this resemblance argument might create a clarifying lens for viewing our love affair with SUVs and other gas-guzzling vehicles.

1. How was life during the era of cheap oil like Paradise?
2. To what extent are Americans "seduced" by gasoline?
3. Is the cartoonist correct in suggesting a theological dimension to the oil crisis?

Here the audience knows what happened at Munich: France and Britain tried to appease Hitler by yielding to his demand for a large part of Czechoslovakia, but Hitler's armies continued their aggression anyway, using Czechoslovakia as a staging area to invade Poland. By arguing that surrender in Vietnam would lead to the same consequences, Johnson brings to his argument about Vietnam the whole weight of his audience's unhappy knowledge of World War II. Administration white papers developed Johnson's precedent argument by pointing toward the similarity of Hitler's promises with those of the Viet Cong: You give us this and we will ask for no more. But Hitler didn't keep his promise. Why should the Viet Cong?

Johnson's Munich precedent persuaded many Americans during the early years of the war and helps explain U.S. involvement in Southeast Asia. Yet many scholars attacked Johnson's reasoning. For example, historian Howard Zinn attacked Johnson's argument by claiming three crucial differences between Europe in 1939 and Southeast Asia in 1965. First, Zinn argued, the Czechs were being attacked from outside by an external aggressor (Germany), whereas Vietnam was being attacked from within by rebels as part of a civil war. Second, Czechoslovakia was a prosperous, effective democracy, whereas the official Vietnam government was corrupt and unpopular. Third, Hitler wanted Czechoslovakia as a base for attacking Poland, whereas the Viet Cong and North Vietnamese aimed at reunification of their country as an end in itself.*

The Munich example shows again how arguments of resemblance depend on emphasizing the similarities between two phenomena and playing down the dissimilarities. One could try to refute the counterargument made by Zinn by arguing first that the Saigon government was more stable than Zinn thinks and second that the Viet Cong and North Vietnamese were driven by goals larger than reunification of Vietnam, namely, communist domination of Asia. Such an argument would once again highlight the similarities between Vietnam and prewar Europe.

■ ■ ■ **FOR CLASS DISCUSSION** **Using Claims of Precedent**

1. Consider the following claims of precedent, and evaluate how effective you think each precedent might be in establishing the claim. How would you develop the argument? How would you cast doubt on it?
   a. Gays should be allowed to serve openly in the U.S. military because they are allowed to serve openly in the militaries of most other Western countries.
   b. Postwar democracy can be created successfully in Iraq because it was created successfully in Germany and Japan following World War II.
2. Advocates for "right to die" legislation legalizing active euthanasia under certain conditions often point to the Netherlands as a country where acceptance of euthanasia works effectively. Assume for the moment that your state has a ballot initiative legalizing euthanasia. Assume further that you are being hired as a lobbyist for (against) the measure and have been assigned to do research on euthanasia in the Netherlands. Working in small groups, make a list of research questions you would want to ask. Your long-range rhetorical goal is to use your research to support (or attack) the ballot initiative by making a precedence argument focusing on the Netherlands.   ■ ■ ■

WRITING ASSIGNMENT A Resemblance Argument

Write a letter to the editor of your campus or local newspaper or a slightly longer guest editorial in which you try to influence public opinion on some issue through the use of a persuasive analogy or precedent. Megan Matthews's argument against the Navy's use of low-frequency sonar to locate submarines is a student piece written for this assignment (see pages 394–400).

Exploring Ideas

Because letters to the editor and guest editorials are typically short, writers often lack space to develop full arguments. Because of their clarifying and emotional power, arguments from analogy or precedent are often effective in these situations.

---

*Based on the summary of Zinn's argument in J. Michael Sproule, *Argument: Language and Its Influence* (New York: McGraw-Hill, 1980), 149–50.

Newspaper editors usually print letters or guest editorials only on current issues or on some current problem to which you can draw attention. For this assignment look through the most recent back issues of your campus or local newspaper, paying particular attention to issues being debated on the op-ed pages. Join one of the ongoing conversations about an existing issue, or draw attention to a current problem or situation that annoys you. In your letter or guest editorial, air your views. As part of your argument, include a persuasive analogy or precedent.

Identifying Your Audience and Determining What's at Stake

Before drafting your argument, identify your targeted audience and determine what's at stake. Consider your responses to the following questions:

- What audience are you targeting? What quick background could you sketch to help them understand your issue? How much do they already care about it?
- Before they read your argument, what stance on your issue do you imagine them holding? What change do you want to bring about in their view?
- What will they find new or surprising about your resemblance argument?
- If you are arguing from precedent, will your audience be familiar with the precedent, or will you have to explain it?
- What dissimilarities or disanalogies might they identify? What clarifications or counterarguments do you need to address to anticipate objections?
- Why does your argument matter? Who might be threatened or made uncomfortable by your views? What is at stake?

Organizing a Resemblance Argument

The most typical way to develop a resemblance argument is shown in the organization plan on page 273. Of course, this structure can be varied in many ways, depending on your issue and rhetorical context. Sometimes writers open an argument with the analogy, which serves as an attention grabber.

Questioning and Critiquing a Resemblance Argument

Once you have written a draft of your letter or guest editorial, you can test its effectiveness by role-playing a skeptical audience. What follows are some typical questions audiences will raise about arguments of resemblance.

- *Will a skeptic say I am putting too much persuasive weight on my analogy or precedent?* The most common mistake people make with resemblance arguments is expecting them to do too much. Too often, an analogy is mistakenly treated as a logical proof rather than a playful figure suggesting tentative but significant insights. The best way to guard against this charge is to qualify your argument and to find other means of persuasion to supplement an analogy or precedent argument.

Organization Plan for a Resemblance Argument

Introduce the issue and state your claim.	• Engage readers' interest in the issue to which you will apply your analogy or precedent. • Show how your issue is controversial or problematic and explain what's at stake. • State your claim.
Develop your analogy or precedent.	• Present the analogy or precedent. • Draw the explicit parallels you want to highlight between your issue and the analogy or precedent. • Help reader transfer insights or emotions derived from the analogy or precedent back to your issue.
Respond to possible objections (if needed).	• Anticipate disanalogies, counter-arguments, or other objections. • Respond to them as appropriate.
Conclusion	• Perhaps sum up your argument. • Help reader return to the "big picture" of what's at stake. • End with something memorable.

■ *Will a skeptic point out disanalogies in my resemblance argument?* To refute a resemblance argument, you can highlight significant differences between the two things being compared rather than similarities. As one example, we have already shown you how Howard Zinn identified disanalogies between Europe in 1939 and Southeast Asia in 1965. Here is another example. When the United States was debating the Twenty-Sixth Amendment, which lowered the voting age from twenty-one to eighteen, supporters of the amendment often argued, "If you are old enough to fight for your country in a war, you are old enough to vote." But conservative rhetorician Richard Weaver claimed that this analogy was true "only if you believe that fighting and voting are the same kind of thing which I, for one, do not. Fighting requires strength, muscular coordination and, in a modern army, instant and automatic response to orders. Voting requires knowledge of men, history, reasoning power; it is essentially a deliberative activity. Army mules and police dogs are used to fight; nobody is interested in giving them the right to vote. The argument rests on a false analogy."* ■

---

*Richard M. Weaver, "A Responsible Rhetoric," *Intercollegiate Review* (Winter 1976–1977), 86–87.

Our first reading is a letter to the editor by student Megan Matthews   **READINGS**
written for the assignment on page 271. The letter responds to a news
story in her local paper about whales damaged by Navy sonar. Notice how Megan uses
an analogy to help readers imagine the effect of human-produced sea noise on marine
mammals. Megan later used this analogy in the introduction to her researched argument shown on pages 394–400.

Whales Need Silence

MEGAN MATTHEWS (STUDENT)

Re: "Whales beach themselves following NATO exercise" (news story, September 26).
Imagine that you are forced to live in an apartment located next to Interstate 5 with its constant roar of engines and tires against concrete, its blaring horns and piercing sirens. When
you open your windows in the summer, you have to shout to be heard. What if you had to
leave your windows open all the time? What if your only housing alternatives were next to
other freeways?

Seems impossible? Not for whales, dolphins, and other marine mammals. Jacques
Cousteau's "world of silence" has been turned into an underwater freeway by the rumbling of cargo ships, the explosions of undersea mineral explorations, and the cacophony of the blasting devices used by fisheries. Now the Navy is adding a more powerful
and dangerous source of sound with its low-frequency active sonar (LFA) for detecting
enemy submarines. Low-frequency waves travel farther than high-frequency waves,
which is why the bumping bass of a car stereo reverberates after the car passes you. In
this case, 215 dB "pings" reflect off submarines—and whales—hundreds of miles away.
The recent beaching incident in the Canary Islands reflects the danger that Navy sonar
systems pose to whales.

Marine mammals depend on sound to avoid predators, to communicate across great
distances between pods and prospective mates, and to establish mother-calf bonds. The
extreme noise of Navy sonar apparently kills whales outright, while background "freeway"
noise throughout the oceans may be threatening their ability to survive as communities.

Congress should not fund further implementation of LFA, which springs from an out-
dated Cold War model of warfare; the risks to our *environmental* security are too great.

Critiquing "Whales Need Silence"

1. What is the analogy in this piece?
2. How effective is this analogy? Does the analogy succeed in moving the readers
   toward a positive identification with the plight of whales and a negative view of
   low-frequency sonar?

3. The letter to the editor genre requires very short arguments that usually focus on one main point, but sometimes include brief summaries of more developed arguments. Compare Megan's letter to the editor with her researched argument on pages 394–400. What is the main point that Megan wishes to drive home in her letter to the editor? Where in the letter does she summarize portions of her longer argument? Based on your reading of Megan's researched argument, what other strategies might Megan have used to write a letter to the editor?

Our second and third readings are a political cartoon and a letter to the editor written in response. The cartoon, by Pulitzer Prize winner Clay Bennett, first appeared in the *Chattanooga Times Free Press* on June 18, 2008, and was reprinted in the *Seattle Times*. The occasion was a California Supreme Court decision legalizing gay marriage in California. The responding letter to the editor, by Beth Reis, appeared in the *Seattle Times* on June 20, 2008.

Just Emancipated

CLAY BENNETT

Toon Offensive

BETH REIS

Don't get me wrong. I'm excited about California recognizing same-sex couples' right to marriage equality. I was a plaintiff in a Washington state marriage lawsuit. But the cartoon car with the words "just emancipated" on it, equating this development to the ending of slavery, especially on Juneteenth—the anniversity of the freeing of slaves after generations of brutality, forced labor, and families being separated and sold—is so offensive!

Yes, I feel a little more equal under the law this week. Yes, it matters that some people are now first-class citizens, entitled to the same rights and held to the same responsibilities as other couples. Yes, the word *marriage* is honorable and understandable and right.

But, please: How is that like outlawing slavery, exactly 146 years ago today? How is it like 143 years ago, when Texans were told that for the last three years they'd been enslaved illegally and were actually free? How is it like being told, nearly a century later, that they could finally vote?

I am proud to be gay, but not at all proud to have this week's small victory equated with the emancipation of slaves and the enfranchisement of their descendants.

Critiquing "Just Emancipated" and "Toon Offensive"

1. How does the cartoon use an analogy to praise the California gay marriage decision? What is the cartoon's implied claim?
2. How does Beth Reis's letter to the editor point out disanalogies as a method of refuting the cartoon's argument?
3. One strategy often used to support the legalization of same-sex marriage is to point out its similarities to earlier court decisions legalizing interracial marriages. What are the analogies and disanalogies between interracial marriage and same-sex marriage?
4. Analyze Beth Reis's rhetorical appeals to *logos, ethos,* and *pathos.*

Our fourth reading is an excerpt fr.om an annual report by the American Association of University Professors (AAUP). Titled "Where Are the Priorities: The Annual Report on the Economic Status of the Profession, 2007–08," this report argues that university administrators often spend students' tuition dollars or taxpayer dollars unwisely rather than focus on the university's primary mission: teaching and research. In the following excerpt, the report focuses on the salaries of football coaches.

Football Coach Salaries

AMERICAN ASSOCIATION OF UNIVERSITY PROFESSORS

Harley-Davidson Motor Company generates profits from the sale of branded T-shirts, jackets, gloves, helmets, boots, vests, sunglasses, even Christmas tree ornaments. But if the company began investing more resources in the manufacture of accessories than in the manufacture of its classic motorcycles, shareholders would demand to know what the company's real priorities were. Ostensibly, the first priority of the universities with Division I-A football programs is higher education. A review of the growing financial resources these universities sink into their football programs might, however, lead one to question the real priorities of the institutions.

USA Today sought to acquire the contracts of the 120 head football coaches leading Division I-A teams during the 2007–08 academic year. Table B compares the newspaper's data on coaches' pay with faculty salary data collected by the AAUP.

The base salaries and other income of fifty of the head coaches are at $1 million or higher. While "other income" includes payments for apparel contracts, public appearances, football camps, and items that may be paid by other sources, universities typically guarantee most of this income. The real number of millionaire coaches climbs substantially higher if one includes bonus payments for securing berths in bowl games or graduating certain percentages of the team's players and other perks such as vehicles, country club memberships, and free tickets for varsity sports events.

Table B presents two years of average salaries for head football coaches, average salaries of full professors, and the ratio of the two for the eleven Division I-A football conferences. In 2007–08, the average salary of the coaches is $1,040,863, a 12.4 percent increase over the $925,683 average paid in 2006–07. By contrast, the average salary of full professors at these universities in 2007–08 is $104,523, 3.5 percent more than the $100,998 paid in 2006–07. In 2006–07, the average head football coach earned 9.2 times the average full professor's salary; that ratio increased to 10 this year. What does this say about the priorities of Division I-A universities?

5   Although head football coaches, on average, earn more than twice the salary of full professors in every conference, the national averages do mask substantial differences between conferences. In the Mid-American Conference, coaches this year are earning 2.4 times the average salary of full professors. This ratio increased from last year because the average salary of full professors increased by only 2.3 percent, while the average salary of head coaches increased by 14.8 percent. By contrast, this year head coaches in the Southeastern Conference are earning 18.6 times the salary of the full professors who carry out the primary functions of their institutions, teaching and research. Full-professor average salaries are up 5.5 percent from last year but are dwarfed by the 36.4 percent increase in average head coach salaries. As we reported last year, new University of Alabama coach Nick Saban made headlines by securing a $3.5 million salary when he returned to the college ranks from the National Football League. But four of his conference colleagues also garnered salaries of more than $2 million this year.

One argument for paying high salaries to head football coaches in Division I-A is that the programs generate profits that can be shared with other university departments, including academic programs. Regarding football in particular, National Collegiate Athletic Association (NCAA) data for 2002–03 indicated that 68 percent of Division I-A programs reported profits, 28 percent reported budget deficits, and 4 percent reported breaking even. While football on average helps to subsidize other sports at Division I-A universities, athletic programs as a whole ran budget deficits. The average athletics deficit of $600,000 is a small amount when compared to a university operating budget in the hundreds of millions of dollars, but even so, NCAA data do not support the promise of football as a source of

TABLE B

Average Salary for Division I-A Football Head Coaches and Full Professors, by Conference, 2006–07 and 2007–08

Conference	Average Head Football Coach Salary						Average Full-Professor Salary						Ratio, Avg. Coach to Avg. Professor	
	2006		2007		Change		2006–07		2007–08		Change		2006–07	2007–08
	Mean	N	Mean	N	(%)		Mean	N	Mean	N	(%)			
Atlantic Coast Conference	$1,215,154	12	$1,363,450	10	12.2		$118,573	12	$125,044	12	5.5		10.2	10.9
Big East Conference	979,706	7	1,184,851	8	20.9		106,168	8	110,263	8	3.9		9.2	10.7
Big Ten Conference	1,431,583	9	1,504,176	9	5.1		113,929	9	118,851	9	4.3		12.6	12.7
Big Twelve	1,577,261	12	1,631,022	12	3.4		100,936	12	105,961	12	5.0		15.6	15.4
Conference USA	552,422	10	649,552	9	17.6		96,486	10	100,074	10	3.7		5.7	6.5
Mid-American Conference	197,319	12	226,475	12	14.8		91,700	10	93,783	12	2.3		2.2	2.4
Pacific-Ten Conference	1,236,604	9	1,311,968	9	6.1		110,331	9	109,654	7	−0.6[a]		11.2	12.0
Southeastern Conference	1,423,565	11	1,941,612	11	36.4		98,788	11	104,229	10	5.5		14.4	18.6
Sun Belt Conference	237,166	8	255,069	9	7.5		85,065	7	87,983	8	3.4		2.8	2.9
Western Athletic Conference	470,748	9	546,508	9	16.1		84,629	9	87,596	9	3.5		5.6	6.2
Mountain West Conference	622,776	8	645,632	8	3.7		96,627	7	102,627	7	6.2		6.4	6.3
Overall Average	$925,683	107	$1,040,863	106	12.4		$100,998	104	$104,523	104	3.5		9.2	10.0

Notes: Coach salary includes base salary and other income, most of which is guaranteed. It does not include performance-based bonuses. Full-professor salary is for full-time instructional faculty, excluding administrators and medical school faculty; base salary adjusted to nine-month basis. Conference figures do not include Pennsylvania State University or independent universities, where data are incomplete.

[a]Faculty salary figures for 2007–08 do not include the University of California, Berkeley, or the University of California, Los Angeles.

revenue for university academic programs. Instead, it appears that any net revenues that may be raised by even the most successful football programs go to subsidize other athletic programs.

When asked by *USA Today* about the enormous salaries commanded by head football coaches, Louisiana State University athletic director Skip Bertman said, "I go back to professional baseball and Alex Rodriguez making $25 million a year. Or to Julia Roberts and $20 million for one movie. Are those people worth it? Of course not. But if that's what the marketplace is and enough people are willing to watch Alex play or Julia Roberts in a movie, they have a right to get that. I don't think this is any different."

While analogies can be enormously useful learning devices, they don't work if they aren't accurate. Alex Rodriguez is paid $25 million by a professional baseball team that is a corporation whose function is to produce a winning team for profit. When Julia Roberts is paid $20 million to make a movie, she is being employed by a media company whose function is to produce entertaining films for profit. By contrast, most of the universities in Division I-A are public and thus subsidized by taxpayers. If the purpose of the institutions were to produce football entertainment for profit and serve as farm teams for the National Football League, then arguments about letting market forces determine college coaches' salaries would make sense. Otherwise, they don't.

In reality, only a few of the college athletes on the field, or of the students in the stands, will find their future success in life determined by what they learned on Saturday afternoons at the game. What will count most in the decades after graduation is what they learned from their professors in the classroom. And it is thus the academic program and the faculty in which taxpayers and alumni and other donors should be investing.

Critiquing "Football Coach Salaries"

1. This excerpt illustrates various kinds of analogy arguments. What points of comparison is the author making in the opening discussion of the Harley-Davidson Motor Company? Do you find the analogy effective? How does it clarify the author's understanding of university priorities?
2. The high salaries of football coaches are often justified by analogy to high-paid professional athletes or movie stars. How does the author rebut this analogy? Do you find the rebuttal persuasive?

Our last reading is from feminist writer Susan Brownmiller's *Against Our Will: Men, Women, and Rape*. First published in 1975, Brownmiller's book was chosen by the *New York Times Book Review* as one of the outstanding books of the year. In the following excerpt, Brownmiller makes an argument from resemblance, claiming that pornography is "antifemale propaganda."

From Against Our Will: Men, Women, and Rape

SUSAN BROWNMILLER

Pornography has been so thickly glossed over with the patina of chic these days in the name of verbal freedom and sophistication that important distinctions between freedom of political expression (a democratic necessity), honest sex education for children (a societal good) and ugly smut (the deliberate devaluation of the role of women through obscene, distorted depictions) have been hopelessly confused. Part of the problem is that those who traditionally have been the most vigorous opponents of porn are often those same people who shudder at the explicit mention of any sexual subject. Under their watchful, vigilante eyes, frank and free dissemination of educational materials relating to abortion, contraception, the act of birth, the female biology in general is also dangerous, subversive and dirty. (I am not unmindful that frank and free discussion of rape, "the unspeakable crime," might well give these righteous vigilantes further cause to shudder.) Because the battle lines were falsely drawn a long time ago, before there was a vocal women's movement, the antipornography forces appear to be, for the most part, religious, Southern, conservative and right-wing, while the pro-porn forces are identified as Eastern, atheistic and liberal.

But a woman's perspective demands a totally new alignment, or at least a fresh appraisal. The majority report of the President's Commission on Obscenity and Pornography (1970), a report that argued strongly for the removal of all legal restrictions on pornography, soft and hard, made plain that 90 percent of all pornographic material is geared to the male heterosexual market (the other 10 percent is geared to the male homosexual taste), that buyers of porn are "predominantly white, middle-class, middle-aged married males" and that the graphic depictions, the meat and potatoes of porn, are of the naked female body and of the multiplicity of acts done to that body.

Discussing the content of stag films, "a familiar and firmly established part of the American scene," the commission report dutifully, if foggily, explained, "Because pornography historically has been thought to be primarily a masculine interest, the emphasis in stag films seems to represent the preferences of the middle-class American male. Thus male homosexuality and bestiality are relatively rare, while lesbianism is rather common."

The commissioners in this instance had merely verified what purveyors of porn have always known: hard-core pornography is not a celebration of sexual freedom; it is a cynical exploitation of female sexual activity through the device of making all such activity, and consequently all females, "dirty." Heterosexual male consumers of pornography are frankly turned on by watching lesbians in action (although never in the final scenes, but always as a curtain raiser); they are turned off with a sudden swiftness of a water faucet by watching naked men act upon each other. One study quoted in the commission report came to the unastounding conclusion that "seeing a stag film in the presence of male peers bolsters masculine esteem." Indeed. The men in groups who watch the films, it is important to note, are *not* naked.

5   When male response to pornography is compared to female response, a pronounced difference in attitude emerges. According to the commission, "Males report being more highly aroused by depictions of nude females, and show more interest in depictions of nude females than [do] females." Quoting the figures of Alfred Kinsey, the commission noted that a majority of males (77 percent) were "aroused" by visual depictions of explicit sex while a majority of females (68 percent) were not aroused. Further, "females more often than males reported 'disgust' and 'offense.'"

From whence comes this female disgust and offense? Are females sexually backward or more conservative by nature? The gut distaste that a majority of women feel when we look at pornography, a distaste that, incredibly, it is no longer fashionable to admit, comes, I think, from the gut knowledge that we and our bodies are being stripped, exposed, and contorted for the purpose of ridicule to bolster that "masculine esteem" which gets its kick and sense of power from viewing females as anonymous, panting playthings, adult toys, dehumanized objects to be used, abused, broken, and discarded.

This, of course, is also the philosophy of rape. It is no accident (for what else could be its purpose?) that females in the pornographic genre are depicted in two cleanly delineated roles: as virgins who are caught and "banged" or as nymphomaniacs who are never sated. The most popular and prevalent pornographic fantasy combines the two: an innocent, untutored female is raped and "subjected to unnatural practices" that turn her into a raving, slobbering nymphomaniac, a dependent sexual slave who can never get enough of the big, male cock.

There can be no "equality" in porn, no female equivalent, no turning of the tables in the name of bawdy fun. Pornography, like rape, is a male invention, designed to dehumanize women, to reduce the female to an object of sexual access, not to free sensuality from moralistic or parental inhibition. The staple of porn will always be the naked female body, breasts and genitals exposed, because as man devised it, her naked body is the female's "shame," her private parts the private property of man, while his are the ancient, holy, universal, patriarchal instrument of his power, his rule by force over *her*.

Pornography is the undiluted essence of antifemale propaganda. Yet the very same liberals who were so quick to understand the method and purpose behind the mighty propaganda machine of Hitler's Third Reich, the consciously spewed-out anti-Semitic caricatures and obscenities that gave an ideological base to the Holocaust and the Final Solution, the very same liberals who, enlightened by blacks, searched their own conscience and came to understand that their tolerance of "nigger" jokes and portrayals of shuffling, rolling-eyed servants in movies perpetuated the degrading myths of black inferiority and gave an ideological base to the continuation of black oppression—these very same liberals now fervidly maintain that the hatred and contempt for women that find expression in four-letter words used as expletives and in what are quaintly called "adult" or "erotic" books and movies are a valid extension of freedom of speech that must be preserved as a Constitutional right.

10   To defend the right of a lone, crazed American Nazi to grind out propaganda calling for the extermination of all Jews, as the ACLU has done in the name of free speech, is, after all, a self-righteous and not particularly courageous stand, for American Jewry is not currently threatened by storm troopers, concentration camps, and imminent extermination, but I wonder if the ACLU's position might change if, come tomorrow morning, the bookstores and movie theaters lining Forty-second Street in New York City were devoted not to the humiliation of women by rape and torture, as they currently are, but to a systematized commercially successful propaganda machine depicting the sadistic pleasures of gassing Jews or lynching blacks?

Is this analogy extreme? Not if you are a woman who is conscious of the ever-present threat of rape and the proliferation of a cultural ideology that makes it sound like "liberated" fun. The majority report of the President's Commission on Obscenity and Pornography tried to pooh-pooh the opinion of law enforcement agencies around the country that claimed their own concrete experience with offenders who were caught with the stuff led them to conclude that pornographic material is a causative factor in crimes of sexual violence. The commission maintained that it was not possible at this time to scientifically prove or disprove such a connection.

But does one need scientific methodology in order to conclude that the antifemale propaganda that permeates our nation's cultural output promotes a climate in which acts of sexual hostility directed against women are not only tolerated but ideologically encouraged? A similar debate has raged for many years over whether or not the extensive glorification of violence (the gangster as hero; the loving treatment accorded bloody shoot-'em-ups in movies, books, and on TV) has a causal effect, a direct relationship to the rising rate of crime, particularly among youth. Interestingly enough, in this area—nonsexual and not specifically related to abuses against women—public opinion seems to be swinging to the position that explicit violence in the entertainment media does have a deleterious effect; it makes violence commonplace, numbingly routine, and no longer morally shocking.

More to the point, those who call for a curtailment of scenes of violence in movies and on television in the name of sensitivity, good taste, and what's best for our children are not accused of being pro-censorship or against freedom of speech. Similarly, minority group organizations, black, Hispanic, Japanese, Italian, Jewish, or American Indian, that campaign against ethnic slurs and demeaning portrayals in movies, on television shows, and in commercials are perceived as waging a just political fight, for if a minority group claims to be offended by a specific portrayal, be it Little Black Sambo or the Frito Bandito, and relates it to a history of ridicule and oppression, few liberals would dare to trot out a Constitutional argument in theoretical opposition, not if they wish to maintain their liberal credentials. Yet when it comes to the treatment of women, the liberal consciousness remains fiercely obdurate, refusing to be budged, for the sin of appearing square or prissy in the age of the so-called sexual revolution has become the worst offense of all.

Critiquing the Passage from *Against Our Will: Men, Women, and Rape*

1. Summarize Brownmiller's argument in your own words.
2. Brownmiller states that pornography degrades and humiliates women the same way that anti-Semitic literature degrades and humiliates Jews or that myths of black inferiority degrade and humiliate blacks. According to Brownmiller, how does pornography degrade and humiliate women?
3. What disanalogies might a skeptic point out between pornography and anti-Semitic or other racist propaganda?
4. One reviewer of Brownmiller's book said, "Get into this book and hardly a single thought to do with sex will come out the way it was." How does this passage from Brownmiller contribute to a public conversation about sexuality? What is thought-provoking about this passage? How does it cause you to view sex differently?

For additional writing, reading, and research resources, go to http://www.mycomplab.com

14 Evaluation and Ethical Arguments

As we explored in Chapter 2, the United States has been embroiled in an ongoing controversy over the influx of illegal immigrants, mostly from Mexico and Central America. While some Americans want to offer citizenship as soon as possible to these immigrants, others want to close off the border between Mexico and the United States and to reduce the number of undocumented workers through deportation or through a crackdown on employers. This marketing image for the movie *A Day Without a Mexican* makes a humorous evaluation argument in favor of Mexican immigrants. It argues that the labor provided by immigrants is valuable—so valuable, in fact, that Californians could hardly endure a day without them. The image of the wealthy white couple having to do their own housekeeping, yard work, and tomato picking is an ironic reminder that the standard of living many Americans take for granted depends on the cheap labor of immigrants.

> ### CASE 2   What Is a "Good Organ" for a Transplant? How Can a Diseased Person Ethically Find an Organ Donor?
>
> In the United States some 87,000 sick people have been waiting as long as six years for an organ transplant, with a portion of these dying before they can find a donor. The problem of organ shortages raises two kinds of evaluation issues. First, doctors are reevaluating the criteria by which they judge a "good organ"—that is, a good lung, kidney, or liver suitable for transplanting. Formerly, people who were elderly or obese or who had engaged in risky behaviors or experienced heart failure or other medical conditions were not considered sources of good organs. Now doctors are reconsidering these sources as well as exploring the use of organs from pigs. Second, the shortage of organs for donation has raised numerous ethical issues: Is it ethical for people to bypass the national waiting list for organs by advertising on billboards and Web sites (see a billboard advertising for a liver on p. 199)? Is it morally right for people to sell their organs? Is it right for patients and families to buy organs or in any way remunerate living organ donors? Some states are passing laws that allow some financial compensation to living organ donors.

An Overview of Evaluation Arguments

In our roles as citizens and professionals, we are continually expected to make difficult evaluations and to persuade others to accept them. In this chapter we explain strategies for conducting two different kinds of evaluation arguments. First, we examine categorical evaluations of the kind "Is this thing a good member of its class?"* (Is Ramon a good committee chair?) In such an evaluation, the writer determines the extent to which a given something fulfills the qualities or standards of its class. Second, we examine ethical arguments of the kind "Is this action right (wrong)?" (Was it right or wrong to drop atomic bombs on Hiroshima and Nagasaki in World War II?) In these arguments, the writer evaluates a given act from the perspective of some system of morality or ethics.

Criteria-Match Structure of Categorical Evaluations

A categorical evaluation follows the same criteria-match structure that we examined in definitional arguments (see Chapter 11). A typical claim for such an argument has the following structure:

> This thing/phenomenon is (is not) a good member of its class because it meets (fails to meet) criteria A, B, and C.

The main conceptual difference between an evaluation argument and a definition argument involves the second term ("a good member of its class"). In a definition argument, one argues whether a particular thing belongs to a certain class or category. (Is this swampy area a *wetland*?) In an evaluation argument, we know what

---

*In addition to the term *good*, a number of other evaluative terms involve the same kind of thinking—*effective, successful, workable, excellent, valuable*, and so forth.

category something belongs to. For example, we know that this 2002 Ford Escort is a *used car.* For an evaluation argument, the question is whether this 2002 Ford Escort is a *good used car.* Or, to place the question within a rhetorical context, is this Ford Escort a *good used car for me to buy for college?*

Toulmin Framework for an Evaluation Argument

As an illustration of the criteria-match structure of an evaluation argument, let's continue with the Ford Escort example. Suppose you get in a debate with Parent or Significant Other about the car you should buy for college. Let's say that Parent or Significant Other argues that the following criteria are particularly important: (1) initial value for the money, (2) dependability, (3) safety, and (4) low maintenance costs. (Note: You would strenuously reject these criteria if you were looking for a muscle car, coolness, or driving excitement. This is why establishing criteria is a crucial part of evaluation arguments.) A Toulmin analysis of how Parent or Significant Other might make the case for "initial value for the money" is shown on page 287. Note how the warrant is a criterion while the stated reason and grounds assert that the specific case meets the criterion.

As the Toulmin analysis shows, Parent or Significant Other needs to argue that getting high value for the initial money is an important consideration (the criterion argument) and that this 2002 Ford Escort meets this criterion better than competing choices (the match argument). If you can't see yourself driving a Ford Escort, you've got to either argue for other criteria (attack the warrant) or accept the criterion but argue that the Ford Escort's projected maintenance costs undermine its initial value (attack the reason and grounds).

Conducting a Categorical Evaluation Argument

Now that you understand the basic criteria-match structure of a categorical evaluation, let's look at some thinking strategies you can use to develop your criteria and to argue whether the thing you are evaluating meets the criteria.

Developing Your Criteria

To help you develop your criteria, we suggest a three-step thinking process:

1. Place the thing you are evaluating in the smallest relevant category so that you don't compare apples to oranges.
2. Develop criteria for your evaluation based on the purpose or function of this category.
3. Determine the relative weight of your criteria.

Let's look at each of these steps in turn.

Step 1: Place the Thing You Are Evaluating in the Smallest Relevant Category   Placing your contested thing in the smallest category is a crucial first step.

Toulmin Analysis of the Ford Escort Argument

ENTHYMEME

CLAIM The Ford Escort is a good used car for you at college

REASON because it provides the most initial value for the money.

GROUNDS

• Evidence that Escorts are dependable

• Evidence that Escorts are not in very high demand, so you can get a 2002 Escort for $5,000 less than a 2002 Honda Civic with the same mileage

• Evidence that a 2002 Civic for the same price would have double the miles

• Low initial mileage means years of dependable use without large repair bills.

CONDITIONS OF REBUTTAL
Attacking the reason and grounds

A 2002 Escort is not as great a value as it seems:

• My research suggests there are high maintenance costs after 60,000 miles.

• The initial savings may be blown on high repair costs.

WARRANT

High value for the initial money is an important criterian for buying your college car.

BACKING

Arguments showing why it is important to get high value for money:

• Money saved on the car can be used for other college expenses.

• Buying in this thrifty way meets our family's image of being careful shoppers.

CONDITIONS OF REBUTTAL
Attacking the warrant and backing

Other criteria are more important to me:

• Great handling and acceleration

• The fun of driving

• The status of having a cool car

Suppose, for example, that you want one of your professors to write you a letter of recommendation for a summer job. The professor will need to know what kind of summer job. Are you applying to become a camp counselor, a law office intern, a retail sales clerk, or a tour guide at a wild animal park in your state? Each of these jobs has different criteria for excellence. Or to take a different example, suppose that you want to evaluate e-mail as a medium of correspondence. To create a stable context for your evaluation, you need to place e-mail in its smallest relevant category. You may choose to evaluate e-mail as medium for business communication (by contrasting e-mail with direct personal contact, phone conversations, or postal mail), as a medium for staying in touch with high school friends (in contrast, say, to text messaging or Facebook), or as a medium for carrying on a long-distance romance (in contrast, say, to old-fashioned "love letters"). Again, criteria will vary across these different categories.

By placing your contested thing in the smallest relevant class you avoid the apples-and-oranges problem. That is, to give a fair evaluation to a perfectly good apple, you need to judge it under the class "apple" and not under the next larger class, "fruit," or a neighboring class such as "orange." And to be even more precise, you may wish to evaluate your apple in the class "eating apple" as opposed to "pie apple" because the latter class is supposed to be tarter and the former class juicier and sweeter.

Step 2: Develop Criteria for Your Evaluation Based on the Purpose or Function of This Category   Suppose that the summer job you are applying for is tour guide at a wild animal park in your state. The function of a tour guide is to drive the tour buses, make people feel welcome, give them interesting information about the wild animals in the park, make their visit pleasant, and so forth. Criteria for a good tour guide would thus include reliability and responsibility, a friendly demeanor, good speaking skills, and knowledge of the kinds of animals in the wild animal park. In our e-mail example, suppose that you want to evaluate e-mail as a medium for business communication. The purpose of this class is to provide a quick and reliable means of communication that increases efficiency, minimizes misunderstandings, protects the confidentiality of internal communications, and so forth. Based on these purposes, you might establish the following criteria:

A good medium for business communication:

- Is easy to use, quick, and reliable
- Increases employee efficiency
- Prevents misunderstandings
- Maintains confidentiality where needed

Step 3: Determine the Relative Weight of Your Criteria   In some evaluations all the criteria are equally important. However, sometimes a phenomenon to be evaluated is strong in one criterion but weak in another—a situation that forces the evaluator to decide which criterion takes precedence. For example, the supervisor interviewing candidates for tour guide at the wild animal park may find one candidate who is very knowledgeable about the wildlife but doesn't have good speaking skills. The supervisor needs to decide which of these two criteria gets more weight.

Making Your Match Argument

Once you've established and weighed your criteria, you'll need to use examples and other evidence to show that the thing being evaluated meets or does not meet the criteria. For example, your professor could argue that you would be a good

EXAMINING VISUAL ARGUMENTS

An Evaluation Claim

This photograph of the "News Team" from *The Daily Show* makes an ironic evaluation argument. On the one hand, it argues that the news you get from *The Daily Show* is just as good (or better than) the news you get on regular news shows. On the other hand, it argues that *The Daily Show* is a spoof. How does this photograph serve to parody network news? What features make it similar to photographs for conventional network news teams? What features make it ironic? Do you think *The Daily Show* is a good source for news?

wildlife park tour guide because you have strong interpersonal skills (based on your work on a college orientation committee), that you have good speaking skills (based on a speech you gave in the professor's class), and that you have quite a bit of knowledge about animals and ecology (based on your major in environmental science).

In our e-mail example, you might establish the following working thesis:

> Despite its being easy to learn, quick, and reliable, e-mail is not an effective medium for business communication because it reduces worker efficiency, leads to frequent misunderstandings, and often lacks confidentiality.

You could develop your last three points as follows:

- *E-mail reduces worker efficiency.* You can use personal anecdotes and research data to show how checking e-mail is addictive and how it eats into worker time (one research article says that the average worker devotes ten minutes of every working hour to reading and responding to e-mail). You might also show how e-mail frequently diverts workers from high-priority to low-priority tasks. Some research even suggests that workers don't relax as much away from work because they are always checking their e-mail.
- *E-mail leads to misunderstandings.* Because an e-mail message is often composed rapidly without revision, e-mail can cause people to state ideas imprecisely, to write something they would never say face-to-face, or to convey an unintended tone. Without the benefits of tone of voice and body language available in face-to-face conversation, e-mail can be easily misread. You could give a personal example of a high-consequence misunderstanding caused by e-mail.
- *E-mail often lacks confidentiality.* You could provide anecdotal or research evidence of cases in which a person clicked on the "reply to all" button rather than the "reply" button, sending a message intended for one person to a whole group of people. Stories also abound of employers who snoop through employees' e-mail messages or workers who forward e-mails without permission from the sender. Perhaps most troubling is the way that e-mail messages are archived forever, so that messages that you thought were deleted may show up years later in a lawsuit.

As these examples illustrate, the key to a successful match argument is to use sufficient examples and other evidence to show how your contested phenomenon meets or does not meet each of your criteria.

■ ■ ■   **FOR CLASS DISCUSSION**   Developing Criteria and Match Arguments

The following small-group exercise can be accomplished in one or two class hours. It gives you a good model of the process you can go through in order to write your own categorical evaluation.

1. Choose a specific controversial person, thing, or event to evaluate (your school's computer services help desk, the invite-a-professor-to-lunch program in your dormitory, Harvey's Hamburger Haven). To help you think of ideas, try brainstorming controversial members of the following categories: *people* (athletes, political leaders, musicians, clergy, entertainers, businesspeople); *science and technology* (weapons systems, word-processing programs, spreadsheets, automotive advancements, treatments for diseases); *media* (a newspaper, a magazine or journal, a TV program, a radio station, a Web site, an advertisement); *government and world affairs* (an economic policy, a Supreme Court decision, a law or legal practice, a government custom or practice, a foreign policy); *the arts* (a movie, a book, a building, a painting, a piece of music); *your college or university* (a course, a teacher, a textbook, a curriculum, an administrative policy, the financial aid system); *the world of work* (a job, a company operation, a dress policy, a merit pay system, a hiring policy, a supervisor); or any other categories of your choice.

2. Place your controversial person or thing within the smallest relevant class, thus providing a rhetorical context for your argument and showing what is at stake. Do you want to evaluate Harvey's Hamburger Haven in the broad category of *restaurants,* in the narrow category of *hamburger joints,* or in a different narrow category such as *late-night study places*? If you are evaluating a recent film, are you evaluating it as *a chick-flick,* as a possible *Academy Award nominee,* or as a *political filmmaking statement*?

3. Make a list of the purposes or functions of that class, and then list the criteria that a good member of that class would need to have in order to accomplish the purpose or function. (What is the purpose or function of a computer services help desk, a late-night study place, or a chick flick? What criteria for excellence can you derive from these purposes or functions?)

4. If necessary, rank your criteria from most to least important. (For a late-night study place, what is more important: good ambience, Wi-Fi availability, good coffee, or convenient location?)

5. Provide examples and other evidence to show how your contested something matches or does not match each of your criteria. (As a late-night study place, Carol's Coffee Closet beats out Harvey's Hamburger Haven. Although Harvey's Hamburger Haven has the most convenient location, Carol's Coffee Closet has Wi-Fi, an ambience conducive to studying, and excellent coffee.)

An Overview of Ethical Arguments

A second kind of evaluation argument focuses on moral or ethical issues, which can often merge or overlap with categorical evaluations. For example, many apparently straightforward categorical evaluations can turn out to have an ethical dimension. Consider again the criteria for buying a car. Most people would base their evaluations on cost, safety, comfort, and so forth. But some people may feel morally obligated to buy the most fuel-efficient car, to buy an American car, or not to buy a car from a manufacturer whose labor policies they find morally repugnant. Depending on how large a role ethical considerations play in the evaluation, we may choose to call this an ethical argument based on moral considerations rather than a categorical evaluation based on the purposes of a class or category.

It is uncertainty about "purpose" that makes ethical evaluations particularly complex. In making a categorical evaluation, we assume that every class or category of being has a purpose, that the purpose should be defined as narrowly as possible, and that the criteria for judgment derive directly from that purpose. For example, the purpose of a computer repairperson is to analyze the problem with my computer, to fix it, and to do so in a timely and cost-efficient manner. Once I formulate this purpose, it is easy for me to define criteria for a good computer repairperson. In ethical evaluations, however, the place of purpose is much fuzzier. In making ethical evaluations, we don't always analyze the function of the class "manager" or "judge" or "computer repairperson." Who people are or what their social function is may make no difference to our ethical assessment of their actions or traits of character. A morally bad person may be a good judge, and a morally good person may be terrible at repairing computers and even worse at being a manager.

As the discussion so far has suggested, disagreements about an ethical issue often stem from different systems of values that make the issue irresolvable. It is precisely this problem—the lack of shared assumptions about value—that makes it so important to confront issues of ethics with rational deliberation. The arguments you produce may not persuade others to your view, but they should make others think seriously about it, and they should help you work out more clearly the reasons and warrants for your own beliefs. By writing about ethical issues, you see more clearly what you believe and why you believe it. Although the arguments demanded by ethical issues require rigorous thought, they force us to articulate our most deeply held beliefs and our richest feelings.

Major Ethical Systems

When we are faced with an ethical issue, we must move from arguments of good or bad to arguments of right or wrong. The terms *right* and *wrong* are clearly different from the terms *good* and *bad* when the latter terms mean simply "effective" (meets purposes of class, as in "This is a good laptop") or "ineffective" (fails to meet purposes of class, as in "This is a bad cookbook"). But *right* and *wrong* often also differ from what seems to be a moral use of the terms *good* and *bad.* We may say, for example, that sunshine is good because it brings pleasure and that cancer is bad because it brings pain and death, but that is not quite the same thing as saying that sunshine is "right" and cancer is "wrong." It is the problem of "right" and "wrong" that ethical arguments confront.

For example, from a nonethical standpoint, you could say that certain people are "good terrorists" in that they fully realize the purpose of the class "terrorist": they cause great anguish and damage with a minimum of resources, and they bring much attention to their cause. However, if we want to condemn terrorism on ethical grounds, we have to say that terrorism is wrong. The ethical question is not whether a person fulfills the purposes of the class "terrorist," but whether it is wrong for such a class to exist.

There are many schools of ethical thought—too many to cover in this brief overview—so we'll limit ourselves to two major systems: arguments from consequences and arguments from principles.

Consequences as the Base of Ethics

Perhaps the best-known example of evaluating acts according to their ethical consequences is utilitarianism, a down-to-earth philosophy that grew out of nineteenth-century British philosophers' concern to demystify ethics and make it work in the practical world. Jeremy Bentham, the originator of utilitarianism, developed the goal of the greatest good for the greatest number, or "greatest happiness," by which he meant the most pleasure for the least pain. John Stuart Mill, another British philosopher, built on Bentham's utilitarianism, using predicted consequences to determine the morality of a proposed action.

Mill's consequentialist approach allows you readily to assess a wide range of acts. You can apply the principle of utility—which says that an action is morally right if it produces a greater net value (benefits minus costs) than any available alternative action—to virtually any situation, and it will help you reach a decision. Obviously, however, it's not always easy to make the calculations called for by the principle, because, like any prediction of the future, an estimate of consequences is conjectural. In particular, it's often very hard to assess the long-term consequences of any action. Too often, utilitarianism seduces us into a short-term analysis of a moral problem simply because long-term consequences are difficult to predict.

Principles as the Base of Ethics

Any ethical system based on principles will ultimately rest on moral tenets that we are duty bound to uphold, no matter what the consequences. Sometimes the moral tenets come from religious faith—for example, the Ten Commandments. At other times, however, the principles are derived from philosophical reasoning, as in the case of German philosopher Immanuel Kant. Kant held that no one should ever use another person as a means to his own ends and that everyone should always act as if his acts were the basis of universal law. In other words, Kant held that we are duty bound to respect other people's sanctity and to act in the same way that we would want all other people to act. The great advantage of such a system is its clarity and precision. We are never overwhelmed by a multiplicity of contradictory and difficult-to-quantify consequences; we simply make sure we are following (or not violating) the principles of our ethical system and proceed accordingly.

Constructing an Ethical Argument

To show you how to conduct an ethical argument, let's now apply these two strategies to an example. In general, you can conduct an ethical evaluation by using the frame for either a principles-based argument or a consequences-based argument or a combination of both.

> *Principles-Based Frame:* An act is right (wrong) because it follows (violates) principles A, B, and C.
> *Consequences-Based Frame:* An act is right (wrong) because it will lead to consequences A, B, and C, which are good (bad).

To illustrate how these frames might help you develop an ethical argument, let's use them to develop arguments for or against capital punishment.

Constructing a Principles-Based Argument

A principles-based argument looks at capital punishment through the lens of one or more guiding principles. Kant's principle that we are duty bound not to violate the sanctity of other human lives could lead to arguments opposing capital punishment. One might argue as follows:

> *Principles-based argument opposing capital punishment:* The death penalty is wrong because it violates the principle of the sanctity of human life.

You could support this principle either by summarizing Kant's argument that one should not violate the selfhood of another person or by pointing to certain religious systems such as Judeo-Christian ethics, where one is told "Vengeance is mine, saith the Lord" or "Thou shalt not kill." To develop this argument further, you might examine two exceptions in which principles-based ethicists may allow killing—self-defense and war—and show how capital punishment does not fall in either category.

Principles-based arguments can also be developed to support capital punishment. You may be surprised to learn that Kant himself—despite his arguments for the sanctity of life—supported capital punishment. To make such an argument, Kant evoked a different principle about the suitability of the punishment to the crime:

> There is no sameness of kind between death and remaining alive even under the most miserable conditions, and consequently there is no equality between the crime and the retribution unless the criminal is judicially condemned and put to death.

Stated as an enthymeme, Kant's argument is as follows:

> *Principles-based argument supporting capital punishment:* Capital punishment is right because it follows the principle that punishments should be proportionate to the crime.

In developing this argument, Kant's burden is to show why the principle of proportionate retribution outweighs the principle of the supreme worth of the individual. Our point is that a principles-based argument can be made both for and against capital punishment. The arguer's duty is to make clear what principle is being evoked and then to show why this principle is more important than opposing principles.

Constructing a Consequences-Based Argument

Unlike a principles-based argument, which appeals to certain guiding maxims or rules, a consequences-based argument looks at the consequences of a decision and measures the positive benefits against the negative costs. Here is the frame that an arguer might use to oppose capital punishment on the basis of negative consequences:

> *Consequences-based argument opposing capital punishment:* Capital punishment is wrong because it leads to the following negative consequences:

- The possibility of executing an innocent person
- The possibility that a murderer who may repent and be redeemed is denied that chance
- The excessive legal and political costs of trials and appeals
- The unfair distribution of executions so that one's chances of being put to death are much greater if one is a minority or is poor

To develop this argument, the reader would need to provide facts, statistics, and other evidence to support each of the stated reasons.

A different arguer might use a consequences-based approach to support capital punishment:

> *Consequences-based argument supporting capital punishment:* Capital punishment is right because it leads to the following positive consequences:

- It may deter violent crime and slow down the rate of murder.
- It saves the cost of lifelong imprisonment.
- It stops criminals who are menaces to society from committing more murders.
- It helps grieving families reach closure and sends a message to victims' families that society recognizes their pain.

It should be evident, then, that adopting an ethical system doesn't lead to automatic answers to one's ethical dilemmas. A system offers a way of proceeding—a way of conducting an argument—but it doesn't relieve you of personal responsibility for thinking through your values and taking a stand. When you face an ethical dilemma, we encourage you to consider both the relevant principles and the possible consequences the dilemma entails. In many arguments, you can use both principles-based and consequences-based reasoning as long as irreconcilable contradictions don't present themselves.

■ ■ ■ **FOR CLASS DISCUSSION** Developing Ethical Arguments

Working as individuals or in small groups, construct an ethical argument (based on principles, consequences, or both) for or against the following actions:

1. Eating meat
2. Buying a hybrid car
3. Legalizing assisted suicide for the terminally ill
4. Selling organs
5. Generating state revenue through lotteries

■ ■ ■

Common Problems in Making Evaluation Arguments

When conducting evaluation arguments (whether categorical or ethical), writers can bump up against recurring problems that are unique to evaluation. In some cases these problems complicate the establishment of criteria; in other cases they complicate the match argument. Let's look briefly at some of these common problems.

- *The problem of standards—what is commonplace versus what is ideal:* In various forms, we experience the dilemma of the commonplace versus the ideal all the time. Is it fair to get a ticket for going seventy miles per hour on a sixty-five-mile-per-hour freeway when most of the drivers go seventy miles per hour or faster? (Does what is *commonplace*—going seventy—override what is *ideal*—obeying the law?) Is it better for high schools to pass out free contraceptives to students because students are having sex anyway (what's *commonplace*), or is it better not to pass them out in order to support abstinence (what's *ideal*)?

- *The problem of mitigating circumstances:* This problem occurs when an arguer claims that unusual circumstances should alter our usual standards of judgment. Ordinarily, it is fair for a teacher to reduce a grade if you turn in a paper late. But what if you were up all night taking care of a crying baby? Does that count as a *mitigating circumstance* to waive the ordinary criterion? When you argue for mitigating circumstances, you will likely assume an especially heavy burden of proof. People assume the rightness of usual standards of judgment unless there are compelling arguments for abnormal circumstances.

- *The problem of choosing between two goods or two bads:* Often an evaluation issue forces us between a rock and a hard place. Should we cut pay or cut people? Put our parents in a nursing home or let them stay at home where they have become a danger to themselves? In such cases one has to weigh conflicting criteria, knowing that the choices are too much alike—either both bad or both good.

- *The problem of seductive empirical measures:* The need to make high-stakes evaluations has led many people to seek quantifiable criteria that can be weighed mathematically. Thus we use grade point averages to select scholarship winners, student evaluation scores to decide merit pay for teachers, and combined scores of judges to judge figure skaters. In some cases, empirical measures can be quite acceptable, but they are often dangerous because they discount important nonquantifiable traits. The problem with empirical measures is that they seduce us into believing that complex judgments can be made mathematically, thus rescuing us from the messiness of alternative points of view and conflicting criteria.

- *The problem of cost:* A final problem in evaluation arguments is cost. Something may be the best possible member of its class, but if it costs too much, we have to go for second or third best. We can avoid this problem somewhat by placing items into different classes on the basis of cost. For example, a Mercedes will exceed a Kia on almost any criterion, but if we can't afford more than a Kia, the comparison is pointless. It is better to compare a Mercedes to a Lexus and a Kia to an equivalent Ford. Whether costs are expressed in dollars, personal discomfort, moral repugnance, or some other terms, our final evaluation of an item must take cost into account.

WRITING ASSIGNMENT An Evaluation or Ethical Argument

Write an argument in which you try to change your reader's mind about the value, worth, or ethics of something. Choose a phenomenon to be evaluated that is controversial so that your readers are likely at first to disagree with your evaluation or at least to be surprised by it. Somewhere in your essay you should summarize alternative views and either refute them or concede to them (see Chapter 7).

Exploring Ideas

Evaluation issues are all around us. Think of disagreements about the value of a person, thing, action, or phenomenon within the various communities to which you belong—your dorm, home, or apartment community; your school community, including clubs or organizations; your academic community, including classes you are currently taking; your work community; and your city, state, national, and world communities. For further ideas, look at the categories listed in the For Class Discussion exercise on page 290. Once you have settled on a controversial thing to be evaluated, place it in its smallest relevant category, determine the purposes of that category, and develop your criteria. If you are making an ethical evaluation, consider your argument from the perspective of both principles and consequences.

Identifying Your Audience and Determining What's at Stake

Before drafting your argument, identify your targeted audience and determine what's at stake. Consider your responses to the following questions:

- What audience are you targeting? What background do they need to understand your issue? How much do they already care about it?
- Before they read your evaluation argument, what stance on your issue do you imagine them holding? What change do you want to bring about in their view?
- What will they find new or surprising about your argument?
- What objections might they raise? What counter-arguments or alternative points of view will you need to address?
- Why does your evaluation matter? Who might be threatened or made uncomfortable by your views? What is at stake?

Organizing an Evaluation Argument

As you write a draft, you may find useful the following prototypical structures for evaluation arguments shown in Organization Plans 1 and 2 on pages 298 and 299. Of course, you can always alter these plans if another structure better fits your material.

Questioning and Critiquing a Categorical Evaluation Argument

Here is a list of questions you can use to critique a categorical evaluation argument:

Will a skeptic accept my criteria? Many evaluative arguments are weak because the writers have simply assumed that readers will accept their criteria. Whenever your audience's acceptance of your criteria is in doubt, you will need to argue for your criteria explicitly.

Are my criteria based on the "smallest relevant class"? For example, the 1999 film *The Blair Witch Project* will certainly be a failure if you evaluate it in the general class "movies," in which it would have to compete with *Citizen Kane* and other great classics. But if you evaluate it as a "horror film" or a "low-budget film," it will have a greater chance for success and hence of yielding an arguable evaluation.

Will a skeptic accept my general weighting of criteria? Another vulnerable spot in an evaluation argument is the relative weight of the criteria. How much anyone weights a given criterion is usually a function of his or her own interests relative to your contested something. You should always ask whether some particular group might not have good reasons for weighting the criteria differently.

Organization Plan 1: Criteria and Match in Separate Sections

Introduce the issue and state your claim.	• Engage reader's interest in your evaluation issue and show why it is controversial or problematic. • Show what's at stake. • Provide background information needed by your audience. • State your claim.
Present your criteria.	• State and develop criterion 1. • State and develop criterion 2. • Continue with the rest of your criteria. • Anticipate and respond to possible objections to the criteria.
Present your match argument.	• Consider restating your claim for clarity. • Argue that your case meets (does not meet) criterion 1. • Argue that your case meets (does not meet) criterion 2. • Continue with the rest of your match argument. • Anticipate and respond to possible objections to the match argument.
Conclude.	• Perhaps sum up your argument. • Help reader return to the "big picture" of what's at stake. • End with something memorable.

Will a skeptic question my standard of reference? In questioning an argument's criteria, a skeptic can also focus on the standard of reference used—what's commonplace versus what's ideal. If you have argued that your something is bad because it doesn't live up to what's ideal, you can expect some readers to defend it on the basis of what's commonplace. Similarly, if you argue that your something is good because it is better than its competitors, you can expect some readers to point out how short it falls from what is ideal.

Will a skeptic criticize my use of empirical measures? The desire to quantify criteria through empirical measures is always open to criticism. As we have discussed earlier, what's most measurable isn't always significant when it comes to assessing the worth of something. A ninety-five-mile-per-hour fastball is certainly an impressive empirical

Organization Plan 2: Criteria and Match Interwoven

Introduce the issue and state your claim.	• Engage reader's interest in your evaluation issue and show why it is controversial or problematic. • Show what's at stake. • Provide background information needed by your audience. • State your claim.
Present series of criterion-match arguments.	• State and develop criterion 1 and argue that your case meets (does not meet) the criterion. • State and develop criterion 2 and argue that your case meets (does not meet) the criterion. • Continue with the rest of your criterion-match arguments.
Respond to possible objections to your argument.	• Anticipate and summarize possible objections. • Respond to the objections through rebuttal or concession.
Conclude.	• Perhaps sum up your argument. • Help reader return to the "big picture" of what's at stake. • End with something memorable.

measure of a pitcher's ability—but if the pitcher doesn't strike batters out, that measure is a misleading gauge of performance.

Will a skeptic accept my criteria but reject my match argument? The other major way of testing an evaluation argument is to anticipate how readers may object to your stated reasons and grounds. Will readers challenge you by showing that you have cherry-picked your examples and evidence? Will they provide counterexamples and counterevidence?

Critiquing an Ethical Argument

Ethical arguments can be critiqued through appeals to consequences or principles. If an argument appeals primarily to principles, it can be vulnerable to a simple cost analysis. What are the costs of adhering to this principle? There will undoubtedly be some, or else there would be no real argument. If the argument is based strictly on consequences, we should ask whether it violates any rules or principles, particularly such commandments as the Golden Rule—"Do unto others as you would have others do unto you"—which most members of our audience adhere to. By failing to mention these alternative ways of thinking about ethical issues, we undercut not only our argument but our credibility as well.

Let's now consider some of the more subtle weaknesses of arguments based on principle. In practice people will sometimes take rigidly "principled" positions because they fear "slippery slopes." If one has an absolutist commitment to the sanctity of life, for example, consider the slippery slope leading from birth control to euthanasia. Once we allow birth control in the form of condoms or the pill, the principled absolutist would say, then we will be forced to accept birth control "abortions" in the first hours after conception (IUDs, "morning after" pills), and then abortions in the first trimester, and then in the second or even the third trimester. And once we have violated the sanctity of human life by allowing abortions, it is only a short step to euthanasia and finally to killing off all undesirables.

One way to refute a slippery-slope argument of this sort is to try to dig a foothold into the side of the hill to show that you don't necessarily have to slide all the way to the bottom. You would thus have to argue that allowing birth control does not mean allowing abortions (by arguing for differences between a fetus after conception and sperm and egg before conception), or that allowing abortions does not mean allowing euthanasia (by arguing for differences between a fetus and a person already living in the world).

Arguments based on consequences have different kinds of difficulties. Have you calculated the consequences accurately? Have you considered all of the possible consequences, particularly unintended ones? Do you offer evidence that the predicted consequences will in fact come to pass? Do you show convincingly that the consequences of any given action are a net good or evil? ■

Our first reading, by student writer Sam Isaacson, was written for the **READINGS**
assignment on page 296. It joins a conversation about whether the legalization
of same-sex marriage would be good for our society. However, Isaacson, a gay writer, limits the question to whether legalization of same-sex marriage would be *good for the gay
community.* Earlier in this text (see Chapter 7, pages 126–127), we discussed Isaacson's
rhetorical choices as he considered the audience for his essay. Isaacson's decision was to
address this paper to the readers of a gay magazine such as *Harvard Gay and Lesbian
Review* or *The Advocate.*

Would Legalization of Gay Marriage Be Good for the Gay Community?

SAM ISAACSON (STUDENT)

For those of us who have been out for a while, nothing seems shocking about a gay
pride parade. Yet at this year's parade, I was struck by the contrast between two groups—
the float for the Toys in Babeland store (with swooning drag queens and leather-clad,
whipwielding, topless dykes) and the Northwest chapters of Integrity and Dignity
(Episcopal and Catholic organizations for lesbians and gays), whose marchers looked as
conservative as the congregation of any American church.

These stark differences in dress are representative of larger philosophical differences in
the gay community. At stake is whether or not we gays and lesbians should act "normal."
Labeled as deviants by many in straight society, we're faced with various opposing methods of response. One option is to insist that we are normal and work to integrate gays into
the cultural mainstream. Another response is to form an alternative gay culture with its
own customs and values; this culture would honor deviancy in response to a society which
seeks to label some as "normal" and some as "abnormal." For the purposes of this paper I
will refer to those who favor the first response as "integrationists" and those who favor the
second response as "liberationists." Politically, this ideological clash is most evident in the
issue of whether legalization of same-sex marriage would be good for the gay community.
Nearly all integrationists would say yes, but many liberationists would say no. My belief is
that while we must take the objections of the liberationists seriously, legalization of same-
sex marriage would benefit both gays and society in general.

Let us first look at what is so threatening about gay marriage to many liberationists.
Many liberationists fear that legalizing gay marriage will reinforce current social pressures
that say monogamous marriage is the normal and right way to live. In straight society,
those who choose not to marry are often viewed as self-indulgent, likely promiscuous, and
shallow—and it is no coincidence these are some of the same stereotypes gays struggle
against. If gays begin to marry, married life will be all the more the norm and subject those
outside of marriage to even greater marginalization. As homosexuals, liberationists argue,
we should be particularly sensitive to the tyranny of the majority. Our sympathies should
lie with the deviants—the transsexual, the fetishist, the drag queen, and the leather-dyke.

By choosing marriage, gays take the easy route into "normal" society; we not only abandon the sexual minorities of our community, we strengthen society's narrow notions of what is "normal" and thereby further confine both straights and gays.

Additionally, liberationists worry that by winning the right to marry gays and lesbians will lose the distinctive and positive characteristics of gay culture. Many gay writers have commented on how as a marginalized group gays have been forced to create different forms of relationships that often allow for a greater and often more fulfilling range of life experiences. Writer Edmund White, for instance, has observed that there is a greater fluidity in the relationships of gays than straights. Gays, he says, are more likely than straights to stay friends with old lovers, are more likely to form close friendships outside the romantic relationship, and are generally less likely to become compartmentalized into isolated couples. It has also been noted that gay relationships are often characterized by more equality and better communication than are straight relationships. Liberationists make the reasonable assumption that if gays win the right to marry they will be subject to the same social pressure to marry that straights are subject to. As more gays are pressured into traditional life patterns, liberationists fear the gay sensibility will be swallowed up by the established attitudes of the broader culture. All of society would be the poorer if this were to happen.

5   I must admit that I concur with many of the arguments of the liberationists that I have outlined above. I do think if given the right, gays would feel social pressure to marry; I agree that gays should be especially sensitive to the most marginalized elements of society; and I also agree that the unique perspectives on human relationships that the gay community offers should not be sacrificed. However, despite these beliefs, I feel that legalizing gay marriage would bring valuable benefits to gays and society as a whole.

First of all, I think it is important to put the attacks the liberationists make on marriage into perspective. The liberationist critique of marriage claims that marriage in itself is a harmful institution (for straights as well as gays) because it needlessly limits and normalizes personal freedom. But it seems clear to me that marriage in some form is necessary for the well-being of society. Children need a stable environment in which to be raised. Studies have shown that children whose parents divorce often suffer long-term effects from the trauma. Studies have also shown that people tend to be happier in stable long-term relationships. We need to have someone to look over us when we're old, when we become depressed, when we fall ill. All people, gay or straight, parents or nonparents, benefit from the stabilizing force of marriage.

Second, we in the gay community should not be too quick to overlook the real benefits that legalizing gay marriage will bring. We are currently denied numerous legal rights of marriage that the straight community enjoys: tax benefits, insurance benefits, inheritance rights, and the right to have a voice in medical treatment or funeral arrangements for a dying partner.

Further, just as important as the legal impacts of being denied the right to marriage is the socially symbolic weight this denial carries. We are sent the message that while gay sex in the privacy of one's home will be tolerated, gay love will not be respected. We are told that it is not important to society whether we form long-term relationships or not. We are told that we are not worthy of forming families of our own. By gaining the same recognitions by the state of our relationships and all the legal and social weight that recognition carries, the new message will be that gay love is just as meaningful as straight love.

Finally, let me address what I think is at the heart of the liberationist argument against marriage—the fear of losing social diversity and our unique gay voice. The liberationists are wary of society's normalizing forces. They fear that if gays win the right to marry gay relationships will simply become imitations of straight relationships—the richness gained through the gay experience will be lost. I feel, however, this argument unintentionally plays into the hands of conservatives. Conservatives argue that marriage is, by definition, the union between man and woman. As a consequence, to the broad culture gay marriage can only be a mockery of marriage. As gays and lesbians we need to argue that conservatives are imposing arbitrary standards on what is normal and not normal in society. To fight the conservative agenda, we must suggest instead that marriage is, in essence, a contract of love and commitment between two people. The liberationists, I think, unwittingly feed into conservative identification and classification by pigeonholing gays as outsiders. Reacting against social norms is simply another way of being held hostage by them.

10   We need to understand that the gay experience and voice will not be lost by gaining the right to marry. Gays will always be the minority by simple biological fact and this will always color the identity of any gay person. But we can only make our voice heard if we are seen as full-fledged members of society. Otherwise we will remain an isolated and marginalized group. And only when we have the right to marry will we have any say in the nature and significance of marriage as an institution. This is not being apologetic to the straight culture, but is a demand that we not be excluded from the central institutions of Western culture. We can help merge the fluidity of gay relationships with the traditionally more compartmentalized married relationship. Further, liberationists should realize that the decision *not* to marry makes a statement only if one has the ability to choose marriage. What would be most radical, most transforming, is two women or two men joined together in the eyes of society.

Critiquing "Would Legalization of Gay Marriage Be Good for the Gay Community?"

1. Who is the audience that Sam Isaacson addresses in this argument?
2. Ordinarily when we think of persons opposing gay marriage, we imagine socially conservative heterosexuals. However, Sam spends little time addressing the anti-gay marriage arguments of straight society. Rather, he addresses the antimarriage arguments made by "liberationist" gay people. What are these arguments? How well does Sam respond to them?
3. What are the criteria Sam uses to argue that legalizing gay marriage would be good for the gay community?
4. How persuasive do you think Sam's argument is to the various audiences he addresses?

Our second reading, by student writer Tiffany Anderson, developed out of discussions of hip-hop music. Tiffany was torn between a general dislike of rap combined with a growing admiration for certain female rappers. This evaluation argument took shape once she formulated her issue question: What makes a good female hip-hop artist?

A Woman's View of Hip-Hop

TIFFANY ANDERSON (STUDENT)

Is there anything good about hip-hop? If you had asked me this question several years ago, I would have said no. I probably disliked hip-hop as much as any typical middle-aged white suburbanite does. I found the aggressive, ego-driven, star-powered, competitive male image of hip-hop devoid of value, especially the beat and the strong language. I also disliked many of the themes explored in gangster rap, such as the derogatory terms for blacks, the treatment of women as sex objects, and the equation of power and money. When some boys at summer camp six years ago first introduced me to hip-hop, we listened to artists like Bone Thugs-n-Harmony, Tupak Shakur, and Biggie Smalls. These boys who liked rap were also sniffing markers and gave me my first encounter with drugs. In my sheltered white world, I associated rap with drugs and gangs, and I gravitated toward the comfort of alternative rock and punk instead.

But my view of rap began to change when I started listening to the female rappers introduced to me by my friends. During my sophomore year in high school I remember going home because of a bomb threat, and we danced to *The Miseducation of Lauryn Hill* in my living room. I liked what Lauryn was saying. Women hip-hop artists have something different to offer in a male-dominated industry, and it has been women artists who have converted me into a hip-hop fan, not the men. What exactly do these women have to offer that is so compelling? What makes a good female hip-hop artist? While many female rappers merely follow in the footsteps of male rappers by rapping about money, sex, or violence, the truly great female artists provide female listeners with a sense of self-empowerment and identity, they offer a woman's perspective on many topics, and they often create a hopeful message that counters the negativity of male rap. Through their songs, good female rappers spread positive, unique messages that not only benefit African Americans, but females of every race.

Very few male artists are able to provide women with a sense of self-empowerment or identity through their music. But excellent female hip-hop artists like Lauryn Hill address women's sense of self, as Hill does in her song "Doo Wop (That Thing)." In the first verse she criticizes a woman who loses her self-respect by doing what men want her to do ("It's silly when girls sell their souls because it's in"). She encourages women who "ain't right within" to take pride in themselves, regain their self-respect, and be true to themselves. The encouragement Lauryn offers her female audience is uplifting in an industry where women are often reduced to sex objects as scantily clad dancers, back-up singers, and eye candy in music videos. Rapper Trina, in her song "Take Me," criticizes the idea that females have to be sex objects: "I

wanna go to a world where I ain't gotta be a freak ho / just so I can be noticed by people."
Perhaps through such urging, girls can take pride in themselves and rebel against stereotypes.
Foxy Brown addresses stereotypes in an entirely different, but equally effective, way. She uses
her explicitly sexual lyrics to objectify men in her songs, where her heroine is always the dominant one. Her songs help break female sexual inhibitions, reverse the typical roles of the
sexes, and allow us to be proud of our sexuality. These songs can be a cathartic release in a
world that is all too often dominated by men. Female artists should address the reality of
derogatory stereotypes and work to foster a positive female image; if this were left to the male
rappers of the industry, females would not be as positively represented in the hip-hop industry.

Another mark of a good female hip-hop artist is that she makes songs that give a woman's
perspective on the world or her songs include topics not usually addressed in hip-hop songs at
all. For example, my favorite song by Lauryn Hill, "To Zion," is about how her world changed
after the birth of her son, Zion. When she sings, "Now the joy of my world is Zion," I am filled
with pride that I am a woman and have the ability to give birth. How often do male artists, like
Nelly or DMX, sing about the joys of parenthood? It is refreshing to hear songs about the mir-
acles of life, as opposed to the death, drugs, and destruction that are often the topics in typical
rap songs. On *Eve-olution,* Eve's most recent album, she criticizes our world where she "can't
trust the air," an allusion to an oncoming ecological crisis. Hip-hop artists are rarely concerned with problems that affect the entire world, but focus more on their communities. Eve
shows her scope as an artist in addressing ecological problems. Another topic not often explored in hip-hop songs is religion. In her song "Confessions," Lady of Rage asks for forgiveness and calls for appreciation of the Lord: "Forgive me, God, for I have forsaken thee / I'm
not gonna say that it's the devil that's makin' me." Hip-hop is so often used to name all the
evils in the world and lay blame, so hearing an artist take responsibility for her actions and explore a religious theme in her music is refreshing. When a female rap artist can offer her listeners something that they don't often hear, she is truly great.

5   Most importantly, the best female rappers often see some kind of hope in life. Some people
might argue that the negativity so blatant in much hip-hop music actually conveys important
social and political messages, addressing racial profiling, police brutality, gun control, violence, the glorification of money and sex, and problems with education and welfare reform.
These people might say that this influential urban folk art exposes economic and social realities that America needs to confront. I agree that sometimes male artists will reveal a heart-
breaking perspective on this empty world by communicating how urban youth struggle with
self-hatred, poverty, lack of education, hopelessness, discrimination, and injustice. For example, in Outkast's song "Git Up, Git Out," the lyrics speak of never-ending cycles of drugs,
negativity, and lack of education that hold African Americans back: "I don't recall, ever grad-
uatin' at all / Sometimes I feel I'm just a disappointment to y'all…Every job I get is cruel and
demeanin' / Sick of taking trash out and toilet bowl cleanin' / But I'm also sick and tired of
strugglin' / I never ever thought I'd have to resort to drug smugglin.'" While male hip-hop often offers a unique, chilling perspective on the problems of urban America, their music often
only serves to strengthen the cycles of despair and self-hatred. Where is hope in songs that often spend verse after verse on the negative aspects of life and the forces that hold people back?

In contrast, female hip-hop artists do identify the problems, but sometimes suggest ways
to overcome the difficulties of their lives. For example, Eve's song "Heaven Only Knows"

talks about the trouble she faced until she overcame her devastating situation by finding peace through music: "Do positive and positive will happen / Stay positive and positive was rapping / It was like my brain was clouded with unnecessary shit / But I chose to see through the negative and make hits." "Heaven Only Knows" demonstrates the power of rap music to heal. Through her songs, Eve encourages her listeners in new paths and reinforces the importance of overcoming the negative aspects of being an African American. In the title track of *The Miseducation of Lauryn Hill,* Lauryn deftly addresses the problems and offers her own personal story of how she overcame life's setbacks: "I look at my environment / And wonder where the fire went / What happened to everything we used to be / I hear so many cry for help / Searching outside themselves / Now I know His strength is within me / And deep in my heart the answer it was in me / And I made up my mind to find my own destiny." Lauryn sings about how she rejected what was expected of her from outside sources, turned to God, and found everything she needed in herself. To impoverished people of urban America, finding inner strength and self-empowerment could be encouraging. Although Lauryn and Eve usually direct their songs to an African American audience, their words of wisdom apply to all races. Every woman alive can benefit from knowing that we can find our "own destiny" within ourselves, as Lauryn raps about.

Because the lyrics of rap are its heart and soul, what a rapper says conveys a powerful worldview. The worldview of male rap for me is too violent, negative, and antiwoman, but female rap often conveys the same gritty sense of urban life without succumbing to hopelessness and without reducing women to sex objects. The best female rappers are able to arouse a sense of pride and self-worth through their thoughtful lyrics, offer a woman's perspective on the world, and include hopeful messages among the harsh realities of urban life. Female artists like Lauryn Hill, Eve, or Trina have taught me that not all hip-hop is bad, and that sometimes, I can even learn a little something from a song. I found hip-hop a surprising source of feminist pride, diversity, and hope, and this discovery served as a reminder that even in a male- and African American–dominated industry, any white girl can find something to relate to and learn from.

Critiquing "A Woman's View of Hip-Hop"

1. Controversies about popular culture can sometimes become purely subjective discussions about likes and dislikes. How effective is Tiffany Anderson at moving her evaluation of hip-hop from the purely private realm into the public arena where reasoned discussion can take place? Whose views of hip-hop do you think Tiffany wants to change?

2. What criteria does she use to evaluate the music of female hip-hop artists? Do you accept these criteria? What other criteria might an arguer offer to evaluate female hip-hop music? Can you think of good hip-hop music by a female artist that doesn't meet Tiffany's criteria?

3. For her categorical evaluation, Tiffany evaluates specific female artists within the category of "women's rap" as opposed to "men's rap." (Her criteria focus primarily on differences between women's and men's rap.) Within what other categories could you evaluate female rappers?

4. Does Tiffany effectively anticipate alternative views? If so, which alternative views does she address?
5. How effective do you find her argument? Why?

Our third reading is a political cartoon by Mike Luckovich that joins the public controversy over supplying the military with enough soldiers to carry out U.S. foreign policy commitments (see Figure 14.3). Currently, U.S. Army standards require recruits to be between the ages of seventeen and thirty-four, to score well on the applicant aptitude test, and to be free of drug use and chronic physical problems. However, the *kairotic* moment of this cartoon is the growing problem of unmet recruitment quotas. The Army and Marines are exploring various incentives and options to increase the number of available soldiers.

Critiquing the Military Recruitment Cartoon

1. Through the use of image and text, political cartoons can powerfully condense a complex argument into a brief statement with a claim and implied line of reasoning. In your own words, what is the claim and implied supporting argument made by this cartoon?
2. How do the drawing, action, and words of the old soldier help convey the argument?

Source: By permission of Mike Luckovich and Creators Syndicate, Inc.

3. What background knowledge about Wal-Mart's hiring practices and wages for employees does this cartoon draw on?
4. What are the implied criteria for "good soldiers" in this cartoon? How does the imagined revision of Army recruitment standards fail to meet these criteria?

Our final reading was posted on the Web site of the Ayn Rand Institute in July 2005. The Ayn Rand Institute in Irvine, California, is an educational organization dedicated to the philosophy of novelist-philosopher Ayn Rand, who believed in "reason, rational self-interest, individual rights and free-market capitalism" (from the Web site, www.aynrand.org). This institute seeks to educate the public about Rand's philosophy, called Objectivism, and to promote a culture informed by its values. The author of this piece, David Holcberg, works for the institute as a media research specialist. In this argument, Holcberg joins the national and global debate about trading and selling human organs.

Human Organs for Sale?

DAVID HOLCBERG

As athletes who have received organ transplants gathered for the 2005 World Transplant Games in the city of London, Canada, a record 87,000 individuals who did not share these athletes' good fortune stood on the U.S. national waiting list for organs. Of the 82,000 waiting for kidneys or livers, about 6,000 will die in the next twelve months. Yet no one is considering a simple way to save many of these people: legalize trade in human organs.

Let's consider it.

Millions of Americans have exercised their right to give away their organs by signing organ donation cards. But very few made the legal arrangements necessary to ensure that their organs can be harvested after death. Many more would make such arrangements if their families were to be paid for the donated organs. It may work as a type of life insurance for the benefit of the deceased's family and would create a mutually advantageous situation: the deceased's family gets needed money while the transplant patient gets a vital organ.

A few people, on the other hand, may choose to sell an organ (or part of one) during their lifetime. This may seem like a radical idea, but it need not be an irrational one.

5   According to the Mayo Clinic, the extraction of a section of liver, for example, carries a risk to the donor's life of less than 1 percent—not negligible, but not overwhelming. In the case of a kidney donation, the *New England Journal of Medicine* reports that the risk to the donor's life is even smaller; just 0.03 percent. Moreover, liver donors can usually count on their healthy liver's ability to regenerate and regain full function. And donors of kidneys usually live normal lives with no reduction of life expectancy.

A person may reasonably decide, after considering all the relevant facts (including the pain, risk and inconvenience of surgery), that selling an organ is actually in his own best interest. A father, for example, may decide that one of his kidneys is worth selling to pay for the best medical treatment available for his child.

But those who object to a free market in organs would deny this father the right to act on his own judgment. Poor people, they claim, are incapable of making rational choices and so must be protected from themselves. The fact, however, is that human beings (poor or rich) do have the capacity to reason, and should be free to exercise it. So long as a person respects the rights of others, he ought to be free to live his life and use his mind and body as he judges best, without interference from the government or anybody else.

Of course, the decision to sell an organ (or part of an organ) is a very serious one, and should not be taken lightly. That some people might make irrational choices, however, is no reason to violate the rights of everyone. If the law recognizes our right to give away an organ, it should also recognize our right to sell an organ.

The objection that people would murder to sell their victims' organs should be dismissed as the scaremongering that it is. (Indeed, the financial lure of such difficult-to-execute criminal action is today far greater than it would be if patients could legally and openly buy the organs they need.)

10   Opponents of a free market in organs argue as well that it would benefit only those who could afford to pay—not necessarily those in most desperate need. This objection should also be rejected. Need does not give anyone the right to damage the lives of other people, by prohibiting a seller from getting the best price for his organ, or a buyer from purchasing an organ to further his life. Those who can afford to buy organs would benefit at no one's expense but their own. Those unable to pay would still be able to rely on charity, as they do today. And a free market would enhance the ability of charitable organizations to procure organs for them.

Ask yourself: if your life depended on getting an organ, say a kidney or a liver, wouldn't you be willing to pay for one? And if you could find a willing seller, shouldn't you have the right to buy it from him?

The right to buy an organ is part of your right to life. The right to life is the right to take all actions a rational being requires to sustain and enhance his life. Your right to life becomes meaningless when the law forbids you to buy a kidney or liver that would preserve your life.

If the government upheld the rights of potential buyers and sellers of organs, many of the 87,000 people now waiting for organs would be spared hideous suffering and an early death. How many?

Let's find out.

Critiquing "Human Organs for Sale?"

1. In this piece, the proposal to legalize the sale of human organs accompanies an ethical argument about the morality of such a law. What reasoning from principles and consequences does David Holcberg offer in support of the legitimacy of this view?
2. What objections does Holcberg address? How well does he refute these opposing views?
3. How does this argument reflect the values of its sponsoring organization?
4. How does Holcberg use appeals to *pathos?* How would Holcberg respond to the billboard advertisement in the photo on page 199? What do you find persuasive about this argument?

For additional writing, reading, and research resources, go to www.mycomplab.com

15 Proposal Arguments

In 2008, the United States imported approximately 70 percent of its oil, much of it from the Middle East. Not only did this dependency threaten our economy and harm the environment by feeding our petroleum addiction, it also threatened national security. The Republican Party proposed addressing this problem by drilling for more domestic oil in offshore sites and in the Arctic National Wildlife Refuge. However, in the summer of 2008 Texas billionaire oilman T. Boone Pickens, one of the staunchest mainstays of the Republican Party, surprised the nation by rejecting the "drilling" plan and proposing instead the "Pickens Plan"—a multibillion-dollar proposal to build enough wind towers and power transmission lines to supply 20 percent of the nation's electricity. Massive use of wind power, Pickens claimed, would free up natural gas to fuel automobiles rather than to generate electricity. Using clean-burning natural gas in cars would substantially reduce our oil imports while lowering Americans' carbon footprint. The Web site for the Pickens Plan illustrates a proposal argument in multimedia style using photographs, videos, graphics, and text.

Case 2   How Can America's Army Recruit Enough Soldiers?

The U.S. Army has had trouble meeting its monthly recruiting goals, leading to a deepening crisis in supplying enough soldiers to meet conflicts throughout the world. The sluggish flow of enlistments meant that army boot camps were less than half full. To address this crisis, analysts proposed a number of possible solutions: increase the number of army recruiters; improve recruitment methods; expand the pool of possible recruits by lowering standards or increasing the upper age limit; double the size of enlistment bonuses for prized recruits from $20,000 to $40,000; eliminate the ban on gay soldiers; keep more first-term soldiers by reducing the discharge rate for drug abuse, poor conduct, or failure to meet fitness standards; reinstate a lottery draft; or mandate a period of national service for all Americans on graduation from high school (with military service one of the options).

An Overview of Proposal Arguments

Although proposal arguments are the last type we examine, they are among the most common arguments that you will encounter or be called on to write. Their essence is that they call for action. In reading a proposal, the audience is enjoined to make a decision and then to act on it—to *do* something. Proposal arguments are sometimes called *should* or *ought* arguments because those helping verbs express the obligation to act: "We *should* do this [action]" or "We *ought* to do this [action]."

For instructional purposes, we will distinguish between two kinds of proposal arguments, even though they are closely related and involve the same basic arguing strategies. The first kind we will call *practical proposals,* which propose an action to solve some kind of local or immediate problem. A student's proposal to change the billing procedures for scholarship students would be an example of a practical proposal, as would an engineering firm's proposal for the design of a new bridge being planned by a city government. The second kind we will call *policy proposals,* in which the writer offers a broad plan of action to solve major social, economic, or political problems affecting the common good. An argument that the United States should adopt a national health insurance plan or that the electoral college should be abolished would be an example of a policy proposal.

The primary difference is the narrowness versus breadth of the concern. *Practical* proposals are narrow, local, and concrete; they focus on the nuts and bolts of getting something done in the here and now. They are often concerned with the exact size of a piece of steel, the precise duties of a new person to be hired, or a close estimate of the cost of paint or computers to be purchased. *Policy* proposals, in contrast, are concerned with the broad outline and shape of a course of action, often on a regional, national, or even international issue. What government should do about overcrowding of prisons would be a problem addressed by policy proposals. How to improve the security alarm system for the county jail would be addressed by a practical proposal.

Learning to write both kinds of proposals is valuable. Researching and writing a *policy* proposal is an excellent way to practice the responsibilities of citizenship, which require the ability to understand complex issues and to weigh positive and negative consequences of policy choices. In your professional life, writing *practical* proposals may well be among your most important duties on the job. Effective proposal writing is the lifeblood of many companies and also constitutes one of the most powerful ways you can identify and help solve problems.

The Structure of Proposal Arguments

Proposal arguments, whether practical proposals or policy proposals, generally have a three-part structure: (1) description of a problem, (2) proposed solution, and (3) justification for the proposed solution. In the justification section of your proposal argument, you develop *because* clauses of the kinds you have practiced throughout this text.

Toulmin Framework for a Proposal Argument

The Toulmin schema is particularly useful for proposal arguments because it helps you find good reasons and link them to your audience's beliefs, assumptions, and values. Suppose that your university is debating whether to banish fraternities and sororities. Suppose further that you are in favor of banishing the Greek system. One of your arguments is that eliminating the Greek system will improve your university's academic reputation. The chart on page 313 shows how you might use the Toulmin schema to make this line of reasoning as persuasive as possible.

Special Concerns for Proposal Arguments

In their call for action, proposal arguments entail certain emphases and audience concerns that you don't generally face with other kinds of arguments. Let's look briefly at some of these special concerns.

- *The need for presence.* To persuade people to *act* on your proposal, particularly if the personal or financial cost of acting is high, you must give your argument presence as well as intellectual force. By *presence* we mean an argument's ability to grip your readers' hearts and imaginations as well as their intellects. You can give presence to an argument through appeals to *pathos* such as effective use of details, provocative statistics, dialogue, illustrative narratives, and compelling examples that show the reader the seriousness of the problem you are addressing or the consequences of not acting on your proposal.

- *The need to overcome people's natural conservatism.* Another difficulty with proposals is the innate conservatism of all human beings, whatever their political persuasion, as suggested by the popular adage "If it ain't broke, don't fix it." The difficulty of proving that something needs fixing is compounded by the fact that frequently the status quo appears to be working. So sometimes when writing a proposal, you can't argue that what we have is bad, but only that what we could have would be better. Often, then, a proposal argument will be based not on present evils but on the evils of lost potential. And getting an audience to accept lost potential may be difficult indeed, given the inherently abstract nature of potentiality.

- *The difficulty of predicting future consequences.* Further, most proposal makers will be forced to predict consequences of their proposed action. As the "law of unintended consequences" suggests, few major decisions lead neatly to their anticipated results without surprises along the way. So when we claim that our proposal will lead to good consequences, we can expect our audience to be skeptical.

Toulmin Analysis of the Greek System Argument

ENTHYMEME

CLAIM Our university should eliminate the Greek system

REASON because doing so will improve our university's academic reputation.

GROUNDS

Evidence that eliminating the Greek system will improve our academic reputation.

- Excessive party atmosphere of some Greek houses emphasizes social life rather than studying—we are known as a party school.

- Last year the average GPA of students in fraternities and sororities was lower than the GPA of non-Greek students.

- New pledges have so many house duties and initiation rites that their studies suffer.

- Many new students think about rush more than about the academic life.

CONDITIONS OF REBUTTAL
Attacking the reason and grounds

- Many of the best students are Greeks. Last year's highest-GPA award went to a sorority woman, and several other Greeks won prestigious graduate school scholarships.

- Statistics on grades are misleading. Many houses had much higher average GPA than the university average. Total GPA was brought down by a few rowdy houses.

- Many other high-prestige universities have Greek systems.

- There are ways to tone down the party atmosphere on campus without abolishing the Greek system.

- Greeks contribute significantly to the community through service projects.

WARRANT

It is good for our university to achieve a better academic reputation.

BACKING

- The school would attract more serious students, leading to increased prestige.

- Campus would be more academically focused and attract better faculty.

- Losing the "party-school" reputation would put us in better light for taxpayers and legislators.

- Students would graduate with more skills and knowledge.

CONDITIONS OF REBUTTAL
Attacking the warrant and backing

- No one will argue that it is not good to have a strong academic reputation.

- However, skeptics may say that eliminating sororities and fraternities won't improve the university's academic reputation but will hurt its social life and its wide range of living options.

■ *The problem of evaluating consequences.* A final problem for proposal writers is the difficulty of evaluating consequences. In government and industry, managers often use a *cost-benefit analysis* to reduce all consequences to a single-scale comparison, usually money. Although this scale may work well in some circumstances, it can lead to grotesquely inappropriate conclusions in other situations. Just how does one balance the environmental benefits of high gasoline prices against the suffering of drivers who can't afford to get to work or the benefits of pollution-free nuclear power against the costs of a potential nuclear accident? Also, what will be a cost for one group will often be a benefit for others. For example, if Social Security benefits are cut, those on Social Security will suffer, but current workers who pay for it with taxes will take home a larger paycheck.

These, then, are some of the general difficulties facing someone who sets out to write a proposal argument. Although these difficulties may seem daunting, the rest of this chapter offers strategies to help you overcome them and produce a successful proposal.

Developing a Proposal Argument

Writers of proposal arguments must focus in turn on three main phases or stages of the argument: showing that a problem exists, explaining the proposed solution, and offering a justification.

Convincing Your Readers That a Problem Exists

There is one argumentative strategy generic to all proposal arguments: calling your reader's attention to a problem. In some situations, your intended audience may already be aware of the problem and may have even asked for solutions. In such cases, you do not need to develop the problem extensively or motivate your audience to solve it. But in most situations, awakening your readers to the existence of a problem—a problem they may well not have recognized before—is your first important challenge. You must give your problem presence through anecdotes, telling statistics, or other means that show readers how the problem affects people or otherwise has important stakes. Your goal is to gain your readers' intellectual assent to the depth, range, and potential seriousness of the problem and thereby motivate them to want to solve it.

Typically, the arguer develops the problem in one of two places in a proposal argument—either in the introduction prior to the presentation of the arguer's proposal claim or in the body of the paper as the first main reason justifying the proposal claim. In the second instance the writer's first *because* clause has the following structure: "We should do this action *because* it addresses a serious problem."

Here is how one student writer gave presence to a proposal, addressed to the chair of the mathematics department at her school, calling for redesign of the first-year calculus curriculum in order to slow its pace. She wants the chair to see a problem from her perspective.

Example Passage Giving Presence to a Problem

For me, who wants to become a high school math teacher, the problem with introductory calculus is not its difficulty but its pace. My own experience in the Calculus 134 and 135 sequence last year showed me that it was not the learning of calculus that was difficult for me. I was able to catch on to the new concepts. My problem was that it went too fast. Just as I was assimilating new concepts and feeling the need to reinforce them, the class was on to a new topic before I had full mastery of the old concept.... Part of the reason for the fast pace is that calculus is a feeder course for computer science and engineering. If prospective engineering students can't learn the calculus rapidly, they drop out of the program. The high dropout rate benefits the Engineering School because they use the math course to weed out an overabundance of engineering applicants. Thus the pace of the calculus course is geared to the needs of the engineering curriculum, not to the needs of someone like me who wants to be a high school mathematics teacher and who believes that my own difficulties with math—combined with my love for it—might make me an excellent math teacher.

By describing the fast pace of the math curriculum from the perspective of a future math teacher rather than an engineering student, this writer brings visibility to a problem. What before didn't look like a problem (it is good to weed out weak engineering majors) suddenly became a problem (it is bad to weed out future math teachers). Establishing herself as a serious student genuinely interested in learning calculus, she gave presence to the problem by calling attention to it in a new way.

Showing the Specifics of Your Proposal

Having decided that there is a problem to be solved, you should lay out your thesis, which is a proposal for solving the problem. Your goal now is to stress the feasibility of your solution, including costs. The art of proposal making is the art of the possible. To be sure, not all proposals require elaborate descriptions of the implementation process. If you are proposing, for example, that a local PTA chapter buy new tumbling mats for the junior high gym classes, the procedures for buying the mats will probably be irrelevant. But in many arguments the specifics of your proposal—the actual step-by-step methods of implementing it—may be instrumental in winning your audience's support.

You will also need to show how your proposal will solve the problem either partially or wholly. Sometimes you may first need to convince your reader that the problem is solvable, not something intractably rooted in "the way things are," such as earthquakes or jealousy. In other words, expect that some members of your audience will be skeptical about the ability of any proposal to solve the problem you are addressing. You may well need, therefore, to "listen" to this point of view in your refutation section and to argue that your problem is at least partially solvable.

In order to persuade your audience that your proposal can work, you can follow any one of several approaches. A typical approach is to lay out a causal argument showing how one consequence will lead to another until your solution is effected. Another approach is to turn to resemblance arguments, either analogy or precedent. You try to show how similar proposals have been successful elsewhere. Or, if similar things have failed in the past, you try to show how the present situation is different.

The Justification: Convincing Your Readers That Your Proposal Should Be Enacted

The justification phase of a proposal argument will need extensive development in some arguments and minimal development in others, again depending on your particular problem and the rhetorical context of your proposal. If your audience already acknowledges the seriousness of the problem you are addressing and has simply been waiting for the right solution to come along, then your argument will be successful so long as you can convince your audience that your solution will work and that it won't cost too much. Such arguments depend on the clarity of your proposal and the feasibility of its being implemented.

But what if the costs are high? What if your readers don't think the problem is serious? What if they don't appreciate the benefits of solving the problem or the bad consequences of not solving it? In such cases you have to develop persuasive reasons for enacting your proposal. You may also have to determine who has the power to act on your proposal and apply arguments directly to that person's or agency's immediate interests. You need to know to whom or to what your power source is beholden or responsive and what values your power source holds that can be appealed to. You're looking, in short, for the best pressure points.

Proposal Arguments as Advocacy Posters or Advertisements

A frequently encountered kind of proposal argument is the one-page newspaper or magazine advertisement often purchased by advocacy groups to promote a cause. Such arguments also appear as Web pages or as posters or fliers. These condensed advocacy arguments are marked by their bold, abbreviated, tightly planned format. The creators of these arguments know they must work fast to capture our attention, give presence to a problem, advocate a solution, and enlist our support. Advocacy advertisements frequently use photographs, images, or icons that appeal to a reader's emotions and imagination. In addition to images, they often use different type sizes and styles. Large-type text in these documents frequently takes the form of slogans or condensed thesis statements written in an arresting style. To outline and justify their solutions, creators of advocacy ads often put main supporting reasons in bulleted lists and sometimes enclose carefully selected facts and quotations in boxed sidebars. To add an authoritative *ethos,* the arguments often include fine-print footnotes and bibliographies. (For more detailed discussion of how advocacy posters and advertisements use images and arrange text for rhetorical effect, see Chapter 9 on visual argument.)

Another prominent feature of these condensed, highly visual arguments is their appeal to the audience through a direct call for a course of action: go to an advocacy Web site to find more information on how to support a cause; cut out a postcardlike form to send to a decision maker; vote for or against the proposition or the candidate; write a letter to a political representative; or donate money to a cause.

What Is Left for Teenagers to Do When the Teen Ordinance Bans Them from Dance Clubs?

Take Ecstasy
at Raves

Drink at Places with
No Adult Supervision

Roam the Streets

Is There an Answer to These Problems?

Yes! Through your support of the All Ages Dance Ordinance, teens will have a safe place to go where:

- **No hard drugs, like ecstasy and cocaine, are present**
- **Responsible adults are watching over everyone**
- **All of their friends can hang out in one place indoors, instead of outside with drug dealers, criminals, and prostitutes**

Give Your Child a Safe Place to Have Fun at Night

Let the Seattle City Committee Know That You Support the All Ages Dance Ordinance

FIGURE 15.1 Student advocacy advertisement

An example of a student-produced advocacy advertisement is shown in Figure 15.1. Here student Lisa Blattner joins a heated debate in her city on whether to close down all-ages dance clubs. Frustrated because the evening dance options for under-twenty-one youth were threatened in Seattle, Lisa directed her ad toward the general readership of regional newspapers with the special intention of reaching adult voters and parents. Lisa's ad uses three documentary-like, emotionally loaded, and disturbing photographs to give immediacy and presence to the problem. The verbal text in the ad states the proposal claim and provides three reasons in support of the claim. Notice how the reasons also pick up the ideas in the three photo images. The final lines of text memorably reiterate the claim and call readers to action. The success of this ad derives from the collaboration of layout, photos, and verbal text in conveying a clear, direct argument.

Now that you have been introduced to the main elements of a proposal argument, including condensed visual arguments, we explain in the next two sections two invention strategies you can use to generate persuasive reasons for a proposal argument and to anticipate your audience's doubts and reservations. We call these the "claim-type strategy" and the "stock issues strategy."

Using the Claim-Types Strategy to Develop a Proposal Argument

In Chapter 10 we explained how claim-type theory can help you generate ideas for an argument. Specifically, we explained how evaluation and proposal claims often depend for their supporting reasons on claims about category, cause, or resemblance. This fact leads to a powerful idea-generating strategy based on arguments from category (which also includes argument from principle), on arguments from consequences, or on arguments from resemblance. This "claim-types" strategy is illustrated in the following chart:

Explanation of Claim-Types Strategy for Supporting a Proposal Claim

Claim Type	Generic Template	Example from Biotechnology Issue
Argument from principle or category	We should do this action ■ because doing so adheres to this good principle [or] ■ because this action belongs to this good category	We should support genetically modified foods ■ because doing so values scientific reason over emotion [or] ■ because genetically modified foods are safe
Argument from consequences	■ because this action will lead to these good consequences	■ because biotech crops can reduce world hunger ■ because biotech crops can improve the environment by reducing use of pesticides
Argument from resemblance	■ because this action has been done successfully elsewhere [or] ■ because this action is like this other good action	■ because genetic modification is like natural crossbreeding that has been accelerated [or] ■ because genetic modification of food is like scientific advancements in medicine

Before we give you some simple strategies for using this approach, let's illustrate it with another example.

Insurance companies should pay for long-term psychological counseling for anorexia (proposal claim)

- because paying for such counseling is a demonstration of commitment to women's health. (principle/category)
- because paying for such counseling may save insurance companies from much more extensive medical costs at a later date. (consequence)
- because paying for anorexia counseling is like paying for alcoholism or drug counseling, which is already covered by insurance. (resemblance)

Note how each of these supporting reasons appeals to the value system of the audience. The writer hopes to show that covering the cost of counseling is within the class of things that the audience already values (commitment to women's health), will lead to consequences desired by the audience (reduced long-term costs), and is similar to something the audience already values (drug and alcohol counseling). The claim-types strategy for generating ideas is easy to apply in practice. The following chart shows you how.

Suggestions for Applying the Claim-Types Strategy to Your Proposal

Claim Type	Your Goal	Thinking Strategy
Argument from principle or category	Show how your proposed action follows a principle valued by your audience or belongs to a category valued by your audience.	<ul><li>Think of how your proposed action adheres to a rule or principle</li><li>Use this template: "because doing this action is _____" and then fill in the blank with a noun or adjective: *kind, just, loving, courageous, merciful, legal, fair, democratic, constitutional, an act of hope, an illustration of the golden rule, faithful to the principle of limited government.*</li><li>If you are opposing a proposal, search for negative rather than positive principles/categories.</li></ul>
Argument from consequences	Show how your proposed action will lead to consequences valued by your audience.	<ul><li>Brainstorm consequences of your proposal and identify those that audience will agree are good.</li><li>If you are opposing a proposal, search for negative consequences.</li></ul>

(Continued)

Claim Type	Your Goal	Thinking Strategy
Argument from resemblance	Show how your proposed action has been done successfully elsewhere or is like another action valued by your audience.	▪ Brainstorm places or times when your proposal (or something similar to it) has been done successfully ▪ Brainstorm analogies that compare your proposed action to something the audience already values. ▪ If you are opposing a proposal, think of places or times where similar actions have failed or construct a negative analogy.

▪ ▪ ▪ **FOR CLASS DISCUSSION**   Generating Ideas Using the Claim-Types Strategy

1. Working individually or in small groups, use the strategies of principle/category, consequence, and resemblance to create *because* clauses that support each of the following claims. Try to have at least one *because* clause from each of the categories, but generate as many reasons as possible. Don't worry about whether any individual reason exactly fits the category. The purpose is to stimulate thinking, not fill in the slots.

Example

People should not own pit bulls (proposal claim)

- because pit bulls are vicious. (category)
- because owning a pit bull leads to conflicts with neighbors. (consequence)
- because owning a pit bull is like having a shell-shocked roommate—mostly they're lovely companions, but they can turn violent if startled. (resemblance)

   a. Marijuana should be legalized.

   b. Division I college athletes should receive salaries.

   c. High schools should pass out free contraceptives.

   d. Violent video games should be made illegal.

   e. Parents should be heavily taxed for having more than two children.

2. Repeat the first exercise, taking a different position on each issue.   ▪ ▪ ▪

Using the "Stock Issues" Strategy to Develop a Proposal Argument

Another effective way to generate ideas for a proposal argument is to ask yourself a series of questions based on the "stock issues" strategy. Suppose, for example, you wanted to develop the following argument: "In order to solve the problem of students who won't take risks with their writing, the faculty should adopt a pass/fail method of grading in all

**When
your right
to an abortion
is taken away,
what are you
going to
do**

Reproductive rights are under attack. The Pro-Choice Public Education Project. It's pro-choice or no choice.
1(688)253-CHOICE or www.protect.choice.org

A Proposal Claim

This ad attempts to counter the influence of the pro-life movement's campaign against abortion rights. Sponsored by the Planned Parenthood Responsible Choices Action Network, the ad appeared in a number of liberal magazines. What policy proposal does this ad make? How would you convert its visual argument into a verbal argument? What action is it asking people to take? How does the image of the coat hanger/question mark appeal simultaneously to both *pathos* and *logos*? How would you evaluate the overall effectiveness of this ad in motivating pro-choice advocates to take action? How might pro-life advocates respond to this ad?

writing courses." The stock issues strategy invites the writer to consider "stock" ways (that is, common, usual, frequently repeated ways) that such arguments can be conducted.

Stock issue 1: *Is there really a problem here that needs to be solved?* Is it really true that a large number of student writers won't take risks in their writing? Is this problem more serious than other writing problems such as undeveloped ideas, lack of organization, and poor sentence structure? This stock issue invites the writer to convince her audience that a true problem exists. Conversely, an opponent to the proposal may argue that a true problem does not exist.

Stock issue 2: *Will the proposed solution really solve this problem?* Is it true that a pass/fail grading system will cause students to take more risks with their writing? Will more interesting, surprising, and creative essays result from pass/fail grading? Or will students simply put less effort into their writing? This stock issue prompts a supporter to demonstrate that the proposal will solve the problem; in contrast, it prompts the opponent to show that the proposal won't work.

Stock issue 3: *Can the problem be solved more simply without disturbing the status quo?* An opponent of the proposal may agree that a problem exists and that the proposed solution might solve it. However, the opponent may say, "Are there not less radical ways to solve this problem? If we want more creative and risk-taking student essays, can't we just change our grading criteria so that we reward risky papers and penalize conventional ones?" This stock issue prompts supporters to show that *only* the proposed solution will solve the problem and that no minor tinkering with the status quo will be adequate. Conversely, opponents will argue that the problem can be solved without acting on the proposal.

Stock issue 4: *Is the proposed solution really practical? Does it stand a chance of actually being enacted?* Here an opponent to the proposal may agree that the proposal would work but that it involves pie-in-the-sky idealism. Nobody will vote to change the existing system so radically; therefore, it is a waste of our time to debate it. Following this prompt, supporters would have to argue that pass/fail grading is workable and that enough faculty members are disposed to it that the proposal is worth debating. Opponents may argue that the faculty is so traditional that pass/fail has utterly no chance of being accepted, despite its merits.

Stock issue 5: *What will be the unforeseen positive and negative consequences of the proposal?* Suppose we do adopt a pass/fail system. What positive or negative consequences may occur that are different from what we at first predicted? Using this prompt, an opponent may argue that pass/fail grading will reduce the effort put forth by students and that the long-range effect will be writing of even lower quality than we have now. Supporters would try to find positive consequences—perhaps a new love of writing for its own sake rather than the sake of a grade.

■ ■ ■   **FOR CLASS DISCUSSION**   Brainstorming Ideas for a Proposal
The following collaborative task takes approximately two class days to complete. The exercise takes you through the process of creating a proposal argument.

1. In small groups, identify and list several major problems facing students in your college or university.
2. Decide among yourselves which are the most important of these problems and rank them in order of importance.
3. Take your group's number one problem and explore answers to the following questions. Group recorders should be prepared to present your group's answers to the class as a whole:
   a. Why is the problem a problem?
   b. For whom is the problem a problem?
   c. How will these people suffer if the problem is not solved? (Give specific examples.)
   d. Who has the power to solve the problem?
   e. Why hasn't the problem been solved up to this point?
   f. How can the problem be solved? (That is, create a proposal.)
   g. What are the probable benefits of acting on your proposal?
   h. What costs are associated with your proposal?
   i. Who will bear those costs?
   j. Why should this proposal be enacted?
   k. Why is it better than alternative proposals?
4. As a group, draft an outline for a proposal argument in which you
   a. describe the problem and its significance.
   b. propose your solution to the problem.
   c. justify your proposal by showing how the benefits of adopting that proposal outweigh the costs.
5. Recorders for each group should write their group's outline on the board and be prepared to explain it to the class.

WRITING ASSIGNMENT A Proposal Argument

Option 1: A Practical Proposal Addressing a Local Problem Write a practical proposal offering a solution to a local problem. Your proposal should have three main sections: (1) description of the problem, (2) proposed solution, and (3) justification. You may include additional sections or subsections as needed. Longer proposals often include an *abstract* at the beginning of the proposal to provide a summary overview of the whole argument. (Sometimes called the *executive summary,* this abstract may be the only portion of the proposal read by high-level managers.) Sometimes proposals are accompanied by a *letter of transmittal*—a one-page business letter that introduces the proposal to its intended audience and provides some needed background about the writer.

Document design is important in practical proposals, which are aimed at busy people who have to make many decisions under time constraints. Because the writer of a practical proposal usually produces the finished document (practical proposals are seldom submitted to newspapers or magazines for publication), the writer must pay particular attention to the attractive design of the document. An effective design helps establish the writer's *ethos* as a quality-oriented professional and helps make the reading of the proposal as easy as possible. Document design includes effective use of headings and subheadings, attractive typeface and layout, flawless editing, and other features enhancing the visual appearance of the document. For a student example of a practical proposal, see Laurel Wilson's argument on pages 328–331.

Option 2: A Policy Proposal as a Guest Editorial   Write a two- to three-page policy proposal suitable for publication as a feature editorial in a college or city newspaper or in some publication associated with a particular group or activity such as a church newsletter or employee bulletin. The voice and style of your argument should be aimed at general readers of your chosen publication. Your editorial should have the following features:

1. The identification of a problem (Persuade your audience that this is a genuine problem that needs solving; give it presence.)
2. A proposal for action that will help alleviate the problem
3. A justification of your solution (the reasons why your audience should accept your proposal and act on it)

Option 3: A Researched Argument Proposing Public Policy   Write an eight- to twelve-page proposal argument as a formal research paper, using research data for development and support. In business and professional life, this kind of research proposal is often called a *white paper,* which recommends a course of action internally within an organization or externally to a client or stakeholder. An example of a researched policy proposal is student writer Juan Vazquez's "Why the United States should Adopt Nuclear Power" on pages 332–337.

Option 4: A One-Page Advocacy Advertisement   Using the strategies of visual argument discussed in Chapter 9 and on pages 316–318 of this chapter, create a one-page advocacy advertisement urging action on a public issue. Your advertisement should be designed for publication in a newspaper or for distribution as a poster or flier. An example of a student-produced advocacy advertisement is shown in Figure 15.1 on page 317.

Exploring Ideas

Because *should* or *ought* issues are among the most common sources of arguments, you may already have ideas for proposal issues. To think of ideas for practical proposals, try making an idea map of local problems you would like to see solved. For initial spokes, try trigger words such as the following:

- Problems at my university (dorms, parking, registration system, financial aid, campus appearance, clubs, curriculum, intramural program, athletic teams)
- Problems in my city or town (dangerous intersections, ugly areas, inadequate lighting, parks, police policy, public transportation, schools)
- Problems at my place of work (office design, flow of customer traffic, merchandise display, company policies)
- Problems related to my future career, hobbies, recreational time, life as a consumer, life as a homeowner

If you can offer a solution to the problem you identify, you may make a valuable contribution to some phase of public life.

To find a topic for policy proposals, stay in touch with the news, which will keep you aware of current debates on regional and national issues. Also, visit the Web sites of your congressional representatives to see what issues they are currently investigating and debating. You might think of your policy proposal as a white paper for one of your legislators.

Once you have decided on a proposal issue, we recommend you explore it by trying one or more of the following activities:

- Explore ideas by using the claim-types strategy (see pp. 318–320).
- Explore ideas by using the "stock issues" strategy (see pp. 320–322).
- Explore ideas using the eleven questions (a–k) on page 323.

Identifying Your Audience and Determining What's at Stake

Before drafting your argument, identify your targeted audience and determine what's at stake. Consider your responses to the following questions:

- What audience are you targeting? What background do they need to understand your problem? How much do they already care about it? How could you motivate them to care?
- After they read your argument, what stance do you imagine them holding? What change do you want to bring about in their view or their behavior?
- What will they find uncomfortable or threatening about your proposal? Particularly, what costs will they incur by acting on your proposal?
- What objections might they raise? What counterarguments or alternative solutions will you need to address?
- Why does your proposal matter? What is at stake?

Organizing a Proposal Argument

When you write your draft, you may find it helpful to have at hand an organization plan for a proposal argument. The plan on page 326 shows a typical structure for a proposal argument. In some cases, you may want to summarize and rebut opposing views before you present the justification for your own proposal.

Designing a One-Page Advocacy Advertisement

As an alternative to a traditional written argument, your instructor may ask you to create a one-page advocacy advertisement. The first stage of your invention process should be the same as for a longer proposal argument. Choose a controversial public issue that needs immediate attention or a neglected issue about which you want to arouse public passion. As with a longer proposal argument, consider your audience in order to identify the values and beliefs on which you will base your appeal.

Organization Plan for a Proposal Argument

Introduce and develop the problem.	• Engage reader's interest in your problem. • Provide background, including previous attempts to solve the problem. • Give the problem "presence" by showing who is affected and what is at stake. • Argue that the problem is solvable (optional).
Present your proposed solution to the problem.	• First, state your proposal concisely to serve as your thesis statement or claim. • Then, explain the specifics of your proposal.
Justify your proposed solution through a series of supporting reasons.	• Restate your claim and forecast your supporting reasons. • Present and develop reason 1. • Present and develop reason 2. • Present and develop additional reasons.
Respond to objections or to alternative proposals.	• Anticipate and summarize possible objections or alternative ways to solve the problem. • Respond appropriately through rebuttal or concession.
Conclude.	• Sum up your argument and help reader return to the "big picture" of what's at stake. • Call readers to action. • End with something memorable.

When you construct your argument, the limited space available demands efficiency in your choice of words and in your use of document design. Your goal is to have a memorable impact on your reader in order to promote the action you advocate. The following questions may help you design and revise your advocacy ad.

1. How could photos or other graphic elements establish and give presence to the problem?
2. How can type size, style, and layout be used to present the core of your proposal, including the justifying reasons, in the most powerful way for the intended audience?
3. Can any part of this argument be presented as a slogan or memorable catchphrase? What key phrases could highlight the parts or the main points of this argument?
4. How can document design clarify the course of action and the direct demand on the audience this argument is proposing?
5. How can use of color enhance the overall impact of your advocacy argument? (Note: One-page advertisements are expensive to reproduce in color, but you

might make effective use of color if your advocacy ad were to appear as a poster or Web page.)

Questioning and Critiquing a Proposal Argument

As we've suggested, proposal arguments need to overcome the innate conservatism of people, the difficulty of anticipating all the consequences of a proposal, and so forth. What questions, then, can we ask about proposal arguments to help us anticipate these problems?

Will a skeptic deny that my problem is really a problem? The first question to ask of your proposal is "What's so wrong with the status quo that change is necessary?" The second question is "Who loses if the status quo is changed?" Be certain not to overlook this second question. Most proposal makers can demonstrate that some sort of problem exists, but often it is a problem only for certain groups of people. Solving the problem will thus prove a benefit to some people but a cost to others. If audience members examine the problem from the perspective of the potential losers rather than the winners, they can often raise doubts about your proposal.

Will a skeptic doubt the effectiveness of my solution? Assuming that you've convinced your audience that a significant problem exists and is worth solving, you then have to convince readers that your solution will work. Skeptics are likely to raise at least two kinds of questions about your proposed solution. First, they may doubt that you have adequately identified the cause of the problem. Perhaps you have mistaken a symptom for a cause or confused two commonly associated but essentially unlinked phenomena for a cause-effect relationship. For example, will paying teachers higher salaries improve the quality of teaching or merely attract greedier rather than brighter people? Maybe more good teachers would be attracted and retained if they were given some other benefit (fewer students? fewer classes? more sabbaticals? more autonomy? more prestige?). Second, skeptics are likely to invoke the phenomenon of unintended consequences—solving one problem merely creates a sequence of new problems. ("Now that we've raised teachers' salaries, we don't have enough tax dollars for highway maintenance; not only that, now firefighters and police are demanding higher salaries also.") As you anticipate audience objections, look again at the potential negative consequences of your proposed solution.

Will a skeptic think my proposal costs too much? The most commonly asked question of any proposal is simply, "Do the benefits of enacting the proposal outweigh the costs?" As we saw earlier, you can't foresee all the consequences of any proposal. It's easy, before the fact, to underestimate the costs and exaggerate the benefits of a proposal. So, in asking how much your proposal will cost, we urge you to make an honest estimate. Will your audience discover costs you hadn't anticipated—extra financial costs or unexpected psychological or environmental or aesthetic costs? As much as you can, anticipate these objections.

Will a skeptic suggest counterproposals? Once you've convinced readers that a problem exists, they are likely to suggest alternative solutions different from yours. If readers acknowledge the seriousness of the problem, yet object to your proposal, they are faced with a dilemma: either they have to offer their own counterproposals or they have to argue that the problem is simply in the nature of things and hence unsolvable. So, given the likelihood that you'll be faced with a counterproposal, it only makes sense to anticipate it and to work out a refutation of it before you have it thrown at you. And who knows, you may end up liking the counterproposal better and changing your mind about what to propose!

READINGS

Our first reading, by student writer Laurel Wilson, is a practical proposal addressing the problem of an inequitable tipping policy for
hosts in a national brewpub restaurant chain.* ("Hosts" are the people who greet
you when you enter a restaurant and escort you to a table.) As a practical proposal,
it uses headings and other elements of document design aimed to give it a finished
and professional appearance. When sent to the intended audience, it is accompanied by a single-spaced letter of transmittal following the conventional format of a
business letter.

A Proposal to Provide Tips for Hosts at Stone's End

LAUREL WILSON (STUDENT)

Paul Smithson

CEO, Stone's End Restaurant and Brewery

1422 Stone Avenue

Certain City,

Certain State, Zip

Dear Mr. Smithson:

Enclosed is a proposal that addresses Stone's End corporate policy forbidding hosts
from receiving tips from servers. My proposal shows the problems associated with this
rule and suggests a workable solution.

The enclosed proposal suggests a modest plan for tipping hosts that would make their
wages more fair. Currently hosts earn only half as much as servers, and yet are expected
not only to work as hard as servers, but also to wear dressy clothes that are quite expensive. Rewarding hosts for their important work in a job that is far from easy should be
supported by management and servers, who benefit from hosts who go above and beyond
the call of duty.

As a former host at Stone's End, I often felt unappreciated by both servers and management. I worked very hard and was not compensated for providing excellent service. I
eventually found a different job because I could not afford to work there without the extra
compensation of tips. I later discovered that many other restaurants not only tipped their
hosts, but also gave them a clothing allowance. I hope my idea is received well and considered as a viable option. A change in corporate policy regarding the tipping of hosts

---

*Laurel Wilson wrote this proposal to an actual company; with the author's permission, we have changed
the names of the manager and brewpub and disguised the location.

might make Stone's End restaurants even more successful than they are now because hosts would feel like appreciated members of the restaurant team.

Thank you for your time.

Sincerely,

Laurel Wilson

A PROPOSAL TO PROVIDE TIPS FOR HOSTS AT STONE'S END
Submitted for Consideration by the Stones End Corporate Office
by
Laurel Wilson, former Stone's End Host in _____
(Address and Phone Number)

If this were the actual proposal, the first page would begin on a new page following the cover page (shown in the box above).

Problem

Because the "no tips" policy for hosts at Stone's End restaurants keeps their wages significantly below those of servers, hosts often feel unnoticed and unappreciated. Hosts at Stone's End currently make a flat wage of $9.00 per hour without tips. Servers make $6.25 per hour plus tips, which range between $50 and $150 per shift. On a busy night, a server can make as much as $31.25 per hour for a four-hour shift if one adds $100 of tips to four hours of wages ($6.25 \times 4 + 100$ divided by 4). Hosts usually have a six-hour shift making $9 per hour. In a four-hour shift a server typically makes $125, while a host makes $54 for a six-hour shift.

Some people might think that hosts shouldn't be tipped because their job is less stressful than that of servers. However, the host's job entails many things that keep the restaurant running smoothly. A host organizes the dining room in a way that accommodates all parties with no customers having to wait more than fifteen minutes for their tables. The host also has to make sure that servers do not have more than one party being seated in their section at the same time. There are usually nine servers in the dining room during the evening shift, each having five tables in his or her section. A good host will clear and wipe down tables of servers who are swamped in order to give them more time and to keep the restaurant running smoothly. At any given time a host will be dealing with cranky customers, answering a four-line phone, taking "to go" orders, trying to organize a dining room that seats over 200 people, and often clearing tables for overwhelmed servers. This is a highly stressful and active job which requires hard work and is often misunderstood by those who do not know all the duties a host performs.

Proposal

I propose that servers give 1 percent of their tips to the host. As it is now, servers give 2 percent of their tips to the bartenders and 1 percent to the expediters (the expo brings the food out to the tables and arranges the servers' trays). If the servers contribute another

1 percent to their host, the cost to servers would average about one dollar per shift to their host. If you add $1 from each server (usually nine) that adds $9 to the host's pay for the shift, raising it from the $54 we figured earlier (based on six hours at $9 per hour) to $63. On a busy night, the host might get $1.50 or even $2.00 from each server—an amount that would help the host immensely while being barely a dent in the server's take-home pay for the shift.

Justification

Some persons might have objections to this proposal. Owners, in setting corporate policy for the national chain of Stone's End restaurants, have most likely researched all aspects of the restaurant business and decided that the "no tips" rule for hosts was the best policy. They probably have reasons for the "no tips" policy that hosts don't understand. But perhaps the owners don't currently recognize the disadvantages of this policy, which leads to disgruntled hosts and a high turnover. Running a successful restaurant hinges on the happiness of all employees. The hosts' contributions are currently disregarded, even though they are a valuable asset to the restaurant. Corporate owners would be caught in a tailspin if they spent just one night doing the job of a host.

Others might point to the plight of the servers. Servers work incredibly hard for their tips and rely on those tips to pay their bills. On a slow night (which is rare), servers might make minimal tips (maybe only $40 per shift). Taking even a small percentage out of their tips might seem painful. Also servers' shifts last about four hours whereas a host usually works a six-hour shift, sometimes even eight. Servers might argue that the host's extra hours, paid at a higher hourly rate than servers receive, give the hosts an adequate income. However, even on a very slow night in which the server makes only $40 in tips, their hourly wage is still $16.25 per hour, more than $7 per hour higher than the host's wage.

Despite the objections that might be raised by owners or servers, the hosts at Stone's End perform a difficult and thankless job that deserves recognition by both servers and the corporate office. My proposal should be enacted for the following reasons:

- Paying a small tip to hosts is a fair way to reward their contributions. As I have noted, the hosts' job entails many tasks that make the server's job more bearable. Moreover, the host makes the first impression on the customer and sets the mood for the customer's experience in the restaurant. Having to wear dressy clothes—a considerable extra expense—is only one part of the host's important job of setting a good first impression for the restaurant. During busy times, a host who goes above and beyond the call of duty helps out the servers by clearing and wiping tables and ensuring the smooth operation of the dining room.
- The current "no tips" policy set by the corporate office places local managers in the unpleasant position of having to defend a corporate policy that they don't personally support. At the Stone's End where I worked (in _____), the manager agreed with the hosts' desire to receive tips as did the servers, who agreed that hosts should be rewarded for all the help they provide servers with their hectic jobs. But the manager had to back the

corporate office's "no tips for hosts" rule, making it difficult for the manager to keep every employee happy. The manager thus had to bear the brunt of the hosts' complaints without having power to change the situation.

- Finally, tipping hosts would make Stone's End more competitive with other restaurants in cities such as _____, where tipping hosts is common practice. For example, in _____, restaurants such as II Fornaio and Pallamino's pay their hosts the same wage as Stone's End, but require that servers tip the hosts. Moreover, each of these restaurants has a clothing allowance for their hosts. Not only do their hosts look nice, but they are happy with their jobs as well.

Conclusion

Asking servers to tip hosts at the low rate of 1 percent of tip income would show Stone's End hosts that they are respected and appreciated by their coworkers and part of the restaurant team whose livelihood depends on happy, satisfied customers. The host works hard to keep everyone happy including servers, managers, and customers. They do not make the money they deserve. In order to keep hosts happy and Stone's End competitive with surrounding restaurants, this policy would provide a satisfactory solution to a significant problem. I believe that corporate owners would be highly pleased with the all-around benefits of having happy hosts.

Critiquing "A Proposal to Provide Tips for Hosts at Stone's End"

1. In your own words, summarize briefly the problem that Laurel Wilson addresses, her proposed solution, and her justifying reasons.
2. Laurel addresses her proposal to the CEO of Stone's End restaurants because the CEO has the power to change policy. To what extent does Laurel develop audience-based reasons for this CEO audience? How effectively does she anticipate and respond to objections her audience might raise?
3. How does Laurel establish a positive *ethos* in this argument and a meaningful picture of the problem?
4. How effective is Laurel's proposal?

Our second reading, by student writer Juan Vazquez, is a researched public policy proposal written in response to the option 3 assignment on page 323. Vazquez's argument is based on library and Internet research he conducted into the problem of fossil fuels and climate change. It is formatted as a formal research paper using the documentation style of the Modern Language Association (MLA). A full explanation of this format is given in Chapter 17.

Vazquez 1

Juan Vazquez

Professor Bean

English 210

July 15, 2008

Why the United States Should Adopt Nuclear Power

Thousands of studies conducted by scientists to measure climate change over the last one hundred years have accumulated substantial evidence that global warming is occurring unequivocally. According to the NASA *Earth Observatory* web site, greenhouse gas emissions have caused the average surface temperature of the Earth to increase by 0.6 to 0.9 degrees Celsius between 1906 and 2006. If fossil fuel energy continues to be burned relentlessly, scientists are predicting that the average surface temperatures could rise between $2°C$ and $6°C$ by the end of the twenty-first century (Riebeek). A prevalent consensus among scientists is that humans are a major culprit in global warming by burning fossil fuels such as coal and petroleum, with coal-fired power plants being one of the major problems. Lately, discussion has focused on what governments in developed countries can do to tackle climate change.

One solution, advocated by scientist William Sweet writing for the magazine *Discover*, is that the United States should expand its long-ignored nuclear power industry. However, many people—especially environmentalists—are afraid of nuclear power and believe that we can solve global warming through other alternatives. Despite these fears and counter-arguments, I believe that Sweet is right about nuclear energy. The United States should as quickly as possible phase out coal-burning power plants and replace them with nuclear power and other green technologies.

Before we look at the advantages of nuclear power, it is important to see why many people are opposed to it. First, opponents argue that nuclear power plants aren't safe. They regularly cite the Three Mile Island accident in 1979 and the disastrous Chernobyl meltdown in 1986. A more exhaustive list of recent small scale but worrisome nuclear accidents is provided by an editorial from the *Los Angeles Times,* which describes how a July 2007 magnitude 6.8 earthquake in Japan "caused dozens of problems at the world's biggest nuclear plant, leading to releases of radioactive elements into the air and ocean and an indefinite shutdown" ("No to Nukes"). Opponents also argue that nuclear plants are attractive terrorist targets. A properly placed explosive could spew radioactive material over wide swathes of densely populated areas. Nuclear power plants also provide opportunities for terrorists to steal plutonium for making their own nuclear weapons.

Second, while agreeing that nuclear power plants don't produce greenhouse gases, opponents remind us that radioactive waste cannot be stored safely and that radioactive waste remains hazardous for tens of thousands of years. The heavy walled concrete containers use to enclose nuclear waste will eventually develop cracks. If the planned disposal facility at Yucca Mountain, Nevada--where wastes would be stored in concrete and steel containers deep underground--ever becomes operational, it would ease the waste issue for the United States but would not eliminate it. The dangerous nuclear waste would still have to be trucked to Nevada, and even the Nevada site might not be completely impervious to earthquake damage or to the possibility that future generations would dig it up accidentally.

5   Finally, opponents claim that nuclear power plants are extremely expensive and the process of building them is extremely slow so that this method won't provide any short-term solutions for climate change. According to the "No to Nukes" editorial from the *Los Angeles Times*, the average nuclear plant is estimated to cost about $4 billion, making nuclear-generated energy about 25% to 75% more expensive than old-fashioned coal. At the same time, the regulatory process for building nuclear power plants is slow and unpredictable, making investors hesitant about supplying the capital needed. Opponents of nuclear energy argue that these high costs and long waiting period would make it impossible to launch a massive construction of nuclear power plants that would have an immediate impact on global warming.

So in the face of these risks, why should we support Sweet's proposal for expanding nuclear technology? One answer is that some of the fears about nuclear plants are overstated, fabricated, or politicized. It is true that in the past there have been accidents at nuclear power plants, but improvements in technology make such disasters in the future very unlikely. According to Sweet, changes in the design of nuclear reactors in the United States make them "virtually immune to the type of accident that occurred at Chernobyl in April 1986" (62). Furthermore, Sweet points out, the oft-cited Three Mile Island accident didn't injure a single person and led to a better regulatory system that makes new reactors much safer than old ones. According to Sweet, today's "coal fired power plants routinely kill tens of thousands of people in the United States each year by way of lung cancer, bronchitis, and other ailments; the U.S. nuclear economy kills virtually no one in a normal year" (62). In addition, management of power plants has improved. As for the fear of terrorist threats and nuclear proliferation, these concerns have been blown out of proportion. As Sweet argues, if any terrorists are seeking to produce bombs, their access to plutonium will not depend on how many nuclear power plants the U.S. is building.

Because nuclear power plants must be housed within concrete containment barriers to prevent damage from earthquakes, hurricanes, and floods, they are also resistant to terrorist attacks. A study carried out by the Electric Power Research Institute and reported in a major study of nuclear power by scientists from MIT showed that an airplane crashing into a U.S. nuclear power plant would not breech the containment barriers (*Future of Nuclear Power* 50). Moreover, nuclear scientists say that the safe containment of nuclear waste is not a technical problem but a political problem.

Although nuclear reactors are not risk free, they are much safer for people's health and for the environment than are coal-fired plants with their pollution-spewing greenhouse gases. According to the MIT study on nuclear power, since the first commercial nuclear reactor was built in the United States in 1957 (there are now currently 100 nuclear reactors in the United States), there has been only one accident that caused core damage (Three Mile Island). Using statistical analysis, the researchers estimate the current safety regulations and design specifications will limit core damage frequency to about 1 accident per 10,000 reactor years. They also believe that the technology exists to reduce the rate of serious accidents to 1 in 100,000 reactor-years (*Future of Nuclear Power* 48). The benefits of nuclear power for reducing global warming therefore outweigh the real but very low risks of using nuclear energy.

As to the problem of nuclear power's expense, it is true that nuclear plants are more expensive than coal, but it is important to understand that the high initial cost of building a nuclear power plant is being compared to the artificially low cost of coal power. If we were to tax coal-burning plants through a cap and trade system so that coal plants would have to pay for social and environmental costs of pollution and production of greenhouse gases, nuclear power would become more competitive. As Sweet argues, we need a tax or equivalent trading scheme that would increase the cost of coal-generated electricity to encourage a switch from cheap coal to more environmental friendly nuclear power plants.

Nuclear power plants are not the perfect or sole alternative to burning coal to generate energy, but they are certainly the most effective for combating global warming. Without nuclear power plants, we can't generate enough electricity to meet U.S. demands while also reducing carbon emissions. There are other alternatives such as wind technology, but this is also more expensive than coal and not nearly as reliable as nuclear power. Wind turbines only generate energy about a third of the time, which would not be enough to meet peak demands, and the problem of building enough wind towers and creating a huge distribution system to transmit the power from remote windy regions to cities where the power is needed is overwhelming. Currently wind power generates less than 1% of the nation's electricity whereas nuclear power currently generates 20 percent (Sweet). According to Jesse Asubel, head of the Program for the Human Environment at Rockefeller University, "To reach the scale at which they would contribute importantly to meeting global energy demand, renewable sources of energy such as wind, water, and biomass cause serious environmental harm. Measuring renewables in watts per square meter, nuclear has astronomical advantages over its competitors."

10   To combat global warming we need to invest in strategies that could make a large difference fairly quickly. The common belief that we can slow global warming by switching to fluorescent light bulbs, taking the bus to work, and advocating for wind or solar energy is simply wrong. According to science writer Matt Jenkins, the climate problem is solvable. "But tackling it is going to be a lot harder than you've been led to believe" (39). Jenkins summarizes the work of Princeton researchers Stephen Pacala and Robert Socolow, who have identified a "package of greenhouse gas reduction measures" (44), each measure of which they call a "stabilization wedge." Each wedge would reduce carbon gas emissions by one gigaton. Pacala and Socolow have identified 15 possible stabilization wedges and have shown that adopting 7 of these wedges will reduce carbon emissions to the levels needed to halt global warming. One of Pacala and Socolow's wedges could be achieved by raising the fuel economy of 2 billion cars from 30 mpg to 60 mpg (Jenkins 44). Another wedge would come from building 50 times more wind turbines than currently exist in the world or 700 times more solar panels. In contrast, we could achieve a wedge simply by doubling the number of nuclear power plants in the world. Nuclear power is clearly not the only solution to climate change. In Pacala and Socolow's scheme, it is at most one-seventh of the solution, still forcing us to take drastic measures to conserve energy, stop the destruction of rain forests, develop clean-burning coal, and create highly fuel-efficient automobiles. But nuclear energy produces the quickest, surest, and most dramatic reduction of the world's carbon footprint. If we do not take advantage of its availability, we will need to get equivalent carbon-free power from other sources, which may not be possible and will certainly be more expensive. Therefore expanded use of nuclear technology has to be part of the solution to stop global warming. We should also note that other countries are already way ahead of us in the use of nuclear technology. France gets almost 80% of its electricity from nuclear power and Sweden almost 50% ("World Statistics"). These

Vazquez 5

countries have accepted the minimal risks of nuclear power in favor of a reduced carbon footprint and a safer environment.

In sum, we should support Sweet's proposal for adopting nuclear power plants as a major national policy. However, there are other questions that we need to pursue. Where are we going to get the other necessary wedges? Are we going to set gas mileage requirements of 60 mpg on the auto industry? Are we going to push research and development for ways to burn coal cleanly by sequestering carbon emissions in the ground? Are we going to stop destruction of the rain forests? Are we going to fill up our land with wind towers to get one more wedge? If all these questions make climate change seem unsolvable, it will be even more difficult if we cannot factor in nuclear technology as a major variable in the equation.

Vazquez 6

Works Cited

Ausubel, Jesse H. "Renewable and Nuclear Heresies." Canadian Nuclear Association. Ottowa, CA. 10 March 2005. Plenary Address. *Nuclear Green.* Web. 20 June 2008.

The Future of Nuclear Power: An Interdisciplinary MIT Study. Massachusetts Institute of Technology, 29 July 2003. Web. 20 June 2008.

Jenkins, Matt. "A Really Inconvenient Truth." *Miller McClune* April-May 2008: 38-49. Print.

"No to Nukes." Editorial. *Los Angeles Times.* Los Angeles Times, 23 July 2007. Web. 1 July 2008.

Riebeek, Holli. "Global Warming." *Earth Observatory.* NASA, 11 May 2007. Web. 18 June 2008.

Sweet, William. "Why Uranium Is the New Green." *Discover* Aug. 2007: 61-62. Print.

"World Statistics: Nuclear Energy around the World." *Resources and Stats.* Nuclear Energy Institute, 2008. Web. 19 June 2008.

MLA

Critiquing "Why the United States Should Adopt Nuclear Power"

1. What are Juan Vazquez's major reasons for building more nuclear power plants? Which of these reasons do you feel is most persuasive?
2. What are your own major objections to building more nuclear power plants? Do you have any objections that Vazquez failed to summarize?
3. To what extent did Vazquez respond persuasively to your objections? Which of his refutations of the anti-nuke arguments is weakest?
4. How effective is Vazquez's use of audience-based reasons? How would you evaluate his overall appeal to *logos, ethos,* and *pathos*?

Our third reading is the one-page paid advocacy advertisement on page 339. This is the second in a series of ads produced by the Center for Children's Health and the Environment located at Mount Sinai School of Medicine in New York. The ads were intended to work in concert with the organization's Web site, http://www.childenvironment.org, which provides backup documentation including access to the scientific studies on which the ads' arguments are based. All the ads can be downloaded as PDF files from the Web site. The ads' purpose is to call public attention to environmental dangers to children and to urge public action.

Critiquing the Advocacy Ad from the Center for Children's Health and the Environment

1. A difficulty faced by many proposal writers is awakening the audience to the existence of the problem. The doctors and researchers who founded the Center for Children's Health and the Environment felt that a series of full-page newspaper ads was the best way to awaken the public to a problem that Americans either denied or didn't know existed.
   a. In your own words, what is the problem that this proposal addresses?
   b. How does the ad give presence to the problem?
2. How does this ad use the strategies of visual argument (use of images, arrangement of text, type size, and so forth) discussed in Chapter 9? The ad makers probably had available thousands of pictures to use in this ad. Why did they choose this photograph? Try to reconstruct the thinking of the ad makers when they decided on their use of type sizes and fonts. How is the message in different parts of the ad connected to the visual presentation of the words?
3. How effective is the verbal argument of this advertisement? Why does it place "Toxic chemicals appear linked to rising rates of some cancers" in boldface type at the beginning of the text?
4. Most of this ad is devoted to presentation of the problem. What does the ad actually propose?

More kids are getting brain cancer.

Why?

Toxic chemicals appear linked to rising rates of some cancers.

As scientists and physicians, we've seen a drop in the death rates of many adult and childhood cancers because of earlier detection and better treatment. But we are also seeing a disturbing rise in the reported *incidence* of cancer among young children and adolescents, especially brain cancer, testicular cancer, and acute lymphocytic leukemia. In fact, after injuries and violence, cancer is the leading cause of death in our children.

The increase in childhood cancers may be explained in part by better detection or better access to medical care. But evidence suggests the rise in these childhood cancers, as well as in cancers like non-Hodgkin's lymphoma and multiple myeloma among adults, may also be partially explained by exposure to chemicals in the environment, chemicals found in many products, from paints and pesticides to dark colored hair dyes.

What We Know

Pound for pound, kids are exposed to more toxic chemicals in food, air, and water than adults, because children breathe twice as much air, eat three to four times more food, and drink as much as two to seven times more water. Recent epidemiologic studies have shown that as children's exposures to home and garden pesticides increase, so does their risk of non-Hodgkin's lymphoma, brain cancer, and leukemia. Yet, right now, you can go to your hardware store and buy lawn pesticides, paint thinner and weed killers, all containing toxic chemicals linked to these diseases.

In both children and adults, the incidence rate for non-Hodgkin's lymphoma has increased thirty percent since 1950. The disease has been linked to industrial chemicals, chemicals found in agricultural, home, and garden pesticides, as well as dark hair dyes.

Studies have shown that Vietnam veterans and chemical workers exposed to Agent Orange, a phenoxy herbicide, are especially at risk for non-Hodgkin's lymphoma. American farmers who use phenoxy herbicides have an increased risk of the cancer. A Swedish study showed that among the general population, the risk of non-Hodgkin's lymphoma rises with increased exposure to these herbicides. And, a study in Southern California found that children of parents who use home pesticides have seven times the risk of non-Hodgkin's lymphoma. Multiple myeloma, a bone marrow cancer,

is also associated with toxic chemicals. Its incidence has tripled since 1950. Farmers are especially at risk: a recent analysis of thirty-two studies worldwide showed "consistent, positive findings" of an association between farming and multiple myeloma.

What We Can Do

There is much that parents can do to protect their children from carcinogenic chemicals, beginning with the elimination of many pesticides both outside and in the home. And, of course, the cessation of smoking. There are more suggestions on our website, www.childenvironment.org.

But more needs to be done. As a society, we've done much to protect people, especially children, from the toxic chemicals in cigarettes. But too many toxic chemicals are being marketed without adequate testing. We should demand that new chemicals undergo the same rigorous testing as medicines before being allowed on the market. And we should phase out those chemicals linked with a wide range of health problems from neurological impairment to cancer in children.

A summary of the supporting scientific evidence, and a list of scientific endorsers, can be found at www.childenvironment.org.

Center for Children's Health and the Environment

MOUNT SINAI SCHOOL OF MEDICINE

Box 1043, One Gustave Levy Place, New York, NY 10029 • **www.childenvironment.org**

5. Overall, how effective do you find this advocacy advertisement? If you were thumbing through a newspaper, would you stop to read this ad? If so, what would hook you?

Our last reading is by Donald Shoup, a professor of urban planning at UCLA and the author of the influential book *The High Cost of Free Parking* (2005). Amazon.com's editorial review for Dr. Shoup's book is as follows:

> American drivers park for free on nearly ninety-nine percent of their car trips, and cities require developers to provide ample off-street parking for every new building. The resulting cost? Today we see sprawling cities that are better suited to cars than people and a nation-wide fleet of motor vehicles that consume one-eighth of the world's total oil production. Donald Shoup contends in *The High Cost of Free Parking* that parking is sorely misunderstood and mismanaged by planners, architects, and politicians. He proposes new ways for cities to regulate parking so that Americans can stop paying for free parking's hidden costs.

This piece appeared in the *New York Times* on March 29, 2007.

Gone Parkin'

DONALD SHOUP

MOST people view traffic with a mixture of rage and resignation: rage because congestion wastes valuable time, resignation because, well, what can anyone do about it? People have places to go, after all; congestion seems inevitable.

But a surprising amount of traffic isn't caused by people who are on their way somewhere. Rather, it is caused by those who have already arrived. Streets are clogged, in part, by drivers searching for a place to park.

Several studies have found that cruising for curb parking generates about 30 percent of the traffic in central business districts. In a recent survey conducted by Bruce Schaller in the SoHo district in Manhattan, 28 percent of drivers interviewed while they were stopped at traffic lights said they were searching for curb parking. A similar study conducted by Transportation

Alternatives in the Park Slope neighborhood in Brooklyn found that 45 percent of drivers were cruising.

When my students and I studied cruising for parking in a 15-block business district in Los Angeles, we found the average cruising time was 3.3 minutes, and the average cruising distance half a mile (about 2.5 times around the block). This may not sound like much, but with 470 parking meters in the district, and a turnover rate for curb parking of 17 cars per space per day, 8,000 cars park at the curb each weekday. Even a small amount of cruising time for each car adds up to a lot of traffic.

5   Over the course of a year, the search for curb parking in this 15-block district created about 950,000 excess vehicle miles of travel—equivalent to 38 trips

around the earth, or four trips to the moon. And here's another inconvenient truth about under-priced curb parking: cruising those 950,000 miles wastes 47,000 gallons of gas and produces 730 tons of the greenhouse gas carbon dioxide. If all this happens in one small business district, imagine the cumulative effect of all cruising in the United States.

What causes this astonishing waste? As is often the case, the prices are wrong. A national study of downtown parking found that the average price of curb parking is only 20 percent that of parking in a garage, giving drivers a strong incentive to cruise. As George Costanza once said on *Seinfeld*: "My father never paid for parking, my mother, my brother, nobody.... It's like going to a prostitute. Why should I pay when, if I apply myself, maybe I could get it for free?"

Like George Costanza, drivers often compare parking at the curb to parking in a garage and decide that the price of garage parking is too high. But the truth is that the price of curb parking is too low. Underpriced curb spaces are like rent-controlled apartments: hard to find and, once you do, crazy to give up. This increases the time costs (and therefore the congestion and pollution costs) of cruising.

And, like rent-controlled apartments, underpriced curb spaces go to the lucky more often than they do to the deserving. While the car owner with good timing can enjoy his space free or cheaply for hours or days, others who are late for a meeting or a job interview are left to circle the block, making themselves— and other drivers—miserable. The solution is to set the right price for curb parking.

To prevent shortages, some cities have begun to adjust their meter rates (using trial and error) to produce about an 85 percent occupancy rate for curb parking. The prices vary by location and the time of day. Drivers can usually find a vacant curb space near their destination, and the search time is zero. Cities can adjust the price of curb parking in response to demand to keep roughly one out of every eight spaces vacant throughout the day. Right-priced curb parking can eliminate cruising.

10   The balance between the varying demand for parking and the fixed supply of curb spaces is the Goldilocks Principle of parking prices: the price is too high if too many spaces are vacant, and too low if no spaces are vacant. But when only a few spaces are vacant, the price is just right, and everyone will see that curb parking is both well used and readily available.

Beyond the transportation and environmental benefits, performance-based prices for curb parking can yield ample revenue. If the city uses a share of this money for added public services on the metered streets, residents and local merchants will be more willing to support charging the right price for curb parking. These funds can be used to clean and maintain sidewalks, plant trees, improve lighting, remove graffiti, bury utility wires, and provide other public improvements. Returning the meter revenue generated by a district to the district can persuade residents, merchants, and property owners to support right-priced curb parking.

Redwood City, California, for example, sets its downtown meter rates to achieve an 85 percent occupancy rate for curb parking (the rates vary by location and time of day, depending on demand). Because the city returns the revenue to pay for added public services in the metered district, the downtown area will receive an estimated $1 million a year for increased police protection and cleaner sidewalks.

The Redwood City merchants and property owners all supported the new policy when they learned what the meter revenue would help pay for, and the city council adopted it unanimously. Performance-based prices create a few curb vacancies so visitors can easily find a space, the added revenue pays to improve public services, and the improved public services create political support for the performance-based prices.

If cities want to reduce congestion, clean the air, save energy, reduce greenhouse gas emissions, and improve neighborhoods—and do it all quickly—they should charge the right price for curb parking, and spend the resulting revenue to improve local public services.

15   Getting that price right will do a world of good.

Critiquing "Gone Parkin'"

1. According to Shoup, what is the problem with the current way that cities price downtown parking spots?
2. What is Shoup's proposed solution? How does this solution help solve the problem he presents in the introduction?

3. How does Shoup justify his proposal? That is, what reasons does he provide to persuade government planners to act on his proposal?
4. Shoup never mentions any specific prices for parking. How high would curb parking rates have to be before you would stop cruising for a curb parking spot?
5. What are the chief objections that you might make to his proposal?
6. How persuasive do you find Shoup's proposal? How would you analyze this article from the perspectives of *logos, ethos, pathos*, and *kairos*?

For additional writing, reading, and research resources, go to
http://www.mycomplab.com

PART FIVE

The Researched Argument

Smart Cars, two-seater vehicles less than nine feet long, can now be seen in dozens of countries. Made by the Mercedes Car Group, these cars get around 40 miles per gallon of gasoline and, with their titanium structure, are purported to have good crash ratings. The Smart Car emerged at the kairotic moment when consumers began rethinking their car-buying habits with respect to fuel economy and concern for the environment. This photo, which juxtaposes a Hummer, the king of the SUVs, with this new "greener" vehicle, emphasizes the parking advantage of going green.

16 Finding and Evaluating Sources

Although the "research paper" is a common writing assignment in college, students are often baffled by their professor's expectations. The problem is that students often think of research writing as presenting information rather than as creating an argument. One of our business school colleagues calls these sorts of research papers "data dumps": The student backs a truckload full of fresh data up to the professor's desk, dumps it, and says: "Here's your load of info on 'world poverty,' Prof. You make sense of it."

But a research paper shouldn't be a data dump. Like any other argument, it should use its information to support a contestable claim. Formal researched arguments have much in common with arguments in a popular magazine. However, there is one major difference between a formal research paper and an informal magazine article—the presence of citations and a bibliography. In academic research, the purpose of in-text citations and a complete bibliography is to enable readers to follow the trail of the author's research. The proper formats for citations and bibliographic entries are simply conventions within an academic discipline to facilitate the reader's retrieval of the original sources.

Fortunately, you will find that writing an argument as a formal research paper draws on the same argumentation skills you have been using all along—the ability to pose a good question at issue within a community, to formulate a contestable claim, and to support your claim with audience-based reasons and evidence. What special skills are required? The main ones are these:

- The ability to use your research effectively to frame your issue and to support your claim, revealing your reputable *ethos* and knowledge of the issue. Sources should be woven seamlessly into your argument, which is written in your own voice throughout.
- The ability to tap the resources of libraries and the Internet.
- The ability to evaluate sources for credibility, bias, and accuracy. Special care is needed to evaluate anything retrieved from the "free-access" portion of the World Wide Web.
- The ability to summarize, quote, or paraphrase sources and to avoid plagiarism through citations and attributive tags such as "according to Jones" or "Peterson says."
- The ability to cite and document sources according to appropriate conventions.

This chapter and the next should help you develop these skills. In Chapter 16 we focus on posing a research question, on unlocking the resources of your library and the Internet, and on developing the rhetorical skills for evaluating sources effectively. In Chapter 17 we explain the more nitty-gritty details of how to incorporate that information into your writing and how to document it properly.

Formulating a Research Question

The best way to avoid writing a data dump is to begin with a good research question—the formulation of a problem or issue that your essay will address. The research question, usually in the form of an issue question, will give you a guiding purpose in doing your library research. Let's say you are interested in how toys affect the development of gender identity in children. You can see that this topic is big and unfocused. Your research will be much easier if you give yourself a clear direction through a focused research question. For example, you might formulate a specific question like one of these:

- Why have Barbie dolls been so continuously popular?
- Does the Barbie doll reinforce traditional ideas of womanhood or challenge them?
- Is culture or biology the stronger force in making little boys interested in trucks and guns?
- Do boys' toys such as video games, complex models, electronic gadgets, and science sets develop intellectual and physical skills more than girls' toys do?

The sooner you can settle on a research question, the easier it will be to find the source materials you need in a time-saving, efficient manner. The exploration methods we suggested in Chapter 2 can help you find a research topic that interests you.

A good way to begin formulating a research question is to freewrite for ten minutes or so, reflecting on recent readings that have stimulated your interest, on recent events that have sparked arguments, or on personal experiences that may open up onto public issues. If you have no idea for a topic, try starting with the trigger question "What possible topics am I interested in?" If you already have an idea for a topic area, explore why you are interested in it. Search for the personal connections or the particular angles that most intrigue you.

When student writer Megan Matthews began brainstorming possible issues for a research project, she was initially interested in the problem of storing nuclear waste, but in the middle of a freewrite she switched her focus to a newspaper article she had seen on how the hearing of whales may be threatened by the Navy's sonar technology for detecting enemy submarines. After a few hours of research, both in the library and on the Web, Megan produced the following freewrite in her research notebook:

A Freewrite from Megan's Research Notebook

I'm really becoming interested in the whale issue. The Navy has its own site with a Q&A that contradicts some of its earlier findings, and NOAA [National Oceanic and Atmospheric Administration] issued approval for the military to "harass and disturb" marine mammals despite expressing earlier reservations. Hmmm. Very interesting. Is this new sonar really necessary for security? No one seems to answer that! How many whales could suffer? How dangerous to whales is this sonar? Have they really done enough testing?

Note how Megan has moved from a topic orientation (I am researching whales and Navy sonar) to a question orientation (I am doing research to find the answers to questions that I have posed). Once you get engaged with questions, then your research has a purpose guided by your own critical thinking.

We'll return to Megan's story occasionally throughout this chapter and the next. Her final argument is reprinted in full at the end of Chapter 17.

Understanding Differences in the Kinds of Sources

To be an effective researcher, you need to understand the differences among the many kinds of books, articles, and Web sites you are apt to encounter. In this section, we explain these different kinds of resources. We summarize our points in two handy tables labeled "A Rhetorical Overview of Print Sources" (Table 16.1) and "A Rhetorical Overview of Web Sites" (Table 16.2). By the term *rhetorical overview,* we indicate a way of looking at sources that makes you fully conscious of the writer's context, bias, and intentions:

- For any given piece, what is the writer's purpose and who is the intended audience?
- What is the writer's bias, perspective, or angle of vision?
- What is being *left out* of this source as well as included?

Once you are aware of the many kinds of sources available—and of the kinds of library or Web search strategies needed to find them—you will be a savvy and responsible researcher.

TABLE 16.1   A Rhetorical Overview of Print Sources

Genre and Publisher	Author and Angle of Vision	How to Recognize Them
	Books	
SCHOLARLY BOOKS		
• University/academic presses • Nonprofit • Selected through peer review	**Author:** Professors, researchers **Angle of vision:** Scholarly advancement of knowledge	• University press on title page • Specialized academic style • Documentation and bibliography
TRADE BOOKS (NONFICTION)		
• Commercial publishers (for example, Penguin Putnam) • Selected for profit potential	**Author:** Journalists, freelancers, scholars aiming at popular audience **Angle of vision:** Varies from informative to persuasive; often well researched sometimes shoddy	• Covers designed for marketing appeal • Popular style • Usually documented in an informal rather than an academic style

Genre and Publisher	Author and Angle of Vision	How to Recognize Them
REFERENCE BOOKS—MANY IN ELECTRONIC FORMAT		
▪ Publishers specializing in reference material ▪ For-profit through library sales	**Author:** Commissioned scholars **Angle of vision:** Balanced, factual overview	▪ Titles containing words such as *encyclopedia, dictionary,* or *guide* ▪ Found in reference section of library or online

Periodicals		
SCHOLARLY JOURNALS		
▪ University/academic presses ▪ Nonprofit ▪ Articles chosen through peer review ▪ Examples: *Journal of Abnormal Psychology, Review of Metaphysics*	**Author:** Professors, researchers, independent scholars **Angle of vision:** Scholarly advancement of knowledge; presentation of research findings; development of new theories and applications	▪ Not sold on magazine racks ▪ No commercial advertising ▪ Specialized academic style ▪ Documentation and bibliography ▪ Cover often has table of contents ▪ Often can be found in online databases or on the Web
PUBLIC AFFAIRS MAGAZINES		
▪ Commercial, "for-profit" presses ▪ Manuscripts reviewed by editors ▪ Examples: *Harper's, Commonweal, National Review*	**Author:** Staff writers, freelancers, scholars for general audiences **Angle of vision:** Aims to deepen public understanding of issues; magazines often have political bias of left, center, or right	▪ Long, well-researched articles ▪ Ads aimed at upscale professionals ▪ Often has reviews of books, theater, film, and the arts ▪ Often can be found in online databases or on the Web
TRADE MAGAZINES		
▪ Commercial, "for-profit" presses ▪ Focused on a profession or trade ▪ Examples: *Advertising Age, Automotive Rebuilder, Farm Journal*	**Author:** Staff writers, industry specialists **Angle of vision:** Informative articles for practitioners; advocacy for the profession or trade	▪ Title indicating trade or profession ▪ Articles on practical job concerns ▪ Ads geared toward a particular trade or profession
NEWSMAGAZINES AND NEWSPAPERS		
▪ Newspaper chains and publishers ▪ Examples: *Time, Newsweek, Washington Post, Los Angeles Times*	**Author:** Staff writers and journalists; occasional freelancers **Angle of vision:** News reports aimed at balance and objectivity; editorial pages reflect perspective of editors; op-ed pieces reflect different perspectives	▪ Readily familiar by name, distinctive cover style ▪ Widely available on newsstands, by subscription, and on the Web ▪ Ads aimed at broad, general audience

(Continued)

Genre and Publisher	Author and Angle of Vision	How to Recognize Them
POPULAR NICHE MAGAZINES		
▪ Large conglomerates or small presses with clear target audience ▪ Focused on special interests of target audience ▪ Examples: *Seventeen, People, TV Guide, Car and Driver, Golf Digest*	**Author:** Staff or freelance writers **Angle of vision:** Varies—in some cases content and point of view are dictated by advertisers or the politics of the publisher	▪ Glossy paper, extensive ads, lots of visuals ▪ Popular; often distinctive style ▪ Short, undocumented articles ▪ Credentials of writer often not mentioned

TABLE 16.2   A Rhetorical Overview of Web Sites

Type of Site	Author/Sponsor and Angle of Vision	Characteristics
COM OR .BIZ (A COMMERCIAL SITE CREATED BY A BUSINESS OR CORPORATION)		
▪ Either of these suffixes signals a for-profit operation; this group includes major periodicals and publishers of reference materials ▪ Purpose is to enhance image, attract customers, market products and services, provide customer service ▪ Creators are paid by salary or fees and often motivated by desire to design innovative sites	**Author:** Difficult to identify individual writers; sponsoring company often considered the author **Angle of vision:** Purpose is to promote the point of view of the corporation or business; links are to sites that promote same values	▪ Links are often to other products and services provided by company ▪ Photographs and other visuals used to enhance corporate image
.ORG (A NONPROFIT ORGANIZATION OR ADVOCACY GROUP)		
▪ May function as a major information portal, such as NPR.org, a think tank, or a museum (for example, the Heritage Foundation or the Museum of Modern Art) ▪ Sometimes purpose is to provide accurate, balanced information (for example, the American Red Cross site) ▪ Frequently, purpose is to advocate for or explain the organization (for example, the Ford Foundation or local charity sites); thus, advocacy for fund-raising or political views is likely (for example, People for the Ethical Treatment of Animals [PETA] site or blog portals [Cursor.org])	**Author:** Often hard to identify individual writers; sponsoring organization often considered the author; some sites produced by amateurs with passionate views; others produced by well-paid professionals **Angle of vision:** Purpose is to promote views of sponsoring organization and influence public opinion and policy; many encourage donations through the site	▪ Advocacy sites sometimes don't announce purpose on home page ▪ You may enter a node of an advocacy site through a link from another site and not realize the political slant ▪ Facts/data selected and filtered by site's angle of vision ▪ Often uses visuals for emotional appeal
.EDU (AN EDUCATIONAL SITE ASSOCIATED WITH A COLLEGE OR UNIVERSITY)		
▪ Wide range of purposes ▪ Home page aimed at attracting prospective students and donors ▪ Inside the site are numerous subsites devoted to research, pedagogy, libraries, student employment, and so forth	**Author:** Professors, staff, students **Angle of vision:** Varies from personal sites of professors and students to sites of research centers and libraries; can vary from scholarly and objective to strong advocacy on issues	▪ Often an .edu site has numerous "subsites" sponsored by the university library, art programs, research units ▪ Links to .pdf documents may make it difficult to determine where you are in the site—e.g., professor's course site, student site, administrative site

Type of Site	Author/Sponsor and Angle of Vision	Characteristics
.GOV OR .MIL (SPONSORED BY A GOVERNMENT AGENCY OR MILITARY UNIT)		
• Provides enormous range of basic data about government policy, bills in Congress, economic forecasts, and so forth • Aims to create good public relations for agency or military unit	**Author:** Development teams employed by the agency; sponsoring agency is usually considered the author	• Typical sites (for example, http://www.energy.gov, the site of the U.S. Dept. of Energy) are extremely layered and complex and provide hundreds of links to other sites
	Angle of vision: Varies—informational sites publish data and government documents with an objective point of view; agency sites also promote agency's agenda—e.g., Dept. of Energy, Dept. of Labor	• Valuable for research • Sites often promote values/assumptions of sponsoring agency
PERSONAL WEB SITES (.NAME OR .NET)		
• An individual contracts with server to publish the site; many personal Web sites have .edu affiliation • Promotes hobbies, politics; provides links according to personal preferences	**Author:** Anyone can create a personal Web site **Angle of vision:** Varies from person to person	• Credentials/bias of author often hard to determine • Irresponsible sites may have links to excellent sites; tracing links is complicated

Books versus Periodicals versus Web Sites

When you conduct library research, you often leave the library with an armload of books and a stack of articles that you have either photocopied from journals or magazines or downloaded from a computer and printed out. At home, you will have no trouble determining who wrote the books and for what purpose, but your photocopied or downloaded articles can pose problems. What is the original source of the article in your hands? If you photocopied the articles from actual journals or magazines in your library, then you can be sure that they are "periodical print sources" (*periodical* means a publication, such as a scholarly journal or magazine, issued at regular intervals—that is, periodically). If you downloaded them from a computer—which may have been connected either to a licensed database leased by the library or to the World Wide Web—they may be electronic copies of periodical print sources or they may be material posted on the Web but never published in a print periodical.

When you download a print article from a computer, you should be aware that you lose many contextual clues about the author's purpose and bias—clues that you can pick up from the original magazine or journal itself by its appearance, title, advertisements (if any), table of contents, and statement of editorial policy. When you download something from the Web that has never appeared in print, you have to be wary about its source. Because print publications are costly to produce, print articles generally go through some level of editorial review. In contrast, anyone can post almost anything on the Web. You need to become savvy at recognizing these distinctions in order to read sources rhetorically and to document them accurately in your bibliography.

Scholarly Books versus Trade Books

Note in Table 16.1 the distinction between scholarly books, which are peer reviewed and published by nonprofit academic presses, and trade books, which are published by for-profit presses with the intention of making money. By "peer reviewed," which is a highly prized concept in academia, we mean the selection process by which scholarly manuscripts get chosen for publication. When manuscripts are submitted to an academic publisher, the editor sends them for independent review to experienced scholars who judge the rigor and accuracy of the research and the significance and value of the argument. The process is highly competitive and weeds out much shoddy or trivial work.

In contrast, trade books are not peer reviewed by independent scholars. Instead, they are selected for publication by editors whose business is to make a profit. Fortunately, it can be profitable for popular presses to publish superbly researched and argued intellectual material because college-educated people, as lifelong learners, create a demand for intellectually satisfying trade books written for the general reader rather than for the highly specialized reader. These can be excellent sources for undergraduate research, but you need to separate the trash from the treasure. Trade books are aimed at many different audiences and market segments and can include sloppy, unreliable, and heavily biased material.

Scholarly Journals versus Magazines

Like scholarly books, scholarly journals are academic, peer-reviewed publications. Although they may look like magazines, they almost never appear on newsstands; they are nonprofit publications subsidized by universities for disseminating high-level research and scholarship.

In contrast, magazines are intended to make a profit through sales and advertising revenues. Fortunately for researchers, a demand exists for intellectually satisfying magazines, just as for sophisticated trade books. Many for-profit magazines publish highly respectable, useful material for undergraduate or professional researchers, but many magazines publish shoddy material. As Table 16.1 shows, magazines fall in various categories aimed at different audiences.

Print Sources versus Cyberspace Sources

Another crucial distinction exists between print sources and cyberspace sources. Much of what you can retrieve from a computer was originally published in print.

What you download is simply an electronic copy of a print source, either from a library-leased database or from someone's Web site. (The next section shows you how to tell the difference.) In such cases, you often need to consider the article's original print origins for appropriate cues about its rhetorical context and purpose. But much cyberspace material, having never appeared in print, may never have undergone either peer review or editorial review. To distinguish between these two kinds of cyberspace sources, we call one kind a "print/cyberspace source" (something that has appeared in print and is made available on the Web or through library-leased databases) and the other a "cyberspace-only source." When you use a cyberspace-only source, you've got to take special care in figuring out who wrote it, why, and for what audience.

■ ■ ■ **FOR CLASS DISCUSSION**   **Identifying Sources**

Your instructor will bring to class a variety of sources—different kinds of books, scholarly journals, magazines, and downloaded material. Working individually or in small groups, try to decide which category in Tables 16.1 and 16.2 each piece belongs to. Be prepared to justify your decisions on the basis of the cues you used to make your decision.

Finding Books: Searching Your Library's Online Catalog

Your library's holdings are listed in its online catalog. Most of the entries are for books, but an academic library also has a wealth of other resources such as periodical collections, government records and reports, newspapers, videos and cassettes, maps, encyclopedias, and hundreds of specialized reference works that your reference librarian can help you use.

Indexed by subject, title, and author, the online catalog gives you titles of books and other library-owned resources relevant to your research area. Note that the catalog lists the titles of journals and magazines in the library's periodical collection (for example, *Journal of Abnormal Psychology, Atlantic Monthly*), but does *not* list the titles of individual articles within these periodicals. As we explain next, you can search the contents of periodicals by using a licensed database. Methods of accessing and using online catalogs vary from institution to institution, so you'll need to learn the specifics of your library's catalog through direct experience.

Finding Articles: Searching a Licensed Database

For many research projects, useful sources are print articles from your library's periodical collection, including scholarly journals, public affairs magazines, newspapers or newsmagazines, and niche magazines related to your research area. Some of these articles are available free on the World Wide Web, but most of them are not. Rather, they may be located physically in your library's periodical collection (or through interlibrary loan) or located electronically in databases leased by your library.

What Is a Licensed Database?

Electronic databases index articles in thousands of periodicals. You can search the database by author, title, subject, keyword, date, genre, and other characteristics. In most cases the database contains an abstract of each article, and in many cases it contains the full text of the article, which you can download and print. Because access to these databases is restricted to fee-paying customers, they can't be searched through Web engines like Yahoo! or Google. Most university libraries allow students to access these databases by using a password. You can therefore use the Internet to connect your computer to licensed databases as well as to the World Wide Web (see Figure 16.1).

Although the methods of accessing licensed databases vary from institution to institution, we can offer some widely applicable guidelines. Most likely your library has online one or more of the following databases:

- *EBSCOhost:* Includes citations and abstracts from journals in most disciplines as well as many full-text articles from more than 3,000 journals; its *Academic Search Elite* function covers material published as long ago as the early 1980s.
- *UMI ProQuest Direct:* Gives access to the full text of articles from journals in a variety of subject areas; includes full-text articles from newspapers.
- *InfoTrac:* Is often called "Expanded Academic Index," and is similar to EBSCOhost and UMI ProQuest in its coverage of interdisciplinary subjects.
- *FirstSearch Databases:* Incorporate multiple specialized databases in many subject areas, including WorldCat, which contains records of books, periodicals, and multimedia formats from libraries worldwide.

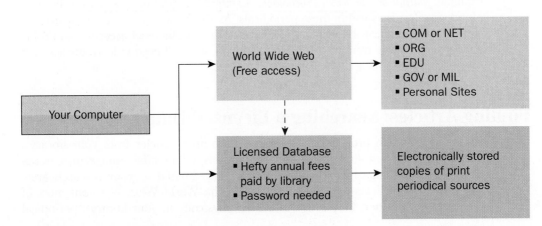

FIGURE 16.1 Licensed database versus free-access portions of Internet

■ *LexisNexis Academic Universe:* Is primarily a full-text database covering current events, business, and financial news; includes company profiles and legal, medical, and reference information.

Generally, one of these databases is the "default database" chosen by your library for most article searches. Your reference librarian will be able to direct you to the most useful licensed database for your purpose.

Keyword Searching

To use an online database, you need to be adept at keyword searching. When you type a word or phrase into a search box, the computer will find sources that contain the same words or phrases. If you want the computer to search for a phrase, put it in quotation marks. Thus if you type "*street people*" using quotation marks, the computer will search for those two words occurring together. If you type in *street people* without quotation marks, the computer will look for the word *street* and the word *people* occurring in the same document but not necessarily together. Use your imagination to try a number of related terms. If you are researching gendered toys and you get too many hits using the keyword *toys,* try *gender toys, Barbie, G.I. Joe, girl toys, boy toys, toys psychology,* and so forth. You can increase the flexibility of your searches by using Boolean terms to expand, narrow, or limit your search (see Table 16.3 for an explanation of Boolean searches).

Illustration of a Database Search

As an illustration of a database search, we'll draw again on Megan's process as she researched the effect of Navy sonar on whales. Using the database EBSCOhost, Megan entered the keywords *Navy sonar* AND *whales,* which revealed the five articles shown in

TABLE 16.3 Boolean Search Commands

Command and Function	Research Example	What to Type	Search Result
X OR Y (Expands your search)	You are researching Barbie dolls and decide to include G.I. Joe figures.	"Barbie doll" OR "GI Joe"	Articles that contain either phrase
X AND Y (Narrows your search)	You are researching the psychological effects of Barbie dolls and are getting too many hits under *Barbie dolls.*	"Barbie dolls" AND psychology	Articles that include both the phrase "Barbie dolls" and the word *psychology*
X NOT Y (Limits your search)	You are researching girls' toys and are tired of reading about Barbie dolls. You want to look at other popular girls' toys.	"girl toys" NOT Barbie	Articles that include the phrase "girl toys" but exclude *Barbie*

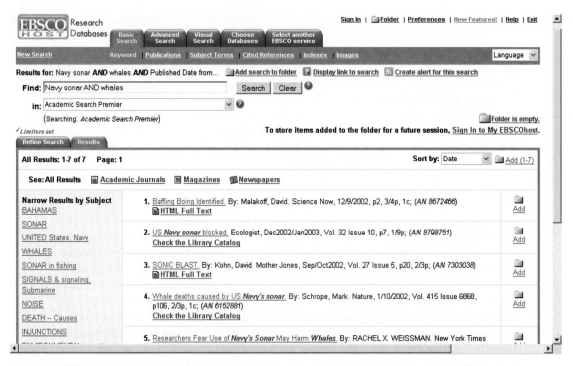

FIGURE 16.2 Results list from a search using EBSCOhost

FIGURE 16.3 Sample display for an article on EBSCOhost

Figure 16.2 on page 354. As the Results list shows, this EBSCO database carries the full text of articles 1 and 3; for articles 2 and 4, Megan will have to check the library's catalog to locate the print periodical in the stacks. To get more information about article 3, "Sonic Blast," Megan clicked on its title, which revealed the screen shown in Figure 16.3 on page 354. This screen gives citation information and provides a brief abstract of the article. If she were interested in reading it, Megan could click on the Full Text link for the whole article.

After you've identified useful articles, locate those available in your library's print periodical collection. (This way you won't lose important contextual cues for reading them rhetorically.) For those unavailable in your library, print, download, or e-mail them from the database or order them from interlibrary loan.

Finding Cyberspace Sources: Searching the World Wide Web

Another valuable resource is the World Wide Web. In this section we begin by explaining in more detail the logic of the Internet—the difference between restricted portions of the Internet, such as licensed databases, and the amorphous, ever-changing, "free-access" portion, commonly called the "World Wide Web" (see again Figure 16.1). We then offer suggestions for searching the Web.

The Logic of the Internet

To understand the logic of Web search engines, you need to know that the Internet is divided into restricted sections open only to those with special access rights and a "free-access" section. Web engines such as Yahoo! or Google search only the free-access portion of the Internet. When you type keywords into a Web search engine, it searches for matches in material made available on the Web by all the users of the world's network of computers—government agencies, corporations, advocacy groups, information services, individuals with their own Web sites, and many others.

The following example will quickly show you the difference between a licensed database search and a Web search. When Megan entered the keywords *Navy sonar* AND *whales* into EBSCOhost, she received five "hits"—the titles of five articles on this subject appearing in print periodicals. In contrast, when she entered the same keywords into the Web search engine Yahoo!, she received 709,000 hits (see Figure 16.4); when she tried the search engine Google, she got even more. The Web search engines are picking up, in addition to articles that someone may have posted on the Web, all references to Navy sonar and whales that appear in advocacy Web sites, government publications, newspapers, blogs, chat rooms, student papers posted on the Web, and so forth.

■ ■ ■ **FOR CLASS DISCUSSION**   Comparing Search Results
Figure 16.4 shows the first screen of hits for the keywords *Navy sonar* AND *whales* retrieved by Yahoo!. Working in small groups or as a whole class, compare these with those retrieved from the EBSCOhost search (Figure 16.2).

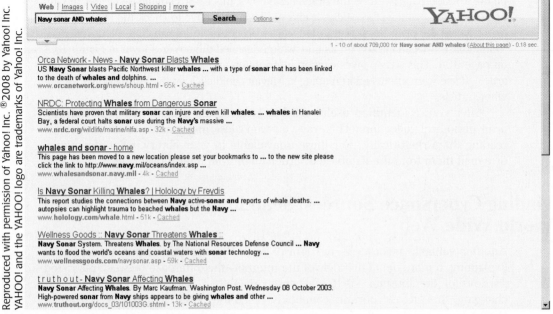

FIGURE 16.4 First screen of hits from Yahoo!

1. Explain why the results for the Web search are different from those of the licensed database search.
2. What do you suspect would be the bias or angle of vision for the first record in the Yahoo! search, "Orca Network—News—Navy Sonar Blasts Whales"?
3. What do you suspect would be the bias or angle of vision of the *Science Now* and *Mother Jones* articles identified in the EBSCOhost search? How could looking at the actual magazines in your college library help you determine the bias? ■ ■ ■

Using Web Search Engines

Although the hits from a Web search frequently include useless, shoddy, trivial, or irrelevant material, the Web's resources are breathtaking. At your fingertips you have access to government documents, legislative and corporate white papers, court cases, persuasive appeals of advocacy groups, consumer information—the list is almost endless.

The World Wide Web can be searched by a variety of engines that collect and categorize individual Web files and search them for keywords. Most of these engines will find not only text files but also graphic, audio, and video files. Different engines search the Web in different ways, so it is important that you try a variety of search engines when you look for information. Again, if you are in doubt, your reference librarian can help you choose the most productive search engine for your needs.

Determining Where You Are on the Web

As you browse the Web looking for resources, clicking from link to link, try to figure out what site you are actually in at any given moment. This information is crucial, both for properly documenting a Web source and for reading the source rhetorically.

To know where you are on the Web, begin by recognizing the codes contained in a site's URL (uniform resource locator). The generic structure of a typical URL looks like this:

Here is a specific example:

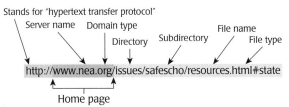

The file name "resources" is linked through a series of directories and subdirectories to the home page of the National Education Association (www.nea.org).

Often, when you click on a link in one site, you will be sent to a totally different site. To determine the home page of this new site, simply note the root URL immediately following the "www."* To view the home page directly, delete the codes to the right of the initial home page URL in your computer's location window and hit Enter. You will then be linked directly to the site's home page. As you will see later in this chapter and in Chapter 17, being able to examine a site's home page helps you read the site rhetorically and document it properly.

Reading Your Sources Rhetorically

Even when you have a research question that interests you, it's easy to feel overwhelmed when you return from a library with a stack of books and magazine or journal articles. How do you begin reading all this material? There is no one right answer to this question. At times you need to read slowly with analytical closeness, as we discussed in Chapter 2. At other times you can skim a source, looking only for its gist or for a needed piece of information.

Reading with Your Own Goals in Mind

How you read a source depends to a certain extent on where you are in the research process. Early in the process, when you are in the thesis-seeking, exploratory stage, your goal is to achieve a basic understanding about your research problem. You need to become aware of different points of view, learn what is unknown or controversial

---

*Not all URLs begin with "www" after the first set of double slashes. Our description doesn't include variations from the most typical URL types. You can generally find the home page of any site by eliminating all codes to the right of the first slash mark following the initial set of double slashes.

about your research question, see what values or assumptions are in conflict, and build up your store of background knowledge.

Given these goals, at the early stages of research you should select, where possible, easy-to-read, overview kinds of sources to get you into the conversation. In some cases, even an encyclopedia or specialized reference work can be a good start for getting general background.

As you get deeper into your research, your questions become more focused, and the sources you read become more specialized. Once you formulate a thesis and plan a structure for your paper, you can determine more clearly the sources you need and read them with purpose and direction.

Reading with Rhetorical Awareness

To read your sources rhetorically, you should keep two basic questions in mind:

(1) What was the source author's purpose in writing this piece?
(2) What might be my purpose in using this piece?

Table 16.4 sums up the kinds of questions a rhetorical reader typically considers.

TABLE 16.4   Questions Asked by Rhetorical Readers

What was the source author's purpose in writing this piece?	What might be my purpose in using this piece in my own argument?
▪ Who is this author? What are his or her credentials and affiliations? ▪ What audience was this person addressing? ▪ What is the genre of this piece? (If you downloaded the piece from the World Wide Web, did it originally appear in print?) ▪ If this piece appeared in print, what is the reputation and bias of the journal, magazine, or press? Was the piece peer reviewed? ▪ If this piece appeared only on the Web, who or what organization sponsors the Web site (check the home page)? What is the reputation and bias of the sponsor? ▪ What is the author's thesis or purpose? ▪ How does this piece try to change his or her audience's view? ▪ What is this writer's angle of vision or bias? ▪ What is omitted or censored from this text? ▪ How reliable and credible is this author? ▪ What facts, data, and other evidence does this author use and what are the sources of these data? ▪ What are this author's underlying values, assumptions, and beliefs?	▪ How has this piece influenced or complicated my own thinking? ▪ How does this piece relate to my research question? ▪ How will my own intended audience react to this author? ▪ How might I use this piece in my own argument? ▪ Is it an opposing view that I might summarize? ▪ Is it an alternative point of view that I might compare to other points of view? ▪ Does it have facts and data that I might use? ▪ Would a summary of all or part of this argument support or oppose one or more of my own points? ▪ Could I use this author for testimony? (If so, how should I indicate this author's credentials?) ▪ If I use this source, will I need to acknowledge the author's bias and angle of vision?

Table 16.4 reinforces a point we've made throughout this text: all writing is produced from an angle of vision that privileges some ways of seeing and filters out other ways. You should guard against reading your sources as if they present hard, undisputed facts or universal truths. For example, if one of your sources says that "Saint John's wort [an herb] has been shown to be an effective treatment for depression," some of your readers might accept that statement as fact—but many wouldn't. Skeptical readers would want to know who the author is, where his views have been published, and what he uses for evidence. Let's say the author is someone named Samuel Jones. Skeptical readers would ask whether Jones is relying on published research, and if so, whether the studies have been peer reviewed in reputable, scholarly journals and whether the research has been replicated by other scientists. They would also want to know whether Jones has financial connections to companies that produce herbal remedies and supplements. Rather than settling the question about Saint John's wort as a treatment for depression, a quotation from Jones may open up a heated controversy about medical research.

Reading rhetorically is thus a way of thinking critically about your sources. It influences the way you take notes, evaluate sources, and shape your argument.

Taking Effective Notes

Taking good research notes serves two functions:

1. Taking notes encourages you to read actively because you must summarize your sources' arguments, record usable information, and extract short quotations.
2. Taking notes encourages you to do exploratory thinking—to write down ideas as they occur to you, to analyze sources as you read them, and to join your sources in conversation.

There are many ways to take notes, but we can offer several techniques that have worked especially well for other writers.

1. You can use a double-entry journal. Divide a page in half, entering your informational notes on one side and your exploratory writing on the other.
2. You can record notes on index cards or in a computer file and then write out your exploratory thinking in a separate research journal.
3. You can record informational notes on your computer in a regular font and then use a boldfaced font for exploratory writing.

No matter the method, your objective is to create a visual way to distinguish your informational notes from your exploratory thinking.

A common practice of beginning researchers—one that experienced researchers almost never use—is *not* taking notes as they read and *not* doing any exploratory writing. We've seen students photocopy a dozen or more articles, but then write nothing as they read (sometimes they highlight passages with a marker), planning to rely later on memory to navigate through the sources. This practice reduces your ability to synthesize your sources and create your argument. When you begin drafting your paper, you'll have no notes to refer to, no record of your thinking-in-progress. Your only recourse is to revisit all your sources, thumbing through them one at a time—a practice that leads to passive cutting and pasting.

TABLE 16.5   Note Taking According to Purpose

How Source Might Be Used in Your Paper	Notes to Take
Background information about research problem or issue	Summarize the information; record specific data.
Part of a section reviewing different points of view on your question	Summarize the source's argument; note its bias and perspective. In exploratory notes, jot down ideas on how and why different sources disagree.
As an opposing view that you must summarize and respond to	Summarize the argument fully and fairly. In and exploratory notes, speculate about why you disagree with the source and whether you can refute the argument, concede to it, or compromise with it.
As data, information, or testimony to be used as evidence to support your thesis	Record the data or information; summarize or paraphrase the supporting argument with occasional quotations of key phrases; directly quote short passages for supporting testimony; note the credentials of the writer or person quoted. In exploratory notes, record new ideas as they occur to you.
As data, information, or testimony that counters your position or raises doubts about your thesis	Take notes on counterevidence. In exploratory notes, speculate on how you might respond to the counterevidence.

To make your notes purposeful, you need to imagine how a given source might be used in your research paper. Table 16.5 shows how notes are a function of your purpose.

When you use a source's exact words, be meticulous in copying them exactly and marking the quoted passage with prominent quotation marks. If you record information without directly quoting it, be sure that you restate it completely in your own words to avoid later problems with plagiarism. Next, check that you have all the bibliographic information you may need for a citation including the page numbers for each entry in your notes and the sponsor of each Web site.

Evaluating Sources

When you read sources for your research project, you need to evaluate them as you go along. As you read each potential source, ask yourself questions about the author's angle of vision, degree of advocacy, reliability, and credibility.

Angle of Vision

By "angle of vision," we mean the way that a piece of writing gets shaped by the underlying values, assumptions, and beliefs of the author so that the text reflects a certain perspective, worldview, or belief system. The angle of vision is revealed by internal factors such as the author's word choice (especially notice the connotations of words), selection and omission of details, overt statements, figurative language, and grammatical emphasis, and by external factors such as the politics of the author, the genre of the source, the politics of the publisher, and so forth.

When reading a source, see whether you can detect underlying assumptions or beliefs that suggest a writer's values or political views: Is this writer conservative or liberal? Predisposed toward traditional "family values" or new family structures? Toward technology or toward the simple life? Toward free markets or regulatory controls on the economy? Toward business interests or labor? Toward the environment or jobs? Toward order or freedom?

You can also get useful clues about a writer's angle of vision by looking at external data. What are the writer's credentials? Is the writer affiliated with an advocacy group or known for a certain ideology? (If you know nothing about an author who seems important to your research, try typing the author's name into a Web search engine. You may discover useful information about the author's other publications or about the writer's reputation in various fields.) Also pay attention to publishing data. Where was this source originally published? What is the reputation and editorial slant of the publication in which the source appears? For example, editorial slants of magazines can range from very liberal to very conservative. Likewise, publications affiliated with advocacy organizations (the Sierra Club, the National Rifle Association) will have a clear editorial bias.* Table 16.6 shows our own assessment of the political biases of various popular magazines and media commentators.

Degree of Advocacy

By "degree of advocacy" we mean the extent to which an author unabashedly takes a persuasive stance on a contested position as opposed to adopting a more neutral, objective, or exploratory stance. When a writer strongly advocates a position, you need to weigh carefully the writer's selection of evidence, interpretation of data, and fairness to opposing views. Although objectivity is itself an "angle of vision" and no one can be completely neutral, it is always useful to seek out authors who offer a balanced assessment of the evidence. Evidence from a more detached and neutral writer may be more trusted by your readers than the arguments of a committed advocate. For example, if you want to persuade corporate executives of the dangers of global warming, evidence from scholarly journals may be more persuasive than evidence from an environmentalist Web site or from a freelance writer in a leftist popular magazine like *Mother Jones.*

---

*If you are uncertain about the editorial bias of a particular magazine or newspaper, consult the *Gale Directory of Publications and Broadcast Media* or *Magazines for Libraries,* which, among other things, identify the intended audience and political biases of a wide range of magazines and newspapers.

TABLE 16.6 Angles of Vision in U.S. Media and Think Tanks: A Sampling Across the Political Spectrum[1]

Commentators

Left	Left Center	Center	Right Center	Right
Barbara Ehrenreich	E.J. Dionne	Amitai Etzioni	David Brooks	Pat Buchanan
Al Franken	Ellen Goodman	Thomas Friedman	Midge Decter	Tucker Carlson
Bob Herbert	Nicholas Kristof	Kathleen Hall Jamieson	William Kristol	Linda Chavez
Michael Moore	William Raspberry	Kevin Phillips	William Safire	Ann Coulter
Bill Moyers	Mark Shields	Leonard Pitts	Andrew Sullivan	Rush Limbaugh
Salim Muwakkil	Fareed Zakaria	William Saletan	George Will	Bill O'Reilly
Daniel Schorr		Bob Woodward		Kathleen Parker

Newspapers and Magazines[2]

Left/Liberal	Center	Right/Conservative
The American Prospect	*Atlantic Monthly*	*American Spectator*
Harper's	*Business Week*	*Fortune*
Los Angeles Times	*Christian Science Monitor*	*National Review*
Mother Jones	*Commentary*	*Reader's Digest*
The Nation	*Commonweal*	*Reason*
New York Times	*Foreign Affairs*	*Wall Street Journal*
Salon	*New Republic*	*Washington Times*
Sojourners	*Slate*	*Weekly Standard*
	Washington Post	

Blogs

Liberal/Left	Moderate/Independent	Right/Conservative
americablog.com	newmoderate.blogspot.com	andrewsullivan.theatlantic.com
atrios.blogspot.com	politics-central.blogspot.com	conservativeblogger.com
crooksandliars.com	rantingbaldhippie.com	instapundit.com
dailykos.com	stevesilven.net	littlegreenfootballs.com
digbysblog.blogspot.com	themoderatevoice.com	michellemalkin.com
firedoglake.com	watchingwashington.blogspot.com	polipundit.com
huffingtonpost.com		powerlineblog.com
mediamatters.com		redstate.com
salon.com/opinion/greenwald/		
talkingpointsmemo.com		

Think Tanks

Left/Liberal	Center	Right/Conservative
Center for Defense Information	The Brookings Institution	American Enterprise Institute
Center for Media and Democracy (sponsors Disinfopedia.org)	Carnegie Endowment for International Peace	Cato Institute (Libertarian)
Institute for Policy Studies	Council on Foreign Relations	Center for Strategic and International Studies
Open Society Institute (Soros Foundation)	Jamestown Foundation	Heritage Foundation (sponsors Townhall.com)
Urban Institute	National Bureau of Economic Research	Project for the New American Century
	Progressive Policy Institute	

[1] *For further information about the political leanings of publications or think tanks, ask your librarian about* Gale Directory of Publications and Broadcast Media *or* NIRA World Directory of Think Tanks.

[2] *Newspapers are categorized according to positions they take on their editorial page.*

Reliability

"Reliability" refers to the accuracy of factual data in a source as determined by external validation. If you check a writer's "facts" against other sources, do you find that the facts are correct? Does the writer distort facts, take them out of context, or otherwise use them unreasonably? In some controversies, key data are highly disputed—for example, the number of homeless people in the United States, the frequency of date rape, or the risk factors for many diseases. A reliable writer acknowledges these controversies and doesn't treat disputed data as fact. Furthermore, if you check out the sources used by a reliable writer, they'll reveal accurate and careful research—respected primary sources rather than hearsay or secondhand reports.

Credibility

"Credibility" is similar to "reliability" but is based on internal rather than external factors. It refers to the reader's trust in the writer's honesty, goodwill, and trustworthiness and is apparent in the writer's tone, reasonableness, fairness in summarizing opposing views, and respect for different perspectives (what we have called *ethos*). Audiences differ in how much credibility they will grant to certain authors. Nevertheless a writer can achieve a reputation for credibility, even among bitter political opponents, by applying to issues a sense of moral courage, integrity, and consistency of principle.

Understanding the Rhetoric of Web Sites

In the previous section we focused on reading sources rhetorically by asking questions about a source's angle of vision, degree of advocacy, reliability, and credibility. In this section we turn to the skills of effectively evaluating and using Web sources by understanding the special rhetoric of Web sites.

The Web as a Unique Rhetorical Environment

Although many Web sites are highly professional and expensive to produce, the Web is also a great vehicle for democracy, giving voice to the otherwise voiceless. Anyone with a cause and a rudimentary knowledge of Web page design can create a Web site. Before the invention of the Web, people with a message had to stand on street corners passing out fliers or put money into newsletters or advocacy advertisements. The Web, in contrast, is cheap. The result is a rhetorical medium that differs in significant ways from print.

Analyzing the Purpose of a Site and Your Own Research Purpose

When you conduct research on the Web, your first question should be, Who placed this piece on the Web and why? You can begin answering this question by analyzing the site's home page, where you will often find navigational buttons linking to "Mission," "About Us," or other identifying information about the site's sponsors. You can also get hints about the site's purpose by asking, What kind of Web site is it? As we explained earlier, different kinds of Web sites have different purposes, often revealed by the domain identifier following the server name (.com, .net, .org, .gov, .mil). As you evaluate the Web site, also consider your own purpose for using it. For instance, are you trying to get an initial understanding of various points of view on an issue, or are you looking for reliable information? An advocacy site may be an excellent place for researching a point of view but a doubtful source of data and evidence for your own argument.

Sorting Sites by Domain Type

One powerful research strategy for reading Web sites rhetorically is to use the "advanced search" feature of a search engine to sort sites by domain type. As an example, consider again Megan's research dilemma when she plugged *Navy sonar* AND *whales* into Yahoo! and received 709,000 "hits." How could she begin to navigate through such a huge number? Using Yahoo!'s "advanced search" feature, Megan sorted through her hits by domain, selecting one type of domain at a time:

- The **.com sites** were primarily the sites of newspapers, news services, and whale-watching tourist sites. These sites tended to repeat the same news stories and offer superficial coverage.
- The **.org sites** were primarily the sites of environmental advocacy groups, such as the National Resources Defense Council, the Sierra Club, the League for Coastal Protection, and the Cetacean Society International—all dedicated to protecting marine life. These advocacy sites were strongly pro-whale; in their arguments against Navy sonar they either discounted or ignored issues of national security.
- The **.edu sites** of colleges and universities were primarily references to course descriptions and syllabi that included this controversy as a source of study. Megan didn't find these helpful.
- The **.gov sites** revealed documents on whales and sonar submitted to congressional hearings; they also revealed key government agencies involved in the sonar dispute: the National Marine Fisheries Service and the National Oceanic and Atmospheric Administration.
- The **.mil sites** gave access to white papers and other documents provided by the Navy to justify its use of low-frequency sonar.

This overview of the territory helped Megan understand the angle of vision or bias of different sources. The .org sites focused on protecting marine life. In contrast, the .mil and the .gov sites helped her understand the national security issue. In the middle, trying to balance the competing demands of the environment, national security, and preservation of commerce, were the sites of government agencies not directly connected to the military. All of these sites provided valuable information, and most of them included links to scientific and research studies.

Criteria for Evaluating a Web Site

Given this overview of the territory, Megan still had to decide which specific sites to use for her research. One of the most challenging parts of using the Web is determining whether a site offers gold or glitter. Sometimes the case may not be clear-cut. How do you sort out reliable, worthwhile sites from unreliable ones? We offer the following criteria developed by scholars and librarians as points to consider when you are using Web sites.

1. Authority

- Is the author or sponsor of the Web site clearly identified?
- Does the site identify the occupation, position, education, experience, and credentials of the site's authors?
- Does the introductory material reveal the author's or sponsor's motivation for publishing this information on the Web?
- Does the site provide contact information for the author or sponsor such as an e-mail or organization address?

2. Objectivity or Clear Disclosure of Advocacy

- Is the site's purpose (to inform, explain, or persuade) clear?
- Is the site explicit about declaring its author's or sponsor's point of view?
- Does the site indicate whether authors are affiliated with a specific organization, institution, or association?
- Does the site indicate whether it is directed toward a specific audience?

3. Coverage

- Are the topics covered by the site clear?
- Does the site exhibit suitable depth and comprehensiveness for its purpose?
- Is sufficient evidence provided to support the ideas and opinions presented?

4. Accuracy

- Are the sources of information stated? Can you tell whether this information is original or taken from someplace else?
- Does the information appear to be accurate? Can you verify this information by comparing this source with other sources in the field?

5. Currency

- Are dates included in the Web site?
- Do the dates apply to the material itself or to its placement on the Web? Is the site regularly revised and updated?
- Is the information current, or at least still relevant, for the site's purpose?

To illustrate how these criteria can help you evaluate a Web site, consider how they could be applied to "Environmental Groups Sue to Stop Global Deployment of Navy Low Frequency Sonar System," a press release Megan found on the site of the

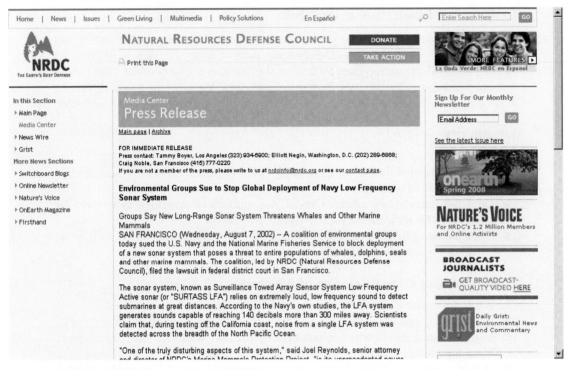

FIGURE 16.5 First screen from article on NRDC Web site

National Resources Defense Council (see Figure 16.5). Is the article trustworthy and reliable, or is it from a fringe environmental group likely to suppress or distort evidence? Using the criteria for evaluating Web sites, Megan was able to identify the strengths and weaknesses of this site in light of her research purpose.

1. *Authority.* The sponsor of the site is clearly the NRDC. Because the NRDC? presents the material as a press release, Megan assumed that their motivation is to provide information for the news media that favors their position on the sonar issue. The site does provide contact information so that journalists and others can get in touch with NRDC staff.

2. *Objectivity or clear disclosure of advocacy.* What type of organization is NRDC? The site is clearly that of an advocacy group, as indicated by the logo and motto in the left-hand panel: "The Earth's Best Defense." Megan located the home page, clicked on "About Us," and discovered that the National Resources Defense Council has been around for almost forty years. The "About Us" section states:

NRDC is the nation's most effective environmental action group, combining the grassroots power of 1.2 million members and online activists with the courtroom clout and expertise of more than 350 lawyers, scientists and other professionals.

The site does very well on the criterion "clear disclosure of advocacy."

3. *Coverage.* The site is unusually broad and deep. It covers hundreds of different environmental issues and has multimedia features, blogs, games for children, and in-depth technical articles written for specialists.
4. *Accuracy.* Megan also determined that the site was accurate. Technical articles had bibliographies, and references to factual data had notes about sources. She discovered that information on this site corroborated well with references to the same data from other sites.
5. *Currency.* The site was current. News items within the site had clear indications of dates. This is an active, ongoing site.

Megan concluded that the site was an excellent source for both arguments and data from a pro-environmental perspective. She could use it to understand potential dangers of Navy sonar to whales and other marine life. However, the site was not helpful for understanding the national security and Navy reasons for needing low-frequency sonar.

Conclusion

Our discussion of the rhetoric of Web sites concludes this chapter's introduction to college-level research. We have talked about the need to establish a good research question; to understand the key differences among different kinds of sources; to use purposeful strategies for searching libraries, databases, and Web sites; to use your rhetorical knowledge when you read and evaluate sources; and to understand the rhetoric of Web sites. In the next chapter we focus on how to integrate research sources into your own prose and how to cite and document them appropriately.

For additional writing, reading, and research resources, go to www.mycomplab.com

17 Using, Citing, and Documenting Sources

The previous chapter helped you pose a good research question and begin unlocking some of the resources of your library and the Internet. This chapter teaches you how to use sources in your own argument—how to incorporate them into your own prose through summary, paraphrase, or quotation; how to cite them using attributive tags and in-text citations; and how to document them using the style and format of the Modern Language Association or the American Psychological Association.

Using Sources for Your Own Purposes

To illustrate the purposeful use of sources, we will use the following short argument from the Web site of the American Council on Science and Health—a conservative organization of doctors and scientists devoted to providing scientific information on health issues and to exposing health fads and myths. Please read the argument carefully in preparation for the discussions that follow.

Is Vegetarianism Healthier than Nonvegetarianism?

Many people become vegetarians because they believe, in error, that vegetarianism is uniquely conducive to good health. The findings of several large epidemiologic studies indeed suggest that the death and chronic-disease rates of vegetarians—primarily vegetarians who consume dairy products or both dairy products and eggs—are lower than those of meat eaters....

The health of vegetarians may be better than that of nonvegetarians partly because of nondietary factors: Many vegetarians are health-conscious. They exercise regularly, maintain a desirable body weight, and abstain from smoking. Although most epidemiologists have attempted to take such factors into account in their analyses, it is possible that they did not adequately control their studies for nondietary effects.

People who are vegetarians by choice may differ from the general population in other ways relevant to health. For example, in Western countries most vegetarians are more affluent than nonvegetarians and thus have better living conditions and more access to medical care.

An authoritative review of vegetarianism and chronic diseases classified the evidence for various alleged health benefits of vegetarianism:

- The evidence is "strong" that vegetarians have (a) a lower risk of becoming alcoholic, constipated, or obese and (b) a lower risk of developing lung cancer.
- The evidence is "good" that vegetarians have a lower risk of developing adult-onset diabetes mellitus, coronary artery disease, hypertension, and gallstones.
- The evidence is "fair to poor" that vegetarianism decreases risk of breast cancer, colon cancer, diverticular disease, kidney-stone formation, osteoporosis, and tooth decay.

For some of the diseases mentioned above, the practice of vegetarianism itself probably is the main protective factor. For example, the low incidence of constipation among vegetarians is almost certainly due to their high intakes of fiber-rich foods. For other conditions, nondietary factors may be more important than diet. For example, the low incidence of lung cancer among vegetarians is attributable primarily to their extremely low rate of cigarette smoking. Diet is but one of many risk factors for most chronic diseases.

What we want to show you is that the way you use this article depends on your own research question and purpose. Sometimes you may decide to summarize a source completely—particularly if the source represents an opposing or alternative view that you intend to address. (See Chapter 2 for a detailed explanation of summary writing; see also Chapter 7, pages 128–129, for the difference between a fair summary and an unfair summary or "straw man.") At other times you may choose to use only parts of a source. To illustrate how your rhetorical purpose governs your use of a source, we show you three different hypothetical examples:

- *Writer 1, arguing for alternative approaches for reducing risk of alcoholism:* On some occasions, you will draw details from a source for use in a different context.

    Another approach to fighting alcoholism is through naturopathy, holistic medicine, and vegetarianism. Vegetarians generally have better health than the rest of the population and particularly have, according to the American Council on Science and Health, "a lower risk of becoming alcoholic."* This lower risk has been borne out by other studies showing that the benefits of the holistic health movement are particularly strong for persons with addictive tendencies.... [goes on to other arguments and sources]

- *Writer 2, arguing for the value of vegetarianism:* Sometimes you can use part of a source for direct support of your own claim. In this case, a summary of relevant parts of the argument can be used as evidence.

    Not only will a vegetarian diet help stop cruelty to animals, but it is also good for your health. According to the American Council on Science and Health, vegetarians have longer life expectancy than nonvegetarians and suffer from fewer chronic diseases. The Council

---

*If the writer had found this quotation in a print source such as a book or magazine, the page number would be placed in parentheses immediately after the quotation, as explained on page 373. Because the writer found this passage in a Web site, no page citation is possible. In a research paper, readers would find full information about the source in the bibliography at the end. In this case, the author would be listed as "American Council on Science and Health," indicated in the attributive tag preceding the quotation.

summarizes evidence from the scientific literature strongly showing that vegetarians have reduced risk of lung cancer, obesity, constipation, and alcoholism. They also cite good evidence that they have a reduced risk of adult-onset diabetes, high blood pressure, gallstones, or hardening of the arteries. Although the evidence isn't nearly as strong, vegetarianism may also lower the risk of certain cancers, kidney stones, loss of bone density, and tooth decay.

■   *Writer 3, arguing for a skeptical view of vegetarianism:* Here writer 3 uses portions of the article consciously excluded by writer 2.

The link between vegetarianism and death rates is a classic instance of correlation rather than causation. While it is true that vegetarians have a longer life expectancy than nonvegetarians and suffer from fewer chronic diseases, the American Council on Science and Health has shown that the causes can mostly be explained by factors other than diet. As the Council suggests, vegetarians are apt to be more health conscious than nonvegetarians and thus get more exercise, stay slender, and avoid smoking. The Council points out that vegetarians also tend to be wealthier than nonvegetarians and see their doctors more regularly. In short, they live longer because they take better care of themselves, not because they avoid meat.

■ ■ ■   **FOR CLASS DISCUSSION**   **Using a Source for Different Purposes**
Each of the hypothetical writers uses this short argument in different ways for different purposes. Working individually or in groups, respond to the following questions; be prepared to elaborate on and defend your answers.

1. How does each writer use the original article differently and why?
2. If you were the author of the article from the American Council on Science and Health, would you think that your article was used fairly and responsibly in each instance?
3. Suppose your goal were simply to summarize the argument from the American Council on Science and Health. Write a brief summary of the argument and then explain how your summary is different from the partial summaries used by writers 2 and 3.   ■ ■ ■

Creating Rhetorically Effective Attributive Tags

In the previous examples we used attributive tags to signal to readers which ideas are the writer's own and which ideas are being taken from another source, in this case the article from the American Council on Science and Health. Attributive tags can also be used rhetorically to shape your reader's response to a source.

Using Attributive Tags to Separate Your Ideas from Your Source's

Attributive tags are phrases such as "according to the American Council on Science and Health…," "Smith claims that…," or "the author continues.…" Such phrases signal to the reader that the material immediately following the tag is from the cited source. Sometimes writers indicate a source only by citing it in parentheses at the end of the borrowed material—a particularly common practice in the social sciences. The more preferred practice when writing to general audiences is to indicate a source with attributive tags. Parentheses after a quotation or at the end of the borrowed material are then used only to indicate page numbers from a print text. The use of attributive tags is generally clearer and often more rhetorically powerful.

Less Preferred: Indicating Source Through Parenthetical Citation

Vegetarians are apt to be more health-conscious than nonvegetarians (American Council on Science and Health).*

More Preferred: Indicating Source Through Attributive Tag

As the American Council on Science and Health has shown, vegetarians are apt to be more health-conscious than nonvegetarians.

Creating Attributive Tags to Shape Reader Response

When you introduce a source for the first time, you can use an attributive tag not only to introduce the source but also to shape your readers' attitude toward the source. For example, if you wanted your readers to respect the expertise of a source, you might say "according to noted chemist Marjorie Casper...." If you wanted your readers to discount Casper's views, you might say "according to Marjorie Casper, an industrial chemist on the payroll of a major corporate polluter...."

When you compose an initial tag, you can add to it any combination of the kinds of information in the chart on page 372, depending on your purpose, your audience's values, and your sense of what the audience already knows about the source.

Our point here is that you can use attributive tags rhetorically to help your readers understand the significance and context of a source when you first introduce it and to guide your readers' attitudes toward the source.

Working Sources into Your Own Prose

As a research writer, you need to incorporate sources gracefully into your own prose. One option is simply to draw factual data from a source. More complex options occur when you choose to summarize the whole or part of an argument, paraphrase a portion of an argument, or quote directly from the source. Let's look at these last three options in more detail.

---

*This parenthetical citation is in MLA form. If this had been a print source rather than a Web source, page numbers would also have been given as follows: (American Council on Science and Health 43). APA form also indicates the date of the source: (American Council on Science and Health, 2002). We explain MLA and APA styles for citing and documenting sources later in this chapter.

Add to Attributive Tag	Example
Author's credentials or relevant specialty (enhances credibility)	Civil engineer David Rockwood, a noted authority on stream flow in rivers, . . .
Author's lack of credentials (decreases credibility)	City council member Dilbert Weasel, a local politician with no expertise in international affairs, . . .
Author's political or social views	Left-wing columnist Alexander Cockburn . . . [has negative feeling]; Alexander Cockburn, a longtime champion of labor . . . [has positive feeling]
Title of source if it provides context	In her book *Fasting Girls: The History of Anorexia Nervosa,* Joan Jacobs Brumberg shows that . . . [establishes credentials for comments on eating disorders]
Publisher of source if it adds prestige or otherwise shapes audience response	Dr. Carl Patrona, in an article published in the prestigious *New England Journal of Medicine,* . . .
Historical or cultural information about a source that provides context or background	In his 1960s book popularizing the hippie movement, Charles Reich claims that . . .
Indication of source's purpose or angle of vision	Feminist author Naomi Wolfe, writing a blistering attack on the beauty industry, argues that . . .

Summarizing

Writing a summary of your source's argument (or of a relevant section) is an appropriate strategy when the source represents an opposing or alternative view or when it supports one of your own points. Summaries can be as short as a single sentence or as long as a paragraph. (See Chapter 2, pages 40–43.)

Paraphrasing

Unlike a summary, which is a condensation of a source's whole argument, a paraphrase translates a short passage from a source into the writer's own words. You often paraphrase when you want to use specific information from a brief passage in the source and don't want to interrupt the flow of your own voice with a needless quotation. Of course, you must still acknowledge the source through an attributive tag or parenthetical citation. When you paraphrase, be careful to avoid the original writer's grammatical structure and syntax. If you mirror the original sentence structure while replacing occasional words with synonyms, you are *plagiarizing* rather than paraphrasing. (See pages 375–376 for an explanation of plagiarism.) Here is an acceptable paraphrase of a short passage from the vegetarian article:

Original

- The evidence is "strong" that vegetarians have (a) a lower risk of becoming alcoholic, constipated, or obese and (b) a lower risk of developing lung cancer.
- The evidence is "good" that vegetarians have a lower risk of developing adult-onset diabetes mellitus, coronary artery disease, hypertension, and gallstones.

Paraphrase

The Council summarizes strong evidence from the scientific literature showing that vegetarians have reduced risk of lung cancer, obesity, constipation, and alcoholism. They also cite good evidence that they have a reduced risk of adult-onset diabetes, high blood pressure, gallstones, or hardening of the arteries.

Note that to avoid plagiarism, the writer has changed the sentence structure substantially. However, the writer still acknowledges the original source with the attributive tag "The Council summarizes."

Quoting

Occasionally, you will wish to quote an author's words directly. Avoid quoting too much because the effect, from your reader's perspective, is to move from an argument to a sequence of cut-and-pasted quotations. Quote only when doing so strengthens your argument. Here are some occasions when a direct quotation is appropriate:

- When the quotation comes from a respected authority and, in a pithy way, supports one of your points. (Your use of the quotation is like expert testimony in a trial.)
- When you are summarizing an opposing or alternative view and want to use brief quotations to show you have listened carefully and accurately.
- When you want to give readers the flavor of a source's voice, particularly if the language is striking or memorable.
- When you want to analyze the writer's choice of words or metaphors. (You would first quote the passage and then begin your analysis.)

When you quote, you must be meticulous in copying the passage *exactly,* including punctuation. When the quoted material takes up more than four lines in your paper, use the block quotation method by indenting the quoted material ten spaces (one inch) in MLA style or five to seven spaces in APA style. When using the block method, do not use quotation marks because the block indentation itself signals a quotation.

When you insert quotations into your own sentences, how you punctuate depends on whether the inserted quotation is a complete sentence or a part of a sentence.

Inserted Quotation When Quotation Is Complete Sentence

Example: According to the American Council on Science and Health, "Many people become vegetarians because they believe, in error, that vegetarianism is uniquely conducive to good health."

Explanation

- Because the quotation is a complete sentence, it starts with a capital letter and is separated from the introductory phrase by a comma.
- If the inserted quotation were taken from a print source, the page number would be indicated in parentheses between the ending quotation mark and the ending punctuation: "…conducive to good health" (43).

Inserted Quotation When Quotation Is Not a Complete Sentence

Example: The American Council on Science and Health argues that the cause of vegetarians' longer life may be "nondietary factors." The Council claims that vegetarians are more "health-conscious" than meat eaters and that they "exercise regularly, maintain a desirable body weight, and abstain from smoking."

Explanation

- Because the material quoted is not a complete sentence, it is worked into the grammar of the writer's own sentence.
- No comma introduces the quotation; commas should be used to fit the grammatical structure of the writer's own sentence.
- If the inserted quotation were taken from a print source, the page number would be indicated in parentheses between the ending quotation mark and the period.

Use Brackets to Indicate Changes in a Quotation

Example: The American Council on Science and Health hypothesizes that vegetarians maintain better health by "exercis[ing] regularly, maintain[ing] a desirable body weight, and abstain[ing] from smoking."

Example: According to the American Council on Science and Health, "They [vegetarians] exercise regularly, maintain a desirable body weight, and abstain from smoking."

Explanation

- In the first example, brackets indicate where the grammar of the original passage has been modified to fit the grammar of the writer's own sentence.
- In the second example, the word "vegetarians" has been added inside brackets to explain what "they" refers to.

Use Ellipses to Indicate Omissions from a Quotation   The ellipsis, which consists of three spaced periods, indicates words omitted from the original. When an omission occurs at the end of a sentence, include a fourth period to mark the end of the sentence.

Example: According to the American Council on Science and Health, "people who are vegetarians by choice may differ... in other ways relevant to health. For example, in Western countries most vegetarians are more affluent than nonvegetarians...."

If you wish to insert a parenthetical citation into the last sentence, insert a space before the first period and place the parentheses in front of the last period, which marks the end of the sentence. Note that the end quotation mark comes before the page number.

Example: "For example, in Western countries most vegetarians are more affluent than nonvegetarians..." (43).

Use Double and Single Quotation Marks to Indicate a Quotation within a Quotation

Example: According to the American Council on Science and Health, "The evidence is 'strong' that vegetarians have (a) a lower risk of becoming alcoholic, constipated, or obese and (b) a lower risk of developing lung cancer."

Explanation

- The original passage has quotation marks around "strong." To indicate those marks within the quotation, the writer has changed the original double marks to single marks.

Avoiding Plagiarism

Plagiarism, a form of academic cheating, is always a serious academic offense. You can plagiarize in one of two ways: (1) by borrowing another person's ideas without indicating the borrowing with attributive tags in the text and a proper citation or (2) by borrowing another person's language without putting the borrowed language in quotation marks or using a block indentation. The first kind of plagiarism is usually outright cheating; the writer usually knows he is stealing material and tries to disguise it.

The second kind of plagiarism, however, often begins in a hazy never-never-land between paraphrasing and copying. We refer to it in our classes as "lazy cheating" and still consider it a serious offense, like stealing from your neighbor's vegetable garden because you are too lazy to do your own planting, weeding, and harvesting. Anyone who appreciates how hard it is to write and revise even a short passage will appreciate why it is wrong to take someone else's language ready-made. Thus, in our classes, we would fail a paper that included the following passage. (Let's call the student "writer 4.")

> The link between vegetarianism and death rates is a classic instance of correlation rather than causation. While it is true that vegetarians have a longer life expectancy than nonvegetarians and suffer from fewer chronic diseases, the American Council on Science and Health has shown that the health of vegetarians may be better than that of nonvegetarians partly because of nondietary factors. Many vegetarians are very conscious of their health. They exercise regularly, keep a desirable body weight, and abstain from smoking. The Council points out that in Western countries most vegetarians are more affluent than nonvegetarians and thus have better living conditions and more access to medical care. In short, they live longer because they take better care of themselves, not because they avoid meat.

■ ■ ■ **FOR CLASS DISCUSSION** **What Is Plagiarism?**

Do you think it was fair to flunk writer 4's essay? He claimed he wasn't cheating because he used attributive tags to indicate his source throughout this passage, and he listed the American Council on Science and Health article accurately in his "Works Cited" list (bibliography) at the end of his paper. Before answering, compare writer 4's passage with the original article on pages 368–369; also compare the passage with writer 3's passage on page 370. What justification is there for giving a high grade to writer 3 and a failing grade to writer 4?

■ ■ ■

The best way to avoid plagiarism is to be especially careful at the note-taking stage. If you copy from your source, copy exactly, word for word, and put quotation marks around the copied material or otherwise indicate that it is not your own wording. If you paraphrase or summarize material, be sure that you don't borrow any of the original wording. Also be sure to change the grammatical structure of the original. Lazy note taking, in which you follow the arrangement and grammatical structure of the original passage and merely substitute occasional synonyms, leads directly to plagiarism.

Also remember that you cannot borrow another writer's ideas without citing them. If you summarize or paraphrase another writer's thinking about a subject, you should indicate in your notes that the ideas are not your own and be sure to record all the information you need for a citation. If you do exploratory reflection to accompany your notes, then the distinction between other writers' ideas and your own should be easy to recognize when it's time to incorporate the source material into your paper.

Understanding Parenthetical Citation Systems with Bibliographies

Not too many years ago, most academic disciplines used footnotes or endnotes to document sources. Today, however, both the MLA (Modern Language Association) system, used primarily in the humanities, and the APA (American Psychological Association) system, used primarily in the social sciences, use parenthetical citations instead of footnotes or endnotes. Before we examine the details of MLA and APA styles, we want to explain the logic of parenthetical citation systems with concluding bibliographies.

In both the MLA and APA systems, the writer places a complete bibliography at the end of the paper. In the MLA system this bibliography is called "Works Cited." In the APA system it is called "References." The bibliography is arranged alphabetically by author or by title (if an author is not named). The key to the system's logic is this:

- Every source in the bibliography must be mentioned in the body of the paper.
- Conversely, every source mentioned in the body of the paper must be listed in the bibliography.
- There must be a one-to-one correspondence between the first word in each bibliographic entry (usually, but not always, an author's last name) and the name used to identify the source in the body of the paper.

Suppose a reader sees this phrase in your paper: "According to Debra Goldstein,…" The reader should be able to turn to your bibliography and find an alphabetized entry beginning with "Goldstein, Debra." Similarly, suppose that in looking over your bibliography, your reader sees an article by "Guillen, Manuel." This means that the name "Guillen" has to occur in the body of your paper in one of two ways:

- As an attributive tag: "Economics professor Manuel Guillen argues that…"
- As a parenthetical citation, often following a quotation: "…changes in fiscal policy" (Guillen 43).

Understanding MLA Style

From this point on, we separate our discussions of the MLA and APA systems. We begin with the MLA system because it is the one most commonly used in writing courses. Our discussion of MLA style and our citation examples are based on the seventh edition of the *MLA Handbook for Writers of Research Papers*, published in 2009, which provides guidelines for undergraduate students. This new edition introduces some major changes to the guidelines found in the *MLA Handbook for Writers of Research Papers,* sixth edition, by Joseph Garibaldi, published in 2003. These changes in style include

- italicizing, rather than underlining, all titles of longer works;
- citing both volume and issue numbers in all journal entries;
- adding the medium of publication (Print, Web, Audio, CD, Film, etc.) to every works-cited entry; and
- a simplified style for all online citations.

Check with your instructor to find out whether you should use the 2009 *Handbook* style (used in this chapter) and visit the MLA Web site for further information about style changes (http://www.mla.org).

The MLA Method of In-Text Citation

To cite sources in your text using the MLA system, place the author's last name and the page reference in parentheses immediately after the material being cited. If an attributive tag already identifies the author, give only the page number in parentheses. Once you have cited the author and it is clear that the same author's material is being used, you need cite only the page references in parentheses.

Basic Parenthetical Citation Format   The following examples show parenthetical documentation with and without an attributive tag. Note that the citation precedes the period. If you are citing a quotation, the parenthetical citation follows the quotation mark but precedes the final period.

> The Spanish tried to reduce the status of Filipina women who had been able to do business, get divorced, and sometimes become village chiefs (Karnow 41).

> According to Karnow, the Spanish tried to reduce the status of Filipina women who had been able to do business, get divorced, and sometimes become village chiefs (41).

> "And, to this day," Karnow continues, "women play a decisive role in Filipino families" (41).

A reader who wishes to look up the source will find the bibliographic information in the "Works Cited" section by looking for the entry under "Karnow." If more than one work by Karnow was used in the paper, the writer would include in the in-text citation an abbreviated title of the book or article following Karnow's name.

(Karnow, "In Our Image" 41)

Citing from an Indirect Source   Occasionally you may wish to use a quotation that you have seen cited in one of your sources. You read Jones, who has a nice quotation from Smith, and you want to use Smith's quotation. What do you do? Whenever possible, find the quotation in its original source and cite that source. But if the original source is not available, cite the source indirectly by using the terms "qtd. in"; and list only the indirect source in your "Works Cited" list. In the following example, the writer wishes to quote a Buddhist monk, Thich Nhat Hanh, who has written a book titled *Living Buddha, Living Christ.* However, the writer is unable to locate the actual book and instead has to quote from a review by newspaper critic Lee Moriwaki. Here is how he would make the in-text citation:

> A Buddhist monk, Thich Nhat Hanh, stresses the importance of inner peace: "If we can learn ways to touch the peace, joy, and happiness that are already there, we will become healthy and strong, and a resource for others" (qtd. in Moriwaki C4).

The "Works Cited" has an entry for "Moriwaki" but not for "Thich Nhat Hanh."

Citing a Work without Page Numbers   If the work you are citing in your paper has no page numbers but does have numbered paragraphs, use *par.* or *pars.* and give the number of the paragraph(s): (Helvarg, par. 10). If the source has neither page nor paragraph numbers, as is typical of many Web sources in HTML format, cite the source in its entirety. (Do not use the page numbers from an HTML printout because they will not be consistent from printer to printer.)

MLA Format for the "Works Cited" List

In the MLA system, you place a complete bibliography, titled "Works Cited," at the end of the paper. The list includes all the sources that you mention in your paper. However, it does not include works you read but did not use. Entries in the Works Cited follow these general guidelines:

- Entries are arranged alphabetically by author, or by title if there is no author.
- Entries must include the publication medium of the source you consulted, for example: *Print, Web, DVD, Performance, Oil on canvas,* and so on.
- If there is more than one entry by the same author, the second and subsequent entries begin with three hyphens followed by a period and the title.

Smith, Roberta. *Body Image in Non-Western Cultures.* London: Bonanza, 1999. Print.
---. *Body Image in Western Cultures, 1750-Present.* London: Bonanza, 1995. Print.
---. "Eating Disorders Reconsidered." *Journal of Appetite Studies* 45.3 (1999): 295-300. Print.

For an example of how to format a "Works Cited" page in MLA style, see the last page of Juan Vazquez's researched argument (p. 337). The remaining pages in this section show examples of MLA "Works Cited" entries for different kinds of sources.

MLA "Works Cited" Citations

Print Articles in Scholarly Journals

General Format for Print Article in Scholarly Journal

Author. "Article Title." *Journal Title* volume number.issue number (year): page numbers. Print.

Note that all scholarly journal entries include both volume number and issue number, regardless of how the journal is paginated. For articles published in a scholarly Web journal, see page 373. For scholarly journal articles retrieved from an online database, see pages 383–384.

One Author

Herrera-Sobek, Maria. "Border Aesthetics: The Politics of Mexican Immigration in Film and Art." *Western Humanities Review* 60.2 (2006): 60–71. Print.

Two or Three Authors

Pollay, Richard W., Jung S. Lee, and David Carter-Whitney. "Separate, but Not Equal: Racial Segmentation in Cigarette Advertising." *Journal of Advertising* 21.1 (1992): 45–57. Print.

Four or More Authors

Either list all the authors in the order in which they appear, or use "et al." (meaning "and others") to replace all but the first author.

Buck, Gayle A., et al. "Examining the Cognitive Processes Used by Adolescent Girls and Women Scientists in Identifying Science Role Models: A Feminist Approach." *Science Education* 92.4 (2008): 688–707. Print.

Print Articles in Magazines and Newspapers

If no author is identified, begin the entry with the title or headline. Distinguish between news stories and editorials by putting the word "Editorial" after the title. If a magazine comes out weekly or biweekly, include the complete date (27 Sept. 2008). If it comes out monthly, then state the month only (Sept. 2008). For magazine and newspaper articles accessed on the Web, see page 383.

General Format for Print Article in Magazines and Newspapers

Author. "Article Title." *Magazine or Newspaper Title* day Month year: page numbers. Print.

If the article continues in another part of the magazine or newspaper, add "+" to indicate the nonsequential pages.

Magazine Article with Named Author

Snyder, Rachel L. "A Daughter of Cambodia Remembers: Loung Ung's Journey."
    Ms. Aug.–Sept. 2001: 62–67. Print.

Hall, Stephen S. "Prescription for Profit." *New York Times Magazine* 11 Mar. 2001: 40+.
    Print.

Magazine Article with No Author Listed

"Daddy, Daddy." *New Republic* 30 July 2001: 2–13. Print.

Newspaper Article

Wims, Meaghan. "More Browsers than Buyers." *Providence Journal* 13 July 2008: A1+. Print.

Review of Book, Film, or Performance

Schwarz, Benjamin. "A Bit of Bunting: A New History of the British Empire Elevates
    Expediency to Principle." Rev. of *Ornamentalism: How the British Saw Their Empire*, by
    David Cannadine. *Atlantic Monthly* Nov. 2001: 126–35. Print.

Kaufman, Stanley. "Polishing a Gem." Rev. of *The Blue Angel*, dir. Josef von Sternberg. *New
    Republic* 30 July 2001: 28–29. Print.

Lahr, John. "Nobody's Darling: Fascism and the Drama of Human Connection in *Ashes to
    Ashes*." Rev. of *Ashes to Ashes*, by Harold Pinter. The Roundabout Theater Co.
    Gramercy Theater, New York. *New Yorker* 22 Feb. 1999: 182–83. Print.

Editorial

"Dr. Frankenstein on the Hill." Editorial. *New York Times* 18 May 2002, natl. ed.: A22. Print.

Letter to the Editor

Tomsovic, Kevin. Letter. *New Yorker* 13 July 1998: 7. Print.

Print Books

General Format for Print Book

Author. *Title*. City of publication: Publisher, year of publication. Print.

One Author

Pollan, Michael. *The Omnivore's Dilemma: A Natural History of Four Meals*. New York:
    Penguin, 2006. Print.

Two or Three Authors

Dombrowski, Daniel A., and Robert J. Deltete. *A Brief, Liberal, Catholic Defense of Abortion*.
    Urbana: U of Illinois P, 2000. Print.

Four or More Authors

Belenky, Mary, et al. *Women's Ways of Knowing: The Development of Self, Voice, and Mind*.
    New York: Basic, 1986. Print.

Second, Later, or Revised Edition

Montagu, Ashley. *Touching: The Human Significance of the Skin.* 3rd ed. New York: Perennial, 1986. Print.

Republished Book (For Example, a Paperback Published after the Original Hardback Edition or a Modern Edition of an Older Work)

Hill, Christopher. *The World Turned Upside Down: Radical Ideas During the English Revolution.* 1972. London: Penguin, 1991. Print.

Wollstonecraft, Mary. *The Vindication of the Rights of Woman, with Strictures on Political and Moral Subjects.* 1792. Rutland: Tuttle, 1995. Print.

Multivolume Work

Churchill, Winston S. *A History of the English-Speaking Peoples.* 4 vols. New York: Dodd, 1956–58. Print.

Churchill, Winston S. *The Great Democracies.* New York: Dodd, 1957. Print. Vol. 4 of *A History of the English-Speaking Peoples.* 4 vols. 1956–58.

Use the first method when you cite the whole work; use the second method when you cite one individually titled volume of the work.

Article in Familiar Reference Book

"Mau Mau." *The New Encyclopædia Britannica.* 15th ed. 2002. Print.

Article in Less Familiar Reference Book

Ling, Trevor O. "Buddhism in Burma." *Dictionary of Comparative Religion.* Ed. S. G. F. Brandon. New York: Scribner's, 1970. Print.

Translation

De Beauvoir, Simone. *The Second Sex.* Trans. H. M. Parshley. New York: Bantam, 1961. Print.

Illustrated Book

Jacques, Brian. *The Great Redwall Feast.* Illus. Christopher Denise. New York: Philomel, 1996. Print.

Graphic Novel

Miyazaki, Hayao. *Nausicaa of the Valley of Wind.* 4 vols. San Francisco: Viz, 1995–97. Print.

Corporate Author (A Commission, Committee, or Other Group)

American Red Cross. *Standard First Aid.* St. Louis: Mosby Lifeline, 1993. Print.

No Author Listed

The New Yorker Cartoon Album: 1975–1985. New York: Penguin, 1987. Print. [Alphabetize under *N*.]

Anthology: Citing the Editor

O'Connell, David F., and Charles N. Alexander, ed. *Self Recovery: Treating Addictions Using Transcendental Meditation and Maharishi Ayur-Veda.* New York: Haworth, 1994. Print.

MLA

Anthology: Citing an Individual Article

Royer, Ann. "The Role of the Transcendental Meditation Technique in Promoting Smoking Cessation: A Longitudinal Study." *Self Recovery: Treating Addictions Using Transcendental Meditation and Maharishi Ayur-Veda.* Ed. David F. O'Connell and Charles N. Alexander. New York: Haworth, 1994. 221–39. Print.

Web and Internet Sources

Because Internet sources vary widely, creating citations for them can sometimes be a puzzling process. To help you create useful, accurate citations, we provide a general format showing the information that needs to be included; we then devote the rest of this section to model citations for types of Internet sources that students frequently use.

General Format for Web Sources

Author, editor, director, narrator, performer, compiler, or producer of the work, if available. *Title of the work, italicized.* OR "Title of the work that is part of a larger work, in quotation marks." *Title of the overall site, usually taken from the home page, if this is distinct from the title of the work.* Publisher or sponsor of the site (if not available, use *N.p.),* day Month year of publication (if not available, use *n.d*). Web. day Month year you accessed the site.

Barrett, John. "*MySpace* Is a Natural Monopoly." *ECommerce Times.* ECT News Network, 17 Jan. 2007. Web. 6 June 2007.

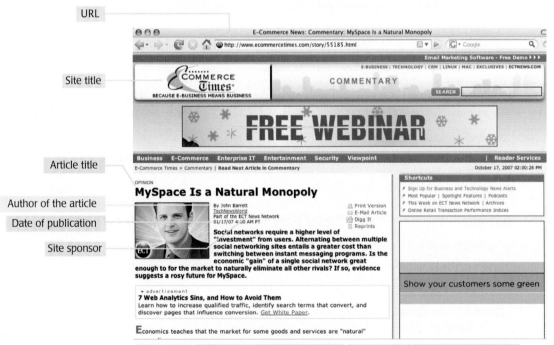

Barrett, John. "*MySpace* Is a Natural Monopoly." *ECommerce Times.* ECT News Network, 17 Jan. 2007. Web. 6 June 2007.

FIGURE 17.1 An article published on the Web, with citation elements identified

Do not include a URL unless you think your reader cannot locate the source without it. If you do include a URL, it goes at the end of the citation, after the access date, enclosed in angle brackets and followed by a period: <http:// www.ecommercetimes.com/story/55185.html>. To see where each element of the Barrett citation comes from, see the Web article in Figure 17.1.

Whole Web Site

MyNRA. National Rifle Association, 2005. Web. 3 Aug. 2005.

Document within a Web Site

Marks, John. "Overview: Letter from the President." *Search for Common Ground.* Search for Common Ground, 25 June 2004. Web. 18 July 2008.

Article from a Scholarly Web Journal

Welch, John R., and Ramon Riley. "Reclaiming Land and Spirit in the Western Apache Homeland." *American Indian Quarterly* 25.4 (2001): n. pag. Web. 19 Dec. 2005.

If page numbers are not available, use "n. pag." for "no pagination."

Article from a Newspaper, News Service, or Magazine Web Site

Bounds, Amy. "Thinking Like Scientists." *Daily Camera* [Boulder]. Scripps Interactive Newspapers Group, 26 June 2007. Web. 27 June 2007.

"Great Lakes: Rwanda Backed Dissident Troops in DRC—UN Panel." *IRIN.* UN Office for the Coordination of Humanitarian Affairs, 21 July 2004. Web. 31 July 2004.

Identify the newspaper's city in brackets only if it is not clear.

Print Article Obtained from Online Database

Beckham II, Jack M. "Placing *Touch of Evil, The Border,* and *Traffic* in the American Imagination." *Journal of Popular Film & Television* 33.3 (2005): 130–41. *Academic Search Premier.* Web. 16 July 2008.

Watanabe, Myrna. "Zoos Act as Sentinels for Infectious Diseases." *Bioscience* 53.4 (2003): 792. *ProQuest.* Web. 26 July 2004.

Show first the original print information, following the formats for print article in scholarly journals, magazines, or newspapers, as relevant. Include the name of the database in italics, and use "Web" as medium of publication, followed by date of access. To see where the information in the Beckham citation comes from, see Figure 17.2.

Article from Online Reference Work

"Doom." *Encyclopaedia Britannica Online.* Encyclopaedia Britannica, 2008. Web. 27 July 2008.

E-Book Also Available in Print

Hanley, Wayne. *The Genesis of Napoleonic Propaganda, 1796–1799.* New York: Columbia UP, 2002. *Gutenberg-e.* Web. 31 July 2004.

Machiavelli, Niccolò. *The Prince.* [1513.] *Bibliomania.* Web. 31 July 2004.

Information about the original print version, including a translator if relevant and available, should be provided. Use brackets for adding information not provided in the source.

MLA

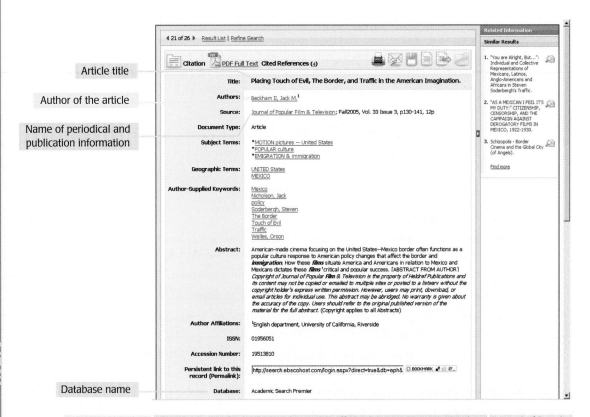

Article title

Author of the article

Name of periodical and publication information

Database name

Beckham II, Jack M. "Placing *Touch of Evil, The Border,* and *Traffic* in the American Imagination." *Journal of Popular Film & Television* 33.3 (2005): 130–41. *Academic Search Premier*. Web. 16 July 2008.

FIGURE 17.2 An article from an online database, with citation elements identified

Posting to a Blog, Electronic Mailing List, Bulletin Board, or Newsgroup

CalEnergyGuy. "Energy Crisis Impacts on the Economy: Changes Since 2001." *California Energy Blog*. N. p., 27 July 2004. Web. 1 Aug. 2007.

Dyer, Bob, and Ella Barnes. "The 'Greening' of the Arctic." *Greenversations*. U.S. Environmental Protection Agency, 7 Oct. 2008. Web. 11 Oct. 2008. <http://blog.epa.gov/blog/2008/10/07/the-greening-of-the-arctic/>.

For less well established blogs, include the URL in angle brackets (< >) at the end of the citation. See Figure 17.3 for the Dyer blog and citation.

Podcast

"The Long and Winding Road: DNA Evidence for Human Migration." *Science Talk*. Scientific American, 7 July 2008. Web. 21 July 2008.

E-Mail

Daffinrud, Sue. "Scoring Guide for Class Participation." Message to the author. 12 Dec. 2001. E-mail.

URL

Site sponsor

Name of blog

Title of posting

Date of posting

Blog author

Dyer, Bob, and Ella Barnes. "The 'Greening' of the Arctic." *Greenversations*, U.S. Environmental Protection Agency, 7 Oct. 2008. Web. 11 Oct. 2008. <http://blog.epa.gov/blog/2008/10/07/the-greening-of-the-arctic/>.

FIGURE 17.3 A blog posting from the Web, with citation elements identified

Miscellaneous Sources

Television or Radio Program

"Lie Like a Rug." *NYPD Blue*. Dir. Steven Bochco and David Milch. ABC. KOMO, Seattle. 6 Nov. 2001. Television.

Ashbrook, Tom. "Turf Wars and the American Lawn." *On Point*. Natl. Public Radio. WBUR, Boston, 22 July 2008. Web. 23 July 2008.

Conan, Neal. "Arab Media." *Talk of the Nation*. With Shibley Telhami. Natl. Public Radio. WGBH, Boston, 4 May 2004. Print. Transcript.

For television and radio broadcasts, use "Television" or "Radio" as the medium of publication. If you watched or listened to a program on the Web, give the basic citation information, drop the original medium of publication, include the Web site name (italicized), and use "Web" as the medium of publication, with an access date. The medium "Print" and label "Transcript" show that a transcript was used. For podcasts, see page 384.

Film or Video Recording

Shakespeare in Love. Dir. John Madden. Perf. Joseph Fiennes and Gwyneth Paltrow.
    Screenplay by Marc Norman and Tom Stoppard. Universal Miramax, 1998. Film.

Beck, Roy. "Immigration Gumballs." *YouTube.* YouTube, 2 Nov. 2006. Web. 23 July 2008.

Use "DVD" or "Videocassette" rather than "Film" as the medium of publication if that is the medium you consulted. If you downloaded the film from the Web, include the Web site or database name (italicized), use "Web" as medium of publication, and include the date of access.

Sound Recording

Dylan, Bob. "Rainy Day Woman." *Bob Dylan MTV Unplugged.* Columbia, 1995. CD.

Begin the entry with what your paper emphasizes—for example, the artist's name, composer's name, or conductor's name—and adjust the elements accordingly. If you downloaded a recording from the Web, include the Web site or database name (italicized), use "Web" as medium of publication, and include the date of access. For podcasts, see page 384.

Visual Art

Picasso, Pablo. *Guernica.* 1937. Oil on canvas. Museo Reina Sofia, Madrid.

If you view a work of art on the Web, omit the original medium. Add the title of the database or Web site (italicized), use "Web" as the medium of publication, and include the date of access.

Cartoon, Comic Strip, or Advertisement

Trudeau, Garry. "Doonesbury." Comic strip. *Seattle Times* 19 Nov. 2001: B4. Print.

Banana Republic. Advertisement. *Details* Oct. 2001: 37. Print.

Interview

Castellucci, Marion. Personal interview. 7 Oct. 2008.

Lecture, Speech, or Conference Presentation

Sharples, Mike. "Authors of the Future." Conference of European Teachers of Academic
    Writing. U of Groningen. Groningen, Neth. 20 June 2001. Lecture.

For the medium of publication, use "Lecture," "Address," "Keynote speech," or "Reading" as appropriate.

Government Publication   Government publications are often difficult to cite because there are so many varieties. In general, follow these guidelines:

■ Usually cite as author the government agency that produced the document. Begin with the highest level and then branch down to the specific agency:

    United States. Dept. of Justice. FBI

    Idaho. Dept. of Motor Vehicles

- Follow this with the title of the document, italicized.
- If a specific person is clearly identified as the author, you may begin the citation with that person's name, or you may list the author (preceded by the word "By") after the title of the document.
- Follow standard formats for citing publication information for print sources or Web sources.

United States. Dept. of Justice. FBI. *The School Shooter: A Threat Assessment Perspective.* By Mary Ellen O'Toole. 2000. Web. 16 Aug. 2001.

Student Example of an MLA-Style Research Paper

For an illustration of a student research paper written in MLA style, see Juan Vazquez's proposal argument on pages 332–337.

Understanding APA Style

In many respects, the APA style and the MLA style are similar and the basic logic is the same. However, the APA style has a few distinguishing features:

- APA style emphasizes dates of books and articles and de-emphasizes the names of authors. Therefore the date of publication appears in parenthetical citations and is the second item mentioned in each entry in the "References" list (the name of the bibliography at the end of a paper). The author's or editor's last name and first initial are the first item in a "References" citation.
- APA style capitalizes only the first word of titles and subtitles of books and articles. It doesn't place titles of articles in quotation marks.
- APA style uses fewer abbreviations and spells out the complete names of university presses. However, it uses an ampersand (&) instead of the word *and* for items in a series in the reference list and in text citations.
- Information about electronic sources such as Web documents and online articles is presented at the end of a citation. If a journal article or other document has been assigned a Digital Object Identifier (DOI), include the DOI at the end of the entry.
- If the Web document or online article has no DOI, then cite the publication's home page URL. (If you found the article through a database like EBSCO's Academic Search Premier, do not cite the database or its URL since readers may find the article elsewhere.) If you need to break a URL at the end of a line, do not use a hyphen. Instead, break it *before* a punctuation mark or *after* http://.
- For electronic sources, retrieval dates are necessary only if the material is likely to be changed or updated. Thus no retrieval dates are needed for journal articles or books.
- For electronic documents without page numbers, APA suggests citing material by heading labels if they are available, and permits the writer to count paragraphs within a section. A parenthetical citation might then read: (Elrod, 2005, Introduction section, para. 7).
- Only published or retrievable documents are included in the "References" list. Personal correspondence, e-mail messages, interviews, and lectures or speeches are referenced in text citations only.

Our discussion of APA style is based on the *Publication Manual of the American Psychological Association*, 6th ed. (2010).

The APA Method of In-Text Citation

When you make an in-text citation in APA style, you place inside the parentheses the author's last name and the year of the source as well as the page number if a particular passage or table is cited. The elements in the citation are separated by commas and a "p." or "pp." precedes the page number(s). If a source has more than one author, use an ampersand (&) to join their names. When the author is mentioned in an attributive tag, you include only the date (and page if applicable). The following examples show parenthetical documentation with and without attributive tags according to APA style.

> The Spanish tried to reduce the status of women who had been able to do business, get divorced, and sometimes become village chiefs (Karnow, 1989, p. 41).

> According to Karnow (1989, p. 41), the Spanish tried to reduce the status of women who had been able to do business, get divorced, and sometimes become village chiefs.

Readers of APA style look for sources in the list of "References" at the end of the paper if they wish to find full bibliographic information. If your sources include two works by the same author published in the same year, place an "a" after the date for the first work and a "b" after the date for the second, ordering the works alphabetically by title in the "References" list. If Karnow had published two different works in 1989, your in-text citation would look like this:

> (Karnow, 1989a, p. 41)

or

> (Karnow, 1989b, p. 41)

APA style also makes provisions for quoting or using data from an indirect source. Use the same procedures as for MLA style (see the example on page 378), and in your parenthetical citation use "as cited in." Here is the APA equivalent of the example on page 378:

> A Buddhist monk, Thich Nhat Hanh, stresses the importance of inner peace: "If we can learn ways to touch the peace, joy, and happiness that are already there, we will become healthy and strong, and a resource for others" (as cited in Moriwaki, 1995, p. C4).

APA Format for the "References" List

Entries in the "References" list are shown alphabetically, with a similar kind of hanging indentation to that used in MLA style. If you list more than one item for an author, repeat the author's name each time and arrange the items in chronological order beginning with the earliest. If two works appeared in the same year, arrange them alphabetically, adding an "a" and a "b" after the year for purposes of in-text citation:

Smith, R. (1995). *Body image in Western cultures, 1750–present.* London, England: Bonanza Press.

Smith, R. (1999a). *Body image in non-Western cultures.* London, England: Bonanza Press.

Smith, R. (1999b). Eating disorders reconsidered. *Journal of Appetite Studies, 45,* 295–300.

APA "References" Citations

Print Articles in Scholarly Journals

General Format for Print Article in Scholarly Journal

Author's last name, initials. (Year of publication). Article title. *Name of Journal, volume number* (issue number if journal restarts page numbering with each issue), inclusive page numbers.

Note that the volume number is italicized along with the title of the journal.

One Author, Scholarly Journal That Numbers Pages Continuously

Barton, E. L. (1993). Evidentials, argumentation, and epistemological stance. *College English, 55,* 745–769.

More than One Author, Scholarly Journal That Restarts Page Numbering with Each Issue

Pollay, R. W., Lee, J. S., & Carter-Whitney, D. (1992). Separate, but not equal: Racial segmentation in cigarette advertising. *Journal of Advertising, 21*(1), 45–57.

Include the names of up to seven authors; use "et al." only when there are more than seven authors of an article or book. The citation includes the issue number in parentheses as well as the volume number.

Print Articles in Magazines and Newspapers

General Format for Print Article in Magazines and Newspapers

Author's last name, initials. (year, Month day of publication). Article title. *Name of Magazine or Newspaper, volume number if stated,* inclusive page numbers.

If page numbers are discontinuous, identify every page.

Magazine Article with Named Author

Snyder, R. L. (2001, August–September). A daughter of Cambodia remembers: Loung Ung's journey. *Ms., 12,* 62–67.

Hall, S. S. (2001, March 11). Prescription for profit. *New York Times Magazine,* 40–45, 59, 91–92, 100.

Magazine Article with No Author Listed

Daddy, daddy. (2001, July 30). *New Republic, 225,* 12–13.

Newspaper Article

Wims, M. (2008, July 13). More browsers than buyers. *Providence Journal,* pp. A1, A15.

Use *p.* or *pp.* to cite newspaper pages.

Review of Book or Film

Schwarz, B. (2001, November). A bit of bunting: A new history of the British empire elevates expediency to principle [Review of the book *Ornamentalism: How the British saw their empire*]. *Atlantic Monthly, 288,* 126–135.

Kaufman, S. (2001, July 30). Polishing a gem [Review of the motion picture *The blue angel*]. *New Republic, 225,* 28–29.

Editorial

Dr. Frankenstein on the hill [Editorial]. (2002, May 18). *The New York Times,* p. A22.

Letter to the Editor

Tomsovic, K. (1998, July 13). Culture clash [Letter to the editor]. *The New Yorker,* 7.

Print Books

General Format for Print Books

Author's last name, initials. (year). *Title of book: Subtitle of book.* Place of publication: Publisher.

One Author

Pollan, M. (2006). *The omnivore's dilemma: A natural history of four meals.* New York, NY: Penguin.

Two or More Authors

Dombrowski, D. A., & Deltete, R. J. (2000). *A brief, liberal, Catholic defense of abortion.* Urbana: University of Illinois Press.

Belenky, M., Clinchy, B. M., Goldberger, N. R., & Tarule, J. M. (1986). *Women's ways of knowing: The development of self, voice, and mind.* New York, NY: Basic Books.

APA style uses "et al." only for books with more than seven authors.

Second, Later, or Revised Edition

Montagu, A. (1986). *Touching: The human significance of the skin* (3rd ed.). New York, NY: Perennial Press.

Republished Book (For Example, a Paperback Published after the Original Hardback Edition or a Modern Edition of an Older Work)

Hill, C. (1991). *The world turned upside down: Radical ideas during the English revolution.* London, England: Penguin. (Original work published 1972)

The in-text citation should read: (Hill, 1972/1991).

Wollstonecraft, M. (1995). *The vindication of the rights of woman, with strictures on political and moral subjects.* Rutland, VT: Tuttle. (Original work published 1792)

The in-text citation should read: (Wollstonecraft, 1792/1995).

Multivolume Work

Churchill, W. S. (1956–1958). *A history of the English-speaking peoples* (Vols. 1–4). New York, NY: Dodd, Mead.

Citation for all the volumes together. The in-text citation should read: (Churchill, 1956–1958).

Churchill, W. S. (1957). *A history of the English-speaking peoples: Vol. 4. The great democracies.* New York, NY: Dodd, Mead.

Citation for a specific volume. The in-text citation should read: (Churchill, 1957).

Article in Reference Book

Ling, T. O. (1970). Buddhism in Burma. In S. G. F. Brandon (Ed.), *Dictionary of comparative religion.* New York, NY: Scribner's.

Translation

De Beauvoir, S. (1961). *The second sex* (H. M. Parshley, Trans.). New York, NY: Bantam Books. (Original work published 1949)

The in-text citation should read: (De Beauvoir, 1949/1961).

Corporate Author (a Commission, Committee, or Other Group)

American Red Cross. (1993). *Standard first aid.* St. Louis, MO: Mosby Lifeline.

No Author Listed

The New Yorker cartoon album: 1975–1985. (1987). New York, NY: Penguin Books.

Alphabetize this entry under *N*. The in-text citation should be a shortened version of the title as follows: (New Yorker cartoon album, 1987).

Anthology: Citing the Editor

O'Connell, D. F., & Alexander, C. N. (Eds.). (1994). *Self recovery: Treating addictions using transcendental meditation and Maharishi Ayur-Veda.* New York, NY: Haworth Press.

Anthology: Citing an Individual Article

Royer, A. (1994). The role of the transcendental meditation technique in promoting smoking cessation: A longitudinal study. In D. F. O'Connell & C. N. Alexander (Eds.), *Self recovery: Treating addictions using transcendental meditation and Maharishi Ayur-Veda* (pp. 221–239). New York, NY: Haworth Press.

Web and Internet Sources

Document or Article within a Web Site

Marks, J. (n.d.). Overview: Letter from the president. Retrieved June 25, 2004, from the Search for Common Ground web site: http://www.sfcg.org/sfcg

Barrett, J. (2007, January 17). MySpace is a natural monopoly. Retrieved from ECommerce Times web site: http://www.ecommercetimes.com

Use "n.d." if no publication date is provided, and include date of access. Do not include date of access if the document has a publication or posting date and is unlikely to change. To see where the information in the Barrett citation comes from, see Figure 17.1.

APA

Article from a Scholarly Web Journal

Welch, J. R., & Riley, R. (2001). Reclaiming land and spirit in the western Apache homeland. *American Indian Quarterly, 25,* 5–14. Retrieved from http://muse.jhu.edu/journals/american_indian_quarterly

Article from a Newspaper Site

Thevenot, B. (2004, July 31). Once in a blue moon. *Times Picayune* [New Orleans]. Retrieved from http://www.nola.com/t-p

Article from Online Database

Beckham II, J. M. (2008). Placing *Touch of evil, The border,* and *Traffic* in the American imagination. *Journal of Popular Film & Television, 33*(3), 130–141. Retrieved from http://www.heldref.org/pubs/jpft

Cite the publication's home page, not the database.

Article from Online Database with DOI

Adelt, U. (2008). Trying to find an identity: Eric Clapton's changing conception of "blackness." *Popular Music & Society, 31,* 433–452. doi: 10.1080/03007760802052809

Article from Online Reference Work

Doom. (2008). *Encyclopædia Britannica.* Retrieved from http://www.britannica.com

E-Book

Hoffman, F. W. (1981). *The literature of rock: 1954–1978.* Retrieved from http://www.netlibrary.com/ebook_info.asl?product_id=24355

Online Posting to a Blog, Electronic Mailing List, Bulletin Board, or Newsgroup

Wright, J. (2006, February 21). MySpace is the new blogosphere [Web log post]. Retrieved from http://www.ensight.org/archives/2006/02/21/myspace-is-the-new -blogosphere/

Podcast

The long and winding road: DNA evidence for human migration [Audio podcast]. (2008, July 7). *Science Talk.* Retrieved from Scientific American web site: http://www.sciam.com

E-Mail, Interviews, and Personal Correspondence

APA guidelines limit the "References" list to publishable or retrievable information. Cite personal correspondence in the body of your text, but not in the "References" list: "Daffinrud (personal communication, December 12, 2001) claims that …"

Miscellaneous Sources

Television or Radio Program

Bochco, S., & Milch, D. (Directors). (2001, November 6). Lie like a rug [Television series episode]. In *NYPD blue.* New York: American Broadcasting Company.

Ashbrook, T. (Anchor). (2008, July 22). Turf wars and the American lawn [Radio program]. *On point.* Retrieved from WBUR web site: http://wbur.org

Conan, N. (Anchor), & Telhami, S. (Guest). (2004, May 4). Arab media [Radio transcript]. *Talk of the nation.* Retrieved from NPR website: http://www.npr.org

Film or Video Recording

Madden, J. (Director). (1998). *Shakespeare in love* [Motion picture]. United States: Universal Miramax.

Beck, R. (2006, Nov. 2). Immigration gumballs [Video file]. Retrieved from http://youtube.com/watch?v=n7WJeqxuOfQ

Sound Recording

Dwarf Music. (1966). Rainy day woman [Recorded by B. Dylan]. On *Bob Dylan MTV unplugged* [CD]. New York, NY: Columbia. (1995)

For podcasts, see page 392.

Unpublished Paper Presented at a Meeting

Sharples, M. (2001, June 20). *Authors of the future.* Paper presented at Conference of European Teachers of Academic Writing, Groningen, the Netherlands.

Government Publication

O'Toole, M. E. (2000). *The school shooter: A threat assessment perspective.* Washington, DC: U.S. Federal Bureau of Investigation. Retrieved from http://www.fbi.gov/publications /school/school2.pdf

Conclusion

This chapter has shown you how to use sources purposively, how to help readers separate your ideas from those of sources through the use of rhetorically effective attributive tags, and how to work sources into your own writing through summarizing, paraphrasing, and quoting. It has also defined plagiarism and shown you how to avoid it. The last half of the chapter has shown you the nuts and bolts of citing and documenting sources in both the MLA and APA styles. It has explained the logic of parenthetical citation systems, showing you how to match sources cited in your text with those in your concluding bibliography. It has also shown you the documentation formats for a wide range of sources in both MLA and APA styles.

Student Example of an APA-Style Research Paper

We conclude with Megan Matthews's researched argument on Navy sonar and whales. We have shown you some of Megan's exploratory thinking leading up to this paper, particularly her "Letter to the Editor" in Chapter 13 (p. 274), and her research notes and database searches in Chapter 16 (pp. 345–346 and 353–354). She uses the APA system for citing and documenting her sources.

APA

Sounding the Alarm:
Navy Sonar and the Survival of Whales
Megan Matthews
English 260
November 1, 2002

SOUNDING THE ALARM   2

Sounding the Alarm:

Navy Sonar and the Survival of Whales

Imagine that you are forced to live in an apartment next to a city freeway with a constant roar of engines and tires against concrete. Cars cruise by on the surface streets with bass systems so powerful that your windows shake and your ears hurt. You tolerate the din day after day, but you and your friends have to shout to be heard. What if you had no alternative place to live?

This scenario is, of course, preposterous. We can move to find the coveted sound of silence. For whales, dolphins, and sea turtles, however, noise is becoming an inescapable catastrophe that threatens far more than their aesthetic sensibilities. The incessant rumbling of cargo ships, the loud explosions of undersea mineral explorations, and the annoying cacophony of the blasting devices used by fisheries have turned Jacques Cousteau's world of silence into an underwater freeway. Now, however, a new and more dangerous source of sound has been approved for use in the oceans—the United States Navy's Low Frequency Active Sonar System (LFA sonar), which will track enemy submarines. The Navy claims that the technology is needed to ensure national security, since it detects submarines at greater distances than previous sonar systems. However, the potential damage to marine life and to the long-term health of the oceans themselves outweighs the Navy's questionable claims about national security. The U.S. Congress should cut funds for further deployment of LFA sonar.

Since the mid-1980s, the Navy has developed and tested LFA sonar systems. LFA is *active* because it does more than just listen for nearby submarines, like our older systems. With LFA, 18 acoustic transmitters the size of bathtubs act like giant woofer speakers suspended beneath the ship on cables. The speakers emit bursts of sound every 6 to 100 seconds. These bursts can be as powerful as 215 decibels, a sound level equivalent to standing 1 meter away from a departing commercial jet (National Marine Fisheries Service [NMFS], 2002a, p. 3). The Navy prefers low-frequency sonar because low-frequency waves travel farther than high-frequency waves, which is why the bumping bass of a car stereo reverberates after the car spins around a street corner. In this case, the sonar's sound waves reflect off objects from hundreds of miles away and alert the ship's crew to the presence of submarines. In its Environmental Impact Statement, the Navy explains that it needs LFA sonar because modern submarines are quieter than clunky Cold War versions. Their ability to run quietly makes the new subs virtually undetectable until they are close by, leaving the Navy only minutes to respond to a potential submarine threat (Department of the Navy

SOUNDING THE ALARM   3

[DON], 2001, p. ES-2). After studying possible solutions, the Navy believes LFA sonar is the only system capable of providing reliable and dependable long-range detection of quieter, harder-to-find submarines (DON, 2001, p. ES-2). Unfortunately, the far-traveling waves that bounce off enemy submarines also can pierce the inner ears of whales and dolphins.

To its credit, the Navy has acted to protect marine mammals and other sea life. The Navy studied existing research reports on the levels of sounds that can cause hearing damage to marine mammals and concluded that protecting whales and dolphins from levels above 180 dB would prevent any harm to their hearing and behavior. Based on these studies, the National Oceanic and Atmospheric Administration's National Marine Fisheries Service determined that the Navy's employment of LFA sonar at levels below 180 dB would have no more than a negligible impact on marine mammal species and stocks (National Oceanic and Atmospheric Administration [NOAA], 2002). The Navy therefore plans to use a maximum volume of 180 dB when marine mammals are nearby. As an initial protective measure, the sonar will not be allowed to operate above 180 dB if it is within 12 nautical miles of coastlines and islands to ensure that coastal stocks of marine mammals and sea turtles will be relatively unaffected by LFA sonar (NMFS, 2002b). This measure protects critically endangered species, like northern right whales, who feed in coastal areas. The Navy also plans to avoid damaging whale hearing and behavior by trying to prevent animals from swimming near the ships. The Navy wants to detect animals that wander within 1 kilometer of the vessel, where they might be exposed to sounds of 180 dB or more. The protective monitoring systems will rely on humans and technology to protect sea animals. Sailors who have been trained to detect and identify marine mammals and sea turtles will stand on deck to look for whales and dolphins (Schregardus, 2002, p. 48149). Underwater microphones will also listen for sounds that whales and dolphins make. Finally, the Navy has developed a second active sonar system called the High Frequency Marine Mammal Monitoring Sonar. It will locate and monitor animals who enter the 180 dB area and will run before and during the LFA sonar transmissions. If whales, dolphins, or sea turtles are observed, the crew will turn off the LFA system until the animals move away.

These efforts to protect sea life are commendable, but current marine research shows that LFA sonar poses a much higher risk to marine mammals than the Navy acknowledges. The conclusions drawn by the Navy about potential hearing damage to marine mammals are open to serious doubt, and their measures to protect the sea environment are inadequate.

To begin, biologists generally agree that hearing is the primary sense of marine mammals. No one knows precisely what functions hearing performs, but it is likely that whales depend on sound to avoid predators, to communicate across great distances between

5

SOUNDING THE ALARM   4

pods and prospective mates, and to establish mother-calf bonds. According to a detailed study by the National Resources Defense Council (Jasny, 1999), significant noise interference could threaten individual mammals or entire populations if biologically important behaviors like these are disrupted. Furthermore, like the members of a rock band, whales and dolphins may experience hearing loss after repeated exposure to sounds at the same frequency. In 1996, two sperm whales residing in a heavily trafficked area of the Canary Islands made no apparent efforts to avoid a collision with a cargo ship and were killed. Autopsies revealed damage to their inner ears, which some environmental scientists believe could have been caused by repeated exposure to the sounds of cargo ships (Jasny, 1999). The Navy's tests of different kinds of sonar systems are also suspected to have caused 16 Cuvier's beaked whales to beach and die in the Bahamas. The Navy had been testing midrange active sonar in the area; autopsies of four whales revealed extensive bleeding in the inner ears and around the brain. The conclusions of the Navy and Fisheries Service interim and final reports named the sonar tests as the most likely cause of the beachings (DON and NMFS, 2001). Although the type of sonar was midrange, rather than low-frequency, the link still implies that whales can be harmed or even killed by sonar—and that the effects can be unanticipated. Beachings also occurred after naval sonar exercises in Greece and the Canary Islands. In Greece, sonar is the likely culprit; scientists cannot establish the cause of death, however, because the initial examination of the bodies was not thorough (Jasny, 1999). Finally, according to Jasny, the long-term effects of noise pollution may not be limited to hearing; noise pollution can increase stress levels, which lead to shorter life spans and lower birth rates—effects that humans may not notice for decades. One ping from a low-frequency system may only *harass* whales, to use the term commonly encountered in Navy or Fisheries Service discussions of low-frequency sonar, but if whales are exposed to LFA sound waves repeatedly, the effects may be long-lasting and even irreversible.

The importance of hearing to marine mammals means that the effect of LFA sonar on the sea environment needs to be extensively studied. Unfortunately, the studies used by the Navy to demonstrate that LFA sonar poses little threat to marine life are scant, scientifically flawed, and inconclusive. No one actually knows how loud or frequent sounds need to be to cause permanent or temporary hearing loss to whales and sea turtles. Most studies have focused on captive species like seals and some dolphins; the data is extrapolated to estimate the hearing capacities of other species. The Navy uses the findings of several scientific workshops that studied the range where serious hearing problems could occur. Based upon these conclusions, as well as the Navy's own examinations of marine mammal inner ear models and extrapolation from human results, the Navy believes that protecting marine mammals from levels above 180 dB will be sufficient (DON, 2001, p. 14). Yet the Navy itself admits, in its own environmental impact statement, that data regarding underwater hearing capabilities of marine mammals are rare and limited to smaller species that can be studied in laboratories (DON, 2001, p. 11). The Navy has tried to dispel fears that mammals are physically and behaviorally harmed by LFA sonar by releasing the results of three separate tests Navy scientists conducted on baleen whale populations in California and Hawaii; these studies concluded that most whales did not alter any observable aspect of their behavior for more than "a few tens of minutes" (DON, 2001, p. 16). Nevertheless, three tests on baleen whales is hardly adequate to conclude that other species of whales, as well as other marine mammals, would react in the same way as the baleen whale. Moreover, none of these studies examined the long-term effects of repeated exposures, nor were whales exposed to sounds above 155 dB, even though the estimated LFA safety level is 180 dB. One has difficulty understanding how the Navy can set 180 dB as their safety threshold when their own tests did not monitor whales at this level. Moreover, some scientists claim that *less intense* sounds can be harmful. Dr. Marsh Green, the president of the Ocean Mammal Institute and an animal behavior specialist, claims that "a significant body of research show[s] that whales avoid underwater sounds starting at 110 to 120 decibels" (Knickerbocker, 2001). If the scientific community continues to debate this issue, it seems unlikely that the Navy could have indisputable evidence that the sonar will not harm whales.

Clearly the Navy's claim that LFA sonar will not hurt marine mammals and other sea life will not survive close scrutiny. Of even greater concern is the dangerous precedent that the U.S. Navy will set if it deploys LFA sonar on its surface ships. There is a strong possibility that other nations might develop LFA sonar systems in order to keep up with the United States. The nuclear weapons race of the past proves that military powers constantly compete with each other to be prepared for armed conflicts. This often results in a frantic struggle to develop the same technologies worldwide with no regard for environmental and social effects. Already, according to Jasny (1999), NATO countries are investigating their own use of similar LFA systems. If additional countries deploy the technology, whales and dolphins will face much greater risks of meeting sonar systems in open water. In addition, the world's governments have not discussed treaties that would require nations to turn off sonar systems in arctic waters, which the Navy currently plans to do. Whales, dolphins, and sea turtles will have no permanent safe havens if other militaries choose to run their systems worldwide.

The Navy justifies developing LFA sonar for the sake of national security; in light of the September 11, 2001, terrorist attacks, this claim almost guarantees

SOUNDING THE ALARM   6

unquestioned public support. Even so, in the age of terrorism, do enemy submarines present significant threats? A confusing array of Navy documents makes it nearly impossible for the general public to find out the facts about potential danger from submarines. The Navy argues that 224 diesel-electric submarines are operated by nonallied nations but never explains who these nations are or how much of a threat they actually pose (Schregardus, 2002, p. 48146). This long-standing anxiety about submarines feels like part of the old Cold War mentality when the nation to fear was the Soviet Union. Perhaps now we should be more concerned about cargo ships than submarines. A large percentage of freight containers are never inspected at our ports, and these seem to be easier targets for terrorists than our Navy ships. Finally, the most recent attack on a Navy ship, the USS *Cole,* came from another boat, not a submarine. The number of terrorists who have sophisticated submarine technology must be smaller than the number who can place a small bomb on a small boat, train, car, or cargo ship.

10   Moreover long-term national security also depends on healthy oceans. Millions of people incorporate fish into their diet, and oceans provide materials for countless human products. Any changes to the balance of marine life could degrade the entire ecosystem. If the health of the oceans is damaged by LFA sonar, it will be only a matter of time before humans feel the effects. Our national environmental security, which never receives much attention in the media, should be as important to the United States as our military readiness. The proposed widespread use of LFA sonar on the Navy's surface ships opens up a range of questions about the long-term effects of our underwater activities. When combined with other sources of human noise pollution, LFA sonar poses dangerous threats to marine life. According to Dr. Sylvia Earle, former chief scientist at the National Oceanic and Atmospheric Administration, undersea noise pollution is like the death of a thousand cuts (as cited in Jasny, 1999, executive summary, first sidebar). Each time we turn up the volume in the oceans, we make it more difficult for marine animals to communicate with each other. We may even diminish their hearing capacities, endangering their abilities to migrate safely and to avoid countless ships that crisscross their routes. Until more is known about the long-term effects of LFA sonar, the Navy should delay operation of LFA sonar voluntarily. If it does not do so, the U.S. Congress should cut off further funding. The debate over LFA sonar cannot be defined as a simple environment-versus-government battle. It is a discussion about whether or not environmental security and ocean health matter to humans. At its core, it is a debate about our futures.

SOUNDING THE ALARM   7

References

Department of the Navy. (2001). *Executive summary: Final overseas environmental impact statement and environmental impact statement for Surveillance Towed Array Sensor System Low Frequency Active (SURTASS LFA) Sonar.* Retrieved from http://www.surtass-lfa-eis.com/docs/EXSUM%20FEIS%201–15.pdf

Department of the Navy and National Marine Fisheries Service. (2001, December 20). *Joint interim report: Bahamas marine mammal stranding event of 15–16 March 2000.* Retrieved from http://www.nmfs.noaa.gov/prot_res/overview/Interim_Bahamas_Report.pdf

Jasny, M. (1999, March). *Sounding the depths: Supertankers, sonar, and the rise of undersea noise.* Retrieved from the National Resources Defense Council Web site: http://www.nrdc.org

Knickerbocker, B. (2001, August 15). Whales to Navy: Less noise, please. *Christian Science Monitor.* Retrieved from http://csmonitor.com

National Marine Fisheries Service. (2002a). *Biological opinion on proposed employment of Surveillance Towed Array Sensor System Low Frequency Active Sonar.* Retrieved from http://www.nmfs.noaa.gov/prot_res/readingrm/ESAsec7/7pr_surtass-2020529.pdf

National Marine Fisheries Service. (2002b). *Final determination and rulemaking on the harassment of marine mammals incidental to Navy operations of Surveillance Towed Array Sensor System Low Frequency Active (SURTASS LFA) Sonar.* Retrieved from http://www.nmfs.noaa.gov/prot_res/readingrm/MMSURTASS/LFAexecsummary.PDF

National Oceanic and Atmospheric Administration. (2002, July 15). *Strong protection measures for marine mammals tied to operation of Low Frequency Sonar* (NOAA news release 2002–90). Retrieved from http://www.publicaffairs.noaa.gov

Schregardus, D. R. (2002, July 16). *Record of decision for Surveillance Towed Array Sensor System Low Frequency Active (SURTASS LFA) Sonar,* Fed Reg 67 (141), pp. 48145–48154. Retrieved from http://www.surtass-lfa-eis.com/docs/LFA%20EIS%20ROD.pdf

APA

Informal Fallacies

In this appendix, we look at ways of assessing the legitimacy of an argument within a real-world context of probabilities rather than within a mathematical world of certainty. Whereas formal logic is a kind of mathematics, the informal fallacies addressed in this appendix are embedded in everyday arguments, sometimes making fallacious reasoning seem deceptively persuasive, especially to unwary audiences. We begin by looking at the problem of conclusiveness in arguments, after which we give you an overview of the most commonly encountered informal fallacies.

The Problem of Conclusiveness in an Argument

In real-world disagreements, we seldom encounter arguments that are absolutely conclusive. Rather, arguments are, to various degrees, "persuasive" or "nonpersuasive." In the pure world of formal logic, however, it is possible to have absolutely conclusive arguments. For example, an Aristotelian syllogism, if it is validly constructed, yields a certain conclusion. Moreover, if the first two premises (called the "major" and "minor" premises) are true, then we are guaranteed that the conclusion is also true. Here is an example:

Valid Syllogism

Major premise: All ducks are feathered animals.

Minor premise: Quacko is a duck.

Conclusion: Therefore Quacko is a feathered animal.

This syllogism is said to be valid because it follows a correct form. Moreover, because its premises are true, the conclusion is guaranteed to be true. However, if the syllogism follows an incorrect form (and is therefore invalid), we can't determine whether the conclusion is true.

Invalid Syllogism

Major premise: All ducks are feathered animals.

Minor premise: Clucko is a feathered animal.

Conclusion: Therefore Clucko is a duck.

In the valid syllogism, we are guaranteed that Quacko is a feathered animal because the minor premise states that Quacko is a duck and the major premise places ducks within the larger class of feathered animals. But in the invalid syllogism, there is no guaranteed conclusion. We know that Clucko is a feathered animal but we can't know whether he is a duck. He may be a duck, but he may also be a buzzard or a chicken. The invalid syllogism thus commits a "formal fallacy" in that its form doesn't guarantee the truth of its conclusion even if the initial premises are true.

From the perspective of real-world argumentation, the problem with formal logic is that it isn't concerned with the truth of premises. For example, the following argument is logically valid even though the premises and conclusion are obviously untrue:

Valid Syllogism with Untrue Major and Minor Premises

Major premise: The blood of insects can be used to lubricate lawn mower engines.

Minor premise: Vampires are insects.

Conclusion: Therefore the blood of vampires can be used to lubricate lawn mower engines.

Even though this syllogism meets the formal requirements for validity, its argument is ludicrous.

In this appendix, therefore, we are concerned with "informal" rather than "formal" fallacies because informal fallacies are embedded within real-world arguments addressing contestable issues of truth and value. Disputants must argue about issues because they can't be resolved with mathematical certainty; any contestable claim always leaves room for doubt and alternative points of view. Disputants can create only more or less persuasive arguments, never conclusive ones.

An Overview of Informal Fallacies

The study of informal fallacies remains the murkiest of all logical endeavors. It's murky because informal fallacies are as unsystematic as formal fallacies are rigid and systematized. Whereas formal fallacies of logic have the force of laws, informal fallacies have little more than explanatory power. Informal fallacies are quirky; they identify classes of less conclusive arguments that recur with some frequency, but they do not contain formal flaws that make their conclusions illegitimate no matter what the terms may say. Informal fallacies require us to look at the meaning of the terms to determine how much we should trust or distrust the conclusion. In evaluating arguments with informal fallacies, we usually find that arguments are "more or less" fallacious, and determining the degree of fallaciousness is a matter of judgment.

Knowledge of informal fallacies is most useful when we run across arguments that we "know" are wrong, but we can't quite say why. They just don't "sound right." They look reasonable enough, but they remain unacceptable to us. Informal fallacies are a sort of compendium of symptoms for arguments flawed in this way. We must be careful, however, to make sure that the particular case before us "fits" the descriptors for the fallacy that seems to explain its problem. It's much easier, for example, to find informal fallacies in a hostile argument than in a friendly one simply because we are more likely to expand the limits of the fallacy to make the disputed case fit.

In arranging the fallacies, we have, for convenience, put them into three categories derived from classical rhetoric: *pathos, ethos,* and *logos.* Fallacies of *pathos* rest on flaws in the way an argument appeals to the audience's emotions and values. Fallacies of *ethos* rest on flaws in the way the argument appeals to the character of opponents or of sources and witnesses within an argument. Fallacies of *logos* rest on flaws in the relationship among statements in an argument.

Fallacies of *Pathos*

Argument to the People (Appealing to Stirring Symbols)   This is perhaps the most generic example of a *pathos* fallacy. Arguments to the people appeal to the fundamental beliefs, biases, and prejudices of the audience in order to sway opinion through a feeling of solidarity among those of the group. Thus a "Support Our Troops" bumper sticker, often including the American flag, creates an initial feeling of solidarity among almost all citizens of goodwill. But the car owner may have the deeper intention of actually meaning "support our president" or "support the war in _____." The stirring symbol of the flag and the desire shared by most people to support our troops is used fallaciously to urge support of a particular political act. Arguments to the people often use visual rhetoric, as in the soaring eagle used in Wal-Mart corporate ads or images of happy families in marketing advertisements.

Appeal to Ignorance   This fallacy persuades an audience to accept as true a claim that hasn't been proved false or vice versa. "Jones must have used steroids to get those bulging biceps because he can't prove that he hasn't used steroids." Appeals to ignorance are particularly common in the murky field of pseudoscience. "UFOs (ghosts, abominable snowmen) do exist because science hasn't proved that they don't exist." Sometimes, however, it is hard to draw a line between a fallacious appeal to ignorance and a legitimate appeal to precaution: "Genetically modified organisms must be dangerous to our health because science hasn't proved that they are safe."

Appeal to Popularity—Bandwagon   To board the bandwagon means (to use a more contemporary metaphor) to board the bus or train of what's popular. Appeals to popularity are fallacious because the popularity of something is irrelevant to its actual merits. "Living together before marriage is the right thing to do because most couples are now doing it." Bandwagon appeals are common in advertising where the claim that a product is popular substitutes for evidence of the product's excellence. There are times, however, when popularity may indeed be relevant: "Global warming is probably caused by human activity because a preponderance of scientists now hold this position." (Here we assume that scientists haven't simply climbed on a bandwagon themselves, but have formed their opinions based on research data and well-vetted, peer-reviewed papers.)

Appeal to Pity   Here the arguer appeals to the audience's sympathetic feelings in order to support a claim that should be decided on more relevant or objective grounds. "Honorable judge, I should not be fined $200 for speeding because I was distraught from hearing news of my brother's illness and was rushing to see him in the hospital." Here the argument is fallacious because the arguer's reason, while evoking sympathy, is not a relevant justification for speeding (as it might have been, for instance, if the arguer had been rushing an injured person to the emergency room). In many cases, however, an arguer can legitimately appeal to pity, as in the case of fund-raising for victims of a tsunami or other disaster.

Red Herring   This fallacy's funny name derives from the practice of using a red herring (a highly odiferous fish) to throw dogs off a scent that they are supposed to be tracking. It refers to the practice of throwing an audience off track by raising an unrelated or irrelevant point. "Debating a gas tax increase is valuable, but I really think there should be an extra tax on SUVs." Here the arguer, apparently uncomfortable with the gas tax issue, diverts the conversation to the emotional issue of SUVs. A conversant who noted how the argument has gotten off track might say, "Stop talking, everyone. The SUV question is a red herring; let's get back to the topic of a gas tax increase."

Fallacies of *Ethos*

Appeal to False Authority   Arguers appeal to false authority when they use famous people (often movie stars or other celebrities) to testify on issues about which these persons have no special competence. "Joe Quarterback says Gooey Oil keeps his old tractor running sharp; therefore, Gooey Oil is a good oil." Real evidence about the quality of Gooey Oil would include technical data about the product rather than testimony from an actor or hired celebrity. However, the distinction between a "false authority" and a legitimate authority can become blurred. Consider the Viagra ads by former senator Bob Dole during the first marketing years of this impotence drug. As a famous person rather than a doctor, Dole would seem to be a false authority. But Dole was also widely known to have survived prostate cancer, and he may well have used Viagra. To the extent a person is an expert in a field, he or she is no longer a "false authority."

Ad Hominem   Literally, *ad hominem* means "to the person." An *ad hominem* argument is directed at the character of an opponent rather than at the quality of the opponent's reasoning. Ideally, arguments are supposed to be *ad rem* ("to the thing"), that is, addressed to the specifics of the case itself. Thus an *ad rem* critique of a politician would focus on her voting record, the consistency and cogency of her public statements, her responsiveness to constituents, and so forth. An *ad hominem* argument would shift attention from her record to features of her personality, life circumstances, or the company she keeps. "Senator Sweetwater's views on the gas tax should be discounted because her husband works for a huge oil company" or "Senator Sweetwater supports tax cuts for the wealthy because she is very wealthy herself and stands to gain." But not all *ad hominem* arguments are *ad hominem* fallacies. Lawyers, for example, when questioning expert witnesses who give damaging testimony, often make an issue of their honesty, credibility, or personal investment in an outcome.

Poisoning the Well This fallacy is closely related to *ad hominem.* Arguers poison the well when they discredit an opponent or an opposing view in advance. "Before I yield the floor to the next speaker, I must remind you that those who oppose my plan do not have the best interests of working people in their hearts."

Straw Man The straw man fallacy occurs when you oversimplify an opponent's argument to make it easier to refute or ridicule. Rather than summarizing an opposing view fairly and completely, you basically make up the argument you wish your opponent had made because it is so much easier to knock over, like knocking over a straw man or scarecrow in a corn field. See pages 128–129 for a fuller discussion of the straw man fallacy.

Fallacies of *Logos*

Hasty Generalization This fallacy occurs when someone makes a broad generalization on the basis of too little evidence. Generally, the evidence needed to support a generalization persuasively must meet the STAR criteria (sufficiency, typicality, accuracy, and relevance) discussed in Chapter 5 (pages 89–90). But what constitutes a sufficient amount of evidence? The generally accepted standards of sufficiency in any given field are difficult to determine. The Food and Drug Administration (FDA), for example, generally proceeds cautiously before certifying a drug as "safe." However, if people are harmed by the side effects of an FDA-approved drug, critics often accuse the FDA of having made a hasty generalization. At the same time, patients eager to have access to a new drug and manufacturers eager to sell a new product may lobby the FDA to quit "dragging its feet" and get the drug to market. Hence, the point at which a hasty generalization passes over into the realm of a prudent generalization is nearly always uncertain and contested.

Part for the Whole Sometimes called by its Latin name *pars pro toto,* this fallacy is closely related to hasty generalization. In this fallacy, arguers pick out a part of the whole or a sample of the whole (often not a typical or representative part or sample) and then claim that what is true of the part is true for the whole. If, say, individuals wanted to get rid of the National Endowment for the Arts (NEA), they might focus on several controversial programs funded by the NEA and use them as justification for wiping out all NEA programs. The flip side of this fallacy occurs when an arguer picks only the best examples to make a case and conveniently forgets about other examples that may weaken the case.

Post Hoc, Ergo Propter Hoc The Latin name of this fallacy means "after this, therefore because of this." The fallacy occurs when a sequential relationship is mistaken for a causal relationship. (See Chapter 12, page 247, where we discuss this fallacy in more depth.) For example, you may be guilty of this fallacy if you say, "Cramming for a test really helps because last week I crammed for my psychology test and I got an A on it." When two events occur frequently in conjunction with each other, we've got a good case for a causal relationship. But until we can show how one causes the other and until we have ruled out other causes, we cannot be certain that a causal relationship is occurring. For example, the A on your psych test may be caused by something other than your cramming. Maybe the exam was easier, or perhaps you were luckier or more mentally alert. It is often difficult to tell when a *post hoc* fallacy occurs. When the New York police department changed its policing tactics in the early 1990s, the crime rate plummeted. Many experts attributed the declining crime rate to the new policing tactics, but some critics proposed other explanations. (See p. 238, where economist Steven Levitt attributes the declining crime rate to the legalization of abortion in the 1970s.)

Begging the Question—Circular Reasoning   Arguers beg the question when they provide a reason that simply restates the claim in different words. Here is an example: "Abortion is murder because it is the intentional taking of the life of a human being." Because "murder" is defined as "the intentional taking of the life of a human being," the argument is circular. It is tantamount to saying, "Abortion is murder because it is murder." In the abortion debate, the crucial issue is whether a fetus is a "human being" in the legal sense. So in this case the arguer has fallaciously "begged the question" by assuming from the start that the fetus is a legal human being. The argument is similar to saying, "That person is obese because he is too fat."

False Dilemma—Either/Or   This fallacy occurs when an arguer oversimplifies a complex issue so that only two choices appear possible. Often one of the choices is made to seem unacceptable, so the only remaining option is the other choice. "It's my way or the highway" is a typical example of a false dilemma. Here is a more subtle one: "Either we allow embryonic stem cell research, or we condemn people with diabetes, Parkinson's disease, or spinal injuries to a life without a cure." Clearly, there may be other options, including other approaches to curing these diseases. A good extended example of the false dilemma fallacy is found in sociologist Kai Erikson's analysis of President Truman's decision to drop the A-bomb on Hiroshima. His analysis suggests that the Truman administration prematurely reduced numerous options to just two: either drop the bomb on a major city, or sustain unacceptable losses in a land invasion of Japan. Erikson, however, shows there were other alternatives.

Slippery Slope   The slippery slope fallacy is based on the fear that once we put a foot on a slippery slope heading in the wrong direction, we're doomed to slide right out of sight. The controlling metaphor is of a slick mountainside without places to hold on rather than of a staircase with numerous stopping places. Here is an example of a slippery slope: "Once we allow medical use of marijuana, we'll eventually legalize it for everyone, after which we're on a slippery slope toward social acceptance of cocaine and heroin." Slippery slope arguments are frequently encountered when individuals request exceptions to bureaucratic rules: "Look, Blotnik, no one feels worse about your need for open-heart surgery than I do. But I still can't let you turn this paper in late. If I were to let you do it, then I'd have to let everyone turn in papers late." Slippery slope arguments can be very persuasive—and often rightfully so because every slippery slope argument isn't necessarily a slippery slope fallacy. Some slopes really are slippery. The slippery slope becomes a fallacy when we forget that we can often dig a foothold into the slope and stop. For example, we can define procedures for exceptions to rules so that Blotnik can turn in his paper late without allowing everyone to turn in a paper late. Likewise, a state could legalize medical use of marijuana without legalizing it for everyone.

False Analogy   In Chapter 13 on resemblance arguments, we explained that no analogy is perfect (see our discussion of disanalogies on page 267). Any two things being compared are similar in some ways and different in other ways. Whether an analogy is persuasive or false often depends on the audience's initial degree of skepticism. For example, people opposed to gun control may find the following argument persuasive: "Banning guns on the basis that guns accidentally kill people is like banning cars on the basis that cars accidentally kill people." In contrast, supporters of gun control are likely to call this argument a false analogy on the basis of dissimilarities between cars and guns. (For example, they might say that banning cars would be far more disruptive on our society than would be banning guns.) Just when a persuasive analogy turns into a false analogy is difficult to say.

Non Sequitur   The name of this fallacy means "it does not follow." *Non sequitur* is a catchall term for any claim that doesn't follow from its premises or is supported by irrelevant premises. Sometimes the arguer seems to make an inexplicably illogical leap: "Genetically modified foods should be outlawed because they are not natural." (Should anything that is not natural be outlawed? In what way are they not natural?) At other times there may be a gap in the chain of reasons: "Violent video games have some social value because the army uses them for recruiting." (There may be an important idea emerging here, but too many logical steps are missing.) At still other times an arguer may support a claim with irrelevant reasons: "I should not receive a C in this course because I currently have a 3.8 GPA." In effect, almost any fallacy could be called a *non sequitur* because fallacious reasoning always indicates some kind of disconnect between the reasons and the claim.

Loaded Label or Definition   Sometimes arguers try to influence their audience's view of something by creating a loaded label or definition. For example, people who oppose the "estate tax" (which calls to mind rich people with estates) have relabeled it the "death tax" in order to give it a negative connotation without any markers of class or wealth. Or to take another example, proponents of organic foods could create definitions like the following: "Organic foods are safe and healthy foods grown without any pesticides, herbicides, or other unhealthy additives." "Safe" and "healthy" are evaluative terms used fallaciously in what purports to be a definition. The intended implication is that nonorganic foods are not safe and healthy.

■ ■ ■   **FOR CLASS DISCUSSION**   Persuasive or Fallacious?

Working individually or in small groups, determine the potential persuasiveness of each of the following argument cores. If fleshed out with supporting evidence, how persuasive do each of these arguments promise to be? If the arguments seemed doomed because of one or more of the fallacies discussed in this appendix, identify the fallacies and explain how they render the argument nonpersuasive. In your discussion, remember that it is often hard to determine the exact point where fallacious reasoning begins to kick in, especially when you consider different kinds of audiences. So in each case, consider also variations in audience. For which audiences would any particular argument appear potentially fallacious? Which audiences would be more likely to consider the argument persuasive?

1. Either we legalize marijuana or we watch a steady increase in the number of our citizens who break the law.
2. Smoking must cause lung cancer because a much higher percentage of smokers get lung cancer than do nonsmokers.
3. Smoking does not cause cancer because my grandfather smoked two packs per day for fifty years and died in his sleep at age ninety.
4. Society has an obligation to provide housing for the homeless because people without adequate shelter have a right to the resources of the community.
5. Based on my observations of the two renters in our neighborhood, I have concluded that people who own their own homes take better care of them than those who rent. [This arguer provided detailed evidence about the house-caring practices of the two renters and of the homeowners in the neighborhood.]
6. Intelligent design must qualify as a scientific theory because hundreds of scientists endorse it.
7. If we pass legislation requiring mandatory registration of handguns, we'll open the door to eventual confiscation of hunting rifles.
8. Those who support gun control are wrong because they believe that no one should have the right to defend himself or herself in any situation.
9. Most other progressive nations have adopted a program of government-provided health insurance. Therefore it is time for the United States to abandon its present employer-funded insurance system and adopt federally funded universal health insurance.
10. You should discount Dr. Smith's objections to federally funded health care because as a doctor he may face a loss of some income.   ■ ■ ■

Small Group Strategies for Practicing Argument Skills

In Chapter 1 we stressed that today truth is typically seen as a product of discussion and persuasion by members of a given community. Instead of seeing "truth" as grounded in some absolute and timeless realm such as Plato's forms or the unchanging laws of logic, many modern thinkers assert that truth is the product of a consensus among a group of knowledgeable peers. Our own belief in the special importance of argumentation in contemporary life follows from our assumption that truth arises out of discussion and debate rather than dogma or pure reason.

In this appendix, we extend that assumption to the classroom itself. We explain a mode of learning often called *collaborative learning*. It involves a combination of learning from an instructor, learning independently, and learning from peers. Mostly it involves a certain spirit—the same sort of inquiring attitude that's required of a good arguer.

From Conflict to Consensus: How to Get the Most Out of the Writing Community

Behind the notion of the writing community lies the notion that thinking and writing are social acts. At first, this notion may contradict certain widely accepted stereotypes of writers and thinkers as solitary souls who retreat to cork-lined studies where they conjure great thoughts and works. But although we agree that every writer at some point in the process requires solitude, we would point out that most writers and thinkers also require periods of talk and social interchange before they retreat to solitude. Poets, novelists, scientists, philosophers, and technological innovators tend to belong to communities of peers with whom they share their ideas, theories, and work. In this section, we try to provide you with some practical advice on how to get the most out of these sorts of communities in developing your writing skills.

Avoiding Bad Habits of Group Behavior

Over the years, most of us have developed certain bad habits that get in the way of efficient group work. Although we use groups all the time to study and accomplish demanding tasks, we tend to do so spontaneously and unreflectively without asking why some groups work and others don't. Many of us, for example, have worked on committees that just didn't get the job done and wasted our time, or else got the job done because one or two tyrannical people dominated the group. Just a couple of bad committee experiences can give us a healthy skepticism about the utility of groups in general. "A committee," according to some people, "is a sort of centipede. It has too many legs, no brain, and moves very slowly."

At their worst, this is indeed how groups function. In particular, they have a tendency to fail in two opposite directions, failures that can be avoided only by conscious effort. Groups can lapse into "clonethink" and produce a safe, superficial consensus whereby everyone agrees with the first opinion expressed in order to avoid conflict or to get on to something more interesting. At the other extreme is a phenomenon we'll call "egothink." In egothink, all members of the group go their own ways and produce a collection of minority views that have nothing to do with each other and would be impossible to act on. Clonethinkers view their task as conformity to a norm; egothinkers see their task as safeguarding the autonomy of individual group members. Both fail to take other people and other ideas seriously.

Successful groups avoid both extremes and achieve unity out of diversity. This means that any successful community of learners must be willing to endure creative conflict. Creative conflict results from an initial agreement to disagree respectfully with each other and to focus that disagreement on ideas, not people. For this reason, we say that the relationship among the members of a learning community is not so much interpersonal or impersonal as *transpersonal,* or "beyond the personal." Each member is personally committed to the development of ideas and does whatever is necessary to achieve that development.

The Value of Group Work for Writers

Because we are basically social animals, we find it natural, pleasurable even, to deal with problems in groups. Proof of this fact can be found on any given morning in any given student union in the country. Around the room you will find many students working in groups. Math, engineering, and business majors will be solving problems together, comparing solutions and their ways of arriving at solutions. Others will be comparing their class notes and testing their understanding of concepts and terms by explaining them to each other and comparing their explanations. Why not ease into the rigors of writing in a similar fashion?

A second major advantage of working on writing in a group is that it provides a real and immediate audience for people's work. Too often, when students write in a school setting, they get caught up in the writing-for-teacher racket, which may distort their notion of audience. Argumentative writing is best aimed either at people who disagree with you or at a neutral "jury" that will be weighing both sides of a controversy. A group of peers gives you a better sense of a real-world audience "out there" than does a single teacher.

There's danger, of course, in having several audiences consider your writing. Your peer audience may well respond differently to your writing than your instructor. You may feel misled if you are praised for something by a peer and then criticized for the same thing by your instructor. These things can and will happen, no matter how much time you spend developing universally accepted criteria for writing. Grades are not facts but judgments, and all judgments involve uncertainty. Students who are still learning the criteria for making judgments will sometimes apply those criteria differently than an instructor who has been working with them for years. But you should know too that two or more instructors may give you conflicting advice, just as two or more doctors may give you different advice on what to do about the torn ligaments in your knee. In our view, the risks of misunderstanding are more than made up for by gains in understanding of the writing process, an understanding that comes from working in writing communities where everyone functions both as a writer and as a writing critic.

A third advantage to working in writing communities is closely related to the second advantage. The act of sharing your writing with other people helps you get beyond the bounds of egocentrism that limit all writers. By egocentrism, we don't mean pride or stuck-upness; we mean the failure to consider the needs of your readers. Unless you share your writing with another person, your audience is always a "mythical group," a fiction or a theory that exists only in your head. You must always try to anticipate the problems others will have in reading your work. But until others actually read it and share their reactions to it with you, you can never be fully sure you have understood your audience's point of view. Until another reads your writing critically, you can't be sure you aren't talking to yourself.

Forming Writing Communities: Skills and Roles

Given that there are advantages to working in groups, just how do we go about forming writing communities in the classroom? We first have to decide how big to make the groups. From our experience, the best groups consist of either five to seven people or simply two people. Groups of three or four tend to polarize and become divisive, and larger groups tend to be unmanageable. Because working in five- to seven-person groups is quite different from working in pairs, we discuss each of these different-size groups in turn.

Working in Groups of Five to Seven People

The trick to successful group work is to consider the maximum number of viewpoints and concerns without losing focus. Because these two basic goals frequently conflict, you need some mechanisms for monitoring your progress. In particular, it's important that each group member is assigned to perform those tasks necessary to effective group functioning. (Some teachers assign roles to individual students, shifting the roles from day to day. Other teachers let the groups themselves determine the roles of individuals.) That is, the group must recognize that it has two objectives at all times: the stated objectives of a given task and the objective of making the group work well. It is very easy to get so involved with the given task that you overlook the second objective, generally known as "group maintenance."

Group Leader   The first role is group leader. We hesitate to call people who fill this role "leaders" because we tend sometimes to think of leaders as know-it-alls who take charge and order people about. In classroom group work, however, being a group leader is a role you play, not a fixed part of your identity. The leader, above all else, keeps the group focused on agreed-on ends and protects the right of every group member to be heard. It's an important function, and group members should share the responsibility from task to task. Here is a list of things for the leader to do during a group discussion:

1. Ensure that everyone understands and agrees on the objectives of any given task and on what sort of final product is expected of the group (for example, a list of criteria, a brief written statement, or an oral response to a question).
2. Ask that the group set an agenda for completing the task, and have some sense of how much time the group will spend at each stage. (Your instructor should always make clear what time limits you have to operate within and when he or she expects your task to be completed. If a time limit isn't specified, you should request a reasonable estimate.)
3. Look for signs of getting off track, and ask individual group members to clarify how their statements relate to agreed-on objectives.
4. Actively solicit everyone's contributions, and take care that all viewpoints are listened to and that the group does not rush to incomplete judgment.
5. Try to determine when the task has been adequately accomplished.

In performing each of these functions, the leader must learn diplomatic ways of facilitating a group. Instead of saying to one silent and bored-looking member of the group, "Hey, Irwin, you haven't said diddly-squat here so far," the leader might say, "Irwin, what's your view here? Do you agree with Beth that the paper is disorganized?" By giving Irwin a graceful way to join in, you will be expanding the number of voices in the group while helping this class member feel valued.

Group Recorder A second crucial role for well-functioning groups is that of recorder. The recorder's function is to provide the group with a record of their deliberations so they can measure their progress. It is particularly important that the recorder write down the agenda and the solution to the problem in precise form. Because the recorder must summarize the deliberations fairly precisely, he must ask for clarifications. In doing this, he ensures that group members don't fall into the "ya know?" syndrome (a subset of clonethink) in which people assent to statements that are in fact cloudy to them. (Ya know?) At the completion of the task, the recorder should also ask whether there are any significant remaining disagreements or unanswered questions. Finally, the recorder is responsible for reporting the group's solutions to the class as a whole.*

---

*There is a debate among experts who study small-group communications about whether the roles of leader and recorder can be collapsed into one job. Your group may need to experiment until it discovers the structure that works best for bringing out the most productive discussions.

Other Group Members   The rest of the group members, though they have no formally defined roles, have an equally important obligation to participate fully. To ensure full participation, group members can do several things. They can make sure that they know all the other group members by their first names and speak to them in a friendly manner. They can practice listening procedures wherein they try not to dissent or disagree without first charitably summarizing the view with which they are taking issue. Most important, they can bring to the group as much information and as many alternative points of view as they can muster. The primary intellectual strength of group work is the ability to generate a more complex view of a subject. But this more complex view cannot emerge unless all individuals contribute their perspectives.

Working in Pairs

Working in pairs is another effective form of community learning. In our classes we use pairs at both the early-draft and the late-draft stages of writing. At the early-draft stage, it serves the very practical purpose of clarifying a student's ideas and sense of direction at the beginning of a new writing project. The interaction best takes place in the form of pair interviews.

Before the First Draft   When you first sit down to interview each other, each of you should have done a fair amount of exploratory writing and thinking about what you want to say in your essay and how you're going to say it. Here is a checklist of questions you can use to guide your interview:

1. "What is your issue?" Your goal here is to help the writer focus an issue by formulating a question that clearly has alternative answers.
2. "What is your position on the issue, and what are alternative positions?" After you have helped your interviewee formulate the issue question, help her clarify this issue by stating her own position and showing how that position differs from opposing ones. Your interviewee may say, for example, that "many of my friends are opposed to building more nuclear power plants, but I think we need to build more of them."
3. "Who is your audience?" Your interviewee may say, "I am addressing this paper to neutral citizens who haven't yet made up their mind about nuclear power."
4. "Can you walk me through your argument step-by-step?" Once you know your interviewee's issue question and intended position, you can best help her by having her walk you through her argument, talking out loud. You can ask prompting questions such as "What are you going to say first?" or "What next?" At this stage your interviewee will probably still be struggling to discover the best way to support the point. You can best help by brainstorming along with her, both of you taking notes on your ideas. Often at this stage you can begin making a schematic plan for the essay and formulating supporting reasons as *because* clauses. Along the way, give your interviewee any information or ideas you have on the issue. It is particularly helpful at this stage if you can provide counterarguments and opposing views.

First Draft Stage   The interview strategy is useful before writers begin their rough drafts. After the first drafts have been written, there are a number of different ways of using pairs to evaluate drafts. One practice that we've found helpful is simply to have writers write a one-paragraph summary of their own drafts and of their partner's. In comparing summaries, writers can often discover which, if any, of their essential ideas are simply not getting across. If a major idea is not in the reader's summary, writer and reader need to decide whether it's due to a careless reading or to problems within the draft. The nice thing about this method is that the criticism is given indirectly and hence isn't as threatening to either party. At other times, your instructor may also devise a checklist of features for you to consider, based on the criteria you have established for the assignment.

Revision Stage   Another powerful strategy late in the writing process is to read your nearly final drafts aloud, either to your pair partner or to larger groups. Doing so is a chance to share the fruits of your labor with others and to hear finished essays that you may have seen in the draft stages. Hearing everyone else's nearly finished products can also help you get a clearer perspective on how your own work is progressing. Listening to the essays read can both reassure you that your work is on par with other people's and challenge you to write up to the level of the best student writing in your group. Your instructor will explain the process he or she finds most valuable for these late peer reviews.

Many of you may find this process a bit frightening at first. But the cause of your fright is precisely the source of the activity's value. In reading your work aloud, you are taking public responsibility for your words. The word has become deed. If you aren't at least a little nervous about reading an essay aloud, you probably haven't invested much in your words. Knowing that you will take public responsibility for your words is an incentive to make that investment—a more real and immediate incentive than grades.

■ ■ ■   **FOR CLASS DISCUSSION**   Working in a Group

This exercise asks you to participate in a thirty-minute small-group task and then to analyze and evaluate your group's process.

> **Part One—Small-group task:** As a small group, identify a significant problem on your campus that inhibits learning or the quality of student life (total time: thirty minutes). Your goal for this task is not to provide a solution to the problem but simply to understand the problem's causes and context and to persuade your audience that the problem is significant and worth solving. Your recorder should be prepared to present to the whole class your group's consensus answers to the following questions:
>
> - What is the problem?
> - What are the stakes in this problem? (For whom is it a problem? Why is it a problem for these people? Who suffers or what opportunities are lost? Give specific examples.)
> - What are the causes of this problem?

- Why hasn't this problem been solved up to this point?
- Who has the power to solve the problem?
- Why is this a significant problem worthy of people's attention?

Part Two—Evaluating your group's process *

a. Working individually (time: five minutes), each student should answer the following questions:

- Overall, how effectively did your group work together on this task? (poorly, adequately, well, extremely well)

- Out of the X members of your group (specify number), how many participated actively most of the time? (none, one, two, three, four, five, six, seven)

- Give one specific example of something you learned from the group or thought about that you probably wouldn't have learned or thought about working alone.

- Give one specific example of something the other group members learned from you or thought about because of your contribution to the discussion.

- Suggest one change the group could make to improve its performance.

b. As a group, share your individual answers to these questions.

c. Reach consensus on one or more things the group could do to improve its performance. Be prepared to report this consensus to the whole class.

Group Project: Holding a "Norming Session" to Define "Good Argumentative Writing"

In this next group task, your problem is to define and identify "good argumentative writing" by creating criteria for evaluating an argument. This is a particularly crucial problem for developing writers insofar as you can't begin to measure your growth as a writer until you have some notion of what you're aiming for. For this task you will rank-order five student essays from best to worst according to criteria you establish within your small groups. College professors use this process regularly (often known as a "norming session") to determine criteria for grading student essays for large-scale assessment projects.

Task 1 (Homework): Preparing for the Group Discussion   Read the five student essays on pages 417–422. These essays were written early in an argument course. Students were asked to develop two or three reasons in support of a claim. Students had studied the argumentative concepts in Chapters 1–6 but had not yet studied

*The questions for this task are adapted from Elizabeth F. Barkely, K. Patricia Cross, and Claire Howell Major, *Collaborative Learning Techniques: A Handbook for College Faculty* (San Francisco: Jossey-Bass, 2005), 93.

refutation strategies. Although the students were familiar with classical argument structure, this introductory assignment did not ask them to summarize and respond to opposing views. The instructor's focus was only on students' developing some good reasons in support of a contestable claim.

After you have looked over the five student essays, concentrate for this task on "Bloody Ice" and "Legalization of Prostitution." Which of these two arguments is the better one? Freewrite your reasons for selecting the better argument, focusing on specific details of what you liked in the better essay and what you saw as problems in the weaker essay. (Note: Both essays have strengths and weaknesses, so you aren't trying to argue that one is excellent and the other is totally awful; you are just trying to determine which of the two more nearly meets the criteria for "good argumentative writing.") When you have finished your freewrite, develop a list of the criteria you used to make your judgment. You will be sharing this list with your classmates.

Task 2 (In-Class Group Work): Developing a Master List of Criteria   As a group, share your evaluations of "Bloody Ice" and "Legalization of Prostitution." Then try to reach group consensus on which of these two is the better essay and why. As a group, justify your evaluation by making a list of criteria you used and a rationale for rating some criteria more important than others. For example, does "quality of reasons" rank higher than "organization and development"? Does "use of evidence" rank higher than "lively style"? Your instructor may then ask each group to report its rankings to the whole class. The goal in this case is to create a class consensus about the two essays along with a master list of criteria.

Task 3 (Homework or Individual In-Class Time): Applying the Criteria to All Five Essays   Read again all five of the essays and rank-order them 1 to 5, best to worst, using the criteria developed during the previous discussions. Freewrite your rationale for ranking each essay as you did.

Task 4 (In-Class Group Work): Reaching Consensus on Ranking of Essays   Your goal now is to reach consensus on how you rank the essays and why you rank them the way you do. Feel free to change the criteria you established earlier if they seem to need some modification. Be careful in your discussions to distinguish between evaluation of the writer's written product and your own personal position on the writer's issue. In other words, there is a crucial difference between saying, "I don't like LeShawn's essay because I disagree with his claim" versus saying, "I don't like LeShawn's essay because he didn't provide adequate evidence to support several of his reasons." As each group reports the results of its deliberations to the whole class, the instructor will highlight discrepancies among the groups' decisions and collate the criteria as they emerge. If the instructor disagrees with the class consensus or wants to add items to the criteria, he or she may choose to make these things known at this time. By the end of this stage, everyone should have a list of criteria for good argumentative writing established by the class.

Bloody Ice

It is March in Alaska. The ocean-side environment is full of life and death. Man and animal share this domain but not in peace. The surrounding iceflows, instead of being cold and white, are steaming from the remains of gutted carcasses and stained red. The men are hunters and the animals are barely six weeks old. A slaughter has just taken place. Thousands of baby harp seals lie dead on the ice and thousands more adult mothers lie groaning over the death of their babies. Every year a total limit of 180,000 seals set by the U.S. Seal Protection Act is filled in a terrifying bloodbath. But Alaska with its limit of 30,000 is not alone. Canadians who hunt seals off the coast of Northern Newfoundland and Quebec are allowed 150,000 seals. The Norwegians are allowed 20,000 and native Eskimos of Canada and Greenland are allowed 10,000 seals per year. Although this act appears heartless and cruel, the men who hunt have done this for 200 years as a tradition for survival. They make many good arguments supporting their traditions. They feel the seals are in no immediate danger of extinction. Also seal furs can be used to line boots and gloves or merely traded for money and turned into robes or fur coats. Sometimes the meat is even used for food in the off hunting months when money is scarce. But are these valid justifications for the unmerciful killings? No, the present limit on harp seal killings should be better regulated because the continued hunting of the seals will lead to eventual extinction and because the method of slaughter is so cruel and inhumane.

The harp seal killing should be better regulated first because eventual extinction is inevitable. According to *Oceans* magazine, before the limit of 180,000 seals was established in 1950, the number of seals had dwindled from 3,300,000 to 1,250,000. Without these limitations hundreds of thousands were killed within weeks of birth. Now, even with this allotment, the seals are being killed off at an almost greater rate than they can remultiply. Adult female seals give birth once every year but due to pollution, disease, predation, whelping success, and malnutrition they are already slowly dying on their own without being hunted. Eighty percent of the seals slaughtered are pups and the remaining twenty percent are adult seals and even sometimes mothers who try attacking the hunters after seeing their babies killed. The hunters, according to the Seal Protection Act, have this right.

Second, I feel the killing should be better regulated because of the inhumane method used. In order to protect the fur value of the seals, guns are not used. Instead, the sealers use metal clubs to bludgeon the seal to death. Almost immediately after being delivered a direct blow, the seals are gutted open and skinned. Although at this stage of life the seal's skull is very fragile, sometimes the seals are not killed by the blows but merely stunned; thus hundreds are skinned alive. Still others are caught in nets and drowned, which, according to

America magazine, the Canadian government continues to deny. But the worst of the methods used is when a hunter gets tired of swinging his club and uses the heel of his boot to kick the seal's skull in. Better regulation is the only way to solve this problem because other attempts seem futile. For example, volunteers who have traveled to hunting sites trying to dye the seals to ruin their fur value have been caught and fined heavily.

The plight of the harp seals has been long and controversial. With the Canadian hunters feeling they have the right to kill the seals because it has been their industry for over two centuries, and on the other hand with humane organizations fearing extinction and strongly opposing the method of slaughter, a compromise must be met among both sides. As I see it, the solution to the problem is simple. Since the Canadians do occasionally use the whole seal and have been sealing for so long they could be allowed to continue but at a more heavily regulated rate. Instead of filling the limit of 180,000 every year and letting the numbers of seals decrease, Canadians could learn to ranch the seals as Montanans do cattle or sheep. The United States has also offered to help them begin farming their land for a new livelihood. The land is adequate for crops and would provide work all year round instead of only once a month every year. As a result of farming, the number of seals killed would be drastically cut down because Canadians would not be so dependent on the seal industry as before. This would in turn lead back to the ranching aspect of sealing and allow the numbers to grow back and keeping the tradition alive for future generations and one more of nature's creatures to enjoy.

RSS Should Not Provide Dorm Room Carpets

Tricia, a University student, came home exhausted from her work- study job. She took a blueberry pie from the refrigerator to satisfy her hunger and a tall glass of milk to quench her thirst. While trying to get comfortable on her bed, she tipped her snack over onto the floor. She cleaned the mess, but the blueberry and milk stains on her brand new carpet could not be removed. She didn't realize that maintaining a clean carpet would be difficult and costly. Tricia bought her own carpet. Some students living in dorm rooms want carpeted rooms provided for them at the expense of the University. They insist that since they pay to live on campus, the rooms should reflect a comfortable home atmosphere. However, Resident Student Services (RSS) should not be required to furnish the carpet because other students do not want carpets. Furthermore, carpeting all the rooms totals into a very expensive project. And lastly, RSS should not have to provide the carpet because many students show lack of respect and responsibility for school property.

Although RSS considers the carpeting of all rooms a strong possibility, students like Tricia oppose the idea. They feel the students should buy their own carpets. Others claim the permanent carpeting would make dorm life more comfortable. The carpet will act as insulation and as a soundproofing system. These are valid arguments, but they should not be the basis for changing the entire residence hall structure. Those students with "cold feet" can purchase house footwear, which cost less than carpet. Unfortunately carpeting doesn't muffle all the noise; therefore, some students will be disturbed. Reasonable quietness should be a matter of respect for other students' privacy and comfort. Those opposed to the idea reason out the fact that students constantly change rooms or move out. The next person may not want carpet. Also, if RSS carpets the rooms, the students will lose the privilege they have of painting their rooms any color. Paint stains cannot be removed. Some students can't afford to replace the carpet. Still another factor, carpet color, may not please everyone. RSS would provide a neutral color like brown or gray. With tile floors, the students can choose and purchase their own carpets to match their taste.

Finally, another reason not to have carpet exists in the fact that the project can be expensive due to material costs, installation cost, and the maintenance cost caused mainly by the irresponsibility of many students. According to Rick Jones, Asst. Director of Housing Services, the cost will be $300 per room for the carpet and installation. RSS would also have to purchase more vacuum cleaners for the students' use. RSS will incur more expense in order to maintain the vacuums. Also, he claims that many accidents resulting from shaving cream fights, food fights, beverage parties, and smoking may damage the carpet permanently. With floor tiles, accidents such as food spills can be cleaned up easier than carpet. The student's behavior plays an important role in deciding against carpeting. Many students don't follow the rules of maintaining their rooms. They drill holes into the walls, break mirrors, beds, and closet doors, and leave their food trays all over the floor. How could they be trusted to take care of school carpet when they violate the current rules? Many students feel they have the "right" to do as they please. This irresponsible and disrespectful behavior reflects their future attitude about carpet care.

In conclusion, the university may be able to afford to supply the carpets in each room, but maintaining them would be difficult. If the students want carpets, they should pay and care for the carpets themselves. Hopefully, they will be more cautious and value it more. They should take the initiative to fundraise or find other financial means of providing this "luxury." They should not rely on the school to provide unnecessary room fixtures such as carpets. Also, they must remember that if RSS provides the carpet and they don't pay for the damages, they and future students will endure the consequences. What will happen???? Room rates will skyrocket!!!!!

Sterling Hall Dorm Food

The quality of Sterling Hall dorm food does not meet the standard needed to justify the high prices University students pay. As I watched a tall, medium-built University student pick up his Mexican burrito from the counter it didn't surprise me to see him turn up his nose. Johnny, our typical University student, waited five minutes before he managed to make it through the line. After he received his bill of $8.50 he turned his back to the cash register and walked away displeased with his meal.

As our neatly groomed University student placed his ValiDine eating card back into his Giorgio wallet, he thought back to the balance left on his account. Johnny had $24 left on his account and six more weeks left of school. He had been eating the cheapest meals he could and still receive a balanced meal, but the money just seemed to disappear. No student, not even a thrifty boy like Johnny, could possibly afford to live healthfully according to the University meal plan system.

Johnny then sat down at a dirty table to find his burrito only halfway cooked. Thinking back to the long-haired cook who served him the burrito, he bit into the burrito and noticed a long hair dangling from his lips. He realized the cook's lack of preparation when preparing his burrito.

Since the food costs so much, yet the quality of the food remains low, University students do not get the quality they deserve. From the information stated I can conclude that using the ValiDine service system University students would be jeopardizing their health and wasting their hard-earned money. University students deserve something more than what they have now.

ROTC Courses Should Not Get College Credit

One of the most lucrative scholarships a student can receive is a four-year ROTC scholarship that pays tuition and books along with a living allowance. It was such a scholarship that allowed me to attend an expensive liberal arts college and to pursue the kind of well-rounded education that matters to me. Of course, I am obligated to spend four years on active duty—an obligation that I accept and look forward to. What I am disappointed in, however, is the necessity to enroll in Military Science classes. Strong ROTC advocates argue that Military Science classes are essential because they produce good citizens, teach leadership skills, and provide practical experience for young cadets. Maybe so. But we could get the same benefits without having to take these courses for credit. Colleges should make ROTC training an extracurricular activity, not a series of academic courses taken for academic credit.

First of all, ROTC courses, unlike other college courses, do not stress inquiry and true questioning. The ROTC program has as its objective the preparation of future officers committed to the ideals and structure of the military. The structure of the military is based upon obediently following the orders of military superiors. Whereas all my other teachers stress critical thinking and doing independent analysis, my ROTC instructors avoid political or social questions saying it is the job of civilian leaders to debate policies and the job of the military to carry them out. We don't even debate what role the military should play in our country. My uncle, who was an ROTC cadet during the Vietnam war, remembers that not only did ROTC classes never discuss the ethics of the war but that cadets were not allowed to protest the war outside of their ROTC courses. This same obedience is demanded in my own ROTC courses, where we are not able to question administration policies and examine openly the complexity of the situation in Iraq and Afghanistan.

A second reason that Army ROTC courses do not deserve academic credit is that the classes are not academically strenuous, thus giving cadets a higher GPA and an unfair advantage over their peers. Much of what a cadet does for academic credit involves nonacademic activities such as physical training for an hour three days a week so that at least some of a cadet's grade is based on physical activity, not mental activity. In conducting an informal survey of 10 upperclassmen, I found out that none of them has ever gotten anything lower than an A in a Military Science class and they do not know of anyone who got anything lower than an A. One third-year cadet stated that "the classes are basic. A monkey coming out of the zoo could get college credit for a Military Science class." He went on to say that most of the information given in his current class is a brush-up to 8th grade U.S. history. In contrast, a typical liberal arts college class requires much thought, questioning, and analysis. The ROTC Military Science class is taught on the basis of "regurgitated knowledge," meaning that once you are given a piece of information you are required to know it and reproduce it at any time without thought or question. A good example is in my class Basic Officership. Our first assignment is to memorize and recite in front of the class the Preamble to the Constitution of the United States. The purpose of doing so doesn't seem to be to understand or analyze the Constitution because we never talk about that. In fact, I don't know what the purpose is. I just do it because I am told to. Because the "A" is so easy to get in my ROTC class, I spend all my time studying for my other classes. I am a step ahead of my peers in the competition for a high GPA, even though I am not getting as good an education.

Finally, having to take ROTC classes means that I can't take other liberal arts courses which would be more valuable. One of the main purposes for ROTC is to give potential officers a liberal education. Many cadets have the credentials to get into an armed forces academy, but they chose ROTC programs because they could combine military training with a well-rounded curriculum. Unfortunately, by taking Military Science classes each quarter, cadets find that their electives are all but eaten up by the time they are seniors. If ROTC classes were valuable in themselves, I wouldn't complain. But they aren't, and they keep me from taking upper division electives in philosophy, literature, and the humanities.

5   All of these reasons lead me to believe that Army ROTC cadets are getting shortchanged when they enroll for Military Science classes. Because cadets receive a lucrative scholarship, they should have to take the required military science courses. But these courses should be treated as extracurricular activities, like a work-study job or like athletics. Just as a student on a full-ride athletic scholarship does not receive academic credit for football practices and games, so should a student on a full-ride ROTC scholarship have to participate in the military education program without getting academic credit. By treating ROTC courses as a type of extracurricular activity like athletics, students can take more elective credits that will expand their minds, better enabling them to have the knowledge to make moral decisions and to enjoy their world more fully.

Legalization of Prostitution

Prostitution...It is the world's oldest profession. It is by definition the act of offering or soliciting sex for payment. It is, to some, evil. Yet the fact is it exists.

Arguments are not necessary to prove the existence of prostitution. Rather, the argument arises when trying to prove something must be done to reduce the problems of this profession. The problems which exist are in the area of crime, of health, and of environment. Crime rates are soaring, diseases are spreading wildly, and the environment on the streets is rapidly decaying. Still, it has been generally conceded that these problems cannot be suppressed. However, they can be reduced. Prostitution should be legalized because it would reduce the wave of epidemics, decrease high crime rates, provide good revenue by treating it like other businesses, and get girls off the streets where sexual crimes often occur.

Of course, there are those who would oppose the legalization of prostitution stating that it is one of the main causes for the spread of venereal diseases. Many argue that it is interrelated with drug trafficking and other organized crimes. And probably the most controversial is the moral aspect of the subject; it is morally wrong, and legalizing it would be enforcing, or even justifying, such an existence.

These points propose good arguments, but I shall counter each point and explain the benefits and advantages of legalizing prostitution. In the case of prostitution being the main cause for the spread of epidemics, I disagree. By legalizing it, houses would be set up which would solve the problem of girls working on the streets and being victims of sexual crimes. It would also provide regular health checks, as is successfully done in Nevada, Germany, and other parts of the United States and Europe, which will therefore cut down on diseases spreading unknowingly.

5   As for the increase of organized crime if prostitution is legalized, I disagree again. Firstly, by treating it like businesses, then that would make good state revenue. Secondly, like all businesses have regulations, so shall these houses. That would put closer and better control in policing the profession, which is presently a problem. Obviously, if the business of prostitution is more closely supervised, that would decrease the crime rates.

Now, I come to one of the most arguable aspects of legalizing prostitution: the moral issue. Is it morally wrong to legalize prostitution? That is up to the individual. To determine whether anything is "right or wrong" in our society is nearly impossible to do since there are various opinions. If a person were to say that prostitution is the root of all evil, that will not make it go away. It exists. Society must begin to realize that fear or denial will not make the "ugliness" disappear. It still exists.

Prostitution can no longer go ignored because of our societal attitudes. Legalizing it is beneficial to our society, and I feel in time people may begin to form an accepting attitude. It would be the beginning of a more open-minded view of what is reality. Prostitution...it is the world's oldest profession. It exists. It is a reality.

PART SIX

An Anthology
of Arguments

Reminding viewers of the inconvenience of heightened airport security since 9/11, this political cartoon humorously suggests that the war on terrorism may have compromised our civil liberties.

Source: Kirk Anderson, www.kirktoons.com

An Overview of the Anthology

Part Six, an anthology of engaging verbal and visual arguments addressing ten important issues, will let you put into practice your new skills of reading and analyzing arguments, conducting inquiry, and joining an argumentative conversation. As we discussed in Chapter 2, writers of arguments come from all walks of life and produce arguments from multiple social contexts within many communities in society. They may be ordinary citizens, members of advocacy groups or lobbyists, media commentators, professional staff writers for magazines and newspapers, scholars and academics, or other kinds of stakeholders within workplaces, neighborhoods, or civic or cultural organizations. Motivated by some occasion, these stakeholders write to an audience for a purpose within a genre, their rhetorical situations influencing their decisions about content, structure, and style.

We chose the articles in this anthology to show this rich variety of argumentative occasions, the multisided nature of argument, and the complexity of issues. The arguments you encounter here represent distinctly divergent angles of vision, different ways of conceptualizing controversies, and different argumentative strategies to influence readers' views and to win over decision makers. Passionate in their own ways, these stakeholders also differ in their commitment to persuasion versus truth-seeking, thereby creating differences in style, tone, and treatment of alternative views. In addition, faced with different rhetorical contexts and purposes, these writers create arguments in many genres: short opinion-editorials, academic arguments grounded in research, advocacy Web sites, public speeches, white papers to set forth the views and policy proposals of organizations, and a rich array of visual arguments, from public affairs advocacy ads, to poster arguments and fliers, to political cartoons and commercial advertisements.

To help you understand the cultural context for each set of readings, we have provided brief introductions to each unit, headnotes for each article, and a concluding set of discussion questions that urge you to see the complexity of the issue and the consequences of different claims. The introductions to each unit sketch key points of background, provide context, and suggest the cultural significance of the issue. The headnotes to each article give original publication data, identify the genre of the piece, and, in most cases, briefly identify the writer and the political perspective.* We encourage you to continue this contextualizing process by using the guide questions we provide in the next section. Finally, we encourage you to consider the class discussion questions at the end of each unit to help you appreciate the multisided views of stakeholders and to acknowledge the consequences, strengths, and limitations of different claims.

As you read through the arguments in this anthology, note how current topical issues (such as whether the federal government should require labeling of genetically engineered food) touch on broad, enduring questions about cultural values such as the rights of consumers versus the rights of corporations. No matter what the specific

---

*For full citation information, see the Credits at the back of the book.

issue is, certain recurring patterns of concern keep cropping up, such as principles versus consequences, spiritual values versus material values, rights of individuals versus rights of society, duties to self versus duties to others, short-range consequences versus long-range consequences, or tradition versus change. One advantage of an anthology of arguments is that in reading through them you can see for yourself how frequently these large issues recur in different guises.

In creating this anthology, we had in mind two main ways you might approach these readings. First, we invite you to enter these argumentative conversations yourself. After listening to and responsibly weighing the alternative views, you will face the responsibility of synthesizing various perspectives to create your own argument for a new context. Often you will need to do more research in order to clarify your views and take a stand. By eliciting your questions and enlarging your perspective—the process of dissent and synthesis at the heart of argument—the arguments in this anthology can challenge you to speak out on your own on these controversies.

A second way to approach these arguments—and one that can be combined with the first way—is to examine these articles for their wide variety of argumentative strategies to see how they can expand your repertoire as an arguer. In studying these arguments, you should ask questions like these: What works or doesn't work to make this argument persuasive? Why might a given argument be effective for its intended audience but not for some other audience? What can this argument teach me about presenting a positive *ethos,* about treating opposing views, about successful uses of evidence, or about appealing to *pathos*? Learning more about your options can empower you as a writer of arguments.

Guide Questions for the Analysis and Evaluation of Arguments

To help you develop skills at analyzing and evaluating arguments, we provide in this section three handy checklists of guide questions. These questions summarize the key principles of argument we have covered throughout the text.

List 1: Questions for Analyzing and Evaluating a Conversation

Whenever you read two or more arguments addressing the same issue, we recommend that you follow the principles of reading described in Chapter 2.

1. What does each argument say? (Reading as a believer, be able to summarize each argument, stating its main claim and supporting reasons in a single sentence if possible.)
2. How can each argument be doubted? (Reading as a doubter, search for weaknesses in the argument, think about what is left out, and articulate important questions that you would like to raise if you could talk to the author.)
3. How have the rhetorical context and genre shaped each argument?

4. Why do the disputants disagree? (Do they disagree about the facts of the case? Do they differ in the selection or interpretation of the facts or other data they use for evidence? Do they disagree about values, assumptions, and beliefs?)

5. Which arguments appear to be stronger? (Which arguments seem most persuasive to you? Before you could take a stand on the issue yourself, what further questions would you need to have answered? Which of your own assumptions, values, and beliefs would you have to examine further and clarify?)

List 2: Questions for Analyzing and Evaluating an Individual Argument Rhetorically

The previous questions ask you to examine arguments in the context of the conversations to which they belong. This next set of questions asks you to look closely at a single argument, examining in detail its structure, its argumentative strategies, and its rhetorical force.

1. What is the writer's purpose and audience?
   - Who are the intended readers? What are their values and beliefs?
   - How does the writer hope to change the intended readers' views on the issue?
   - What was the occasion for writing? What motivated the writer to produce this piece?
2. What genre is the piece?
   - Where was this piece published?
   - How does the genre of the piece—or its place of publication—influence its content, point of view, or style?
   - How can certain features of the text be explained by genre?
3. What seems to be the writer's perspective, bias, or angle of vision?
   - What does the text reveal about the author's values and beliefs?
   - What does the author omit?
   - How committed is the author to his or her claim?
   - What views does the author oppose? Why?
4. Does the argument have a strong logical core?
   - What is the writer's claim? Where is it explicitly stated or where is it implied?
   - What are the main reasons in support of the claim? Are the reasons audience-based?
5. How effective is the writer's use of evidence?
   - Is the evidence relevant, sufficient, and appropriately up-to-date?
   - Does the evidence come from reputable sources?
   - What kind of evidence is used?
   - How is the argument reasonably supported and developed? Are there any obvious flaws or fallacies in the argument?
6. How effective is the writer at making ethical appeals?
   - What *ethos* does the writer project?
   - How does the writer try to seem credible and trustworthy to the intended audience?

7. How effective is the writer at creating pathetic appeals?
   - How effective is the writer at using audience-based reasons?
   - How effective is the writer's use of concrete language, word choice, examples, and analogies for giving the argument emotional presence?
8. How could the writer's argument be refuted?
   - Can the writer's reasons and grounds be called into question?
   - Can the writer's warrants and backing be called into question?
9. If used, how effective are the author's use of images, graphics, or other visuals?
   - Why did the author choose or design these particular images, graphics, or visuals?
   - How do font sizes and styles, the layout of images and text, and the use of color contribute to the effectiveness of the visual?
   - How does the composition of images—such as setting, props, clothing, poses of characters, and so forth—contribute to the effectiveness of the visual?
   - How are graphics used to tell a particular story with numbers? Why does the author focus on this particular story rather than another story?

List 3: Questions for Responding to a Reading and Forming Your Own Views

This final set of questions is designed to help you speak back to a text in order to form your own views.

1. Which of the author's points do you agree with?
2. What new insights has the reading given you?
3. Which of the author's points do you disagree with?
4. What gaps or omissions do you see in the text? What has the author overlooked?
5. What questions or problems does the text raise for you? How has it troubled you or expanded your views?
6. In terms of your own evolving views on this issue, how useful is this reading? How might you use it in your own argument?

Web 2.0 and Online Identity

Over the short but remarkable history of the Internet, its uses and consequently the sources of controversies related to it have evolved. In the early days—incredibly, less than two decades ago—the most common uses of the Internet were consumption based: We downloaded information and received email. Internet controversies were consumption oriented as well: Is it legal to download or share music files? What copyright laws apply to Internet content? How do users avoid receiving unsolicited spam, pornography, and viruses? While some of these issues remain, many have been addressed: Following the highly publicized prosecution of college students caught file sharing illegally, young people began to buy inexpensive music and download it to their computers and portable devices; Internet service providers now use effective spam and virus blocking technologies that quarantine damaging emails, and so on.

Meanwhile, especially among younger people, the Internet allows increasing collaboration, permitting users to create and upload content easily and to make that content accessible to others around the globe. This next generation of the World Wide Web has been dubbed "Web 2.0," a name attributed to software mogul Tim O'Reilly, who defines it as "the new participatory version of the Web" that supports the sharing of content through blogs (web logs), vlogs (video logs), wikis (sites that allow all users to create and alter content), photo and video uploading sites such as *Flickr* and *YouTube*, and social networking spaces such as *MySpace* and *Facebook*. Such options offer exciting opportunities for users to create and share text, graphic, video, and audio content. Not surprisingly, these options have created their own controversies, particularly surrounding content authenticity, user privacy and safety, and online identities.

The readings, cartoon, and photograph in this unit ask you to consider the following questions: How is Web 2.0 changing how we read and write, especially for young people? What are the implications for educators of these changes? What are the ethics of creating false content or fictional identities online? Should such creations be considered "art"? What are the dangers of widespread access to personal information, and what should be the role of colleges and other institutions in protecting users who post such information? Your analysis of the readings in this unit will be enriched by your self-reflections on your own use of the Internet.

"Tomorrow Will Not Be Like Today": Literacy and Identity in a World of Multiliteracies

BRONWYN T. WILLIAMS

Bronwyn T. Williams is an Associate Professor in the Department of English at the University of Louisville, Kentucky. He researches and writes on issues of literacy and popular culture. He has also written a regular column on literacy and identity for the Journal of Adolescent and Adult Literacy, *in which this article appeared as his last column in May 2008. In it, he suggests that rapidly changing technologies have altered students' literacy practices and allowed them to play with identities in ways that have implications for classroom teaching.*

Five years ago, when I began writing this column, the following either hadn't been invented or were not yet widely in use: *MySpace, Facebook, YouTube, Second Life, Pandora,* iPhones, and cellphone cameras. This list is only a small portion of the technologies that have changed the way young people communicate in the last five years, and five years from now the items on my list might be obsolete memories (anyone remember *Friendster?*). I've always tended to be skeptical of dramatic claims of change whether they are social or technological. I'm old enough to have seen true change as a more incremental process—easier to recognize in hindsight than as it is happening. Yet the change in communication technologies that seems to happen almost daily is both real and dramatic in the ways it is changing how young people read and write with words and images. Consider this statement from a young adolescent girl about her routine online practices:

> Sarah and I go home and she calls me on the phone when she's ready to log on later. We keep the phone conversations going while we log on and decide where to go. We're always on the talker, but sometimes we go idle to visit other places. I keep telling dad I need a bigger monitor, because I end up with so many windows open that I can't always follow what's going on in each one. Then we do about six different things at the same time. We'll have my talker open, our ICQ on, we have the role-playing MOO we've just joined open, we have our homework open (which I'm pleased to report, we both get done at the end of the night, and it's soooo much more fun doing it this way!), we have the palace open, we have our own private conversation windows open for different friends and we have our phone conversations going on at the same time. (Thomas, 2007, p. 167)

Many of the adolescents I talk with describe their lives in similar ways (and if you don't understand all the references and abbreviations, that is just another example of the differences between generations). There seem to be few ways of escaping the fact that we are living through a moment in which literacy practices are being fundamentally altered. Kress (1997) said, "We know that tomorrow will not be like today. That is one of the few certainties of the present period. We can perceive only dimly what the day after that tomorrow is likely to be like" (p. 157). Such changes are in some ways quite heartening; today's online technologies have young people reading and writing far more than they were 20 years or even a decade ago. Words are an integral part of today's online world, along with images and sound, and young people read and write thousands of words online each week. For many adolescents, "life on the screen is an everyday, natural practice—they know no other way of being" (Kress, 1997, p. 167). At the same time, the online world in which they read and write is a fast, multitasking, multi-literate world that seems disconcerting and overwhelming to many teachers and parents.

It is clear that the changes in literacy practices created by rapidly evolving, online technologies have many implications for how we teach reading and writing. My interest in this column, as always, is how these changes alter issues of identity as well as how they create new challenges when students read and write.

Playing with Online Identities

One of the more intriguing developments has been the way online technologies allow young people to manipulate and play with their identities. The idea that individuals can create online personas that are in some ways different from the way they present themselves in their face-to-face encounters is well known. The idea was even parodied in a popular cartoon from the early 1990s, reminding us that "on the Internet, nobody knows you're a dog" (Steiner, 1993). In some ways, however, this creation of a particular identity in writing is as old as literacy itself. Novelists, playwrights, and other writers have been creating identities on the page for hundreds of years. The difference in writing online is not in the ability to create a new persona, it is in the ease with which that writing can be distributed to an audience of readers and that such an audience may very well write back.

5   With the advent of both online technologies and an increasing number of young people with their own computers, the days when people write only for an audience of teachers or nearby friends are over. Our students can now compose material that is instantly available to a global audience.

What's more, students can create and maintain a variety of these texts and personas for a variety of different audiences. As Thomas (2007) noted about the young girl previously quoted, her "transition between roles is quick and spontaneous, and as for many young people like her, she is able to engage in multiple scripts, playing multiple roles (both online and offline) simultaneously" (p. 168). For example, the students I talk with often have personal pages on several of the popular social networking sites such as *MySpace* and *Facebook* and also participate in discussion forums, online games, and interactive fan fiction. For those not familiar with social networking sites (and all literacy teachers should be), they allow users to create personal pages that display photographs, lists of favorite movies and music, pop culture images and videos, blogs, and other information. These pages can then be linked to the pages of friends, and messages can be sent around the social network. The page a person composes, then, has very real consequences for the kinds of responses that people offer when reading the page. The identities students perform on each different website may be quite different from one another. The creation and revision of each personal page is up to the student. She or he must engage in complex rhetorical choices, often many times a day, about how to portray her or his identity to a real audience. If identity is a matter of matching our performance of self to the appropriate cultural context, then these young people are negotiating such moments daily through writing and reading. As a consequence, they are gaining literacy experiences in issues of identity and audience that are far more complex than previous generations.

The interactive nature of online reading and writing makes clear how misplaced the concern is that young people sitting at their computers for hours on end are always socially isolated. Instead, they may very well be communicating with people they know in a variety of different social contexts and locations with a variety of literacy practices. (Indeed, the online social interactions of young people raise a different set of concerns that may be legitimate but are not the focus of this column.) In teaching reading and writing, we have come to accept that literacy is not a standalone set of skills but social practices influenced by context and culture. It is important that we recognize how real and rich the experiences of many young people are in negotiating different identities in different social situations online.

Composing a Performance of Self

A number of scholars have discovered (Black, 2007; Davies, 2006; Thomas, 2007) that young people today are learning by experience how to enter a new community through their reading and writing. They quickly figure out through trial and error and observation how to refer to themselves, what kinds of comments are appropriate for the context, how best to establish a convincing ethos, how to determine whose comments and ideas they can trust, and many other complex rhetorical and literacy practices that we want very much for them to learn in school. For example, young people engage in online discussion groups covering subjects from television programs to relationships to computer technology. Upon entering these groups, they not only need to understand the general textual conventions that govern these groups but also to figure out the context-specific customs of messages and responses for each group. Learning to negotiate such literacy situations teaches students valuable lessons about reading and writing. Davies (2006) maintained, "The development of self within communities…involves a sense of empowerment. As a sense of writing the self develops, a sense of possibility as an active agent in one's own life emerges" (p. 227). If, as Gee (2004) argued, literacy skills are learned through this kind of experience and acquisition more thoroughly than through direct instruction then it is essential that we pay more attention to how our students are creating their online identities through reading and writing.

To say that writing online allows students to create different identities is not to say that the identity issues that shape our daily lives—such as race, gender, social class, religion, ethnicity, or sexual orientation—disappear completely in the virtual world. Although such forces may manifest themselves in ways that are less familiar to those who don't spend as much time online, the same cultural contexts that influence our other literacy practices are at work when any of us are online. For example, much of the reading and writing that young people do online is either concerned with or connected to popular culture. The websites they visit and the online discussions they are involved in are, more often than not, connected to movies, music, television programs, and video games. Their *MySpace* and *Facebook* pages are covered in popular culture images and references. Students I have talked with tell me that the song a person has playing on a *MySpace* page, or the list of that person's favorite movies, may be a decisive factor in determining whether to interact with the person online. In fact, some scholars (Jenkins, 2006; Livingstone, 2002) have pointed out that popular culture is one of the most powerful organizing forces in determining where young people go online and with whom they interact.

10   When asked how they determine their popular cultural preferences, young people (and for that matter many older people) often shrug the question off as a matter of individual taste. Yet our taste in popular culture is not innate but learned from the culture around us. And, like all the culture around us, what we learn, both online and in the face-to-face world, is influenced by social constructions of identity such as gender, ethnicity, and class. Students may not be thinking about how they are portraying themselves in terms of gender or social class when they put together their *MySpace* pages or post on discussion forums. Yet they are negotiating their identities in these virtual spaces in the contexts of social forces. Their decisions to put images of Orlando Bloom or Jessica Alba on *MySpace* pages or to list songs by hip-hop artists or teen pop bands shape the identities they perform on-line and how those identities are read by others.

New Conversations in the Classroom

Regardless of our personal feelings toward online communication, we must think seri-ously about how identity figures into the literacy practices of students. Many of them spend much more time reading and writing online than they do in the classroom. The most important thing we can do is talk with our students about how and why they read and write online. What I'm advocating is not a lecture about how much better it would be to read a novel than a blog but a respectful and extended dialogue about what sites they visit, how they make sense of the material on those sites, and what they write in any online setting. We need to find out from them what rhetorical and literacy practices they have learned when reading and writing in diverse online settings from one day to the next. Of course, we must be prepared for students to be initially hesitant to engage in such a conversation. They've been told too often that their online activities are a waste of time, and they may be understandably reluctant to volunteer such information until we convince them that we are not out to scold them. Students may also not talk about their online literacy practices in the academic language we recognize. If we listen closely we will find that their experiences and resulting knowledge may surprise us and offer new opportunities for connecting our pedagogies with their lives.

If we talk to students and let them show us what they read and write online not only can we discover how much our students may have learned about traditional literacy concepts, but also we can get a better understanding of the social skills students have learned online, such as collaboration and knowledge sharing. We can take that knowledge and build on it to teach both traditional practices of reading and writing and new literacy practices such as appropriation of media content, networking, negotiation of social contexts, and working with multiple media (Jenkins, 2006).

As one example, teachers could start a class *MySpace* page and ask students to collabo-rate on how the class will chose to represent itself, how it will determine audience concerns, how best to combine multiple media, and so on. This exercise in the classroom would also help students rethink their activities outside of class. Or, when engaging in a research project, students could each keep a wiki in which they build their knowledge of a subject using multiple media. (A wiki is software that allows users to create, edit, and link collaborative websites.) Each student then could visit and contribute to the wikis of other students in the class, building their collaborative literacy skills.

Innovation in the Classroom

These ideas for activities offer only the slightest glimpse of what can be accomplished in the literacy classroom through the use of online technologies. Many other teachers and scholars around the world are creating innovative pedagogical strategies in their classrooms every day. The strategies teachers are trying with their students and the knowledge that students are bringing to the classroom from their daily experiences emphasize the necessity of an ongoing, open-minded conversation about the ways in which evolving online technologies are changing literacy practices.

The changing world of new technologies can be unnerving to me. In the first writing classes I taught, students wrote either by hand or on typewriters. I am convinced that young people growing up reading and writing in online, collaborative situations—using multiple screens and multiple media—think and feel about literacy and communication in fundamentally different ways than I do. When I am trying to negotiate reading and writing online, I often feel like I'm waist deep in fast water, watching my students swim comfortably around me. Yet I realize these changes, rapid and unpredictable as they can be, offer all of us exciting opportunities to rethink how we communicate in words, images, and sound.

The evolving possibilities of online literacy practices may change a great deal about how we perceive and teach reading and writing. What will not change, however, is the importance of identity in terms of literacy practices. If anything, new literacies reveal to us how important it will be to continue to consider how people position themselves in changing cultural contexts and how that influences their ability to communicate with others. Issues of identity and culture will reinforce dominant relations of power and confront those who, through their reading and writing, challenge those relations and seek to have their voices heard. Because identities are ever shifting, as are technologies of literacy, we must resist the inclination to believe that we have somehow solved problems of power and inequality in the literacy classroom. Instead, we must continue to reflect on the ways in which identity and power affect our teaching strategies and the efforts of our students.

At the same time, however, we should not see issues of literacy and identity as necessarily divisive. In our conversations, with our students and with one another, we can create the opportunities for greater understanding of all of our needs, concerns, and desires. Reading and writing offer distinct opportunities for connecting our minds and hearts to those around us. As we teach reading and writing to young people we can help them understand the potential for connection and how, even as it raises our awareness of what divides us, it reveals our hope in our common humanity.

References

Black, R. W. (2007). Digital design: English language learners and reader reviews in online fiction. In M. Knobel & C. Lankshear (Eds.), *A new literacies sampler* (pp. 115–136). New York: Peter Lang.

Davies, J. (2006). "Hello newbie! **big welcome hugs** hope u like it here as much as i do!" An exploration of teenagers' informal online learning. In D. Buckingham & R. Willett (Eds.), *Digital generations: Children, young people, and new media* (pp. 211–228). Mahwah, NJ: Erlbaum.

Gee, J. P. (2004). *Situated language and learning: A critique of traditional schooling.* New York: Routledge.

Jenkins, H. (with K. Clinton, R. Purushotma, A. J. Robison, & M. Weigel). (2006). *Confronting the challenges of participatory culture: Media education for the 21st century.* Chicago: The John D. and Catherine T. MacArthur Foundation.

Kress, G. (1997). *Before writing: Rethinking paths to literacy.* London: Routledge.

Livingstone, S. (2002). *Young people and new media: Childhood and the changing media environment.* London: Sage.

Steiner, P. (1993). On the Internet, nobody knows you're a dog. The New Yorker, 69(20), 61.

Thomas, A. (2007). *Youth online: Identity and literacy in the digital age.* New York: Peter Lang.

You Wanna Take This Online?

JEFF CHU

Text messaging, instant messaging, and Web journals are shaping today's youth in drastic and unanticipated ways, according to this feature article, which appeared in the August 8, 2005, edition of Time, *a weekly news commentary magazine for a general readership. Jeff Chu writes regularly for* Time.

What does 13-year-old Taylor Hern ♥? Lots of things: the actor Ewan McGregor, the color pink, the band My Chemical Romance, her boyfriend Alex. You would know all that if you visited her Xanga, a blog-home-page hybrid that is the modern teen's public and interactive equivalent of a diary. You could even leave a comment on her Xanga or send her an "eProp" if, say, you ♥ Ewan McGregor too.

On April 18, Taylor, who is about to enter eighth grade at Lost Mountain Middle School in Kennesaw, Ga., got an instant message (IM) from her friend Sydney Meyer that said, "OMG [Oh, my God] OMG OMG go to your xanga." Someone using the screen name Immsgirlsgot2hell had left Taylor a comment that read, "Go to my Xanga, bitch." Taylor did—and found a List of Hos. Her name was on it. The list was hurtful, but Taylor says she wasn't as bothered as other girls. "A bunch of the cheerleading chicks spazzed," she says. "Me and all my friends thought it was stupid. Who would actually make time in their schedule to do something like that?"

Turns out, many of her peers would. Technology has transformed the lives of teens, including the ways they pick on one another. If parents and teachers think it's hard to control mean girls and bullying boys in school, they haven't reckoned with cyberspace.

Cyberbullying can mean anything from posting pejorative items like the List of Hos to spreading rumors by e-mail to harassing by instant message. It was experienced in the preceding two months by 18% of 3,700 middle schoolers surveyed by researchers at Clemson University. Their study is scheduled to be presented at this month's American Psychological Association meeting. The phenomenon peaks at about age 13; 21% of eighth-graders surveyed reported being cyberbullied recently. And incidents of online bullying are like roaches: for every one that's reported, many more go unrecorded. "Our statistics are conservative," says Clemson psychologist Robin Kowalski. "Part of the problem is kids not recognizing that what's happening is a form of bullying."

5   Online bullying follows a gender pattern that's the opposite of what happens offline, the Clemson study found. On playgrounds and in school hallways, boys are the primary perpetrators and victims; online, girls rule. Nearly a third of the eighth-grade girls surveyed reported being bullied online in the previous two months, compared with 10% of boys; 17% of the girls said they had bullied online, but only 10% of the boys said they had. Such stats get an eye roll from teens. "Girls make up stuff and sooooooo much drama," Taylor said (by IM, of course). "Drama queens."

On the Internet, you can wear any mask you like—and that can be harrowing for the victim of a cyberbully. A few weeks after the List of Hos was posted, Taylor's classmate Courtney Katasak got an IM from someone using the screen name ToastIsYummy. Courtney thought it might be a friend with a new screen name, so she asked, WHO IS THIS? ToastIsYummy responded with teasing lines and a link to a porn site. "Then they kept sending me these inappropriate messages," she says. "I blocked the screen name so they couldn't talk to me, but I didn't know who this person was or what they were trying to do. It freaked me out."

"Anonymity emboldens the person doing it— and it increases the fear factor for the victim," says Kowalski. Parry Aftab, founder of an online nonprofit called WiredSafety.org, says teens "are exploring who they are—and they role-play by

being mean, horrible and hateful in ways they would never be offline." Aftab recalls meeting a New Jersey 13-year-old with a preppie-perfect appearance—khakis, button-down shirt, penny loafers complete with pennies—and a creepy hobby of making online death threats against strangers. He would gather information from chat rooms or people's websites, then threaten them as if he knew them. Says Aftab: "He said to me, 'I would never do anything in real life. I'm a good kid. But I can do it online because it doesn't matter.'"

Actually, it does. When a cyberbully lashes out, it can be a sign of emotional or psychological problems. And cyberbullying is viral. The Clemson study found that kids who are victimized "seem to be heavily involved in bullying others," says psychologist Sue Limber. In the real world, physical intimidation may keep those who are bullied from retaliating, but that's not a problem online. "Cyberbullying can also lead to other forms of victimization," Limber says. If someone insults a classmate on a Xanga, the effects could include ostracization at school. "Passing notes or writing on lockers was nothing," says Limber. "This takes public to a whole other level."

It can be especially embarrassing since cyberbullying often has sexual overtones. "It's raging hormones, and 13 is the heart of it," says Aftab. "We tell adults they can't operate heavy machinery under the influence. These kids are under the influence of hormones 24/7."

10   A parent's instinctive response may be to apply an electronic tourniquet, cutting off a teen's access. But experts agree that severing online links is not the solution. "The Internet is no longer just an advantage. A child is at a disadvantage not having it," says Brittany Bacon, an FBI-trained WiredSafety.org volunteer. She says teens need to learn boundaries and manners in cyberspace just as they must in other venues of society.

It's also the parents' responsibility to be aware of a child's life online. "Kids know so much about the computer that some parents just throw up their hands," says Patti Agatston, a counselor with Cobb

County Schools' prevention-intervention program in Georgia. "Don't do that," she says. Instead, parents should keep their eyes open. "Parents are totally clueless that some of this even exists," Aftab says.

Taylor Hern's mother Caryn counts herself in that number. "I am absolutely an idiot when it comes to that kind of stuff," she says. But Taylor's cyberbullying experience convinced Hern that she had to get Netsavvy. She has signed up for lessons from an expert: her son David, who is 19. "You read about what kids do to other kids, but you don't think it's going to happen to yours," she says. "Who knows what happens online after I go to bed at 10? I need to find out."

A False Wikipedia "Biography"

JOHN SEIGENTHALER, SR.

John Seigenthaler spent forty-three years as a journalist for the Nashville Tennessean *newspaper, retiring as editor, publisher, and CEO in 1991. He was also the founding editorial director of* USA Today, *in which the following appeared in November 2005. In the 1960s he worked briefly as an administrative assistant to Attorney General Robert F. Kennedy in the U.S. Justice Department—a biographical detail that was the basis for the* Wikipedia *entry on which this op-ed is based. Upon his retirement from journalism, Seigenthaler founded The First Amendment Center to foster national discussion about First Amendment rights and freedoms through information and education.*

"John Seigenthaler Sr. was the assistant to Attorney General Robert Kennedy in the early 1960's. For a brief time, he was thought to have been directly involved in the Kennedy assassinations of both John, and his brother, Bobby. Nothing was ever proven."

—Wikipedia

This is a highly personal story about Internet character assassination. It could be your story.

I have no idea whose sick mind conceived the false, malicious "biography" that appeared under my name for 132 days on *Wikipedia*, the popular, online, free encyclopedia whose authors are unknown and virtually untraceable. There was more:

"John Seigenthaler moved to the Soviet Union in 1971, and returned to the United States in 1984," *Wikipedia* said. "He started one of the country's largest public relations firms shortly thereafter."

At age 78, I thought I was beyond surprise or hurt at anything negative said about me. I was wrong. One sentence in the biography was true. I was Robert Kennedy's administrative assistant in the early 1960s. I also was his pallbearer. It was mind-boggling when my son, John Seigenthaler, journalist with NBC News, phoned later to say he found the same scurrilous text on *Reference.com* and *Answers.com.*

5   I had heard for weeks from teachers, journalists and historians about "the wonderful world of *Wikipedia*," where millions of people worldwide visit daily for quick reference "facts," composed and posted by people with no special expertise or knowledge—and sometimes by people with malice.

At my request, executives of the three websites now have removed the false content about me. But they don't know, and can't find out, who wrote the toxic sentences.

Anonymous Author

I phoned Jimmy Wales, Wikipedia's founder and asked,

"Do you...have any way to know who wrote that?"

"No, we don't," he said. Representatives of the other two websites said their computers are programmed to copy data verbatim from *Wikipedia*, never checking whether it is false or factual.

Naturally, I want to unmask my "biographer." And, I am interested in letting many people know that *Wikipedia* is a flawed and irresponsible research tool.

10   But searching cyberspace for the identity of people who post spurious information can be frustrating. I found on *Wikipedia* the registered IP (Internet Protocol) number of my "biographer"—65-81-97-208. I traced it to a customer of BellSouth Internet. That company advertises a phone number to report "Abuse Issues." An electronic voice said all complaints must be e-mailed. My two e-mails were answered by identical form letters, advising me that the company would conduct an investigation but might not tell me the results. It was signed "Abuse Team."

Wales, *Wikipedia*'s founder, told me that BellSouth would not be helpful. "We have trouble with people posting abusive things over and over and over," he said. "We block their IP numbers, and they sneak in another way. So we contact the service providers, and they are not very responsive."

After three weeks, hearing nothing further about the Abuse Team investigation, I phoned BellSouth's Atlanta corporate headquarters, which led to conversations between my lawyer and BellSouth's counsel. My only remote chance of getting the name, I learned, was to file a "John or Jane Doe" lawsuit against my "biographer." Major communications Internet companies are bound by federal privacy laws that protect the identity of their customers, even those who defame online. Only if a lawsuit resulted in a court subpoena would BellSouth give up the name.

Little Legal Recourse

Federal law also protects online corporations—BellSouth, AOL, MCI, *Wikipedia*, etc.—from libel lawsuits. Section 230 of the Communications Decency Act, passed in 1996, specifically states that "no provider or user of an interactive computer service shall be treated as the publisher or speaker." That legalese means that, unlike print and broadcast companies, online service providers cannot be sued for disseminating defamatory attacks on citizens posted by others.

Recent low-profile court decisions document that Congress effectively has barred defamation in cyberspace. *Wikipedia*'s website acknowledges that it is not responsible for inaccurate information, but Wales, in a recent C-Span interview with Brian Lamb, insisted that his website is accountable and that his community of thousands of volunteer editors (he said he has

only one paid employee) corrects mistakes within minutes.

15   My experience refutes that. My "biography" was posted May 26. On May 29, one of Wales' volunteers "edited" it only by correcting the misspelling of the word "early." For four months, *Wikipedia* depicted me as a suspected assassin before Wales erased it from his website's history Oct. 5. The falsehoods remained on *Answers.com* and *Reference.com* for three more weeks.

In the C-Span interview, Wales said *Wikipedia* has "millions" of daily global visitors and is one of the world's busiest websites. His volunteer community runs the *Wikipedia* operation, he said. He funds his website through a nonprofit foundation and estimated a 2006 budget of "about a million dollars."

And so we live in a universe of new media with phenomenal opportunities for worldwide communications and research—but populated by volunteer vandals with poison-pen intellects. Congress has enabled them and protects them.

When I was a child, my mother lectured me on the evils of "gossip." She held a feather pillow and said, "If I tear this open, the feathers will fly to the four winds, and I could never get them back in the pillow. That's how it is when you spread mean things about people."

For me, that pillow is a metaphor for *Wikipedia*.

The Fakebook Generation

ALICE MATHIAS

Alice Mathias is a 2007 graduate of Dartmouth College in Hanover, New Hampshire. She was one of eight college students selected to blog about life as a near-college graduate for the New York Times *feature "The Graduates: Eight College Seniors Face the Future." The following piece was published in the* Times *on October 6, 2007.*

The time-chugging Web site *Facebook.com* first appeared during my freshman year as the exclusive domain of college students. This spring, *Facebook* opened its pearly gates, enabling myself and other members of the class of '07 to graduate from our college networks into those of the real world.

In no time at all, the Web site has convinced its rapidly assembling adult population that it is a forum for genuine personal and professional connections. Its founder, Mark Zuckerberg, has even declared his quest to chart a "social graph" of human relationships the way that cartographers once charted the world.

Just a warning: if you're planning on following the corner of this map that's been digitally doodled by my 659 *Facebook* friends, you are going to end up in the middle of nowhere. All the rhetoric about human connectivity misses the real reason this popular online study buddy has so distracted college students for the past four years.

Facebook did not become popular because it was a functional tool—after all, most college students live in close quarters with the majority of their *Facebook* friends and have no need for social networking. Instead, we log into the Web site because it's entertaining to watch a constantly evolving narrative starring the other people in the library.

5   I've always thought of *Facebook* as online community theater. In costumes we customize in a backstage makeup room—the Edit Profile page, where we can add a few Favorite Books or touch up our About Me section—we deliver our lines on the very public stage of friends' walls or photo albums. And because every time we join a network, post a link or make another friend it's immediately made visible to others via the News Feed, every *Facebook* act is a soliloquy to our anonymous audience.

It's all comedy: making one another laugh matters more than providing useful updates about ourselves, which is why entirely phony profiles were all the rage before the grown-ups signed in. One friend announced her status as In a Relationship with Chinese Food, whose profile picture was a carry-out box and whose personal information personified the cuisine of China.

We even make a joke out of how we know one another—claiming to have met in "Intro to Super Mario Re-enactments," which I seriously doubt is a real course at Wesleyan, or to have lived together in a "spay and neuter clinic" instead of the dorm. Still, these humor bits often reveal more about our personalities and interests than any honest answers.

Facebook administrators have since exiled at least the flagrantly fake profiles, the Greta Garbos and the I Can't Believe It's Not Butters, in an effort to have the site grow up from a farce into the serious social networking tool promised to its new adult users, who earnestly type in their actual personal information and precisely label everyone they know as former co-workers or current colleagues, family members or former lovers.

But does this more reverent incarnation of *Facebook* actually enrich adult relationships? What do these constellations of work colleagues and long-lost friends amount to? An online office mixer? A reunion with that one other guy from your high school who has a *Facebook* profile? Oh! You get to see pictures of your former college sweetheart's family! (Only depressing possibilities are coming to mind for some reason.)

10   My generation has long been bizarrely comfortable with being looked at, and as performers on the *Facebook* stage, we upload pictures of ourselves cooking dinner for our parents or doing keg stands at last night's party; we are reckless with our personal information. But there is one area of privacy that we won't surrender:

the secrecy of how and whom we search.

A friend of mine was recently in a panic over rumors of a hacker application that would allow *Facebook* users to see who's been visiting their profiles. She'd spent the day ogling a love interest's page and was horrified at the idea that he knew she'd been looking at him. But there's no way *Facebook* would allow such a program to exist: the site is popular largely because it enables us to indulge our gazes anonymously. (We might feel invulnerable in the spotlight, but we don't want to be caught sitting in someone else's audience.) If our ability to privately search is ever jeopardized, *Facebook* will turn into a ghost town.

Facebook purports to be a place for human connectivity, but it's made us more wary of real human confrontation. When I was in college, people always warned against the dangers of "*Facebook* stalking" at a library computer—the person

whose profile you're perusing might be right behind you. Dwelling online is a cowardly and utterly enjoyable alternative to real interaction.

So even though *Facebook* offers an elaborate menu of privacy settings, many of my friends admit that the only setting they use is the one that prevents people from seeing that they are Currently Logged In. Perhaps we fear that the Currently Logged In feature advertises to everyone else that we (too!) are Currently Bored, Lustful, Socially Unfulfilled or Generally Avoiding Real Life.

For young people, *Facebook* is yet another form of escapism; we can turn our lives into stage dramas and relationships into comedy routines. Make believe is not part of the postgraduate *Facebook* user's agenda. As more and more older users try to turn *Facebook* into a legitimate social reference guide, younger people may follow suit and stop treating it as a circus ring. But let's hope not.

I Can't Wait...

PAUL NOTH

Paul Noth's cartoons appear regularly in the New Yorker *and other publications, including the* Wall Street Journal. *He has been a writer for* Late Night with Conan O'Brien *and CBS's* The Late Late Show *and is working on a graphic novel,* The Milwaukee Apocalypse. *View his Web site at www.paulnoth.com.*

"I can't wait to see what you're like online."

Youthful Indiscretions: Should Colleges Protect Social Network Users from Themselves and Others?

DANA L. FLEMING

Dana L. Fleming is a Boston area attorney specializing in higher education law. The following article appeared in the Winter 2008 issue of the New England Journal of Higher Education.

Counting members in the hundreds of millions, online social networking communities such as *MySpace* and *Facebook* may prove nearly as transformative as the 1876 invention of the telephone. Creating a *MySpace* or *Facebook* profile is free and making online "friends" is easy—if you're under 30. But students' online identities and friendships come at a price, as job recruiters, school administrators, law enforcement officers and sexual predators sign on and start searching.

MySpace is routinely ranked among the top three most popular websites in America. The site was founded in 2003 by Tom Anderson, a graduate student at UCLA. Two years later, Rupert Murdoch's News Corp. purchased *MySpace* for a reported $327 million.

Beyond its financial success, *MySpace* boasts an international audience with more users than any other networking site in the world.

In New England, however, *Facebook* is a local favorite among college students and recent graduates, perhaps because it was founded in the region, by then Harvard sophomore Mark Zuckerberg. The first month the site went "live" in 2004, half of Harvard's undergraduates signed up. Its popularity spread to other Boston-area campuses including MIT, Boston University and Boston College. By December 2004, the number of registered *Facebook* users surpassed one million. *Facebook* began by catering to undergraduates and for many years restricted membership by requiring all users to have a ".edu" email account. In recent years, *Facebook* has opened its site to a wider audience in order to serve the growing demand for online social networking. Yet, *Facebook* remains the most popular site among New England college students.

Other sites such as *Friendster, LiveJournal* and *YouTube* offer additional means for users to "broadcast" their innermost thoughts and secrets across the World Wide Web. To join, a user needs only an email address and a willingness to share his or her "profile" with other users. Profiles usually include pictures and personal descriptions, music and video clips, plus information about the user's relationship status, school affiliations, interests and hometown. "Friending" someone (yes, it's a verb now) is as easy as searching for a name and clicking on it. This automatically sends a "friend request" to the other user, which that user can then accept, simply by clicking on the request. Perhaps not surprisingly, it is commonplace for users to have hundreds, even thousands of friends. Thirty percent of students report accepting "friend" requests from total strangers.

5   Joining or forming groups on these networks is easy too. With just a few clicks, users can join "Drunks United," "Sexy and Single on MySpace," or "My B.A.C. is Higher Than Your GPA." All of these groups have memberships in the tens of thousands. While privacy settings allow users to restrict who may view their profiles and group affiliations, such settings are rarely enabled by the user. Even when access is restricted to a user's so-called "friends," when students have hundreds or even thousands of "friends," anonymity can be hard to come by.

The explosion in online social networking sites and attendant loss of anonymity carries a cost. One University of Chicago student ruined his chances at a summer internship when an executive from the company viewed his *Facebook* profile, only to discover that his interests included "smoking blunts" (cigars stuffed with marijuana), shooting people, and obsessive sex. A chemical engineering major sabotaged his career in a similar manner by confessing in his online bio that he liked to "blow things up."

Recruiters are not the only ones checking up on students' profiles. In May 2005, two swimmers at Louisiana State University lost athletic scholarships for making disparaging comments about their coach on *Facebook*. In October 2005, a student at Boston's Fisher College was reportedly expelled for defaming a college police officer on *Facebook*. In an ongoing dispute at Millersville University in Pennsylvania, a young woman was denied her teaching degree after a fellow student brought one of her *MySpace* photos to the attention of school administrators. The photo, which has spurred a lawsuit, features the young woman wearing a pirate hat, drinking from an opaque plastic cup. The photo is suggestively captioned "Drunken Pirate."

A private Christian university in Virginia got creative when it found out that one of its law students posted an unflattering video of the school's founder, Pat Robertson, on *Facebook* and *YouTube*. (In the video, Pat Robertson appears to scratch his face with his middle finger.) The university has demanded that the law student publicly apologize for the posting or submit a legal brief defending it as satire protected under the First Amendment. Reports indicate that the student has chosen the latter punishment.

The dangers of online social networking transcend disciplinary actions and reputational harm. A 17-year-old Rhode Island girl was reportedly drugged and raped by three men she befriended on *MySpace*. Detectives in Colorado recently used *MySpace* to identify six men involved in the brutal rape and robbery of one of their online "friends." And the parents of a 13-year-old girl from Texas blame *MySpace* for their daughter's sexual assault and tried unsuccessfully to sue the company for negligence. The girl, "Julie Doe," lied about her age on her *MySpace* profile, then agreed to meet one of her "friends" in a restaurant parking lot where her friend, a 19-year-old male, sexually assaulted her. A U.S. District Court Judge dismissed the suit, stating: "If anyone had a duty to protect Julie Doe, it was her parents, not *MySpace*."

10   Parents groups, attorneys general and legislators are grappling with how to protect young users from other users and, still more challenging, how to protect young users from themselves. Forty-five attorneys general are pushing *MySpace* to adopt more parental controls and an age-verification system. For example, Connecticut Attorney General Richard Blumenthal wants to see *MySpace* raise its minimum age limit from 14 to 16. Several bills in Congress have included provisions barring schools and libraries that receive federal funding from allowing minors to access networking sites like *MySpace* and *Facebook*.

Like lawmakers, college administrators have not yet determined how to handle the unique issues posed by the public display of their students' indiscretions. While some are starting to develop very thoughtful policies about these sites, many still wonder what all the fuss is about. Some schools use material from *MySpace* and *Facebook* in their judiciary proceedings while others turn a blind eye to the site. Some address the risks associated with these sites during freshman orientation, while others let students proceed at their own risk.

The office of student affairs at the University of Maine warns that while "the administrators are not monitoring *Facebook*," they may act on any violations of law or University policy if it is brought to their attention. As the school candidly puts it: "Just because you don't want them [the administrators] to look at your page doesn't mean they can't or won't." Norwich University offers this reminder to its students: "As an institution of higher learning, Norwich University recognizes the importance of free speech and the use of information technology in the pursuit of educational goals. Nonetheless…we are all expected to behave—on campus, in public and online—in a manner consistent with the University's Honor Code and Guiding Values."

The Norwich policy, like many others across the country, is followed by a series of practical tips for online networkers, such as: "Don't post anything you wouldn't be comfortable with your grandmother seeing." Good advice, to be sure, but even a cursory perusal of these sites suggests that many students are not listening.

There is no practical way for colleges to monitor the content of these sites, as students' profiles and postings are changing constantly. It would take a full-time staff working around the clock to scratch the surface of a single network. An aggressive monitoring approach can also backfire. When students find out that a network is being monitored by administrators, they frequently change networks, password-protect their profile or group or post misleading information to confuse and frustrate administrators, (e.g., one student advertised a frat party at a specific dorm room, only to leave a "gotcha" note for campus police).

15   While a blanket monitoring approach is unfeasible, if not counterproductive, a targeted review of online social networking sites can be a good thing. For example, when a student exhibits signs of distress, a review of his or her online profile or blog may be appropriate. A review of a student's profile may also be appropriate where that student is involved in a disciplinary proceeding. Courts treat people's online postings as evidence in criminal proceedings, and college and university lawyers routinely check students' online profiles. It stands to reason then, that schools are free to use content from these sites in their own judiciary proceedings. Colleges that wish to create a policy specially tailored to online social networking policies should review Cornell's University's "Thoughts on *Facebook*," which cautions students about the personal risks and legal ramifications of online social networking, while at the same time acknowledging the benefits and popular appeal of such sites. In this era of aggressive date-mining and total information access, students' privacy is in peril. Advertisers are particularly interested in students' personal information, as they try to tailor ads to individual users. For example, a restaurant may create an online advertisement based not only on the student's geographic location, but also by noting that one of their "friends" is a regular customer. This type of targeted advertising helps to explain the financial success of sites like *MySpace* and *Facebook* where online advertisers can pay as much for online advertising space as they do for commercial slots on primetime TV.

Under the Family Educational Rights and Privacy Act (FERPA), colleges have a responsibility not to divulge students' personal information, sell their names, phone numbers and email addresses to advertisers or otherwise violate their privacy rights. But when students post their most intimate secrets online, how can schools protect students' privacy?

Though many students believe that the information they post online is "private," it's not—and the simplest way to address the liabilities posed by these sites is to treat them like any other university activity, subject to the school's code of conduct and applicable state and federal laws.

Hey There, Lonelygirl

ADAM STERNBERGH

Adam Sternbergh writes about popular culture for New York Magazine. *In August 2006, he wrote the following article about a video blog (vlog) posted to* YouTube, *purportedly by a fifteen-year-old girl. The vlogger's dramatic musings captured the attention of millions of followers prior to the revelation that Lonelygirl15 was, in fact, an actress apparently hoping to be discovered and that the video diary was—as Sternbergh predicted in this article—a hoax.*

There are thousands of people who post video diaries on *YouTube*, and, by all rights, Lonelygirl 15 should be just as annoying as the rest of them. Even more so, actually, since in all likelihood, Lonelygirl 15 is a fake. She's a suspiciously photogenic teen who films first-person confessionals in her bedroom, detailing the dramas of her so-called life. Most of them revolve around her study-buddy Daniel, who secretly (okay, not so secretly—is anything a secret in the *YouTube* world?) has a crush on her. This is all supposedly done without the knowledge of her religious, homeschooling parents. From her first video, posted June 16, she's doled out new chapters in two-minute chunks, each with an alluring title such as "Boy Problems," "Dad 'Talks' to Daniel," and "What Did Daniel and Dad Talk About?" And lots of viewers are caught up in her micro-soap; her videos have totaled almost 2 million views, her "channel" is the fourth most popular on *YouTube*, and the *New York Times*' Virginia Heffernan recently lobbied for her to get her own TV show.

Along the way, people have started questioning whether she even exists, and for good reason: She's just a little *too* charming, her videos a little *too* well edited, and her story a little *too* neatly laid out. As such, her saga's taken on the brimstone whiff of viral marketing. Some skeptical YouTubers are posting short films dedicated to debunking her, while others wave a smoking gun: The domain name for her fan site was registered a month before her first video went up.

Ironically, her most prominent critic—a YouTuber named Gohepcat, a film-geek hipster in mirrored sunglasses and a cowboy hat—has become a mini–*YouTube* star in his own right. And because anyone on *YouTube* can post responses or theories about Lonelygirl (and plenty have), her story now has its own metastasizing, David Lynch–worthy cast: Not just Lonelygirl, Daniel, and their monkey puppet (don't ask), but the Javert-like Mirrored Cowboy; her defender, Nerd With the Headset; a nemesis called Lazydork; and Richard Feynman. (Yes, Richard Feynman, the famous physicist. He doesn't appear personally—it's a long story.)

But wait a minute—what if the Mirrored Cowboy is in on it, too? After all, networks routinely spray the Internet with fake reality-show spoilers to throw intrepid fans off the scent. Wouldn't this be the ultimate viral-marketing technique—to create not only the cute-girl phenomenon but the she's-a-fake controversy as well? And what about the other characters? *Et tu*, Headset Nerd?

5   Of course, not everyone commenting on Lonelygirl can be part of the hoax (if it is a hoax). But they're all, in their own way, now part of her story.

And presto: Just like that, Lonelygirl's tale goes from Web-based melodrama or viral-marketing trickery toward something like a brand-new art form. It's the birth of WikiTV: a television show created by a broad community of participants and built not of sequential, hour-long episodes, but of two-minute interconnected parcels. The story line is both linear (will Daniel get the girl?) and expansive (enter the Mirrored Cowboy!), and anyone can join in. I, for example, could don a tuxedo and eye patch, and post a video claiming that the Cowboy's a double agent. Then someone could post a video refuting me, now known as the Dapper Pirate.

Which means that, of all the possible outcomes to the Lonelygirl story, the one in which she actually turns out to be just some cute teen with preternatural editing skills will be the least interesting of all. The second-least-interesting outcome—and the one I dread, and half-expect—is that once her page views reach critical mass, she'll start popping open the Mountain Dews and talking about how deliciously refreshing they are.

The best scenario is that she's a sleeper agent in the employ of MTV, or VH1, or some as-yet-unidentified entity, and that others will follow her fictional lead. Imagine how much fun J. J. Abrams of *Lost* could have with a *YouTube*-based conspiracy story. Or forget that—imagine what fun *you* could have with a camera, a computer, and a catchy idea. Of course, as a necessary side effect, *YouTube* will be flooded with crap. (Or even more flooded with crap.) But the weak story lines will wither and the smartly crafted ones will blossom, just as Lonelygirl's have. And maybe this, and not some NBC shows for sale on iTunes, is the future of television—or the promised land of a new narrative form. If so, we might look back at Lonelygirl 15 as Moses with a monkey puppet.

A Message from the Creators

THE CREATORS

Once the Lonelygirl15 video drama was revealed to be fiction, the creators of the drama issued the following letter on the Lonelygirl Web site. The letter appeared on September 7, 2006. The Web site mentioned in the letter, complete with Lonelygirl videos and active discussion forums, is at http://www.lonelygirl15.com.

To Our Incredible Fans,

Thank you so much for enjoying our show so far. We are amazed by the overwhelmingly positive response to our videos; it has exceeded our wildest expectations. With your help we believe we are witnessing the birth of a new art form. Our intention from the outset has been to tell a story—A story that could only be told using the medium of video blogs and the distribution power of the internet. A story that is interactive and constantly evolving with the audience.

Right now, the biggest mystery of Lonelygirl15 is "who is she?" We think this is an oversimplification. Lonelygirl15 is a reflection of everyone. She is no more real or fictitious than the portions of our personalities that we choose to show (or hide) when we interact with the people around us. Regardless, there are deeper mysteries buried within the plot, dialogue, and background of the Lonelygirl15 videos, and many of our tireless and dedicated fans have unearthed some of these. There are many more to come.

To enhance the community experience of Lonelygirl15, which you have already helped to create, we are in the process of building a website centered around video and interactivity. This website will allow everyone to enjoy the full potential of this new medium. Unfortunately, we aren't programmers. We are filmmakers. We are working furiously to complete the website, and hope to have it up and running shortly.

5   So, sit tight. You are the only reason for our success, and we appreciate your devotion. We want you to know that we aren't a big corporation. We are just like you. A few people who love good stories. We hope that you will join us in the continuing story of

Lonelygirl15, and help us usher in an era of interactive storytelling where the line between "fan" and "star" has been removed, and dedicated fans like yourselves are paid for their efforts. This is an incredible time for the creator inside all of us.

Thank you.

The Thinker, Reimagined

YASUHIDE FUMOTO

Auguste Rodin's sculpture The Thinker *is an iconic representation of human introspection carried out in isolation. What argument is suggested by photographer Yasuhide Fumoto's resizing the enormous statue? By placing it in close juxtaposition with the Internet-connected laptop? What does the image suggest about the evolution of human intellectual activity?*

■ ■ ■ **FOR CLASS DISCUSSION** Web 2.0 and Online Identity

1. Think about the articles in this unit as well as your own experiences with the Internet. In what specific ways do you think the Internet is affecting interpersonal relationships, for better or worse? How has the Internet changed or extended the use of such words as "relationship" or "friend"? What kinds of real damage are possible as a result of faking online identities?

2. Log your own Internet use for twenty-four hours. Come to class prepared to discuss the ways in which you use the Internet—specifically, the percentage of time you spent

creating as opposed to consuming content, and the various ways you spend your time online (e.g., news, education, movies, music, gaming, consumer activity, communication, etc.). To what extent are these activities improving your literacy skills?

3. As a class, brainstorm and make a list of the ways your teachers have used or are using Web 2.0 applications in the classroom. Then review Bronwyn T. Williams's suggestions for incorporating online literacy practices into teaching. Under what conditions might such online practices succeed as extensions of the classroom? Under what conditions would they be likely to fail?

4. While John Seigenthaler, Sr., is furious at finding false information in his *Wikipedia* biography, Alice Mathias, Paul Noth, Adam Sternbergh, and the creators of Lonelygirl15 all suggest that creating false identities online may have positive aspects. Compare and contrast the arguments presented by Mathias, Sternbergh, and The Creators. When is it unethical to create and post false information or false identities online? Under what circumstances is it acceptable?

5. Much has been made in the mainstream media about the dangers of revealing too much personal information on social networking sites such as *Facebook* and *MySpace*. Discuss your own experiences of identity sharing on social networking spaces: What do you reveal? What do you conceal? What responsibility, if any, do schools or colleges and universities have to ensure the safety of students who post personal information over their servers? Do you agree with Dana L. Fleming that "a targeted review of [students'] social networking sites can be a good thing"? Should students be required to make their social networking sites conform to a school's code of conduct?

6. Choose one of the readings from this unit and analyze it carefully using the List 2 guide questions on pages 426–427.

WRITING ASSIGNMENT Researched Argument

If your school has published any guidelines for using social networking spaces, review their policy. Such information might be available on your school's "information technology" or "computer services" Web site or in the student handbook, or you might have to contact your school's computer center or Dean of Students office. Conduct some research to find such policies at other schools; for example, see "Thoughts on Facebook" on the Cornell University Web site, http://www.cit.cornell.edu/policy/memos/facebook.html. You might also want to review recommendations for safe use of such sites at onguardonline.gov/socialnetworking.html or at http://www.ftc.gov/bcp/edu/pubs/consumer/tech/tec13.shtm. Then, write a researched argument for or against school oversight of students' publicly posted content, or write a set of guidelines appropriate for use by your school. ■

For additional writing, reading, and research resources, go to
www.mycomplab.com

Video Games and Their Influence

Since the earliest days of video games, their popularity has been met with criticism and concern—the more complex and violent the games, the more vocal the concern. In the 1970s critics worried about the apparent mindlessness of games like *Pong, Asteroids,* and *Pac-Man,* fearing the intellect-numbing effects of hours spent manipulating dots on the screen. As the complexity and popularity of games has increased, so has the realism and the violence of their content, and the enormous success of such games as *Grand Theft Auto* has led to claims of frightening links between violent games and aggressive or even murderous behavior. Yet as it has evolved, the gaming industry seems to have recognized that users are also hungry for challenging intellectual and athletic content. Many online games now require intense concentration and keen strategy, involving collaboration among team members and taking days or even months to play. Gaming, once a predominantly masculine realm, has become co-ed and draws in people of all ages and interests. Currently *Dance, Dance Revolution,* and *Guitar Hero* vie with *Grand Theft Auto* on college campuses for top game status, while senior citizens are getting the hang of Wii Sports to stay fit.

Despite these improvements, apprehension continues over the possible negative effects of hours spent gaming. Researchers and critics have expressed concerns about appropriate socialization and even addiction of young people who spend too much time alone, staring at a screen. Some studies have identified a cause-effect relationship between violent games and dangerous aggression, while others discount these studies as flawed. Other critics have worried about the games' frequent sexism and racism or their tendency to make targets of law enforcement officials or foreigners, fearing the inculcation of undesirable prejudices and stereotypes.

The readings in this unit—as well as the video game screen captures on pages 59 and 182 and Carmen Tieu's writing in Chapters 3 through 5—ask you to think about the following questions: What, if any, are the real dangers of video games? What, if anything, should be done to prevent damaging consequences of video games? Can video games actually be useful or beneficial? As you read, be aware of what counts as evidence in the various arguments.

ISU Psychologists Publish Three New Studies on Violent Video Game Effects on Youths

IOWA STATE UNIVERSITY NEWS SERVICE

The following article highlights the work of Craig Anderson and Douglas Gentile, both professors in the Department of Psychology at Iowa State University, and Katherine Buckley, a doctoral student. Anderson's research interests include social cognition and aggression, and he has published widely on the subject of violent video games. Gentile runs the Media Research Lab at Iowa State, which studies the effects of media, including video games, on children and adults. This news item was released by Iowa State University's News Service in March 2007.

New research by Iowa State University psychologists provides more concrete evidence of the adverse effects of violent video game exposure on the behavior of children and adolescents.

ISU Distinguished Professor of Psychology Craig Anderson, Assistant Professor of Psychology Douglas Gentile, and doctoral student Katherine Buckley share the results of three new studies in their book, *Violent Video Game Effects on Children and Adolescents* (Oxford University Press, 2007). It is the first book to unite empirical research and public policy related to violent video games.

Anderson and Gentile will present their findings at the Society for Research in Child Development Biennial Meeting in Boston March 29 through April 1.

Study One: Kids' Games Still Have Behavioral Effect

The book's first study found that even exposure to cartoonish children's violent video games had the same short-term effects on increasing aggressive behavior as the

more graphic teen (T-rated) violent games. The study tested 161 9- to 12-year-olds, and 354 college students. Each participant was randomly assigned to play either a violent or non-violent video game. "Violent" games were defined as those in which intentional harm is done to a character motivated to avoid that harm. The definition was not an indication of the graphic or gory nature of any violence depicted in a game.

5   The researchers selected one children's non-violent game ("Oh No! More Lemmings!"), two children's violent video games with happy music and cartoonish game characters ("Captain Bumper" and "Otto Matic"), and two violent T-rated video games ("Future Cop" and "Street Fighter"). For ethical reasons, the T-rated games were played only by the college-aged participants.

The participants subsequently played another computer game designed to measure aggressive behavior in which they set punishment levels in the form of noise blasts to be delivered to another

person participating in the study. Additional information was also gathered on each participant's history of violent behavior and previous violent media viewing habits.

The researchers found that participants who played the violent video games—even if they were children's games—punished their opponents with significantly more high-noise blasts than those who played the non-violent games. They also found that habitual exposure to violent media was associated with higher levels of recent violent behavior—with the newer interactive form of media violence found in video games more strongly related to violent behavior than exposure to non-interactive media violence found in television and movies.

"Even the children's violent video games—which are more cartoonish and often show no blood—had the same size effect on children and college students as the much more graphic games have on college students," said Gentile. "What seems to matter is whether the players are practicing intentional harm to another character in the game. That's what increases immediate aggression—more than how graphic or gory the game is."

Study Two: The Violent Video Game Effect

Another study detailed in the book surveyed 189 high school students. The authors found that respondents who had more exposure to violent video games held more pro-violent attitudes, had more hostile personalities, were less forgiving, believed violence to be more typical, and behaved more aggressively in their everyday lives. The survey measured students' violent TV, movie and video game exposure; attitudes toward violence; personality trait hostility; personality trait forgiveness; beliefs about the normality of violence; and the frequency of various verbally and physically aggressive behaviors.

10   The researchers were surprised that the relation to violent video games was so strong.

"We were surprised to find that exposure to violent video games was a better predictor of the students' own violent behavior than their gender or their beliefs about violence," said Anderson. "Although gender aggressive personality and beliefs about violence all predict aggressive and violent behavior, violent video game play still made an additional difference.

"We were also somewhat surprised that there was no apparent difference in the video game violence effect between boys and girls or adolescents with already aggressive attitudes," he said.

The study found that one variable—trait forgiveness—appeared to make that person less affected by exposure to violent video games in terms of subsequent violent behavior, but this protective effect did not occur for less extreme forms of physical aggression.

Study Three: Violent Video Games and School

A third new study in the book assessed 430 third-, fourth- and fifth-graders, their peers, and their teachers twice during a five-month period in the school year. It found that children who played more violent video games early in the school year changed to see the world in a more aggressive way, and became more verbally and physically aggressive later in the school year—even after controlling for how aggressive they were at the beginning of the study. Higher aggression and lower pro-social behavior were in turn related to those children being more rejected by their peers.

15   "I was startled to find those changes in such a short amount of time," said Gentile. "Children's aggression in school did increase with greater exposure to violent video games, and this effect was big enough to be noticed by their teachers and peers within five months."

The study additionally found an apparent lack of "immunity" to the effects of media violence exposure. TV and video game screen time was also found to be a significant negative predictor of grades.

The book's final chapter offers "Helpful Advice for Parents and Other Caregivers on Choosing and Using Video Games." The authors say that providing clear, science-based information to parents and caregivers about the harmful effects of exposure to violent video games is the first step in helping educate the people who are best able to use the information. The advice includes links to Web sites about entertainment media and parenting issues, including Anderson's and Gentile's Web pages at http://www.psychology. iastate.edu/faculty/caa/ and http:// www.psychology.iastate.edu/faculty/ dgentile/.

Reality Bytes: Eight Myths about Video Games Debunked

HENRY JENKINS

Henry Jenkins is a literature professor and director of the Comparative Media Studies Program at Massachusetts Institute of Technology. He has written widely on popular culture and computer games and, with Kurt Squire, has co-authored articles for Computer Games Magazine. *The essay that follows was written to accompany a PBS television program,* The Video Game Revolution, *which traced the history, impact, and future of video games. The accompanying Web site can be viewed at http://www.pbs.org/kcts/videogamerevolution/index.html.*

A large gap exists between the public's perception of video games and what the research actually shows. The following is an attempt to separate fact from fiction.

1. The Availability of Video Games Has Led to an Epidemic of Youth Violence.

According to federal crime statistics, the rate of juvenile violent crime in the United States is at a 30-year low. Researchers find that people serving time for violent crimes typically consume less media before committing their crimes than the average person in the general population. It's true that young offenders who have committed school shootings in America have also been game players. But young people in general are more likely to be gamers—90 percent of boys and 40 percent of girls play. The overwhelming majority of kids who play do NOT commit antisocial acts. According to a 2001 U.S. Surgeon General's report, the strongest risk factors for school shootings centered on mental stability and the quality of home life, not media exposure. The moral panic over violent video games is doubly harmful. It has led adult authorities to be more suspicious and hostile to many kids who already feel cut off from the system. It also misdirects energy away from eliminating the actual causes of youth violence and allows problems to continue to fester.

2. Scientific Evidence Links Violent Game Play With Youth Aggression.

Claims like this are based on the work of researchers who represent one relatively narrow school of research, "media effects." This research includes some 300 studies of media violence. But most of those studies are inconclusive and many have been criticized on methodological grounds. In these studies, media images are removed from any narrative context. Subjects are asked to engage with content that they would not normally consume and may not understand. Finally, the laboratory context is radically different from the environments where games would normally be played. Most studies found a correlation, not a causal relationship, which means the research could simply show that aggressive people like aggressive entertainment. That's why the vague term "links" is used here. If there is a consensus emerging around this research, it is that violent video games may be one risk factor—when coupled with other more immediate, real-world influences—which can contribute to anti-social behavior. But no research has found that video games are a primary factor or that violent video game play could turn an otherwise normal person into a killer.

3. Children Are the Primary Market for Video Games.

While most American kids do play video games, the center of the video game market has shifted older as the first generation of gamers continues to play into adulthood. Already 62 percent of the console market and 66 percent of the PC market is age 18 or older. The game industry caters to adult tastes. Meanwhile, a sizable number of parents ignore game ratings because they assume that games are for kids. One quarter of children ages 11 to 16 identify an M-Rated (Mature Content) game as among their favorites.

Clearly, more should be done to restrict advertising and marketing that targets young consumers with mature content, and to educate parents about the media choices they are facing. But parents need to share some of the responsibility for making decisions about what is appropriate for their children. The news on this front is not all bad. The Federal Trade Commission has found that 83 percent of game purchases for underage consumers are made by parents or by parents and children together.

4. Almost No Girls Play Computer Games.

5   Historically, the video game market has been predominantly male. However, the percentage of women playing games has steadily increased over the past decade. Women now slightly outnumber men playing Web-based games. Spurred by the belief that games were an important gateway into other kinds of digital literacy, efforts were made in the mid-90s to build games that appealed to girls. More recent games such as *The Sims* were huge crossover successes that attracted many women who had never played games before. Given the historic imbalance in the game market (and among people working inside the game industry), the presence of sexist stereotyping in games is hardly surprising. Yet it's also important to note that female game characters are often portrayed as powerful and independent. In his book *Killing Monsters,* Gerard Jones argues that young girls often build upon these representations of strong women warriors as a means of building up their self confidence in confronting challenges in their everyday lives.

5. Because Games Are Used to Train Soldiers to Kill, They Have the Same Impact on the Kids Who Play Them.

Former military psychologist and moral reformer David Grossman argues that because the military uses games in training (including, he claims, training soldiers to shoot and kill), the generation of young people who play such games are similarly being brutalized and conditioned to be aggressive in their everyday social interactions.

Grossman's model only works if:

- we remove training and education from a meaningful cultural context.
- we assume learners have no conscious goals and that they show no resistance to what they are being taught.
- we assume that they unwittingly apply what they learn in a fantasy environment to real world spaces.

The military uses games as part of a specific curriculum, with clearly defined goals, in a context where students actively want to learn and have a need for the information being transmitted. There are consequences for not mastering those skills. That being said, a growing body of research does suggest that games can enhance learning. In his recent book, *What Video Games Have to Teach Us About Learning and Literacy,* James Gee describes game players as active problem solvers who do not see mistakes as errors, but as opportunities for improvement. Players search for newer, better solutions to problems and challenges, he says. And they are encouraged to constantly form and test hypotheses. This research points to a fundamentally different model of how and what players learn from games.

6. Video Games Are Not a Meaningful Form of Expression.

On April 19, 2002, U.S. District Judge Stephen N. Limbaugh Sr. ruled that video games do not convey ideas and thus enjoy no constitutional protection. As evidence, Saint Louis County presented the judge with videotaped excerpts from four games, all within a narrow range of genres, and all the subject of previous controversy. Overturning a similar decision in Indianapolis, Federal Court of Appeals Judge Richard Posner noted: "Violence has always been and remains a central interest of humankind and a recurrent, even obsessive theme of culture both high and low. It engages the interest of children from an early age, as anyone familiar with the classic fairy tales collected by Grimm, Andersen, and Perrault are aware." Posner adds, "To shield children right up to the age of 18 from exposure to violent descriptions and images would not only be quixotic, but deforming; it would leave them unequipped to cope with the world as we know it." Many early games were little more than shooting galleries where players were encouraged to blast everything that moved. Many current games are designed to be ethical testing grounds. They allow players to navigate an expansive and open-ended world, make their own choices and witness their consequences. *The Sims* designer Will Wright argues that games are perhaps the only medium that allows us to experience guilt over the actions of fictional characters. In a movie, one can always pull back and condemn the character or the artist when they cross certain social boundaries. But in playing a game, we choose what happens to the characters. In the right circumstances, we can be encouraged to examine our own values by seeing how we behave within virtual space.

10 7. Video Game Play Is Socially Isolating.

Much video game play is social. Almost 60 percent of frequent gamers play with friends. Thirty-three percent play with siblings and 25 percent play with spouses or parents. Even games designed for single players are often played socially, with one person giving advice to another holding a joystick. A growing number of games are designed for multiple players—for either cooperative play in the same space or online play with distributed players. Sociologist Talmadge Wright has logged many hours observing online communities interact with and react to violent video games, concluding that metagaming (conversation about game content) provides a context for thinking about rules and rule-breaking. In this way there are really two games taking place simultaneously: one, the explicit conflict and combat on the screen; the other, the implicit cooperation and comradeship between the players. Two players may be fighting to death on screen and growing closer as friends off screen. Social expectations are reaffirmed through the social contract governing play, even as they are symbolically cast aside within the transgressive fantasies represented onscreen.

8. Video Game Play Is Desensitizing.

Classic studies of play behavior among primates suggest that apes make basic distinctions between play fighting and actual combat. In some circumstances, they seem to take pleasure wrestling and tousling with each other. In others, they might rip each other apart in mortal combat. Game designer and play theorist Eric Zimmerman describes the ways we understand play as distinctive from reality as entering the "magic circle." The same action—say, sweeping a floor—may take on different meanings in play (as in playing house) than in reality (housework). Play allows kids to express feelings and impulses that have to be carefully held in check in their real-world interactions. Media reformers argue that playing violent video games can cause a lack of empathy for real-world victims. Yet, a child who responds to a video game the same way he or she responds to a real-world tragedy could be showing symptoms of being severely emotionally disturbed. Here's where the media effects research, which often uses punching rubber dolls as a marker of real-world aggression, becomes problematic. The kid who is punching a toy designed for this purpose is still within the "magic circle" of play and understands her actions on those terms. Such research shows us only that violent play leads to more violent play.

Sources

Entertainment Software Association. "Top Ten Industry Facts." 2003. http://www.theesa.com/pressroom.html.

Gee, James. *What Video Games Have to Tell Us About Learning and Literacy.* New York: Palgrave, 2001.

Grossman, David. "Teaching Kids to Kill." *Phi Kappa Phi National Forum 2000.* http://www.killology.org/article_teachkid.htm.

Heins, Marjorie. Brief Amica Curiae of Thirty Media Scholars, submitted to the United States Court of Appeals, Eighth Circuit, Interactive Digital Software Association et al. vs. St. Louis County et al. 2002. http://www.fepproject.org/courtbriefs/stlouissummary.html.

Jenkins, Henry. "Coming Up Next: Ambushed on 'Donahue'." *Salon* 2002. http://www.salon.com/tech/feature/2002/08/20/jenkins_on_donahue/.

Jenkins, Henry. "Lessons From Littleton: What Congress Doesn't Want to Hear About Youth and Media." *Independent Schools* 2002. http://www.nais.org/pubs/ismag.cfm?file_id=537&ismag_id=14.

Jones, Gerard. *Killing Monsters: Why Children Need Fantasy, Super Heroes, and Make-believe Violence.* New York: Basic, 2002.

Salen, Katie and Eric Zimmerman. *Rules of Play: Game Design Fundamentals.* Cambridge: MIT Press, 2003.

Sternheimer, Karen. *It's Not the Media: The Truth About Popular Culture's Influence on Children.* New York: Westview, 2003.

Wright, Talmadge."Creative Player Actions in FPS Online Video Games: Playing Counter-Strike." *Game Studies* Dec. 2002. http://www.gamestudies.org/0202/wright/.

Brain Candy: Is Pop Culture Dumbing Us Down or Smartening Us Up?

MALCOLM GLADWELL

Malcolm Gladwell is a longtime staff writer for the New Yorker *magazine and the author of two best-selling books:* The Tipping Point: How Little Things Make a Big Difference *(2000); and* Blink: The Power of Thinking without Thinking *(2005). In 2005 he was named one of the 100 Most Influential People by* Time *magazine. The following review of Steven Johnson's book,* Everything Bad Is Good for You, *appeared in the* New Yorker *in May 2005.*

Twenty years ago, a political philosopher named James Flynn uncovered a curious fact. Americans—at least, as measured by I.Q. tests—were getting smarter. This fact had been obscured for years, because the people who give I.Q. tests continually recalibrate the scoring system to keep the average at 100. But if you took out the recalibration, Flynn found, I.Q. scores showed a steady upward trajectory, rising by about three points per decade, which means that a person whose I.Q. placed him in the top ten per cent of the American population in 1920 would today fall in the bottom third. Some of that effect, no doubt, is a simple by-product of economic progress: in the surge of prosperity during the middle part of the last century, people in the West became better fed, better educated, and more familiar with things like I.Q. tests. But, even as that wave of change has subsided, test scores have continued to rise—not just in America but all over the developed world. What's more, the increases have not been confined to children who go to enriched day-care centers and private schools. The middle part of the curve—the people who have supposedly been suffering from a deteriorating public-school system and a steady diet of lowest-common-denominator television and mindless pop music—has increased just as much. What on earth is happening? In the wonderfully entertaining "Everything Bad Is Good for You" (Riverhead; $23.95), Steven Johnson proposes that what is making us smarter is precisely what we thought was making us dumber: popular culture.

Johnson is the former editor of the online magazine *Feed* and the author of a number of books on science and technology. There is a pleasing eclecticism to his thinking. He is as happy analyzing "Finding Nemo" as he is dissecting the intricacies of a piece of software, and he's perfectly capable of using Nietzsche's notion of eternal recurrence to discuss the new creative rules of television shows. Johnson wants to understand popular culture—not in the postmodern, academic sense of wondering what "The Dukes of Hazzard" tells us about

Southern male alienation but in the very practical sense of wondering what watching something like "The Dukes of Hazzard" does to the way our minds work.

As Johnson points out, television is very different now from what it was thirty years ago. It's *harder.* A typical episode of "Starsky and Hutch," in the nineteen-seventies, followed an essentially linear path: two characters, engaged in a single story line, moving toward a decisive conclusion. To watch an episode of "Dallas" today is to be stunned by its glacial pace—by the arduous attempts to establish social relationships, by the excruciating simplicity of the plotline, by how *obvious* it was. A single episode of "The Sopranos," by contrast, might follow five narrative threads, involving a dozen characters who weave in and out of the plot. Modern television also requires the viewer to do a lot of what Johnson calls "filling in," as in a "Seinfeld" episode that subtly parodies the Kennedy assassination conspiracists, or a typical "Simpsons" episode, which may contain numerous allusions to politics or cinema or pop culture. The extraordinary amount of money now being made in the television aftermarket—DVD sales and syndication—means that the creators of television shows now have an incentive to make programming that can sustain two or three or four viewings. Even reality shows like "Survivor," Johnson argues, engage the viewer in a way that television rarely has in the past:

> When we watch these shows, the part of our brain that monitors the emotional lives of the people around us—the part that tracks subtle shifts in intonation and gesture and facial expression—scrutinizes the action on the screen, looking for clues....The phrase "Monday-morning quarterbacking" was coined to describe the engaged feeling spectators have in relation to games as opposed to stories. We absorb stories, but we second-guess games. Reality programming has brought that second-guessing to prime time, only the game in question revolves around social dexterity rather than the physical kind.

How can the greater cognitive demands that television makes on us now, he wonders, not *matter*?

5 Johnson develops the same argument about video games. Most of the people who denounce video games, he says, haven't actually played them—at least, not recently. Twenty years ago, games like *Tetris* or *Pac-Man* were simple exercises in motor coordination and pattern recognition. Today's games belong to another realm. Johnson points out that one of the "walk-throughs" for "*Grand Theft Auto III*"—that is, the informal guides that break down the games and help players navigate their complexities—is fifty-three thousand words long, about the length of his book. The contemporary video game involves a fully realized imaginary world, dense with detail and levels of complexity.

Indeed, video games are not games in the sense of those pastimes—like Monopoly or gin rummy or chess—which most of us grew up with. They don't have a set of unambiguous rules that have to be learned and then followed during the course of play. This is why many of us find modern video games baffling: we're not used to being in a situation where we have to figure out what to do. We think we only have to learn how to press the buttons faster. But these games withhold critical information from the player. Players have to explore and sort through hypotheses in order to make sense of the game's environment, which is why a modern video game can take forty hours to complete. Far from being engines of instant gratification, as they are often described, video games are actually, Johnson writes, "all about delayed gratification—sometimes so long delayed that you wonder if the gratification is ever going to show."

At the same time, players are required to manage a dizzying array of information and options. The game presents the player with a series of puzzles, and you can't succeed at the game simply by solving the puzzles one at a time. You have to craft a longer-term strategy, in order to juggle and coordinate competing interests. In denigrating the video game, Johnson argues, we have confused it with other phenomena in teen-age life, like multitasking—simultaneously e-mailing and listening to music and talking on the telephone and surfing the Internet. Playing a video game is, in fact, an exercise in "constructing the proper hierarchy of tasks and moving through the tasks in the correct sequence," he writes. "It's about finding order and meaning in the world, and making decisions that help create that order."

It doesn't seem right, of course, that watching "24" or playing a video game could be as important cognitively as reading a book. Isn't the extraordinary success of the "Harry Potter" novels better news for the culture than the equivalent success of "Grand Theft Auto III"? Johnson's response is to imagine what cultural critics might have said had video games been invented hundreds of years ago, and only recently had something called the book been marketed aggressively to children:

> Reading books chronically understimulates the senses. Unlike the longstanding tradition of gameplaying—which engages the child in a vivid, three-dimensional world filled with moving images and musical soundscapes, navigated and controlled with complex muscular movements—books are simply a barren string of words on the page....
>
> Books are also tragically isolating. While games have for many years engaged the young in complex social relationships with their peers, building and exploring worlds together, books force the child to sequester him or herself in a quiet space, shut off from interaction with other children....
>
> But perhaps the most dangerous property of these books is the fact that they follow a fixed linear path. You can't control their narratives in any fashion—you simply sit back and have the story dictated to you.... This risks instilling a general passivity in our children, making them feel as though they're powerless to change their circumstances. Reading is not an active, participatory process; it's a submissive one.

He's joking, of course, but only in part. The point is that books and video games represent two very different kinds of learning. When you read a biology textbook, the content of what you read is what matters. Reading is a form of explicit learning. When you play a video game, the value is in how it makes you think. Video games are an example of collateral learning, which is no less important.

Being "smart" involves facility in both kinds of thinking—the kind of fluid problem solving that matters in things like video games and I.Q. tests, but also the kind of crystallized knowledge that comes from explicit learning. If Johnson's book has a flaw, it is that he sometimes speaks of our culture being "smarter" when he's really referring just to that fluid problem-solving facility. When it comes to the other kind of intelligence, it is not clear at all what kind of progress we are making, as anyone who has read, say, the Gettysburg Address alongside any Presidential speech from the past twenty years can attest. The real question is what the right balance of these two forms of intelligence might look like. "Everything Bad Is Good for You" doesn't answer that question. But Johnson does something nearly as important, which is to remind us that we shouldn't fall into the trap of thinking that explicit learning is the only kind of learning that matters.

In recent years, for example, a number of elementary schools have phased out or reduced recess and replaced it with extra math or English instruction. This is the triumph of the explicit over the collateral. After all, recess is "play" for a ten-year-old in precisely the sense that Johnson describes video games as play for an adolescent: an unstructured environment that requires the child actively to intervene, to look for the hidden logic, to find order and meaning in chaos.

One of the ongoing debates in the educational community, similarly, is over the value of homework. Meta-analysis of hundreds of studies done on the effects of homework shows that the evidence supporting the practice is, at best, modest. Homework seems to be most useful in high school and for subjects like math. At the elementary-school level, homework seems to be of marginal or no academic value. Its effect on discipline and personal responsibility is unproved. And the causal relation between high-school homework and achievement is unclear: it hasn't been firmly established whether spending more time on homework in high school makes you a better student or whether better students, finding homework more pleasurable, spend more time doing it. So why, as a society, are we so enamored of homework? Perhaps because we have so little faith in the value of the things that children would otherwise be doing with their time. They could go out for a walk, and get some exercise; they could spend time with their peers, and reap the rewards of friendship. Or, Johnson suggests, they could be playing a video game, and giving their minds a rigorous workout.

ICED (I Can End Deportation)

ICED (I Can End Deportation) is a game available via the Games for Change (G4C) *Web site. G4C supports the use of games to advance social change. It describes itself as "the primary community of practice for those interested in making digital games about the most pressing issues of our day, from poverty to race and the environment." The object of ICED is "to become a citizen of the United States."*

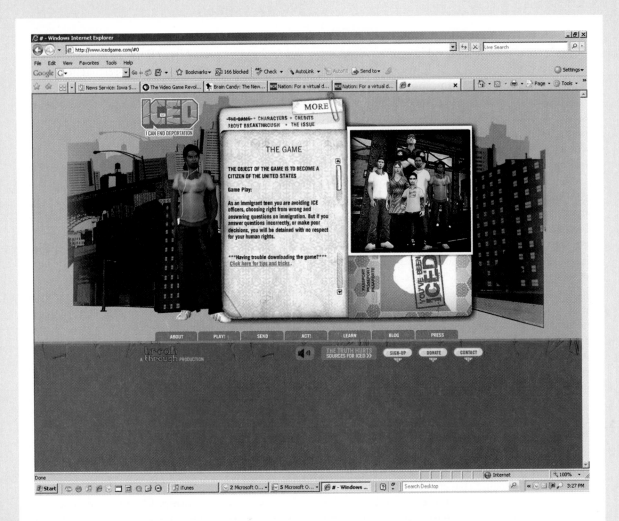

For a Virtual Dose of Reality, a Different Kind of Video Game

MICHAEL HUMPHREY

Michael Humphrey is a freelance writer who lives in Kansas City, Missouri. This article about the organization Games for Change, which promotes digital games for social awareness and change, appeared in March 2008 in the National Catholic Reporter.

The sit-in, the boycott, the prayer vigil and the video game— no, it's not a Sesame Street exercise about which of the four doesn't belong. This is a wake-up call to activists about what is going to create social change in the digital age.

"Games are a young medium and they are evolving, they are growing up and becoming more able to sustain a different kind of content," says Suzanne Seggerman, president and cofounder of Games for Change (G4C) (www.gamesforchange.org).

The New York City–based nonprofit has been called the "Sundance" of digital games for social change. It educates organizations and foundations interested in entering the field.

"Our biggest goal is to activate the nonprofit sector," Seggerman says, "to let them know that games are really good in engaging young people, especially, in social issues."

5 Understandably, resistance to the idea abounds. It's reasonable to ask whether kids accustomed to shooting their way through virtual dangers will suddenly be willing to adopt more worthy gaming goals: save the environment, feed the hungry or help an immigrant get her U.S. citizenship, say.

If market testing for ICED (I Can End Deportation) is any indication, the answer is yes. ICED is a free, Web-based game created by Breakthrough, a human rights organization that uses pop culture to advocate for their causes (www.breakthrough.tv).

ICED was conceived by Breakthrough staff in collaboration with Hunter College's Integrated Media Arts program. Initially, the students wanted to create an art installation that looked like a deportation detention center. The idea evolved from there.

"An installation is only going to have a limited number of people [as viewers]," says Mallika Dutt, founder and executive director of Breakthrough. "A video game is going to reach a much larger number of people. And it has the same first-person immersive component to it."

Over two years, with just $50,000 (a paltry amount to create a video game), Breakthrough was able to create a product that looks and sounds professional and makes the social points without appearing overly preachy.

There are several characters to 10 choose from in ICED, most of whom are not illegal immigrants. Some have green cards, some have asylum, one is a veteran in the U.S. Army. But each has to keep a low profile, stay out of trouble and avoid deportation.

While testing the game, Dutt says, Breakthrough learned that gaming has to look beyond the problems, and even the potential solutions. It has to look at the vision for a better world.

"The young people came back to us and said, 'The game is a real bummer, because there's nothing you can do to win,' " Dutt says. "So we added the outcome of becoming a U.S. citizen in almost the last iteration—because current laws are such that it is extremely unlikely that you're going to end up with citizenship. However, adding the goal of citizenship reinforced the values we were trying to communicate."

But will ICED change attitudes toward immigration?

"The range of audience that we're reaching out to has been quite astonishing," Dutt says. "Whether that translates into changed attitudes, it's really too early to know that."

Games for Change has com- 15 piled a list of best games on its Web site. You can raise a family in rural Haiti (Ayiti: The Cost of Life), you can play the role of child in a wheelchair (Pete Arm Strong), you can solve problems through nonviolent means (A Force More Powerful and Peacemaker), you can play the role of your U.S. congressman (My US Rep) or you can be a farmer in a developing country (3rd World Farmer).

The objective, Seggerman says, is for gaming titles to merge into the mainstream and compete with Grand Theft Auto or Madden 2008.

"This gaming model is only getting bigger. There will someday be a game like An Inconvenient Truth," based on Al Gore's global warming products, "or a game like Nickel and Dimed," based on Barbara Ehrenreich's book about living on the low end of the economic scale, says Seggerman, who is working with corporations such as Microsoft and MTV on creating a viable market of socially aware games.

Perhaps the most notable resistance is coming from the very organizations that could use video games for added outreach. Activists, advocacy groups and especially foundations have been resistant, or just as likely, unaware of gaming's reach.

To continue raising awareness, G4C is building buzz through its own Games for Change Festival, now in its fifth year. This year's event, scheduled for June 2–4 in New York City, will include "Let the Games Begin: 101 Workshop on Making Social Issue Games." The workshop was funded through an award in the first Digital Media and Learning Competition of the John D. and Catherine T. MacArthur Foundation.

20   "More and more people, once they play a game like ICED, and they see the richness of the experience, they are going to see that things are shifting," Seggerman says.

Violent Video Games Recruit American Youth

WILLIAM LUGO

William Lugo is assistant professor of sociology at Eastern Connecticut State University in Willimantic. His research interests are video games and their intersection with race, gender, and violence. The article below appeared in March 2006 in Reclaiming Children and Youth, *a journal whose mission is to reclaim and empower children and youth who are in conflict with family, school, and community.*

On May 12, 2004, Black Hawk helicopters converged on downtown Los Angeles, surrounding the city's convention center. Troops rappelled down nearby buildings, and armed with machine guns, soldiers ran through the street. Most people remained motionless, fixated on the surreal events. Others, possibly out of fear of a terrorist attack, ran for cover. It was not until an Army spokesman made an announcement that individuals breathed easier. There were no terrorist activities occurring. In fact, there were no immediate threats in the area. So what did the Army want? They were there to encourage everyone to download the latest version of *America's Army* off the internet. Simply put, the operation was a promotional event.

For those unfamiliar with *America's Army,* it is one of the most technologically advanced military games available. Since its release in 2002, the game has been a resounding success, with over five million registered players (U.S. Army 2005). The goals of the game are fairly simple. Individuals are first required to complete basic training. There they practice marksmanship, go through ropes courses, and learn the basic tenets of Army doctrine. Upon completion of basic training, gamers then engage in more complex counter terrorist missions, such as *Special Forces Pipeline,* where they, along with other teammates, defend an Alaskan oil pumping station from a terrorist attack. While the missions within *America's Army* are not unique, there are two things that separate it from other video games. First, it's free. That's right, free. It costs nothing to play one of the newest, graphically amazing games at any time. It sounds almost too good to be true. After all, why would someone spend millions of dollars developing and marketing a game, just to give it away for free? This is the second distinguishing characteristic of *America's Army*—it is made by the United States military. According to the military, the game is used as a recruitment tool (Downing, 2004). The game has been a success, not only in terms of recruitment, but also in its cost effectiveness. For example, while the military currently spends almost $4 billion annually on recruitment (General Accounting Office, 2003), it spends only $4 million annually upgrading and marketing *America's Army* (Gwinn, 2003). For these reasons, in January 2004, the Army set up its own video game studio in Cary, North Carolina.

Unfortunately, any discussion of the military's involvement in video games begins and ends with *America's Army.* All discussions have remained fixated on this game. However, the military's presence within the video game industry extends well beyond *America's Army.* Most notably, in the summer of 2004, the training simulator used by the Army for urban combat became available for purchase, under the title *Full Spectrum Warrior.* The goal of the game is to command two units of soldiers through the fictional country of Zekistan, trying to remove a brutal dictator who was involved in the ethnic cleansing of his own people—the Zekis. According to the game, the U.S., along with NATO, invaded Zekistan, but only "after repeated warnings and failed diplomatic relations in the U.N." (FSW Instruction Manual, 2004). Fusing fiction and reality, the game was an instant bestseller. Gamers lauded the realistic visuals, complex combat maneuvers, and contemporary storyline. However, a considerable amount of realism was also absent from the game, particularly in the combat environment. As students in my Sociology of Video Games class commented, "Where are all the women and children? Aren't we supposed to be in a city?" Apparently the only inhabitants of Zekistan cities consist of the enemy or NATO soldiers. The opportunity for innocent bystanders to die is a virtual impossibility. This is an interesting phenomenon as the game's combat environment takes place in a city and the original purpose of the game was to serve as an authentic urban combat simulator. One would think that to recreate such an environment would necessitate the presence of many women and children. Apparently, that kind of realism was deemed either irrelevant or too intense for potential recruits to handle.

It should be noted that unlike *America's Army,* the military does not own the rights to *Full Spectrum Warrior.* Instead, the game is owned and marketed by Pandemic Studios and THQ. In fact, on the back of the game box, in fine print, reads "This game is not sponsored or endorsed by the United States Army." Why would Pandemic Studios and THQ make this lack of a relationship so explicit? The answer to this question is found on the very same box. Written above the previous statement, large, bold print reads "based on a training aid developed for the U.S. Army." The relationship between *Full Spectrum Warrior* and the Army is popularized in every review and press release about the game and no doubt adds an element of legitimacy the game would not have had if it were not in some way related to the military. The message from THQ and Pandemic is clear: for an authentic military experience, buy *Full Spectrum Warrior.* And to the Army's credit, there is no game like it. People who have played the game have commented on the unique, deliberate, and methodical movements necessary to complete it. Any attempt to rush through the game is a near impossibility This is in contrast to other military games which rely on one individual, many times with unlimited ammunition and health. Because of the commercial and recruiting success of *Full Spectrum Warrior,* the Marines have now released their own training simulator. *Close Combat: First to Fight,* in April 2005. Not to be left behind, the Air Force is also developing a video game which they will offer for free.

5   The dire implications of this new recruitment strategy are compounded by the reality that the military are now making all of their games in-house. Prior to this, recruitment goals were consistently tempered by the pursuit of profit. Private companies jointly developing games with the military had to first think about meeting their bottom lines before adhering to recruiting strategies. After all, gamers are just like any other consumer. They are influenced by the same market forces, in particular, the greatest market force—price. This is why the average price of video games has not increased for the last 15 years, despite the fact that production values have risen dramatically. To price a game above $49.99 is virtual suicide. Thus, the research, development, and marketing costs of all video games revolve around this magic number, placing limits and boundaries on the types of games that can be made. Such a scenario is alien to *America's Army,* as profit ceases to be a constraining factor (as evidenced by the game's $0 price tag, yet high development costs). Now with their own video games studio, recruiting can stand as a top priority (and perhaps the only priority) throughout the development and distribution phase of a video game. The impact that this has can already be seen in games like *America's Army.*

One way is through game difficulty. For example, developers not only have to make games affordable, but also enjoyable. And part of this enjoyment comes from how challenging a game is. If the game is too easy, individuals will not purchase it; the short time it would take to complete the game would not justify its purchase price. If the game is too hard, individuals will become frustrated and discourage others from purchasing it. Thus, developers must find an appropriate level of difficulty. However, when profits are not a priority, game difficulty becomes a much more pliable characteristic. For example, during basic training in *America's Army,* the MOUT mission involves throwing a flash bang grenade into a room and shooting the targets inside, all within eight seconds. In a typical game (i.e., one made with profits as the top priority), failing to meet level objectives would result in mission failure. However, during the MOUT mission, if one fails to complete the objectives, the clock simply starts over, offering an unlimited amount of time to complete the mission. Why might the Army design levels in such a way? If the primary goal is recruitment, it is likely the game design fulfills such a goal, and by making basic training a relatively easy, pain free experience, one's opinion of the Army, and more specifically basic training, might be similarly impacted.

A similar situation exists in *Full Spectrum Warrior.* However, instead of ease of difficulty being the anomaly, the uniqueness is in the few ethical dilemmas that exist. As mentioned earlier, even though the game takes place in an urban environment, virtually no women and children walk the streets. Thus, the possibility of killing innocent people does not exist. This situation is unique to *Full Spectrum Warrior,* as most video games do not censor the opportunity to kill innocent civilians. For example, in the *Splinter Cell* game series, one takes on the role of Sam Fisher, a covert operations field agent. In the game. Fisher has the "fifth freedom" or the right to kill anyone at anytime, although needlessly killing innocent civilians often results in mission failure. In other video games, killing innocent civilians is a game objective. For example, in *Burnout 3: Takedown,* the goal of the game is to smash into busy city intersections at high speeds, causing as much damage as possible. After each accident occurs, a damage total is calculated—the more damage, the more rewards. Finally, a game which takes death and destruction to another level is *Grand Theft Auto: San Andreas.* The fifth game in the *Grand*

Theft Auto franchise, *San Andreas* was one of the biggest games of 2004, selling over 12 million copies. The objective within the game is to build a crime empire and take over the town. All people, pedestrians, friends, enemies, police officers, are potential targets. As long as one is able to escape the repercussions of killing someone (e.g., if a cop is killed, more cops will come after the guilty gamer), then casualties are acceptable. Many times it is advantageous to kill innocent people. For example, if one needs money, killing pedestrians is a quick way to steal a few dollars. Overall, the message from video games is clear—killing innocent people is not an experience to keep from gamers. In fact, it can actually be used to increase game sales. So why would a military game, which takes place in a city, shy away from the possibility? Could it be that the Army did not want potential recruits having to face difficult ethical decisions? Could this also be the reason that all enemies in *Full Spectrum Warrior* are referred to as "Tangos" (a military term for enemy), further shielding the gamer from having to kill a real person?

Another way recruitment goals can alter game development is in "load times." Load times are brief pauses in a game that the computer uses to load in new material (e.g., a special character, level, or cinematic sequence). Such pauses are universally hated among gamers as they break into the action of the game. Furthermore, because of rapid improvements in technology, it is an increasing expectation that games will have no load times, or they will be hardly noticeable. Developers have answered this expectation with load times that often last less than a second, sometimes appearing only as a momentary glitch. This is an area where *America's Army,* by not having profit as a primary motivation in its development, deviates significantly from the norm. Instead of long load times being taboo, they become a necessity and an opportunity. This is evidenced by the fact that *America's Army* is riddled with load times, often lasting for over twenty seconds! During load times the following message is displayed:

> I am an American Soldier.
> I am a Warrior and a member of a team.
> I serve the people of the United States and
> live the Army Values.
> I will always place the mission first.
> I will never accept defeat.
> I will never quit.
> I will never leave a fallen comrade.
> I am disciplined, physically and mentally tough,
> trained and proficient in my warrior tasks and
> drills. I always maintain my arms,
> my equipment and myself.
> I am an expert and I am a professional.
> I stand ready to deploy, engage, and destroy
> the enemies of the United States of America
> in close combat.
> I am a guardian of freedom and the
> American way of life.
> I am an American Soldier.

For those unfamiliar with the previous passage, it is known as the *Soldier's Creed.* Only recently created, in November 2003, the *Soldier's Creed* is given to every soldier (as a wallet insert) to ensure they remember the Army's values. Lines 4-7 of the *Soldier's Creed,* also known as the *Warrior's Ethos,* are printed on all Army dogtags, and thus must be worn at all times. According to Colonel Kevin A. Shwedo, G-3 of the United States Army Accessions Command at Fort Monroe:

> The sooner we proliferate the *Soldier's Creed* throughout the Army, the faster we will start to blur the lines of MOS loyalties and we start understanding that we're a Soldier and we're a warrior first. The faster we implement this program and we've got Soldiers who are well-trained and can back up the issues that are addressed in the *Soldier's Creed,* the better off we'll be as an Army. (Rogers, 2004)

Since 2003, the Chief of Staff of the Army General Petter J. Schoomaker, has made it clear that the *Soldier's Creed* is to be an essential part of Army training, in particular to ensure the proper psychological mindset of the soldier (Burlas, 2004). And while the Army cannot use the exact same psychological training on every gamer (i.e., by giving them dogtags), they are able to pass their message onto potential recruits hour after hour through *America's Army.* And, unlike television, there is no way to change the channel.

10   Examples such as these offer insights into the types of games the Army will be producing in their new video games studio. And it is games like *America's Army* and *Full Spectrum Warrior,* and more generally the entire practice of the military making video games, that is completely unethical. Our country is in a state of war and desperately short of soldiers. In October 2004, House Resolution 163 was introduced which attempted to reinstate the draft. Even President Bush has issued "Stop-Loss Orders" on active military personnel, extending tours of duty beyond their required time. Finally, the Army has openly admitted it is falling drastically short of recruiting goals and has responded by targeting high school dropouts (Savage, 2004). Given these realities, the military has a serious conflict of interest in making video games. Is it possible for them to balance their ethical responsibility to be honest about the purpose of the games against their desperate need for higher recruitment? For example, while the military has admitted that *America's Army* is a recruitment tool, on the game's very website, they refer to it only as a "communications strategy" and that it "provides virtual insights about the Army" (U.S. Army, 2005). Teenagers have no idea they are being recruited and neither do their parents. Furthermore, when a recruiting commercial airs on television, individuals know they are being recruited and the experience lasts for only thirty seconds. In games like *America's Army,* the players do not realize they are being recruited, and the process can last for over a hundred hours! How is it possible for someone who is undecided about joining the military not to be impacted by an enjoyable, one hundred-hour recruitment session?

In the end, while using video games to recruit youth is unethical, it is also brilliant. The process begins similarly to other advertising campaigns—by offering a product for free. During this trial process, potential recruits are "conditioned." They are taught company values, techniques, and etiquette. The next step puts new recruits through the same training as current employees. In the case of gamers, offering them products like *Full Spectrum Warrior* makes players ready for combat by the time they finish the last level. And, if all goes as planned, reality and fiction will become so blurred, gamers will not know the difference, nor will they even understand how they ended up in the middle of the desert, fighting an enemy they know nothing about. However, unlike a game, this time there will be women and children walking the streets.

References

Burlas, J. (2004, March 4). Army chief of staff stresses warrior ethos for all soldiers. *Army Nezus Service.* Retrieved September 9, 2005 from: http://www.dcmilitary.com/army/standard/9_05/national news /

Downing, J. (2004, December 7). Army to potential recruits: Wanna play? *Seattle Times, p. AI.*

Full Spectrum Warrior. (2004). *Instruction manual.* Los Angeles: Pandemic Studios.

Gee, J. P. (2004). *What video games have to teach us about learning and literacy.* New York: Macmillan.

General Accounting Office. (2003). *Military recruiting: DOD needs to establish objectives and measures to better evaluate advertising's effectiveness.* Washington DC: Author.

Gwinn, E. (2003, November 7). Army targets recruits with new game. *Chicago Tribune,* p. Al.

Rogers, R. P. (2004, May 26). Army to issue new soldier's creed and warrior ethos ID cards, dogtags. *TRADOC News Service.* Retrieved May 4, 2005 from: http://www-tradoc.army.mil/pao /TNSarchi ves/MayO4/055304.htm

Savage, C. (2004, November 29). Military recruiters target schools strategically. *Boston Globe,* p. Al.

U.S. Army. (2005). *Is this a recruiting tool?* Retrieved April 23, 2005 from: http:// www.americasarmy.com /support/faq_win.php#faq2

U.S. Army. (2005). *Marksmanship totals: America's Army.* Retrieved April 21, 2005 from: http://www.americasarmy.com/

■ ■ ■ **FOR CLASS DISCUSSION** Video Games and Their Influence

1. Anderson and Gentile's Iowa State studies seem to suggest some very negative effects of video gaming, while Jenkins argues that such studies overrate the dangers of video games. Carefully analyze the arguments in each case. Then discuss: Are the two articles addressing precisely the same question? Does Jenkins contradict the results of Anderson and Gentile's research, or does he just weaken their claims? What counts as evidence in each case? Which do you find more convincing, and why?

2. Malcolm Gladwell explains the distinction Steven Johnson makes between "explicit learning" and "collateral learning." Reread this discussion. From the context, what do you understand the difference to be? How do video games provide collateral learning, and of what kinds? What other activities, in addition to the ones Gladwell names, similarly provide such learning? What is the connection between collateral learning and recess or homework, according to Gladwell? How might an understanding of collateral learning lead to a reimagined school curriculum?

3. Michael Humphrey states that "perhaps the most notable resistance [to games for social change] is coming from the very organizations that could use video games for added outreach"—specifically, "activists, advocacy groups and especially foundations."

Discuss this observation: why would these organizations, in particular, resist such games? Brainstorm as many reasons as you can, explaining why such groups would resist. How might you answer their concerns?

4. Analyze William Lugo's argument about video games as recruitment tools using the List 2 guide questions on pages 426–427.

WRITING ASSIGNMENT   Evaluation Argument or Opinion Piece

Option 1: An Evaluation Argument   Write an argument in which you argue the value or risks of a specific video or computer game or category of games. Aim your argument at people who are likely to disagree with you; for example, if you are arguing about the dangers of a particular game, construct your argument in such a way that people who enjoy the game will nevertheless want to have a conversation with you about it. Somewhere in your argument, recognize alternative views and refute them or concede to them. You may want to conduct additional research to support your argument.

Option 2: An Opinion Piece   Write an opinion piece for your local newspaper supporting or objecting to the use of taxpayers' money to develop video games for use in military recruitment. You may want to review the *America's Army* Web site at http://www.americasarmy.com/ and possibly conduct additional research to learn the arguments on all sides. ■

For additional writing, reading, and research resources, go to www.mycomplab.com

The News Media
Responsible Production, Responsible Consumption

On July 7, 2005, when terrorist bombs exploded in the London subway, Britain and the world experienced what the British newspaper the *Guardian* has called "the democratization of the news process, the true birth of the 'citizen reporter.'" The public watched live coverage from the scene through mobile phone pictures and video clips sent by nonjournalists. Text messaging and blogging also helped to shape the professional news coverage of the crisis. Similarly, news and images sent by soldiers from Iraq or posted on the Web have also influenced the world's understanding of this war, as have the gruesome videos of beheadings posted on the Web by terrorists. Although the United States' government sought initially to censor the now famous flag-draped coffin photo and photos of prisoner abuse in Abu Ghraib, these images have circulated widely, thereby affecting peoples' view of the war. The fact that images can easily be digitally altered and manipulated in terms of presentation and context further complicates the power of images to shape viewers' understanding of events.

In addition to these new problems, the media itself is conducting heated discussions of challenges facing the media and journalists—problems such as corporate control and bias in news media; journalistic credibility; reporters' use of confidential sources versus full disclosure of their sources; the proliferation of venues from which people get their news; political advertising; and shallow versus in-depth coverage of critical issues.

The readings in this unit surround two major questions: What constitutes "responsible journalism" in an era of instant news? And what are the responsibilities of citizen/consumers to follow, be selective or discerning about, or even help create and disseminate the news?

The Massless Media

WILLIAM POWERS

A former reporter for the Washington Post, *William Powers is currently a regular columnist for the* National Journal, *a magazine committed to nonpartisan, reliable reporting. His chosen subject matter centers on the media, politics, and culture, as does this article from the January/February 2005 edition of the* Atlantic Monthly.

One day last June, as a hot political summer was just warming up, a new poll was released. This one wasn't about which candidate voters favored for the White House. It was about which news channels they were choosing with their TV remotes.

"Political polarization is increasingly reflected in the public's news viewing habits," the Pew Research Center for the People and the Press reported.

Since 2000, the Fox News Channel's gains have been greatest among political conservatives and Republicans. More than half of regular Fox viewers describe themselves as politically conservative (52%), up from 40% four years ago. At the same time, CNN, Fox's principal rival, has a more Democrat-leaning audience than in the past.

It's no surprise, of course, that Fox News viewers are more conservative than CNN viewers. But it is rather surprising that even as the network's audience is growing in sheer numbers, it is also growing increasingly conservative. The months following the poll offered further evidence of the ideological sorting of cable-news viewers. During the Democratic National Convention, in July, CNN came in first in the cable ratings, prompting a Fox spokesman to say, "They were playing to their core audience." Weeks later, during the Republican National Convention, Fox News played to its core audience and scored ratings that beat not only CNN and the other cable channels but even the broadcast networks—a historical first. When election day came around and George Bush won, it wasn't hard to predict that Fox News would again be the cable ratings victor: the conservative candidate took the prize, and so, naturally, did the news channel favored by conservatives.

5   Committed partisans on the left and the right have always had ideological media outlets they could turn to (*The Nation* and *National Review,* for example), but for most Americans political affiliation was not the determining factor in choosing where they got their news. The three national networks, CBS, NBC, and ABC, offered pretty much the same product and the same establishment point of view. That product was something you shared with all Americans—not just friends, neighbors, and others like you but millions of people you would never meet, many of them very unlike you.

For some time now Americans have been leaving those vast media spaces where they used to come together and have instead been clustering in smaller units. The most broad-based media outlets, the networks and metropolitan newspapers, have been losing viewers and readers for years. But lately, thanks to the proliferation of new cable channels and the rise of digital and wireless technology, the disaggregation of the old mass audience has taken on a furious momentum. And the tribalization is not just about political ideology. In the post-mass-media era audiences are sorting themselves by ethnicity, language, religion, profession, socioeconomic status, sexual orientation, and numerous other factors.

"The country has atomized into countless market segments defined not only by demography, but by increasingly nuanced and insistent product preferences," *BusinessWeek* reported last July, in a cover story called "The Vanishing Mass Market." To survive in this environment even old mass-media companies have had to learn the art of "niching down." Though national magazines have produced targeted subeditions for years, the slicing grows ever thinner. Time, Inc., the grand-daddy of print media for the masses, has launched a new women's magazine just for Wal-Mart shoppers. Radio now has satellite and Web variants that let listeners choose their taste pods with exceptional precision. The fast-growing XM Satellite Radio has not just one "urban" music channel but seven, each serving up a different subgenre twenty-four hours a day.

Some niches are so small they're approaching the vanishing point. There are now hundreds of thousands of bloggers, individuals who publish news, commentary, and other content on their own idiosyncratic Web sites. Some boast readerships exceeding those of prestigious print magazines, but most number their faithful in the double and triple digits. Find the one who shares your tastes and leanings, and you'll have attained the *ne plus ultra* of bespoke media: the ghostly double of yourself.

To sensibilities shaped by the past fifty years, the emerging media landscape seems not just chaotic but baleful. Common sense would suggest that as the vast village green of the broadcast era is chopped up into tiny plots, divisions in the culture will only multiply. If everyone tunes in to a different channel, and discourse happens only among like minds, is there any hope for social and political cohesion? Oh, for a cozy living room with one screen and Walter Cronkite signing off with his authoritative, unifying "That's the way it is."

10   It's instructive to remember, however, that the centralized, homogeneous mass-media environment of Cronkite's day was really an anomaly, an exception to the historical rule. For two centuries before the arrival of television America had a wild, cacophonous, emphatically decentralized media culture that mirrored society itself. And something like that media culture seems to be returning right now.

When primitive newspapers first appeared in seventeenth-century London, they were just official bulletins about the doings of the monarchy. Royally sanctioned and censored, they had no ideology other than that of the throne. The first real American newspaper, the *Boston News-Letter,* came straight from this mold. It was put out by an imperial official, the postmaster of colonial Boston, and stamped with the same seal of governmental approval worn by its British predecessors: "Published by Authority."

That timid approach didn't last long in America, however. In 1721 a Boston printer named James Franklin, older brother of Benjamin, founded a paper called the *New England Courant,* which brashly questioned the policies of the colony's ruling elite. The very first issue attacked Cotton Mather and other worthies for their support of smallpox inoculations. The paper was on the wrong side of that argument, but the real news was that it made the

argument at all. The *Courant* was "America's first fiercely independent newspaper, a bold, antiestablishment journal that helped to create the nation's tradition of an irreverent press," Walter Isaacson writes in his recent biography of Benjamin Franklin (whose first published writings appeared in his brother's paper).

Franklin's paper set the tone for the evolution of the media in this country. Outspoken newspapers played a crucial role in the Revolutionary War, and when it was over the leaders of the young republic consciously used public policy to nurture a free press. As the Princeton sociologist Paul Starr notes in his recent book, *The Creation of the Media: Political Origins of Modern Communications,* the United States dispensed with the European tradition of licensing papers and policing their content. Congress even granted American publishers lower rates for postal delivery, a valuable subsidy that made starting up and running a paper more economical.

Such policies, combined with the freewheeling ethos that had already taken root in the press, set off a wild journalistic flowering in the nineteenth century. By the 1830s newspapers were everywhere, and they spoke in a myriad of voices about all manner of issues. Alexis de Tocqueville, who was accustomed to the reined-in newspapers of France, marveled at all the variety.

15   The number of periodical and semi-periodical publications in the United States is almost incredibly large. It may readily be imagined that neither discipline nor unity of action can be established among so many combatants, and each one consequently writes under his own standard. All the political journals of the United States are, indeed, arrayed on the side of the administration or against it; but they attack and defend it in a thousand different ways.

In this the media reflected the political scene. The nineteenth century was a time of intense national growth and fervent argument about what direction the country should take. Numerous political parties appeared (Democratic, Whig, Republican, Free Soil, Know-Nothing), and the views and programs they advocated all found expression in sympathetic papers. In fact, the parties themselves financially supported newspapers, as did the White House for a time. Starr notes that according to a U.S. Census estimate, by the middle of the nineteenth century 80 percent of American newspapers were avowedly partisan.

This partisanship was not typically expressed in high-minded appeals to readers' better instincts. As Tocqueville wrote, "The characteristics of the American journalist consist in an open and coarse appeal to the passions of his readers; he abandons principles to assail the characters of individuals, to track them into private life and disclose all their weaknesses and vices." When Martin Chuzzlewit, the central character of the Dickens novel by the same name, arrives in the New York City of the early 1840s, he is greeted by newsboys hawking papers with names like the *New York Stabber* and the *New York Keyhole Reporter*. "Here's the *New York Sewer!*," one newsie shouts. "Here's the *Sewer*'s exposure of the Wall Street Gang, and the *Sewer*'s exposure of the Washington Gang, and the *Sewer*'s exclusive account of a flagrant act of dishonesty committed by the Secretary of State when he was eight years old."

Yet even though the media of this period were profuse, partisan, and scandalously downmarket, they were at the same time a powerful amalgamator that encouraged participatory democracy and forged a sense of national identity. Michael Schudson, a professor of communication and sociology at the University of California at San Diego and the author of *The Sociology of News* (2003), says that the rampant partisanship displayed by newspapers "encouraged people to be attentive to their common enterprise of electing representatives or presidents." Commenting that "politics was the best entertainment in town in the middle of the 19th century," Schudson compares its effect to that of sports today.

"Professional baseball is an integrative mechanism even though it works by arousing very partisan loyalties," he says. In other words, newspapers helped pull the country together not by playing down differences and pretending everyone agreed but by celebrating and exploiting the fact that people didn't. It's the oldest American paradox: nothing unifies like individualism.

We tend to think of the rise of the modern mass media as primarily a function of technology: the advent of television, for example, enabled broadcasters to reach tens of millions of Americans, but the cost of entry was high enough to sharply limit the number of networks. However, technology was only one of several factors that determined the character of the media establishment that arose in the United States after World War II. Beginning in the nineteenth century the idea of objectivity began to cross over from science into business and popular culture. As the historian Scott Sandage notes in his new book, *Born Losers: A History of Failure in America,* a whole new industry rose up in nineteenth-century New York when a handful of creative entrepreneurs discovered they could gather "objective" information about businesses and people (the precursor of modern-day credit ratings) and sell it to other businesses for a profit. Soon journalists, including the muckrakers of the Progressive Era, were embracing a similar notion of objective, irrefutable fact. When the Washington journalist Walter Lippmann wrote in the 1920s that "good reporting requires the exercise of the highest of scientific virtues," and called for the founding of journalistic research institutes, he was, as Starr notes, codifying a standard of disinterested inquiry that would influence generations of journalists to come.

20   At the same time, a federal government that had once used policy to encourage the growth of a free press now faced a very different challenge. Unlike

newspapers, the public airwaves were a finite resource, and someone had to decide how to dole it out. The solution was a federal regulatory structure that sought to ensure fairness but could never offer the ease of access or the expressive freedom of the press. (Not that the networks necessarily wanted the latter; in order to pull in the large audiences that ad buyers demanded, all strove for a safe neutrality that offended no one.) For these reasons, although the broadcast media reached more people, the range of content they offered was actually more constricted than that of the print media that preceded them.

Finally, the political culture of the 1940s and 1950s discouraged extremism. The two major political parties of that period certainly had their differences, but they shared a basic set of beliefs about the country's priorities. Politics hewed to the center, and the media both reflected and reinforced this tendency. The centrist, "objective" networks and large newspapers didn't just cover the political establishment; they were an essential part of it. The anchormen who appeared on television and the columnists of the great papers were effectively spokesmen for the ruling postwar elite. (On occasion literally so: Lippmann, the great proponent of objectivity, worked with his fellow reporter James Reston on a famous speech by Senator Arthur Vandenberg; both journalists then turned around to write about the speech for their respective papers.)

That establishment consensus exploded in the 1960s and 1970s, with Vietnam and Watergate, but the mass media hung on for a few decades, a vestigial reminder of what had been. The Reagan era and the end of the Cold War dealt the old politico-media structure the final blows. In the 1990s partisan politics really took hold in Washington, and again the news media followed suit. The demise of the postwar consensus made the mass media's centrism obsolete. Long-simmering conservative resentment of the mainstream

25

media fueled the rise of Rush Limbaugh and Fox News. Their success, in turn, has lately inspired efforts on the left to create avowedly liberal radio and cable outlets.

Socially, too, our fragmented media are to this era what James Franklin's newspaper was to the 1720s and the CBS evening news was to the 1950s. The cultural sameness and conformity that prevailed after World War II—the era of Father Knows Best and Betty Crocker—have been replaced by a popular pursuit of difference and self-expression. In explaining why McDonald's has shifted a significant portion of its advertising into niches, an executive of the company told *BusinessWeek,* "From the consumer point of view, we've had a change from 'I want to be normal' to 'I want to be special.' " In a mass-media world it's hard to be special. But in the land of niches it's easy. What is blogging if not a celebration of the self?

The "Trust us, we know better" ethos that undergirded the broadcast era today seems increasingly antique. If red and blue America agree on anything, it's that they don't believe the media. To traditionalists worried about the future of news, this attitude reflects a corrosive cynicism. But in another way it's much like the skepticism that animates great journalism. As the media have become more transparent, and suffered their own scandals, the public has learned to think about the news the same way a good journalist would—that is, to doubt everything it's told.

Although network ratings continue to plummet, there's still evidence elsewhere of an enduring demand for the sort of connectedness that only broad-based media can offer. For the six months that ended last September 30 many of America's largest newspapers saw the now customary declines in circulation. But among those that saw increases were the only three with a national subscriber base: *The New York Times, The Wall Street Journal,* and *USA Today.* The presidential debates last year drew impressive audiences to the broadcast networks, suggesting that although Americans no longer go to mass outlets out of habit, they will go by choice when there's good reason. In one of those debates Senator John Kerry cracked a Tony Soprano joke, and it was safe to assume that most viewers got the allusion. When we rue the passing of mass togetherness, we often forget that the strongest connective tissue in modern culture is entertainment—a mass medium if ever there was one.

Moreover, for all the pointed criticism and dismissive eye-rolling that niche and mass outlets direct each other's way, the two are becoming more and more symbiotic. Where would the Drudge Report and the blogging horde be without *The New York Times,* CBS News, and *The Washington Post*? Were it not for the firsthand reporting offered by those media dinosaurs, the Internet crowd would have nothing to talk about. Conversely, where would the Web versions of mass outlets be without the traffic that is directed their way by the smaller players? If there's a new media establishment taking form, it's shaped like a pyramid, with a handful of mass outlets at the top and innumerable niches supporting them from below, barking upward.

Whenever critics of the new media worry about the public's clustering in niches, there's an unspoken assumption that viewers watch only one outlet, as was common thirty years ago—that is, that there are Fox people and CNN people, and never the twain shall meet. But the same Pew poll that showed the increasingly ideological grouping of cable audiences revealed that most Americans watch the news with remote at the ready, poised to dart away at any moment. Pew also detected an enormous affinity for "inadvertent" news consumption: a large majority of Internet users from almost all demographic groups say that while online they encounter news unexpectedly, when they aren't even looking for it. "Fully 73% of Internet users come across the news this way," Pew reported, "up from 65% two years ago, and 55% as recently as 1999." Thus it appears that one of the great joys of newspaper reading—serendipitous discovery—lives on.

And although much changes in the media over time, there are some eternal truths. Most outlets crave two things, money and impact, and the easiest path to both is the old-fashioned one: grow your audience. Ambitious niches will always seek to become larger, and in so doing to attract a more diverse audience. It's only a matter of time before the first mass blog is identified, celebrated, and showered with minivan ads.

Finally, there's no substantive evidence yet that the rise of the niches is bad for democracy. The fractious, disunited, politically partisan media of the nineteenth century heightened public awareness of politics, and taught the denizens of a new democracy how to be citizens. Fast forward to the present. The United States just held an election that was covered by noisy, divisive, often thoroughly disreputable post-broadcast-era media. And 120 million people, 60 percent of eligible voters, showed up to cast their ballots—a higher percentage than have voted in any election since 1968. Maybe we're on to something.

Yahoo! Home Page

Internet users often encounter news unintentionally, on their way to search, email, instant message, or perform other tasks online, as illustrated in this screen capture from Yahoo.com. What elements of visual argument are evident here?

Reproduced with permission of Yahoo! Inc. ®2008 by Yahoo! Inc. YAHOO! and the YAHOO! logo are trademarks of Yahoo! Inc.

Plugged In, Tuned Out: Young Americans Are Embracing New Media but Failing to Develop an Appetite for News

DAN KENNEDY

Dan Kennedy is an Assistant Professor at Northeastern University's School of Journalism in Boston, where he specializes in new media trends. He is a regular contributor to the Guardian, *the* Boston Phoenix, *and* CommonWealth Magazine, *in which this article appeared in the fall of 2007.* CommonWealth *focuses on politics, ideas, and civic life in Massachusetts, and particularly on public policy questions as they affect the middle class. Kennedy maintains a blog,* MediaNation, *at MediaNation.blogspot.com.*

It's morning in Boston. Take a look around. Whether you're on the subway, walking through downtown, or standing in line at Starbucks or Dunkin' Donuts, you're surrounded by young people—twentysomethings, thirtysomethings, maybe a few teenagers, all of them getting ready for work or for school.

Now look more closely. What are they doing? Maybe a few (a very few) are flipping through the section fronts of *The Boston Globe,* or carrying a folded-up *New York Times.* You might see a couple of *Boston Herald* readers poring over news about the Patriots. Quite a few more might be glancing at the *Metro,* or possibly the newer *BostonNOW*—thin weekday freebies with a distinctly lite approach to the news.

Most, though, will be staying as far away from the news as they can. They might be talking to one another. They might be keeping to themselves, staring into space or reading a book. Or they might be wearing the distinctive white earbuds of an iPod. And if you assume they're not listening to a podcast of *All Things Considered* or *The NBC Nightly News,* you would most likely be correct.

For some years now, media executives and social scientists alike have been fretting over the disconnect between young people and the news. It's not just that those under 40 are less attuned to current events than older people are. It's also that they pay dramatically less attention to what's going on in the world than did people of the same age a generation or two ago.

5   "What's happening, I think, is that many more of them are entering adulthood without a news habit," says Tom Patterson, the Bradlee Professor of Government and the Press at Harvard's Kennedy School of Government. "As they age, they'll probably consume a bit more news, but it's not going to get up there to the level of older people today."

This past July, Patterson and the Kennedy School's Joan Shorenstein Center on the Press, Politics, and Public Policy released a study called *Young People and News,* which asked why most

young adults—despite spending as much as six hours a day with media of various kinds—are unable, for example, to identify the secretary of state by name. The answer: Despite being saturated with media, young people, when surveyed, evince a notable aversion to *news* media. For instance, just 16 percent of young adults (ages 18 to 30) read a newspaper every day, compared with 35 percent of those older than 30. Despite the rise of the Internet, young adults are more likely to watch a national newscast (31 percent) or local newscast (36 percent) every day than to read online news (22 percent)—although, again, they're far less likely to watch television news than are older adults. And a whopping 24 percent of young adults "paid almost no attention to news, whatever the source."

If you suspect it's ever been thus, you're wrong. Because, the study notes, in the late 1950s, some 53 percent of Americans in their 20s read newspaper coverage of national politics, a proportion not much lower than that of older adults during that era. A study of television news in 1967 found roughly the same pattern.

To Patterson, the culprit is obvious: cable television and a concomitant rise in choices. The typical household news habit of a newspaper on the doorstep every morning and Walter Cronkite on television every evening has given way to all entertainment, all the time. "I think we've broken the link between adult and child, or parent and child, in the transmission of the news habit," says Patterson.

That broken link represents a threat not just to the news media, which are losing readers, viewers, and listeners, but to civic life, the ideal of an informed citizenry, and our ability to govern ourselves.

10   Steve Babcock is a self-professed news junkie. As one of my students at Northeastern University, from which he graduated earlier this year, he read the *Globe* and the *Times,* the *New Yorker, Harper's,* and the *New York Review of Books,* and he listened to National Public Radio whenever he found himself in

a car. But Babcock was unusual, and he realized it whenever he would try to engage his friends in a conversation about the news.

"I'm the kind of person who wants to know what's going on in Sri Lanka. I never found many people who have that kind of knowledge," says Babcock, 23, who's now working as a reporter for the weekly *Rio Grande Sun*, in Española, N.M. "I think college is when your consciousness about the world gets raised. If you come up in an environment where you haven't been exposed to these things, you don't understand that keeping up with the news is important."

It's also a leading indicator of community well-being. In his oft-cited 2000 book, *Bowling Alone: The Collapse and Revival of American Community*, the scholar Robert Putnam found that young adults were far less likely than older people not just to read a newspaper, but also to attend religious services, sign a petition, go to a public meeting, write to an elected official, or serve as an officer in a local organization. "Newspaper readers are older, more educated, and more rooted in their communities than is the average American," Putnam wrote.

Similarly, Peter Levine, director of the Center for Information and Research on Civic Learning and Engagement, at the University of Maryland, observes that there is a direct correlation between voting and news awareness, and that young people are distinctly lacking in both. In his new book, *The Future of Democracy: Developing the Next Generation of American Citizens*, Levine writes that "you cannot vote unless you know whom you will support, and you cannot know that unless you are aware, at least, of the candidates or parties and a few fundamental issues."

Earlier this year, veteran television journalist Judy Woodruff hosted an hour-long documentary on PBS called *Generation Next*, which examined the lives of people between the ages of 16 and 25. The program was accompanied by a lengthy survey conducted by the Pew Research Center for the People and the Press, which found that there had been a slight uptick in news interest among young people since the late 1980s, but that their knowledge of current affairs was dismal nevertheless.

15 Even so, Woodruff expresses some hope, saying that critics are too focused on the traditional media, and that alternative venues such as *The Daily Show with Jon Stewart* and even cartoons such as *Family Guy* are reaching young people with substantive critiques of politics and public affairs in ways that, say, *The New York Times* or the network news can't, or won't. With about 1.4 million viewers, *The Daily Show* is hardly a threat to the Big Three network newscasts, whose combined audience can reach as high as 30 million. But its viewers' median age (35) is considerably lower than that of the audience for traditional news outlets.

"Much of the news young people see is not presented in a way that's relevant to them," says Woodruff in a telephone interview. "It's presented in a way that makes sense to people who are older, who know what Medicaid Part B is, or who know what the Kyoto Accord is, or McCain-Feingold. There's a lot of jargon in the news, and there's an adult framing of the news, if you will."

Woodruff adds: "I think we need to put ourselves in their shoes. I'm not at all saying we should dumb stories down, because young people today are smart. They're better educated than any generation that preceded them. But we need to find out what they're interested in and address the news to them. They're young. They're not at a stage in their lives where they own property and are home by 6 or 6:30 at night."

Woodruff is far from alone in pointing to Jon Stewart as a way of commenting on serious news so that it's entertaining without being aimed at the lowest common denominator. For instance, Saint Michael's College journalism professor David T. Z. Mindich, a former CNN assignment editor and the author of *Tuned Out: Why Americans Under 40 Don't Follow the News* (2005), says that *The Daily Show* is considerably more intelligent than a lot of what passes for news programming on television these days, especially on cable.

The Daily Show Is Seen as a Smarter Alternative to CNN

"If you can contrast *The Daily Show* with a typical hour on CNN now," Mindich says, citing the evening talk shows hosted by Glenn Beck and Nancy Grace, as well as *Showbiz Tonight*, "the only conclusion that we can reach is that the CNN executives think that we're idiots. In contrast, *The Daily Show* assumes that we're intelligent people capable of sophisticated thought."

20   Surveys show that news interest and voter turnout among young people was up slightly in 2004 and '06, a likely reflection of worries over the war in Iraq. Mindich says that's borne out by conversations he's had with young people since writing his book—and he notes that the consequences of not paying attention to the news can be a government whose officials do not fear having to suffer any consequences for their actions.

"One of the clearest examples of this is Abu Ghraib," Mindich says, referring to the notorious abuse of Iraqi prisoners by American soldiers. "You'd think that days after Abu Ghraib, [then–secretary of defense Donald] Rumsfeld would have been out. But the Bush administration was operating under the assumption—perhaps the correct assumption—that bad news would just blow over. So nobody in power was held accountable."

If there's one downward trend that appears irreversible, it is the cratering circulation of daily newspapers, caused in large part by the near-total abandonment of daily papers by young adults.

Peter Kadzis, executive editor of the weekly *Phoenix* newspapers, in Boston, Providence, and Portland, says studies of the *Phoenix's* core demographic—readers in their late 20s and early 30s—show two trends. First, with Americans marrying, having children, and buying their first houses later than ever, they have less need for the nuts-and-bolts news about government and community goings-on that are the typical fare of daily papers. Second, young adults are accustomed to using media that are well-designed and easy to use—cell phones, laptops, and iPods. The broadsheet newspaper (though not as broad as it used to be) is seen by this age group as a 19th-century relic, says Kadzis, who presided over a 2005 redesign to make the *Phoenix* papers more magazine-like in appearance.

"We're in the trenches with this age group, because if we lose them, we've got no one else to get," says Kadzis. (Disclosure: I worked with Kadzis at the *Phoenix* from 1991 through 2005, and continue to be an occasional contributor to the paper.)

25   Daily newspaper executives understand the problem, which is why they've been so aggressive about pursuing younger readers online. It's a difficult challenge; despite the long hours young adults spend on the Internet, they're not necessarily looking for news. And even if they are, that doesn't necessarily mean they're going to visit the Web sites of local newspapers.

Still, the region's two biggest dailies, the *Globe* and the *Herald*, have enjoyed some success on the Internet. Nielsen/ NetRatings reports that the *Globe's* Boston.com site attracted 4.2 million unique users in June, making it the fifth-most-popular news site in the country, and that BostonHerald.com drew 1.2 million unique users, good for 30th place. (A technical aside: BostonHerald.com's internal count showed 4.4 million unique users in June. Experts say such a disparity is not unusual, and there's widespread frustration with Nielsen's methodology, which is based on surveying people by phone. Nevertheless, the Nielsen numbers are the only ones available for making apples-to-apples comparisons.) The evidence also suggests that the papers' Web sites are attracting a younger audience than their print versions are. Boston.com, for example, reports that 54 percent of its users are between 25 and 44; by contrast, the median reader of the *Globe's* print edition is 46, according to the paper.

Both Boston.com and BostonHerald.com rely heavily on blogs, multimedia, interactivity, and feature material. Much of this might appear fluffier than what's in print. But is it condescending?

No, says Dave Beard, the editor of Boston.com, who argues that members of a generation who've been putting together PowerPoint presentations since they were in grade school aren't necessarily going to sit still and read a long story on a computer screen. He's focused on pulling in readers for the *Globe's* longer stories through online features such as a slide show on what you could buy with the $456 billion spent on the war in Iraq. (Some answers: 30 Big Digs; 52,615 years of Daisuke Matsuzaka's contract; or five and a half years of feeding and educating the world's poor.) "I think the impact of that is much more than another 2,000-word article on what we're doing in Iraq," says Beard.

Young Readers Can Get More Involved through More User-Generated Content

Adds Kerry Purcell, director of content development for Herald Interactive: "It's very difficult to get younger people involved in reading newspapers, even getting online to learn what is happening. But I think most news organizations ought to, first of all, get the readers involved with more user-generated content." For instance, BostonHerald.com (which underwent a spiffy redesign in September) published reader reviews of the Police concert earlier this year, and posted a survey asking users whether they would read "spoilers" giving away the ending of the last Harry Potter novel. The site also had a notable success with posting the payrolls of public employees this past spring—so much so that the Web traffic crashed the paper's server.

30   Two other 24-hour news organizations in Boston—WBUR radio (90.9 FM) and New England Cable News—don't have any specific strategies for attracting young people but are pursuing on-demand delivery systems that younger users would presumably find attractive.

Some of WBUR's programs are already available via free podcasts through outlets such as Apple's iTunes online store. Also, the new weekly *Radio Boston* program, hosted by former WCVB-TV (Channel 5) reporter David Boeri, had a strong Web presence even before its on-air debut. "You walk down Commonwealth Avenue, and all you see are white earbuds, and those people aren't listening to the radio. Those people are listening to downloaded content," says John Davidow, the station's news director and managing editor. According to Sam Fleming, managing director of news and programming, 18 percent of WBUR's audience is under 35, and another 22 percent is under 45. With an average age of 48, he says, WBUR listeners are about four years younger than those of news-oriented NPR affiliates nationwide.

Much of the news video at NECN is available online (the station is a content partner with the *Globe* at Boston.com) and can even be accessed through cell phones and personal digital assistants. But Tom Melville, NECN's assistant news director, resists the idea that young people need to be approached differently from the rest of the television news audience. "The people who are dying in Iraq right now are young people," he says. "We're very committed to covering, from a local angle, the war in Iraq. I think it's the most important story of our time, and we get a very positive response."

But even if local news organizations are doing a reasonably good job of repositioning their content for digital delivery, is that enough? The buzz phrase in online media for the past year or so has been "Web 2.0." Get past the hype, and it means this: Increasingly, users of online media see themselves not as passive consumers but as members of a community who create, share, and discuss content. If news organizations want to engage young people on their own turf, then that is the paradigm they're going to have to embrace.

What does a successful Web 2.0 news outlet look like? Well, it might look something like Blue Mass. Group, a liberal political site started in 2004 by three youngish Democratic activists. Blue Mass. Group is small (it attracts 2,500 to 3,000 unique users a day). It does little in the way of original reporting, relying mainly on links to the mainstream media (though it does include some on-the-ground accounts). And it's noncommercial, despite the presence of a few ads.

35   But Blue Mass. Group is built on a software platform that has enabled a community essentially to assemble itself. It's a group blog. Anyone can post items, and any of the site's three co-editors can promote those items to the "front page," making them more readily available to casual readers. The comments are as lively as the posts. Blue Mass. Group can be engaging or enraging, and it can be criticized for giving Gov. Deval Patrick the benefit of the doubt even though he doesn't always deserve it. (To be fair, Patrick does take an occasional hit.) But it's rarely dull.

David Kravitz, one of the co-editors, says he has no way of knowing Blue Mass. Group's demographics, but he suspects they skew young based on some of the live events the site has sponsored. "I think that younger people are just more accustomed to interacting with the world through a medium like the Internet than through a medium like radio [or TV or newspapers], which is more like other people talking to you," says Kravitz, a lawyer who is himself a not-particularly-young 43. "To the extent that blogs are able to bring in a somewhat younger demographic than *The CBS Evening News*, maybe that's why, because it does become a conversation."

Can mainstream news organizations reinvent themselves through conversation and community? John Wilpers thinks so. The founding editor of *BostonNOW* (he was let go in August, though he's still consulting on Web projects), Wilpers helped put together the paper's unusual hybrid model—letting readers set up blogs on the paper's Web site, and running excerpts from those blogs, as well as from other blogs in Greater Boston, in the print edition.

To be sure, the paper itself is pretty uninspiring, but the model is interesting, potentially giving readers what Wilpers describes as a sense of ownership in the newspaper. "If they feel they have a stake in something, if they're a member of something and have a say in its direction and they get their viewpoints out there, I think that's really powerful," Wilpers says. "And it can bring people back to the print medium."

Young people are already involved in non-news-related social media. Social-networking sites, especially *MySpace* and *Facebook*, have been enormously successful, with their mostly young users spending hours tweaking their profiles with photos, videos, blogs, and lists of their favorite musicians and movies. Politicians have also been quicker to embrace social media than have news organizations, and most of the current presidential candidates have set up shop on both sites. *YouTube*, another type of social network that allows users to share videos, has become the go-to site for raw political content, whether it's former US Sen. George Allen's "macaca" meltdown or positive footage posted by the campaigns themselves. Pauline Millard, a 30-year-old former Associated Press reporter who's now online editor for the newspaper trade magazine *Editor & Publisher*, believes news sites need to adopt some of those participatory features.

40   "I think it works because the young people actually get to participate in it," she says. "And one of the big things that newspapers are overlooking is that if you're a young person, you already create content all the time."

Perhaps the most popular example of social-media-meet-the-news is *Digg.com*, a site that allows users to submit news stories that are then rated by other members of the community. The more people who "digg" a story, the higher it moves toward the top of the list. *Digg* tends to be heavy on tech stories, and the most popular political items are often silly or of dubious provenance. But the idea of a community forming itself around the news is compelling.

In fact, shortly after issuing his *Young People and News* report, the Kennedy School's Tom Patterson put out another Shorenstein study showing that *Digg* and news sites based on other kinds of participatory models, such as *Newsvine* and *Reddit*, were growing exponentially faster than traditional news sites—with *Digg* exploding from fewer than 2 million unique users in April 2006 to more than 15 million in April 2007. *Digg* could conceivably pave the way for more serious attempts to build news communities, such as *NewsTrust*, an experimental site whose users are asked to rate stories on such journalistic values as importance, sourcing, and fairness.

Tom Rosenstiel, director of the Washington–based Project for Excellence in Journalism, is optimistic about the power of technology and community to revitalize the news business. "I think that, to some extent, these Web sites like *Digg* and *Reddit* represent something really meaningful," Rosenstiel says. "*Digg's* got really big numbers. There's something going on there." The idea, Rosenstiel adds, is to "make it participatory—it's a dialogue now, not a lecture. People don't just want to be able to complain afterwards, they want to converse." Social media, he says, allows users to "re-edit the agenda," adding that news organizations need to "give up some control and give up some of that omniscient-narrator pose."

None of this, of course, is meant to suggest that transforming a typical 25-year-old news ignoramus into a well-informed citizen is simply a matter of persuading her to watch Jon Stewart, check in on a few news sites, and then turn her loose on a social-media network or two to discuss what she's learned with like-minded young people. The news is a hard sell, especially in a time of affluence and a war that,

thanks to the all-volunteer military, can seem very distant from the life of a typical young adult living in Massachusetts.

45   The ongoing reinvention of the media that's being driven by the Internet could lead to a better, more democratic, more decentralized way of staying informed—a type of participatory news that could evolve into an example of civic engagement in and of itself. But for participatory news to work, you need participants. And the evidence suggests that young adults (most of them, anyway) are not using these new tools to learn about the world around them.

When Matt Storin was editor of the *Globe*, he once told me there was nothing wrong with newspaper circulation that a depression and a draft wouldn't cure. Indeed, in many ways the disconnect between young people and the news is a product of prosperity and, if not exactly peace, then at least the security of knowing that the government can't compel you to fight and die in a foreign land.

Even so, we need a certain amount of information in order to govern ourselves, to be full participants in civic life, to vote knowledgeably on matters of more significance than who ought to win the latest version of *American Idol*. The late social critic Neil Postman warned us a quarter-century ago that we were "amusing ourselves to death." If anything has changed, it's that the trends he warned of then have accelerated. Yes, the news media need to evolve. But young people—and all of us—also need to get over our self-absorption and start paying attention to what's going on, too.

Should Killers Be Given Air Time?

CHRIS SHAW

Chris Shaw is a senior program controller for news and current affairs at British television's Channel Five and a regular columnist for the Guardian, *a British newspaper founded in 1821 that prides itself on editorial and political independence. The article here appeared in the* Guardian *on April 19, 2007, three days after a gunman opened fire on the campus of Virginia Tech University in Blacksburg, Virginia, killing more than thirty people.*

The chilling suicide video and digital photo album sent to NBC by the Virginia Tech mass murderer and then broadcast and rebroadcast instantly around the world on TV and online represents the sinister side of user generated content.

Cho Seung-hui's insane self-justifying monologue and the gun-toting posturing has become an inevitable internet hit, going straight to the top of the click charts on virtually every news website I checked.

The NBC video is the most visited story on the BBC news website and dominates the front page of the Sky News site—which incidentally relaunched today.

It will quite probably remain the most visited video posting for several weeks.

5   This is exactly the kind of instant notoriety sought by the disturbed spree killers, from Dunblane through to Columbine and now Virginia Tech. Fears of copy-cat killings seeking instant cyber celebrity are not unfounded.

At Columbine, the young killers filmed their shooting practice in the woods—it was part of their private conspiracy to record their premeditated killing spree.

However, Cho went even further by apparently preparing a complete electronic press kit to send to NBC while he was carrying out his massacre of fellow students. It is surprising that he chose to mail it rather than download it straight to the newsroom.

Terrorists have long understood the importance and power of using digital media. Arguably, the dissemination of the film of a terror attack has become as important to the perpetrators as the act itself.

We're all familiar with the gruesome images of internet executions and many of the bomb attacks on coalition troops in Iraq are filmed with more than one camera so they can be edited into even more distressing propaganda for the terrorist cause.

10   This kind of user generated content does present some serious ethical issues for news organizations that choose to rebroadcast the material.

The news value of this stuff was irresistible to NBC despite any qualms about its impact on the survivors and the bereaved, not to mention any future spree killers.

All news organizations in the UK have followed suit and they, like NBC, will see massive spikes in their internet traffic.

In the end, news organizations did not have much choice about showing the material but the implications are quite scary.

Cho's motivation may never be fully understood but he certainly recognized the power of digital media. His massacre at Virginia Tech may be remembered as the first *YouTube* killing spree.

Those Terrible Virginia Tech Cartoons

DARYL CAGLE

Daryl Cagle is a syndicated cartoonist whose cartoons appear in over 700 newspapers. Cagle also writes a blog, The Cagle Post *in which the following appeared on April 20, 2007—four days after the Virginia Tech shooting spree. The cartoon targets NBC's decision to release to the public a media package sent to the network by the shooter himself.*

When a lunatic killed 32 people at Virginia Tech University earlier this week I knew what to expect from political cartoonists, who don't react well to tragedy. Some of the cartoons seemed insensitive, as today's generation of jokesters struggled to respond to a story with no lighter side.

I have some sympathy for the editorial cartoonists who have a daily deadline and must respond to the headline of the day. The first cartoons were predictable: Uncle Sam or the Virginia Tech mascot, with bowed heads and flags or the school pennant at half-mast. There were lots of riffs on the school logo (the letters "VT"), including one depicting the school logo in dead bodies. Some cartoonists launched immediately into gun control cartoons—"how terrible it is that guns are so widely available" and "what a shame it is that none of the victims were toting firearms to protect themselves."

I run a syndicate that distributes editorial cartoons to newspapers, and our editors were not happy. The day after the tragedy one editor from Georgia wrote: "As a Cagle subscriber, I have to tell you the cartoons sent today about the Virginia Tech shootings showed a deplorable lack of sensitivity and taste. Can't you find (someone) who isn't so quick to try to be funny or cute at innocent people's expense?"

As bad as this week was for cartoonists, it was worse for television. An army of aggressive TV reporters descended on little Blacksburg, Va., asking everyone they could find, "How do you feel?" and "Did you know him?" The television coverage reached new heights of ugliness when NBC released the killer's "Multimedia Manifesto" and all we could see on cable news was 24 hours of "non-stop nut-case." It took a day for the wallpaper killer coverage to devolve into finger pointing among the media about whether they were doing the right thing in publicizing the killer's message.

5   When I first heard about the massacre, I wrote in my blog that I would not be drawing any cartoons about it. But after only two days the story had matured into something I wanted to draw cartoons about because there was something for me to criticize. I

drew two cartoons bashing NBC; one showed the NBC peacock dressed up as the network of gun-brandishing Seung-Hui Cho. I drew another showing two kids dressed like Cho, because "He's the only guy we see on TV now." I drew another one generally bashing people who didn't see that Cho was a psychopath, with Cho painting the giant words "STOP ME" on the ground while two oblivious college professors walk by saying, "How can we know something like this is going to happen?"

Political cartooning is a negative art form. Cartoonists and columnists work best when bashing hypocrites or speaking to issues where opinion is divided. I am fortunate to have no daily deadline. When I don't want to draw on a subject, I don't have to; that was a luxury for me with the Virginia Tech story. Unfortunately, the deadlines of the 24-hour news cycle demand that most cartoonists, reporters and commentators chime in right away.

Sometimes it pays to take a step back and hold your breath without writing, drawing or reporting anything for a couple of days—until there is something constructive to say.

Not a Pretty Picture

SYDNEY H. SCHANBERG

Best known for his coverage of the war in Cambodia, Sydney H. Schanberg won a Pulitzer Prize for international reporting in 1976 for his contributions to the New York Times. *Until 2006, he wrote regularly for the* Village Voice, *a liberal, New York–based publication, where this article appeared on May 17, 2005.*

"History," Hegel said, "is a slaughterhouse." And war is how the slaughter is carried out.

If we believe that the present war in Iraq is just and necessary, why do we shrink from looking at the damage it wreaks? Why does the government that ordered the war and hails it as an instrument of good then ask us to respect those who died in the cause by not describing and depicting how they died? And why, in response, have newspapers gone along with Washington and grown timid

about showing photos of the killing and maiming? What kind of honor does this bestow on those who are sent to fight in the nation's name?

The Iraq war inspires these questions.

The government has blocked the press from soldiers' funerals at Arlington National Cemetery. The government has prevented the press from taking pictures of the caskets that arrive day after day at the Dover Air Force Base military mortuary in Delaware, the world's

largest funeral home. And the government, by inferring that citizens who question its justifications for this war are disloyal Americans, has intimidated a compliant press from making full use of pictures of the dead and wounded. Also worth noting: President Bush's latest rationale for the war is that he is trying to "spread democracy" through the world. He says these new democracies must have a "free press." Yet he says all this while continuing to restrict and limit the American press.

5　　There's a huge disconnect here.

More than 1,600 American soldiers have died in this war that began a little over two years ago. Wounded Americans number about 12,000. No formal count is kept of the Iraqi civilian dead and wounded, but it is far greater than the military toll. But can you recall the last time your hometown newspaper ran a picture spread of these human beings lying crumpled at the scene of the slaughter? And when was the last time you saw a picture of a single fallen American soldier at such a scene?

Yes, some photos of such bloodshed have been published at times over the span of this war. But they have become sparser and sparser, while the casualty rate has stayed the same or, frequently, shot higher. At the moment, five GIs die every two days.

Some readers may object to my use of the word slaughter. I do respect other points of view. But I served in the military, and as a reporter I covered several wars—in India, Vietnam, and Cambodia. I came away persuaded that whether one considers a particular war necessary or misguided, the military goal in armed combat is always to kill and thus render helpless those on the other side. That being the case, what is a government's basis for depriving the public of candid press coverage of what war is all about? How else can voters make informed decisions about a war their government has led them into? The true reason why a government—in this case, the Bush administration—tries to censor and sanitize coverage is to prevent a public outcry against the war, an outcry that might bring down the administration.

The photographs that accompany this piece [omitted here] are not gratuitously violent. They are merely real. All but one were taken by David Leeson, a highly regarded photographer at *The Dallas Morning News.* He and his *Morning News* colleague Cheryl Diaz Meyer were awarded the 2004 Pulitzer Prize in breaking-news photography "for their eloquent photographs depicting both the violence and poignancy of the war with Iraq."

10　　I realize there are other sides to the story. One is the government's side. President Bush says that none of the government's actions can be characterized as censorship or intimidation of the press. He says he is merely honoring the fallen by protecting the privacy of their families in their time of grief. A *New York Times* columnist—his name is not needed; the issue is what's important—offered another slant a week ago. He called for less coverage of the war's violence because the press was "frantically competing to get gruesome pictures and details for broadcasts and front pages" at a time when there is "really nothing new to say." He seemed to think the use of these "gruesome pictures" was on the rise—though others in the media-watching industry, such as Howard Kurtz of *The Washington Post,* have been recording a decline. The *Times* columnist said the press was, wittingly or not, assisting the "media strategy" of the suicide bombers and their leaders.

A columnist, of course, is permitted to offer up pretty much any opinion he or she chooses, but still it's very odd to see a journalist—since we historically have always pressed for transparency—recommending that information be left out of stories. He insisted he was "not advocating official censorship" but simply asking the media for "a little restraint." Also, he cited the press controls used by former New York mayor Rudolph Giuliani as a model for achieving "restraint." Giuliani, the column said, had told his police department "to stop giving out details of daily crime in time for reporters' deadlines," in order to keep "the day's most grisly crime" off the 11 o'clock television news.

I don't hold much esteem for the usual crime-and-catastrophe formula on most late-news shows, but I have even less for contentions that withholding information from the public is good for them. Because we are a country of diverse culture groupings, there will always be differences of view, about war photographs and stories, over matters of taste and "shock" issues. But, while the reporter or photographer must consider these impact and shock issues his primary mission has to be one of getting the story right. And getting it right means not omitting anything important out of timidity or squeamishness. When I would return from a war scene, I always felt I had to write the story first for myself and then for the reader. The goal was to come as close as possible to make the reader smell, feel, see, and touch what I had witnessed that day. "Pay attention," was my mental message to the reader. "People are dying. This is important."

A generation later, the photographer David Leeson, whom I talked with on the phone, has similar passions.

He said: "I understand the criticisms about blood and gore. I don't seek that. When I approach a body on the ground after a battle, I'm determined to give dignity to that person's life and photograph him with respect. But sometimes, as with my pictures of child victims, the greatest dignity and respect you can give them is to show the horror

they have suffered, the absolutely gruesome horror." Leeson went on: "War is madness. Often when I was in it, I would think of my work as dedicated to stopping it. But I know that's unrealistic. When I considered the readers who would see my photos, I felt I was saying to them: 'If I hurt inside, I want you to hurt too. If something brings me to tears, I want to bring you to tears too.'"

I don't see any place for "restraint" in this picture.

■ ■ ■   **FOR CLASS DISCUSSION**   **The News Media**

1. Shaw, Cagle, and Schanberg all address the issue of whether or when it is appropriate to air graphic or violent and disturbing photos, videos, and images. What arguments can be made for making such materials public? What are the arguments for keeping them from public view? Why do you think the graphic photos that originally accompanied the Schanberg article have been omitted in this textbook?

2. Discuss the connotations of the following terms used in these articles to describe some journalistic practices. Consider who might choose each term, and in what rhetorical context: "journalistic restraint," "censorship," "gruesome pictures," "candid press coverage," "disinterested inquiry," "safe neutrality," "establishment consensus," "objectivity," "fragmented media," "niche media," "rampant partisanship," "ideological polarization," "participatory news," "wallpaper killer coverage."

3. William Powers writes that the history of American news is largely one of fragmented interests and partisanship and notes, "It's the oldest American paradox: nothing unifies like individualism." What do you understand this paradox to mean? Do you think that present-day "niche news" has helped to bring the country together, or to divide it? What support can you provide for your response?

4. Together, the Powers and Kennedy articles sketch a profile of the twenty-first century news consumer in very specific terms. Working in groups or as a whole class, list as many characteristics of present-day news consumers as you can recall. Then discuss: Does this profile ring true for you and your friends or family? Is Kennedy's concern about young people not developing a taste for news justified? What responsibility, if any, do citizens have to follow the news?

5. Shaw's and Cagle's concerns arise from the news media's coverage of the Virginia Tech shootings in April 2007. Review the two opinions and the cartoon; what arguments are stated outright? What implicit arguments does each text make?
6. Choose one of the arguments in this unit for closer analysis, using the List 2 guide questions on pages 426–427.

WRITING ASSIGNMENT Definition Argument

Review the readings and visuals in this unit, noting particularly any direct or implied arguments about the role and responsibilities of journalists. Write a paper in which you define "responsible journalism" for a college student considering journalism as a career. Quote or cite from these readings. Your teacher may want you to conduct additional research in specialized journalism sources or online. See, for example, the *Society of Professional Journalists' Code of Ethics* at http://www.spj.org/ethics.asp, or the Project for Excellence in Journalism, which collects ethics guidelines from around the world, at http://journalism.org/resources/ethics_codes. ∎

> For additional writing, reading, and research resources, go to
> www.mycomplab.com

Immigration in the Twenty-First Century
Accommodation and Change

We are accustomed to discussing immigration as a political issue. Candidates for public office and politicians debate immigration policy or strategies for stopping the flow of illegal immigrants across our borders. We are also accustomed to media coverage of marches and protests by illegal immigrants petitioning for rights—to drive, to receive an education, to obtain health care—and we are well aware of efforts to build a wall to stem the flow of Mexican citizens into the United States. Legal immigrants make headlines less regularly, but the fact is that streams of immigrants, many of them young people, continue to arrive in the United States through legal as well as illegal means. The latest U. S. Census showed that there are 2.84 million foreign-born U.S. residents under age eighteen. As the articles in this unit suggest, there is tremendous national, ethnic, and cultural diversity within this population. Nor do these census figures account for the vast numbers of first-generation Americans, the children of immigrants. These children may have been born in the United States or may have arrived here at a young age; they are being educated in American schools but may go home to families whose first language is not English and whose religious and cultural practices are outside the American mainstream.

The readings in this unit (as well as those in Chapter 2) ask you to consider the issues and challenges of immigration in a country that prides itself on its immigrant origins but sometimes has trouble welcoming people with unfamiliar appearances, languages, and practices. In particular, this unit asks you to consider the following questions: How well is the United States accommodating its immigrant populations? What are the particular issues and challenges facing immigrant youth? To what extent should immigrants be expected to adapt or acculturate to a new country? Is it possible, or even advisable, to preserve elements of one culture while adapting to another?

Understanding and Responding to the Needs of Newcomer Immigrant Youth and Families

FRANCISCO X. GAYTÁN, AVARY CARHILL, AND CAROLA SUÁREZ-OROZCO

Francisco X. Gaytán is a doctoral candidate in applied psychology in the Steinhardt School of Culture, Education, and Human Development of New York University. He studies how social networks affect acculturation, particularly among Mexican immigrant students in New York City. Avary Carhill is a researcher in immigration studies at New York University; her research focuses on the roles of peer social networks and school contexts in individual language learning among adolescent immigrants. Carola Suárez-Orozco is a professor of applied psychology in the Steinhardt School of New York University and is co-director of Immigration Studies@NYU, *which studies immigration issues as they affect children, youth, and families. This article, which reports on a five-year longitudinal study of diverse immigrant students, appeared in November 2007 in* Prevention Researcher, *a newsletter for professionals who work with at-risk youth.*

In 2000 there were 2.84 million foreign-born U.S. residents under the age of 18 (U.S. Census Bureau, 2001). Although many common themes are embodied in the immigrant experience, enormous diversity exists among newcomer families with important implications for the development and adaptation of youth. Immigrant youth come from dozens of countries for different reasons, follow different paths of migration, and once in the U.S., they encounter vastly different circumstances. The public debate about immigration has largely failed to notice the children of immigrants and the fundamental differences within this group. While some immigrant youth out-perform their American-born peers in educational achievement, health, and happiness, many struggle to thrive in schools and communities that do not provide the resources they most need (Portes & Rumbaut, 2001; Suárez-Orozco, Suárez-Orozco & Todorova, in press).

Immigrant youth and their families migrate for a myriad of reasons. The adaptation experience of immigrant youth can vary greatly depending upon their lives in their country of origin, the availability of internal and external resources and the welcome they receive. Understanding the varied resources and experiences that immigrants have is critical for service professionals trying to meet the needs of immigrant youth as they adapt to life in the United States.

In this article we present quantitative and qualitative data that our research team collected and analyzed as part of the Longitudinal Immigrant Student Adaptation Study (LISA), a 5-year longitudinal study, which documents the patterns of adaptation among 407 recently-arrived youth from China, Central America, the Dominican Republic, Haiti, and Mexico (See Table 3.1). The participants in this study were all foreign-born and had parents who were born in the same country. At recruitment, participants had spent at least two-thirds of their lives in their country of origin and spoke a native language other than English. The participants were between the ages of 9 and 14 during the first year of the study, meaning that not only were they of an age range that allowed them to experience schooling abroad and the U.S., it also allowed them to reflect on their experiences of migration and development. In addition to student data, this study collected data from parents and teachers. The findings of this research project highlight the complexity and diversity of experiences among newcomer youth and the need for developing policy, prevention, and intervention that are relevant for them.

TABLE 3.1   LISA Study: Sample Characteristics

	Total Sample N=407	China [N=80]	Haiti [N=75]	Dominican Republic [N=83]	Central America [N=78]	Mexico [N=91]
Gender—Males [N=191]	46.9%	40.0%	42.7%	44.6%	47.4%	58.2%
Gender—Females [N=216]	53.07%	60.0%	57.3%	55.4%	52.6%	41.8%
Age at Year 1 of Study (years)	11.8	12.0	11.3	12.3	11.9	11.3

Family Separation and Reunification

For many newcomers, the driving motivation for migration is to be reunited with family members who emigrated earlier. For immigrant children, a period of separation from one or both parents is normative. In the LISA sample 85% of the 385 immigrant children participants reported being separated from at least one of their parents during the migration process. These separations, whether from both (49%) or only one parent (36%), had a significant effect on mental health; children who underwent separations reported significantly more depressive symptoms than those that did not. Aracell[1], a 14-year-old Dominican girl describes this sadness:

> "The day I left my mother I felt like my heart was staying behind. Because she was the only person I trusted—she was my life. I felt as if a light had extinguished. I still have not been able to get used to living without her."

5   Youth who were left with a loving caretaker for an extended period of time, often became attached to that caretaker. Although children would be happy about the prospect of "regaining" parents when called on to rejoin them, they would also "lose" contact with the caretakers to whom they had become attached. Ricardo, an 11-year-old Central American boy captured the feelings caused by simultaneous gains and losses:

> "Once I was in the plane they told me to be calm, not to be nervous, not to cry. I was crying because I was leaving my grandfather. I had conflicting feelings. On the one side I wanted to see my mother, but on the other I did not want to leave my grandfather."

During reunification in the new country, family relationships need to be renegotiated. After a long period of separation, the reunited child must first get reacquainted with family members. Often, the children encounter new family constellations that may

---

[1]All names are pseudonyms and identifying information has been changed to protect the confidentiality of study participants.

include stepparents, stepsiblings, and siblings they have never met. The father of Enrique, a 13-year-old Mexican boy explained:

> "My son and my daughter are not warm towards me. They are still mad that I left them and was separated from them for years. Even when I explain to them that I came here for them, they don't hear, they don't understand. My daughter acted strangely when she first got here, she got jealous when I hugged my wife. She just wanted my attention for herself. Now, that's changed and things are getting back to normal."

Youth respond in a variety of ways to these family separations. If the migrating family prepared the children and youth emotionally and psychologically for the separation and discussed the separation as temporary, necessary, and undertaken for the good of the family, the separation was more manageable than if the child felt abandoned. If parents and caretakers manage the separation cooperatively and if the accompanying losses are minimized, the youth, though changed, may not necessarily be damaged by the experience. The mother of Rosario, a 13-year-old Mexican girl described how her family managed their separation:

> "In spite of everything, we have a good relationship because [her grandmother] always spoke well of me. She always told [my daughter] where I was and that some day I would come for her. So there's a certain respect."

Family Conflict

Based on the LISA study, immigrant youth who reported fewer family problems felt better and did better in school. Research has demonstrated that family conflict plays a central role in undesirable psychosocial and educational outcomes (Alva & de los Reyes, 1999; Buehler & Gerard, 2002; Conger, Ge, Elder, Lorenz, & Simons, 1994). To establish whether newcomer adolescents found family conflict to be a significant factor in their lives, we asked students about issues that were a problem in their family after youth had been in the U.S. for almost 7 years, on average; these included conflicts about parents working long hours, grades, friends, household responsibilities, changing family constellations due to migration, and conflicting plans for the future. While some of these conflicts are part of adolescent development regardless of immigration status, understanding their impact on immigrant youth in particular is important.

Most students responded to the bulk of these potential family tensions with "not a problem." This corresponded to previous research suggesting that newcomer immigrant youth generally view family as an important resource in their lives that builds resilience despite the stresses of migration (Suárez-Orozco & Suárez-Orozco, 1995). However, those students who reported family problems were more likely to report lower levels of wellbeing and lower academic performance.

10   While outright conflicts and problems were not especially an issue for most of these students, the qualitative data revealed a general drift over time in intimacy and ease of communication within the family. As the children matured and as they spent more time in

the new country, parents worried about a growing distance between their children and themselves. For some families, this was a result of the natural changes that take place during adolescence. For many, as the children's native language skills atrophied, communication about anything more than basic exchanges declined. For others, cultural changes (often fashion and dating practices) the youth brought into the home appalled immigrant parents. For still others, as the gap between the parents and their children's educational and cultural competence increased, they found less and less in common. Xie, a 14 year-old Chinese boy remarked:

> "[My mother] isn't good at my schoolwork. It is impossible for me to ask her to help me with my English. She, herself, is going to night school right now. Her English is not that good."

The participants readily acknowledged that their parents had different rules than those of American parents, although conflicts resulting from these differences were not as pronounced as one might expect. Eighty percent said yes to the question: "Do you think parents from [your country of origin] have different rules than American parents?" This did not seem to create a lot of dissonance within the participants' families, however. We asked our participants: "Sometimes parents want their kids to behave the way they would in [their country of origin] but their kids want to behave more like Americans. How often do you think this happens in your family?" Twenty percent said that these tensions happened often or all the time, while most participants (79%) acknowledged that this was infrequently or never an issue. About half the youth (48%) said that their parents used the standards of expectations from their country of origin and an equal amount (48%) disclosed that their parents used a mix of rules from the country of origin and the U.S. Interestingly, most youth in our sample preferred a mix of both country of origin rules and American rules (64%); only 11% would have preferred mostly American rules and 21% indicated preference to be raised largely by the standards of their native country. We believe that the fact that the youth were immigrants themselves who had lived in the U.S. for a relatively short period of time resulted in less conflict than might be seen between American-born children and their immigrant parents.

Linguistic and Cultural Challenges

Immigration is one of the most stressful transitions a family can undergo. Immigrants are stripped of significant relationships with extended family members, best friends, and neighbors. Additionally, immigrants who were esteemed members of the community prior to migration may take on low-status jobs after migrating to the U.S. and youth who were good students may struggle to keep up in school as they learn English. These changes in contexts, relationships, and roles are disorienting and generally lead to a sense of loss. Immigrant youth in particular face many changes that can have a lasting impact on their development.

The shared repertoires of social and cultural practices that make the flow of life predictable are dramatically interrupted following migration; without a sense of cultural competence, control, and belonging, immigrants often feel disoriented. Immigrant youth typically come into contact with American culture more intimately and intensely than their parents do. Schools are sites of cultural change for immigrant youth because they meet teachers—often members of the dominant culture—as well as peers from other backgrounds. Immigrant parents, however, are often removed from American culture, particularly if they work with other immigrants and live in enclaves with others from their country of origin. The relative speed of the child's absorption into the new culture can create opportunities but also cause tensions. Immigrant adolescents may feel vague to intense embarrassment about their parents' cultural practices, while immigrant parents may fear that acculturation will lead to their children acting "like Americans."

Proficiency in the new language is frequently viewed as a measure of acculturation. Students were asked: "What do you think are the main obstacles to getting ahead in the United States?" Fifty-six percent spontaneously offered "learning English" as a response—more often than any other obstacle such as discrimination, lack of resources, or not being documented. Language learning takes a much longer time than many teachers and policy makers may realize. Although learning English was clearly important to students in our sample, after 7 years in the U.S. on average, only 7% demonstrated academic English proficiency equivalent to native English-speaking students their age. Many immigrant youth feel isolated by their developing English skills. Lotus, a 15-year-old Chinese girl, related the impact of her language proficiency on school participation:

> "I don't have much to say in class. I'm afraid to raise my hand. I worry that I would say something wrong and people will laugh at me."

15   Many immigrant parents are unable to help with homework given their own limited educational history as well as their language challenges. As a result, newcomer students struggle with the language and the content of homework alone. Marieli, a 16-year-old Dominican girl, shared the frustration of not being able to count on her parents for help with homework:

> "If I don't understand, there isn't anybody in the house to help me. So why bother?"

As a result of greater exposure to the new culture in school, the media, and for some, on the streets, youth frequently learn the new language more quickly than their parents. The child's relative mastery of the new language often leads to a complex negotiation of roles for parents, children and the institutions of the new culture (Orellana, Dorner, & Pulido, 2003). The majority of participants reported translating for family members: 42% reported translating once in a while and a third reported translating for their family daily or nearly daily.

Family responsibilities such as translation can be a double-edged sword. Youth who are called upon to be responsible at home may develop a set of soft skills that can serve them well at school—a sense of responsibility, organization, work ethic and being someone that can be counted on (Faulstich-Orellana, 2001). On the other hand, excessive responsibility can distract students from academic performance—helping parents translate documents or facilitate doctor's visits takes time away from completing homework and sometimes from attending school. In this study, high-performing students were significantly less likely to report that they had to miss school because they were called upon to help out their family (7.8%) than were low-achieving students (26.8%).

Though immigrant youth may continue to speak their native language, the level of fluency is likely to diminish over time. Without a concerted effort, oral and literacy skills in the home language will not keep pace with psychosocial development, particularly during adolescence. As time passes, although immigrant youth may easily communicate basic needs in their native language, many youth do not develop the ability to communicate the age-appropriate subtleties of their thoughts and emotions. The opposite is often true for parents who continue to rely on the native language to discuss their most intimate and important life issues. Consequently, misunderstandings and reduced communication can result. Lotus, a Chinese immigrant who was 17 years old at the end of our study, illustrated the dilemma of the generational and cultural gap that can occur between immigrant parents and children. Fieldworkers noted that her father was frequently unavailable, and when she encountered questions with her homework, she could not seek help at home. Over the duration of the study, partly because of a hectic work schedule and partly because he did not feel confident in his ability to help Lotus, he became less involved in his children's lives.

Implications for Policy and Intervention

Sadly, we found that the vast majority of recently arrived immigrant youth were quite isolated in their schools and neighborhoods. Only 37% reported participating in any kind of regularly scheduled after-school activities that were supervised by adults. Further, high-achieving students were much more likely to participate in these activities than low achieving students (55% vs. 34%, respectively). Thus, a domain that is ripe for creative policy work that could help immigrant families enormously is the area of community supports and mentorship. Our ethnographic observations revealed that immigrant children and youth by and large do not have access to supportive after-school programs, mentoring opportunities, and community-based organizations. Ideally, these programs would be culturally appropriate and sensitive, although they were rare in any form.

20   Carefully planned and well-staffed programs designed to meet the needs of immigrant families may play an especially important role in the lives of disoriented or isolated newcomer youth. Service professionals and mentors can act as cultural guides to families by helping them find their way during the turmoil-filled years of adolescence in a new country. Staff at community organizations can ease youth's adjustment to new family structures after long separations. Knowledgeable counselors can ameliorate some of the generational and cultural conflicts that occur as children and parents in immigrant families adapt to their new culture at different rates. Peer and adult tutors and adult mentors can support newcorner students in homework and continued language development when parents cannot. Caring adults can serve newcomer immigrant parents and youth by navigating the convoluted path to college that even native-born middle-class parents can find daunting.

Behind nearly every successful immigrant youth journey we found a mentor (e.g., from the church, the athletic team, or the local community center) who took a youngster under his or her wing. But in nearly every case these mentorship relationships started by accidental encounter. Thus, a much more coordinated effort to link immigrant youth and families with caring and knowledgeable adults, service professionals, and mentors, is essential.

References

Alva, S.A., & de los Reyes, R. (1999). Psychosocial stress, internalized symptoms, and the academic achievement of Hispanic adolescents. *Journal of Adolescent Research*, 14, 343–358.

Buchler, C., & Gerard, J.M. (2002). Marital conflict, ineffective parenting, and children's and adolescents' maladjustment. *Journal of Marriage and Family*, 64, 78–92.

Conger, R.D., Ge, X., Elder, G.H., Lorenz, F.O., & Simons, R.L. (1994) Economic stress, coercive family process, and developmental problems of adolescents. *Child Development*, 65, 541–561.

Faulstich-Orellana, M. (2001). The work kids do: Mexican and Central American Immigrant children's contributions to households and schools in California. *Harward Educational Review*, 71, 366–389.

Orellana, M.F., Dorner, L., & Pulido, L. (2003). Accessing assets: Immigrant youth's work as family translators or "para-phrasers." *Social Problems,* 50, 505–524.

Portes, A., & Rumbaut, R. (2001). *Legacies: The Story of the Immigrant Second Generation.* Berkeley, CA: University of California Press.

Suárez-Orozco, C., & Suárez-Orozco, M. (1995). *Transformations: Immigration, Family Life, and Achievement Motivation Among Latino Adolescents.* Standford, CA: Standford University Press.

Suárez-Orozco, C., Suárez-Orozco, M., & Todorova, I. (in press). *Learning a New Land: Immigrant Students in American Society.* Cambridge, MA: Harvard University Press.

U.S. Census Bureau, (2001). *Profile of the Foreign-born Population in the United States: 2000.* (Current Population Reports No. P23–206). Washington, D.C.: U.S. Government Printing Office.

A Note to Young Immigrants

MITALI PERKINS

Mitali Perkins was born in India and immigrated to the United States when she was six years old. At first she lived in New York, but later, as a seventh-grader in a California suburb, Perkins was the only person in her class who was not white and not born in America. This experience, of living in what she calls the "strange space between cultures," has inspired her fiction, including Monsoon Summer *and* The Not-so-star-spangled Life of Sunita Sen. *Mitali Perkins maintains a blog on* MySpace *that includes a "fire escape," which, she hopes, is "a safe place to think, chat, and read about life between cultures." This article appeared in the magazine* Teaching Tolerance *in the Fall of 2005.*

Be ready: You lose a lot once you're tossed into the mainstream. You lose a place that feels like home, a community where the basics are understood, where conversations can begin at a deeper level. No easy havens await you, no places to slip into with a sigh of relief, saying, "At last, a place where everybody is like me." In the neighborhood, you're like a pinch of chili tossed into a creamy pot.

You lose the sharpness of your ethnic flavor quickly but find that you can never fully dissolve.

You lose the ability to forget about race. You're aware of it everywhere in town, like a woman aware of her gender in a roomful of men. You dodge stereotypes at school by underperforming or overachieving. You wonder if you're invisible to the opposite sex because you're foreign or because you're unattractive.

You lose a language. You still speak your parents' language, but it will soon begin to feel foreign to lips, pen and mind. Your heart won't forget as quickly; it will reserve a space for this mother tongue, your instructor of emotion, whispered in love and hurled in anger. Your heart language will speak words that tremble through tears; it will join you with others in the camaraderie of uncontrollable laughter. In your new language, English, you enjoy the lyrical cadence of poetry and glimpse the depth of ancient epics, but your heart will remain insatiable.

You lose the advantage of parents who can interpret the secrets of society. Your friends learn the art of conversation, the habits of mealtimes, the nuances of relationships, even the basics of bathroom behavior, from their parents. Your own parents' social etiquette sometimes leads to confusion or embarrassment in the outside world. You begin to take on the responsibility of buffering your parents from a culture that is even more foreign to them. You translate this new world's secrets for them.

5   You lose the stabilizing power of traditions. The year is not punctuated by rituals your grandmother and great-grandmother celebrated. Holidays in this new place lack the power to evoke nostalgia and renew childlike wonder. Your parents' feasts of celebration fall on days when you have to go to school.

You lose the chance to disappear into the majority anywhere in your new world. In the new neighborhood, you draw reactions common to minorities—outright racism, patronizing tokenism, enthusiasm from curious culture-seekers. If you travel across the seas to neighborhoods where your parents grew up, you're greeted with curious, appraising stares. You're too tall or too short; you move your arms and hips differently when you walk; you smile too often or not often enough; you employ the confusing nonverbal gestures from another world.

But don't get discouraged. In fact, you should feel quite the opposite. There is good news about life in the melting pot. There are gains to offset the losses, if you manage not to melt away altogether. You're boiled down, refined to your own distinctiveness. You realize early that virtues are not the property of one heritage; you discover a self powerful enough to balance the best of many worlds.

A part of you rises above the steamy confusion of diversity to glimpse the common and universal. You recognize the ache that makes us all feel like strangers, even in the middle of comfortable homogeneity. You understand the soul's craving for a real home because yours is never sated with a counterfeit version.

So take time to mourn your losses, but remember to revel in the gains. Learn to embrace a litany of genuine labels—words like *stranger, pilgrim, sojourner, wayfarer*. Stride past the lure of false destinations, intent on traveling to a place where, at last, everyone can feel at home.

My Turn: Being American

MAILEEN HAMTO

Maileen Hamto is Senior Communications Manager for the United Way of Columbia-Willamette. She lists her passions as "photography and ethnic journalism," and she believes that being bilingual and bicultural makes her better able to communicate across cultures. This essay appeared in January 2008 in the Asian Reporter, *to which she has been a regular contributor.*

Why do immigrants in the U.S. still hang on to their home culture? Why can't they simply adopt an American identity?

It's funny, the things that get discussed at a diversity workshop.

Funnier still: Such questions are asked by Americans, of Americans, in our United States, a nation of immigrants.

The topic at hand was neighborhood organizing. Held in Portland, the workshop included participants from Colorado, Pennsylvania, Utah, New York, and California. The man who posed the question manages a nonprofit in Utah. He was born in New Mexico to parents of Mexican descent. Now in his late 40s, he professes that he never learned to speak Spanish, although it was spoken in his home.

5   I was one of only two women of color in the room, with immigrant roots. The instructor came to the United States via Ecuador. The questions were directed at me, because I had earlier talked about my experience immigrating to the United States as a teenager. I shared that all of my "growing up" was done in Texas, before moving to Oregon.

Where does one begin to address such remarks? American History 101 seemed like a good place to start. Perhaps start with the Puritans who left England to escape religious persecution, then fast-forward to Jamestown and the pilgrims. Talk about the forced migration of Africans who powered the rise of the United States as a military and economic power. Then go off on lessons about waves of Irish and Italian immigration throughout the Industrial Revolution. Underscore the contributions of the Chinese in building the railroads that bridged the eastern and western parts of the new country.

But we didn't have time for a history lesson, and it wouldn't have mattered anyhow. Despite mounds of evidence to the contrary, the questions reflect bias toward the belief that the United States is a melting pot of cultures. People come here, shed the gifts of their own cultures and identities, and voila! Instant Americans.

Is that how assimilation and acculturation happen? Of course not.

Throughout American history, each and every immigrant community—no matter which continent they come from—has made efforts to preserve and honor the cultural traditions from the old country. Ethnic enclaves are not a new phenomenon. Until World War I, German and English were co-official languages in Pennsylvania. Many Italian Americans continue to retain aspects of their culture. New York City still has more people who claim Irish heritage than the entire population of Dublin. About four percent of the U.S. population has Scandinavian heritage, with about 160,000 who speak a Scandinavian language.

10   What is different is that in recent decades, more and more newcomers are people of color—immigrants from Asia, Latin America, and Africa. For the most part, the dominant culture views traditions and social mores of these newcomers as foreign. Throughout our history as a nation, fear and apprehension about "the other"—especially in times of economic uncertainty—have fuelled anti-immigration sentiment.

So how did I respond? For the sake of preserving diplomacy and a conducive learning environment, I took a few deep breaths before addressing his concerns. In so many words, my response was brief and pointed.

"For many immigrants, becoming an American means that we subscribe to the tenets of hard work, sense of community, and a spirit of independence and self-sufficiency. The wonderful thing about living in the United States is that we don't expect people who want to make a life here to check their cultures at the customs office."

Rather than a melting pot, *Being American* is akin to halo-halo, a popular Filipino dessert made up of a variety of ingredients: ice cream, shaved ice, a mixture of sweetened beans, and fruits. There is no hard-and-fast recipe, and each ingredient retains its original flavor to create a truly unique experience.

Miss or Diss?

SCARF ACE

This excerpt is taken from the blog Scarf Ace: Wearing a Muslim Head Scarf in America, *whose masthead describes the subject matter as follows: "An American Muslim wears the Islamic headscarf in middle America. Issues: Hijab, Modesty, Religion, Law, Faith, and Beauty." The blogger's profile identifies her as "a Pakistani-American Muslim mother" and lists her interests as "Islam, Muslims, Women's rights, America, and Motherhood." The images are two of several posted on the blog at* http://scarfacewearingaheadscarfinamerica.blogspot.com/.

May 24, 2008

So it's been a year with the scarf. The weather is getting so hot and humid now, it's a big ordeal to get dressed and go out, especially being all covered up. I apologize in advance if this post is offensive, hurtful, confusing, etc. to anyone who loves wearing a headscarf. I started this blog as a way to cope with all the frustrations involved in starting hijab. And having an outlet has helped me to keep it on. Also, since I'm not an "all or nothing" type of person, getting comments from people that tell me that it is understandable to wear it while at the same time still have doubts and struggle and dislike for it also has helped me keep it on. Being able to be open and honest about my mental rumblings helps me feel less "two-faced" when it comes to wearing the headscarf, since the general assumption is that a hijabi has it all figured out in a very solid, committed way. It makes me think, what comes

first, the chicken or the egg? In other words, should a Muslim girl wear the headscarf AFTER she's got her beliefs all figured out, or BEFORE as a way to help her solidify her beliefs? Anyhoo…

I miss the relief of cool breezes on my neck.

I miss having a good hair day and/or a great fitting outfit showing off whatever's left of my decreasing physical assets to get that ego boost.

5   I miss not wondering what other people are thinking when they see me.

If it weren't for 2 main things, I think I would have stopped wearing it by now:

1. My husband's high regard for hijab
2. Being a stay-at-home mom, I have the freedom to choose when and where I go (unlike at work or school).

When I struggle, these are the voices I hear in my head:

GOD: It's OK. I am Most Merciful, Gracious, Oft Forgiving. Remember Me and I will remember you.

HIJABI POLICE: She really should figure out who she is. What is her point?

10   NON-MUSLIM, IGNORANT: 1. I should watch her/stare at her/glance at her to figure her out.
2. I've got her figured out and it ain't good.

NON-MUSLIM, ENLIGHTENED: 1. There is a woman with a scarf. Perhaps she is Muslim.
2. It's refreshing to see diversity!

And, what I don't miss about not wearing a scarf: that nagging feeling of inconsistency when I thought about being all covered up to pray but not when out in public.

Sometimes when I'm sitting in traffic at an intersection, watching all the cars buzz by me, looking inside them to see people who dress nothing like me, I wonder, "Why am I here?" Shouldn't I be somewhere where the people, the women, dress like me, with headscarves and covered-up-ness? Why do I live here? Is there anywhere I can go and not feel like odd-man out all the time? Yup, sure, Iran, Pakistan, Indonesia, India…Dearborn, Michigan?…places where covered heads are the norm. So why did my family and other families come to America? Hmm…But I know that this kind of attitude is dangerous for America, it leads to the "Love it or Leave it" thing or "Go home!" or "Act like an American!" There is a part of America that says there is no one way to **look like** an American. But then there's another part that says, yes there is, and it doesn't include a Muslim headscarf, a Sikh turban, or a Hindu dot on the forehead. But it does seem to include a Nun's Habit. Hmm…It's interesting. It reminds me of how in some parts of Pakistani culture, the words, "American" and "Christian" are interchangeable.

I saw this Christian channel program in which they were sponsoring a "return the Jews to Israel" campaign, showing clips of people saying, "As a Christian, I feel very connected to my Jewish brothers." I thought…what about your Muslim brothers? Why is there no brotherly love for us?! I'm not going to get into the political problems/history of this issue here, but my point is that I was insecure for a moment, imagining a world with

Jews and Christians against the Muslims, but then I felt this strength inside, a sort of "Well, if it's us against them, then, I will go down with this ship," which is a sort of nice feeling to have, instead of the insecure one I often feel when I think of those people who would rather not have Muslims around...

Anyway, back to my point about being in traffic. I'm just desperate to see some other hijabis when I go out, especially if it was a common thing to always see head-scarves wherever I go.

Scarfing It Down

FATEMEH FAKHRAIE

Fatemeh Fakhraie maintains a Web site called Muslimah Media Watch: Looking at Muslim Women in the Media and in Pop Culture, *a forum for critiquing images of Muslim women. "We're tired," says the site, "of seeing ourselves portrayed in the media in ways that are one-dimensional and misleading." She has also been a regular contributor to the blog* Racialicious.com. *Her research interests revolve around identity, appearance, and style, especially regarding Islamic attire.*

Even before Pakistani-Canadian teen Aqsa Parvez was killed by her father last December because of her alleged refusal to wear hijab, provinces in Canada were hopping on the headscarf-banning bandwagon set in motion by countries like France and Turkey where women in hijab are not allowed in public institutions like schools and government buildings. Exclusionary rulings have also affected non-governmental entities: Many female sports teams (in both Canada and the United States) with members who wear hijab have been subject to short- or long-term rulings by sports federations banning them from playing on the basis that hijab is unsafe, despite the development of sport-safe hijabs. This past January, Washington, D.C. high-school track competitor Juashaunna Kelly was disqualified from a meet after officials deemed her custom-made uniform unfit for competition—even though she'd worn it the previous three seasons.

The idea of banning the hijab is an exclusionary and ignorant one. But a good share of the ignorance comes as much from the media's coverage of these bans as from those implementing them. News stories on hijab bans are always ready to skew the issue by focusing on the hijab ban as a "freedom of religion" issue. More important, the stories nearly always take away the voices of those who should have a say in these bans—namely, Muslim women themselves. How can we know what a particular person or group thinks about something that concerns them if we don't talk to them about it?

Another problem with the coverage is that the stories often call the hijab "a traditional Muslim garment" or "an Islamic obligation." While many Muslims do see hijab as a mandatory obligation, others do not. There are many devout women who don't observe hijab for whatever reason, and decrying hijab bans on the pretext of religious freedom leaves these women out—are they not Muslims, despite the fact that they don't wear a headscarf?

When you get right down to it, banning a headscarf is banning an item of clothing, which is an issue of personal, not religious, freedom. But banning the hijab specifically targets women. It's kind of like not allowing women to wear long-sleeved shirts; or, if you want to add a religious dimension to it, it's like banning Christmas sweaters. (A tempting idea sometimes, but not one most people would take seriously.)

5   So the next time you hear about a hijab ban (and sadly, there will be a next time), think about your best pair of jeans or your faded t-shirt with the logo of your favorite band. Then think about being forbidden by law to wear them.

Student Advocates for Immigration Reform

Immigration reform is an ongoing issue in national politics with many stakeholders, including immigrant students. Of particular interest to students is the DREAM Act, a bill that has been introduced in Congress several times in the last few years, most recently in May 2007 as part of a comprehensive immigration reform bill in the Senate (S.1348). The DREAM (Development, Relief, and Education for Alien Minors) Act would provide a path to citizenship for illegal immigrants under the age of 18 who either go to college in the United States or serve in the U.S. armed forces. It would also allow the states to determine whether undocumented students could receive in-state tuition rates at state colleges. Despite having the support of President George W. Bush, this effort at immigration reform never even came to a vote in the Senate. The photo shown on page 500 was taken before an immigration reform rally in New York City on March 14, 2007.

Bassackwards: Construction Spanish and Other Signs of the Times

JAY NORDLINGER

Jay Nordlinger is a senior editor at the National Review, *a conservative magazine, where he writes on such topics as politics, foreign affairs, and music. His column, "Impromptus," appears in the* National Review Online. *He is also a music critic for the* New Criterion *and the* New York Sun. *Some of his writings appear in the publication* Here, There, and Everywhere: Collected Writings of Jay Nordlinger (2007). *This opinion piece appeared in January 2007 in the* National Review Online.

America, of course, has always been a place of many languages, along with our common tongue, English. German, its cousin Yiddish, Chinese, Italian, Polish—they have all been spoken here, especially in homes and community centers. But Spanish in today's America is something else: a language coddled, bowed to, enshrined.

We could talk about "bilingual education," which too often turns out to be monolingual education, and in the wrong tongue. We could talk about Spanish-language election ballots. We could talk about "For English, press 1. *Para español, oprima el dos.*" But let's talk, instead, about Construction Spanish.

Classes in—shall we call it "Con. Span."?—have sprouted up all over America. These are classes designed to teach contractors, supervisors, and other bosses in the construction business how to speak to their Hispanic workers. The bosses aren't learning Spanish, exactly; they will not be reading *Don Quixote.* This is a specialized language: *casco* for hard hat; *montacarga* for forklift; *pistola de clavos* for nail gun.

But wouldn't it be better, for all concerned, if the workers learned "hard hat," "forklift," and "nail gun"? We must put off such foolish questions, for the moment.

5   Construction Spanish is an example of what has been called "Survival Spanish," or "Command Spanish"—bits of Spanish acquired for a specific purpose. You can get trained in Restaurant Spanish, Fireman Spanish, or Health Care Spanish. And this last Spanish has sub-branches, such as Dental Spanish and Physical Therapy Spanish. Also, you can buy books and tapes that tell you how to converse with your gardener or maid, if that is your need.

But Construction Spanish has loomed especially large lately, for an obvious reason: the predominance of Hispanics in that field. Go into a Lowe's or Home Depot—stores that sell building materials—and you will see signs in Spanish (quite naturally). And you can buy any number of glossaries or handbooks. My favorite is *Spanish on the Job,* for its ad copy:

> No previous knowledge of Spanish is necessary. All words are phonetically spelled out to assure correct pronunciation. Trust me, yelling in English isn't going to help.

Let me yell, just a little bit. The old deal was, you came to America and you assimilated into the culture. You presumably wanted to, otherwise you wouldn't have immigrated. You retained your mother tongue, of course, and you figured your children would know it, and you hoped your grandchildren would be interested (although that was no guarantee). But you were in America, and America included English. Hooray!

And what of now? Forgetting an immigrant mindset, what is the general American mindset? An article published in the *Washington Post* a few years ago shed some light. It concerned a Northern Virginia county, Fairfax, which had trained 450 of its employees in Spanish. A Fairfax official explained, "As we saw the changing demographics of the county, we said, 'How are we responding to the needs of new residents of the county?'" Not by encouraging their assimilation, that's for sure.

Hispanic immigrants had joined the sanitation department, so an assistant superintendent there took Spanish for Garbage Workers. (Really.) He said, "In our type of business, it's something we're gonna have to learn." It was not too long ago that immigrants thought English was something they had to learn. They did not expect their employers or supervisors to take Survival Polish or Survival Serbian; they saw to it that they acquired some Survival English.

10   The *Post*'s reporter found one person, a middle-aged "supervisor on building projects in downtown Washington," who was not too happy about the new order. He acknowledged to

the reporter that he wished his workers would simply learn English. But they were not—so he enrolled in Construction Spanish. "I'm not saying I like what's happening," he said. "But I figure I can't fight it."

Which is a near-perfect expression of cultural defeatism.

There is always a tug between the pragmatic and the idealistic, or the short term and the long term. You want assimilation and acculturation; but you also want to do business in the here and now, in whatever language. You want to be considerate of the immigrant, who has enough challenges, without a new language; but you are not pleased to see him trapped in a linguistic ghetto—barrio-ization, some people have called it.

I consider myself a veteran of the Spanish wars, although I participated in the most minor of ways. Years ago, I was working at a firm in Washington, D.C. We were told that, when we wanted boxes thrown away, we had to mark them "BASURA." *Basura* is the Spanish word for *trash*. And all of our janitors were Hispanic.

Everything in my traditional-American soul rebelled at writing "BASURA," thinking it a gross act of separatism, and probably an insult to the workers. "Why don't we write 'TRASH'?" I asked. "We're in America, and we don't want anyone walled off. We want them to join the American family. How will they ever rise in our society if they don't learn English? In Guatemala, we would write 'BASURA.' But here we write 'TRASH.'"

15   That didn't go over terribly well, and I made no headway. But I took to writing "BASURA/TRASH" on my boxes to be thrown out. That was my pathetic little stand: a word, a slash, and another word. But I liked it.

A while back, I wrote about this experience in a *National Review Online* column, and the subject provoked a ton of mail. I seemed to have touched some national nerve. Many Hispanics wrote of their frustration and resentment at having been shunted into Spanish-only classes, or "bilingual" classes that were the usual Spanish-preservation rackets. And a former manager of custodial crews in Phoenix wrote the following:

> I once spent a few months trying to convince people in the corporate offices of a major insurance company that my employees didn't need orders in Spanish. They may have been willing to do menial labor, but that didn't mean that they were stupid, and it was condescending to think they couldn't learn a simple five-letter word in the English language.

Namely, "trash."

Another correspondent added a twist, saying, "Here in Chicago, the big offices distribute stickers to be placed on garbage items. They read, 'GARBAGE/BASURA/SMIECI,'" laying it out in English, Spanish, and Polish.

20   Still another reader contributed this:

> An acquaintance once told me that, years ago, when he was preparing for a job that involved supervising an office cleaning crew, the guy he was replacing suggested that he come in a half-hour early each day of the following week so he could learn enough Spanish to deal with the crew. The new guy replied: "I've got a better idea: Why don't you have them come in a half-hour early each day to learn enough English to deal with me?"

A stirring protest against the ass-backwardness of contemporary American life.

At that Washington firm, a young janitor and I became friends, and I learned that he had no dictionary: no English-Spanish, Spanish-English dictionary. I got him one. That night, he left me a note that contained one word: "Grasias." Mainly because of the misspelling, I'm sure, it was one of the most touching notes I had ever received.

Yet I am under no illusion that everyone who comes to America is dying to melt into the pot. Is aching to bear out the national motto, *E pluribus unum.* Years before I worked at the Washington firm, I worked at a public golf course in Michigan, and we had many leagues, one of which was "the Korean League." I was appalled at this, mortified for those good Americans of Korean origin who played every Wednesday afternoon.

So, brimming with idealism, I said to the leader of the group, "We should call it the Korean-American League or something else, right? Because you are fellow Americans, and it's not right to call it the Korean League." He looked at me blankly and said, "No, we're Koreans." Oh.

25   In any case, I tried—and so should all Americans, I dare say (native and immigrant alike). Of course, when you talk as I have, in this piece, someone always accuses you of being a jingo, boob, or xenophobe. People who can't find their way to the toilet in any European capital will paint you as a foe of languages. Will say that you're "afraid of the Other."

This even happened to S. I. Hayakawa, the famed linguist and politician. He was the fellow who founded U.S. English, the lobbying group. Hayakawa liked to say, "Bilingualism for the individual is fine, but not for a country." I imagine he spoke more languages than most people have toes. Yet that did not spare him the usual accusations.

I assure the reader that I like Spanish as much as the next guy—actually, considerably more. And Con. Span., Dental Span., and all the rest of the Spans. are hardly the worst threat we face. Moreover, I trust that Americanization will sometime kick in, for the masses of newly arrived Hispanics. But if it doesn't, we will lose a lot—all of us will.

■ ■ ■ ■ **FOR CLASS DISCUSSION** **Immigration in the Twenty-First Century**

1. Gaytán, Carhill, and Suárez-Orozco observe that "Behind nearly every successful immigrant youth journey we found a mentor," but that in almost every case, the mentorship was "accidental." What kinds of assistance programs for immigrants are you aware of in your community or school? After reading Gaytán, Carhill, and Suárez-Orozco's study, what kinds of knowledge or understanding do you think you would need to be a successful mentor? With your classmates, brainstorm ways that you and your classmates might use your skills to mentor immigrants in your community.

2. Mitali Perkins and Maileen Hamto each make reference to the "melting pot" metaphor in discussing immigrant assimilation in the United States. Review their discussions: do the two writers view the metaphor differently? In your opinion, does "melting pot" still work as a metaphor for immigration in the United States? Why or why not? What other metaphors do writers in this unit use? What other metaphors do you suggest?

3. Do you think that Scarf Ace would agree with Fatemeh Fakhraie's contention that the decision to wear hijab is "an issue of personal, not religious freedom"?

Do you agree with the analogy Fakhraie draws between hijab and long-sleeved shirts or Christmas sweaters? If not, what other analogies would be more appropriate?

4. Brainstorm: Besides headscarves, what other items of clothing or body adornment mark a person as a member of a religious, ethnic, cultural, or other group? Which of these go largely unnoticed in mainstream American society? Which are controversial, and why?

5. Read Jay Nordlinger's essay, "Bassackwards," as both a believer and a doubter. Working in small groups or as a class, discuss: What are the warrants for *believing* his argument—that is, what other beliefs or values must one hold in order to buy his contention that immigrant workers should learn to speak more than just "construction Spanish"? What beliefs and values would enable one to *doubt* Nordlinger's argument?

WRITING ASSIGNMENT   White Paper Summarizing the Arguments about a Policy Proposal

Although the readings in this unit do not deal specifically with U.S. immigration laws and policies, the people discussed in these readings are affected by those policies on a daily basis. Research one recent proposal to change federal immigration laws and read about it in three to five sources. Identify and characterize the stakeholders in the debate: Who are they? What do they stand to gain or lose? Then analyze the arguments used by these stakeholders. What are their strengths and weaknesses? Finally, write a white paper in which you summarize the proposal and the arguments for and against it for a citizen wanting to be better informed. You might find the following resources helpful as a starting place: the White House Web site on immigration reform at http://www.whitehouse.gov/infocus/immigration/, the Federation for American Immigration Reform site at www.fairus.org, the National Immigration Law Center at www.nilc.org, or the League of Women Voters at www.lwv.org/immigrationstudy. ■

For additional writing, reading, and research resources, go to www.mycomplab.com

Women in Math and Science

The puzzling relationship between biology and culture in the formation of gender identity has triggered extensive research with important consequences for parents, educators, and each of us individually as we try to make sense of our own gendered lives. Why do girls tend to play with dolls and boys with trucks? Are boys who push and shove each other in junior high school halls ramped up on testosterone or simply acting out cultural expectations for males? Are little girls who hold tea parties for their teddy bears imitating cultural stereotypes or living out some kind of biological hardwiring? Some research points heavily toward "nature" (gendered behavior is influenced by sex differences in genes, brain structure, hormone production, and exposure to prenatal hormones in utero), while other research points just as heavily toward "nurture" (boys and girls are socialized into different gender roles). Most scientists resist choosing either nature or nurture as the sole determinate of gendered behavior; they point rather to complex interactions between biology and the environment. Science writer Deborah Blum uses the metaphor of radio signals to suggest this relationship: biology produces "faint signals" that get "amplified by culture."[1]

The readings in this unit and in Chapter 12 connect the nature/nurture controversy about gender differences to the phenomenon that women are currently underrepresented in the career fields of mathematics, physics, and engineering. The nature/nurture controversy exploded into an international debate following the January 2005 remarks of Lawrence Summers, then president of Harvard University, at an economics conference on diversifying the engineering and science workforce. Summers hypothesized that the under-representation of female professors on tenured faculties in math, science, and engineering at prestigious universities might be caused by innate differences between the sexes (nature) rather than by patterns of discrimination and socialization that discouraged women from entering these fields (nurture). Summers's remarks—which led several female scientists to leave the room—made instant headlines, serving as the kairotic moment for the debate that followed. Op-ed writers and bloggers voiced their views on Summers' hypothesis, often reflecting their own political perspectives on feminism, family values, and women's roles in society. Some prominent scientists took time from their scholarly work to write "public intellectual" articles on this issue. The general flavor of this cultural debate is represented in the articles that follow. The originating question is why women are under-represented in mathematics, physics, and engineering, but this question broadens quickly into disagreements about the nature of scientific evidence, about the interpretation of statistical data, and about the value we ascribe to different gender roles in a just society.

[1]Blum, Deborah. "The Gender Blur." *Utne Reader* Sept.-Oct. 1998: 45–48.

A Note on Lawrence Summers's Speech

All the readings in this unit refer to Lawrence Summers's controversial speech on January 14, 2005, at an economic conference entitled "Diversifying the Science and Engineering Workforce." Unfortunately, Dr. Summers would not give us permission to reprint his speech. However, the transcript is available on the Harvard University Web site at http://www.president.harvard.edu/speeches/2005/nber.html, and we urge you to read it as background for the articles and cartoon in this unit.

In lieu of printing the speech itself, we'll give you a quick background on Summers and then briefly summarize his speech. Lawrence H. Summers, born in 1954, was Secretary of the Treasury under President Bill Clinton until he became president of Harvard University from 2001–2006. An economist by training (Ph.D. Harvard), Summers won the prestigious John Bates Clark medal in 1993 for his work in macro-economics. His speech at the economics conference addressed the question of why women are underrepresented among tenured professors of mathematics, physics, and engineering at prestigious research universities. Summers offered three hypotheses. The first he called the "high powered job hypothesis." Here he suggested that women might be underrepresented in math and science because women are more inclined than men to seek careers that permit a balance between family and career. Under this hypothesis, women who have the talent for high-powered careers in science and math voluntarily choose other careers that require fewer nights and weekends at work on research projects that take "near total commitments to their work." The second he called the "different availability of aptitude at the high end" hypothesis. This is the bio-logical hypothesis that caused the uproar; we will return in a moment to summarize it in more detail. His third hypothesis he called "different socialization and patterns of discrimination." This hypothesis embraces the arguments from "nurture" that women are socialized to be less competitive than men, especially in math and science, and that men are socialized into patterns of discrimination against women that are often subconsciously internalized rather than consciously overt. Summers downplayed the discrimination hypothesis, believing that other factors, particularly the biological expla-nations, were at play.

It was Summers's second hypothesis—focusing on biological differences between the genders—that sparked the heated reaction. Summers's biological argument is subtle in that it focuses not on mean scores but on standard deviations. Summers did not say that men are better than women in math and science or that men on average are better than women in math and science. He said rather that in tests of math and science aptitude the distribution curves are different for men and women, with more men scoring at both the high and low ends (or tails) of the distribution curve. Thus a higher percentage of men than women score in both the genius range and the dunce range of math ability. A female math genius is just as brilliant as a male math genius, but there are more male math geniuses (just as there are more male math dunces). Summers's argument, then, is that the talent pool for highly prestigious math and science positions at distinguished universities (requiring genius levels of aptitude) contains a much higher proportion of men than women. As evidence he pointed at the statistical results from numerous studies of gender differences. Often these show similar mean scores but greater variability for males than females.

For the international reaction to Summers's second hypothesis, we invite you now to turn to the readings that follow.

Harvard Prez's Admission: Men and Women Are Different

LINDA CHAVEZ

This op-ed piece by Linda Chavez appeared in the Jewish World Review *on January 19, 2005, just four days after Summers's speech. Linda Chavez is a highly regarded conservative columnist whose books such as* Out of the Barrio: Toward a New Politics of Hispanic Assimilation *(1991) and* An Unlikely Conservative: The Transformation of an Ex-Liberal *(2002) have made her a prominent leader in the Republican Party.* Jewish World Review *is a free online magazine aimed at promoting serious discussion of a revitalized Judaism. It publishes a wide range of opinion columns, but is weighted heavily toward the conservative viewpoint.*

The president of Harvard University is the last person you'd expect to venture politically incorrect opinions on gender and intelligence, but then Lawrence H. Summers is no ordinary Ivy League president. Last week, at a conference organized by the National Bureau of Economic Research (NBER), Summers questioned whether discrimination is entirely responsible for the dearth of female professors in science and engineering at America's elite universities. According to some participants at the conference, Summers suggested that innate differences in math and science aptitude between men and women might be partly responsible. The remarks caused one participant, Massachusetts Institute of Technology (MIT) biologist Nancy Hopkins, to walk out, later telling reporters that she would have "either blacked out or thrown up" if she had remained to listen to Summers. So much for rigorous intellectual debate.

But as uncomfortable as it might make feminists, the empirical evidence points to small but important differences in scientific and mathematical abilities between men and women. On average, women perform better on verbal tests, while men demonstrate greater visual-spatial capabilities, and these differences are more striking at both the lower and upper extremes of intellectual ability. Boys outnumber girls in remedial reading classes—by large ratios, in most studies—but they are even more likely to outnumber girls among the most gifted in math and science. In one study of gifted pre-adolescent students conducted by Johns Hopkins University, boys outperformed girls among the top scoring students on math by 13-to-1.

For years, feminists have tried to explain away these achievement differences by suggesting that girls are not encouraged properly to pursue math and science. Lately, some have even started blaming the way in which these subjects are taught: too much emphasis on competition and being "right," too little on collaborative learning and nurturing self-esteem. But socialization alone can't explain the wide differences in ability, especially at the highest levels of mathematical and scientific achievement. Summers was really just articulating what most researchers in this area believe—that biology plays a bigger role in explaining these differences than socialization does.

Although Summers' original comments were made in closed sessions to an academic group—and are therefore not available for public scrutiny—critics were quick to take to the barricades. For example, Hopkins later told the *Boston Globe,* "It is so upsetting that all these brilliant young women [at Harvard] are being led by a man who views them this way." She went on to describe studies that, according to the *Globe,* "indicate that women score higher on math tests if there are fewer men in the room while they are taking the test." Perhaps the *Globe* misrepresented Hopkins' statement; Hopkins is an accomplished scientist who should know better than to attribute a cause-and-effect relationship to such specious data.

5   But Hopkins is also an outspoken feminist. She made a name for herself in the mid-1990s by charging that MIT discriminated against female scientists, allotting them less lab space and giving them fewer plum assignments. Hopkins later led a university-appointed group to study her own charges, which—surprise, surprise—found gender discrimination at MIT "subtle but pervasive," even though the group's report fell short of offering evidence of such discrimination in differential salaries, for example. The report nonetheless concluded that gender bias "stems largely from unconscious ways of thinking that have been socialized into all of us, men and women alike."

Summers, an economist, would have trouble accepting that kind of explanation. As he explained to the NBER conferees, if a school practiced that kind of discrimination against women, another school would gain an advantage by hiring them away. Since there is no evidence that is happening, Summer told the *Globe* "the real issue is the overall size of the pool, and it's less clear how much the size of the pool was held down by discrimination."

He may not have won any friends among the women-as-perennial-victims set, but Summers deserves high marks for opening up for debate some of the shibboleths of academe.

Amazing Facts about the Fairer, Yet Equal Sex

BRIAN MCFADDEN

Brian McFadden, a member of Cartoonists with Attitude, produces "Big Fat Whale," a weekly humor comic strip that satirizes current politics and popular culture. His comic strip appears in the Cleveland Free Times, Boston Phoenix, *and many other publications. You can visit his work at www.bigfatwhale.com. The comic strip here appeared in 2005 at the height of the Lawrence Summers controversy.*

Separating Science from Stereotype

NATURE NEUROSCIENCE EDITORIAL

This editorial appeared in March 2005 in Nature Neuroscience, *a peer-reviewed multidisciplinary scientific journal. "In addition to primary research," according to its Web site, "*Nature Neuroscience *publishes news and views, reviews, editorials, commentaries, perspectives, book reviews and correspondence. In this way, the journal aims to be the voice of the worldwide neuroscience community."*

Harvard University president Lawrence Summers stirred up a hornet's nest in January when he suggested that innate biological differences may help explain why men have more career success in science and mathematics than women. His speech at a National Bureau of Economics conference, which was off the record, set off a storm of protest, and Summers has spent the last several weeks clarifying and apologizing for his remarks. Journalists have had a field day debating the incident, and although some have criticized Summers as being almost neanderthal in his thinking, others have portrayed him as a victim of political correctness.

There is no doubt that Summers' comments were impolitic. There is no official record of what he said, but his reported implication that men are biologically predisposed to outperform women at the upper end of the math and science spectrum has captured the media's fancy. Unfortunately, however, most of his supporters have not been preoccupied with evaluating whether this argument has any scientific merit. Are there neurobiological differences between men and women that may explain the gender gap in science and mathematics? The evidence to support this hypothesis of 'innate difference' turns out to be quite slim.

In his talk, Summers apparently cited a gender difference in Scholastic Aptitude Test (SAT) mathematics scores: boys are more likely than girls to score on the tail ends of the bell curve. (That is, the worst performers and the highest scorers tend to be male.) Similarly, in a 2003 study of teenagers by the Programme for International Student Assessment, boys outperformed girls in math by a statistically small margin (http://www.pisa.oecd.org/dataoecd/1/63/34002454.pdf). However, in 7 of 43 countries, boys and girls had similar scores, and in Iceland girls outscored boys, suggesting that cultural factors can influence this gender difference.

The meaning of this overrepresentation at the high end is anyone's guess. Summers apparently mused that it may explain why there are many more gifted male mathematicians than female. However, aptitude tests are not very good predictors of future educational success. In particular, for reasons that are unclear, the SAT tends to underpredict female and overpredict male academic performance. On average, males score 33 points higher on the math section of the SAT than females who earn the same grades in the same college math courses (www.FairTest.org). Similarly, Chinese nationals tend to do very well on the Graduate Record Examination (GRE) subject tests, although they do not perform much differently in graduate school from their American counterparts, indicating that test score differences do not necessarily translate to meaningful professional distinctions.

5   In terms of neuroscience, there is evidence that male and female brains differ anatomically in subtle ways, but no one knows how (or even if) these anatomical differences relate to cognitive performance. Women have greater gyrification of the brain surface (and by inference,

increased cortical surface area) in frontal and parietal regions[1]. Boys were reported to have an increased gray matter volume relative to girls (even correcting for total cerebral volume), but other authors[2] have contradicted these findings, reporting that this difference in gray matter volume can be accounted for by differences in brain size and is unrelated to gender. A related problem is that studies reporting gender differences in anatomy, no matter how small, are more likely to be published and reported in the press than those that fail to find such differences. And despite these differences, males and females score equally well on IQ tests[3].

One of the clearest cognitive gender differences is in spatial reasoning and navigation, which some media reports have linked to mathematical ability. Spatial cognition is organized differently in male and female rats. In the Morris water maze, female rats rely more on frontal cortex for spatial navigation, whereas male rats rely more on entorhinal cortex. Human males and females use different neural strategies to maneuver through unfamiliar environments as well, with men showing a greater activation of left hippocampus[4]. Men and women also use different behavioral strategies—women are thought to focus on landmarks, whereas men tend to assess the euclidean properties of the environment. Similarly, men outperform women on mental rotation tasks. Some of these differences are linked to hormones—a single testosterone injection improves women's performance on a visuospatial task[5]. Although this difference may well have a biological basis, it seems much too narrow to account for the dramatic overrepresentation of men in science departments at top universities.

Social scientists find that changing a female name to a male name on otherwise identical work increases its perceived value. In addition, female and minority students who are aware of gender and racial stereotypes score lower on tests such as the SAT. In the early years of the SAT, females scored higher on the verbal section, until male test scores were raised by selective inclusion of questions on which males performed better, such as those on politics, business and sports[6]. No similar attempt has been made to 'balance' the math section of the SAT. In light of such evidence that gender bias influences test scores and academic success, it is difficult to take seriously the enshrinement of the test score gap as reflecting biological differences.

In a world of perfectly equal opportunity, what proportion of Harvard's mathematics professors would be female? No one knows, and no studies can be done to find out because humans cannot be examined in a culture-free state. What does seem clear is that we do not live in such a perfect world. In this one, Summers' comments as Harvard's president—and the resulting media hype—are likely to make the road tougher for aspiring female mathematicians and scientists, who now must confront the additional handicap of being told that they are at a biological disadvantage. Putting less faith in aptitude differences and more belief in hard work and individual evaluation of performance seems like a more productive way forward.

[1] Luders, E. *et al. Net. Neurosci,* 7, 799–800 (2004).

[2] Luders, E., Steinmetz, H. & Jancke, L. *Neuroreport* 13, 2371–2374 (2002).

[3] Haier, R.J., Jung, R.E., Yeo, R.A., Head, K. & Alkire, M.T. *Neuroimage* 23, 425–433 (2004).

[4] Gron, G. *et al. Nat. Neurosci.* 3, 404–408 (2000).

[5] Alernan, A., Bronk, E., Kessels, R.P., Koppeschaar, H.P. & van Honk, J. *Psychoneuroendocrinology* 29, 612–617 (2004).

[6] Tavris, C. *The Mismeasure of Woman* (Simon and Schuster, New York, 1992).

Solving for XX

DEBORAH BLUM

Deborah Blum is a professor of journalism at the University of Wisconsin and a past president of the National Association of Science Writers. She won the 1992 Pulitzer prize for her book The Monkey Wars *on the ethical dilemmas of primate research. Her 1998 book* Sex on the Brain *was named a New York Times Notable Book of the Year. The following article appeared in the* Boston Globe *on January 23, 2005.*

Some time back, when I began reporting on the science of sex differences, I had the privilege of interviewing Richard Lynn, an Irish scientist whose views on mental differences between the races had been enshrined in a then-best-seller titled "The Bell Curve."

We had an unspoken contest going throughout the conversation. He was trying to make me lose my temper. I was trying to keep it. I won, sort of.

Even when he informed me that women lacked the brains to perform sophisticated math calculations and to handle strategy, I simply wrote it down. When he used the example of his daughter—she would never be able to beat him in chess, she lacked the necessary intellectual equipment— I merely pointed out that some people would find that statement offensive.

No matter what he said, I politely continued asking my questions. Apparently, however, I was polite in an increasingly loud voice because afterward people from across the newsroom stopped to tell me that I did the most *interesting* interviews.

5 OK, perhaps we should call that contest a draw.

This is not meant to yoke Lynn with Harvard president Lawrence H. Summers, who received international attention last week for his speculation, made at an academic conference, that a difference in "innate ability" might be one reason that women still lag substantially in the field of science and math.

Summers later explained that he intended only to be provocative, not to imply that women were, well, dumb. But for many women—including myself—the first reaction to these remarks was a sense of dismayed deja vu.

Spend any time at all studying the biology of behavior and you will find it riddled with similar, nature-based defenses of the often less-than-perfect status quo. In the days before women were admitted to college, male scientists insisted that girls were born too fragile and emotional to even handle higher education. Only a few weeks ago, a University of Michigan study concluded that men are less attracted to assertive and successful women, which the authors called a natural biological response.

As Marlene Zuk, a University of California-Riverside biologist specializing in sex-linked behaviors, wearily said to me this week: "I don't find Summers's statements either offensive or provocative— they trot out the same old lines we've heard for decades if not centuries, and they just aren't supported by good data."

10 But before considering the data, I'd like to begin on a note of superficial agreement with Summers.

According to a number of irate women who heard the speech, Harvard's president used a particular anecdote to illustrate the case for sex-specific biology. He'd once given his young daughter a pair of toy trucks as a gift. She turned them into a rather charming single-parent truck family, naming them "Daddy Truck" and "Baby Truck." I can't claim to be offended by that story since I tell the same kind of tales on my two sons, although mine tend to involve dismembering Barbies. There's nothing like being the parent of a small child to convince you that biology is a powerful influence on behavior—and vice versa.

The research to support the latter idea is getting better all the time. There are some terrific studies from the National Institutes of Health showing that parenting style itself can affect the way behavioral genes are expressed; countless others demonstrate that the way we behave helps shape both the structure and function of our brain. Behavioral researchers have found, for instance, that constant anxiety can alter pathways in the brain that produce stress hormones, raising the levels to such an extent that the body resets into a constant nervous state. Further, the compounds produced in that stress-chain reaction can cause damage to certain parts of the brain, such as the hippocampus, which helps regulate memory. In other words, if you suffer from memory problems during stress, chances are it's because stress has altered your brain.

So, nature impacts nurture—and vice versa. They dance together throughout our lives, so closely intertwined in their particular waltz, that it becomes simplistic to argue that a behavior is just one or the other.

But according to members of his audience, Summers took the simplistic approach, using his truck anecdote to imply that little girls' lack of interest in the mechanical aspects of toy trucks preordained their future failure in the analytical world of math and science. This, he said, helps explain the fact that while women make up 35 percent

of the faculty in American universities, they constitute only 20 percent of the science and engineering departments.

15 He's right about those numbers, and it's to his credit that he sees them as a problem. It's also true that there are some good studies on childhood play, which indicate that hormones, such as testosterone, contribute to the stereotypical rough-and-tumble style of boys. Other research shows that girls with unusually high levels of testosterone often play rough, disdain dolls, and prefer trucks to be trucks.

But I've never seen research showing that those girls all became brilliant scientists—or that testosterone- influenced play has anything to do with math ability. In fact, comparable male-female math ability has been well documented for many years. In 1990, University of Wisconsin psychologist Janet Hyde and her colleagues did the first national meta-analysis showing that adolescent boys and girls were barely a few percentage points apart in average math performance—a conclusion that has been repeatedly confirmed. Hyde later found that most "gender effect differences" in all areas, from math or verbal ability to musical talent—fall in the small or "close to zero" range.

There is a twist to those average results—one actually raised by Summers. Although overall scores in math, for instance, are

comparable, males seem to cluster at the high and low ends of the results, and women more consistently in the middle. For decades, psychologists have been puzzled over this "male variability"; the first papers pointing it out surfaced in 1914. No one knows for sure what those results mean. Do men have more potential for genius or failure? Or more of a tendency to test extremely badly or extremely well? In any case, almost everyone agrees that this is an area deserving of more research.

Hyde points out that some of the mythologies of gender difference—such as the myth about math-challenged women perpetuated by Summers—can and do influence performance. Surveys have found that both parents and teachers admit that they expect more from boys, based on the impression of greater talent. Not surprisingly, she finds Summers's foray into gender biology unimpressive: "Offensive and stupid, both. Worse, with his level of education and intelligence, he has no excuse."

That is, unless we want to argue that the male brain, due to some innate failure of ability, just cannot quite grasp the complex interaction between nature and nurture. In the interest of fairness, that could make a good story; kind of provocative, don't you think? I might enjoy doing the interviews—and I could promise to keep my voice down during the process.

The Science of Difference: Sex Ed

STEVEN PINKER

In this article published in the New Republic Online *in February 2005, psychologist Steven Pinker argues that research from cognitive science and evolutionary biology supports Lawrence Summers's hypothesis that innate differences between males and females can influence mathematical aptitude. Pinker is the Johnstone Family Professor of Psychology at Harvard and has also served on the faculty at MIT. He is a leading authority on language acquisition in children and is especially interested in the neural basis of consciousness.*

When I was an undergraduate in the early 1970s, I was assigned a classic paper published in *Scientific American* that began: "There is an experiment in psychology that you can perform easily in your home.…Buy two presents for your wife, choosing things…she will find equally attractive." Just ten years after those words were written, the author's blithe assumption that his readers were male struck me as comically archaic. By the early '70s, women in science were no longer an oddity or a joke but a given. Today, in my own field, the study of language development in children, a majority of the scientists are women. Even in scientific fields with a higher proportion of men, the contributions of women are so indispensable that any talk of turning back the clock would be morally heinous and scientifically ruinous.

Yet to hear the reaction to Harvard President Lawrence Summers's remarks at a conference on gender imbalances in science, in which he raised the possibility of innate sex differences, one might guess that he had proposed exactly that. Nancy Hopkins, the eminent MIT biologist and advocate for women in science, stormed out of the room to avoid, she said, passing out from shock. An engineering dean called his remarks "an intellectual tsunami," and, with equal tastelessness, a *Boston Globe* columnist compared him to people who utter racial epithets or wear swastikas. Alumnae threatened to withhold donations, and the National Organization of Women called for his resignation. Summers was raked in a letter signed by more than 100 Harvard faculty members and shamed into issuing serial apologies.

Summers did not, of course, say that women are "natively inferior," that "they just can't cut it," that they suffer "an inherent cognitive deficit in the sciences," or that men have "a monopoly on basic math ability," as many academics and journalists assumed. Only a madman could believe such things. Summers's analysis of why there might be fewer women in mathematics and science is commonplace among economists who study gender disparities in employment, though it is rarely mentioned in the press or in academia when it comes to discussions of the gender gap in science and engineering. The fact that women make up only 20 percent of the workforce in science, engineering, and technology development has at least three possible (and not mutually exclusive) explanations. One is the persistence of discrimination, discouragement, and other barriers. In popular discussions of gender imbalances in the workforce, this is the explanation most mentioned. Although no one can deny that women in science still face these injustices, there are reasons to doubt they are the only explanation. A second possibility is that gender disparities can arise in the absence of discrimination as long as men and women differ, on average, in their mixture of talents, temperaments, and interests—whether this difference is the result of biology, socialization, or an interaction of the two. A third explanation is that child-rearing, still disproportionately shouldered by women, does not easily co-exist with professions that demand Herculean commitments of time. These considerations speak against the reflex of attributing every gender disparity to gender discrimination and call for research aimed at evaluating the explanations.

The analysis should have been unexceptionable. Anyone who has fled a cluster of men at a party debating the fine points of flat-screen televisions can appreciate that fewer women than men might choose engineering, even in the absence of arbitrary barriers. (As one female social scientist noted in *Science Magazine,* "Reinventing the curriculum will not make me more interested in learning how my dishwasher works.") To what degree these and other differences originate in biology must be determined by research, not fatwa. History tells us that how much we want to believe a proposition is not a reliable guide as to whether it is true.

5   Nor is a better understanding of the causes of gender disparities inconsequential. Overestimating the extent of sex discrimination is not without costs. Unprejudiced people of both sexes who are responsible for hiring and promotion decisions may be falsely charged with sexism. Young women may be pressured into choosing lines of work they don't enjoy. Some proposed cures may do more harm than good; for example, gender quotas for grants could put deserving grantees under a cloud of suspicion, and forcing women onto all university committees would drag them from their labs into endless meetings. An exclusive focus on overt discrimination also diverts attention from policies that penalize women inadvertently because of the fact that, as the legal theorist Susan Estrich has put it, "Waiting for the connection between gender and parenting to be broken is waiting for Godot." A tenure clock that conflicts with women's biological clocks, and family-unfriendly demands like evening seminars and weekend retreats, are obvious examples. The regrettably low proportion of women who have received tenured job offers from Harvard during Summers's presidency may be an unintended consequence of his policy of granting tenure to scholars early in their careers, when women are more likely to be bearing the full burdens of parenthood.

Conservative columnists have had a field day pointing to the Harvard hullabaloo as a sign of runaway political correctness at elite universities. Indeed, the quality of discussion among the nation's leading scholars and pundits is not a pretty sight. Summers's critics have repeatedly mangled his suggestion that innate differences might be one cause of gender disparities (a suggestion that he drew partly from a literature review in my book, *The Blank Slate*) into the claim that they must be the only cause. And they have converted his suggestion that the statistical distributions of men's and women's abilities are not identical to the claim that all men are talented and all women are not—as if someone heard that women typically live longer than men and concluded that every woman lives longer than every man. Just as depressing is an apparent unfamiliarity with the rationale behind political equality, as when Hopkins sarcastically remarked that, if Summers were right, Harvard should amend its admissions policy, presumably to accept fewer women. This is a classic confusion between the factual claim that men and women are not indistinguishable and the moral claim that we ought to judge people by their individual merits rather than the statistics of their group.

Many of Summers's critics believe that talk of innate gender differences is a relic of Victorian pseudoscience, such as the old theory that cogitation harms women by diverting blood from their ovaries to their brains. In fact, much of the scientific literature has reported numerous statistical differences between men and women. As I noted in *The Blank Slate,* for instance, men are, on average, better at mental rotation and mathematical word problems; women are better at remembering locations and at mathematical calculation. Women match shapes more quickly, are better at reading faces, are better spellers, retrieve words more fluently, and have a better memory for verbal material. Men take greater risks and place a higher premium on status; women are more solicitous to their children.

Of course, just because men and women are different does not mean that the differences are triggered by genes. People develop their talents and personalities in response to their social milieu, which can change rapidly. So some of today's sex differences in cognition could be as culturally determined as sex differences in hair and clothing. But the belief, still popular among some academics (particularly outside the biological sciences), that children are born unisex and are molded into male and female roles by their parents and society is becoming less credible. Many sex differences are universal across cultures (the twentieth-century belief in sex-reversed tribes is as specious as the nineteenth-century belief in blood-deprived ovaries), and some are found in other primates. Men's and women's brains vary in numerous ways, including the receptors for sex hormones. Variations in these hormones, especially before birth, can exaggerate or minimize the typical male and female patterns in cognition and personality. Boys with defective genitals who are surgically feminized and raised as girls have been known to report feeling like they are trapped in the wrong body and to show characteristically male attitudes and interests. And a meta-analysis of 172 studies by psychologists Hugh Lytton and David Romney in 1991 found virtually no consistent difference in the way contemporary Americans socialize their sons and daughters. Regardless of whether it explains the gender disparity in science, the idea that some sex differences have biological roots cannot be dismissed as Neanderthal ignorance.

Since most sex differences are small and many favor women, they don't necessarily give an advantage to men in school or on the job. But Summers invoked yet another difference that may be more consequential. In many traits, men show greater variance than women, and are disproportionately found at both the low and high ends of the distribution. Boys are more likely to be learning disabled or retarded but also more likely to reach the top percentiles in assessments of mathematical ability, even though boys and girls are similar in the bulk of the bell curve. The pattern is readily explained by evolutionary biology. Since a male can have more offspring than a female–but also has a greater chance of being childless (the victims of other males who impregnate the available females)—natural selection favors a slightly more conservative and reliable baby- building process for females and a slightly more ambitious and error-prone process for males. That is because the advantage of an exceptional daughter (who still can have only as many children as a female can bear and nurse in a lifetime) would be canceled out by her unexceptional sisters, whereas an exceptional son who might sire several dozen grandchildren can more than make up for his dull childless brothers. One doesn't have to accept the evolutionary explanation to appreciate how greater male variability could explain, in part, why more men end up with extreme levels of achievement.

10   What are we to make of the breakdown of standards of intellectual discourse in this affair—the statistical innumeracy, the confusion of fairness with sameness, the refusal to glance at the scientific literature? It is not a disease of tenured radicals; comparable lapses can be found among the political right (just look at its treatment of evolution). Instead, we may be seeing the operation of a fascinating bit of human psychology.

The psychologist Philip Tetlock has argued that the mentality of taboo—the belief that certain ideas are so dangerous that it is sinful even to think them—is not a quirk of Polynesian culture or religious superstition but is ingrained into our moral sense. In 2000, he reported asking university students their opinions of unpopular but defensible proposals, such as allowing people to buy and sell organs or auctioning adoption licenses to the highest-bidding parents. He found that most of his respondents did not even try to refute the proposals but expressed shock and outrage at having been asked to entertain them. They refused to consider positive arguments for the proposals and sought to cleanse themselves by volunteering for campaigns to oppose them. Sound familiar?

The psychology of taboo is not completely irrational. In maintaining our most precious relationships, it is not enough to say and do the right thing. We have to show that our heart is in the right place and that we don't weigh the costs and benefits of selling out those who trust us. If someone offers to buy your child or your spouse or your vote, the appropriate response is not to think it over or to ask how much. The appropriate response is to refuse even to consider the possibility. Anything less emphatic would betray the awful truth that you don't understand what it means to be a genuine parent or spouse or citizen. (The logic of taboo underlies the horrific fascination of plots whose protagonists are agonized by unthinkable thoughts, such as *Indecent Proposal* and *Sophie's Choice*.) Sacred and tabooed beliefs also work as membership badges in coalitions. To believe something with a perfect faith, to be incapable of apostasy, is a sign of fidelity to the group and loyalty to the cause. Unfortunately, the psychology of taboo is incompatible with the ideal of scholarship, which is that any idea is worth thinking about, if only to determine whether it is wrong.

At some point in the history of the modern women's movement, the belief that men and women are psychologically indistinguishable became sacred. The reasons are understandable: Women really had been held back by bogus claims of essential differences. Now anyone who so much as raises the question of innate sex differences is seen as "not getting it" when it comes to equality between the sexes. The tragedy is that this mentality of taboo needlessly puts a laudable cause on a collision course with the findings of science and the spirit of free inquiry.

Does Gender Matter?

BEN A. BARRES

Stanford neurobiologist Ben A. Barres argues that the current dearth of women in math and science is caused by socialization, discrimination, and patriarchal hegemony. Drawing on social science research, statistical studies, and his own experience as a female-to-male transgendered person, Barres explores the forces that discourage women from excelling in math and science. This article was published in July 2006 in the commentary section of the British journal Nature, *a prestigious interdisciplinary journal of science that publishes peer-reviewed research articles as well as news and commentary related to science and public affairs.*

When I was 14 years old, I had an unusually talented maths teacher. One day after school, I excitedly pointed him out to my mother. To my amazement, she looked at him with shock and said with disgust: "You never told me that he was black". I looked over at my teacher and, for the first time, realized that he was an African-American. I had somehow never noticed his skin color before, only his spectacular teaching ability. I would like to think that my parents' sincere efforts to teach me prejudice were unsuccessful. I don't know why this lesson takes for some and not for others. But now that I am 51, as a female-to-male transgendered person, I still wonder about it, particularly when I hear male gym teachers telling young boys "not to be like girls" in that same derogatory tone.

Hypothesis Testing

Last year, Harvard University president Larry Summers suggested that differences in innate aptitude rather than discrimination were more likely to be to blame for the failure of women to advance in scientific careers.[1] Harvard professor Steven Pinker then put forth a similar argument in an online debate[2], and an almost identical view was elaborated in a 2006 essay by Peter Lawrence entitled "Men, Women and Ghosts in Science"[3]. Whereas Summers prefaced his statements by saying he was trying to be provocative, Lawrence did not. Whereas Summers talked about "different availability of aptitude at the high end," Lawrence talked about average aptitudes differing. Lawrence argued that, even in a utopian world free of bias, women would still be under-represented in science because they are innately different from men.

Lawrence draws from the work of Simon Baron-Cohen[4] in arguing that males are "on average" biologically predisposed to systematize, to analyze and to be more forgetful of others, whereas females are "on average" innately designed to empathize, to communicate and to care for others. He further argues that men are innately better equipped to aggressively compete in the "vicious struggle to survive" in science. Similarly, Harvard professor Harvey Mansfield states in his new book, *Manliness*[5], that women don't like to compete, are risk adverse, less abstract and too emotional.

I will refer to this view—that women are not advancing because of innate inability rather than because of bias or other factors—as the Larry Summers Hypothesis. It is a view that seems to have resonated widely with male, but not female, scientists. Here, I will argue that available scientific data do not provide credible support for the hypothesis but instead support an alternative one: that women are not advancing because of discrimination. You might call this the "Stephen Jay Gould Hypothesis"

> Few tragedies can be more extensive than the stunting of life, few injustices deeper than the denial of an opportunity to strive or even to hope, by a limit imposed from without, but falsely identified as lying within.

I have no desire to make men into villains (as Henry Kissinger once said, "Nobody will ever win the battle of the sexes; there's just too much fraternizing with the enemy"). As to who the practitioners of this bias are, I will be pointing my finger at women as much as men. I am certain that all the proponents of the Larry Summers Hypothesis are well-meaning and fair-minded people, who agree that treatment of individuals should be based on merit rather than on race, gender or religion stereotypes.

The Sums Don't Add Up

5   Like many women and minorities, however, I am suspicious when those who are at an advantage proclaim that a disadvantaged group of people is innately less able. Historically, claims that disadvantaged groups are innately inferior have been based on junk science and intolerance[6]. Despite powerful social factors that discourage women from studying maths and science from a very young age[7], there is little evidence that gender differences in maths abilities exist, are innate or are even relevant to the lack of advancement of women in science[8]. A study of nearly 20,000 maths scores of children aged 4 to 18, for instance, found little difference between the genders (Fig. 1)[9], and, despite all the social forces that hold women

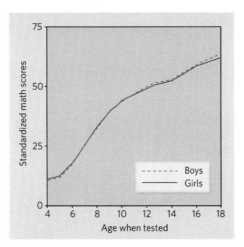

FIGURE 1 MATHS-TEST SCORES FOR AGES 4 TO 18.

In the United States there is little to distinguish the maths-test scores of boys and girls throughout school.

back from an early age, one-third of the winners of the elite Putnam Math Competition last year were women. Moreover, differences in maths-test results are not correlated with the gender divide between those who choose to leave science[10]. I will explain why I believe that the Larry Summers Hypothesis amounts to nothing more than blaming the victim, why it is so harmful to women, and what can and should be done to help women advance in science.

If innate intellectual abilities are not to blame for women's slow advance in science careers, then what is? The foremost factor, I believe, is the societal assumption that women are innately less able than men. Many studies, summarized in Virginia Valian's excellent book *Why So Slow?*[11], have demonstrated a substantial degree of bias against women—more than is sufficient to block women's advancement in many professions. Here are a few examples of bias from my own life as a young woman. As an undergrad at the Massachusetts Institute of Technology (MIT), I was the only person in a large class of nearly all men to solve a hard maths problem, only to be told by the professor that my boyfriend must have solved it for me. I was not given any credit. I am still disappointed about the prestigious fellowship competition I later lost to a male contemporary when I was a PhD student, even though the Harvard dean who had read both applications assured me that my application was much stronger (I had published six high-impact papers whereas my male competitor had published only one). Shortly after I changed sex, a faculty member was heard to say "Ben Barres gave a great seminar today, but then his work is much better than his sister's."

Anecdotes, however, are not data, which is why gender-blinding studies are so important[11]. These studies reveal that in many selection processes, the bar is unconsciously raised so high for women and minority candidates that few emerge as winners. For instance, one study found that women applying for a research grant needed to be 2.5 times more productive than men in order to be considered equally competent (Fig. 2)[12]. Even for women lucky enough to obtain an academic job, gender biases can influence the relative resources allocated to faculty, as Nancy

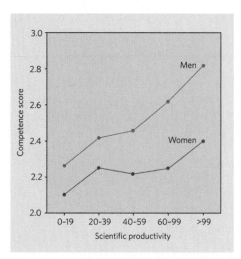

FIGURE 2 COMPETENCE SCORES AWARDED AFTER PEER REVIEW.
Peer reviewers in Sweden award lower competence scores to female scientists than to similarly productive male scientists.

Hopkins discovered when she and a senior faculty committee studied this problem at MIT. The data were so convincing that MIT president Charles Vest publicly admitted that discrimination was responsible. For talented women, academia is all too often not a meritocracy.

In Denial

Despite these studies, very few men or women are willing to admit that discrimination is a serious problem in science. How is that possible? Valian suggests that we all have a strong desire to believe that the world is fair[11]. Remarkably, women are as likely as men to deny the existence of gender-based bias[13]. Accomplished women who manage to make it to the top may 'pull up the ladder behind them; perversely believing that if other women are less successful, then one's own success seems even greater. Another explanation is a phenomenon known as "denial of personal disadvantage," in which women compare their advancement with other women rather than with men[11].

My own denial of the situation persisted until last year, when, at the age of 50, several events opened my eyes to the barriers that women and minorities still face in academia. In addition to the Summers speech, the National Institutes of Health (NIH) began the most prestigious competition they have ever run, the Pioneer Award, but with a nomination process that favoured male applicants[14]. To their credit, in response to concerns that 60 of 64 judges and all 9 winners were men, the NIH has revamped their Pioneer Award selection process to make it fairer. I hope that the Howard Hughes Medical Institute (HHMI) will address similar problems with their investigator competitions. When it comes to bias, it seems that the desire to believe in a meritocracy is so powerful that until a person has experienced sufficient career-harming bias themselves they simply do not believe it exists.

10   My main purpose in writing this commentary is that I would like female students to feel that they will have equal opportunity in their scientific careers. Until intolerance is addressed, women will continue to advance only slowly. Of course, this feeling is also deeply personal to me (see 'Personal Experiences'). The comments of Summers, Mansfield, Pinker and Lawrence about women's lesser innate abilities are all wrongful and personal attacks on my character and capabilities, as well as on my colleagues' and students' abilities and self esteem. I will certainly not sit around silently and endure them.

Mansfield and others claim that women are more emotional than men. There is absolutely no science to support this contention. On the contrary, it is men that commit the most violent crimes in anger—for example, 25 times more murders than women. The only hysteria that exceeded MIT professor Nancy Hopkins' (well-founded) outrage after Larry Summers' comments was the shockingly vicious news coverage by male reporters and commentators. Hopkins also received hundreds of hateful and even pornographic messages, nearly all from men, that were all highly emotional.

Taboo or Untrue?

There is no scientific support, either, for the contention that women are innately less competitive (although I believe powerful curiosity and the drive to create sustain most scientists far more than the love of competition). However, many girls are discouraged from sports for fear of being labelled tomboys. A 2002 study did find a gender gap in competitiveness in financial tournaments, but the authors suggested that this was due to differences in self confidence rather than ability[15]. Indeed, again and again, self confidence has been pointed to as a factor influencing why women

Personal Experiences

As a transgendered person, no one understands more deeply than I do that there are innate differences between men and women. I suspect that my transgendered identity was caused by fetal exposure to high doses of a testosterone-like drug. But there is no evidence that sexually dimorphic brain wiring is at all relevant to the abilities needed to be successful in a chosen academic career. I underwent intensive cognitive testing before and after starting testosterone treatment about 10 years ago. This showed that my spatial abilities have increased as a consequence of taking testosterone. Alas, it has been to no avail; I still get lost all the time when driving (although I am no longer willing to ask for directions). There was one innate difference that I was surprised to learn is apparently under direct control of testosterone in adults—the ability to cry easily, which I largely lost upon starting hormone treatment. Likewise, male-to-female transgendered individuals gain the ability to cry more readily. By far, the main difference that I have noticed is that people who don't know I am transgendered treat me with much more respect: I can even complete a whole sentence without being interrupted by a man.

"choose" to leave science and engineering programs. When women are repeatedly told they are less good, their self confidence falls and their ambitions dim[16]. This is why Valian has concluded that simply raising expectations for women in science may be the single most important factor in helping them make it to the top[11].

Steven Pinker has responded to critics of the Larry Summers Hypothesis by suggesting that they are angry because they feel the idea that women are innately inferior is so dangerous that it is sinful even to think about it[17]. Harvard Law School professor Alan Dershowitz sympathizes so strongly with this view that he plans to teach a course next year called "Taboo." At Harvard we must have veritas; all ideas are fair game. I completely agree. I welcome any future studies that will provide a better understanding of why women and minorities are not advancing at the expected rate in science and so many other professions.

But it is not the idea alone that has sparked anger. Disadvantaged people are wondering why privileged people are brushing the truth under the carpet. If a famous scientist or a president of a prestigious university is going to pronounce in public that women are likely to be innately inferior, would it be too much to ask that they be aware of the relevant data? It would seem that just as the bar goes way up for women applicants in academic selection processes, it goes way down when men are evaluating the evidence for why women are not advancing in science. That is why women are angry. It is incumbent upon those proclaiming gender differences in abilities to rigorously address whether suspected differences are real before suggesting that a whole group of people is innately wired to fail.

15   What happens at Harvard and other universities serves as a model for many other institutions, so it would be good to get it right. To anyone who is upset at the thought that free speech is not fully protected on university campuses, I would like to ask, as did third-year Harvard Law student Tammy Pettinato: what is the difference between a faculty member calling their African-American students lazy and one pronouncing that women are innately inferior? Some have suggested that those who are angry at Larry Summers' comments should simply fight words with more words (hence this essay). In my view, when faculty tell their students that they are innately inferior based on race, religion, gender or sexual orientation, they are crossing a line that should not be crossed—the line that divides free speech from verbal violence—and it should not be tolerated at Harvard or anywhere else. In a culture where women's abilities are not respected, women cannot effectively learn, advance, lead or participate in society in a fulfilling way.

Take Action

Although I have argued that the Larry Summers Hypothesis is incorrect and harmful, the academic community is one of the most tolerant around. But, as tolerant as academics are, we are still human beings influenced by our culture. Comments by Summers and others have made it clear that discrimination remains an under-recognized problem that is far from solved. The progress of science increasingly depends on the global community, but only 10% of the world's population is male and caucasian. To paraphrase Martin Luther King, a first-class scientific enterprise cannot be built upon a foundation of second-class citizens. If women and minorities are to achieve their full potential, all of us need to be far more proactive. So what can be done?

First, enhance leadership diversity in academic and scientific institutions. Diversity provides a substantially broader point of view, with more sensitivity and respect for different perspectives, which is invaluable to any organization. More female leadership is vital in lessening the hostile working environment that young women scientists often encounter. In addition to women and under-represented minority groups, we must not forget Asians and lesbian, gay, bisexual and transgendered folks. There are enough outstanding scientific leaders in these racial and gender groups that anyone with a will to achieve a diverse leadership in their organization could easily attain it.

Speak Out

Second, the importance of diverse faculty role models cannot be overstated. There is much talk about equal opportunity, but, in practice, serious attention still needs to be directed at how to run fair job searches. Open searches often seem to be bypassed entirely for top leadership positions, just when it matters most—search committees should not always be chaired by men and the committee itself should be highly diverse[14,18]. Implementation of special hiring strategies and strong deans willing to push department chairs to recruit top women scientists are especially effective. It is crucial in the promotion process that merit be decided by the quality, not quantity, of papers published.

Women faculty, in particular, need help from their institutions in balancing career and family responsibilities. In an increasingly competitive environment, women with children must be able to compete for funding and thrive. Why can't young faculty have the option of using their tuition benefits, in which some universities pay part of the college tuition fees for the children of faculty, for day care instead? Tuition benefits will be of no help if female scientists don't make tenure. And institutions that have the financial capability, such as HHMI, could help by making more career-transition fellowships available for talented women scientists.

Third, there should be less silence in the face of discrimination. Academic leadership has a particular responsibility to speak out, but we all share this responsibility. It takes minimal effort to send a brief message to the relevant authority when you note a lack of diversity in an organization or an act of discrimination. I don't know why more women don't speak out about sexism at their institutions, but I do know that they are often reluctant, even when they have the security of a tenured faculty position. Nancy Hopkins is an admirable role model, and it is time that others share the burden. It doesn't only have to be women that support women. I was deeply touched by the eloquent words of Greg Petsko[19] following Summers' comments. And it has been 30 years since I was a medical student, but I still recall with gratitude the young male student who immediately complained to a professor who had shown a slide of a nude pin-up in his anatomy lecture.

Fourth, enhance fairness in competitive selection processes. Because of evaluation bias, women and minorities are at a profound disadvantage in such competitive selection unless the processes are properly designed[11,12,14,18]. As the revamped NIH Pioneer Award demonstrates, a few small changes can make a significant difference in outcome. By simply changing the procedure so that anyone can self-nominate and by ensuring a highly diverse selection committee, the number of women and minority winners went up to more than 50% from zero. This lesson can and should now be applied to other similar processes for scientific awards, grants and faculty positions. Alas, too many selection committees still show a striking lack of diversity—with typically greater than 90% white males. When selection processes are run fairly, reverse discrimination is not needed to attain a fair outcome.

At school, girls and boys show similar levels of ability in the sciences.

Confidence Booster

Finally, we can teach young scientists how to survive in a prejudiced world. Self-confidence is crucial in advancing and enjoying a research career. From an early age, girls receive messages that they are not good enough to do science subjects or will be less liked if they are good at them. The messages come from many sources, including parents, friends, fellow students and, alas, teachers. When teachers have lower expectations of them, students do less well. But we are all at fault for sending these messages and for remaining silent when we encounter them. Teachers need to provide much more encouragement to young people, regardless of sex, at all stages of training. Occasional words of encouragement can have enormous effects.

All students, male and female, would benefit from training in how to be more skillful presenters, to exert a presence at meetings by asking questions, to make connections with faculty members who may help them to obtain grants and a job, and to have the leadership skills necessary to survive and advance in academia. Because women and minorities tend to be less confident in these areas, their mentors in particular need to encourage them to be more proactive. I vividly recall my PhD supervisor coming with me to the talks of famous scientists and forcing me to introduce myself and to ask them questions. There is a great deal of hallway mentoring that goes on for young men that I am not sure many women and minorities receive (I wish that someone had mentioned to me when I was younger that life, even in science, is a popularity contest—a message that Larry Summers might have found helpful as well). It is incumbent on all of us who are senior faculty to keep a look out for highly talented young people, including women and minority students, and help them in whatever way possible with their careers.

1 Summers, L. *Letter to the Faculty Regarding NBER Remarks* www.president.harvard.edu/speeches/summers/2005/facletter.html(2005).

2 *The Science of Gender and Science. Pinker vs. Spelke: A Debate* www.edge.org/3rd_culture/debate05/debate05_index.html(2005).

3 Lawrence, P.A. *PLoS Biol.* 4, 13–15 (2006).

4 Baron-Cohen, S. *The Essential Difference: Men, Women, and the Extreme Male Brain* (Allen Lane, London, 2003).

5 Mansfield, H. *Manliness* (Yale Univ. Press, New Haven, 2006).

6 Gould, S. J. *The Mismeasure of Man* (W. W. Norton & Co, New York, 1996).

7 Steele, C. M. *Am. Psychol.* 52, 613–629 (1997).

8 Spelke, E. S. *Am. Psychol.* 60, 950–958 (2005).

9 Leahey, E. & Guo, G. *Soc. Forces* 80. 2, 713–732 (2001).

10 Xie, Y. & Shauman, K. *Women in Science: Career Processes and Outcomes* (Harvard Univ. Press, Cambridge, 2003).

11 Valian, V. *Why So Slow?* (MIT Press, Cambridge, 1998).

12 Wenneras, C. & Wold, A. *Nature* 387, 341–343 (1997).

13 Rhode, D. L. *Speaking of Sex: The Denial of Gender Inequality* (Harvard Univ. Press, Cambridge, 1997).

14 Carnes, M. *et al. J. Womens Health* 14, 684–691 (2005).

15 Gneezy, U., Niederle, M. & Rustichini, A. Q. *J. Econ.* 18, 1049–1074 (2003).

16 Fels, A. *Necessary Dreams* (Pantheon Press, New York, 2004).

17 Pinker, S. *New Repub.* 15 (14 Feb. 2005).

18 Moody, J. *Faculty Diversity: Problems and Solutions* (Taylor and Francis, New York, 2004).

19 Petsko, G. A.*Genome Biol. 6,* 1–3(2005).

Girls = Boys at Math

DAVID MALAKOFF

David Malakoff is a freelance science writer and occasional contributor to ScienceNow
Daily News, *an online daily news service for the prestigious peer-reviewed journal* Science.
*This brief article, posted in July 2008, summarizes for popular audiences a technical
research report that refutes Summer's comments.*

Zip. Zilch. Nada. There's no real difference between the scores of U.S. boys and girls on common math tests, according to a massive new study. Educators hope the finding will finally dispel lingering perceptions that girls don't measure up to boys when it comes to crunching numbers.

"This shows there's no issue of intellectual ability—and that's a message we still need to get out to some of our parents and teachers," says Henry "Hank" Kepner, president of the National Council of Teachers of Mathematics in Reston, Virginia.

It won't be a new message. Nearly 20 years ago, a large-scale study led by psychologist Janet Hyde of the University of Wisconsin, Madison, found a "trivial" gap in math test scores between boys and girls in elementary and middle school. But it did suggest that boys were better at solving more complex problems by the time they got to high school.

Now, even that small gap has disappeared, Hyde reports in tomorrow's issue of *Science*. Her team sifted through scores from standardized tests taken in 2005, 2006, and 2007 by nearly 7 million students in 10 states. Overall, the researchers found "no gender difference" in scores among children in grades two through 11. Among students with the highest test scores, the team did find that white boys outnumbered white girls by about two to one. Among Asians, however, that result was nearly reversed. Hyde says that suggests that cultural and social factors, not gender alone, influence how well students perform on tests.

5   Another portion of the study did confirm that boys still tend to outscore girls on the mathematics section of the SAT test taken by 1.5 million students interested in attending college. In 2007, for instance, boys' scores were about 7% higher on average than girls'. But Hyde's team argues that the gap is a statistical illusion, created by the fact that more girls take the test. "You're dipping farther down into the distribution of female talent, which brings down the score," Hyde says. It's not clear that statisticians at the College Board, which produces the SAT, will agree with that explanation. But Hyde says it's good news, because it means the test isn't biased against girls.

The study's most disturbing finding, the authors say, is that neither boys nor girls get many tough math questions on state tests now required to measure a school district's progress under the 2002 federal No Child Left Behind law. Using a four-level rating scale, with level one being easiest, the authors said that they found no challenging level-three or -four questions on most state tests. The authors worry that means that teachers may start dropping harder math from their curriculums, because "more teachers are gearing their instruction to the test."

The results "essentially confirm" earlier studies—and they should finally put to rest the idea that girls aren't going into technical fields because they can't do the math, says Ann Gallagher, a psychologist who studies testing at the Law School Admission Council in Newtown, Pennsylvania. But she still thinks there may be cultural or psychological reasons for why girls still tend to lag behind boys on high-stakes tests such as the SAT. Among students she's observed, she says "the boys tend to be a little more idiosyncratic in solving problems, the girls more conservative in following what they've been taught."

■ ■ ■   **FOR CLASS DISCUSSION**   Women in Math and Science

1. As you analyze the various reactions to Summers's speech, return to our summary of what he actually said.
   a. What hypotheses did he propose to explain the underrepresentation of women on the tenured faculties in math, physics, and engineering at prestigious universities?
   b. Concerning Summers's biological hypothesis: What is the difference between saying "On average, men are better at math than women" and saying "Men show greater variability in the distribution of test scores than do women?" Which of these statements more closely represents Summers's point about innate differences between the sexes?
   c. Why does it matter which of the two statements most represents Summers's view? What is at stake?
2. Among the persons who responded to Summers's speech, what variations do you find in the way they summarized his innate-differences argument? Do you think some commentators treated Summers more fairly than others? How so?
3. Many of the writers in this unit refer to specific scientific studies. Working in small groups or as a whole class, try to place these studies in one of three columns:
   a. Research studies/experiments that support the nature hypothesis
   b. Research studies/experiments that support the nurture hypothesis

    c. Research studies/experiments that are ambiguous or open to different interpretations

4. From a broad cultural perspective, what is at stake in the controversy over Summers's speech?

    a. What important values and beliefs are reinforced or threatened by different positions on this controversy?

    b. What ideologies or world views makes some commentators apt to accept Summers' biological hypothesis and others apt to oppose it?

    c. Where do you stand and why?

5. In June 2006, Lawrence Summers resigned as president of Harvard, having received votes of "no confidence" from the faculty. One of the contributing causes of the no-confidence vote was the accusation of sexism stemming from his innate-differences speech. Conservative media commentators accused the liberal Harvard faculty of railroading Summers from office, preferring political correctness over truth-seeking scientific inquiry. Where do you stand on this issue?

WRITING ASSIGNMENT Summary and Response

Within the readings in this unit, find a writer with whom you particularly disagree. Your disagreement could focus on your chosen writer's stand on the nature/nurture controversy about math aptitude or on the assumptions, beliefs, or values that your chosen writer brings to the discussion. Also, your disagreement might focus on your writer's main thesis or on some subpoint or sidepoint raised in the argument. What you are looking for is a hot-spot that sparks your own entry into this controversy.

Write an argument that accurately and fairly summarizes the view that you are pushing against and then create your best argument persuading readers to your alternative point of view. In many cases, you might need to do further research into the scientific controversy on gender differences. An example of a student paper on this issue is Julee Christianson's "Why Lawrence Summers Was Wrong: Culture Rather Than Biology Explains the Under-Representation of Women in Science and Mathematics" on pp. 254–257. ■

For additional writing, reading, and research resources, go to www.mycomplab.com

Finding Soldiers
The Volunteer Army, Recruitment, and the Draft

As the United States' involvement in Iraq stretches on, the military is facing critical recruitment problems. In addition, the military is drawing heavily on the National Guard and the Army Reserve, returning troops to Iraq for enlistments of indefinite length and employing a large number of contractors, or mercenaries, to play quasi-military roles in Iraq. The military is also using multiple strategies to find soldiers: lowering its recruitment standards, being more innovative and aggressive in its recruitment campaigns—including trying to interest high school students and get early commitments from them—and offering larger financial incentives and benefits.

Since the Vietnam War and the unpopular draft that supplied soldiers for it, the country has relied on an "all-volunteer Army" and on the principle that a smaller but highly trained, highly technologically equipped fighting force is better than an Army composed of less-skilled draftees. However, the current Army is not designed for prolonged engagements like Iraq, nor is the size of the Army sufficient to handle multiple global conflicts. Although polls show that a majority of Americans are opposed to a draft and the Bush administration repeatedly said it would not reinstitute conscription, many analysts suggest that a draft is needed. The problem of filling the Army has taken the form of many questions being debated by journalists, analysts, military strategists, policymakers, and citizens: What size Army does the United States need to maintain its global superpower status? Can an all-volunteer Army supplemented with military contractors serve our national security and foreign policy needs, or should the United States reinstate a draft? Who should be in the military for our national security? Citizen soldiers? Professional military? Mercenaries? Drafted soldiers? Should citizens be required to serve their country? What are the fairest and most effective ways to fill military quotas? How can the responsibility of defending the country be equitably spread among classes, ethnic groups, and genders? Which of the present recruitment and retention strategies are the most effective?

The readings and visuals in this unit—in addition to the screen captures from the Army's online video game, America's Army (p. 182), and the recruitment cartoon (p. 307)—introduce you to the controversy about these urgent questions, asking you to consider your own values and views on these issues.

New Model Army

DONALD RUMSFELD

Secretary of defense for the Bush administration, from 2001 to 2006, Donald Rumsfeld has had a long career of political posts, including U.S. congressman, White House chief of staff, and U.S.

ambassador to NATO. He also served as CEO of two Fortune 500 companies. This brief to the Pentagon, expressing his vision for the United States Army, was released on March 15, 2005.

In just 28 months, U.S. forces, with our Coalition partners, have overthrown two terrorist regimes, captured or killed thousands of terrorist leaders and operatives, disrupted terrorist cells on virtually every continent, and undoubtedly prevented a number of additional terrorist attacks. Our troops have performed magnificently—despite the significant increase in operational tempo of the global war on terror, which has increased the demand on the force.

Managing that demand is one of the Department of Defense's top priorities. Doing so means being clear about the problem, and fashioning the most appropriate solutions. Much of the current increase in demand on the force is most likely a temporary spike caused by the deployment of nearly 115,000 troops to Iraq. We do not expect to have 115,000 troops permanently deployed in any one campaign.

Nevertheless, for the moment, the increased demand is real, and over the past two years we have taken a number of immediate actions to alleviate it. We are increasing international military participation in Iraq and Afghanistan. We are accelerating the training of Iraqi security forces—now over 200,000—so Iraqis will increasingly take responsibility for their own security and stability, and we are hunting down those who threaten Iraq's transition to self-government and self-reliance.

Another way of relieving the increased demand on the force is to add more people— and we have done that as well. Using the emergency powers granted to the president by Congress, since September 2001 we have increased active force levels above authorized levels—by 33,000, or more at times. If the situation demands it, we will not hesitate to add still more—whatever is needed. However, the fact that we have to increase force levels at all should give us pause. U.S. Armed Forces currently total about 2.6 million men and women—1.4 million active forces, 876,000 guard and reserve in units, and 287,000 individual ready reserves. Yet despite these large numbers, the deployment of 115,000 troops to Iraq has required that we temporarily increase the size of the force.

5 That should tell us something. It tells us that the real problem is not necessarily the size of our active and reserve military components, per se, but rather how forces have been managed, and the mix of capabilities at our disposal.

Army Chief of Staff Gen. Pete Schoomaker compares the problem to a barrel of rainwater on which the spigot is placed too high up. The result: when you turn it on, it only draws water off the top, while the water at the bottom is not accessible or used. Our real problem is that the way our total force is presently managed, we have to use many of the same people over and over again. In Gen. Schoomaker's analogy, the answer is not a bigger barrel of more than the current 2.6 million men and women available, but to move the spigot down, so more of the potentially available troops are accessible, usable, and available to defend our nation. The department must promptly reorganize to gain better access to the fine men and women who make up the all-volunteer force, and to ensure we have the skills needed available as and when needed. Clearly, we are not doing so today.

Take the Guard and Reserve for example. Since Sept. 11, 2001, we have mobilized roughly 36% of the Selected Reserve. Those mobilizations have concentrated on certain skill sets: installation security forces, air crews, military police, Special Forces, civil affairs, and intelligence officers. Yet even now, we have not mobilized over 60% of the Selected Reserve to fight the global war on terror. Indeed, 58% of the current Guard and Reserve force have not been involuntarily mobilized in the past decade. Clearly they have not been stressed. That suggests that our problem is certainly not too few forces. Rather, it is that we have too few forces with the skill sets that are in high demand, and too many forces with skills that are not in high demand.

We are working hard to fix that—by rebalancing skill sets within the Reserve component and between the active and reserve force. In 2003, we rebalanced some 10,000 positions. We expect to have rebalanced a total of 50,000 positions by the end of next year. Simultaneously, the services are transforming to increase combat capability while relieving demand on the forces. For example, the Army has put forward a plan that, when implemented, will use our emergency authorities to bring the Army's temporary strength up by nearly 30,000 troops above its peacetime statutory limit—it is today about 7,000 above that limit. But the proposal is to use that increase, and all the movement in the system during the force deployments and redeployments, to increase the Army's combat power by up to 30%. How? Instead of simply adding more Divisions, the Army is focusing instead on creating a "Modular Army" comprised of smaller, self-contained brigades that would be interchangeable, available to work for any Division.

The new more "Modular Army" will be appropriate for the 21st century. In the event of a crisis, the 4th Infantry Division commander, for example, could gather two of his own brigades, combine them with available brigades from, say, the 1st Armored Division and the National Guard, and deploy them together. The result is improved interoperability within the Army, even as the Army is becoming more interoperable with the other services, as we saw in Iraq. This is a bold proposal and the DoD leadership is working with Congress on it.

10   In addition, other initiatives are underway to improve force management and increase capability: We are taking military personnel out of civilian jobs to free them up for military tasks. We are reducing the number of troops and dependents that are constantly being rotated in and out of foreign bases and facilities. And we are fixing the mobilization process to make it more respectful of troops, families, and employers.

The key to these initiatives is flexibility—to be able to increase or decrease as demand requires, and to manage the force as the security circumstances permit. Today, with authority granted by Congress, the DoD has the flexibility to adjust troop levels as the security situation requires—and we are doing so. A permanent increase in statutory end-strength, as many are proposing, would significantly reduce flexibility.

The president charged us with the responsibility of transforming the department for the challenges our nation faces in this century. The American people expect this: that we maintain the best force in the world, and that we be respectful of the people in that force and of the taxpayers who support it. And that is what we are doing.

The Case for the Draft

PHILLIP CARTER AND PAUL GLASTRIS

Paul Glastris served as a speechwriter to the Clinton administration from 1998 to 2001 and is currently the editor-in-chief of the Washington Monthly. *He is also a senior fellow at the Western Policy Center, a foreign policy institute that focuses on United States policy and action in Eastern Europe. Phillip Carter is a former U.S. Army officer who now writes on national security issues for the* Washington Monthly. *He also practices international and contract law. This article appeared in the March 2005 issue of the* Washington Monthly, *an independent magazine devoted to politics and government.*

The United States has occupied many foreign lands over the last half century—Germany and Japan in World War II, and, on a much smaller scale, Haiti, Bosnia, and Kosovo in the 1990s. In all these cases, we sponsored elections and handed-off to democratic governments control of countries that were relatively stable, secure, and reasonably peaceful.

In Iraq, we failed to do this, despite heroic efforts by U.S. and coalition troops. The newly-elected Iraqi government inherits a country in which assassinations, kidnappings, suicide bombings, pipeline sabotages, and beheadings of foreigners are daily occurrences. For the last eight months, the ranks of the insurgency have been growing faster than those of the security forces of the provisional Iraqi government—and an alarming number of those government forces are secretly working for the insurgency. American-led combat operations in Ramadi and Fallujah killed large numbers of the enemy, but at the price of fanning the flames of anti-American hatred and dispersing the insurrection throughout Iraq. Despite nearly two years of effort, American troops and civilian administrators have failed to restore basic services to much of the central part of the country where a majority of Iraqis live. The U.S. military has not even been able to secure the 7-mile stretch of highway leading from the Baghdad airport to the Green Zone where America's own embassy and the seat of the Iraqi government are headquartered.

How we got to this point is by now quite obvious. Even many of the war's strongest supporters admit that the Bush administration grievously miscalculated by invading Iraq with too few troops and then by stubbornly refusing to augment troop numbers as the country descended into violent mayhem after the fall of Saddam.

This analysis, of course, presumes that it was ever possible to invade and quickly pacify Iraq, given the country's religious–ethnic divisions and history of tyranny. But it also presumes that the fault is primarily one of judgment: that the president and key senior military officials made a mistake by accepting Defense Secretary Donald Rumsfeld's theory that a "transformed" American military can prevail in war without great masses of ground troops. That judgment was indeed foolish; events have shown that, while a relatively modest American force can win a stunning battlefield victory, such a force is not enough to secure the peace.

5   But there's a deeper problem, one that any president who chose to invade a country the size of Iraq would have faced. In short, America's all-volunteer military simply cannot deploy and sustain enough troops to succeed in places like Iraq while still deterring threats elsewhere in the world. Simply adding more soldiers to the active duty force, as some in Washington are now suggesting, may sound like a good solution. But it's not, for sound operational and pragmatic reasons. America doesn't need a bigger standing army; it needs a deep bench of trained soldiers held in reserve who can be mobilized to handle the unpredictable but inevitable wars and humanitarian interventions of the future. And while there are several ways the all-volunteer force can create some extra surge capacity, all of them are limited.

The only effective solution to the manpower crunch is the one America has turned to again and again in its history: the draft. Not the mass combat mobilizations of World War II, nor the inequitable conscription of Vietnam—for just as threats change and war-fighting advances, so too must the draft. A modernized draft would demand that the privileged participate. It would give all who serve a choice over how they serve. And it would provide the military, on a "just in time" basis, large numbers of deployable ground troops, particularly the peacekeepers we'll need to meet the security challenges of the 21st century.

America has a choice. It can be the world's superpower, or it can maintain the current all-volunteer military, but it probably can't do both.

Plowing a Field with a Ferrari

Before the invasion of Iraq, Army Chief of Staff Eric Shinseki and Army Secretary Thomas White advised Rumsfeld that many more troops would be needed to secure Iraq (something on the order of 250,000 to 300,000). Secretary of State Colin Powell, whose State Department was shut out of the post-war planning process, also privately argued for a bigger force. A RAND Corporation analysis, published in summer 2003, offered a range of estimates for what size force would be necessary in Iraq. Using troops-to-population ratios from previous occupations, RAND projected that, two years after the invasion, it would take anywhere from 258,000 troops (the Bosnia model), to 321,000 (post–World War II Germany), to 526,000 (Kosovo) to secure the peace.

None of these figures seems, at first glance, unachievable for a U.S. military comprised of 14 million active-duty troops, 870,900 reservists, and 110,000 individual ready reservists (soldiers who have served their tour of duty and are not training with the reserves but who can by statute still be called up for service). And yet an Iraq deployment that has never exceeded 153,000 ground personnel has put so much stress on the military that a senior Army Reserve official has candidly stated that current rotation policies will lead to a "broken force." How can that be?

10   To answer that question, begin by deducting virtually the entire Navy and Air Force from the head count; the Iraq occupation has been almost exclusively a ground game, hence an Army and Marine

operation. Next, consider that the United States sends into combat not individual soldiers but units, complete with unit equipment sets, unit leaders, and an organizational structure that facilitates command, control, and logistical support. So instead of counting individual soldiers—a meaningless exercise—one must look at how many *units* the United States could theoretically put on the ground if it wanted to mobilize every active and reserve soldier available. And if you do that, you come to a figure of roughly 600,000 troops. That's the total number of deployable soldiers that the United States could theoretically have called upon to man the initial invasion.

In practice, however, the Pentagon would never have sent that many troops to Iraq, for good reasons: It would have left the defense cupboard bare and served as an open invitation to America's enemies to make trouble elsewhere in the world. Massing a 600,000 force would have meant not only pulling nearly all front-line troops out of Korea, but also mobilizing the poorly-resourced divisions of the National Guard, the third-string crew that the president can call on when the first string (active troops) and the second string (the Guard's elite "enhanced" reserve brigades) are depleted.

Given the need to hold troops in reserve for deterrence purposes, the Pentagon had perhaps 400,000 troops available for the invasion. Yet that number includes many troops in specialized fields that are of little or no use in desert warfare or peacekeeping—off-loading equipment in sea ports, for instance. Such troops could have been reshaped into provisional infantry units, as the Army has done with artillery and air-defense formations, but that would've taken time. The number of troops with units that would actually have been of use in Iraq was probably closer to the figures that Gen. Shinseki and Secretary White have suggested: 250,000 to 300,000—in other words, the lower end of what RAND estimated would be required for success.

But even that number is deceptive. It is the size of the force that could have been initially sent into

Iraq, not the number that could have realistically been *sustained* there. Because so many soldiers in the all-volunteer military are married with families (compared to conscript armies), and because soldiers must periodically be induced or persuaded to voluntarily reenlist, the Pentagon must rotate its forces in and out of theater every 12 months or so in order to maintain morale and reenlistment. Thus, just as a civilian police department must hire three to four police officers for every one cop on the beat, so too must the U.S. military have three to four soldiers for every one serving in Iraq.

The Pentagon, then, could have realistically kept those initial 250,000 to 300,000 troops in place only for a limited time—perhaps a year, certainly not more than two. That might have been enough time to pacify the country, especially if higher troop numbers at the outset would have quelled the early looting and disorder. Then again, a year or two might not have been sufficient time to beat back an insurgency which, we now know, was to some extent planned in advance of the invasion. In that case, keeping 250,000 to 300,000 troops in Iraq for two years or longer would have risked so lowering morale and reenlistment rates as to destroy the all-volunteer force. It would have been like plowing a field with a Ferrari; it could have been done, but only once.

15 Taking the need for rotations into account, then, the U.S. military can comfortably handle something like 80,000 troops in Iraq at any one time. The actual number on the ground has averaged 133,286 for the last two years, and more than 150,000 soldiers are in Iraq now.

That's a woefully insufficient number for the task. Yet it is pushing the outside limits of what the current force structure can handle. It has meant imposing "stop-loss" emergency measures to prevent soldiers from exiting the service. It has required deploying nearly every active-duty brigade, including one previously committed elsewhere in Korea. It has meant raiding the seed corn of military readiness by deploying the Army's elite "opposing force" training units—seasoned soldiers who play the enemy in mock exercises to build the skills of greener troops before they are sent into battle. It has necessitated calling up all 15 of the National Guard's enhanced readiness brigades, as well as poorly-resourced National Guard divisions that have not been mobilized *en masse* since the Korean War. It has led the Army Reserve Chief Lt. Gen. James Helmly to write in a recent memo that the Reserve will be unable to meet its commitments without substantial use of the Army's *involuntary* mobilization authorities under federal law. As of Dec. 15, 2004, the Army Reserve retained just 37,515 deployable soldiers out of a total of 200,366—almost no cushion at all. And in the final two months of last year, the Reserves missed their enlistment targets last year by 30 percent—a sign of even greater problems to come.

All this for a war that most planners consider to be a medium-sized conflict—nothing like what the United States faced in World War I, World War II, or the Cold War. And while threats of that magnitude aren't anywhere on the horizon, there are plenty of quite possible scenarios that could quickly overwhelm us—an implosion of the North Korean regime, a Chinese attack on Taiwan, worsening of the ethnic cleansing in the Sudan, or some unforeseen humanitarian nightmare. Already we have signaled to bad actors everywhere the limits of our power. Military threats might never have convinced the Iranians to give up their nuclear program. But it's more than a little troubling that ruling Iranian mullahs can publicly and credibly dismiss recent administration saber-rattling by pointing to the fact that our forces are pinned down in Iraq.

Stress Test

Every 20 years or so for the past century, America has found it necessary, for national security reasons, to send at least half a million troops overseas into harm's way, and to keep them there for years at a time. It did so in World War I, sending 4.1 million doughboys and Marines to Europe.

In World War II, it mobilized 16 million for the war effort. America sent more than 3 million grunts to fight in Korea against the North Koreans and Chinese, in the first hot war of the Cold War. It rotated 5.1 million soldiers and Marines through Vietnam over a decade, with 543,400 stationed there at the height of that war in April 1969. And more recently, America sent 550,000 ground troops to eject Saddam's forces from Kuwait, as part of a ground force which totaled 831,500 with allied contributions from dozens of nations. Along the way, the United States military simultaneously fought small wars in Greece, Lebanon, El Salvador, Somalia, Haiti, Bosnia, and Kosovo, requiring the commitment of thousands more. This ability to deploy large numbers of troops overseas for long periods of time has been the price of America's superpower status—what President John Kennedy alluded to in his inaugural address when he said America would bear any burden to assure the survival and the success of liberty.

There's no reason to think that America will be exempt from paying that price in the future. Even those who don't support the Bush policy of using unilateral force to democratize the Middle East (and we don't), and who prefer to work through military alliances whenever possible (and we do), should understand the need to increase American troop strength. The international community failed to act in Rwanda largely because the United States chose not to send troops; our NATO allies sent soldiers into Bosnia and Kosovo only because we put substantial numbers of ours in, too. The same will hold true for just about any other major war or humanitarian intervention in the future.

20   What we're increasingly learning from Iraq is that the all-volunteer force, as presently built, cannot do that—indeed, it was consciously designed to be incapable of such deployments. Today's force was built for precisely the kinds of wars that Caspar Weinberger and Colin Powell envisioned in their doctrines: wars with explicit purposes, narrow parameters, and clear exit strategies. In other words, it

was built for the kinds of wars the military prefers to fight, not necessarily the kinds of wars we have, as a nation, historically fought.

The evolution of this force owes much to Vietnam. After that war ended, the nation's senior generals devised a military structure called the "total force" concept to circumvent two of the great moral hazards they identified with Vietnam: the failure to mobilize the nation, with all of its strata and segments, for the war; and the reliance on young American conscripts, who were coerced by the state to kill or be killed.

Vietnam had been fought almost entirely by active-duty volunteers and conscripts. A great number of young men, including many from the nation's privileged classes, sought refuge in the reserves as a way out of duty in Vietnam. The total force concept entailed, first of all, the splitting of lay war-fighting and support functions. Henceforth, active-duty troops would perform nearly all the traditional combat roles; reservists would provide most of the support functions, such as logistics and military policing. This ensured that future wars could not be fought without the heavy involvement of the reserves. Army Gen. Creighton Abrams and other leaders felt that this would be a check on the power of presidents to go to war because mass reserve call-ups typically require a great deal of political capital.

Second, Pentagon leaders replaced the conscripted military with an all-volunteer force that would recruit enlistees with pay and benefits like the civilian world. This all-volunteer model, they believed, would improve morale for the simple reason that all soldiers would be in the service by choice. It would also improve military effectiveness because if soldiers could be lured to stay longer by reenlisting, they could acquire higher levels of skill. The mantra of the new military became "send a bullet, not a man"; the modern American military came to embrace precision firepower over manpower in what historian Russell Weigley called the "American way of war."

This all-volunteer military made good on nearly all these promises. After a rough period in the late 1970s, the U.S. military emerged a leaner, better force in the 1980s, proving itself in the small wars of that decade—Grenada, Libya, and Panama. Then came the first Gulf War—the apothesis of the all-volunteer, total force model. Coming off the Cold War, the Army had 18 divisions on active duty, in comparison to 10 today, and had little in the way of a pressing commission with the imminent collapse of the Soviet Union. By mobilizing seven of

these Army divisions and two Marine divisions, in addition to the reserves and ready reserves, military leaders were able to send half a million troops to the Saudi desert. But because that war lasted just months, largely due to U.S. reluctance to invade and occupy Iraq, the system worked. Active-duty soldiers deployed for less than a year, without fear of immediately being sent back to fight; reservists were similarly tapped just once. Desert Storm did not break the all-volunteer force because that war was precisely the kind that the force had been designed to fight: a limited campaign for limited ends, of limited duration, and with a defined exit strategy.

25   Unfortunately, national security threats don't always conform to the military's precise specifications. The 1990s brought two wars, in Bosnia and Kosovo, requiring the long-term commitment of U.S. troops for peacekeeping. These were relatively modest-sized deployments. Yet the military leadership complained that they put undo stress on the system, and, indeed, then-Gov. George Bush lambasted the Clinton administration in 2000 for the way it managed military readiness, charging that the Kosovo war put two of the Army's 10 divisions out of action, hurting the nation's ability to respond to threats abroad. In the wake of September 11, the U.S. military mobilized tens of thousands of reservists for homeland security and sent thousands of elite infantrymen and special forces into the mountains of Afghanistan; neither mission conformed to the model of past wars.

Then came Operation Iraqi Freedom, and the real stress test began.

Five Bad Options

In theory, there are several ways to get out of the military manpower bind we find ourselves in. In reality, there are inherent limits to almost all of them.

The first option—at least the one Democrats and moderate Republicans have talked most about—is to convince other countries to share the burden in Iraq. But that's not likely. Even if the security situation in Iraq improves and the Bush administration begins to share decision-making—something it's so far refused to do—European leaders would be extremely wary of trying to sell their citizens on sending troops to keep the peace in a war they expressly opposed. It may be possible to convince the Europeans and other developed nations to be more willing to contribute troops the next time there's an international need. But that, as we've seen, will require more U.S. troops, not fewer. Nor should it be the policy of the United States to have to rely on other countries' troops. We must be prepared to intervene unilaterally if necessary.

A second solution to the manpower crisis would be to rely more on private military contractors whose use has exploded in recent years. Currently, more than 40,000 government contractors are on duty in Iraq, working in myriad jobs from security to reconstruction. The advantage of using contractors is that they provide surge capacity; they are hired only for the duration of an engagement. But according to Peter W. Singer, a research fellow at the Brookings Institution, these private armies also create problems. First, all costs considered, they're not necessarily less expensive for the military. Second, private military contractors often compete with the military for personnel, so any growth in these contractors usually results in tension between military retention and contractor recruiting efforts. Third, contractors operate in a legal gray area where their financial and accounting activities are heavily regulated, but their operations are barely looked at. It's one thing to contract for truck drivers; it's another to hire contractors to guard Afghan President Hamid Karzai or work as interrogation linguists in the Abu Ghraib prison because the military has too few commandos or linguists in its own ranks. The military has probably already pushed the contractor concept about as far as it will go; expecting much more surge capacity from private industry is probably unrealistic.

30   A third possibility might be to follow the advice of several cutting-edge military reformers to radically transform today's military. According to these reformers, today's force was drawn up for a bygone age of massed superpower armies; it does not reflect today's threats. These visionaries would downsize the Navy, scrap some of the Army's mechanized divisions, and in these and other ways free up tens of thousands of troops to be redeployed into "soldier centric" units capable

of doing everything along the spectrum from humanitarian relief in Banda Aceh to combat patrols in Baghdad. Under pressure from the Iraq mission, the military has taken some steps in this direction—for instance, by retraining and reequipping some army artillery and air defense units into military police units. But such moves have been incremental in nature thus far; the true scope of the problem is orders of magnitude larger than the Pentagon's current solution. And some day, a war may come which requires all kinds of combat power—from large land-based formations to ships capable of sailing through the Taiwan strait to legions of peacekeepers. The military cannot build additional capability simply by playing a shell game with its personnel; at some point, it must genuinely add more soldiers too, and in large numbers.

A fourth option, and the most obvious one, would be to simply increase the size of the active-duty force. This too has been discussed. During the 2004 campaign, Sen. John Kerry called for increasing the active-duty force by 40,000 troops. More recently a bipartisan group of hawkish defense intellectuals published an open letter on *The Weekly Standard* Web site calling on Congress to add 25,000 ground troops each year for the next several years. And the Pentagon has announced some money for extra troops in the administration's latest budget. The problem with such proposals is that they underestimate both current manpower needs and the cost of forcing the all-volunteer military to grow.

In theory, one can always lure the next recruit, or retain the next soldier, by offering a marginally higher monetary incentive—but in reality, there are practical limits to such measures. The pool of people who might be convinced to join the Army is mainly comprised of healthy young people with high school degrees but no college plans. That pool is inherently limited, especially when the economy is heating up and there's a shooting war

on. Last year, despite signing bonuses in the tens of thousands and other perks, military recruiters had to lower entry standards to meet their enlistment goals. The active force met its recruiting targets for 2004, but the reserves have found themselves increasingly struggling to bring enough soldiers in the door.

But it's the long-term cost issues that most militate against making the all-volunteer force bigger. Generals today are fond of saying that you recruit a soldier, but you retain their families. One reason the Army has resisted Congress' attempts to raise its end strength is that it does not want to embrace all of the costs associated with permanently increasing the size of the military, because it sees each soldier as a 30-year commitment—both to the soldier and his (or her) family. According to the Congressional Budget Office, each soldier costs $99,000 per year—a figure which includes medical care, housing, and family benefits.

The United States does not necessarily need a massive standing military all the time. What it needs is a highly trained professional force of a certain size—what we have right now is fine—backed by a massive surge capacity of troops in reserve to quickly augment the active-duty force in times of emergency. Sure, right now, the Army is light several hundred thousand deployable ground troops. But over the long term, the demands of Iraq will subside, the need for troops will decline, and it could be another decade or two before another mission that big comes along.

35 The problem is that under the all-volunteer system it's hard to fix the short-term problem (too few troops now) without creating long-term problems (too many troops later). And so, paying for the salaries and benefits and families of 50,000 or 500,000 extra soldiers on active duty over the course of their careers doesn't, from a military standpoint, make sense. Politically, it would put the senior military leadership in the position of convincing the American people to

keep military budgets extremely high to pay for a huge standing army that isn't being used and might not be for years. It might be possible now to convince the public to add another 100,000 soldiers (annual cost: about $10 billion in personnel costs alone, not including equipment and training). But the generals rightly worry that this support will evaporate after Iraq stabilizes. Indeed, Americans have a long tradition dating back to the writing of Constitution, of refusing to support a large standing military unless the need is apparent. (The public paid for a much bigger all-volunteer military in the 1970s and 1980s, but only because of the obvious need to deter a massive Soviet army from threatening Europe; after the Berlin Wall fell, both political parties supported big cuts in troop strength). What we really need is the capability to rapidly mobilize and deploy a half million troops to project U.S. power abroad, and to be able to sustain them indefinitely while maintaining a reserve with which to simultaneously engage other enemies.

A fifth option would be to build this surge capacity into the reserves, instead of the active force. Under this plan, which some military personnel planners are already discussing, the army would radically bump up enlistment bonuses and other incentives to lure vastly more young people directly into the reserves than are being recruited now. Such a plan would have the advantage of creating the surge capacity the nation needs without saddling the nation with a large, standing professional army. But the disadvantages are substantial, too. For such a plan to work, the military would have to make a commitment, which thus far it never has, to fix the legendary resources problems and anemic readiness of the reserves. A great many reservists have gone through the crucible of combat in Afghanistan and Iraq, and yet still cope with vehicles that lack armor, weapons older than they are, and a paucity of training dollars. Also, the

army would always (and rightly) insist that signing bonuses for reservists be substantially below those offered by to active-duty recruits. And even if bonuses and other renumeration for both the active-duty and the reserves were to rise substantially, it is hard to see how the reserves could lure in a sufficient number of recruits without significantly lowering admissions standards. The real advantage of the all-volunteer force is its quality. If the military tries to recruit so many soldiers that it must substantially lower its entry requirements, then the all-volunteer force will lose its qualitative edge. This decrease in quality will have a cascade effect on discipline within the ranks, degrading combat effectiveness for these units.

A 21st-Century Draft

That leaves one option left for providing the military with sufficient numbers of high-quality deployable ground forces: conscription. America has nearly always chosen this option to staff its military in times of war. Today, no leading politician in either party will come anywhere near the idea—the draft having replaced Social Security as the third rail of American politics. This will have to change if the United States is to remain the world's preeminent power.

Traditional conscription has its obvious downsides. On a practical level, draftees tend to be less motivated than volunteers. Because they serve for relatively short periods of time (typically two years), any investment made in their training is lost to the military once the draftees return to civilian life. And despite the current manpower shortage, there's no foreseeable scenario in which all 28 million young Americans currently of draft age would be needed.

Above all else, there's the serious ethical problem that conscription means government compelling young adults to risk death, and to kill—an act of the state that seems contrary to the basic notions of liberty which animate our society.

40   In practice, however, our republic has decided many times throughout its history that a draft was necessary to protect those basic liberties. Even if you disagreed with the decision to invade Iraq, or think the president's rhetoric is demagogic and his policies disastrous, it is hard to argue that Islamic terrorism isn't a threat to freedom and security, at home and abroad. Moreover, any American, liberal or conservative, ought to have moral qualms about basing our nation's security on an all-volunteer force drawn disproportionately, as ours is, from America's lower socioeconomic classes. And the cost of today's war is being borne by an extremely narrow slice of America. Camp Pendleton, Calif., home to the 1st Marine Expeditionary Force, is also home to approximately one-seventh of the U.S. fatalities from Iraq. In theory, our democracy will not fight unpopular wars because the people who must bear the casualties can impose their will on our elected leaders to end a war they do not support. But when such a small fraction of America shoulders the burden—and pays the cost—of America's wars, this democratic system breaks down.

Nor are the practical considerations of a draft impossible to overcome. A draft lottery, of the kind that existed in the peacetime draft of the 1950s, with no exemptions for college students, would provide the military an appropriate and manageable amount of manpower without the class inequities that poisoned the national culture during Vietnam. Such a system, however, would not avoid the problem of flooding the military with less-than-fully-motivated conscripts.

A better solution would fix the weaknesses of the all-volunteer force without undermining its strengths. Here's how such a plan might work. Instead of a lottery, the federal government would impose a requirement that no four-year college or university be allowed to accept a student, male or female, unless and until that student had completed a 12-month to two-year term of service. Unlike an old-fashioned draft, this 21st-century service requirement would provide a vital element of personal choice. Students could choose to fulfill their obligations in any of three ways: in national service programs like AmeriCorps (tutoring disadvantaged children), in homeland security assignments (guarding ports), or in the military. Those who chose the latter could serve as military police officers, truck drivers, or other non-combat specialists requiring only modest levels of training. (It should be noted that the Army currently offers two-year enlistments for all of these jobs, as well as for the infantry.) They would be deployed as needed for peacekeeping or nation-building missions. They would serve for 12-months to two years, with modest follow-on reserve obligations.

Whichever option they choose, all who serve would receive modest stipends and GI Bill-type college grants. Those who sign up for lengthier and riskier duty, however, would receive higher pay and larger college grants. Most would no doubt pick the less dangerous options. But some would certainly select the military—out of patriotism, a sense of adventure, or to test their mettle. Even if only 10 percent of the one-million young people who annually start at four-year colleges and universities were to choose the military option, the armed forces would receive 100,000 fresh recruits every year. These would be motivated recruits, having chosen the military over other, less demanding forms of service. And because they would all be college-grade and college-bound, they would have—to a greater extent than your average volunteer recruit—the savvy and inclination to pick up foreign languages and other skills that are often the key to effective peacekeeping work.

A 21st-century draft like this would create a cascading series of benefits for society. It would instill a new ethic of service in that sector of society, the college-bound, most likely to reap the fruits of American prosperity. It would mobilize an army of young people for vital domestic missions, such as helping a growing population of seniors who want to avoid nursing homes but need help with simple daily tasks like grocery shopping. It would give more of America's elite an experience of the military. Above all, it would provide the all-important surge capacity now missing from our force structure, insuring that the military would never again lack for manpower. And it would do all this without requiring any American to carry a gun who did not choose to do so.

45   The war in Iraq has shown us, and the world, many things: the bloody costs of inept leadership; the courage of the average American soldier; the hunger for democracy among some of the earth's most oppressed people. But perhaps more than anything, Iraq has shown that our military power has limits. As currently constituted, the U.S. military can win the wars, but it cannot win the peace, nor can it commit for the long term to the stability and security of a nation such as Iraq. Our enemies have learned this, and they will use that knowledge to their advantage in the next war to tie us down and bleed us until we lose the political will to fight.

If America wishes to retain its mantle of global leadership, it must develop a military force structure capable of persevering under these circumstances. Fortunately, we know how to build such a force. We have done it many times in the past. The question is: Do we have the will to do so again?

How the Draft Has Changed

SELECTIVE SERVICE SYSTEM

After the 2001 attacks on the United States, the Selective Service System felt the need to update its Web site with an explanation of how a possible new draft would differ from the lottery system used during the Vietnam War. Note the emphasis on equity in consideration of race, national origin, and education.

An All-Volunteer Army? Recruitment and Its Problems

LAWRENCE J. KORB AND SEAN E. DUGGAN

Lawrence J. Korb is a Senior Fellow at the Center for American Progress, a progressive think tank, and is a Senior Advisor to the Center for Defense Information. He was

Assistant Secretary of Defense in the Reagan administration. Sean E. Duggan is a research assistant at the Center for American Progress. The two write frequently on national security issues. In this article, which appeared in the July 2007 issue of PS: Political Science and Politics, *they argue for maintaining an all-volunteer army.*

The current condition of Army manpower, like the situation in Iraq, is grave and deteriorating. The January 2007 decision by the George W. Bush administration to send additional ground combat and support troops to the wars in Iraq and Afghanistan has thrown the Army's manpower shortages into stark relief. This latest escalation, however, not only runs the risk of breaking the all-volunteer Army but also undermines our national security. Several questions must therefore be addressed: Is an all-volunteer Army desirable? What are the current difficulties facing Army recruitment and retention? What consequences have the wars in Iraq and Afghanistan had on the service? Before engaging a more substantive discussion which includes the present demographics of the force and the recruitment process, one point should be made clear. We believe the all-volunteer model is the right one and should be maintained if at all possible.

The Case for Maintaining the All-Volunteer Army

The president and the Congress should make every effort to maintain the total Army on an all-volunteer basis. While the Army is composed of over a million volunteers, only about a half is on full-time active duty. The other half is in the reserve component, which is composed of the selected reserve and the individual ready reserve. These three groups comprise the total Army. Returning to the draft would not address the manpower and capability problems the total Army currently faces. Rather, a return to the draft would diminish the Army's overall experience and education level, leading to an Army that is not as well-suited to today's challenges. In addition, a mixed force of draftees and volunteers would be more expensive due to increases in turnover and, therefore, much higher training costs.

Any discussion of a reinstatement of the draft introduces several problems, both logistical and political. While the average volunteer enlists for four years and about half of them reenlist, draftees typically served for only two years and less than 10% of those drafted from 1948 to 1973 reenlisted (Rostker 2007). Moreover, Pentagon studies show that recruits need up to three years to reach full competency in combat, combat support, and combat service support skills. In addition, reinstating a draft at this time would open up a whole host of issues that this nation has not addressed satisfactorily since the 1960s—in particular, the question of who shall serve when not all must serve. Reinstating the draft would also further isolate the United States from our NATO allies, most of whom have abolished conscription at our urging.

Force Demographics

It is important to note that the goal of the all-volunteer force (AVF) is to maintain high standards for its soldiers so as to ensure a professional and competent force. Ideally, the AVF should be broadly representative of the population it defends. Yet, the rising American death toll nearly four years after the beginning of the war in Iraq has brought criticism that it is mainly uneducated, poor, and minority soldiers who are enlisting for wartime duty and paying the greatest toll in the war effort. Recent studies on the AVF suggest otherwise.

5   A report by the Heritage Foundation entitled, "Who Are the Recruits? The Demographic Characteristics of U.S. Military Enlistment, 2003–2005," (Kane 2006) supports the finding that U.S. military recruits are more similar than dissimilar to the overall American youth population. The slight difference between new military enlistees and the average youth population is, surprisingly, that wartime U.S. military recruits and soldiers are better educated and wealthier but also more rural on average than their civilian peers.

Another study by the Center for American Progress entitled, "Two Years and Counting," also contradicts claims that minorities and the underprivileged are disproportionately paying the highest price for the war in Iraq. Of those soldiers killed in Iraq, 96% had graduated from high school versus 94% of all military personnel and 86% of all Americans 18 to 44 years old. Similarly, 73% of these fallen have been White, a higher figure than the 67% of all military personnel who are White (12% of those killed in Iraq have been Hispanic as compared to 9% of military personnel, 11% of those killed have been African American as compared to 19% of all military personnel). Finally, roughly 29% of those soldiers killed in Iraq come from public high schools in neighborhoods above the average poverty rate as compared to the national average of 30%. However, as shown in Chart 1, while the poor and uneducated are not bearing the burden of this war, neither is the upper-middle class or the elite. And, overall, the people of this nation do not have the same emotional or material involvement in our current wars as they did in Vietnam. This is the first extended war in the nation's history when we have not had a draft or raised taxes—instead we have reduced them.

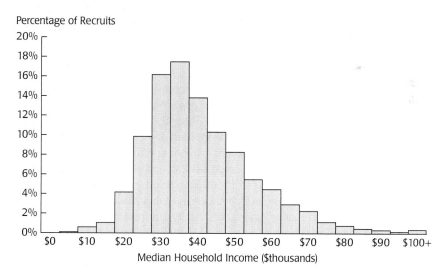

Current Difficulties

Current Difficulties

While trying to achieve the goal of an AVF, the Army is finding out how difficult recruiting can be while soldiers and marines are dying in an unpopular war which is increasingly viewed by the public as unnecessary. Indeed, this is the first time the military has had to recruit for the AVF during a time of protracted war. As a result the Army has resorted to various strategies including lowering enlistment standards, augmenting age restrictions, manipulating drop-out rates, offering extremely large cash bonus and incentive programs, using pressure and coercion tactics, and implementing a "back-door draft" Stop-Loss policy in order to keep the ranks filled.

It is important to note that except for the total Army, the current manpower situation of the four armed services is in good shape. The Navy and the Air Force, which are not heavily involved in the war in Iraq, are actually forcing people to leave because fewer personnel are needed to operate their new high-tech weapons. The Marine Corps, which furnishes about 20% of the force in Iraq but is only one-fifth the size of the Army, has so far been able to maintain its quality standards.

Questionable Recruiting Practices
Relaxing Enlistment Standards, Age Restrictions, and Drop-Out Rates

The Army has made much of its ability to meet its fiscal year 2006 recruitment goals. Upon closer inspection, such self congratulation is not merited. In an effort to prevent the overstretched forces from breaking, the Army has not only raised its maximum age for enlistment (from 35 to 42), it has shortened the enlistment period for some recruits from four years to 15 months, and it has reduced basic training drop-out rates in the first six months of 2006 (8% of recruits failed basic training, down from 18% in May 2005). Further, other recruitment standards have been relaxed. The number of Army recruits who scored below average on the ASVAB aptitude test doubled in 2005, as did the number of high school drop-outs in the first half of 2006. According to a recent report (*New York Times* 2007), even with these relaxed standards, the Army still had to give more than 8,000 of its new recruits moral waivers, some for criminal convictions, including 900 for felons. While such measures have ensured that the Army achieves the quantity of recruits it needs, they have resulted in a decrease in the quality the nation demands.

Cash Bonuses and Incentives

10   The Army has resorted to large cash bonuses and incentives in order to retain and lure new recruits. Last year alone, the Pentagon's struggle to keep soldiers (and Marines) in the military became a $1.03 campaign (Associated Press, 2007). Recently, the Army has offered as much as $40,000 for high-demand military occupational specialty assignments; generally for special forces, as well as advanced linguistic and specific civilian skills. It also is paying bonuses of up to $50,000 to senior enlisted soldiers in 16 hard-to-fill job categories, including truck drivers and bomb-disposal specialists. According to a *USA Today* investigation (Moniz 2005) into military recruitment, the "Pentagon is using cash bonuses on an unprecedented scale to try to boost re-enlistments, recruiting and morale among active-duty and reservist troops." Examples of such programs include offering bonuses of up to $150,000 for long-serving Army (as well as Air Force and Navy special operations) troops who agree to stay in the military for up to six more years. It is also offering re-enlistment payments of up to $15,000 to soldiers in 49% of its enlisted job categories—regardless of rank or where they are stationed; it is offering the same bonus to any soldier who agrees to re-enlist while serving in a combat zone (Moniz 2005).

Coercion and Manipulation

The state of manpower affairs is such that the Army has had to scramble for new recruits, prompting allegations of Army recruiters' misleading students in order to fill their quota.

A November 2006 ABC investigative report provides some evidence that recruiters, under pressure, are misleading young people. ABC showed Army enlistment officers lying to students from New York, New Jersey, and Connecticut who had been given hidden cameras. The recruiters claimed that, "We are not at war. War ended a long time ago," and that the Army was in fact, "Bringing people back" from Iraq. In the report several recruiters were filmed telling students that if they enlisted, there was little chance that they would go to Iraq. On his own initiative, one Colorado student taped a recruiting session while posing as a drug addicted dropout. When the student brought up the subject of drugs and asked if he was, "Going to get in trouble" for it, the recruiter told him "No", and according to the report, "helped him cheat to sign up."

ABC News even found one recruiter who went so far as to claim that if you did not like the Army, you could just quit. "It's called a 'Failure to Adapt' discharge," the recruiter said. "It's an entry-level discharge so it won't affect anything on your record. It'll just be like it never happened." Robert Manning, the U.S. Army Colonel responsible for recruitment throughout the Northeast, said "It's hard to believe some of things they are telling prospective applicants." He added, "I still believe that this is the exception more than the norm....I've visited many stations myself, and I know that we have many wonderful Americans serving in uniform as recruiters."

According to a recent recruiting investigation, this exception has become more frequent. WTVF, a CBS affiliate in Nashville, recently conducted a similar hidden-camera report showing Army recruiters instructing potential recruits how to lie on medical screening forms. "Bottom line is I take Zoloft," the investigative producer told each recruiter—re-enacting the real life story of Pvt. Jay Mallard, who killed himself during basic training after, his family says, a recruiter urged him to lie about his long-term dependence on antidepressants. When presented with this information, the sergeant told the potential recruit that, "There's ways around the system." The recruiter went one step further to speak with his commander who told the sergeant, "the only thing they (the Army) know about you is what you tell them."

Stop-Loss

While the Army insists that this strategy of lying to recruits is not the norm, the service has employed several strategies in order to get and keep soldiers in uniform. Perhaps the most questionable of these tactics has been the Army's Stop-Loss policy; essentially a "back-door draft" practice which has prevented more than 70,000 soldiers from retiring or leaving the Army when their enlistment contract expires (Thompson 2007). Were it not for the Stop-Loss policy, which even high-ranking officials admit is inconsistent with the principles of voluntary service, the all-volunteer Army would be in even more jeopardy than it already is. There simply would not be enough personnel for the Army to complete its missions. For example, one infantry battalion commander deployed in Kuwait and headed for Iraq commented that he would have lost a quarter of his unit at the time if were it not for the order (Tice and Cox 2003).

Tail-End Effects

15   An often overlooked consequence of the wars in Iraq and Afghanistan is the burden placed on the equipment used in the wars and the tail-end cost it is having on our troops. The toll of attrition coupled with the effects of the harsh environment in both Iraq and Afghanistan has only added to the beleaguered state of manpower and equipment readiness. The Army's

preferred measure of equipment usage is operational tempo, or "OPTEMPO." Not surprisingly, high OPTEMPOs have resulted in an accelerated aging of equipment, in some cases producing OPTEMPOs as high as six times their peacetime rate (as with the Army's M1A2 Abrams tank and the M2 Bradley tracked fighting vehicle). This results not only from the frequency of use but also the unforgiving conditions in both Iraq and Afghanistan. To ensure that troops on the ground in both theatres are supplied with proper equipment, the military has been forced to transfer new or refurbished equipment from non-deployed active units and National Guard and Reserve units training at home to troops forwardly deployed—a process known as "cross-leveling." Consequentially, some active troops and most Guard and Reserve troops being called to duty in both Iraq and Afghanistan are frequently trained with aged and inadequate equipment different from what they will eventually be using.

The 3,500 soldiers of the Third Infantry Division's First Brigade scheduled to deploy to Iraq in the spring of 2007 demonstrate a different training problem. In place of learning vital knowledge about Iraq and its peoples that could help them defeat the insurgency and quell sectarian violence, these soldiers have instead had to use their training time on equipment that commanders say should have been available to them eight months earlier. According to the *Wall Street Journal* (Jaffe 2006), Lt. Col. Clifford Wheeler, who commands one of the brigade's 800-soldier units, has stated that, "We haven't spent as much time as I would like on learning the local culture, language, and politics—all the stuff that takes a while to really get good at." Again, rather than intensive language and cultural immersion programs, vital to success in any counterinsurgency mission, soldiers have been occupied with training on such essential equipment as their M-4 rifles and rifle sights for the first time. Some soldiers being deployed still lack experience with the machine guns and long-range surveillance systems that they will use in Iraq. They have been told that they would get their training with that equipment only upon arrival in Iraq.

Resetting the gutted Army in the wake of the ongoing wars in Iraq and Afghanistan will be a challenging task, especially in the face of pressures from the administration and the Congress to hold down overall spending. Adding to the difficulty of the budgetary situation is the dilemma the Pentagon is facing because of its desire to look to the future and to "transform" the services even while financing and resetting the Army in the midst of two costly wars.

Moreover, the Department of Defense apparently does not see the necessity of making difficult trade-offs. In fact, neither the 2006 Quadrennial Defense Review or the Fiscal Year 2008 defense budget, both issued by the Pentagon, called for the cancellation of a single major weapons program, despite the fact that the wars in Iraq and Afghanistan show the irrelevancy of some of these weapons to current threats. As noted by Ike Wilson in this symposium, the Department of Defense should seek funding for the weapons systems that combat the actual twenty-first century threats, and that it should cease development and production of unnecessary weapons systems and/or those that do not meet performance standards. Such weapons include the F/A 22 Raptor, the SSN-774 Virginia class submarine, the DD(X) destroyer, the V-22 Osprey, the C-130J transport aircraft, and offensive space-based weapons, as well as further deployment of the National Missile Defense System.

Avoiding these hard choices will restrict the Army's ability to continuously repair, rebuild, and replace equipment worn out or destroyed by the war effort and will only exacerbate the spiral of tail-end consequences outlined above.

Conclusion

20   Addressing the Army's glaring manpower and equipment problems will be a daunting task. Its difficulties in recruiting and maintaining the nation's Army at existing levels will be exacerbated by the recent decision to add over 92,000 service men and women to the Army and Marines. While the war in Iraq has demonstrated the necessity for these additional ground forces, even a cursory understanding of the hardships plaguing the Army outlined above indicates the difficulty of raising such numbers on an all-volunteer basis. Still, reinstituting the draft does not seem to be an option supported by the military leadership or the American people. Therefore, the Department of Defense must make the difficult decisions necessary to ensure the strength and quality of its Army. One decision must be to emphasize manpower over hardware; people not hardware must be our highest priority. That could mean transferring resources from the Navy and Air Force to the Army—an argument it is difficult for the Army to make.

A second will require new ideas and options related to recruitment. Should the Army have a pay scale different from the Air Force and Navy? Will better advertising help? A promise of more rapid advancement?

A third would be to institute a program of national service, along the lines suggested by Congressman Charles Rangel (D-NY), which would require every American to spend two years serving the country, either in the armed forces or in a non-defense agency such as the Peace Corps or AmeriCorps.

The country must provide the all-volunteer Army with the best equipment and the qualified men and women it needs to prepare for, fight, and win the nation's wars and secure the peace. To do any less would endanger our national security.

Appendix: Force Demographics

Educational Level of U.S. Military Recruits

Educational Level	2003 Recruits[*]	2004 Recruits	2005 Recruits	2004 Population
No high school credentials	1.85%	1.85%	1.95%	20.20%
High school senior	1.37%	1.37%	1.33%	
General Equivalency Diploma	7.03%	7.03%	9.40%	33.80%
High school diploma graduate	82.66%	82.66%	80.43%	
Associate's degree	1.23%	1.23%	1.26%	46.00%
Greater than high school credentials	5.87%	5.87%	5.63%	
High school graduation rate	96.78%	96.78%	96.72%	79.80%

[*]Some of the values for fiscal year 2003 may not directly correspond with the percentages in the previous Heritage Foundation study, which examined the last three quarters of fiscal year 2003 (January–September). The data here were obtained from the U.S. Department of Defense in a format consistent with the educational categories in the 2004 and 2005 fiscal years data sets.

Sources: Heritage Foundation calculations based on data from U.S. Department of Defense, Office of the Under Secretary of Defense for Personnel and Readiness, October 2002–September 2005 Non-Prior Service Active Duty Accessions, and U.S. Census Bureau, 2004 American Community Survey, Table S1501, at factfinder.census.gov/servlet/STTable?_bm=y&geo_id=01000US&-qr_name=ACS_2004_EST_G00_S1501&-ds_name=ACS_2004_EST_G00_(August 9, 2006).

U.S. Military Recruits by Race

Race	2004 U.S. Population Percent	2004 Data				2005 Data			
		Recruit Percent	Army Percent	Recruit/ Population Ratio	Army/ Population Ratio	Recruit Percent	Army Percent	Recruit/ Population Ratio	Army/ Population Ratio
American Indian/Alaska Native	0.75%	2.01%	1.14%	2.68	1.52	2.62%	1.17%	3.49	1.56
Asian	4.23%	2.82%	2.39%	0.67	0.57	2.92%	2.07%	0.69	0.49
Black or African American	12.17%	14.54%	14.25%	1.19	1.17	12.99%	11.74%	1.07	0.96
Native Hawai/on or Other Pacific Islander	0.14%	1.05%	0.93%	7.48	6.62	1.05%	0.90%	7.49	6.41
White	75.62%	73.12%	72.53%	0.97	0.96	73.12%	71.94%	0.97	0.95
Other	5.19%	–	–	–	–	–	–	–	–
Combination of two or more races	1.89%	1.52%	1.16%	0.80	0.61	0.93%	0.54%	0.18	0.10
Declined to Respond	–	4.94%	7.61%	–	–	6.37%	11.64%	–	–

Sources: Heritage Foundation calculations based on data from U.S. Department of Defense, Office of the Under Secretary of Defense for Personnel and Readiness, October 2002–September 2005 Non-Prior Service Active Duty Accessions, and U.S. Census Bureau, 2004 American Community Survey, Table B02001, at factfinder.census.gov/servlet/DTTable?_bm=y&geo_id=01000US&-ds_name=ACS_2004_EST_G00_&-mt_name=ACS_2004_EST_G2000_B02001 (August 9, 2006).

References

ABC News. 2006. "Army Accused of Misleading Students to Get Them to Enlist." November 3. Available at http://abcnews.go.com/GMA/story?id=2626032&page=1.

Associated Press. 2007. "Military Spending to Retain Troops Skyrockets." April 11. Available at www.msnbc.msn.com/id/18053235/.

Bergmann, Max, Lawrence J. Korb, and Pete Ogden. 2006. "Bush Has Mismanaged the Military." *New Republic,* September 13.

CBS News. 2007. "Dishonorable Deception," May 8. Available at www.newschannel5.com/Global/category.asp?C=99556.

Farsetta, Diane. 2007. "How PR Plows Fill the Pentagon's Recruiting Quotas." Center for Media and Democracy, February.

"Gates Calls for 92,000 More Soldiers, Marines." 2007. www.defenselink.com, January 11.

Hockstader, Lee. 2003. "Army Stops Many Soldiers From Quitting." *Washington Post,* Dec. 29.

Jaffe, Greg. 2006. "Despite a $168B Budget, Army Faces a Cash Crunch." *Wall Street Journal,* December 12.

Kane, Tim. 2006. "Who Are the Recruits? The Demographic Characteristics of U.S. Military Enlistment, 2003–2005." *Heritage Foundation,* October 27.

Korb, Lawrence J. 2005a. "Two Years and Counting." Center for American Progress, May.

Korb, Lawrence J. 2005b "For Soldier and Country: Saving the All-Volunteer Army." Progressive Priorities.

Korb, Lawrence J., and Max Bergmann. 2006. "Marine Corps Equipment after Iraq." Center for American Progress, Lexington Institute, August.

Korb, Lawrence J., Caroline P. Wadhams, and Andrew J. Grotto. 2006. "Restoring American Military Power: A Progressive Quadrennial Defense Review." Center for American Progress, January.

Moniz, Dave. 2005. "Military Offering More, and Bigger, Bonuses." *USA Today,* February 20.

Rostker, Bernard. 2007. "America Goes to War: Managing the Force During Times of Uncertainty." RAND.

Shanker, Thom. 2006. "Army and Ground Forces Meet '06 Recruiting Goals." *New York Times,* October 10.

Shanker, Thom. 2004. "Need for Draft is Dismissed by Pentagon Officials." *New York Times,* October 31, A22.

Shukovsky, Paul. 2005. "U.S. Court Upholds Extending Enlistments." *Seattle Post-Intelligencer,* April 7.

Thompson, Mark. 2007. "America's Broken Down Army." *Time,* April 16.

Tice, Jim, and Matthew Cox. 2003. "Deploying? Then You're on Stop-Loss; With New Order, Soldiers Put their Plans on Hold." *Army Times,* Dec. 1, 18.

Thompson, Lauren B., Lawrence J. Korb, and Caroline P. Wadhams. 2006. "Army Equipment after Iraq." Center for American Progress, Lexington Institute, April.

Wilson, Isaiah III. 2007. "What Weapons Do We Have and What Can They Do?" *PS: Political Science and Politics* 40 (July): 473–8.

Heroes

U.S. DEPARTMENT OF DEFENSE

Since 2006 the United States Department of Defense Web site has profiled individuals who have served with distinction in the Global War on Terror. The profiles appear as clickable, downloadable trading cards. The soldier's photo appears on the card "front," with a capsule version of the hero's story on the "reverse" next to a more detailed pop-up story. See more such trading cards at http://www.defenselink.mil/heroes/.

Military Service

LOUIS CALDERA

Louis Caldera has held a number of political and public service positions, including secretary of the army under the Clinton administration from 1998 to 2001, and presidency of the University of New Mexico. His opinion piece appeared in the Fall 2002 issue of the Brookings Review, *published by the Brookings Institution, an independent, nonpartisan think tank.*

Military service can be a transformative life experience. It was for me, and it continues to be so for today's young servicemen and women. As young Americans consider their options for national and community service today, however, military service is rarely even on the agenda. What must we do to increase the interest of our young people in serving their country in uniform?

I volunteered to serve driven by the immigrant spirit to give something back to the country that had given so much to my family and to me. Bookish, shy, a sheltered son of struggling, Spanish-speaking parents, I knew little of the world outside my own cloistered neighborhood. The military, with its emphasis on leadership development, moral and physical courage, and command presence and voice, opened my eyes to the vast possibilities of life. I learned that the world had much more to offer me than I had ever imagined and that no doors were closed to me except the ones I chose not to open. Our mission in the army—to be prepared to defend the nation and to serve wherever called in support of our nation's interests in the world—gave me a deeper appreciation for the forces, events, and people that shape the world we live in. Inchoate notions of duty, service, and citizenship began to become tangible and permanent.

Throughout my recent tenure as secretary of the army, I heard young men and women express what service means to them. Often deployed far from home, they would say there was no place they would rather be, because they knew they were making a difference. Whether helping to save lives and leading recovery efforts in Central America after Hurricane Mitch or preventing genocide in Bosnia-Herzegovina, they could palpably feel the gratitude of those for whom their presence and aid meant hope for a better life for themselves and for their children. Standing watch on the world's hot spots or training to deploy there if necessary, they knew that what they were prepared to do was essential to protecting our nation. These young people did not come, by and large, from America's most privileged families. Yet they were the ones who had internalized the sense that we are abundantly blessed as Americans and called, out of our own principles and enlightened self-interest, to lead and to help others in places riven by hatred and calamity.

Why does military service not figure more prominently in calls for a renewed commitment to service? In part, it is the benign result of the structure of such service initiatives as AmeriCorps and America's Promise, which address urgent domestic needs. In part, it results from the end of the draft a generation ago: relatively few parents, teachers, and other role models of today have ever worn the uniform of our country. It may also come from misconceptions about the nature of modern military service, discomfort with the fundamental role of the military, lingering suspicion and hostility arising from an antiwar movement that spanned three decades, and unhappiness with current policies toward openly gay service members. Whatever the reasons, few adults challenge today's young people to consider serving their country in uniform.

5   President Bush has included the military in his recent national service proposals, but creating new opportunities for military service that parallel civilian service will not be easy. The military itself has struggled to find ways to embrace the concept of more young people serving shorter tours of duty without compromising the requirements of military cohesiveness and readiness, particularly in the era of the high-tech battlefield. Today's recruitment and training costs are high. Because service members often train for a year or more before arriving at their first unit, the military services prefer four- to six-year enlistment contracts and put a premium on retaining skilled careerists. Moreover, high personnel turnover at the unit level degrades unit cohesiveness. Teams never quite gel as new recruits keep moving in and out of the ranks. Trainers and leaders rarely get to hone higher-order team competencies as they constantly work to rebuild basic ones. So it will not be as simple as mandating shorter tour options—a proposal that many in the military suspect will bring into the ranks soldiers who are not really committed to the proposition that they must train as if war is imminent and that they will be the ones to fight it.

Despite these difficulties, we should try to create some workable opportunities for shorter-term military service, and we should work with employers, educators, and government leaders to create an enhanced framework of realistic enlistment and reenlistment incentives. Above all, we should make military service an important part of the national conversation about the obligations and benefits of service. Young Americans deserve to know about this opportunity to see firsthand our country's principles put into action, to work with people of all backgrounds and walks of life, to challenge themselves to live by the high standards the military demands of those who respond to the call of duty. For them, as for me and for so many others, military service can be the foundation for a life-long commitment to public service and the source of a deep appreciation for the importance of civic engagement in a democracy.

Stop-Loss

(ARMY)WIFE

Stop-loss is a policy that permits the military, during times of war, to "halt voluntary separa-tions and retirements" and redeploy soldiers for additional tours of active duty once their initial terms of enlistment are through. Criticized by opponents as a "back-door draft," the policy has been used widely to meet the need for soldiers in Iraq. Here, the wife a National Guardsman weighs in on the issue on her blog, "More Than an (Army) Wife." The blog, she writes, is "about our life with the National Guard, but it's also about more than that," noting, in particular, the couple's fondness for Thai food, movies, and playing with their three pups. http://morethananarmywife.blogspot.com/2008/01/stop-loss.html.

11 January 2008
Stop-Loss

As I briefly mentioned in my last post, there is new movie coming out in March called *Stop-Loss.* I think the title of the movie and the previews give you a pretty good idea of what the movie is about. I haven't seen the movie yet, but I'll take the shot in dark here and say it is about the controversial stop-loss policy. (I'll admit, I read a spoiler for the movie. I'll just say that the movie sounds amazing and I was pleased with the ending, but that's all I'll say. I don't want to ruin it for anyone.)

Along with the official movie website, Paramount has launched another website called *Stop-Loss Sound Off.* This site is for service members and their families to post comments and videos about their experiences with the policy and with the military in general. The movie's director, Kimberly Peirce, also posted on the site and she has made it clear that the movie isn't simply about the stop-[loss] policy, but also about a soldier's journey and expe-riences when he is stop-lossed.

Okay, now for me and my opinion. For the record, I whole-heartedly believe that the stop-loss policy will always be a source of tension and turmoil in our military simply be-cause there are two very distinct sides to this issue. The need to have soldiers in our mili-tary and the need of the soldiers to move forward in their lives. I believe that both sides have valid points and neither side will ever be fully right. However, in this issue I side with our military and the need to use the stop-loss policy.

To many this policy seems unfair. A contract for so many number of years is signed, but at the end of those years, you're told you still can't leave. Let's face it, in the real world if you signed a lease, a contract, to live in an apartment for 1 year, at the end of the year the owner cannot make you stay in that apartment longer. However, as most military families will tell you, the military is not the "real world" nor is it always fair. I've been married to a soldier for just less than a year and already I need more fingers and toes to count how many Army policies/rules/ behaviors seem to be unfair.

5   Here's the thing though, the contract a soldier signs does say that he/she can be stop-lossed. At no point is this policy a surprise to the soldier. When that contract is signed you are signing on for so many years at a minimum. After those minimum amount of years are complete, the military can choose to extend your contract because you agreed that they could. It's a part of being in the military. Just like camo, MREs, war, kissing someone's ass to get a promotion, Tricare and saluting are also a part of the military. You take the good with the bad. The Stop-Loss policy is considered one of the bad, but it is there for a reason.

Many states are creating a new unit called the PTAE, Pre-mobilization Training Assistance Element. One of the purposes of this unit is to make sure deploying units are trained as fully as they can be. One of the reasons this type of unit is necessary is because soldiers and their families are trying to sue the military, and this includes unit Commanders such as Stonewall, for not properly training them before sending them to war.

Stonewall is National Guard. When he found out his unit was set to deploy, drill weekends became a life line. He sees his soldiers once a month and 2-3 weeks during the summer. Between announcement time and deployment time, that left Stonewall with approximately 30 days of face-time and training time with his soldiers. 30 days, and not 30 consecutive days, to train soldiers to fight and survive.

Now here is where stop-loss comes into play and ties these two units together. In the National Guard soldiers can be stop-lossed 90 days prior to deployment. We have not reached those 90 days yet. Every drill weekend Stonewall is losing soldiers who have decided they no longer want to be in the military because they do not want to go to Iraq and so they are trying to find loopholes and ways to get out of the military.

While these soldiers will eventually be replaced and the new soldiers will be deployed with the unit, these are soldiers who have trained with the unit for less than a month. Is that enough time to fully prepare for deployment? I don't know; some would say it is, some would say it isn't enough time. All of the soldiers will be trained as best as they can be and that will be considered good enough to send them to Iraq, but like I mentioned, soldiers are trying to sue the military for improper training. But whose fault is it that these soldiers are not getting the training they feel they should get?

10   The blame cannot be put entirely on the military. Stonewall is doing the best he can to train his soldiers. It is not his fault soldiers are leaving and new soldiers are being sent to him at the last minute. Whether anyone likes it or not we are at war and we need to send soldiers to Iraq. We cannot stop sending units to Iraq because some quit and force more work and responsibility on others. Our military must train our soldiers as best it can in a very short amount of time. It is the soldiers who run that put the undue pressure and responsibility on the unit leaders, the remaining unit, and the new soldiers.

The Stop-Loss policy takes some of that pressure to deploy fully trained off of Stonewall and the other leaders of the unit and puts it on the rest of the unit. In fact, Stonewall would rather stop-loss go into effect the day they learn they will be deployed. Then he knows that his soldiers are trained to the best of his and their abilities. There is no questioning whether a new soldier has learned all the ropes. Instead, Stonewall would lead soldiers that he has worked with for the past year.

Stop-loss exists to protect the soldiers. More fully trained and experienced soldiers are sent to Iraq because they have best ability to stay alive over there and complete the mission, so that all the soldiers can come home. Yes, it is true that there will be soldiers who do not come home safely or at all, but that is the reality we face in the military. It is a reality all soldiers must face. In the long run though, I think stop-loss saves more lives because it's the experienced soldiers that are re-sent to Iraq and it is the soldiers who have had more valuable training time before being deployed.

My husband was essentially stop-lossed the day he took command of his unit. It was agreed that he would not leave this unit until after the deployment. The deployment has been pushed back 3 times now and so he remains with his unit. I do not feel sorry for the others who will be stop-lossed. It is their experience and their time that will help bring my soldier home, along with the soldier whose wife is having a baby in a few months, the soldier who has 3 children all under the age of 5, and the soldier whose Mom gives all her free time to our FRG. They do not leave the unit because they want to fight, it is what they agreed to do when they signed their contract and took their oath and they will do it until the military agrees their time in the NG is finished.

There are two sides to this coin. In a few years, I may prefer the other side. Are those who fight stop-loss dishonorable or anti-America? I do not believe so. I have never been to Iraq, but I can't imagine there are many who want to go back after they made it home safely the first time. I know I do not want Stonewall to have to go back, but it's what he does, what he agreed to do. When I married him, I signed up for the military and the deployments as well, whether it was within his 4 years or not.

POSTED BY (ARMY)WIFE AT 09:48

I Need You

MATT CARMODY

Matt Carmody is a freelance editorial cartoonist and the political cartoons editor of Free World Syndicate, a network that encourages political dialogue and the use of the Internet to fight corporate control of information. This cartoon appeared on the Web site Artizans—the World's Best Cartoons, Caricatures, Graphic Art & Illustrations *(http://zone.artizans/com) for February 25, 2005.*

Source: Matt Carmody/artizans.com

■ ■ ■ **FOR CLASS DISCUSSION** **Finding Soldiers**
1. What different arguments can you sketch out for each of the following positions on the issue of military recruitment and the draft?
   ■ In favor of reinstituting a draft (consider the perspectives of citizen soldiers, military leaders, practical utilitarian thinkers, liberals, conservative patriots, feminists)
   ■ Against reinstituting a draft (consider the views of military experts, political leaders/Rumsfeld, liberals, feminists)

2. Some of the readings in this unit and a number of the visuals illustrate U.S. military recruitment strategies and problems. The army is using computer simulation games, offering free cosmetic surgery to military personnel and their families, and advertising at sports events that attract daring young people. Although the Army claims that *America's Army,* the free online action game that simulates Army experience and that is one of the top five or six most popular games, is simply a public relations tool, it too clearly has a recruitment agenda. How effective do you find the Army's recruitment strategies? (You may need to do some additional research, such as reading William Lugo's piece on p. 460, and logging on to *America's Army,* to the National Guard Web site, or to *DefenseLink News* to see the new ad campaign posters.) What values do these recruiting campaigns appeal to? How have the creators of this strategy designed their approach to appeal to specific audiences? Do you think the Army is justified in spending large amounts of taxpayers' money to fund these recruitment venues?

3. Concern about the possibility of a draft has fired up the energy of many advocacy groups. After investigating one of the following Web sites, list what you see as the primary argument this site is making against the draft: www.citizen-soldier.org (*Citizen Soldier*); www.objector.org (*The Central Committee for Conscientious Objectors*); or www.mothersagainstthedraft.org/ (*Mothers against the Draft*).

4. A provocative conversation about military recruitment is taking place within the genre of political cartoons. Find a political cartoon and bring it to class. Then, working individually or in groups, sketch out the argument the cartoon makes and discuss how the image and text work to make this cartoon effective. What insight does it contribute to the controversy over recruitment?

5. Choose one of the readings in this unit and analyze it carefully using the List 2 guide questions on pages 426–427.

WRITING ASSIGNMENT Letter to Congress

Write a letter to your congressional representative arguing for your informed view on how the United States Army should fill the military. Show that you understand the problems from political leaders' perspectives. ■

For additional writing, reading, and research resources, go to www.mycomplab.com

Wal-Mart and the Public Good

Wal-Mart, the super discount corporation, is the biggest retail company in the world with more than 7,000 stores, nearly 2 million employees, and annual sales of around $374 billion. In fact, Wal-Mart's profits make it richer than a number of countries. All this growth, wealth, and national and global dominance have put Wal-Mart at the center of a number of heated controversies. On the one hand, Wal-Mart is known for its range of merchandise; its "everyday low prices" affordable by low-income Americans; and its friendly, folksy, American image. On the other hand, Wal-Mart has the reputation of driving local and smaller retailers out of business, discriminating against female employees, underpaying its workers, not providing affordable medical coverage, fiercely preventing unionizing, driving the wages of competitor companies lower, and endlessly expanding to ever-more communities around the United States and the world. At stake in all these conflicts are Wal-Mart's own employer-employee-consumer relationships; its powerful effect on markets, competitors, and communities; and the influence of its business model as a successful big-box store.

The controversies surrounding Wal-Mart have taken a number of specific forms. Currently, Wal-Mart is engaged in a massive class-action suit involving 1.5 million women (*Dukes v. Wal-Mart Stores*), and communities across the country—often galvanized by anti-Wal-Mart and anti-sprawl Web sites—have launched campaigns to prevent Wal-Mart from building new stores. In recent countermoves, Wal-Mart has sought to change its negative image by building up its reputation for social contributions (see its Web site *Wal-Mart Facts* at www.walmartfacts.com) and by sponsoring an environmental program, "Acres for America," in partnership with the National Fish and Wildlife Foundation.

The readings and visuals in this unit (as well as the poster on page 188) invite you to explore questions about these conflicting images of Wal-Mart: Is Wal-Mart's economic and social influence on the United States positive or negative? What should Americans do as citizens and consumers to influence Wal-Mart's business practices? Should communities oppose the building of new Wal-Mart stores? Should Americans stop patronizing this super-discount chain?

A Downward Push
The Impact of Wal-Mart Stores on Retail Wages and Benefits
ARINDRAJIT DUBE, T. WILLIAM LESTER, AND BARRY EIDLIN

The Center for Labor Research and Education is a public service project that strives to connect academic resources with working people through research and education on employment issues. In this article the authors summarize a study suggesting that the presence of a Wal-Mart in a community has a negative impact on wages and benefits for retail workers in the entire area. Arindrajit Dube is with the Institute for Research on Labor and Employment at the University of California at Berkeley; he has published widely on labor and wage issues. T. William Lester is with the Department of City and Regional Planning, and Barry Eidlin is with the Department of Sociology, both at UC Berkeley.

Executive Summary

Empirical evidence suggests that employees at Wal-Mart earn lower average wages and receive less generous benefits than workers employed by many other large retailers. But controversy has persisted on the question of Wal-Mart's effect on local pay scales. Our research finds that Wal-Mart store openings lead to the replacement of better paying jobs with jobs that pay less. Wal-Mart's entry also drives wages down for workers in competing industry segments such as grocery stores.

Looking at the period between 1992 and 2000, we find that the opening of a single Wal-Mart store in a county lowered average retail wages in that county by between 0.5 and 0.9 percent. In the general merchandise sector, wages fell by 1 percent for each new Wal-Mart. And for grocery store employees, the effect of a single new Wal-Mart was a 1.5 percent reduction in earnings.

When Wal-Mart entered a county, the total wage bill declined along with the average wage. Factoring in both the impact on wages and jobs, the total amount of retail earnings in a county fell by 1.5 percent for every new Wal-Mart store. Similar effects appeared at the state level.

With an average of 50 Wal-Mart stores per state, the average wages for retail workers were 10 percent lower, and their job-based health coverage rate was 5 percentage points less than they would have been without Wal-Mart's presence. Nationally, the retail wage bill in 2000 was estimated to be $4.5 billion less in nominal terms due to Wal-Mart's presence.

5   The study addressed a number of methodological issues that have plagued previous attempts to assess the effect of Wal-Mart on local labor markets. A less sophisticated statistical model risks confounding the effects of Wal-Mart openings with unobserved economic factors (positive or negative) that might have drawn the retailer to specific locations. We use the spatial pattern of Wal-Mart's growth (radiating out of Arkansas over time) to identify Wal-Mart store openings

that are not driven by local economic conditions. This helps ensure we are measuring the results of store openings, not preexisting conditions.

Further, we investigate (and reject) the possibility that wage declines were an artifact of changes in demographics of the retail workforce. If Wal-Mart jobs bring more minorities, women, young people or workers with lower educational attainment into the retail work force, the wage decline could be accounted for by the lower earning potential of these groups. But controlling for age, gender, ethnicity and education did not change the results. Overall, the results strongly support the hypothesis that Wal-Mart entry lowers wages and benefits of retail workers.

Wal-Mart Wages

Wal-Mart's size and growth over the past two decades, and its contribution to re-shaping retailing in America, means that it may be an important force in shaping wages for low-end workers. Existing evidence suggests that Wal-Mart pays lower wages and benefits than other large retailers. In 2005, the company reported an average hourly wage of $9.68 per hour.[1] An earlier study of pay scales in California found that Wal-Mart employees earned 26 percent less than workers in comparable jobs, defined as retail firms with 1,000 or more workers.[2] A national study found a 25 percent earnings gap with retailers overall, and 28 percent with large retailers, though wages did not look significantly different from those paid by other discount stores.[3]

There are two general problems with comparing Wal-Mart workers' wages with those of other retailers. Wal-Mart started and has its greatest presence in lower-wage and more rural areas, which will account for some part of the wage differential. Second, Wal-Mart makes up a large share of general merchandise workers, giving it a significant impact on the average wage of these workers. Its employees account for 55 percent of all general merchandise workers, and 71 percent of employees who work for large general merchandise companies in the country. To get a valid comparison with *other* general merchandisers, we adjusted retail wages in the Current Population Survey to match Wal-Mart's location and adjusted for Wal-Mart's contribution to the average general merchandise wage.

The results still found a sizeable wage gap between Wal-Mart and *other* general merchandising employers: 17.4 percent. The gap is smaller when compared to all grocery workers (7.5 percent) but larger when compared to large grocers (17.5 percent). In the area of large general merchandise companies, meaning businesses with more than 1,000 employees, Wal-Mart employees earned more than 25 percent less than workers in competing stores.[4]

[1]Wal-Mart Stores, Inc. 2005. http://www.walmartfacts.com/associates/default.aspx#a41.
[2]Dube, Arindrajit and Ken Jacobs, 2004. *Hidden Cost of Wal-Mart Jobs: Use of Safety Net Programs by Wal-Mart Workers in California.* University of California-Berkeley, Center for Labor Research and Education.
[3]Bernhardt, Annette, Anmol Chaddha and Siobhan McGrath, 2005. *What Do We Know About Wal-Mart?* New York University Brennan Center for Justice.
[4]Dube, Arindrajit and Steve Wertheim, 2005. *Wal-Mart and Job Quality: What Do We Know, and Should We Care?* University of California-Berkeley, Center for Labor Research and Education.

Research Methods

10   Anecdotal evidence suggests that competitors perceive the need to lower wages and reduce benefits to compete with Wal-Mart. In 2003, as Southern California unions negotiated their contracts with grocery chains, competition with Wal-Mart came up repeatedly as a rationale for lowering wages and cutting benefits.[5] Although such anecdotal accounts are common and reported often in the media, there is not much in the way of rigorous academic research on this question. We sought to test the hypothesis that Wal-Mart store openings depress local wages and benefits. Our research investigated the effect that a new Wal-Mart store had on the economy of the surrounding county and state by comparing how wages for retail workers, especially grocery and general merchandise employees, changed over time in response to a store opening.

Any effort to estimate the impact of individual store openings in a credible way encounters a fundamental methodological obstacle: Wal-Mart does not randomly choose where to expand. In deciding where to open a new store, management may take into account several factors, including the cost of labor. If the company selects areas where wages are already falling in order to minimize competition for employees, the results might artificially indicate that Wal-Mart's arrival in a county *caused* wages to fall. Alternatively, and more important in reality, Wal-Mart may choose sites with strong economic prospects to take advantage of a healthy consumer market. Such local booms usually lead to an uptick in workers' wages. When Wal-Mart store openings are correlated with local economic booms, the results would mistakenly indicate that Wal-Mart raised wages or had no effect on local wages—*even when its entry caused wages to be lower than they would have been.* In either case, there is the danger of confusing the factors enticing Wal-Mart to open a particular store with the effects of the store's arrival in the local economy. This problem is what economists call selection bias.

In order to resolve this problem, our research began with the fact that Wal-Mart has spread out over time from its initial headquarters. The first Wal-Mart store in 1962 was in Rogers, Arkansas. Since then, new stores have sprung up at increasing distances from the center, like a circular ripple spreading away from a drop of water. The farther a county is from Benton County, Arkansas (ground zero for Wal-Mart), the later it experienced the Wal-Mart growth spurt (see Figure 1). This pattern of expansion allowed the company to take full advantage of distribution networks and lower the overall costs of expansion.[6]

By following the ripple of store openings across the country and over time, we are able to test whether retail wages fell in its wake. Looking at store openings based on both how far the county is from Wal-Mart's "ground zero" and the year in question, our estimates avoid the selection bias that can be a problem for similar studies. We also subject our results to a number of different tests of internal and external validity, which all indicate that our methodology is robust.

[5]Goldman, Abigail and Nancy Cleeland, 2003. "An Empire Built on Bargains Remakes the Working World," *Los Angeles Times* (November 23, 2003). Pearlstein, Steven, 2003. "Wal-Mart's Hidden Costs," *Washington Post* (October 29, 2003).

[6]Graff, Thomas O., 1998. "The Locations of Wal-Mart and Kmart Supercenters: Contrasting Corporate Strategies," *The Professional Geographer* 50(1): 46–57. Holmes, Thomas J. 2005. *The Diffusion of Wal-Mart and Economics of Density.* Unpublished manuscript.

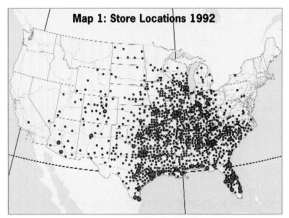

Map 1: Store Locations 1992

Number of Wal-Mart stores

- • 1–2
- • 3–6
- ● 7–12
- ● 13–19
- —— Interstates

Map 2: Store Locations 1996

Map 3: Store Locations 2000

FIGURE 1 Wal-Mart store locations 1992, 1996 and 2000

Our study uses two sources for data on wages: the Quarterly Census of Employment and Wages, employed by the US Bureau of Labor Statistics, which provides county-level information; and the March Supplement to the Current Population Survey, which provides greater detail about wages and benefits, but only at the state level.

Wal-Mart's National Expansion

15   The study focuses on the period 1992–2000, the time period when Wal-Mart expanded outside the South and exploded into major metropolitan areas. During this time, Wal-Mart grew from 1,800 US stores to 2,500, an increase of almost 40 percent. During the 1990s, the corporation expanded from the South to the Midwest, and then to the West and Northeast. By the end of the 1990s, more than half the counties in America had a Wal-Mart in them, and some had many more.

In 1992, half the Wal-Mart stores were in rural counties. But during the next eight years, three-quarters of new stores were in metropolitan counties, as Wal-Mart expanded from its rural starting point.

Wal-Mart Openings Put Downward Pressure on County Wages

When Wal-Mart's timing of expansion is taken into account, we find strong evidence that each new Wal-Mart lowered retail wages (see Table 1). Opening a single Wal-Mart store lowers the average retail wage in the surrounding county between 0.5 and 0.9 percent. In the category of general merchandise, wages fell about 1 percent for each new store, while workers in grocery stores saw average wages decline about 1.5 percent. As we would expect, there was no noticeable effect on wages in other low-paying economic sectors that did not compete with Wal-Mart. Restaurant workers, for example, saw no change in their take-home pay as a result of big box entry into their county.

Several independent factors explain the fall in wages associated with Wal-Mart openings. First is the substitution effect: a new Wal-Mart store replaces better paying jobs with lower-paying ones. Since Wal-Mart workers account for more than half of general merchandising employees, mixing lower-paid Wal-Mart jobs in with higher-paid jobs reduces average wages noticeably. A second factor is competition: Wal-Mart pushes down wages in competing businesses. This is most evident for grocery stores, where the effect on wages is purely a result of competitors cutting costs in response to Wal-Mart (see sidebar.)

TABLE 1   County-level effects from the entry of a single Wal-Mart store

Average Wage		Aggregate Wage Bill	
Retail workers:	0.5–0.9% lower	Retail sector:	1.5% lower
General merchandise workers	1% lower		
Grocery employees:	1.5% lower		

Some research suggests that Wal-Mart may be responsible for a small net increase in jobs.[8] Our study demonstrates that the opening of new Wal-Mart stores produces a decline not just in average wages but in the total wage bill of a county. Every new Wal-Mart in a county reduced the combined or aggregate earnings of retail workers by around 1.5 percent. Given that the fall in total wages was greater than the decline in average wages, it is highly unlikely that there is compensating positive employment growth associated with a Wal-Mart store opening. This is consistent with research by Neumark et al.,[9] who find that once the timing of store openings is taken into account, there is no evidence of job gains.

20   At the national level, our study concludes that in 2000, total earnings of retail workers nationwide were reduced by $4.5 billion due to Wal-Mart's presence, and these losses were concentrated in metropolitan areas.[10]

Wal-Mart Openings Reduced State-Level Earnings and Benefits Potential Impact on Firms' Costs

We also perform a state-level analysis of Wal-Mart's impact. By the year 2000, there were 2,500 Wal-Mart stores in the US, an average of 50 per state. Our study finds that each new Wal-Mart lowered the average hourly wage of retail workers in the surrounding state by two-tenths of a percent (see Table 2). Fifty new Wal-Mart stores would mean a 10 percent average wage reduction.

The study was also able to measure the effect of Wal-Mart stores on healthcare benefits using the Current Population Survey. While employees in the retail sector typically do not enjoy good healthcare benefits, anecdotal evidence suggests that Wal-Mart employees receive employer-sponsored health insurance at a lower level

---

Wal-Mart and Supermarket Employees

Wal-Mart's effect on earnings of grocery workers is particularly striking. The opening of a single Wal-Mart store lowered grocery wages by 1.5 percent. This is in large part because supermarkets typically pay higher wages and have higher rates of unionization than other retail businesses. In 2005, the unionization rate in supermarkets was 21 percent, compared to 5 percent in general merchandising and 6 percent in retail overall. Wages of unionized supermarket workers are 27 percent higher than their nonunion counterparts, as compared to a 6 percent union wage premium for general merchandise and 8 percent for all retail workers.[7] Because of higher wages and the greater advantage to union membership, competition with a large low-wage, non-union employer like Wal-Mart is particularly significant in the grocery sector.

Wal-Mart sells groceries and competes with grocery stores, but its workers are categorized as general merchandise employees, not grocery workers. The average wages for grocery workers does not include Wal-Mart workers. Hence, the decline in grocery worker wages found in the research results must be due to a decline in wages among Wal-Mart's competitors in the grocery industry.

---

[7]Current Population Survey, 2005.

[8]Basker, Emek, 2005. "Job Creation or Destruction: Labor Market Effects of Wal-Mart Expansion," *Review of Economics and Statistics* 87(1): 174–183.

[9]Neumark, David, Junfu Zhan and Stephen Ciccarella, 2005. "The Effects of Wal-Mart on Local Labor Markets," *NBER Working Paper* No. 11782.

[10]On average, a single store reduced the retail wage bill by 1 percent in a metro county. In 2000, metro counties had an average of 1.5 Wal-Mart stores, and had a total retail wage bill of $300 billion. This produced an annual reduction in the nominal wage bill by $4.5 billion.

TABLE 2 State-level effects of Wal-Mart openings on retail workers

	Average Retail Wages	Employer-Sponsored Health Insurance
Effects of a single store opening	0.2 percent lower	0.1 percentage point lower
Effects of 10 store openings	2 percent lower	1 percentage point lower
Effects of 50 Wal-Marts (the average number per state)	10 percent lower	5 percentage points lower

than workers in competing businesses. Our data indicates Wal-Mart's job-based coverage rate was higher than retailers in general, but lower than large retailers, including large general merchandisers and large grocery stores.[11]

Just as Wal-Mart's low wages depressed wages in competing businesses, we found similar effects on the rate of health insurance. The research demonstrates that 10 new Wal-Mart store openings in a state translated to a 1 percentage point reduction in the proportion of retail workers who received health insurance from their employer.

Effect on Metropolitan Counties

Wal-Mart's effect on county wages appeared only in metropolitan statistical areas. The strong decline in earnings that was evident in metropolitan counties did not show up in rural counties. This result is consistent with other research that shows that rural areas are more likely to have low-wage firms.[12] Where wages are low to begin with, the arrival of the retail chain is less significant. This is especially true because the minimum wage becomes binding at low wage levels, which is more likely in rural areas. In metro areas with better-paying jobs and a higher rate of unionization, Wal-Mart's entry was more likely to have an impact on the labor market. This is particularly important since the large majority of new Wal-Mart stores are located in metro areas. This also explains the greater resistance to Wal-Mart store locations in metropolitan compared to rural areas, since workers and unions have more to lose in urban settings.

Controlling for Demographics

25   One possible explanation for the apparent reduction in wages is a change in the mix of the workforce. If Wal-Mart hires more minorities, women and young-people than its competitors, then the wage difference could be explained by the lower earnings of these groups, regardless of where they work. A related possibility could be a change in hours of work, skills of workers and fringe benefits. If Wal-Mart hires disproportionately more part-time workers or less skilled workers, for example, then the apparent decline in average wages might not result from a reduction in wages for comparable employees.

---

[11]Dube and Wertheim, 2005.
[12]Anderrson, Fredrik, Harry Holzer and Julia Lane, 2002. "The Interaction of Workers and Firms in the Low-Wage Labor Market," *LEHD Working Paper*.

In order to investigate this possibility, we use the Current Population Survey data (from the Annual Demographic Supplement), which provides details on individual worker characteristics. We look at the impact of Wal-Mart expansion in a state on the average hourly wages for retail workers (as opposed to earnings per worker in our other dataset, the QCEW), and control for the demographics of the workforce, i.e., gender, age, education and race, as well as the average wage of workers without a college education.[13] Controlling for these factors does not change the overall conclusion. Wal-Mart's effects on wages in surrounding areas created lower wages for a set of retail workers, not a change in who was working retail.

Conclusions

Until now there have been few studies documenting the effects on compensation from Wal-Mart's entry into a new labor market. The few studies that do address the question focus on a small set of counties in primarily rural states. Because of methodological limitations, none are able to distinguish the effects of Wal-Mart's arrival from the particular conditions that attracted the retailer to open in a given area in the first place.

The new research strongly suggests that Wal-Mart entry lowers wages for employees in competing businesses, and the effect can be seen at both the county and state levels. Controlling for demographic or skill mix of the workforce cannot explain the results. Wal-Mart openings depress average and aggregate wages and reduce the proportion of the workforce that is covered by employer-sponsored health insurance.

Of course, Wal-Mart's presence is also likely to bring lower prices. Existing research shows big-box stores like Wal-Mart can use their distribution systems and leverage with suppliers to produce substantial savings to consumers.[14] However, to the extent that competing on cost produces negative effects on low-wage workers, this is an important consideration when deciding the "rules of the game" that big-box retailers need to abide by. And since wage and benefit savings are not the main part of the cost advantage for a company like Wal-Mart, it could continue to pass on most of these savings while paying higher wages and benefits. These factors should be taken into account by policy makers in their decision-making on economic development.

[13]To be sure, whether or not lower wages bring in more disadvantaged groups does not change the fact that wages are reduced for retail jobs. Our analysis further shows that this cannot "explain" the fall in wages.
[14]Hausman, Jerry and Ephraim Leibtag, 2005. "Consumer Benefits from Increased Competition in Shopping Outlets: Measuring the Effect of Wal-Mart," *NBER Working Paper No. 11809.*

Bizarro, "Greeter Gone Wild"

DAN PIRARO

Dan Piraro's comic strip, Bizarro, *is distributed internationally to over 250 newspapers. Piraro focuses, in his own words, on the "incredibly surreal things that happen to us in our so-called 'normal' lives." To emphasize the surreal elements, Piraro inserts odd and unexpected images into his cartoons. See more of Piraro's work on his web site: http://www.bizarro.com/.*

Don't Blame Wal-Mart

ROBERT B. REICH

Formerly on the faculty of Harvard University's John F. Kennedy School of Government, Robert B. Reich was the secretary of labor during the presidency of Bill Clinton. He is the author of ten books on history, politics, economics, and business. This op-ed piece appeared in the New York Times *on February 28, 2005.*

Bowing to intense pressure from neighborhood and labor groups, a real estate developer has just given up plans to include a Wal-Mart store in a mall in Queens, thereby blocking Wal-Mart's plan to open its first store in New York City. In the eyes of Wal-Mart's detractors, the Arkansas-based chain embodies the worst kind of economic exploitation: it pays its 1.2 million American workers an average of only $9.68 an hour, doesn't provide most of them with health insurance, keeps out unions, has a checkered history on labor law and turns main streets into ghost towns by sucking business away from small retailers.

But isn't Wal-Mart really being punished for our sins? After all, it's not as if Wal-Mart's founder, Sam Walton, and his successors created the world's largest retailer by putting a gun to our heads and forcing us to shop there.

Instead, Wal-Mart has lured customers with low prices. "We expect our suppliers to drive the costs out of the supply chain," a spokeswoman for Wal-Mart said. "It's good for us and good for them."

Wal-Mart may have perfected this technique, but you can find it almost everywhere these days. Corporations are in fierce competition to get and keep customers, so they pass the bulk of their cost cuts through to consumers as lower prices. Products are manufactured in China at a fraction of the cost of making them here, and American consumers get great deals. Back-office work, along with computer programming and data crunching, is "offshored" to India, so our dollars go even further.

5 Meanwhile, many of us pressure companies to give us even better bargains. I look on the Internet to find the lowest price I can and buy airline tickets, books, merchandise from just about anywhere with a click of a mouse. Don't you?

The fact is, today's economy offers us a Faustian bargain: it can give consumers deals largely because it hammers workers and communities.

We can blame big corporations, but we're mostly making this bargain with ourselves. The easier it is for us to get great deals, the stronger the downward pressure on wages and benefits. Last year, the real wages of hourly workers, who make up about 80 percent of the work force, actually dropped for the first time in more than a decade; hourly workers' health and pension benefits are in free fall. The easier it is for us to find better professional services, the harder professionals have to hustle to attract and keep clients. The more efficiently we can summon products from anywhere on the globe, the more stress we put on our own communities.

But you and I aren't just consumers. We're also workers and citizens. How do we strike the right balance? To claim that people shouldn't have access to Wal-Mart or to cut-rate airfares or services from India or to Internet shopping, because these somehow reduce their quality of life, is paternalistic tripe. No one is a better judge of what people want than they themselves.

The problem is, the choices we make in the market don't fully reflect our values as workers or as citizens. I didn't want our community bookstore in Cambridge, Mass., to close (as it did last fall) yet I still bought lots of books from Amazon.com. In addition, we may not see the larger bargain when our own job or community isn't directly at stake. I don't like what's happening to airline workers, but I still try for the cheapest fare I can get.

10 The only way for the workers or citizens in us to trump the consumers in us is through laws and regulations that make our purchases a social choice as well as a personal one. A requirement that companies with more than 50 employees offer their workers affordable health insurance, for example, might increase slightly the price of their goods and services. My inner consumer won't like that very much, but the worker in me thinks it a fair price to pay. Same with an increase in the minimum wage or a change in labor laws making it easier for employees to organize and negotiate better terms.

I wouldn't go so far as to re-regulate the airline industry or hobble free trade with China and India—that would cost me as a consumer far too much—but I'd like the government to offer wage insurance to ease the pain of sudden losses of pay. And I'd support labor standards that make trade agreements a bit more fair.

These provisions might end up costing me some money, but the citizen in me thinks they are worth the price. You might think differently, but as a nation we aren't even having this sort of discussion. Instead, our debates about economic change take place between two warring camps: those who want the best consumer deals, and those who want to preserve jobs and communities much as they are. Instead of finding ways to soften the blows, compensate the losers or slow the pace of change—so the consumers in us can enjoy lower prices and better products without wreaking too much damage on us in our role as workers and citizens—we go to battle.

I don't know if Wal-Mart will ever make it into New York City. I do know that New Yorkers, like most other Americans, want the great deals that can be had in a rapidly globalizing high-tech economy. Yet the prices on sales tags don't reflect the full prices we have to pay as workers and citizens. A sensible public debate would focus on how to make that total price as low as possible.

Why Wal-Mart Is Good

STEVE MAICH

Steve Maich is a business columnist for the Canadian public affairs magazine Maclean's, *which published this article in July 2005. Maich maintains a popular Web log "All Business," in which he comments on globalized economics from a Canadian perspective.*

There's a place on the western edge of Cleveland that encapsulates the story of the city—its proud industrial past, its slow depressing decline, its hopes for a brighter future. But the battle now being waged over that patch of land tells an even bigger tale.

It's called the steelyard flats, a 130-acre plot of barren wasteland at the intersection of Interstates 90 and 71, in what was once the heart of Cleveland's thriving steel industry. The site has sat idle since 2000, when LTV Steel went bankrupt. The finishing mill was torn down, and the shells of a few remaining buildings have been crumbling here ever since. The place is now littered with dis-carded scrap metal, concrete and junk: a dozen old tires here, a shattered TV there.

Soon, however, this site will also be a symbol of renewal. In May, work began on what will be the first big-box shopping center in this city of 500,000 people. It's called Steelyard Commons, and will include a Target store, a Home Depot, a Staples, plus restaurants and smaller businesses. It's expected to bring close to 2,000 jobs to the city identified as the most impoverished urban area in the U.S. in the 2004 census. Unemployment here runs at 11 percent—roughly double the national average.

But there's a problem. Wal-Mart Stores, the world's biggest retailer, will be the anchor tenant of Steelyard Commons, and that has transformed this place into another front in North America's most bitter retail cold war. Wal-Mart's critics say the company destroys local economies, putting small competitors out of business; that it abuses workers with low wages and paltry benefits; and that it drives urban sprawl and all the environmental damage that goes with it. And so, a coalition of labor leaders, activists and city councillors have banded together, vowing to keep Wal-Mart out even if it means killing the whole project.

5   It's a divisive political standoff that's been mirrored in communities throughout North America over the past few years. To the project's advocates in City Hall, this is just the kind of development Cleveland so desperately needs. Aside from precious jobs, the mall will spin off US$3 million in property taxes annually, US$1.8 million of which will go to the city's struggling school system, plus US$700,000 in local payroll tax. It will also give city residents a place to shop near home, rather than travelling to the suburbs. Officials estimate local residents spend US$4 billion a year in retail shops, a third of which currently goes outside the city. If ever there was a Wal-Mart that deserves support, they say, this is it.

But that's just the point: Wal-Mart isn't engaged in a series of messy local zoning disputes. It's at war with a well-financed, well-organized opposition, determined to fight it on every front. From Los Angeles to the Saguenay, from Hartford, Conn., to Vancouver, a broad array of activist groups and unions have launched protests, lawsuits and ad campaigns, all aimed at discrediting Wal-Mart, halting its growth, and unionizing its workforce.

Like most wars, it's about money and power, and the first casualty is truth. Because even after all the scrutiny and analysis of the Wal-Mart phenomenon, most of what we've been told—about worker abuse, destroyed small-town economies, crushed suppliers and greedy management—is wrong.

To Carol Foote, it just didn't make sense. It was near the end of the summer of 2000, and most of her neighbours in Miramichi, N.B., were planning to drive to Moncton, an hour and a half away, to buy school supplies for their kids at Wal-Mart. Foote knew that many in town already made regular trips there to buy household goods, clothes and electronics. And she knew every carload took more money from the local economy. But the prices, they said, were just too good to pass up.

So, Foote and her friend Paula Beaulieu decided to make it their mission to bring Wal-Mart to Miramichi. They organized a petition, and within six weeks they'd gathered 11,276 signatures in and around the town of about 19,000 residents. "The whole talk of the Miramichi was this petition," Foote remembers. "Lots of people would say, 'I'll sign, but we'll never get one,' and I'd say, 'C'mon, you've got to believe!' "

10   It took almost five years of trying, but last January Wal-Mart finally opened an outlet in Miramichi. Aside from creating dozens of jobs, Foote says the store has brought new life to the town's small commercial district. Pennington's has opened a store, Staples is on the way, and there is talk of a Quizno's sandwich shop. To city dwellers, the arrival of such mass-market brands is no big deal, but in a little town like Miramichi, they represent investment that would've seemed impossible a few years ago.

This is how the Wal-Mart revolution was built: on small towns like Miramichi. The numbers are truly staggering. Wal-Mart had sales of US$288.2 billion last year—meaning, if it were a country, it would be the world's 33rd biggest economy, ahead of Sweden, Switzerland and Hong Kong. It has 1.7 million employees worldwide, slightly less than the population of Montreal. The company's stock has risen 79 percent in the past decade, giving it a market value just north of US$200 billion—more than the total combined value of Canada's Big Five banks. And profit rose 13 percent last year, to US$10.3 billion, making it the undisputed Goliath of retail.

In Canada, the growth is no less impressive. Wal-Mart first arrived here in 1994, buying 122 Woolco stores with about 15 percent of the department store market. Over the next decade, it more than doubled its number of outlets and increased its market share to about 52 percent. And while critics portray this as the work of a ravenous invading force, the truth is most communities reached out to Wal-Mart and embraced it.

Foote heard lots of grousing about Wal-Mart, but when she looks at what it has brought to her town, she has no regrets. "We weren't trying to hurt our city, we just wanted it to grow," she says. "The stores here charged so much, people had to go to Moncton. And when they did, they'd buy their fuel there, they'd eat there. All our money was leaving town. I thought, 'This has got to stop.'" Rather than Wal-Mart crushing the few local businesses like the critics warned, she suspected the store would invigorate them, because that's just what has happened in hundreds of places across the country.

In 2002, Ryerson University completed the first major study on the company's impact on nearby small retailers, and found the opening of a new outlet is generally an economic boon for the whole area—attracting other retailers and driving up sales at nearby stores. In metropolitan areas, a new Wal-Mart was generally followed by an increase of $56.8 million in local sales, and the opening of 12.9 new stores. In rural areas, the commercial boost was $74.1 million and 16.7 new stores on average. Meanwhile, economic growth in areas with Wal-Mart stores far outpaced growth in places without them. The final line of the study said it all: "It is difficult to make the case that a Wal-Mart store actually puts other retailers out of business."

15   That study confirmed what Wal-Mart had long claimed: that its stores are economic generators, not predators. And, it seems, even small-business owners are coming around to that view. A 2004 Canadian Imperial Bank of Commerce survey of more than 1,800 small-business owners across Canada found that just 16 percent of respondents said they had been hurt by competition from big-box retailers like Wal-Mart and Home Depot. Five percent said the big boxes had actually helped them, while the vast majority claimed little or no impact.

Andy Grossman, however, doesn't buy any of that. Grossman is executive director of Wal-Mart Watch, a lobbying and publicity organization that coordinates the efforts of several anti-Wal-Mart groups. In April, it launched a two-week media blitz across the U.S., with full-page ads in major newspapers like the *New York Times* alleging a by-now familiar litany of misdeeds. "Wal-Mart needs to become a better corporate citizen, a better neighbour and a better employer," Grossman says. And at the very top of his list of grievances is Wal-Mart's purported ill-treatment of its workers. But there again, research suggests the criticism is overblown.

To be sure, nobody is claiming that being a Wal-Mart associate is a job many would aspire to. It's a low-wage gig, with only moderate opportunity for advancement, and it's not easy. The average full-time Wal-Mart worker in the U.S. makes US$9.68 an hour, which works out to roughly US$17,500 a year before taxes. If that worker is a sole earner trying to support a spouse and child, it puts him only about US$1,500 above the federal poverty line. Labor advocates say that in light of Wal-Mart's US$10-billion profit, the company should pay higher wages. But a closer look at the numbers paints a different picture. Wal-Mart's 2004 profit works out to a little more than US$6,000 per employee, compared to US$54,000 at General Electric, and US$143,000 per employee at Microsoft. Despite mammoth earnings, Wal-Mart doesn't have as much room for generosity as it first appears.

Health care is another oft-cited complaint. Only about 48 percent of Wal-Mart's workers buy into the company's health care plan, and critics say that's because it's too expensive: US$40 a month for an individual and US$155 for a family, plus a US$1,000 deductible. A recent study by researchers at the University of California at Berkeley concluded Wal-Mart's wages and benefits are so low that its workers in California rely on about US$86 million in public assistance every year. On the other hand, Wal-Mart points out that only about 36 percent of all retail workers get employee-sponsored health care in the U.S.—meaning its plan is better than most in its industry. And while unions say the company should provide big benefits like those offered by General Motors, financial analysts point out that skyrocketing health care costs now threaten the stability of GM's business and have contributed to massive layoffs—hardly a model to emulate.

Even in Canada, where the health care issue is largely moot, it would still be difficult to raise a family on an associate's wage. But very few are in that position. While the majority of Wal-Mart employees work full time, the company also employs many students, seniors and people collecting a second income. And Wal-Mart says only seven percent of its staff are supporting a family.

20   Perhaps most telling is the fact that most Wal-Mart workers seem content. Human resources consulting firm Hewitt Associates issues an annual ranking of Canadian employers based largely on worker satisfaction surveys, and for three of the past four years Wal-Mart has been named best retailer, due mainly to incentives like profit sharing and a discounted stock purchase program. And despite union claims of widespread mistreatment, Andrew Pelletier, director of corporate affairs with Wal-Mart Canada, says new stores usually receive between six and 10 applications for every available job.

The various campaigns to paint Wal-Mart as an avaricious and abusive employer simply don't hold up to scrutiny, says Elisa Sumanski, a legal analyst with the National Right to Work Legal Defense Foundation, a Virginia-based group that represents workers in disputes with their unions, and which has received grants from Wal-Mart's founding Walton family. "We think it's really pretty simple— if Wal-Mart is such a terrible place to work, then why are so many thousands of people so eager to work there?" she says.

But when it comes to Wal-Mart, perception and myth are powerful. In spite of all the evidence to the contrary, the company is still struggling with the consequences of its increasingly tainted image. For much of the past year debate raged in Vancouver's city council over plans to build the city's first Wal-Mart. Opponents complained the store would be an energy-hogging blight on the environment. Wal-Mart responded by designing perhaps the most environmentally progressive big-box store ever—lit with skylights, cooled with shade trees, with rainwater running the toilets, and a geothermal heating

system run by wind-turbine power. But nothing could convince the critics. "Big-box stores create traffic congestion, cause air pollution and harm small businesses," said councillor Anne Roberts, who led the anti-Wal-Mart campaign. Last month, city council rejected the plan by eight to three.

Shortly after, Wal-Mart received its second B.C. rejection in a week, this time when the town council of the Vancouver Island city of Campbell River voted 7–0 against a rezoning application that would have paved the way for the retailer. More than 300 people spoke against Wal-Mart during three days of hearings, most saying the proposed riverside site should be used for a park. Pushing the development was the Campbell River Indian Band, which was hoping to buy the parcel of land from a logging company and had applied to have its status changed. After being turned down, some band members said racism had played a part in the rejection.

As far as Bruce Bartlett is concerned, people who hate Wal-Mart don't understand it.

25   Bartlett, a former deputy assistant secretary for economic policy at the U.S. Treasury Department, now serves as senior fellow at the National Center for Policy Analysis, a conservative Washington think tank. Over the past two decades, he has watched the company's astonishing rise with admiration, and the recent public backlash with dismay.

His concern is not primarily for the company or its executives. Nor is he worried for the descendants of founder Sam Walton—by far the wealthiest clan in North America. Rather, Bartlett worries about the impact the war on Wal-Mart will have on the poor families who have come to rely on the stores. "The problem with this debate is that there's no one out there representing the people who've benefited from Wal-Mart, which is primarily the poor people," Bartlett says. "If you're stuck with a low income and you can reduce the amount you pay for basic items, then your real income goes up."

Those savings are substantial. In 2002, a study by the New England Consulting Group estimated that Wal-Mart's "everyday low prices" on a wide range of groceries and household goods saves U.S. consumers US$100 billion annually, or US$600 a year for the average American family. That's because not only does Wal-Mart sell for less, it forces competitors to cut prices in order to compete. UBS Warburg analysts measured grocery prices in various markets across the country and found that basic food items are 10 to 15 percent cheaper in areas where Wal-Mart competes. So it's far from being an insidious influence: those savings are a godsend for consumers, especially for working-poor families. As W. Michael Cox, chief economist for the Federal Reserve Bank of Dallas, said in 2003: "Wal-Mart is the greatest thing that ever happened to low-income Americans."

As Wal-Mart has grown, those savings have sent ripple effects through every corner of the North American economy, even benefiting consumers who've never set foot in one of its stores. In 2002, the consulting firm McKinsey & Co. delved into the so-called "Wal-Mart effect" and found it was the biggest single contributor to the growth of economic productivity across the U.S. between 1995 and 1999. According to McKinsey, Wal-Mart's pioneering approach to computerized inventory management, and analysis of store traffic patterns to better deploy its staff in peak hours, improved the efficiency of thousands of companies. The U.S. National Bureau of Economic Research has found that Wal-Mart's prices have a significant impact on holding down the rate of inflation. That, in turn, helps keep interest rates low, and helps fuel economic growth.

All this isn't some happy accident, but a fundamental part of what makes the company tick. Ever since Sam Walton opened his first store in Arkansas in 1962, Wal-Mart has dedicated itself to providing the lowest possible price for people living on a budget. "The underpinning of everyday low prices is a commitment to lowering the cost of living," says Wal-Mart Canada's Pelletier. "That was Sam Walton's vision, and it permeates the company today. The only way we can do that is by driving waste out."

30 Even now, 13 years after Walton died, his obsession with cost is still evident in every aspect of the business. Head offices are spartan and basic. Company officials fly economy, and stay at bargain hotels. And every person, in every division, is constantly encouraged to look for less expensive ways of doing everything. Critics say this obsession with price has put relentless pressure on suppliers, even driving some out of business as they failed to meet Wal-Mart's demands for efficiency. But the company makes no apologies. It offers suppliers full access to sales data on every item sold, right to the minute and the penny. And every year thousands of small suppliers line up for the chance to get their products on Wal-Mart's shelves.

That helps explain why, for the past several years, Wal-Mart has ranked among the world's most admired companies, according to *Fortune* magazine's annual rankings. This year's survey of thousands of executives and industry analysts put the company first among retailers for innovation, employee talent, quality of management, financial soundness, and second for social responsibility.

So, last year, when Bruce Bartlett saw opponents in his own city of Washington defeat plans for a Wal-Mart, he shook his head. "It's just stupid and frankly insane if you really care about the well-being of your constituents," he says. "They're shooting themselves in the foot, and they're just showing that they really don't care about people at all. They'd rather cater to a few squeaky wheels."

But the wheels turning against Wal-Mart are more than squeaky. They're coordinated, tireless, and deeply committed to their cause. For them, defeating Wal-Mart is a matter of life or death.

Tom Robertson is a guy who wears his passions on his sleeve.

35 Sitting in his wood-panelled office near downtown Cleveland, the head of the northern Ohio chapter of the United Food and Commercial Workers union lays out his objections to Cleveland's proposed Wal-Mart, but he finds it hard to contain his contempt. "My mission isn't to

organize Wal-Mart when they come to town. My mission is to keep them the hell out of town so they won't drive wages down," he explains, gaining steam as he speaks. "They just fuckin' destroy jobs, period, because they replace high-paying jobs with low-paying jobs." 40

Robertson is paid to defend the unionized workers at a chain of small local grocery stores that will be threatened by Wal-Mart's arrival. But, he acknowledges, this fight is about more than just this city and his roughly 1,600 local members. It's about saving the union movement itself, and that's why so many labor organizations and their political allies have joined the fight. "If Wal-Mart continues to grow and expand based on their terms and conditions, with nobody overseeing the way they treat people and compete, yes—it could destroy the labor movement," Robertson says.

The plight of Robertson's own union illustrates why. Over the past three years, his local has lost 3,000 members—a decline of more than 10 percent—and he says Wal-Mart is the number 1 reason for it. Unionized stores have had to cut staff and wages to compete, and other companies have increased efforts to prevent unionization.

The UFCW's membership crisis is but one example of a larger trend unfolding throughout the continent, as traditionally union-heavy industrial companies downsize, and as mostly non-union sectors like services, technology and retail become a much larger portion of the economy. The same phenomenon is happening in Canada, where private sector unionization has fallen from 26 percent in the early 1970s to just 18 percent in 2003. In short, organized labor is dying a slow death and its financial strength and political influence are waning as a result.

The fight over Wal-Mart is really a fight to halt organized labor's gradual death spiral. If the unions are to turn the tide, they need to be in retail, and if they are going to get into retail, they have to get into Wal-Mart—union leaders themselves acknowledge as much. As Stuart Acuff, organizing

director of the AFL-CIO, America's umbrella organization for trade unions, told *Fortune* last year, "If we want to survive, labor has no choice but to organize Wal-Mart."

They've spared no expense to do it. For the past five years, the UFCW has sent organizers around Canada and the U.S., trying to get Wal-Mart workers to sign union cards and force certification votes. It waged a four-year effort, at a cost of about US$3 million a year, to certify a single Las Vegas store. But so far, they've had no luck.

Wal-Mart has been equally aggressive in keeping the unions out. Managers are encouraged to report union activity, and the UFCW points to dozens of cases in which it accuses the company of firing workers for working on behalf of the union. When the UFCW was able to get a unit certified in Jonquiére, Que., the company responded by shutting down the store. Pelletier insists, however, that this is not a fight over worker rights. "At the end of the day, this campaign is all about money for the union," he says. "The union is looking for dues to finance their operations. If they could collect union dues from our thousands of associates across the country, this would amount to millions of dollars a year into the union and out of the pockets of our workers."

Lately, though, the unions and their allies have changed their approach. Efforts to unionize have been stymied, so they've decided to focus on discrediting the company and slowing its growth. Hence Wal-Mart Watch's publicity campaign, and the union-supported zoning fights cropping up everywhere. "It's an effort to destroy Wal-Mart because the company's continued growth and success is really an argument against the need for unionization," Sumanski says.

But Andy Grossman says the union fight is only part of the picture. As he sees it, Wal-Mart is driving a vicious cycle: it starts with lower prices, and leads over time to a single player essentially rewriting the economics of the industry for everybody. Pretty soon, there are fewer employers, lower wages, less medical coverage, more poverty—all widening the gap between the rich owners of Wal-Mart stock and the poor who shop and work there. "This is a societal fight," Grossman explains. "Wal-Mart is a symbol, because they're so good at what they do, others have to emulate them. This company's reach is so broad, we need to change the relationship between it and the communities it seeks to do business in, otherwise it's going to continue to destroy our societies."

For Grossman, those are the stakes: social destruction. Never mind that most of the research refutes this view. Never mind that millions more consumers vote with their feet and their wallets every year, opting for the financial freedom Wal-Mart affords. The point is that Grossman, and thousands of others, believe with near-religious zeal that Wal-Mart is dangerous. And the war drags on.

45 Back in Cleveland, Chris Ronayne is still a little baffled by the whole controversy. As chief of staff to Democratic Mayor Jane Campbell and former head of the city planning commission, he knew enough to expect opposition to any plan to bring Wal-Mart to the city. And he knew his boss would be locking horns with the very union bosses that helped put her in office in 2001.

Still, he didn't expect the debate to be so nasty. Opponents tried, and failed, to pass a change to zoning laws to keep the company out, and protesters recently tried to crash Campbell's re-election campaign kickoff. Former supporters have denounced the mayor for selling out to the Great Satan of Corporate America. "We see this as a first step toward a bigger turnaround, toward making Cleveland into a city that can attract residents."

Ronayne says. "We know these are starter jobs, but this city has seen a serious erosion of our employment base and a starter job is better than no job, from our perspective. We need jobs, period."

And while there is certainly a vocal faction, led by the UFCW, vowing to keep fighting Wal-Mart every step of the way, it remains in the minority. With the support of about 78 percent of residents in a recent poll and with a legal building permit in hand, it appears Wal-Mart has won this battle. The war, though, is less certain, and the company knows it. Already it's getting much more difficult and expensive for Wal-Mart to build stores. It is sued thousands of times every year by local activists, disgruntled ex-employees, and unions. Thanks to a steady stream of negative press, thousands of consumers would sooner go barefoot than buy shoes there.

The company, as always, puts a positive spin on things. Pelletier says all the scrutiny will only make Wal-Mart stronger and more responsive. He says it will keep listening to the complaints, and acting to address what it can. But the one thing that will not change is Sam Walton's admonition to put the customer first, always. Carol Foote likes it that way. "I think sometimes it's just easier for people to blame the other guy," she says. "If your customers aren't coming back, maybe you should look at why they're not coming back rather than trying to point the finger."

But the war on Wal-Mart raises more complicated questions. If the company helps poor families, creates decent jobs and fuels economic growth, what does it say that so many are so determined to stop it? More important—if Wal-Mart loses this fight, who wins?

Shopping for a Nobel

JOHN TIERNEY

John Tierney, now a science columnist for The New York Times, *writes extensively on science, technology, and the environment, usually from a libertarian point of view. This column was published in the* Times *on October 17, 2006, when Tierney was writing a general opinion column for the Op-Ed page.*

I don't want to begrudge the Nobel Peace Prize won last week by the Grameen Bank and its founder, Muhammad Yunus. They deserve it. The Grameen Bank has done more than the World Bank to help the poor, and Yunus has done more than Jimmy Carter or Bono or any philanthropist.

But has he done more good than someone who never got the prize: Sam Walton? Has any organization in the world lifted more people out of poverty than Wal-Mart?

The Grameen Bank is both an inspiration and a lesson in limits. Compared with other development programs, it's remarkable for its large scale. Since it was started three decades ago in Bangladesh, it has expanded to more than 2,000 branches. Its micro-loans, typically less than $150, have helped millions of villagers start small businesses, like peddling incense or handicrafts at the local market, or selling milk and eggs.

The economist William Easterly, who was afraid Bono was going to get this year's Nobel, calls the bank's prize "a victory for the one-step-at-a-time homegrown bottom-up approach" to development. That approach is a welcome contrast to the grandiose foreign-aid schemes that do more harm than good, as Easterly documents in his book, "The White Man's Burden."

5   But there's a limit to how much money villagers can make selling eggs to one another— a thatched ceiling, as Michael Strong calls it. Strong, the head of Flow, a nonprofit group promoting entrepreneurship abroad, is a fan of the Grameen Bank, but he figures that villagers can lift themselves out of poverty much faster by getting a job in a factory.

The best way for third world villagers to tap "the vast pipeline of wealth from the developed world," he argued in a recent TCSDaily.com article, is to sell their products to the world's largest retailer, Wal-Mart. Strong challenged anyone to name an organization that is doing more to alleviate third world poverty than Wal-Mart.

So far he's gotten a lot of angry responses from Wal-Mart's critics, but nobody has come up with a convincing nomination for a more effective antipoverty organization. And certainly none that saves money for Americans at the same time it's helping foreigners.

Making toys or shoes for Wal-Mart in a Chinese or Latin American factory may sound like hell to American college students—and some factories should treat their workers much better, as Strong readily concedes. But there are good reasons that villagers will move hundreds of miles for a job.

Most "sweatshop" jobs—even ones paying just $2 per day—provide enough to lift a worker above the poverty level, and often far above it, according to a study of 10 Asian and Latin American countries by Benjamin Powell and David Skarbek. In Honduras, the economists note, the average apparel worker makes $13 a day, while nearly half the population makes less than $2 a day.

10   In America, the economic debate on Wal-Mart mostly concerns its effect on American workers. The best evidence is that, while Wal-Mart's competition might (or might not) depress the wages of some workers, on balance Americans come out well ahead because they save so much money by shopping there.

Some critics, particularly ones allied with American labor unions, argue that the consumer savings don't justify the social dislocations caused by Wal-Mart's relentless cost-cutting. They'd rather see Wal-Mart and other retailers paying higher wages to their employees, and selling more products made by Americans instead of foreigners.

But this argument makes moral sense only if your overriding concern is saving the jobs and protecting the salaries of American workers who are already far better off than most of the planet's population. If you're committed to Bono's vision of "making poverty history," shouldn't you take a less parochial view? Shouldn't you be more worried about villagers overseas subsisting on a dollar a day?

Some of them prefer to keep farming or to run small local businesses, and they're lucky to get loans from the Grameen Bank and its many emulators. But other villagers would prefer to make more money by working in a factory. If you want to help them, remember the new social justice slogan proposed by Strong: "Act locally, think globally: Shop Wal-Mart."

A New World to Conquer

DAVID HORSEY

David Horsey, a nationally syndicated political cartoonist, has won two Pulitzer Prizes for editorial cartooning (in 1999 and again in 2003). This cartoon, which we found in the Seattle Post-Intelligencer, *appeared in newspapers around the country in January 2004.*

· A NEW WORLD TO CONQUER ·

■ ■ ■ **FOR CLASS DISCUSSION** Wal-Mart and the Public Good

1. The readings in this unit as well as the political cartoons and the movie poster have looked at Wal-Mart from multiple perspectives. What are some of the main views these articles present on each of the following issues?
   - Wal-Mart's labor practices (employee wages, medical insurance, gender equity, compensation insurance, career opportunities)
   - Wal-Mart's effect on local businesses
   - Wal-Mart's contribution to the appearance of a community
   - Wal-Mart's benefits for consumers
   - Wal-Mart's benefits for the world's poor

2. Which of the views of Wal-Mart that you sketched out in Question 1 do you find most persuasive as an argument? In other words, which argument offers the most compelling and reliable evidence as well as the most effective appeals to *ethos* and *pathos*?

3. Some of the articles in this unit emphasize consumers' responsibility, claiming that Americans' demand for low prices is a major cause of Wal-Mart's success. What points could you offer in support of this idea? What points can you think of against it?

4. Some opponents of Wal-Mart have particularly objected to these statements:
   - Wal-Mart is a patriotic, true-American company.
   - Wal-Mart is an environmentally conscious company.

   What is the strongest evidence in favor of and against these claims?

5. Some journalists and economic analysts have compared Wal-Mart to other big-box retail chains such as Costco, Home Depot, Lowe's, and Target. In many cases, Costco is said to balance its treatment of its employees, its appeals to customers, and its returns for shareholders more effectively than Wal-Mart. After doing some research on Costco or another big-box retailer, what do you see as the main similarities and differences between it and Wal-Mart?

6. Choose one of the readings in this unit and analyze it carefully using the List 2 questions on pages 426–427.

WRITING ASSIGNMENT   Email to a Friend

Write a persuasive email message to a friend in which you urge him or her to give up (or continue) shopping at Wal-Mart. Build the most compelling case for this friend by tapping into your friend's values and needs. To gather more evidence for your message, you might consult Wal-Mart's Web site (www.walmartfacts.com) or some of the anti-Wal-Mart sites (*Sprawl-Busters,* www.sprawl-busters.com; *Wal-Mart Watch.com,* www.walmartwatch.com, or *Wake Up Wal-Mart,* www.wakeupwalmart.com). ■

For additional writing, reading, and research resources, go to www.mycomplab.com

Sustainability and the Search for Clean Energy

Since the publication of the U.N. Intergovernmental Panel on Climate Change's report, *Climate Change 2007*, which affirms the scientific conclusion that human-influenced climate change threatens our global environment, much of the public debate has shifted from arguing about causes of global warming to arguing about potential consequences and solutions. The dominant question is no longer whether climate change is happening but whether we can reverse the change or adapt to it. How will climate change affect rich countries, poor countries, agriculture, water supplies, animal life, or other aspects of life on earth? What can we do about these consequences? Another question raised by climate change concerns the search for alternatives to fossil fuels. Much controversy now swirls round the feasibility of nuclear energy and wind, solar, and geothermal power.

In addition to the discussions over alternative sources of energy, public concern over climate change has expanded to include the whole issue of sustainable living. A memorable definition of sustainability has been expressed in these words: "leave the world better than you found it, take no more than you need, try not to harm [the] life of the environment, make amends if you do" (from Fifth Town Artisan Cheese Company). When people focus on sustainability, they recognize that the earth's resources are limited, that these resources are being overdrawn, and that some countries such as the United States and China are responsible for a much larger percentage of environmental damage than others.

Furthermore, as climate change, alternative sources of energy, and sustainability have gained traction as important issues, the words "environmentally friendly," "green," and "sustainable" have become trendy concepts and useful marketing tools, prompting many to call for more stringent environmental regulations. The readings and images in this unit invite you to enter these controversies as you explore the questions, Who should take responsibility for the effects of climate change? What sources of energy and which environmental practices appear to be the most sustainable?

Our Gas Guzzlers, Their Lives

NICHOLAS KRISTOF

Nicholas D. Kristof is a two-time Pulitzer Prize-winning journalist who writes regular columns for the New York Times *and who is known for his eloquence about human suffering in third-world countries. Kristof, a world traveler and reporter, authored, along with with his wife Sheryl WuDunn, also a journalist,* China Wakes: the Struggle for the Soul of a Rising Power *(1994) and* Thunder from the East: Portrait of a Rising Asia *(2000). Each year he takes a student and a teacher who win an essay contest on a reporting trip. In this op-ed piece, written during the 2007 trip, Kristof employs his knowledge of Africa and world economics to build a case for greater environmental responsibility on the part of wealthy countries.*

BUJUMBURA, Burundi—If we need any more proof that life is unfair, it is that subsistence villagers here in Africa will pay with their lives for our refusal to curb greenhouse gas emissions.

When we think of climate change, we tend to focus on Alaskan villages or New Orleans hurricanes. But the people who will suffer the worst will be those living in countries like this, even though they don't contribute at all to global warming.

My win-a-trip journey with a student and a teacher has taken us to Burundi, which the World Bank's latest report shows to be the poorest country in the world. People in Burundi have an annual average income of $100, nearly one child in five dies before the age of five, and life expectancy is 45.

Against that grim backdrop, changing weather patterns in recent years have already caused crop failures—and when the crops fail here, people starve. In short, our greenhouse gases are killing people here.

5 "If the harvest fails in the West, then you have stocks and can get by," said Gerard Rusuku, an agriculture scientist here who has been studying the impact of global warming in Africa. "Here, we're much more vulnerable. If climate change causes a crop failure here, there's famine."

Guillaume Foliot of the World Food Program notes that farmers here overwhelmingly agree that the weather has already become more erratic, leading to lost crops. And any visitor can see that something is amiss: Africa's "great lakes" are shrinking.

Burundi is on Lake Tanganyika, which is still a vast expanse of water. But the shoreline has retreated 50 feet in the last four years, and ships can no longer reach the port.

"Even the hippos are unhappy," said Alexander Mbarubukeye, a fisherman on the lake, referring to the hippos that occasionally waddled into town before the lake retreated.

The biggest of Africa's great lakes, Lake Victoria, was dropping by a vertical half-inch a day for much of last year. And far to the north, once enormous Lake Chad has nearly vanished. The reasons for the dipping lake levels seem to include climate change.

10 Greenhouse gases actually have the greatest impact at high latitudes—the Arctic and Antarctica. But the impact there isn't all bad (Canada will gain a northwest passage), and the countries there are rich enough to absorb the shocks.

In contrast, the Intergovernmental Panel on Climate Change warned this year that the consequences for Africa will be particularly harsh because of the region's poverty and vulnerability. It foresees water shortages and crop failures in much of Africa.

"Projected reductions in yield in some countries could be as much as 50 percent by 2020, and crop net revenues could fall as much as 90 percent," the panel warned. It also cautioned that warming temperatures could lead malaria to spread to highland areas. Another concern is that scarcities of food and water will trigger wars. More than five million lives have already been lost since 1994 in wars in Rwanda, Burundi and Congo, and one factor was competition for scarce resources.

"It seems to me rather like pouring petrol onto a burning fire," Jock Stirrup, the chief of the British defense staff, told a meeting in London this month. He noted that climate change could cause weak states to collapse.

Yoweri Museveni, Uganda's president, describes climate change as "the latest form of aggression" by rich countries against Africa. He has a point. Charles Ehrhart, a Care staff member in Kenya who works full time on climate-change issues, says that the negative impact of the West's carbon emissions will overwhelm the positive effects of aid.

15   "It's at the least disastrous and quite possibly catastrophic," Mr. Ehrhart said of the climate effects on Africa. "Life was difficult, but with climate change it turns deadly."

"That's what hits the alarm bells for an organization like Care," he added. "How can we ever achieve our mission in this situation?"

All this makes it utterly reckless that we fail to institute a carbon tax or at least a cap-and-trade system for emissions. The cost of our environmental irresponsibility will be measured in thousands of children dying of hunger, malaria and war.

Carbon-Neutral Is Hip, but Is It Green?

ANDREW C. REVKIN

Andrew C. Revkin has authored three books about environmental issues: The Burning Season *(1990) about an Amazon rain forest activist who was killed;* Global Warming: Understanding the Forecast *(1992); and most recently,* The North Pole Was Here: Puzzles and Perils at the Top of the World *(2006). An environmental reporter for the* New York Times, *Revkin has won the American Association for the Advancement of Science Journalism Award, and he holds degrees in biology and journalism. This exploratory piece, which was first published in the* New York Times *on April 29, 2007, questions the effectiveness of carbon-neutral practices. The carbon-neutral movement seeks to cut the carbon emissions of individuals and businesses largely by encouraging activities and purchases that in some way cancel out the negative effects of burning carbons: for example, buying and planting trees to counter the emissions caused by flying in jets or driving cars.*

In addition to the celebrities—Leo, Brad, George—politicians like John Edwards and Hillary Clinton are now running, at least part of the time, carbon-neutral campaigns. A lengthening list of big businesses—international banks, London's taxi fleet, luxury airlines—also claim "carbon neutrality." Silverjet, a plush new trans-Atlantic carrier, bills itself as the first fully carbon-neutral airline. It puts about $28 of each round-trip ticket into a fund for global projects that, in theory, squelch as much carbon dioxide as the airline generates—about 1.2 tons per passenger, the airline says.

Also, a largely unregulated carbon-cutting business has sprung up. In this market, consultants or companies estimate a person's or

company's output of greenhouse gases. Then, these businesses sell "offsets," which pay for projects elsewhere that void or sop up an equal amount of emissions—say, by planting trees or, as one new company proposes, fertilizing the ocean so algae can pull the gas out of the air. Recent counts by *Business Week* magazine and several environmental watchdog groups tally the trade in offsets at more than $100 million a year and growing blazingly fast.

But is the carbon-neutral movement just a gimmick?

On this, environmentalists aren't neutral, and they don't agree. Some believe it helps build support, but others argue that these purchases don't accomplish anything meaningful—other than giving someone a slightly better feeling (or greener reputation) after buying a 6,000-square-foot house or passing the million-mile mark in a frequent-flier program. In fact, to many environmentalists, the carbon-neutral campaign is a sign of the times—easy on the sacrifice and big on the consumerism.

5   As long as the use of fossil fuels keeps climbing—which is happening relentlessly around the world—the emission of greenhouse gases will keep rising. The average American, by several estimates, generates more than 20 tons of carbon dioxide or related gases a year; the average resident of the planet about 4.5 tons.

At this rate, environmentalists say, buying someone else's squelched emissions is all but insignificant.

"The worst of the carbon-offset programs resemble the Catholic Church's sale of indulgences back before the Reformation," said Denis Hayes, the president of the Bullitt Foundation, an environmental grant-making group. "Instead of reducing their carbon footprints, people take private jets and stretch limos, and then think they can buy an indulgence to forgive their sins."

"This whole game is badly in need of a modern Martin Luther," Mr. Hayes added.

Some environmental campaigners defend this marketplace as a legitimate, if imperfect, way to support an environmental ethic and political movement, even if the numbers don't all add up.

10 "We can't stop global warming with voluntary offsets, but they offer an option for individuals looking for a way to contribute to the solution in addition to reducing their own emissions and urging their elected representatives to support good policy," said Daniel A. Lashof, the science director of the climate center at the Natural Resources Defense Council.

But he and others agree that more oversight is needed. Voluntary standards and codes of conduct are evolving in Europe and the United States to ensure that a ton of carbon dioxide purchased is actually a ton of carbon dioxide avoided.

The first attempt at an industry report card, commissioned by the environmental group Clean Air/Cool Planet (which has some involvement in the business), gave decidedly mixed reviews to the field, selecting eight sellers of carbon offsets that it concluded were reasonably reliable.

But the report, "A Consumer's Guide to Retail Carbon-Offset Providers," concluded that this market was no different than any other, saying, "if something sounds too good to be true, it probably is."

Prices vary widely for offsetting the carbon dioxide tonnage released by a long plane flight, S.U.V. commute or energy-hungry house. The report suggested that the cheapest offsets may not be legitimate.

15 For example, depending on where you shop for carbon credits, avoiding the ton of carbon dioxide released by driving a midsize car about 2,000 miles could cost $5 or $25, according to data in the report.

Mr. Hayes said there were legitimate companies and organizations that help people and companies measure their emissions and find ways to cut them, both directly and indirectly by purchasing certain kinds of credits. But overall, he said, an investment in such credits—given the questions about their reliability—should be looked at more as conventional charity (presuming you check to be sure the projects are real) and less as something like a license to binge on private jet travel.

Better Energy

GWYNETH CRAVENS

Gwyneth Cravens is the author of the recently published Power to Save the World: The Truth About Nuclear Energy. *In addition to writing opinion pieces for many publications, Cravens has published five novels. In this article, published in* Discover *in May 2008, Cravens makes a case for environmentally sound nuclear energy.*

Four years ago this month, James Lovelock upset a lot of his fans. Lovelock was revered in the green movement for developing the Gaia hypothesis, which links everything on earth to a dynamic, organic whole. Writing in the British newspaper *The Independent*, Lovelock stated in an op-ed: "We have no time to experiment with visionary energy sources; civilization is in imminent danger and has to use nuclear—the one safe, available energy source—now or suffer the pain soon to be inflicted by our outraged planet."

Lovelock explained that his decision to endorse nuclear power was motivated by his fear of the consequences of global warming and by reports of increasing fossil-fuel emissions that drive the warming. Jesse Ausubel, head of the Program for the Human Environment at Rockefeller University, recently echoed Lovelock's sentiment. "As a green, I care intensely about land-sparing, about leaving land for nature," he wrote. "To reach the scale at which they would contribute importantly to meeting global energy demand, renewable sources of energy such as wind, water, and biomass cause serious environmental harm. Measuring renewables in watts per square meter, nuclear has astronomical advantages over its competitors." All of this has led several other prominent environmentalists to publicly favor new nuclear plants. I had a similar change of heart. For years I opposed nuclear power, but while I was researching my book *Power to Save the World: The Truth About Nuclear Energy*, my views completely turned around.

According to the Department of Energy, just to maintain nuclear's 20 percent share of the energy supply, the United States would need to add three or four new nuclear power plants a year starting in 2015. (There are 104 nuclear power plants currently in operation in the United States.) But no new nuclear power plants have been built here in 30 years, partly because of the public's aversion to nuclear power after the Three Mile Island accident in 1979 and the Chernobyl disaster in 1986. Now NRG Energy, based in Princeton, New Jersey, is sticking its neck out with plans to build two new nuclear reactors at the South Texas Project facility near Bay City. The new reactors will be able to steadily generate a total of 2,700 megawatts—enough to light up 2 million households.

The United States alone pumped the equivalent of nearly 7 billion tons of carbon dioxide into the atmosphere in 2005. More than 2 billion tons of that came from electricity generation—not surprising, considering that we burn fossil fuels for 70 percent of our electricity. About half of all our electricity comes from more than 500 coal-fired plants. Besides contributing to global warming, their pollution has a serious health impact. Burning coal releases fine particulates that kill 24,000 Americans annually and cause hundreds of thousands of cases of lung and heart problems.

5   America's electricity demand is expected to increase by almost 50 percent by 2030, according to the Department of Energy. Unfortunately, renewable energy sources, such as the wind and sun, are highly unlikely to meet that need. Wind and solar installations today supply less than 1 percent of electricity in the United States, do so intermittently, and are decades away from providing more than a small boost to the electric grid. "To meet the 2005 U.S. electricity demand of about 4 million megawatt-hours with around-the-clock wind would have required wind farms covering over 780,000 square kilometers," Ausubel notes. For context, 780,000 square kilometers (301,000 square miles) is greater than the area of Texas. Solar power fares badly too, in Ausubel's analysis: "The amount of energy generated in [one quart] of the core of a nuclear reactor requires [2.5 acres] of solar cells." Geothermal power also is decades away from making a significant contribution to America's electricity budget.

"Nuclear has the power to move the needle in the fight against global warming," says NRG's president and CEO, David Crane. "While the up-front costs of building new nuclear generation are not cheap, in the long run it's one of the most economical ways to make electricity." NRG is already the target of vocal opposition. National environmental groups, and some in Texas like the Sierra Club and Public Citizen, do not want new electrical demand met by nuclear power. "We're all very much in opposition," says Karen Hadden, director of the Sustainable Energy and Economic Development Coalition, which has rallied other groups to the battle. "We'll fight the reactors." She, like other opponents, insists that nuclear power is unsafe and costly and diverts dollars from conservation, energy efficiency, wind, solar, and energy-storage technologies.

Public concerns about nuclear power have traditionally centered on two issues: the risk of widespread radioactive fallout from an accident and the hazards of nuclear waste. (Since 9/11, security risk has emerged as a third major worry.) My research shows such fears are unfounded. A Chernobyl cannot happen here—a survey by the Nuclear Regulatory Commission (NRC) established that our reactors are free of the design flaws that permitted Chernobyl to explode, and in the United States a typical reactor core is surrounded by multiple enclosures to block the escape of radioactive material even in the event of an accident. Chernobyl had no such containment.

Our worst commercial reactor accident, at Three Mile Island 2, was said to be successfully contained despite a partial meltdown, according to the NRC's investigation. A minute quantity of radioactive gas was intentionally vented from the reactor building, but several independent, peer-reviewed studies have not ascertained any health effects attributable to exposure. Since then, U.S. regulations have instituted many additional safety measures. The reactors that will be used by NRG in the South Texas Project are of a type dubbed the Advanced Boiling Water Reactor, the latest iteration of a thoroughly vetted design that has been safely used for a decades, the light water reactor. These reactors have the intriguing feature that the water used to cool the core and run the generating turbine is also essential to maintaining a nuclear chain reaction. Briefly, fissioning atoms in the nuclear reactor's fuel emit neutrons that are traveling too fast to efficiently cause other atoms to fission. The water slows the neutrons, allowing the chain reaction to continue at a steady pace. In case of an accident, multiple systems would keep cooling water flowing to the core, and control rods would quickly drop, automatically shutting down the nuclear reactions.

What about the waste? Uranium is an extremely dense source of energy, and the volume of waste is therefore small. According to David Bradish, a data analyst at the Nuclear Energy Institute, a nuclear fuel pellet measures 0.07 cubic inch (about the size of your fingertip) and contains the energy equivalent of 1,780 pounds of coal. The nation's 104 reactors generate roughly 800 billion kilowatt-hours a year and contribute about 2,000 tons of spent nuclear fuel a year. By contrast, U.S. coal combustion produces some 100 million tons of toxic material annually.

10   At nuclear plants, spent fuel is currently being transferred from pools to robust concrete casks, where it can be secured for about a century. But this spent fuel, which retains more than 95 percent of its energy, can be reprocessed to make new fuel, reducing the ultimate volume of waste by more than 60 percent. The National Academy of Sciences has given the nod to long-term disposal of spent fuel in canisters that will be sealed deep inside a mountain near the vast, remote Nevada Test Site, where hundreds of atomic bombs were once exploded.

NRG is currently waiting for a go-ahead from the NRC to construct and operate its new pair of reactors, scheduled to come online in 2014 and 2015. Several other companies are now lining up to submit their own new reactor plans. NRG's approval is expected no sooner than 2011, but should it come, it could signal the start of a nuclear renaissance and of substantial reductions in America's carbon footprint.

Save the Planet, Let Someone Else Drill

CHARLES KRAUTHAMMER

A well-known psychiatrist in his earlier life, Charles Krauthammer has become a Pulitzer Prize-winning columnist who writes for the Washington Post, Time *magazine, and* The New Republic. *He is known as a conservative policy analyst whose articulate commentaries influence national affairs, from foreign policy as to bioethics. His columns are widely reprinted in U.S. newspapers and around the world. In this op-ed piece, which appeared in the* Washington Post *on August 1, 2008, Krauthammer contends that opening up the Arctic National Wildlife Refuge in northern Alaska for oil drilling is more environmentally sustainable than using oil produced in foreign countries.*

WASHINGTON—House Speaker Nancy Pelosi opposes lifting the moratorium on drilling in the Arctic National Wildlife Refuge and on the Outer Continental Shelf. She won't even allow it to come to a vote.

With $4 gas having massively shifted public opinion in favor of domestic production, she wants to protect her Democratic members from having to cast an anti-drilling election-year vote. Moreover, given the public mood, she might even lose. This cannot be permitted. Why? Because as she explained to Politico: "I'm trying to save the planet; I'm trying to save the planet."

A lovely sentiment. But has Pelosi actually thought through the moratorium's actual effects on the planet?

Consider: 25 years ago, nearly 60 percent of U.S. petroleum was produced domestically. Today it's 25 percent. From its peak in 1970, U.S. production has declined a staggering 47 percent. The world consumes 86 million barrels a day; the United States, roughly 20 million. We need the stuff to run our cars and planes and economy. Where does it come from?

5 Places like Nigeria, where chronic corruption, environmental neglect and resulting unrest and instability lead to pipeline explosions, oil spills and illegal siphoning by the poverty-stricken population—which leads to more spills and explosions. Just last week, two Royal Dutch Shell pipelines had to be shut down because bombings by local militants were causing leaks into the ground.

Compare the Niger Delta to the Gulf of Mexico, where deep-sea U.S. oil rigs withstood Hurricanes Katrina and Rita without a single undersea well suffering a significant spill.

The United States has the highest technology to ensure the safest drilling. Today, directional drilling—essentially drilling down, then sideways—allows access to oil that in 1970 would have required a surface footprint more than three times as large. Additionally, the U.S. has one of the most extensive and least corrupt regulatory systems on the planet.

Does Pelosi imagine that with so much of America declared off-limits, the planet is less injured as drilling shifts to Kazakhstan and Venezuela and Equatorial Guinea? That Russia will be more environmentally scrupulous than we in drilling in *its* Arctic?

The net environmental effect of Pelosi's no-drilling willfulness is *negative*. Outsourcing U.S. oil production does nothing to lessen worldwide environmental despoliation. It simply exports it to more corrupt, less efficient, more unstable parts of the world—thereby increasing net planetary damage.

10 Democrats want no oil from the American OCS or ANWR. But of course they do want more oil. From OPEC. From where Americans don't vote. From places Democratic legislators can't see.

On May 13, Sen. Chuck Schumer—deeply committed to saving just those pieces of the planet that might have huge reserves of American oil—demanded that the Saudis increase production by a million barrels a day. It doesn't occur to him that by eschewing the slightest disturbance of the mating habits of the Arctic caribou, he is calling for the further exploitation of the pristine deserts of Arabia. In the name of the planet, mind you.

The other panacea, yesterday's rage, is biofuels: We can't drill our way out of the crisis, it seems, but we can greenly grow our way out. By now, however, it is blindingly obvious even to Democrats that biofuels are a devastating force for environmental degradation. It has led to the rape of "lungs of the world" rainforests in Indonesia and Brazil as huge tracts have been destroyed to make room for palm oil and sugar plantations.

Here in the U.S., one out of every three ears of corn is stuffed into a gas tank (by way of ethanol), causing not just food shortages abroad and high prices at home, but intensive increases in farming with all of the attendant environmental problems (soil erosion, insecticide pollution, water consumption, etc.).

This to prevent drilling on an area in the Arctic one-sixth the size of Dulles Airport that leaves untouched a refuge one-third the size of Britain.

15 There are a dizzying number of economic and national-security arguments for drilling at home: a $700 billion oil balance-of-payment deficit, a gas tax (equivalent) levied on the paychecks of American workers and poured into the treasuries of enemy and terror-supporting

regimes, growing dependence on unstable states of the Persian Gulf and Caspian basin. Pelosi and the Democrats stand athwart

shouting: We don't care. We come to save the planet!

They seem blissfully unaware that the argument for their

drill-there-not-here policy collapses on its own environmental terms.

Fuel for Thought: All Biofuels Are Not Created Equal

DAVID TILMAN AND JASON HILL

David Tillman is Regents Professor and McKnight Presidential Professor of Ecology at the University of Minnesota. In his academic biographical sketch, Tillman describes his interest in "the benefits that society receives from natural and managed ecosystems, and in the ways to assure environmental and social sustainability in the face of global increases in human consumption and population." He has written numerous scholarly articles and books on resource and plant competition and on biofuels. At the same university, Jason Hill works as a research associate in the Department of Applied Economics. This editorial, which was published in the Seattle Times *on April 15, 2007, shows Tillman and Hill in the role of public intellectuals, translating their research into understandable terms for general readers.*

The world has come full circle. A century ago our first transportation biofuels—the hay and oats fed to our horses—were replaced by gasoline. Today, ethanol from corn and biodiesel from soybeans have begun edging out gasoline and diesel.

This has been hailed as an overwhelmingly positive development that will help us reduce the threat of climate change and ease our dependence on foreign oil. In political circles, ethanol is the flavor of the day, and presidential candidates have been cycling through Iowa extolling its benefits. Lost in the ethanol-induced euphoria, however, is the fact that three of our most fundamental needs—food, energy, and a livable

and sustainable environment—are now in direct conflict. Moreover, our recent analyses of the full costs and benefits of various biofuels, performed at the University of Minnesota, present a markedly different and more nuanced picture than has been heard on the campaign trail.

Some biofuels, if properly produced, do have the potential to provide climate-friendly energy, but where and how can we grow them? Our most fertile lands are already dedicated to food production. As demand for both food and energy increases, competition for fertile lands could raise food prices enough to drive the poorer third of the globe into malnourishment. The destruction of

rainforests and other ecosystems to make new farmland would threaten the continued existence of countless animal and plant species and would increase the amount of climate-changing carbon dioxide in the atmosphere.

Finding and implementing solutions to the food, fuel and environment conflict is one of the greatest challenges facing humanity. But solutions will be neither adopted nor sought until we understand the interlinked problems we face.

5   Fossil-fuel use has pushed atmospheric carbon dioxide higher than at any time during the past half-million years. The global population has increased threefold in the past century and will

increase by half again, to 9 billion people, by 2050. Global food and fossil energy consumption are on trajectories to double by 2050.

Biofuels, such as ethanol made from corn, have the potential to provide us with cleaner energy. But because of how corn ethanol currently is made, only about 20 percent of each gallon is "new" energy. That is because it takes a lot of "old" fossil energy to make it: diesel to run tractors, natural gas to make fertilizer and, of course, fuel to run the refineries that convert corn to ethanol.

For this reason, if every one of the 70 million acres on which corn was grown in 2006 was used for ethanol, the amount produced would displace only 12 percent of the U.S. gasoline market. Moreover, the "new" (non-fossil) energy gained would be very small—just 2.4 percent of the market. Car tune-ups and proper tire air pressure would save more energy.

There is another problem with relying on a food-based biofuel, such as corn ethanol, as the poor of Mexico can attest. In recent months, soaring corn prices, sparked by demand from ethanol plants, have doubled the price of tortillas, a staple food. Tens of thousands of Mexico City's poor recently protested this "ethanol tax" in the streets.

In the United States, the protests have also begun—in Congress. Representatives of the dairy, poultry and livestock industries, which rely on corn as a principal animal feed, are seeking an end to subsidies for corn ethanol in the hope of stabilizing corn prices. (It takes about three pounds of corn to produce a pound of chicken, and seven or eight pounds to grow a pound of beef.) Profit margins are being squeezed, and meat prices are rising.

U.S. soybeans, which are used to make biodiesel, may be about to follow corn's trajectory, escalating the food-vs.-fuel conflict. The National Biodiesel Board recently reported that 77 biodiesel production plants are under construction and that eight established plants are expanding capacity.

In terms of environmental impact, all biofuels are not created equal. Ethanol is the same chemical product no matter what its source. But ethanol made from prairie grasses, from corn grown in Illinois and from sugar cane grown on newly cleared land in Brazil have radically different impacts on greenhouse gases.

Corn, like all plants, is a natural part of the global carbon cycle. The growing crop absorbs carbon dioxide from the atmosphere, so burning corn ethanol does not directly create any additional carbon. But that is only part of the story. All of the fossil fuels used to grow corn and change it into ethanol release new carbon dioxide and other greenhouse gases. The net effect is that ethanol from corn grown in the Corn Belt does increase atmospheric greenhouse gases, and this increase is only about 15 percent less than the increase caused by an equivalent amount of gasoline. Soybean biodiesel does better, causing a greenhouse-gas increase that is about 40 percent less than that from petroleum diesel.

In Brazil, Sugar Cane

In Brazil, ethanol made from sugar cane produces about twice as much ethanol per acre as corn. Brazilian ethanol refineries get their power from burning cane residue, in effect recycling carbon from the atmosphere. The environmental benefit is large. Sugar-cane ethanol grown on established soils releases 80 percent less greenhouse gases than gasoline.

But that isn't the case for sugar-cane ethanol or soybean biodiesel from Brazil's newly cleared lands, including tropical forests and savannas. Clearing land releases immense amounts of greenhouse gases into the air, because much of the material in the plants and soil is broken down into carbon dioxide.

Plants and soil contain three times more carbon than the atmosphere. The trees and soil of an acre of rainforest—which, once cleared, is suitable for growing soybeans—contain about 120 tons of organic carbon. An acre of tropical woodland or savanna, suitable for sugar cane, contains about half this amount. About a fourth of the carbon in an ecosystem is released to the atmosphere as carbon dioxide when trees are clear-cut, brush and branches are burned or rot, and roots decay. Even more is lost during the first 20 to 50 years of farming, as soil carbon decomposes into carbon dioxide and as wood products are burned or decay.

This means that when tropical woodland is cleared to produce sugar cane for ethanol, the greenhouse gas released is about 50 percent greater than what occurs from the production and use of the same amount of gasoline. And that statistic holds for at least two decades.

Simply being "renewable" does not automatically make a fuel better for the atmosphere than the fossil fuel it replaces, nor guarantee that society gains any new energy by its production. The European Union was recently shocked to learn that some of its imported biodiesel, derived from palm trees planted on rain-forest lands, was more than twice as bad for climate warming as petroleum diesel. So much for the "benefits" of that form of biodiesel.

Although current Brazilian ethanol is environmentally friendly, the long-term environmental implications of buying more ethanol and biodiesel from Brazil, a possibility raised recently during President Bush's trip to that country, are cloudy. It could be harmful to both the climate and the preservation of tropical plant and animal species if it involved, directly or indirectly, additional clearing of native ecosystems.

Concerns about the environmental effects of ethanol production are starting to be felt in the United States as well. It appears that American farmers may add 10 million acres of corn this year to meet booming demand for ethanol. Some of this land could come from millions of acres now set aside nationwide for conservation under a government-subsidized program. Those uncultivated acres absorb atmospheric carbon, so farming them and converting the corn into ethanol could release more carbon dioxide into the air than would burning gasoline.

Alternative Crops

There are biofuel crops that can be grown with much less energy and chemicals than the food crops we currently use for biofuels. And they can be grown on our less fertile land, especially land that has been degraded by farming. This would decrease competition between food and biofuel. The United States has about 60 million acres of such land—in the Conservation Reserve Program, road edge rights-of-way and abandoned farmlands.

In a 10-year experiment reported in Science magazine in December, we explored how much bioenergy could be produced by 18 different native prairie plant species grown on highly degraded and infertile soil. We planted 172 plots in central Minnesota with various combinations of these species, randomly chosen. We found, on this highly degraded land, that the plots planted with mixtures of many native prairie perennial species yielded 238 percent more bioenergy than those planted with single species. High plant diversity led to high productivity, and little fertilizer or chemical weed or pest killer was required.

The prairie "hay" harvested from these plots can be used to create high-value energy sources. For instance, it can be mixed with coal and burned for electricity generation. It can be "gasified," then chemically combined to make ethanol or synthetic gasoline. Or it can be burned in a turbine engine to make electricity. A technique that is undergoing rapid development involves bioengineering enzymes that digest parts of plants (the cellulose) into sugars that are then fermented into ethanol.

Whether converted into electricity, ethanol or synthetic gasoline, the high-diversity hay from infertile land produced as much or more new usable energy per acre as did fertile land planted with corn for ethanol. And it could be harvested year after year.

Even more surprising were the greenhouse-gas benefits. When high-diversity mixtures of native plants are grown on degraded soils, they remove carbon dioxide from the air. Much of this carbon ends up stored in the soil. In essence, mixtures of native plants gradually restore the carbon levels that degraded soils had before being cleared and farmed. This benefit lasts for about a century.

25 Across the full process of growing high-diversity prairie hay, converting it into an energy source and using that energy, we found a net removal and storage of about a ton and a half of atmospheric carbon dioxide per acre. The net effect is that ethanol or synthetic gasoline produced from high-diversity prairie hay grown on degraded land can provide energy that actually reduces atmospheric levels of carbon dioxide.

Carbon-Negative Biofuels

When one of these carbon-negative biofuels is mixed with gasoline, the resulting blend releases less carbon dioxide than traditional gasoline.

Biofuels, if used properly, can help us balance our need for food, energy and a habitable and sustainable environment. To help this happen, though, we need a national biofuels policy that favors our best options. We must determine the carbon impacts of each method of making these fuels, then mandate fuel blending that achieves a prescribed greenhouse-gas reduction. We have the knowledge and technology to start solving these problems.

Two Ways to Show You Care about Our Forests

SUSTAINABLE FORESTRY INITIATIVE

Sustainable Forestry Initiative is a program designed to ensure that forests are managed so they are not depleted. Founded in 1994 by members of the American Forest and Paper Association, the program became independent in 2007. This advocacy ad appeared in newspapers in 2007.

Two ways to show you care about our forests.

Ever since the recycling symbol appeared, more and more paper products have been recycled. Today, there's another symbol to look for when you shop for wood and paper products: the symbol of the Sustainable Forestry Initiative.® The SFI® symbol on a product means it has wood or paper content from well-managed forests certified to the SFI Standard. To find SFI-certified products, visit *www.sfiprogram.org*.

SUSTAINABLE FORESTRY INITIATIVE
Good for you. Good for our forests.™

Time to Recycle Recycling?

IAIN MURRAY

Iain Murray is the Director of Projects and Analysis and Senior Fellow in Energy, Science and Technology at the Competitive Enterprise Institute, a libertarian think tank known for its advocacy as well as its research, and committed to the philosophy that "individuals are best helped not by government intervention, but by making their own choices in a free marketplace." A conservative media commentator, Murray frequently writes about scientific issues and global warming for The New York Post, *the* Financial Times, *and the* Wall Street Journal, *among other newspapers. This editorial was published in the* Washington Times *on June 16, 2008 and posted on the CEI Web site.*

One of the curious things about global warming alarmism is that so many of the other features of traditional environmentalism are actually at odds with it. Nuclear power is perhaps the best source of low carbon electricity. Genetically modified organisms can dramatically lower the energy needed to grow crops. And in fact, striking at the base of institutionalized environmentalism, it appears recycling can produce more carbon than new manufacture.

Let's face it, there is probably no more widespread example of what some people have termed "everyday environmentalism" than recycling. Many of us do it as a matter of course because the recycling company comes round at the same time as the garbage truck. Or we have "green" receptacles in our offices for the paper that seems to abound in our "paperless" offices. It is also pushed as a solution for global warming.

For instance, one environmental organization's Web site lists four steps to lowering one's carbon emissions (note: descriptions are shortened slightly from full Web site text):

1. Reduce every form of energy use that derives ultimately from fossil fuel.
2. Reuse as much of every product as possible.
3. Recycle all paper, cardboard and wood products.
4. Purchase personal carbon offsets.

If only it was that simple.

What this group, Al Gore and many other environmentalists may not appreciate is that recycling paper is actually a carbon positive process. Fossil fuels are required to de-ink recovered paper and sanitize paper headed for close consumer use. Compare this to virgin trees—which produce no net carbon provided a new tree is planted to replace each one that is harvested, as is generally the case.

5   Contrary to received wisdom, paper is one of the least recyclable materials in circulation. Each time paper is recycled, it loses part of its physical construction. Structure is crucial to paper's performance—lose it, and performance plummets.

Paper is often recycled far more than once. According to a study for the Corporate Forum on Paper and the Environment, the first time paper is recycled, it retains about 85 percent of its strength. By the time it is recycled the sixth time, that drops to 38 percent. Yet each time, it is using the same energy and emitting more and more carbon for the value you get from it.

This makes very little sense from an environmental point of view. In fact, recycling of the type that is so common—the curbside pick-up, the "green bins"—can be counterproductive.

As my colleague Angela Logomasini wrote in the *Wall Street Journal* on March 18, 2002: "Isn't recycling supposed to save money and resources? Some recycling does—when driven by market forces. Private parties don't voluntarily recycle unless they know it will save money, and, hence, resources. But forced recycling can be a waste of both because recycling itself entails using energy, water and labor to collect, sort, clean and process the materials. There are also air emissions, traffic and wear on streets from the second set of trucks prowling for recyclables. The bottom line is that most mandated recycling hurts, not helps, the environment."

At this point someone will probably accuse me of being against all recycling and compare me—unfavorably—to Lord Voldemort. As it happens, I'm not against recycling, just against recycling that doesn't make sense. It should even be possible to achieve an economically sensible form of carbon "Zendom" by eliminating the most intensive processes. Recovered paper actually makes sense for things like packaging (i.e., corrugated cardboard in shipping boxes), but not so much in expensive consumer products like seventh-generation bath tissue.

10   This is unlikely to be attractive to environmentalists, for whom recycling is a sacred cow, despite the evidence.

There is another option, of course, and it lies in the fourth recommendation repeated above. Perhaps the recycling companies could sell carbon offsets with their inefficient, energy-intensive, expensive products. When the gas-guzzling recycling trucks come round in the morning, we could buy an offset each time for that. And every time we drop an unread memo in the recycling box at work, we could have our wages garnished by the Environmental Protection Agency. I would prefer to just buy the economically efficient, low-cost paper. But, trust me, someone will think this is a good idea.

Nobel Lecture

AL GORE

The final reading in this unit is Al Gore's Nobel Peace Prize acceptance speech delivered on December 10, 2007, in Oslo, Norway. Along with the U.N. Intergovernmental Panel on Climate Change, Gore, a former U.S. representative, senator, and vice-president, won this prize for his work raising awareness of and combating global warming. His film, An Inconvenient Truth, *which won the 2007 Academy Award for best documentary, warns of humans' contribution to climate change. Gore has authored three books seeking to galvanize individual, corporate, and government action:* Earth in the Balance: Ecology and the Human Spirit *(2000);* An Inconvenient Truth: The Planetary Emergency of Global Warming and What We Can Do about It *(2006); and* The Assault on Reason *(2007).*

Your Majesties, Your Royal Highnesses, Honorable members of the Norwegian Nobel Committee, Excellencies, Ladies and gentlemen.

I have a purpose here today. It is a purpose I have tried to serve for many years. I have prayed that God would show me a way to accomplish it.

Sometimes, without warning, the future knocks on our door with a precious and painful vision of what might be. One hundred and nineteen years ago, a wealthy inventor read his own obituary, mistakenly published years before his death. Wrongly believing the inventor had just died, a newspaper printed a harsh judgment of his life's work, unfairly labeling him "The Merchant of Death" because of his invention—dynamite. Shaken by this condemnation, the inventor made a fateful choice to serve the cause of peace.

Seven years later, Alfred Nobel created this prize and the others that bear his name.

5   Seven years ago tomorrow, I read my own political obituary in a judgment that seemed to me harsh and mistaken—if not premature. But that unwelcome verdict also brought a precious if painful gift: an opportunity to search for fresh new ways to serve my purpose.

Unexpectedly, that quest has brought me here. Even though I fear my words cannot match this moment, I pray what I am feeling in my heart will be communicated clearly enough that those who hear me will say, "We must act."

The distinguished scientists with whom it is the greatest honor of my life to share this award have laid before us a choice between two different futures—a choice that to my ears echoes the words of an ancient prophet: "Life or death, blessings or curses. Therefore, choose life, that both thou and thy seed may live."

We, the human species, are confronting a planetary emergency—a threat to the survival of our civilization that is gathering ominous and destructive potential even as we gather here. But there is hopeful news as well: we have the ability to solve this crisis and avoid the worst—though not all—of its consequences, if we act boldly, decisively and quickly.

However, despite a growing number of honorable exceptions, too many of the world's leaders are still best described in the words Winston Churchill applied to those who ignored Adolf Hitler's threat: "They go on in strange paradox, decided only to be undecided, resolved to be irresolute, adamant for drift, solid for fluidity, all powerful to be impotent."

10   So today, we dumped another 70 million tons of global-warming pollution into the thin shell of atmosphere surrounding our planet, as if it were an open sewer. And tomorrow, we will dump a slightly larger amount, with the cumulative concentrations now trapping more and more heat from the sun.

As a result, the earth has a fever. And the fever is rising. The experts have told us it is not a passing affliction that will heal by itself. We asked for a second opinion. And a third. And a fourth. And the consistent conclusion, restated with increasing alarm, is that something basic is wrong.

We are what is wrong, and we must make it right.

Last September 21, as the Northern Hemisphere tilted away from the sun, scientists reported with unprecedented distress that the North Polar ice cap is "falling off a cliff." One study estimated that it could be completely gone during summer in less than 22 years. Another new study, to be presented by U.S. Navy researchers later this week, warns it could happen in as little as 7 years.

Seven years from now.

15   In the last few months, it has been harder and harder to misinterpret the signs that our world is spinning out of kilter. Major cities in North and South America, Asia and Australia are nearly out of water due to massive droughts and melting glaciers. Desperate farmers are losing their livelihoods. Peoples in the frozen Arctic and on low-lying Pacific islands are planning evacuations of places they have long called home. Unprecedented wildfires have forced a half million people from their homes in one country and caused a national emergency that almost brought down the government in another. Climate refugees have migrated into areas already inhabited by people with different cultures, religions, and traditions, increasing the potential for conflict. Stronger storms in the Pacific and Atlantic have threatened whole cities. Millions have been displaced by massive flooding in South Asia, Mexico, and 18 countries in

Africa. As temperature extremes have increased, tens of thousands have lost their lives. We are recklessly burning and clearing our forests and driving more and more species into extinction. The very web of life on which we depend is being ripped and frayed.

We never intended to cause all this destruction, just as Alfred Nobel never intended that dynamite be used for waging war. He had hoped his invention would promote human progress. We shared that same worthy goal when we began burning massive quantities of coal, then oil and methane.

Even in Nobel's time, there were a few warnings of the likely consequences. One of the very first winners of the Prize in chemistry worried that, "We are evaporating our coal mines into the air." After performing 10,000 equations by hand, Svante Arrhenius calculated that the earth's average temperature would increase by many degrees if we doubled the amount of CO_2 in the atmosphere.

Seventy years later, my teacher, Roger Revelle, and his colleague, Dave Keeling, began to precisely document the increasing CO_2 levels day by day.

But unlike most other forms of pollution, CO_2 is invisible, tasteless, and odorless—which has helped keep the truth about what it is doing to our climate out of sight and out of mind. Moreover, the catastrophe now threatening us is unprecedented—and we often confuse the unprecedented with the improbable.

20 We also find it hard to imagine making the massive changes that are now necessary to solve the crisis. And when large truths are genuinely inconvenient, whole societies can, at least for a time, ignore them. Yet as George Orwell reminds us: "Sooner or later a false belief bumps up against solid reality, usually on a battlefield."

In the years since this prize was first awarded, the entire relationship between humankind and the earth has been radically transformed. And still, we have remained largely oblivious to the impact of our cumulative actions.

Indeed, without realizing it, we have begun to wage war on the earth itself. Now, we and the earth's climate are locked in a relationship familiar to war planners: "Mutually assured destruction."

More than two decades ago, scientists calculated that nuclear war could throw so much debris and smoke into the air that it would block life-giving sunlight from our atmosphere, causing a "nuclear winter." Their eloquent warnings here in Oslo helped galvanize the world's resolve to halt the nuclear arms race.

Now science is warning us that if we do not quickly reduce the global warming pollution that is trapping so much of the heat our planet normally radiates back out of the atmosphere, we are in danger of creating a permanent "carbon summer."

25 As the American poet Robert Frost wrote, " Some say the world will end in fire; some say in ice." Either, he notes, "would suffice."

But neither need be our fate. It is time to make peace with the planet.

We must quickly mobilize our civilization with the urgency and resolve that has previously been seen only when nations mobilized for war. These prior struggles for survival were won when leaders found words at the 11th hour that released a mighty surge of courage, hope and readiness to sacrifice for a protracted and mortal challenge.

These were not comforting and misleading assurances that the threat was not real or imminent; that it would affect others but not ourselves; that ordinary life might be lived even in the presence of extraordinary threat; that Providence could be trusted to do for us what we would not do for ourselves.

No, these were calls to come to the defense of the common future. They were calls upon the courage, generosity and strength of entire peoples, citizens of every class and condition who were ready to stand against the threat once asked to do so. Our enemies in those times calculated that free people would not rise to the challenge; they were, of course, catastrophically wrong.

30   Now comes the threat of climate crisis—a threat that is real, rising, imminent, and universal. Once again, it is the 11th hour. The penalties for ignoring this challenge are immense and growing, and at some near point would be unsustainable and unrecoverable. For now we still have the power to choose our fate, and the remaining question is only this: Have we the will to act vigorously and in time, or will we remain imprisoned by a dangerous illusion?

Mahatma Gandhi awakened the largest democracy on earth and forged a shared resolve with what he called "Satyagraha"—or "truth force."

In every land, the truth—once known—has the power to set us free.

Truth also has the power to unite us and bridge the distance between "me" and "we," creating the basis for common effort and shared responsibility.

There is an African proverb that says, "If you want to go quickly, go alone. If you want to go far, go together." We need to go far, quickly.

35   We must abandon the conceit that individual, isolated, private actions are the answer. They can and do help. But they will not take us far enough without collective action. At the same time, we must ensure that in mobilizing globally, we do not invite the establishment of ideological conformity and a new lock-step "ism."

That means adopting principles, values, laws, and treaties that release creativity and initiative at every level of society in multifold responses originating concurrently and spontaneously.

This new consciousness requires expanding the possibilities inherent in all humanity. The innovators who will devise a new way to harness the sun's energy for pennies or invent an engine that's carbon negative may live in Lagos or Mumbai or Montevideo. We must ensure that entrepreneurs and inventors everywhere on the globe have the chance to change the world.

When we unite for a moral purpose that is manifestly good and true, the spiritual energy unleashed can transform us. The generation that defeated fascism throughout the world in the 1940s found, in rising to meet their awesome challenge, that they had gained the moral authority and long-term vision to launch the Marshall Plan, the United Nations, and a new level of global cooperation and foresight that unified Europe and facilitated the emergence of democracy and prosperity in Germany, Japan, Italy and much of the world. One of their visionary leaders said, "It is time we steered by the stars and not by the lights of every passing ship."

In the last year of that war, you gave the Peace Prize to a man from my hometown of 2000 people, Carthage, Tennessee. Cordell Hull was described by Franklin Roosevelt as the "Father of the United Nations." He was an inspiration and hero to my own father, who followed Hull in the Congress and the U.S. Senate and in his commitment to world peace and global cooperation.

40   My parents spoke often of Hull, always in tones of reverence and admiration. Eight weeks ago, when you announced this prize, the deepest emotion I felt was when I saw the headline

in my hometown paper that simply noted I had won the same prize that Cordell Hull had won. In that moment, I knew what my father and mother would have felt were they alive.

Just as Hull's generation found moral authority in rising to solve the world crisis caused by fascism, so too can we find our greatest opportunity in rising to solve the climate crisis. In the Kanji characters used in both Chinese and Japanese, "crisis" is written with two symbols, the first meaning "danger," the second "opportunity." By facing and removing the danger of the climate crisis, we have the opportunity to gain the moral authority and vision to vastly increase our own capacity to solve other crises that have been too long ignored.

We must understand the connections between the climate crisis and the afflictions of poverty, hunger, HIV-Aids and other pandemics. As these problems are linked, so too must be their solutions. We must begin by making the common rescue of the global environment the central organizing principle of the world community.

Fifteen years ago, I made that case at the "Earth Summit" in Rio de Janeiro. Ten years ago, I presented it in Kyoto. This week, I will urge the delegates in Bali to adopt a bold mandate for a treaty that establishes a universal global cap on emissions and uses the market in emissions trading to efficiently allocate resources to the most effective opportunities for speedy reductions.

This treaty should be ratified and brought into effect everywhere in the world by the beginning of 2010—two years sooner than presently contemplated. The pace of our response must be accelerated to match the accelerating pace of the crisis itself.

45   Heads of state should meet early next year to review what was accomplished in Bali and take personal responsibility for addressing this crisis. It is not unreasonable to ask, given the gravity of our circumstances, that these heads of state meet every three months until the treaty is completed.

We also need a moratorium on the construction of any new generating facility that burns coal without the capacity to safely trap and store carbon dioxide.

And most important of all, we need to put a *price* on carbon—with a CO_2 tax that is then rebated back to the people, progressively, according to the laws of each nation, in ways that shift the burden of taxation from employment to pollution. This is by far the most effective and simplest way to accelerate solutions to this crisis.

The world needs an alliance—especially of those nations that weigh heaviest in the scales where earth is in the balance. I salute Europe and Japan for the steps they've taken in recent years to meet the challenge, and the new government in Australia, which has made solving the climate crisis its first priority.

But the outcome will be decisively influenced by two nations that are now failing to do enough: the United States and China. While India is also growing fast in importance, it should be absolutely clear that it is the two largest CO_2 emitters—most of all, my own country—that will need to make the boldest moves, or stand accountable before history for their failure to act.

50   Both countries should stop using the other's behavior as an excuse for stalemate and instead develop an agenda for mutual survival in a shared global environment.

These are the last few years of decision, but they can be the first years of a bright and hopeful future if we do what we must. No one should believe a solution will be found without effort, without cost, without change. Let us acknowledge that if we wish to redeem squandered time and speak again with moral authority, then these are the hard truths:

The way ahead is difficult. The outer boundary of what we currently believe is feasible is still far short of what we actually must do. Moreover, between here and there, across the unknown, falls the shadow. That is just another way of saying that we have to expand the boundaries of what is possible. In the words of the Spanish poet, Antonio Machado, "Pathwalker, there is no path. You must make the path as you walk."

We are standing at the most fateful fork in that path. So I want to end as I began, with a vision of two futures—each a palpable possibility—and with a prayer that we will see with vivid clarity the necessity of choosing between those two futures, and the urgency of making the right choice now.

The great Norwegian playwright, Henrik Ibsen, wrote, "One of these days, the younger generation will come knocking at my door."

55 The future is knocking at our door right now. Make no mistake, the next generation *will* ask us one of two questions. Either they will ask: "What were you thinking; why didn't you act? "

Or they will ask instead: "How did you find the moral courage to rise and successfully resolve a crisis that so many said was impossible to solve?"

We have everything we need to get started, save perhaps political will, but political will is a renewable resource.

So let us renew it, and say together: "We have a purpose. We are many. For this purpose we will rise, and we will act."

■ ■ ■ **FOR CLASS DISCUSSION** Sustainability and the Search for Clean Energy

1. In this unit, many of the arguments are causal arguments. Working individually or in a group, choose one of the arguments that relies heavily on causal reasoning. Trace the causal chain the writer constructs. How well does the writer support each link in the chain? Where might readers challenge this causal reasoning? What do you see as the most persuasive part of this argument and why?

2. As the readings in this unit illustrate, the problem of cutting down and replacing the use of fossil fuels is complex. Gwyneth Cravens confronts problems with wind and solar power; Andrew Revkin questions the effectiveness of carbon trading; and Tillman and Hill call for a rethinking of biofuel. After reconstructing the main claim and reasons in each argument, discuss what you think each argument contributes to the search for sustainable energy.

3. Charles Krauthammer and Iain Murray, particularly, challenge supposedly beneficial environmental practices. Krauthammer opposes the moratorium on oil drilling in the Arctic National Wildlife Refuge, and Iain Murray attacks the value of recycling. Examine the *logos* of these arguments. What assumptions underlie their arguments? What evidence do they use to support their claim and reasons?

4. The Sustainable Forestry Initiative appeals to consumers to let environmental values guide their buying practices. Where have you seen these two symbols? How meaningful and effective are these symbols? If you were asked to create a poster campaign to raise consciousness about "well managed forests," how would you design this advocacy piece to reach college student consumers?

5. Al Gore's Nobel lecture differs from other arguments in this unit in its purpose, tone, and argument structure. What is Gore's argument in this speech and how are its features tailored to its motivating occasion and genre? Think particularly about Gore's war imagery.

WRITING ASSIGNMENT Rhetorical Analysis or Rogerian Response to an Argument

Option 1: Rhetorical Analysis of an Argument. Write a thesis-driven analysis of one of the arguments in this unit in which you analyze the writer's appeals to *logos*, *ethos*, and *pathos*. Consider how the writer's angle of vision shapes the argument and how persuasive this argument is for a general audience.

Option 2: Rogerian Response to an Argument. Write a Rogerian response addressed to one of the writers of the readings in this unit. Begin your argument by setting up the problem the writer is addressing. Then write an accurate summary of the writer's argument and identify the values you share with the writer to establish common ground. Use the last third to half of your argument to motivate the writer to listen to your view of the problem by pointing out ideas you think the writer should consider in his/her approach to the problem. ∎

> For additional writing, reading, and research resources, go to
> www.mycomplab.com

Biotech Agriculture and the Ethics of Food Production

If you have eaten any processed foods lately, you have probably eaten food from genetically modified crops. Pervaded by much uncertainty, confusion, fear, and optimism, the multiple controversies surrounding genetically modified foods involve numerous stakeholders. Proponents of biotech agriculture point to its potential to increase crop yield, reduce the need for pesticides and herbicides and thereby reduce the impact of these chemicals on the environment, lower production costs, add nutritional content to foods, and grow crops in formerly unsuitable conditions. Skeptics and opponents, however, consider genetically engineered foods highly experimental, even mutant, and object to the unleashing of new genetic material into the environment, to the rapid commercialization of products that may have unforeseen long-term consequences, and to food growers' and producers' lack of accountability to consumers concerning the ingredients of the food they are buying. Finally, lawmakers, policymakers, businesses, scientists, and public interest groups also argue about the driving forces behind the push for biotech foods, about the control of patents, and about international policy.

The arguments in this unit focus primarily on the ethics of biotech foods as they connect to problems of world hunger, the preservation of the environment, the safety of consumers, and the just distribution of knowledge and wealth.

Will Frankenfood Save the Planet?

JONATHAN RAUCH

This influential article arguing for the humanitarian and environmental benefits of biotech agriculture appeared in the Atlantic *in October 2003. Its author, Jonathan Rauch, is a senior writer and columnist for* National Journal *magazine in Washington and a correspondent for the* Atlantic. *He is the author of several books and many articles on public policy, culture, and economics. He is also a visiting scholar at the Brookings Institution, a leading Washington think tank. In 2005 he received the National Magazine Award for columns and commentary. Note that he is not a scientist. This article is based on his own field research conducted by visiting biotech sites and interviewing scientists and agricultural experts.*

That genetic engineering may be the most environmentally beneficial technology to have emerged in decades, or possibly centuries, is not immediately obvious. Certainly, at least, it is not obvious to the many U.S. and foreign environmental groups that regard biotechnology as a bête noire. Nor is it necessarily obvious to people who grew up in cities, and who have only an inkling of what happens on a modern farm. Being agriculturally illiterate myself, I set out to look at what may be, if the planet is fortunate, the farming of the future.

It was baking hot that April day. I traveled with two Virginia state soil-and-water-conservation officers and an agricultural- extension agent to an area not far from Richmond. The farmers there are national (and therefore world) leaders in the application of what is known as continuous no-till farming. In plain English, they don't plough. For thousands of years, since the dawn of the agricultural revolution, farmers have ploughed, often several times a year; and with ploughing has come runoff that pollutes rivers and blights aquatic habitat, erosion that wears away the land, and the release into the atmosphere of greenhouse gases stored in the soil. Today, at last, farmers are working out methods that have begun to make ploughing obsolete.

At about one-thirty we arrived at a 200-acre patch of farmland known as the Good Luck Tract. No one seemed to know the provenance of the name, but the best guess was that somebody had said something like "You intend to farm this? Good luck!" The land was rolling, rather than flat, and its slopes came together to form natural troughs for rainwater. Ordinarily this highly erodible land would be suitable for cows, not crops. Yet it was dense with wheat—wheat yielding almost twice what could normally be expected, and in soil that had grown richer in organic matter, and thus more nourishing to crops, even as the land was farmed. Perhaps most striking was the almost complete absence of any chemical or soil runoff. Even the beating administered in 1999 by Hurricane Floyd, which lashed the ground with nineteen inches of rain in less than twenty-four hours, produced no significant runoff or erosion. The land simply absorbed the sheets of water before they could course downhill.

At another site, a few miles away, I saw why. On land planted in corn whose shoots had only just broken the surface, Paul Davis, the extension agent, wedged a shovel into the ground and dislodged about eight inches of topsoil. Then he reached down and picked up a clump. Ploughed soil, having been stirred up and turned over again and again, becomes lifeless and homogeneous, but the clump that Davis held out was alive. I immediately noticed three squirming earthworms, one grub, and quantities of tiny white insects that looked very busy. As if in greeting, a worm defecated. "Plant-available food!" a delighted Davis exclaimed.

5   This soil, like that of the Good Luck Tract, had not been ploughed for years, allowing the underground ecosystem to return. Insects and roots and microorganisms had given the soil an elaborate architecture, which held the earth in place and made it a sponge for water. That was why erosion and runoff had been reduced to practically nil. Crops thrived because worms were doing the ploughing. Crop residue that was left on the ground, rather than ploughed under as usual, provided nourishment for the soil's biota and, as it decayed, enriched the soil. The farmer saved the fuel he would have used driving back and forth with a heavy plough. That saved money, and of course it also saved energy and reduced pollution. On top of all that, crop yields were better than with conventional methods.

The conservation people in Virginia were full of excitement over no-till farming. Their job was to clean up the James and York Rivers and the rest of the Chesapeake Bay watershed. Most of the sediment that clogs and clouds the rivers, and most of the fertilizer runoff that causes the algae blooms that kill fish, comes from farmland. By all but eliminating agricultural erosion and runoff—so Brian Noyes, the local conservation-district manager, told me—continuous no-till could "revolutionize" the area's water quality.

Even granting that Noyes is an enthusiast, from an environmental point of view no-till farming looks like a dramatic advance. The rub—if it is a rub—is that the widespread elimination of the plough depends on genetically modified crops.

It is only a modest exaggeration to say that as goes agriculture, so goes the planet. Of all the human activities that shape the environment, agriculture is the single most important, and it is well ahead of whatever comes second. Today about 38 percent of the earth's land area is cropland or pasture—a total that has crept upward over the past few decades as global population has grown. The increase has been gradual, only about 0.3 percent a year; but that still translates into an additional Greece or Nicaragua cultivated or grazed every year.

Farming does not go easy on the earth, and never has. To farm is to make war upon millions of plants (weeds, so-called) and animals (pests, so-called) that in the ordinary course of things would crowd out or eat or infest whatever it is a farmer is growing. Crop monocultures, as whole fields of only wheat or corn or any other single plant are called, make poor habitat and are vulnerable to disease and disaster. Although fertilizer runs off and pollutes water, farming without fertilizer will deplete and eventually exhaust the soil. Pesticides can harm the health of human beings and kill desirable or harmless bugs along with pests. Irrigation leaves behind trace elements that can accumulate and poison the soil. And on and on.

10   The trade-offs are fundamental. Organic farming, for example, uses no artificial fertilizer, but it does use a lot of manure, which can pollute water and contaminate food. Traditional farmers may use less herbicide, but they also do more ploughing, with all the ensuing environmental complications. Low-input agriculture uses fewer chemicals but more land. The point is not that farming is an environmental crime—it is not—but that there is no escaping the pressure it puts on the planet.

In the next half century the pressure will intensify. The United Nations, in its midrange projections, estimates that the earth's human population will grow by more than 40 percent, from 6.3 billion people today to 8.9 billion in 2050. Feeding all those people, and feeding their billion or so hungry pets (a dog or a cat is one of the first things people want once they move beyond a subsistence lifestyle), and providing the increasingly protein-rich diets that an increasingly wealthy world will expect—doing all of that will require food output to at least double, and possibly triple.

But then the story will change. According to the UN's midrange projections (which may, if anything, err somewhat on the high side), around 2050 the world's population will more or less level off. Even if the growth does not stop, it will slow. The crunch will be over. In fact, if in 2050 crop yields are still increasing, if most of the world is economically developed, and if population pressures are declining or even reversing—all of which seems reasonably likely—then the human species may at long last be able to feed itself, year in and year out, without putting any additional net stress on the environment. We might even be able to grow everything we need while *reducing* our agricultural footprint: returning cropland to wilderness, repairing damaged soils, restoring ecosystems, and so on. In other words, human agriculture might be placed on a sustainable footing forever: a breathtaking prospect.

The great problem, then, is to get through the next four or five decades with as little environmental damage as possible. That is where biotechnology comes in.

One day recently I drove down to southern Virginia to visit Dennis Avery and his son, Alex. The older Avery, a man in late middle age with a chinstrap beard, droopy eyes, and an intent, scholarly manner, lives on ninety-seven acres that he shares with horses, chickens, fish, cats, dogs, bluebirds, ducks, transient geese, and assorted other creatures. He is the director of global food issues at the Hudson Institute, a conservative think tank; Alex works with him, and is trained as a plant physiologist. We sat in a sunroom at the back of the house, our afternoon conversation punctuated every so often by dog snores and rooster crows. We talked for a little while about the Green Revolution, a dramatic advance in farm productivity that fed the world's burgeoning population over the past four decades, and then I asked if the challenge of the next four decades could be met.

15 "Well," Dennis replied, "we have tripled the world's farm output since 1960. And we're feeding twice as many people from the same land. That was a heroic achievement. But we have to do what some think is an even more difficult thing in this next forty years, because the Green Revolution had more land per person and more water per person—"

"—and more potential for increases," Alex added, "because the base that we were starting from was so much lower."

"By and large," Dennis went on, "the world's civilizations have been built around its best farmland. And we have used most of the world's good farmland. Most of the good land is already heavily fertilized. Most of the good land is already being planted with high-yield seeds. [Africa is the important exception.] Most of the good irrigation sites are used. We can't triple yields again with the technologies we're already using. And we might be lucky to get a fifty percent yield increase if we froze our technology short of biotech."

"Biotech" can refer to a number of things, but the relevant application here is genetic modification: the selective transfer of genes from one organism to another. Ordinary breeding can cross related varieties, but it cannot take a gene from a bacterium, for instance, and transfer it to a wheat plant. The organisms resulting from gene transfers are called "transgenic" by scientists—and "Frankenfood" by many greens.

Gene transfer poses risks, unquestionably. So, for that matter, does traditional crossbreeding. But many people worry that transgenic organisms might prove more unpredictable. One possibility is that transgenic crops would spread from fields into forests or other wild lands and there become envi-

ronmental nuisances, or worse. A further risk is that transgenic plants might cross-pollinate with neighboring wild plants, producing "superweeds" or other invasive or destructive varieties in the wild. Those risks are real enough that even most biotech enthusiasts—including Dennis Avery, for example—favor some government regulation of transgenic crops.

20 What is much less widely appreciated is biotech's potential to do the environment good. Take as an example continuous no-till farming, which really works best with the help of transgenic crops. Human beings have been ploughing for so long that we tend to forget why we started doing it in the first place. The short answer: weed control. Turning over the soil between plantings smothers weeds and their seeds. If you don't plough, your land becomes a weed garden—unless you use herbicides to kill the weeds. Herbicides, however, are expensive, and can be complicated to apply. And they tend to kill the good with the bad.

In the mid-1990s the agricultural-products company Monsanto introduced a transgenic soybean variety called Roundup Ready. As the name implies, these soybeans tolerate Roundup, an herbicide (also made by Monsanto) that kills many kinds of weeds and then quickly breaks down into harmless ingredients. Equipped with Roundup Ready crops, farmers found that they could retire their ploughs and control weeds with just a few applications of a single, relatively benign herbicide—instead of many applications of a complex and expensive menu of chemicals. More than a third of all U.S. soybeans are now grown without ploughing, mostly owing to the introduction of Roundup Ready varieties. Ploughless cotton farming has likewise received a big boost from the advent of bioengineered varieties. No-till farming without biotech is possible, but it's more difficult and expensive, which is why no-till and biotech are advancing in tandem.

In 2001 a group of scientists announced that they had engineered a transgenic tomato plant able to thrive on salty water—water, in fact, almost half as salty as seawater, and fifty times as salty as tomatoes can ordinarily abide. One of the researchers was quoted as saying, "I've already transformed tomato, tobacco, and canola. I believe I can transform any crop with this gene"—just the sort of Frankenstein hubris that makes environmentalists shudder. But consider the environmental implications. Irrigation has for millennia been a cornerstone of agriculture, but it comes at a price. As irrigation water evaporates, it leaves behind traces of salt, which accumulate in the soil and gradually render it infertile. (As any Roman legion knows, to destroy a nation's agricultural base you salt the soil.) Every year the world loses about 25 million acres—an area equivalent to a fifth of California—to salinity; 40 percent of the world's irrigated land, and 25 percent of America's, has been hurt to some degree. For decades traditional plant breeders tried to create salt-tolerant crop plants, and for decades they failed.

Salt-tolerant crops might bring millions of acres of wounded or crippled land back into production. "And it gets better," Alex Avery told me. The transgenic tomato plants take up and sequester in their leaves as much as six or seven percent of their weight in sodium. "Theoretically," Alex said, "you could reclaim a saltcontaminated field by growing enough of these crops to remove the salts from the soil."

His father chimed in: "We've worried about being able to keep these salt-contaminated fields going even for decades. We can now think about *centuries*."

25　One of the first biotech crops to reach the market, in the mid-1990s, was a cotton plant that makes its own pesticide. Scientists incorporated into the plant a toxin-producing gene from a soil bacterium known as *Bacillus thuringiensis*. With Bt cotton, as it is called, farmers can spray much less, and the poison contained in the plant is delivered only to bugs that actually eat the crop. As any environmentalist can tell you, insecticide is not very nice stuff—especially if you breathe it, which many Third World farmers do as they walk through their fields with backpack sprayers.

Transgenic cotton reduced pesticide use by more than two million pounds in the United States from 1996 to 2000, and it has reduced pesticide sprayings in parts of China by more than half. Earlier this year the Environmental Protection Agency approved a genetically modified corn that resists a beetle larva known as rootworm. Because rootworm is American corn's most voracious enemy, this new variety has the potential to reduce annual pesticide use in America by more than 14 million pounds. It could reduce or eliminate the spraying of pesticide on 23 million acres of U.S. land.

All of that is the beginning, not the end. Bioengineers are also working, for instance, on crops that tolerate aluminum, another major contaminant of soil, especially in the tropics. Return an acre of farmland to productivity, or double yields on an already productive acre, and, other things being equal, you reduce by an acre the amount of virgin forest or savannah that will be stripped and cultivated. That may be the most important benefit of all.

Of the many people I have interviewed in my twenty years as a journalist, Norman Borlaug must be the one who has saved the most lives. Today he is an unprepossessing eighty-nine-year-old man of middling height, with crystal-bright blue eyes and thinning white hair. He still loves to talk about plant breeding, the discipline that won him the 1970 Nobel Peace Prize: Borlaug led efforts to breed the staples of the Green Revolution. (See "Forgotten Benefactor of Humanity," by Gregg Easterbrook, an article on Borlaug in the January 1997 *Atlantic*.) Yet the renowned plant breeder is quick to mention that he began his career, in the 1930s, in forestry, and that forest conservation has never been far from his thoughts. In the 1960s, while he was working to improve crop yields in India and Pakistan, he made a mental connection. He would create tables detailing acres under cultivation and average yields—and then, in another column, he would estimate how much land had been saved by higher farm productivity. Later, in the 1980s and 1990s, he and others began paying increased attention to what some agricultural economists now call the Borlaug hypothesis: that the Green Revolution has saved not only many human lives but, by improving the productivity of existing farmland, also millions of acres of tropical forest and other habitat—and so has saved countless animal lives.

From the 1960s through the 1980s, for example, Green Revolution advances saved more than 100 million acres of wild lands in India. More recently, higher yields in rice, coffee, vegetables, and other crops have reduced or in some cases stopped forest- clearing in Honduras, the Philippines, and elsewhere. Dennis Avery estimates that if farming techniques and yields had not improved since 1950, the world would have lost an additional 20 million or so square miles of wildlife habitat, most of it forest. About 16 million square miles of forest exists today. "What I'm saying," Avery said, in response to my puzzled expression, "is that we have saved every square mile of forest on the planet."

30   Habitat destruction remains a serious environmental problem; in some respects it is the most serious. The savannahs and tropical forests of Central and South America, Asia, and Africa by and large make poor farmland, but they are the earth's storehouses of biodiversity, and the forests are the earth's lungs. Since 1972 about 200,000 square miles of Amazon rain forest have been cleared for crops and pasture; from 1966 to 1994 all but three of the Central American countries cleared more forest than they left standing. Mexico is losing more than 4,000 square miles of forest a year to peasant farms; sub-Saharan Africa is losing more than 19,000.

That is why the great challenge of the next four or five decades is not to feed an additional three billion people (and their pets) but to do so without converting much of the world's prime habitat into second- or third-rate farmland. Now, most agronomists agree that some substantial yield improvements are still to be had from advances in conventional breeding, fertilizers, herbicides, and other Green Revolution standbys. But it seems pretty clear that biotechnology holds more promise—probably much more. Recall that world food output will need to at least double and possibly triple over the next several decades. Even if production could be increased that much using con-

ventional technology, which is doubtful, the required amounts of pesticide and fertilizer and other polluting chemicals would be immense. If properly developed, disseminated, and used, genetically modified crops might well be the best hope the planet has got.

If properly developed, disseminated, and used. That tripartite qualification turns out to be important, and it brings the environmental community squarely, and at the moment rather jarringly, into the picture.

Not long ago I went to see David Sandalow in his office at the World Wildlife Fund, in Washington, D.C. Sandalow, the organization's executive vice-president in charge of conservation programs, is a tall, affable, polished, and slightly reticent man in his forties who holds degrees from Yale and the University of Michigan Law School.

Some weeks earlier, over lunch, I had mentioned Dennis Avery's claim that genetic modification had great environmental potential. I was surprised when Sandalow told me he agreed. Later, in our interview in his office, I asked him to elaborate. "With biotechnology," he said, "there are no simple answers. Biotechnology has huge potential benefits and huge risks, and we need to address both as we move forward. The huge potential benefits include increased productivity of arable land, which could relieve pressure on forests. They include decreased pesticide usage. But the huge risks include severe ecological disruptions—from gene flow and from enhanced invasiveness, which is a very antiseptic word for some very scary stuff."

35   I asked if he thought that, absent biotechnology, the world could feed everybody over the next forty or fifty years without ploughing down the rain forests. Instead of answering directly he said, "Biotechnology could be part of our arsenal if we can overcome some of the barriers. It will never be a panacea or a magic bullet. But nor should we remove it from our tool kit."

Sandalow is unusual. Very few credentialed greens talk the way he does about biotechnology, at least publicly. They would readily agree with him about the huge risks, but they wouldn't be caught dead speaking of huge potential benefits—a point I will come back to. From an ecological point of view, a very great deal depends on other environmentalists' coming to think more the way Sandalow does.

Biotech companies are in business to make money. That is fitting and proper. But developing and testing new transgenic crops is expensive and commercially risky, to say nothing of politically controversial. When they decide how to invest their research-and-development money, biotech companies will naturally seek products for which farmers and consumers will pay top dollar. Roundup Ready products, for instance, are well suited to U.S. farming, with its high levels of capital spending on such things as herbicides and automated sprayers. Poor farmers in the developing world, of course, have much less buying power. Creating, say, salt-tolerant cassava suitable for growing on hardscrabble African farms might save habitat as well as lives—but commercial enterprises are not likely to fall over one another in a rush to do it.

If earth-friendly transgenics are developed, the next problem is disseminating them. As a number of the farmers and experts I talked to were quick to mention, switching to an unfamiliar new technology—something like no-till—is not easy. It requires capital investment in new seed and equipment, mastery of new skills and methods, a fragile transition period as farmer and ecology readjust, and an often considerable amount of trial and error to find out what works best on any given field. Such problems are only magnified in the Third World, where the learning curve is steeper and capital cushions are thin to nonexistent. Just handing a peasant farmer a bag of newfangled seed is not enough. In many cases peasant farmers will need one-on-one attention. Many will need help to pay for the seed, too.

Finally there is the matter of using biotech in a way that actually benefits the environment. Often the technological blade can cut either way, especially in the short run. A salt-tolerant or drought-resistant rice that allowed farmers to keep land in production might also induce them to plough up virgin land that

40

previously was too salty or too dry to farm. If the effect of improved seed is to make farming more profitable, farmers may respond, at least temporarily, by bringing more land into production. If a farm becomes more productive, it may require fewer workers; and if local labor markets cannot provide jobs for them, displaced workers may move to a nearby patch of rain forest and burn it down to make way for subsistence farming. Such transition problems are solvable, but they need money and attention.

In short, realizing the great—probably unique—environmental potential of biotech will require stewardship. "It's a tool," Sara Scherr, an agricultural economist with the conservation group Forest Trends, told me, "but it's absolutely not going to happen automatically."

So now ask a question: Who is the natural constituency for earth-friendly biotechnology? Who cares enough to lobby governments to underwrite research—frequently unprofitable research—on transgenic crops that might restore soils or cut down on pesticides in poor countries? Who cares enough to teach Asian or African farmers, one by one, how to farm without ploughing? Who cares enough to help poor farmers afford high-tech, earth-friendly seed? Who cares enough to agitate for programs and reforms that might steer displaced peasants and profit-seeking farmers away from sensitive lands? Not politicians, for the most part. Not farmers. Not corporations. Not consumers.

At the World Resources Institute, an environmental think tank in Washington, the molecular biologist Don Doering envisions transgenic crops designed specifically to solve environmental problems: crops that might fertilize the soil, crops that could clean water, crops tailored to remedy the ecological problems of specific places. "Suddenly you might find yourself with a virtually chemical-free agriculture, where your cropland itself is filtering the water, it's protecting the watershed, it's providing habitat," Doering told me. "There is still so little investment in what I call design-for-environment." The natural constituency for such investment is, of course, environmentalists.

But environmentalists are not acting as such a constituency today. They are doing the opposite. For example, Greenpeace declares on its Web site: "The introduction of genetically engineered (GE) organisms into the complex ecosystems of our environment is a dangerous global experiment with nature and evolution…GE organisms must not be released into the environment. They pose unacceptable risks to ecosystems, and have the potential to threaten biodiversity, wildlife and sustainable forms of agriculture."

Other groups argue for what they call the Precautionary Principle, under which no transgenic crop could be used until proven benign in virtually all respects. The Sierra Club says on its Web site,

> In accordance with this Precautionary Principle, we call for a moratorium on the planting of all genetically engineered crops and the release of all GEOs [genetically engineered organisms] into the environment, *including those now approved*. Releases should be delayed until extensive, rigorous research is done which determines the long-term environmental and health impacts of each GEO and there is public debate to ascertain the need for the use of each GEO intended for release into the environment. [italics added]

Under this policy the cleaner water and healthier soil that continuous no-till farming has already brought to the Chesapeake Bay watershed would be undone, and countless tons of polluted runoff and eroded topsoil would accumulate in Virginia rivers and streams while debaters debated and researchers researched. Recall David Sandalow: "Biotechnology has huge potential benefits and huge risks, and we need to address both as we move forward." A lot of environmentalists would say instead, "*before* we move forward." That is an important difference, particularly because the big population squeeze will happen not in the distant future but over the next several decades.

45 For reasons having more to do with politics than with logic, the modern environmental movement was to a large extent founded on suspicion of markets and artificial substances. Markets exploit the earth; chemicals poison it. Biotech touches both hot buttons. It is being pushed forward by greedy corporations, and it seems to be the very epitome of the unnatural.

Still, I hereby hazard a prediction. In ten years or less, most American environmentalists (European ones are more dogmatic) will regard genetic modification as one of their most powerful tools. In only the past ten years or so, after all, environmentalists have reversed field and embraced market mechanisms—tradable emissions permits and the like—as useful in the fight against pollution. The environmental logic of biotechnology is, if anything, even more compelling. The potential upside of genetic modification is simply too large to ignore—and therefore environmentalists will not ignore it. Biotechnology will transform agriculture, and in doing so will transform American environmentalism.

Would It Surprise You to Know that Growing Soybeans Can Help the Environment?

COUNCIL FOR BIOTECHNOLOGY INFORMATION

The Council for Biotechnology Information is an advocacy group that "communicates science-based information about the benefits and safety of agricultural biotechnology and its contributions to sustainable development," according to the "About Us" section of their Web site. This ad appeared in magazines in 2002.

WOULD IT
SURPRISE YOU TO KNOW
THAT GROWING SOYBEANS CAN
HELP THE ENVIRONMENT?

Biotech soybeans have been widely
planted by American farmers and they
help preserve our natural resources.
Plant biotechnology makes it easier to
control weeds and plow soybean fields
less—which means less soil erosion.

But before those soybean seeds could
be planted, it took years of research and
testing to ensure that biotech crops
were safe for people and the environment. Extensive testing by scientists
shows foods derived from plant
biotechnology are as safe to eat as
traditional foods.

In fact, three government agencies
share the authority to evaluate the safety
of new biotech products from incep-
tion to approval—the U.S.
Department of Agriculture
(USDA), the Environmental Protection
Agency (EPA), and the Food and Drug
Administration (FDA). If you want to
learn more, we invite you to call or
visit our Web site.

Biotech
Soybean

WWW.WHYBIOTECH.COM
1-800-980-8660

Ten Reasons Why Biotechnology Will Not Ensure Food Security, Protect the Environment, and Reduce Poverty in the Developing World

MIGUEL A. ALTIERI AND PETER ROSSET

This scholarly policy argument appeared first in the academic journal AgBioForum *in 1999 and was subsequently posted on the Web site for that publication. The article has also been published in* Sierra Magazine. *Miguel A. Altieri, Ph.D., teaches agroecology in the Department of Environmental Science, Policy and Management at the University of California at Berkeley and is a technical advisor to the Latin American Consortium on Agroecology and Development in Santiago. Peter Rosset is the executive director of the Institute for Food and Development Policy, www.foodfirst.org.*

Biotechnology companies often claim that genetically modified organisms (GMOs)—specifically, genetically altered seeds—are essential scientific breakthroughs needed to feed the world, protect the environment, and reduce poverty in developing countries. The Consultative Group on International Agricultural Research (CGIAR) and its constellation of international centers around the world charged with research to enhance food security in the developing world echo this view, which rests on two critical assumptions. The first is that hunger is due to a gap between food production and human population density or growth rate. The second is that genetic engineering is the only or best way to increase agricultural production and, thus, meet future food needs.

Our objective is to challenge the notion of biotechnology as a magic bullet solution to all of agriculture's ills, by clarifying misconceptions concerning these underlying assumptions.

1. There is no relationship between the prevalence of hunger in a given country and its population. For every densely populated and hungry nation like Bangladesh or Haiti, there is a sparsely populated and hungry nation like Brazil and Indonesia. The world today produces more food per inhabitant than ever before. Enough food is available to provide 4.3 pounds for every person every day: 2.5 pounds of grain, beans and nuts, about a pound of meat, milk and eggs and another of fruits and vegetables. The real causes of hunger are poverty, inequality and lack of access to food and land. Too many people are too poor to buy the food that is available (but often poorly distributed) or lack the land and resources to grow it themselves (*Lappe, Collins & Rosset, 1998*).

2. Most innovations in agricultural biotechnology have been profit-driven rather than need-driven. The real thrust of the genetic engineering industry is not to make third world agriculture more productive, but rather to generate profits (*Busch et al., 1990*). This is illustrated by reviewing the principle technologies on the market today: (1) herbicide resistant crops, such as Monsanto's "Roundup Ready" soybeans, seeds that are tolerant to Monsanto's herbicide Roundup, and (2) "Bt" (*Bacillus thuringiensis*) crops which are engineered to produce their own insecticide. In the first instance, the goal is to win a greater herbicide market-share for a proprietary product and, in the second, to boost seed sales at the cost of damaging the usefulness of a key pest management product (the

Bacillus thuringiensis based microbial insecticide) relied upon by many farmers, including most organic farmers, as a powerful alternative to insecticides. These technologies respond to the need of biotechnology companies to intensify farmers' dependence upon seeds protected by so-called "intellectual property rights" which conflict directly with the age-old rights of farmers to reproduce, share or store seeds (*Hobbelink, 1991*). Whenever possible corporations will require farmers to buy a company's brand of inputs and will forbid farmers from keeping or selling seed. By controlling germplasm from seed to sale, and by forcing farmers to pay inflated prices for seed-chemical packages, companies are determined to extract the most profit from their investment (*Krimsky & Wrubel, 1996*).

5   **3. The integration of the seed and chemical industries appears destined to accelerate increases in per acre expenditures for seeds plus chemicals, delivering significantly lower returns to growers.** Companies developing herbicide tolerant crops are trying to shift as much per acre cost as possible from the herbicide onto the seed via seed costs and technology charges. Increasingly price reductions for herbicides will be limited to growers purchasing technology packages. In Illinois, the adoption of herbicide resistant crops makes for the most expensive soybean seed-plus-weed management system in modern history—between $40.00 and $60.00 per acre depending on fee rates, weed pressure, and so on. Three years ago, the average seed-plus-weed control costs on Illinois farms was $26 per acre, and represented 23% of variable costs; today they represent 35–40% (*Benbrook, 1999*). Many farmers are willing to pay for the simplicity and robustness of the new weed management system, but such advantages may be short-lived as ecological problems arise.

4. Recent experimental trials have shown that genetically engineered seeds do not increase the yield of crops. A recent study by the United States Department of Agriculture (USDA) Economic Research Service shows that in 1998 yields were not significantly different in engineered versus non-engineered crops in 12 of 18 crop/region combinations. In the six crop/region combinations where Bt crops or herbicide tolerant crops (HTCs) fared better, they exhibited increased yields between 5–30%. Glyphosphate tolerant cotton showed no significant yield increase in either region where it was surveyed. This was confirmed in another study examining more than 8,000 field trials, where it was found that Roundup Ready soybean seeds produced fewer bushels of soybeans than similar conventionally bred varieties (*USDA, 1999*).

5. Many scientists claim that the ingestion of genetically engineered food is harmless. Recent evidence, however, shows that there are potential risks of eating such foods as the new proteins produced in such foods could: (1) act themselves as allergens or toxins; (2) alter the metabolism of the food producing plant or animal, causing it to produce new allergens or toxins; or (3) reduce its nutritional quality or value. In the case of (3), herbicide resistant soybeans can contain less isoflavones, an important phytoestrogen present in soybeans, believed to protect women from a number of cancers. At present, developing countries are importing soybean and corn from the United States, Argentina, and Brazil. Genetically engineered foods are beginning to flood the markets in the importing countries, yet no one can predict all their health effects on consumers, who are unaware that they are eating such food. Because genetically engineered food remains unlabeled, consumers cannot discriminate between genetically engineered (GE) and non-GE food, and should serious health problems arise, it will be extremely difficult to trace them to their source. Lack of labeling also helps to shield the corporations that could be potentially responsible from liability (*Lappe & Bailey, 1998*).

6. Transgenic plants which produce their own insecticides closely follow the pesticide paradigm, which is itself rapidly failing due to pest resistance to insecticides. Instead of the failed "one pest-one chemical" model, genetic engineering emphasizes a "one pest-one gene" approach, shown over and over again in laboratory trials to fail, as pest species rapidly adapt and develop resistance to the insecticide present in the plant (*Alstad & Andow, 1995*). Not only will the new varieties fail over the short-to-medium term, despite so-called voluntary resistance management schemes (*Mallet & Porter, 1992*), but in the process may render useless the natural Bt-pesticide which is relied upon by organic farmers and others desiring to reduce chemical dependence. Bt crops violate the basic and widely accepted principle of integrated pest management (IPM), which is that reliance on any single pest management technology tends to trigger shifts in pest species or the evolution of resistance through one or more mechanisms (*NRC, 1996*). In general, the greater the selection pressure across time and space, the quicker and more profound the pests' evolutionary response. An obvious reason for adopting this principle is that it reduces pest exposure to pesticides, retarding the evolution of resistance. But when the product is engineered into the plant itself, pest exposure leaps from minimal and occasional to massive and continuous exposure, dramatically accelerating resistance (*Gould, 1994*). *Bacillus thuringiensis* will rapidly become useless, both as a feature of the new seeds and as an old standby sprayed when needed by farmers that want out of the pesticide treadmill (*Pimentel et al., 1989*).

7. The global fight for market share is leading companies to massively deploy transgenic crops around the world (more than 30 million hectares in 1998) without proper advance testing of short-or long-term impacts on human health and ecosystems. In the United States, private sector pressure led the White House to decree "no substantial difference" between altered and normal seeds, thus evading normal Food and Drug Administration (FDA) and Environmental Protection Agency (EPA) testing. Confidential documents made public in an on-going class action lawsuit have revealed that the FDA's own scientists do not agree with this determination. One reason is that many scientists are concerned that the large scale use of transgenic crops poses a series of environmental risks that threaten the sustainability of agriculture (*Goldberg, 1992; Paoletti & Pimentel, 1996; Snow & Moran, 1997; Rissler & Mellon, 1996; Kendall et al., 1997; Royal Society, 1998*). These risk areas are as follows:

- The trend to create broad international markets for single products is simplifying cropping systems and creating genetic uniformity in rural landscapes. History has shown that a huge area planted to a single crop variety is very vulnerable to new matching strains of pathogens or insect pests. Furthermore, the widespread use of homogeneous transgenic varieties will unavoidably lead to "genetic erosion," as the local varieties used by thousands of farmers in the developing world are replaced by the new seeds (*Robinson, 1996*).

- The use of herbicide resistant crops undermines the possibilities of crop diversification, thus, reducing agrobiodiversity in time and space (*Altieri, 1994*).
- The potential transfer through gene flow of genes from herbicide resistant crops to wild or semidomesticated relatives can lead to the creation of superweeds (*Lutman, 1999*).
- There is potential for herbicide resistant varieties to become serious weeds in other crops (*Duke, 1996; Holt & Le Baron, 1990*).
- Massive use of Bt crops affects non-target organisms and ecological processes. Recent evidence shows that the Bt toxin can affect beneficial insect predators that feed on insect pests present on Bt crops (*Hilbeck et al., 1998*). In addition, windblown pollen from Bt crops, found on natural vegetation surrounding transgenic fields, can kill non-target insects such as the monarch butterfly (*Losey et al., 1999*). Moreover, Bt toxin present in crop foliage plowed under after harvest can adhere to soil colloids for up to 3 months, negatively affecting the soil invertebrate populations that break down organic matter and play other ecological roles (*Donnegan et al., 1995; Palm et al., 1996*).
- There is potential for vector recombination to generate new virulent strains of viruses, especially in transgenic plants engineered for viral resistance with viral genes. In plants containing coat protein genes, there is a possibility that such genes will be taken up by unrelated viruses infecting the plant. In such situations, the foreign gene changes the coat structure of the viruses and may confer properties, such as changed method of transmission between plants. The second potential risk is that recombination between RNA virus and a viral RNA inside the transgenic crop could produce a new pathogen leading to more severe disease problems. Some researchers have shown that recombination occurs in transgenic plants and that under certain conditions it produces a new viral strain with altered host range (*Steinbrecher, 1996*).

10   Ecological theory predicts that the large-scale landscape homogenization with transgenic crops will exacerbate the ecological problems already associated with monoculture agriculture. Unquestioned expansion of this technology into developing countries may not be wise or desirable. There is strength in the agricultural diversity of many of these countries, and it should not be inhibited or reduced by extensive monoculture, especially when consequences of doing so result in serious social and environmental problems (*Altieri, 1996*).

Although the ecological risks issue has received some discussion in government, international, and scientific circles, discussions have often been pursued from a narrow perspective that has downplayed the seriousness of the risks (*Kendall et al., 1997; Royal Society, 1998*). In fact, methods for risk assessment of transgenic crops are not well developed (*Kjellsson & Simonsen, 1994*) and there is justifiable concern that current field biosafety tests tell little about potential environmental risks associated with commercial-scale production of transgenic crops. A main concern is that international pressures to gain markets and profits is resulting in companies releasing transgenic crops too fast, without proper consideration for the long-term impacts on people or the ecosystem.

8. There are many unanswered ecological questions regarding the impact of transgenic crops. Many environmental groups have argued for the creation of suitable regulation to mediate the testing and release of transgenic crops to offset environmental risks and demand a much better assessment and understanding of ecological issues associated with genetic engineering. This is crucial, as many results emerging from the environmental performance of released transgenic crops suggest that in the development of resistant crops not only is there a need to test direct effects on the target insect or weed, but the indirect effects on the plant. Plant growth, nutrient content, metabolic changes, and effects on the soil and non-target organisms should all be examined. Unfortunately, funds for research on environmental risk assessment are very limited. For example, the USDA spends only 1% of the funds allocated to biotechnology research on risk assessment, about $1–2 million per year. Given the current level of deployment of genetically engineered plants, such resources are not enough to even discover the "tip of the iceberg." It is a tragedy-in-the-making that so many millions of hectares have been planted without proper biosafety standards. Worldwide such acreage expanded considerably in 1998 with transgenic cotton reaching 6.3 million acres, transgenic corn reaching 20.8 million acres, and transgenic soybean 36.3 million acres. This expansion has been helped along by marketing and distribution agreements entered into by corporations and marketers (i.e., Ciba Seeds with Growmark and Mycogen Plant Sciences with Cargill), and in the absence of regulations in many developing countries. Genetic pollution, unlike oil spills, cannot be controlled by throwing a boom around it.

9. **As the private sector has exerted more and more dominance in advancing new biotechnologies, the public sector has had to invest a growing share of its scarce resources in enhancing biotechnological capacities in public institutions, including the CGIAR, and in evaluating and responding to the challenges posed by incorporating private sector technologies into existing farming systems.** Such funds would be much better used to expand support for ecologically based agricultural research, as all the biological problems that biotechnology aims at can be solved using agroecological approaches. The dramatic effects of rotations and intercropping on crop health and productivity, as well as of the use of biological control agents on pest regulation have been confirmed repeatedly by scientific research. The problem is that research at public institutions increasingly reflects the interests of private funders at the expense of public good research, such as biological control, organic production systems and general agroecological techniques. Civil society must request for more research on alternatives to biotechnology by universities and other public organizations (*Krimsky & Wrubel, 1996*). There is also an urgent need to challenge the patent system and intellectual property rights intrinsic to the World Trade Organization (WTO) which not only provide multinational corporations with the right to seize and patent genetic resources, but will also accelerate the rate at which market forces already encourage monocultural cropping with genetically uniform transgenic varieties. Based on history and ecological theory, it is not difficult to predict the negative impacts of such environmental simplification on the health of modern agriculture (*Altieri, 1996*).

10. **Much of the needed food can be produced by small farmers located throughout the world using agroecological technologies (Uphoff & Altieri, 1999).** In fact, new rural development approaches and low-input technologies spearheaded by farmers and non-governmental organizations (NGOs) around the world are already making a significant contribution to food security at the household, national, and regional levels in Africa, Asia and Latin America

(*Pretty, 1995*). Yield increases are being achieved by using technological approaches, based on agroecological principles that emphasize diversity, synergy, recycling and integration; and social processes that emphasize community participation and empowerment (*Rosset, 1999*). When such features are optimized, yield enhancement and stability of production are achieved, as well as a series of ecological services such as conservation of biodiversity, soil and water restoration and conservation, improved natural pest regulation mechanisms, and so on (*Altieri et al., 1998*). These results are a breakthrough for achieving food security and environmental preservation in the developing world, but their potential and further spread depends on investments, policies, institutional support, and attitude changes on the part of policy makers and the scientific community; especially the CGIAR who should devote much of its efforts to the 320 million poor farmers living in marginal environments. Failure to promote such people-centered agricultural research and development due to the diversion of funds and expertise towards biotechnology will forego an historical opportunity to raise agricultural productivity in economically viable, environmentally benign, and socially uplifting ways.

References

Alstad, D. N., and Andow, D. A. (1995). Managing the evolution of insect resistance to transgenic plants. *Science, 268,* 1894–1896.

Altieri, M. A. (1994). *Biodiversity and pest management in agroecosystems.* New York: Haworth Press.

Altieri, M. A. (1996). *Agroecology: The science of sustainable agriculture.* Boulder, CO: Westview Press.

Altieri, M. A., Rosset, P., and Thrupp, L. A. (1998). *The potential of agroecology to combat hunger in the developing world* (2020 Brief No. 55). Washington, DC: International Food Policy Research Institute.

Benbrook, C. (1999). *World food system challenges and opportunities: GMOs, biodiversity and lessons from America's heartland.* Unpublished manuscript.

Busch, L., Lacey, W. B., Burkhardt, J., and Lacey, L. (1990). *Plants, power and profit.* Oxford, England: Basil Blackwell.

Casper, R., and Landsmann, J. (1992). The biosafety results of field tests of genetically modified plants and microorganisms. P. K. Landers (Ed.), *Proceedings of the Second International Symposium Goslar,* pp. 89–97, Germany.

Donnegan, K. K., Palm, C. J., Fieland, V. J., Porteous, L. A., Ganis, L. M., Scheller, D. L., and Seidler, R. J. (1995). Changes in levels, species, and DNA fingerprints of soil microorganisms associated with cotton expressing the Bacillus thuringiensis var. Kurstaki endotoxin. *Applied Soil Ecology, 2,* 111–124.

Duke, S. O. (1996). *Herbicide resistant crops: Agricultural, environmental, economic, regulatory, and technical aspects.* Boca Raton: Lewis Publishers.

Goldberg, R. J. (1992). Environmental concerns with the development of herbicide-tolerant plants. *Weed Technology, 6,* 647–652.

Gould, F. (1994). Potential and problems with high-dose strategies for pesticidal engineered crops. *Biocontrol Science and Technology, 4,* 451–461.

Hilbeck, A., Baumgartner, M., Fried, P. M., and Bigler, F. (1998). Effects of transgenic Bacillus thuringiensis corn fed prey on mortality and development time of immature Chrysoperla carnea Neuroptera: Chrysopidae. *Environmental Entomology, 27,* 460–487.

Hobbelink, H. (1991). *Biotechnology and the future of world agriculture.* London: Zed Books, Ltd.

Holt, J. S., and Le Baron, H. M. (1990). Significance and distribution of herbicide resistance. *Weed Technology, 4,* 141–149.

James, C. (1997). *Global status of transgenic crops in 1997* (ISAAA Briefs No. 5.). Ithaca, NY: International Service for the Acquisition of Agri-Biotech Application (ISAAA). Available on the World Wide Web: http://www.isaaa.org/frbrief5.htm

Kendall, H. W., Beachy, R., Eismer, T., Gould, F., Herdt, R., Ravon, P. H., Schell, J., and Swaminathan, M. S. (1997). *Bioengineering of crops* (Report of the World Bank Panel on Transgenic Crops, pp. 1–30). Washington, DC: World Bank.

Kennedy, G. G., and Whalon, M. E. (1995). Managing pest resistance to Bacillus thuringiensis endotoxins: Constraints and incentives to implementation. *Journal of Economic Entomology, 88,* 454–460.

Kjellsson, G., and Simonsen, V. (1994). *Methods for risk assessment of transgenic plants.* Basil, Germany: Birkhauser Verlag.

Krimsky, S., and Wrubel, R. P. (1996). Agricultural biotechnology and the environment: Science, policy and social issues. Urbana, IL: University of Illinois Press.

Lappe, F. M., Collins, J., and Rosset, P. (1998). *World hunger: Twelve myths.* New York: Grove Press.

Lappe, M., and Bailey, B. (1998). *Against the grain: Biotechnology and the corporate takeover of food.* Monroe, ME: Common Courage Press.

Liu, Y. B., Tabashnik, B. E., Dennehy, T. J., Patin, A. L., and Bartlett A. C. (1999). Development time and resistance to Bt crops. *Nature, 400,* 519.

Losey, J. J. E., Rayor, L. S., and Carter, M. E. (1999). Transgenic pollen harms monarch larvae. *Nature, 399,* 214.

Lutman, P. J. W. (1999). (Ed.). Gene flow and agriculture: Relevance for transgenic crops. *British Crop Protection Council Symposium Proceedings, 72,* 43–64.

Mallet, J., and Porter, P. (1992). Preventing insect adaptations to insect resistant crops: Are seed mixtures or refugia the best strategy? *Proceedings of the Royal Society of London Series B Biology Science, 250,* 165–169.

National Research Council (NRC). (1996). *Ecologically based pest management.* Washington, DC: National Academy of Sciences.

Palm, C. J., Schaller, D. L., Donegan, K. K., and Seidler, R. J. (1996). Persistence in soil of transgenic plant produced bacillus thuringiensis var. kustaki-endotoxin. *Canadian Journal of Microbiology, 42,* 1258–1262.

Paoletti, M. G., and Pimentel, D. (1996). Genetic engineering in agriculture and the environment: Assessing risks and benefits. *BioScience, 46,* 665–671.

Pimentel, D., Hunter, M. S., LaGro, J. A., Efroymson, R. A., Landers, J. C., Mervis, F. T., McCarthy, C. A., and Boyd, A. E. (1989). Benefits and risks of genetic engineering in agriculture. *BioScience, 39,* 606–614.

Pretty, J. (1995). Regenerating agriculture: Policies and practices for sustainability and self-reliance. London: Earthscan.

Rissler, J., and Mellon, M. (1996). *The ecological risks of engineered crops.* Cambridge, MA: MIT Press.

Robinson, R. A. (1996). Return to resistance: Breeding crops to reduce pesticide resistance. Davis, CA: AgAccess.

Rosset, P. (1999). *The multiple functions and benefits of small farm agriculture in the context of global trade negotiations* (IFDP Food First Policy Brief No. 4). Washington, DC: Institute for Food and Development Policy.

Royal Society. (1998, February). Genetically modified plants for food use. *Statement 2/98.* London: Royal Society.

Snow, A. A., and Moran, P. (1997). Commercialization of transgenic plants: Potential ecological risks. *BioScience, 47,* 86–96.

Steinbrecher, R. A. (1996). From green to gene revolution: The environmental risks of genetically engineered crops. *The Ecologist, 26,* 273–282.

United States Department of Agriculture (USDA). (1999). *Genetically engineered crops for pest management*. Washington, DC: USDA Economic Research Service.

Uphoff, N., and Altieri, M. A. (1999). *Alternatives to conventional modern agriculture for meeting world food needs in the next century* (Report of a Bellagio Conference). Ithaca, NY: Cornell International Institute for Food, Agriculture and Development.

Monsantoland

This poster image has appeared on numerous Web sites protesting the major biotech food company, Monsanto. Note the impact of its claim and its powerful appeals to pathos.

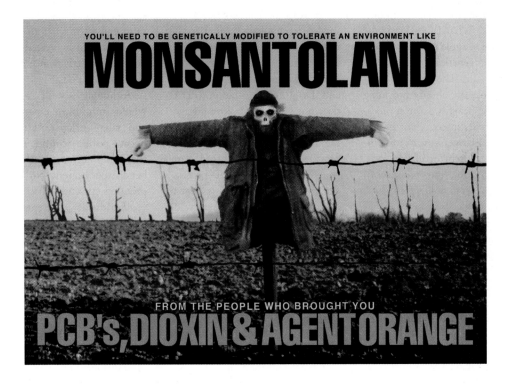

Lessen the Fear of Genetically Engineered Crops

GREGORY A. JAFFE

This middle-ground policy argument appeared in the Christian Science Monitor *on August 8, 2001. Gregory A. Jaffe is codirector for the Project on Biotechnology for the Center for Science in the Public Interest.*

Protesters carrying signs stating "Biocide is Homicide" and shouting concerns about the risks of eating genetically engineered foods recently demonstrated outside the biotechnology industry's annual convention. Inside the convention center, the industry extolled the safety of genetically engineered foods and the benefits of future crops like "golden rice."

Neither corporate hyperbole nor radical slogans do much to inform the public. What is needed is the shaping of sensible measures to ensure that genetically engineered foods are safe. The first few engineered crops are already providing remarkable benefits. Cotton modified to kill insects has greatly diminished farmers' use of toxic insecticides, thereby reducing costs, increasing yields, and, presumably, reducing harm to nontarget species. Likewise, biotech soybeans facilitate no-till farming, which reduces soil erosion and water pollution.

Despite such benefits, agricultural biotechnology is under siege for reasons good and bad. Activists have burned fields and bombed labs. Farmers will not plant genetically engineered sweet corn, sugar beets, and apples, for fear of consumer rejection. And countries in Europe and Asia refuse to import US-grown genetically engineered crops. Some countries now require labeling of foods containing engineered ingredients. Those requirements have spurred food processors, who want to avoid negative-sounding labels, to eliminate bioengineered ingredients.

Buffeted by the polarized debate, many Americans oppose biotech foods, in part because farmers and seed companies get the benefits while consumers bear the risk. If anti-genetically engineered sentiment increases, US farmers may be forced to forgo the advantages of engineered crops. And most public and private investment in agricultural biotechnology would dry up.

5   To reap the benefits of agricultural biotechnology, minimize the risks, and boost public confidence, the US must upgrade its flawed regulatory system. Currently, the Food and Drug Administration (FDA) does not formally approve any genetically engineered crops as safe to eat. Instead, it reviews safety data provided voluntarily by seed companies. That consultation process, which the FDA admits is "not a comprehensive scientific review of the data," culminates with the FDA stating only that it has "no further questions…at this time." Although no health problems with genetically engineered crops have been detected, that industry-driven process is weak insurance. The recent FDA proposal requiring a formal notification before marketing a biotech food is an improvement.

All biotech foods should go through a mandatory approval process with specific testing and data requirements. The National Academy of Sciences should be commissioned to recommend a precise method of assessment.

Genetically engineered crops also raise environmental concerns.

They could lead to pesticide-resistant insects and weeds and might contaminate plants that are close relatives of the crops. To safeguard our ecosystem, the current laws need fixing. Congress should close regulatory gaps to ensure that all future applications of biotechnology, ranging from fast-growing fish to corn plants that produce industrial chemicals, receive thorough environmental reviews. Also, the Environmental Protection Agency must enforce restrictions it has imposed on bioengineered crops to help prevent emergence of insecticide-resistant pests.

Although strong regulations would minimize environmental and safety risks, nothing would boost public confidence more than engineered products that benefit consumers. No beneficial products currently exist.

Worldwide acceptance of biotechnology will only occur when other countries reap benefits from this technology. Instead of spending millions of dollars on feel-good advertising campaigns, the biotech industry should train developing-country scientists and fund research in those countries. Companies—and universities—should donate patented crops and processes to developing countries. Agricultural biotechnology is not a panacea for all agricultural problems here or abroad, nor is it free from risk. But, with adequate safeguards, it could provide tremendous benefits for an ever-populous, pesticide-drenched, and water- deficient globe.

Food Industry Should Modify Its Stance on Altered Food

FROMA HARROP

This op-ed piece by nationally syndicated columnist Froma Harrop appeared in news-papers across the United States in November 2002. The immediate context for Harrop's argument was an Oregon referendum—defeated by voters at the polls—to require label-ing of genetically modified foods. The presence of the referendum on the Oregon ballot stimulated a corporate advertising blitz by the major growers of genetically modified foods, who outspent their opponents 25 to 1.

My primitive response to ge-netically modified foods is to ask, "What's wrong with the grub of the last 250,000 years?" Mucking around with genetic material to create new kinds of fruits, vegeta-bles and animals seems somehow unnecessary. Cows have produced pretty good milk over the millen-nia using their cow genes. So why insert rat genes into a perfectly ac-ceptable cow?

Call me old-fashioned, but given a choice between a traditional tomato and a tomato carrying fish DNA, I will select the former.

Are these genetically modified organisms (GMOs) safe to eat? I don't know. But regardless of the science, I remain an anchor in the stream of progress. I do not want GMOs on my plate for moral, eth-ical, emotional, religious, aesthetic, sentimental and other reasons I haven't thought of yet.

Monsanto, I'm obviously not your customer. But I'd like to make a deal with you and the other food/biotech companies pushing all this gene splicing. Let me decide whether or not to buy genetically engineered foods at the store. Don't force me onto a farm in the woods where I must sit guard over my organic vegetable patch with a shotgun and a crazed look on my face. In other words, stop fighting proposals to label foods for GMO content.

The biotech-food-industrial complex opposes such labeling for sound business reasons: The world is full of people like me. Polls con-sistently show Americans objecting to genetically manipulated food by solid majorities. Some 93 percent of the respondents to a poll conducted for ABCNEWS.com wanted mandatory labeling of bio-engineered products.

That's why the complex pounced on a potentially path-clearing referendum in Oregon that would have required labels. Monsanto joined Kraft, Unilever and other opponents to outspend supporters 25-to-1. The proposal was soundly defeated following ludicrous claims that a labeling law would cost the average Oregon family $550 a year. (Similar laws in Europe, Japan and Australia have not noticeably raised the price of food.)

Actually, the U.S. trade represen-tative will soon decide whether to drag Europe before the World Trade Organization over its restrictions on importing genetically modified corn and soybeans. Right now, 34 per-cent of corn and 75 percent of soy-beans in America are grown from genetically manipulated seed.

With Europeans already in-flamed by U.S. environmental policies, this seems a swell time for the Bush administration to bully them over their food supply, Europe's No. 1 cultural issue. Prince Charles is going around the kingdom condemning geneti-cally engineered food as some-thing that "takes mankind into realms that belong to God and God alone."

The Bush administration and Monsanto like each other a great deal, which is why we can't trust our government to give us the straight story on GMOs. Of course, they will never conquer dine-o-saurs like me. But if they want to win over folks concerned only about how GMOs might affect health and the environment, they're going about it the wrong way.

10 A U.S. Food and Drug Administration confident about the safety of these products would not have weighed in so loudly against the Oregon labeling proposal. And what possessed the administration to name Monsanto's former Washington lobbyist for GMOs as second in command at the Environmental Protection Agency?

Over at the National Academy of Sciences, a panel sung the praises of federal efforts to regulate geneti-cally engineered foods. It turned out that six of the 12 panel members had ties to the biotech industry.

The complex showers the public with rather impressive claims for GMOs. GMO farm-ers can up food production for a hungry world. GMO crops re-duce pesticide use. GMO cows (the ones with rat genes) pro-duce milk that's better for the heart. Hey, they may be right in some cases.

All this matters not to me. Others may forge ahead with new culinary traditions. I won't chow down on GMOs and I will echo Prince Charles' call for "strong and sustained pressure from consumers to ensure that they keep the right not to eat them."

Our farmers produce beautiful and abundant food without put-ting moth genes into catfish. Why mess with success?

What Is the FDA Trying to Feed Us?

SUSTAINUSA.ORG

Using the "piranhaberry" as its main image, Sustainusa.org, a "non-profit organization that promotes a healthy, sustainable environment through innovative communication strategies" (from its Web page), launched a "Keep Nature Natural" campaign against Monsanto and other biotechnology companies. This striking image appeared on the campaign's fliers, posters, postcards, and magazine ads.

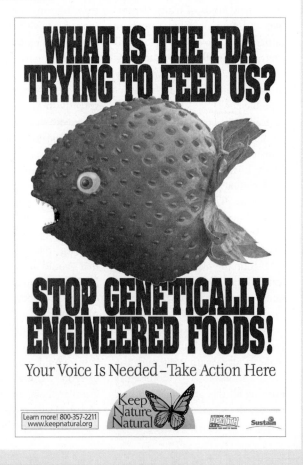

Is Genetic Engineering the Answer to Hunger?

GERALD D. COLEMAN

This article focuses on differing ethical views of genetic engineering in the light of Roman Catholic social teaching, which calls on people from rich nations to stand in solidarity with the world's poor. It was published in America, *one of the nation's leading Catholic intellectual magazines. Its author, Gerald D. Coleman, is a professor of moral theology at St. Patrick's Seminary and University in Menlo Park, California.*

Both the developed and developing worlds are facing a critical moral choice in the controversial issue of genetically modified food, also known as genetically modified organisms and genetically engineered crops. Critics of these modifications speak dismissively of biotech foods and genetic pollution. On the other hand, proponents like Nina Federoff and Nancy Marie Brown, authors of *Mendel in the Kitchen: A Scientist's View of Genetically Modified Foods* (2004), promote genetically modified organisms (G.M.'s or G.M.O.'s) as "the miracle of seed science and fertilizers."

To mark the 20th anniversary of U.S. diplomatic relations with the Holy See, the U.S. Embassy to the Holy See, in cooperation with the Pontifical Academy of Sciences, hosted a conference last fall at Rome's Gregorian University on "Feeding a Hungry World: The Moral Imperative of Biotechnology." Archbishop Renato Martino, who heads the Pontifical Council for Justice and Peace and has been a strong and outspoken proponent of G.M.O.'s, told Vatican Radio: "The problem of hunger involves the conscience of every man. For this reason the Catholic Church follows with special interest and solicitude every development in science to help the solution of a plight that affects...humanity."

Americans have grown accustomed, perhaps unwittingly, to G.M.O. products. In the United States, for example, 68 percent of the soybeans, 70 percent of the cotton crop, 26 percent of corn and 55 percent of canola are genetically engineered. G.M.O.'s represent an estimated 60 percent of all American processed foods. A recent study by the National Center for Food and Agriculture found that farmers in the United States investing in biotech products harvested 5.3 billion additional pounds of crops and realized $22 billion in increased income. Most of the world's beer and cheese is made with G.M.O.'s, as are hundreds of medications. In an article published last October, James Nicholson, then U.S. Ambassador to the Vatican and an aggressive promoter of U.S. policy in Vatican circles, wrote that "millions of Americans, Canadians, Australians, Argentines and other people have been eating genetically modified food for nearly a decade—without one proven case of an illness, allergic reaction or even the hiccups....Mankind has been genetically altering food throughout human history." And according to its supporters, biotechnology helps the environment by reducing the use of pesticides and tilling.

The World Health Association recently reported that more than 3.7 billion people around the world are now malnourished, the largest number in history. To this, opponents of G.M.O.'s reply that the "real problems" causing hunger, especially in the developing world, are poverty, lack of education and training, unequal land distribution and lack of access to markets. The moral point they advance is that distribution, not production, is the key to solving hunger. Another significant moral issue relates to "intellectual property policies" and the interest of companies in licensing potentially valuable discoveries. The Rev. Giulio Albanese, head of the Missionary News Agency, insists that unless the problem of intellectual property is resolved in favor of the poor, it represents a "provocation" to developing countries: "The concern of many in the missionary world over the property rights to

G.M. seeds . . . cannot but accentuate the dependence of the poor nations on the rich ones." In response to this concern, a proposal was made recently (reported in *Science* magazine on March 19) that research universities cooperate to seek open licensing provisions that would allow them to share their intellectual property through a "developing-country license." Universities would still retain rights for research and education and maintain negotiating power with the biotechnology and pharmaceutical industries. Catholic social ethics would support this type of proposal, since it places the good of people over amassing profit. Three moral paths suggest themselves:

1. Favor the use of G.M.O.'s. Nobel Prize winner Norman Borlaug, who developed the Green Revolution wheat and rice strains, recently wrote: "Biotechnology absolutely should be part of Africa's agricultural reform. African leaders would be making a grievous error if they turn their back on it." Proponents at the Rome conference agreed, arguing that the use of G.M.O.'s decreases pesticide-use, creates more nutrient-filled crops that require less water and have greater drought resistance, produces more food at a lower cost and uses less land. One small-scale South African farmer concluded, "We need this technology. We don't want always to be fed food aid. We want access to this technology so that one day we can also become commercial farmers."

    This position concludes that the use of G.M.O.'s amounts to a moral obligation.

2. Condemn the use of G.M.O.'s. Many Catholic bishops take an opposing stance. Perhaps the clearest statement comes from the National Conference of Bishops of Brazil and their Pastoral Land Commission. Their argument is threefold: the use of G.M.O.'s involves potential risks to human health; a small group of large corporations will be the greatest beneficiaries, with grave damage to the family farmers; and the environment will be gravely damaged.

The bishops of Botswana, South Africa and Swaziland agree: "We do not believe that agrocompanies or gene technologies will help our farmers to produce the food that is needed in the 21st century." Roland Lesseps and Peter Henriot, two Jesuits working in Zambia who are experts on agriculture in the developing world, state their opposition on principle: "Nature is not just useful to us as humans, but is valued and loved in itself, for itself, by God in Christ. . . . The right to use other creatures does not give us the right to abuse them."

In a similar but distinct criticism, the executive director of the U.S. National Catholic Rural Conference, David Andrews, C.S.C., feels that "the Pontifical Academy of Sciences has allowed itself to be subordinated to the U.S. government's insistent advocacy of biotechnology and the companies which market it." Sean McDonagh states: "With patents [on genetically engineered food], farmers will never own their own food. . . ." He believes that "corporate greed" is at the heart of the G.M.O. controversy. Biowatch's Elfrieda Pschorn-Strauss agrees: "With G.M. crops, small-scale farmers will become completely reliant on and controlled by big foreign companies for their food supply."

This position concludes that the use of G.M.O.'s is morally irresponsible.

3. Approach the use of G.M.O.'s with caution. Two years ago Pope John Paul II declared that G.M.O. agriculture could not be judged solely on the basis of "short-term economic interests," but needed to be subject to "a rigorous scientific and ethical process of verification." This cautionary stance has been adopted by the Catholic Bishops Conference of the Philippines in urging its government to postpone authorization of G.M.O. corn until comprehensive studies have been made: "We have to be careful because, once it is there, how can we remedy its consequences?"

In 2003 the Rural Life Committee of the North Dakota Conference of Churches also called for "rigorous examination" to understand fully the outcomes of the use of G.M.O.'s. This document endorses the "Precautionary Principle" formulated in 1992 by the United Nations Conference on Environment and Development in order to avoid "potential harm and unforeseen and unintended consequences."

This view mandates restraint and places the fundamental burden on demonstrating safety. The arguments are based on three areas of concern: the impact on the natural environment, the size of the benefit to the small farmer if the owners and distributors are giant companies like Bristol-Myers and Monsanto and the long-term effects of G.M.O.'s on human and animal health and nutrition.

This position concludes that the use of G.M.O.'s should be approached with caution. While the "Precautionary Principle" seems prudent, there is simultaneously a strong moral argument that a war on hunger is a grave, universal need. Last year, 10 million people died of starvation. Every 3.6 seconds someone dies from hunger—24,000 people each day. Half of sub-Saharan Africans are malnourished, and this number is expected to increase to 70 percent by 2010. It was a moral disgrace that in 2002 African governments gave in to G.M.O. opponents and returned to the World Food Program tons of G.M.O. corn simply because it was produced in the U.S. by biotechnology.

The Roman conference gives solid reasons that G.M.O.'s are useful, healthful and nonharmful. After all, organisms have been exchanging genetic information for centuries. The tomato, corn and potato would not exist today if human engineering had not transferred genes between species.

The Catechism of the Catholic Church teaches that we have a duty to "make accessible to each what is needed to lead a truly human life." The very first example given is food. In *Populorum Progressio* (1967), *Sollicitude Rei Socialis* (1987) and *Centesimus Annus* (1991), Paul VI and later John Paul II forcefully insisted that rich countries have an obligation to help the poor, just as global economic interdependence places us on a moral obligation to be in solidarity with poor nations. Likewise, The Challenge of Faithful Citizenship, published by the U.S. bishops in 2004, argues that the church's preferential option for the poor entails "a moral responsibility to commit ourselves to the common good at all levels."

At the same time, it is critical that farmers in developing countries not become dependent on G.M.O. seeds patented by a small number of companies. Intellectual knowledge must be considered the common patrimony of the entire human family. As the U.S. bishops have stated, "Both public and private entities have an obligation to use their property, including intellectual and scientific property, to promote the good of all people" (*For I Was Hungry and You Gave Me Food,* 2003).

The Catholic Church sees deep sacramental significance in wheat and bread, and insists on the absolute imperative to feed and care for the poor of the world. A vital way to promote and ensure the dignity of every human being is to enable them to have their daily bread.

■ ■ ■ **FOR CLASS DISCUSSION** **Biotech Agriculture**

1. The readings and visuals in this unit reveal a complex network of issues related to the genetic engineering of food. Working in small groups or as a whole class, identify specific areas of disagreement or controversy among the authors represented in this unit. Then create as many specific issue questions connected to the genetic engineering of food as you can.

2. Some of the disagreement about biotech food involves the concept of "natural." When is a food natural as opposed to unnatural or artificial? Do the terms "natural/

unnatural" have a scientific meaning or a cultural meaning? In written or visual arguments, how do anti-biotech advocates portray biotech food as "unnatural"? How have supporters of biotech foods attempted to answer the accusations that GMOs are unnatural?

3. At the end of "Will Frankenfood Save the Planet?" Jonathan Rauch calls on Greenpeace, the Sierra Club, and other environmental organizations to change their anti-biotech agendas. Examine the Sierra Club's policy statement on genetic engineering as stated on its Web site, http://www.sierraclub.org/policy/conservation/biotech.asp. To what extent do you think that some of the Sierra Club's policies on genetically modified foods should be revised in light of the readings in this unit?

4. Choose one of the arguments for closer analysis, applying the List 2 questions on pages 426–427.

WRITING ASSIGNMENT Letter Taking a Stand

Many of the advocacy Web sites on all sides of the controversy over biotech agriculture elicit consumer feedback, suggesting that we tell our lawmakers and also our local supermarkets what we think about the labeling and the selling of genetically engineered foods. Write a letter to (a) one of your state's representatives to Congress, (b) the sponsors of an advocacy web site, or (c) the CEO of the supermarket where you or your family regularly buy groceries. In your letter, take a stand on some aspect of biotech foods and urge them to adopt your position. If you are writing to your legislator, you might argue for more rigorous, systematic, and extensive testing of genetically modified products, for a moratorium on the sale of genetically modified foods, or for government support of genetic engineering of foods. If you are writing to an advocacy Web site, you might urge them to change some of their beliefs, policies, or calls to action. If you are writing to the CEO of your favorite supermarket chain, you might argue that the supermarket change its buying practices, provide more consumer information about sources of food, or lobby for or against the labeling of genetically modified ingredients in food products. ■

> For additional writing, reading, and research resources, go to
> www.mycomplab.com

Argument Classics

In this unit we present five arguments that have been particularly effective at influencing public opinion, presenting uncomfortable truths to their audiences, and demonstrating powerful strategies of persuasion. Each of these arguments has made a difference in the world, either because it has persuaded people of the justice of its claims or has evoked powerful resistance and counterargument. Each of these arguments is also richly suitable for classroom analysis. Widely reprinted in anthologies, each argument has achieved classic status in its ability to engage students in discussion, promote critical thinking about important issues, and move students and teachers alike to introspection and to agreement or dissent.

Letter from Birmingham Jail

MARTIN LUTHER KING, JR.

Martin Luther King's "Letter from a Birmingham Jail," is one of the world's most famous arguments. It accelerated the U.S. civil rights movement in the 1960s and inspired protests against racism and oppression throughout the world. On April 3, 1963, Dr. King, as leader of the Southern Christian Leadership Conference, helped organize a series of sit-ins in Birmingham, Alabama, to protest segregation. On April 6 and 7, the demonstrations escalated when 45 protesters were arrested and two police dogs attacked and mauled a 19-year-old protester. The city then obtained an injunction forbidding King from organizing more demonstrations. When King refused to call off the demonstrations, he was arrested on Good Friday, April 12, and placed in solitary confinement in the Birmingham jail. While in jail he read a newspaper ad "A Call for Unity" signed by eight Alabama clergymen, urging demonstrators to make their case in the courts, not on the streets. These eight clergymen comprise the immediate audience for King's open letter, which he began writing in the margins of the newspaper and later finished on a yellow pad provided by a friendly jailer. "A Letter from a Birmingham Jail" elegantly illustrates the power of audience-based reasons.

A Call for Unity
12 April 1963

We the undersigned clergymen are among those who, in January, issued "An Appeal for Law and Order and Common Sense," in dealing with racial problems in Alabama. We expressed understanding that honest convictions in racial matters could properly be pursued in the courts, but urged that decisions of those courts should in the meantime be peacefully obeyed.

Since that time there had been some evidence of increased forbearance and a willingness to face facts. Responsible citizens have undertaken to work on various problems which cause racial friction and unrest. In Birmingham, recent public events have given indication that we will have opportunity for a new constructive and realistic approach to racial problems.

However, we are now confronted by a series of demonstrations by some of our Negro citizens, directed and led in part by outsiders. We recognize the natural impatience of people who feel that their hopes are slow in being realized. But we are convinced that these demonstrations are unwise and untimely.

We agree rather with certain local Negro leadership which has called for honest and open negotiation of racial issues in our area. And we believe this kind of facing of issues can best be accomplished by citizens of our own metropolitan area, white and Negro, meeting with their knowledge and experience of the local situation. All of us need to face that responsibility and find proper channels for its accomplishment.

Just as we formerly pointed out that "hatred and violence have no sanction in our religious and political traditions," we also point out that such actions as incite to hatred and violence, however technically peaceful those actions may be, have not contributed to the resolution of our local problems. We do not believe that these days of new hope are days when extreme measures are justified in Birmingham.

We commend the community as a whole, and the local news media and law enforcement officials in particular, on the calm manner in which these demonstrations have been handled. We urge the public to continue to show restraint should the demonstrations continue, and the law enforcement officials to remain calm and continue to protect our city from violence.

We further strongly urge our own Negro community to withdraw support from these demonstrations, and to unite locally in working peacefully for a better Birmingham. When rights are consistently denied, a cause should be pressed in the courts and in negotiations among local leaders, and not in the streets. We appeal to both our white and Negro citizenry to observe the principles of law and order and common sense.

Signed by:
C.C.J. Carpenter, D.D., LL.D., Bishop of Alabama
Joseph A. Durick, D.D., Auxiliary Bishop, Diocese of Mobile-Birmingham
Rabbi Milton L. Grafman, Temple Emanu-El, Birmingham, Alabama
Bishop Paul Hardin, Bishop of the Alabama-West Florida Conference of the Methodist Church
Bishop Nolan B. Harmon, Bishop of the North Alabama Conference of the Methodist Church
George M. Murray, D.D., LL.D., Bishop Coadjutor, Episcopal Diocese of Alabama
Edward V. Ramage, Moderator, Synod of the Alabama Presbyterian Church in the United States
Earl Stallings, Pastor, First Baptist Church, Birmingham, Alabama

Letter from Birmingham Jail
16 April 1963

My Dear Fellow Clergymen:

While confined here in the Birmingham city jail, I came across your recent statement calling my present activities "unwise and untimely." Seldom do I pause to answer criticism of my work and ideas. If I sought to answer all the criticisms that cross my desk, my secretaries would have little time for anything other than such correspondence in the course of the day, and I would have no time for constructive work. But since I feel that you are men of genuine good will and that your criticisms are sincerely set forth, I want to try to answer your statement in what I hope will be patient and reasonable terms.

I think I should indicate why I am here in Birmingham, since you have been influenced by the view which argues against "outsiders coming in." I have the honor of serving as president of the Southern Christian Leadership Conference, an organization operating in every southern state, with headquarters in Atlanta, Georgia. We have some eighty-five affiliated organizations across the South, and one of them is the Alabama Christian Movement for Human Rights. Frequently we share staff, educational and financial resources with our affiliates. Several months ago the affiliate here in Birmingham asked us to be on call to engage in a non-violent direct-action program if such were deemed necessary. We readily consented, and when the hour came we lived up to our promise. So I, along with several members of my staff, am here because I was invited here. I am here because I have organizational ties here.

But more basically, I am in Birmingham because injustice is here. Just as the prophets of the eighth century B.C. left their villages and carried their "thus saith the Lord" far beyond the boundaries of their home towns, and just as the Apostle Paul left his village of Tarsus and carried the gospel of Jesus Christ to the far corners of the Greco-Roman world, so am I compelled to carry the gospel of freedom beyond my own home town. Like Paul, I must constantly respond to the Macedonian call for aid.

Moreover, I am cognizant of the interrelatedness of all communities and states. I cannot sit idly by in Atlanta and not be concerned about what happens in Birmingham. Injustice anywhere is a threat to justice everywhere. We are caught in an inescapable network of mutuality, tied in a single garment of destiny. Whatever affects one directly, affects all indirectly. Never again can we afford to live with the narrow, provincial "outside agitator" idea. Anyone who lives inside the United States can never be considered an outsider anywhere within its bounds.

5   You deplore the demonstrations taking place in Birmingham. But your statement, I am sorry to say, fails to express a similar concern for the conditions that brought about the demonstrations. I am sure that none of you would want to rest content with the superficial kind of social analysis that deals merely with effects and does not grapple with underlying causes. It is unfortunate that demonstrations are taking place in Birmingham, but it is even more unfortunate that the city's white power structure left the Negro community with no alternative.

In any nonviolent campaign there are four basic steps: collection of the facts to determine whether injustices exist; negotiation; self-purification; and direct action. We have gone through all these steps in Birmingham. There can be no gainsaying the fact that racial injustice engulfs this community. Birmingham is probably the most thoroughly segregated city in the United States. Its ugly record of brutality is widely known. Negroes have experienced grossly unjust treatment in the courts. There have been more unsolved bombings of Negro homes and churches in Birmingham than in any other city in the nation. These are the hard, brutal facts of the case. On the basis of these conditions, Negro leaders sought to negotiate with the city fathers. But the latter consistently refused to engage in good-faith negotiation.

Then, last September, came the opportunity to talk with leaders of Birmingham's economic community. In the course of the negotiations, certain promises were made by the merchants—for example, to remove the stores' humiliating racial signs. On the basis of these promises, the Reverend Fred Shuttlesworth and the leaders of the Alabama Christian Movement for Human Rights agreed to a moratorium on all demonstrations. As the weeks and months went by, we realized that we were the victims of a broken promise. A few signs, briefly removed, returned; the others remained.

As in so many past experiences, our hopes had been blasted, and the shadow of deep disappointment settled upon us. We had no alternative except to prepare for direct action, whereby we would present our very bodies as a means of laying our case before the conscience of the local and the national community. Mindful of the difficulties involved, we decided to undertake a process of self-purification. We began a series of workshops on nonviolence, and we repeatedly asked ourselves: "Are you able to accept blows without retaliating?" "Are you able to endure the ordeal of jail?" We decided to schedule our direct-action program for the Easter season, realizing that except for Christmas, this is the main shopping period of the year. Knowing that a strong economic-withdrawal program would be the by-product of direct action, we felt that this would be the best time to bring pressure to bear on the merchants for the needed change.

Then it occurred to us that Birmingham's mayoral election was coming up in March, and we speedily decided to postpone action until after election day. When we discovered that the Commissioner of Public Safety, Eugene "Bull" Connor, had piled up enough votes to be in the run-off, we decided again to postpone action until the day after the run-off so that the demonstrations could not be used to cloud the issues. Like many others, we waited to see Mr. Connor defeated, and to this end we endured postponement after postponement. Having aided in this community need, we felt that our direct-action program could be delayed no longer.

10   You may well ask: "Why direct action? Why sit-ins, marches and so forth? Isn't negotiation a better path?" You are quite right in calling for negotiation. Indeed, this is the very purpose of direct action. Nonviolent direct action seeks to create such a crisis and foster such a tension that a community which has constantly refused to negotiate is forced to confront the issue. It seeks so to dramatize the issue that it can no longer be ignored. My citing the creation of tension as part of the work of the nonviolent-resister may sound rather shocking. But I must confess that I am not afraid of the word "tension." I have earnestly opposed violent tension, but there is a type of constructive, nonviolent tension which is necessary for growth. Just as Socrates felt that it was necessary to create a tension in the mind so that individuals could rise from the bondage of myths and half-truths to the unfettered realm of creative analysis and objective appraisal, so must we see the need for nonviolent gadflies to create the kind of tension in society that will help men rise from the dark depths of prejudice and racism to the majestic heights of understanding and brotherhood.

The purpose of our direct-action program is to create a situation so crisis-packed that it will inevitably open the door to negotiation. I therefore concur with you in your call for negotiation.

Too long has our beloved Southland been bogged down in a tragic effort to live in monologue rather than dialogue.

One of the basic points in your statement is that the action that I and my associates have taken in Birmingham is untimely. Some have asked: "Why didn't you give the new city administration time to act?" The only answer that I can give to this query is that the new Birmingham administration must be prodded about as much as the outgoing one, before it will act. We are sadly mistaken if we feel that the election of Albert Boutwell as mayor will bring the millennium to Birmingham. While Mr. Boutwell is a much more gentle person than Mr. Connor, they are both segregationists, dedicated to maintenance of the status quo. I have hope that Mr. Boutwell will be reasonable enough to see the futility of massive resistance to desegregation. But he will not see this without pressure from devotees of civil rights. My friends, I must say to you that we have not made a single gain in civil rights without determined legal and nonviolent pressure. Lamentably, it is an historical fact that privileged groups seldom give up their privileges voluntarily. Individuals may see the moral light and voluntarily give up their unjust posture; but, as Reinhold Niebuhr has reminded us, groups tend to be more immoral than individuals.

We know through painful experience that freedom is never voluntarily given by the oppressor; it must be demanded by the oppressed. Frankly, I have yet to engage in a direct-action campaign that was "well timed" in the view of those who have not suffered unduly from the disease of segregation. For years now I have heard the word "Wait!" It rings in the ear of every Negro with piercing familiarity. This "Wait" has almost always meant "Never." We must come to see, with one of our distinguished jurists, that "justice too long delayed is justice denied."

We have waited for more than 340 years for our constitutional God-given rights. The nations of Asia and Africa are moving with jetlike speed toward gaining political independence, but we still creep at horse-and-buggy pace toward gaining a cup of coffee at a lunch counter. Perhaps it is easy for those who have never felt the stinging darts of segregation to say, "Wait." But when you have seen vicious mobs lynch your mothers and fathers at will and drown your sisters and brothers at whim; when you have seen hate-filled policemen curse, kick, and even kill your black brothers and sisters; when you see the vast majority of your twenty million Negro brothers smothering in an airtight cage of poverty in the midst of an affluent society; when you suddenly find your tongue twisted and your speech stammering as you seek to explain to your six-year-old daughter why she can't go to the public amusement park that has just been advertised on television, and see tears welling up in her eyes when she is told that Funtown is closed to colored children, and see ominous clouds of inferiority beginning to form in her little mental sky, and see her beginning to distort her personality by developing an unconscious bitterness toward white people; when you have to concoct an answer for a five-year-old son who is asking: "Daddy, why do white people treat colored people so mean?"; when you take a cross-country drive and find it necessary to sleep night after night in the uncomfortable corners of your automobile because no motel will accept you; when you are humiliated day in and day out by nagging signs reading "white" and "colored"; when your first name becomes "nigger," your middle name becomes "boy" (however old you are) and your last name becomes "John," and your wife and mother are never given the respected title "Mrs."; when you are harried by day and haunted by night by the fact that you are a Negro, living constantly at tiptoe stance, never quite knowing what to expect next, and are plagued with inner fears and outer resentments; when you are forever fighting a degenerating sense of "nobodiness"—then you will understand why we find it difficult to wait. There comes a time when the cup of endurance runs over, and men are no longer willing to be plunged into the abyss of despair. I hope, sirs, you can understand our legitimate and unavoidable impatience.

15   You express a great deal of anxiety over our willingness to break laws. This is certainly a legitimate concern. Since we so diligently urge people to obey the Supreme Court's decision of 1954 outlawing segregation in the public schools, at first glance it may seem rather paradoxical for us consciously to break laws. One may well ask: "How can you advocate breaking some laws and obeying others?" The answer lies in the fact that there are two types of laws: just and unjust. I would be the first to advocate obeying just laws. One has not only a legal but a moral responsibility to obey just laws. Conversely, one has a moral responsibility to disobey unjust laws. I would agree with St. Augustine that "an unjust law is no law at all."

Now, what is the difference between the two? How does one determine whether a law is just or unjust? A just law is a man-made code that squares with the moral law or the law of God. An unjust law is a code that is out of harmony with the moral law. To put it in the terms of St. Thomas Aquinas: An unjust law is a human law that is not rooted in eternal law and natural law. Any law that uplifts human personality is just. Any law that degrades human personality is unjust. All segregation statutes are unjust because segregation distorts the soul and damages the personality. It gives the segregator a false sense of superiority and the segregated a false sense of inferiority. Segregation, to use the terminology of the Jewish philosopher Martin Buber, substitutes an "I–it" relationship for an "I–thou" relationship and ends up relegating persons to the status of things. Hence, segregation is not only politically, economically and sociologically unsound, it is morally wrong and sinful. Paul Tillich has said that sin is separation. Is not segregation an existential expression of man's tragic separation, his awful estrangement, his terrible sinfulness? Thus it is that I can urge men to obey the 1954 decision of the Supreme Court, for it is morally right; and I can urge them to disobey segregation ordinances, for they are morally wrong.

Let us consider a more concrete example of just and unjust laws. An unjust law is a code that a numerical or power majority group compels a minority group to obey but does not make binding on itself. This is *difference* made legal. By the same token, a just law is a code that a majority compels a minority to follow and that it is willing to follow itself. This is *sameness* made legal.

Let me give another explanation. A law is unjust if it is inflicted on a minority that, as a result of being denied the right to vote, had no part in enacting or devising the law. Who can say that the legislature of Alabama which set up that state's segregation laws was democratically elected? Throughout Alabama all sorts of devious methods are used to prevent Negroes from becoming registered voters, and there are some counties in which, even though Negroes constitute a majority of the population, not a single Negro is registered. Can any law enacted under such circumstances be considered democratically structured?

Sometimes a law is just on its face and unjust in its application. For instance, I have been arrested on a charge of parading without a permit. Now, there is nothing wrong in having an ordinance which requires a permit for a parade. But such an ordinance becomes unjust when it is used to maintain segregation and to deny citizens the First-Amendment privilege of peaceful assembly and protest.

20   I hope you are able to see the distinction I am trying to point out. In no sense do I advocate evading or defying the law, as would the rabid segregationist. That would lead to anarchy. One who breaks an unjust law must do so openly, lovingly, and with a willingness to accept the penalty. I submit that an individual who breaks a law that conscience tells him is unjust, and who willingly accepts the penalty of imprisonment in order to arouse the conscience of the community over its injustice, is in reality expressing the highest respect for law.

Of course, there is nothing new about this kind of civil disobedience. It was evidenced sublimely in the refusal of Shadrach, Meshach and Abednego to obey the laws of Nebuchadnezzar, on the ground that a higher moral law was at stake. It was practiced superbly by the early Christians, who were willing to face hungry lions and the excruciating pain of chopping blocks rather than submit to certain unjust laws of the Roman Empire. To a degree, academic freedom is a reality today because Socrates practiced civil disobedience. In our own nation, the Boston Tea Party represented a massive act of civil disobedience.

We should never forget that everything Adolf Hitler did in Germany was "legal" and everything the Hungarian freedom fighters did in Hungary was "illegal." It was "illegal" to aid and comfort a Jew in Hitler's Germany. Even so, I am sure that, had I lived in Germany at the time, I would have aided and comforted my Jewish brothers. If today I lived in a Communist country where certain principles dear to the Christian faith are suppressed I would openly advocate disobeying that country's antireligious laws.

I must make two honest confessions to you, my Christian and Jewish brothers. First, I must confess that over the past few years I have been gravely disappointed with the white moderate. I have almost reached the regrettable conclusion that the Negro's great stumbling block in his stride toward freedom is not the White Citizen's Counciler or the Ku Klux Klanner, but the white moderate, who is more devoted to "order" than to justice; who prefers a negative peace which is the presence of tension to a positive peace which is the presence of justice; who constantly says, "I agree with you in the goal you seek, but I cannot agree with your methods of direct action"; who paternalistically believes he can set the timetable for another man's freedom; who lives by a mythical concept of time and who constantly advises the Negro to wait for a "more convenient season." Shallow understanding from people of good will is more frustrating than absolute misunderstanding from people of ill will. Lukewarm acceptance is much more bewildering than outright rejection.

I had hoped that the white moderate would understand that law and order exist for the purpose of establishing justice and that when they fail in this purpose they become the dangerously structured dams that block the flow of social progress. I had hoped that the white moderate would understand that the present tension in the South is a necessary phase of the transition from an obnoxious negative peace, in which the Negro passively accepted his unjust plight, to a substantive and positive peace, in which all men will respect the dignity and worth of human personality. Actually, we who engage in nonviolent direct action are not the creators of tension. We merely bring to the surface the hidden tension that is already alive. We bring it out in the open, where it can be seen and dealt with. Like a boil that can never be cured so long as it is covered up but must be opened with all its ugliness to the natural medicines of air and light, injustice must be exposed, with all the tension its exposure creates, to the light of human conscience and the air of national opinion before it can be cured.

25   In your statement you assert that our actions, even though peaceful, must be condemned because they precipitate violence. But is this a logical assertion? Isn't this like condemning a robbed man because his possession of money precipitated the evil act of robbery? Isn't this like condemning Socrates because his unswerving commitment to truth and his philosophical inquiries precipitated the act by the misguided populace in which they made him drink hemlock? Isn't this like condemning Jesus because his unique God-consciousness and never-ceasing devotion to God's will precipitated the evil act of crucifixion? We must come to see that, as the federal courts have consistently affirmed, it is wrong to urge an individual to cease his efforts to gain his basic constitutional rights because the quest may precipitate violence. Society must protect the robbed and punish the robber.

I had also hoped that the white moderate would reject the myth concerning time in relation to the struggle for freedom. I have just received a letter from a white brother in Texas. He writes: "All Christians know that the colored people will receive equal rights eventually, but it is possible that you are in too great a religious hurry. It has taken Christianity almost two thousand years to accomplish what it has. The teachings of Christ take time to come to earth." Such an attitude stems from a tragic misconception of time, from the strangely irrational notion that there is something in the very flow of time that will inevitably cure all ills. Actually, time itself is neutral; it can be used either destructively or constructively. More and more I feel that the people of ill will have used time much more effectively than have the people of good will. We will have to repent in this generation not merely for the hateful words and actions of the bad people but for the appalling silence of the good people. Human progress never rolls in on wheels of inevitability; it comes through the tireless efforts of men willing to be co-workers with God, and without this hard work, time itself becomes an ally of the forces of social stagnation. We must use time creatively, in the knowledge that the time is always ripe to do right. Now is the time to make real the promise of democracy and transform our pending national elegy into a creative psalm of brotherhood. Now is the time to lift our national policy from the quicksand of racial injustice to the solid rock of human dignity.

You speak of our activity in Birmingham as extreme. At first I was rather disappointed that fellow clergymen would see my nonviolent efforts as those of an extremist. I began thinking about the fact that I stand in the middle of two opposing forces in the Negro community. One is a force of complacency, made up in part of Negroes who, as a result of long years of oppression, are so drained of self-respect and a sense of "somebodiness" that they have adjusted to segregation; and in part of a few middle-class Negroes who, because of a degree of academic and economic security and because in some ways they profit by segregation, have become insensitive to the problems of the masses. The other force is one of bitterness and hatred, and it comes perilously close to advocating violence. It is expressed in the various black nationalist groups that are springing up across the nation, the largest and best-known being Elijah Muhammad's Muslim movement. Nourished by the Negro's frustration over the continued existence of racial discrimination, this movement is made up of people who have lost faith in America, who have absolutely repudiated Christianity, and who have concluded that the white man is an incorrigible "devil."

I have tried to stand between these two forces, saying that we need emulate neither the "do-nothingism" of the complacent nor the hatred and despair of the black nationalist. For there is the more excellent way of love and nonviolent protest. I am grateful to God that, through the influence of the Negro church, the way of nonviolence became an integral part of our struggle.

If this philosophy had not emerged, by now many streets of the South would, I am convinced, be flowing with blood. And I am further convinced that if our white brothers dismiss as "rabble-rousers" and "outside agitators" those of us who employ nonviolent direct action, and if they refuse to support our nonviolent efforts, millions of the Negroes will, out of frustration and despair, seek solace and security in black-nationalist ideologies—a development that would inevitably lead to a frightening racial nightmare.

30   Oppressed people cannot remain oppressed forever. The yearning for freedom eventually manifests itself, and that is what has happened to the American Negro. Something within has reminded him of his birthright of freedom, and something without has reminded him that it can be gained. Consciously or unconsciously, he has been caught up by the *Zeitgeist*, and with his black brothers of Africa and his brown and yellow brothers of Asia, South America and the Caribbean, the United States Negro is moving with a sense of great urgency toward the promised land of racial justice. If one recognizes this vital urge that has engulfed the Negro community, one should readily understand why public demonstrations are taking place. The Negro has many pent-up resentments and latent frustrations, and he must release them. So let him march; let him make prayer pilgrimages to the city hall; let him go on freedom rides—and try to understand why he must do so. If his repressed emotions are not released in nonviolent ways, they will seek expression through violence; this is not a threat but a fact of history. So I have not said to my people: "Get rid of your discontent." Rather, I have tried to say that this normal and healthy discontent can be channeled into the creative outlet of nonviolent direct action. And now this approach is being termed extremist.

But though I was initially disappointed at being categorized as an extremist, as I continued to think about the matter I gradually gained a measure of satisfaction from the label. Was not Jesus an extremist for love: "Love your enemies, bless them that curse you, and persecute you." Was not Amos an extremist for justice: "Let justice roll down like waters and righteousness like an ever-flowing stream." Was not Paul an extremist for the Christian gospel: "I bear in my body the marks of the Lord Jesus." Was not Martin Luther an extremist: "Here I stand; I cannot do otherwise, so help me God." And John Bunyan: "I will stay in jail to the end of my days before I make a butchery of my conscience." And Abraham Lincoln: "This nation cannot survive half slave and half free." And Thomas Jefferson: "We hold these truths to be self-evident, that all men are created equal...." So the question is not whether we will be extremists, but what kind of extremists we will be. Will we be extremists for hate or for love? Will we be extremists for the preservation of injustice or for the extension of justice? In that dramatic scene on Calvary's hill three men were crucified. We must never forget that all three were crucified for the same crime—the crime of extremism. Two were extremists for immorality, and thus fell below their environment. The other, Jesus Christ, was an extremist for love, truth and goodness, and thereby rose above his environment. Perhaps the South, the nation and the world are in dire need of creative extremists.

I had hoped that the white moderate would see this need. Perhaps I was too optimistic; perhaps I expected too much. I suppose I should have realized that few members of the oppressor race can understand the deep groans and passionate yearnings of the oppressed race, and still fewer have the vision to see that injustice must be rooted out by strong, persistent and determined action. I am thankful, however, that some of our white brothers in the South have grasped the meaning of this social revolution and committed themselves to it. They are still all too few in quantity, but they are big in quality. Some—such as Ralph McGill, Lillian Smith, Harry Golden, James McBride Dabbs, Ann Braden and Sarah Patton Boyle—have written about our struggle in eloquent and prophetic terms. Others have marched with us down nameless streets of the South. They have languished in filthy, roach-infested jails, suffering the abuse and brutality of policemen who view them as "dirty nigger-lovers." Unlike so many of their moderate brothers and sisters, they have recognized the urgency of the moment and sensed the need for powerful "action" antidotes to combat the disease of segregation.

Let me take note of my other major disappointment. I have been so greatly disappointed with the white church and its leadership. Of course, there are some notable exceptions. I am not unmindful of the fact that each of you has taken some significant stands on this issue. I commend you, Reverend Stallings, for your Christian stand on this past Sunday, in welcoming Negroes to your worship service on a nonsegregated basis. I commend the Catholic leaders of this state for integrating Spring Hill College several years ago.

But despite these notable exceptions, I must honestly reiterate that I have been disappointed with the church. I do not say this as one of those negative critics who can always find something wrong with the church. I say this as a minister of the gospel, who loves the church; who was nurtured in its bosom; who has been sustained by its spiritual blessings and who will remain true to it as long as the cord of life shall lengthen.

35   When I was suddenly catapulted into the leadership of the bus protest in Montgomery, Alabama, a few years ago, I felt we would be supported by the white church. I felt that the white ministers, priests and rabbis of the South would be among our strongest allies. Instead, some have been outright opponents, refusing to understand the freedom movement and misrepresenting its leaders; all too many others have been more cautious than courageous and have remained silent behind the anesthetizing security of stained-glass windows.

In spite of my shattered dreams, I came to Birmingham with the hope that the white religious leadership of this community would see the justice of our cause and, with deep moral concern, would serve as the channel through which our just grievances could reach the power structure. I had hoped that each of you would understand. But again I have been disappointed.

I have heard numerous southern religious leaders admonish their worshipers to comply with a desegregation decision because it is the law, but I have longed to hear white ministers declare: "Follow this decree because integration is morally right and because the Negro is your brother." In the midst of blatant injustices inflicted upon the Negro, I have watched white churchmen stand on the sideline and mouth pious irrelevancies and sanctimonious trivialities. In the midst of a mighty struggle to rid our nation of racial and economic injustice, I have heard many ministers say: "Those are social issues, with which the gospel has no real concern." And I have watched many churches commit themselves to a completely otherworldly religion which makes a strange, un-Biblical distinction between body and soul, between the sacred and the secular.

I have traveled the length and breadth of Alabama, Mississippi and all the other southern states. On sweltering summer days and crisp autumn mornings I have looked at the South's beautiful churches with their lofty spires pointing heavenward. I have beheld the impressive outlines of her massive religious-education buildings. Over and over I have found myself asking: "What kind of people worship here? Who is their God? Where were their voices when the lips of

Governor Barnett dripped with words of interposition and nullification? Where were they when Governor Wallace gave a clarion call for defiance and hatred? Where were their voices of support when bruised and weary Negro men and women decided to rise from the dark dungeons of complacency to the bright hills of creative protest?"

Yes, these questions are still in my mind. In deep disappointment I have wept over the laxity of the church. But be assured that my tears have been tears of love. There can be no deep disappointment where there is not deep love. Yes, I love the church. How could I do otherwise? I am in the rather unique position of being the son, the grandson, and the great-grandson of preachers. Yes, I see the church as the body of Christ. But, oh! How we have blemished and scarred that body through social neglect and through fear of being nonconformists.

40   There was a time when the church was very powerful—in the time when the early Christians rejoiced at being deemed worthy to suffer for what they believed. In those days the church was not merely a thermometer that recorded the ideas and principles of popular opinion; it was a thermostat that transformed the mores of society. Whenever the early Christians entered a town, the people in power became disturbed and immediately sought to convict the Christians for being "disturbers of the peace" and "outside agitators." But the Christians pressed on, in the conviction that they were "a colony of heaven," called to obey God rather than man. Small in number, they were big in commitment. They were too God-intoxicated to be "astronomically intimidated." By their effort and example they brought an end to such ancient evils as infanticide and gladiatorial contests.

Things are different now. So often the contemporary church is a weak, ineffectual voice with an uncertain sound. So often it is an archdefender of the status quo. Far from being disturbed by the presence of the church, the power structure of the average community is consoled by the church's silent—and often even vocal—sanction of things as they are.

But the judgment of God is upon the church as never before. If today's church does not recapture the sacrificial spirit of the early church, it will lose its authenticity, forfeit the loyalty of millions, and be dismissed as an irrelevant social club with no meaning for the twentieth century. Every day I meet young people whose disappointment with the church has turned into outright disgust.

Perhaps I have once again been too optimistic. Is organized religion too inextricably bound to the status quo to save our nation and the world? Perhaps I must turn my faith to the inner spiritual church, the church within the church, as the true *ekklesia* and the hope of the world. But again I am thankful to God that some noble souls from the ranks of organized religion have broken loose from the paralyzing chains of conformity and joined us as active partners in the struggle for freedom. They have left their secure congregations and walked the streets of Albany, Georgia, with us. They have gone down the highways of the South on tortuous rides for freedom. Yes, they have gone to jail with us. Some have been dismissed from their churches, have lost the support of their bishops and fellow ministers. But they have acted in the faith that right defeated is stronger than evil triumphant. Their witness has been the spiritual salt that has preserved the true meaning of the gospel in these troubled times. They have carved a tunnel of hope through the dark mountain of disappointment.

I hope the church as a whole will meet the challenge of this decisive hour. But even if the church does not come to the aid of justice, I have no despair about the future. I have no fear about the outcome of our struggle in Birmingham, even if our motives are at present misunderstood. We will reach the goal of freedom in Birmingham and all over the nation, because the goal of America is freedom. Abused and scorned though we may be, our destiny is tied up with America's destiny. Before the pilgrims landed at Plymouth, we were here. Before the pen of Jefferson etched the majestic words of the Declaration of Independence across the pages of history, we were here. For more than two centuries our forebears labored in this country without wages; they made cotton king; they built the homes of their masters while suffering gross injustice and shameful humiliation—and yet out of a bottomless vitality they continued to thrive and develop. If the inexpressible cruelties of slavery could not stop us, the opposition we now face will surely fail. We will win our freedom because the sacred heritage of our nation and the eternal will of God are embodied in our echoing demands.

45   Before closing I feel impelled to mention one other point in your statement that has troubled me profoundly. You warmly commended the Birmingham police force for keeping "order" and "preventing violence." I doubt that you would have so warmly commended the police force if you had seen its dogs sinking their teeth into unarmed, nonviolent Negroes. I doubt that you would so quickly commend the policemen if you were to observe their ugly and inhumane treatment of Negroes here in the city jail; if you were to watch them push and curse old Negro women and young Negro girls; if you were to see them slap and kick old Negro men and young boys; if you were to observe them, as they did on two occasions, refuse to give us food because we wanted to sing our grace together. I cannot join you in your praise of the Birmingham police department.

It is true that police have exercised a degree of discipline in handling the demonstrators. In this sense they have conducted themselves rather "nonviolently" in public. But for what purpose? To preserve the evil system of segregation. Over the past few years I have consistently preached that nonviolence demands that the means we use must be as pure as the ends we seek. I have tried to make clear that it is wrong to use immoral means to attain moral ends. But now I must affirm that it is just as wrong, or perhaps even more so, to use moral means to preserve immoral ends. Perhaps Mr. Connor and his policemen have been rather nonviolent in public, as was Chief Pritchett in Albany, Georgia, but they have used the moral means of nonviolence to maintain the immoral end of racial injustice. As T. S. Eliot has said: "The last temptation is the greatest treason: To do the right deed for the wrong reason."

I wish you had commended the Negro sit-inners and demonstrators of Birmingham for their sublime courage, their willingness to suffer and their amazing discipline in the midst of great provocation. One day the South will recognize its real heroes. They will be the James Merediths, with the noble sense of purpose that enables them to face jeering and hostile mobs, and with the agonizing loneliness that characterizes the life of the pioneer. They will be old, oppressed, battered Negro women, symbolized in a seventy-two-year-old woman in Montgomery, Alabama, who rose up with a sense of dignity and with her people decided not to ride segregated buses, and who responded with ungrammatical profundity to one who inquired about her weariness: "My feets is tired, but my soul is at rest." They will be the young high school and college students, the young ministers of the gospel and a host of their elders, courageously and nonviolently sitting in at lunch counters and willingly going to jail for conscience' sake. One day the South will know that when these disinherited children of God sat down at lunch counters, they were in reality standing up for what is best in the American dream and for the most sacred values in our Judaeo-Christian heritage, thereby bringing our nation back to those great wells of democracy which were dug deep by the founding fathers in their formulation of the Constitution and the Declaration of Independence.

Never before have I written so long a letter. I'm afraid it is much too long to take your precious time. I can assure you that it would have been much shorter if I had been writing from a comfortable desk, but what else can one do when he is alone in a narrow jail cell, other than write long letters, think long thoughts and pray long prayers?

If I have said anything in this letter that overstates the truth and indicates an unreasonable impatience, I beg you to forgive me. If I have said anything that understates the truth and indicates my having a patience that allows me to settle for anything less than brotherhood, I beg God to forgive me.

50   I hope this letter finds you strong in faith. I also hope that circumstances will soon make it possible for me to meet each of you, not as an integrationist or a civil-rights leader but as a fellow clergyman and a Christian brother. Let us all hope that the dark clouds of racial prejudice will soon pass away and the deep fog of misunderstanding will be lifted from our fear-drenched communities, and in some not too distant tomorrow the radiant stars of love and brotherhood will shine over our great nation with all their scintillating beauty.

Yours for the cause of Peace and Brotherhood
MARTIN LUTHER KING, JR.

Lifeboat Ethics: The Case Against Aid That Does Harm

GARRETT HARDIN

Garrett Hardin's "Lifeboat Ethics: The Case Against Aid That Does Harm" is not as widely known as King's "Letter from a Birmingham Jail," but it has been influential in changing the debate about foreign aid, in stimulating new thinking about the causes of poverty and about ways to combat it, and in promoting wider understanding of the "tragedy of the commons." It has also sparked dozens of impassioned counterarguments. Based on an unflinching analysis of consequences, Hardin presents his anti-liberal thesis against foreign aid and open borders. Rhetorically, Hardin's argument is famous for its extended use of analogy—in this case a lifeboat filled with people representing rich countries and an ocean of swimmers (poor countries) clamoring to get in the boat. The article was originally published in Psychology Today *in 1974.*

Environmentalists use the metaphor of the earth as a "spaceship" in trying to persuade countries, industries and people to stop wasting and polluting our natural resources. Since we all share life on this planet, they argue, no single person or institution has the right to destroy, waste, or use more than a fair share of its resources.

But does everyone on earth have an equal right to an equal share of its resources? The spaceship metaphor can be dangerous when used by misguided idealists to justify suicidal policies for sharing our resources through uncontrolled immigration and foreign aid. In their enthusiastic but unrealistic generosity, they confuse the ethics of a spaceship with those of a lifeboat.

A true spaceship would have to be under the control of a captain, since no ship could possibly survive if its course were determined by committee. Spaceship Earth certainly has no captain; the United Nations is merely a toothless tiger, with little power to enforce any policy upon its bickering members.

If we divide the world crudely into rich nations and poor nations, two thirds of them are desperately poor, and only one third comparatively rich, with the United States the wealthiest of all. Metaphorically each rich nation can be seen as a lifeboat full of comparatively rich people. In the ocean outside each lifeboat swim the poor of the world, who would like to get in, or at least to share some of the wealth. What should the lifeboat passengers do?

First, we must recognize the limited capacity of any lifeboat. For example, a nation's land has a limited capacity to support a population and as the current energy crisis has shown us, in some ways we have already exceeded the carrying capacity of our land.

Adrift in a Moral Sea

So here we sit, say 50 people in our lifeboat. To be generous, let us assume it has room for 10 more, making a total capacity of 60. Suppose the 50 of us in the lifeboat see 100 others swimming in the water outside, begging for admission to our boat or for handouts. We have several options: we may be tempted to try to live by the Christian ideal of being "our brother's keeper," or by the Marxist ideal of "to each according to his needs." Since the needs of all in the water are the same, and since they can all be seen as "our brothers," we could take them all into our boat, making a total of 150 in a boat designed for 60. The boat swamps, everyone drowns. Complete justice, complete catastrophe.

Since the boat has an unused excess capacity of 10 more passengers, we could admit just 10 more to it. But which 10 do we let in? How do we choose? Do we pick the best 10, "first come, first served"? And what do we say to the 90 we exclude? If we do let an extra 10 into our lifeboat, we will have lost our "safety factor," an engineering principle of critical importance. For example, if we don't leave room for excess capacity as a safety factor in our country's agriculture, a new plant disease or a bad change in the weather could have disastrous consequences.

Suppose we decide to preserve our small safety factor and admit no more to the lifeboat. Our survival is then possible although we shall have to be constantly on guard against boarding parties.

While this last solution clearly offers the only means of our survival, it is morally abhorrent to many people. Some say they feel guilty about their good luck. My reply is simple: "Get out and yield your place to others." This may solve the problem of the guilt-ridden person's conscience, but it does not change the ethics of the lifeboat. The needy person to whom the guilt-ridden person yields his place will not himself feel guilty about his good luck. If he did, he would not climb aboard. The net result of conscience-stricken people giving up their unjustly held seats is the elimination of that sort of conscience from the lifeboat.

This is the basic metaphor within which we must work out our solutions. Let us now enrich the image, step by step, with substantive additions from the real world, a world that must solve real and pressing problems of overpopulation and hunger.

The harsh ethics of the lifeboat become even harsher when we consider the reproductive differences between the rich nations and the poor nations. The people inside the lifeboats are doubling in numbers every 87 years; those swimming around outside are doubling, on the average, every 35 years, more than twice as fast as the rich. And since the world's resources are dwindling, the difference in prosperity between the rich and the poor can only increase.

As of 1973, the U.S. had a population of 210 million people, who were increasing by 0.8 percent per year. Outside our lifeboat, let us imagine another 210 million people (say the combined populations of Colombia, Ecuador, Venezuela, Morocco, Pakistan, Thailand and the Philippines) who are increasing at a rate of 3.3 percent per year. Put differently, the doubling time for this aggregate population is 21 years, compared to 87 years for the U.S.

The harsh ethics of the lifeboat become harsher when we consider the reproductive differences between rich and poor.

Multiplying the Rich and the Poor

Now suppose the U.S. agreed to pool its resources with those seven countries, with everyone receiving an equal share. Initially the ratio of Americans to non-Americans in this model would be one-to-one. But consider what the ratio would be after 87 years, by which time the Americans would have doubled to a population of 420 million. By then, doubling every 21 years, the other group would have swollen to 3.54 billion. Each American would have to share the available resources with more than eight people.

But, one could argue, this discussion assumes that current population trends will continue, and they may not. Quite so. Most likely the rate of population increase will decline much faster in the U.S. than it will in the other countries, and there does not seem to be much we can do about it. In sharing with "each according to his needs," we must recognize that needs are determined by population size, which is determined by the rate of reproduction, which at present is regarded as a sovereign right of every nation, poor or not. This being so, the philanthropic load created by the sharing ethic of the spaceship can only increase.

The Tragedy of the Commons

The fundamental error of spaceship ethics, and the sharing it requires, is that it leads to what I call "the tragedy of the commons." Under a system of private property, the men who own property recognize their responsibility to care for it, for if they don't they will eventually suffer. A farmer, for instance, will allow no more cattle in a pasture than its carrying capacity justifies. If he overloads it, erosion sets in, weeds take over, and he loses the use of the pasture.

If a pasture becomes a commons open to all, the right of each to use it may not be matched by a corresponding responsibility to protect it. Asking everyone to use it with discretion will hardly do, for the considerate herdsman who refrains from overloading the commons suffers more than a selfish one who says his needs are greater. If everyone would restrain himself, all would be well; but it takes only one less than everyone to ruin a system of voluntary restraint. In a crowded world of less than perfect human beings, mutual ruin is inevitable if there are no controls. This is the tragedy of the commons.

One of the major tasks of education today should be the creation of such an acute awareness of the dangers of the commons that people will recognize its many varieties. For example, the air and water have become polluted because they are treated as commons. Further growth in the population or per-capita conversion of natural resources into pollutants will only make the problem worse. The same holds true for the fish of the oceans. Fishing fleets have nearly disappeared in many parts of the world, technological improvements in the art of fishing are hastening the day of complete ruin. Only the replacement of the system of the commons with a responsible system of control will save the land, air, water and oceanic fisheries.

The World Food Bank

In recent years there has been a push to create a new commons called a World Food Bank, an international depository of food reserves to which nations would contribute according to their abilities and from which they would draw according to their needs. This humanitarian proposal has received support from many liberal international groups, and from such prominent citizens as Margaret Mead, U.N. Secretary General Kurt Waldheim, and Senators Edward Kennedy and George McGovern.

A world food bank appeals powerfully to our humanitarian impulses. But before we rush ahead with such a plan, let us recognize where the greatest political push comes from, lest we be disillusioned later. Our experience with the "Food for Peace program," or Public Law 480, gives us the answer. This program moved billions of dollars worth of U.S. surplus grain to food-short, population-long countries during the past two decades. But when P.L. 480 first became law, a headline in the business magazine *Forbes* revealed the real power behind it: "Feeding the World's Hungry Millions: How It Will Mean Billions for U.S. Business."

And indeed it did. In the years 1960 to 1970, U.S. taxpayers spent a total of $7.9 billion on the Food for Peace program. Between 1948 and 1970, they also paid an additional $50 billion for other economic-aid programs, some of which went for food and food-producing machinery and technology. Though all U.S. taxpayers were forced to contribute to the cost of P.L. 480 certain special interest groups gained handsomely under the program. Farmers did not have to contribute the grain; the Government or rather the taxpayers, bought it from them at full market prices. The increased demand raised prices of farm products generally. The manufacturers of farm machinery, fertilizers and pesticides benefited by the farmers' extra efforts to grow more food. Grain elevators profited from storing the surplus until it could be shipped. Railroads made money hauling it to ports, and shipping lines profited from carrying it overseas. The implementation of P.L. 480 required the creation of a vast Government bureaucracy, which then acquired its own vested interest in continuing the program regardless of its merits.

Extracting Dollars

Those who proposed and defended the Food for Peace program in public rarely mentioned its importance to any of these special interests. The public emphasis was always on its humanitarian effects. The combination of silent selfish interests and highly vocal humanitarian apologists made a powerful and successful lobby for extracting money from taxpayers. We can expect the same lobby to push now for the creation of a World Food Bank.

However great the potential benefit to selfish interests, it should not be a decisive argument against a truly humanitarian program. We must ask if such a program would actually do more good than harm, not only momentarily but also in the long run. Those who propose the food bank usually refer to a current "emergency" or "crisis" in terms of world food supply. But what is an emergency? Although they may be infrequent and sudden, everyone knows that emergencies will occur from time to time. A well-run family, company, organization or country prepares for the likelihood of accidents and emergencies. It expects them, it budgets for them, it saves for them.

Learning the Hard Way

What happens if some organizations or countries budget for accidents and others do not? If each country is solely responsible for its own well-being, poorly managed ones will suffer. But they can learn from experience. They may mend their ways, and learn to budget for infrequent but certain emergencies. For example, the weather varies from year to year, and periodic crop failures are certain. A wise and competent government saves out of the production of the good years in anticipation of bad years to come. Joseph taught this policy to Pharaoh in Egypt more than 2,000 years ago. Yet the great majority of the governments in the world today do not follow such a policy.

They lack either the wisdom or the competence, or both. Should those nations that do manage to put something aside be forced to come to the rescue each time an emergency occurs among the poor nations?

"But it isn't their fault!" Some kind-hearted liberals argue. "How can we blame the poor people who are caught in an emergency? Why must they suffer for the sins of their governments?" The concept of blame is simply not relevant here. The real question is, what are the operational consequences of establishing a world food bank? If it is open to every country every time a need develops, slovenly rulers will not be motivated to take Joseph's advice. Someone will always come to their aid. Some countries will deposit food in the world food bank, and others will withdraw it. There will be almost no overlap. As a result of such solutions to food shortage emergencies, the poor countries will not learn to mend their ways, and will suffer progressively greater emergencies as their populations grow.

Population Control the Crude Way

On the average poor countries undergo a 2.5 percent increase in population each year; rich countries, about 0.8 percent. Only rich countries have anything in the way of food reserves set aside, and even they do not have as much as they should. Poor countries have none. If poor countries received no food from the outside, the rate of their population growth would be periodically checked by crop failures and famines. But if they can always draw on a world food bank in time of need, their population can continue to grow unchecked, and so will their "need" for aid. In the short run, a world food bank may diminish that need, but in the long run it actually increases the need without limit.

Without some system of worldwide food sharing, the proportion of people in the rich and poor nations might eventually stabilize. The overpopulated poor countries would decrease in numbers, while the rich countries that had room for more people would increase. But with a well-meaning system of sharing, such as a world food bank, the growth differential between the rich and the poor countries will not only persist, it will increase. Because of the higher rate of population growth in the poor countries of the world, 88 percent of today's children are born poor, and only 12 percent rich. Year by year the ratio becomes worse, as the fast-reproducing poor outnumber the slow-reproducing rich.

A world food bank is thus a commons in disguise. People will have more motivation to draw from it than to add to any common store. The less provident and less able will multiply at the expense of the abler and more provident, bringing eventual ruin upon all who share in the commons. Besides, any system of "sharing" that amounts to foreign aid from the rich nations to the poor nations will carry the taint of charity, which will contribute little to the world peace so devoutly desired by those who support the idea of a world food bank.

As past U.S. foreign-aid programs have amply and depressingly demonstrated, international charity frequently inspires mistrust and antagonism rather than gratitude on the part of the recipient nation [see "What Other Nations Hear When the Eagle Screams," by Kenneth J. and Mary M. Gergen, PT, June].

Chinese Fish and Miracle Rice

The modern approach to foreign aid stresses the export of technology and advice, rather than money and food. As an ancient Chinese proverb goes: "Give a man a fish and he will eat for a day; teach him how to fish and he will eat for the rest of his days." Acting on this advice, the Rockefeller and Ford Foundations have financed a number of programs for improving agriculture in the hungry nations. Known as the "Green Revolution," these programs have led to the development of "miracle rice" and "miracle wheat," new strains that offer bigger harvests and greater resistance to crop damage. Norman Borlaug, the Nobel Prize winning agronomist who, supported by the Rockefeller Foundation, developed "miracle wheat," is one of the most prominent advocates of a world food bank.

Whether or not the Green Revolution can increase food production as much as its champions claim is a debatable but possibly irrelevant point. Those who support this well-intended humanitarian effort should first consider some of the fundamentals of human ecology. Ironically, one man who did was the late Alan Gregg, a vice president of the Rockefeller Foundation. Two decades ago he expressed strong doubts about the wisdom of such attempts to increase food production. He likened the growth and spread of humanity over the surface of the earth to the spread of cancer in the human body, remarking that "cancerous growths demand food; but, as far as I know, they have never been cured by getting it."

Overloading the Environment

Every human born constitutes a draft on all aspects of the environment: food, air, water, forests, beaches, wildlife, scenery and solitude. Food can, perhaps, be significantly increased to meet a growing demand. But what about clean beaches, unspoiled forests, and solitude? If we satisfy a growing population's need for food, we necessarily decrease its per capita supply of the other resources needed by men.

India, for example, now has a population of 600 million, which increases by 15 million each year. This population already puts a huge load on a relatively impoverished environment. The country's forests are now only a small fraction of what they were three centuries ago and floods and erosion continually destroy the insufficient farmland that remains. Every one of the 15 million new lives added to India's population puts an additional burden on the environment, and increases the economic and social costs of crowding. However humanitarian our intent, every Indian life saved through medical or nutritional assistance from abroad diminishes the quality of life for those who remain, and for subsequent generations. If rich countries make it possible, through foreign aid, for

600 million Indians to swell to 1.2 billion in a mere 28 years, as their current growth rate threatens, will future generations of Indians thank us for hastening the destruction of their environment? Will our good intentions be sufficient excuse for the consequences of our actions?

My final example of a commons in action is one for which the public has the least desire for rational discussion—immigration. Anyone who publicly questions the wisdom of current U.S. immigration policy is promptly charged with bigotry, prejudice, ethnocentrism, chauvinism, isolationism or selfishness. Rather than encounter such accusations, one would rather talk about other matters leaving immigration policy to wallow in the crosscurrents of special interests that take no account of the good of the whole, or the interests of posterity.

Perhaps we still feel guilty about things we said in the past. Two generations ago the popular press frequently referred to Dagos, Wops, Polacks, Chinks and Krauts in articles about how America was being "overrun" by foreigners of supposedly inferior genetic stock [see "The Politics of Genetic Engineering: Who Decides Who's Defective?" PT, June]. But because the implied inferiority of foreigners was used then as justification for keeping them out, people now assume that restrictive policies could only be based on such misguided notions. There are other grounds.

A Nation of Immigrants

Just consider the numbers involved. Our Government acknowledges a net inflow of 400,000 immigrants a year. While we have no hard data on the extent of illegal entries, educated guesses put the figure at about 600,000 a year. Since the natural increase (excess of births over deaths) of the resident population now runs about 1.7 million per year, the yearly gain from immigration amounts to at least 19 percent of the total annual increase, and may be as much as 37 percent if we include the estimate for illegal immigrants. Considering the growing use of birth-control devices, the potential effect of education campaigns by such organizations as Planned Parenthood Federation of America and Zero Population Growth, and the influence of inflation and the housing shortage, the fertility rate of American women may decline so much that immigration could account for all the yearly increase in population. Should we not at least ask if that is what we want?

For the sake of those who worry about whether the "quality" of the average immigrant compares favorably with the quality of the average resident, let us assume that immigrants and native-born citizens are of exactly equal quality, however one defines that term. We will focus here only on quantity; and since our conclusions will depend on nothing else, all charges of bigotry and chauvinism become irrelevant.

Immigration vs. Food Supply

World food banks move food to the people, hastening the exhaustion of the environment of the poor countries. Unrestricted immigration, on the other hand, moves people to the food, thus speeding up the destruction of the environment of the rich countries. We can easily understand why poor people should want to make this latter transfer, but why should rich hosts encourage it?

As in the case of foreign-aid programs, immigration receives support from selfish interests and humanitarian impulses. The primary selfish interest in unimpeded immigration is the desire of employers for cheap labor, particularly in industries and trades that offer degrading work. In the past, one wave of foreigners after another was brought into the U.S. to work at wretched jobs for wretched wages. In recent years the Cubans, Puerto Ricans and Mexicans have had this dubious honor. The interests of the employers of cheap labor mesh well with the guilty silence of the country's liberal intelligentsia. White Anglo-Saxon Protestants are particularly reluctant to call for a closing of the doors to immigration for fear of being called bigots.

But not all countries have such reluctant leadership. Most educated Hawaiians, for example, are keenly aware of the limits of their environment, particularly in terms of population growth. There is only so much room on the islands, and the islanders know it. To Hawaiians, immigrants from the other 49 states present as great a threat as those from other nations. At a recent meeting of Hawaiian government officials in Honolulu, I had the ironic delight of hearing a speaker who like most of his audience was of Japanese ancestry, ask how the country might practically and constitutionally close its doors to further immigration. One member of the audience countered: "How can we shut the doors now? We have many friends and relatives in Japan that we'd like to bring here some day so that they can enjoy Hawaii too." The Japanese-American speaker smiled sympathetically and answered: "Yes, but we have children now, and someday we'll have grandchildren too. We can bring more people here from Japan only by giving away some of the land that we hope to pass on to our grandchildren some day. What right do we have to do that?"

At this point, I can hear U.S. liberals asking: "How can you justify slamming the door once you're inside? You say that immigrants should be kept out. But aren't we all immigrants, or the descendants of immigrants? If we insist on staying, must we not admit all others?" Our craving for intellectual order leads us to seek and prefer symmetrical rules and morals: a single rule for me and everybody else; the same rule yesterday, today and tomorrow. Justice, we feel, should not change with time and place.

We Americans of non-Indian ancestry can look upon ourselves as the descendants of thieves who are guilty morally, if not legally, of stealing this land from its Indian owners. Should we then give back the land to the now living American descendants of those Indians? However morally or logically sound this proposal may be, I, for one, am unwilling to live by it and I know no one else who is. Besides, the logical consequence would be absurd. Suppose that, intoxicated with a sense of pure justice, we should decide to turn our land over to the Indians. Since all our other wealth has also been derived from the land, wouldn't we be morally obliged to give that back to the Indians too?

Pure Justice vs. Reality

Clearly, the concept of pure justice produces an infinite regression to absurdity. Centuries ago, wise men invented statutes of limitations to justify the rejection of such pure justice, in the interest of preventing continual disorder. The law zealously defends property rights, but only relatively recent property rights. Drawing a line after an arbitrary time has elapsed may be unjust, but the alternatives are worse.

We are all the descendants of thieves, and the world's resources are inequitably distributed. But we must begin the journey to tomorrow from the point where we are today. We cannot remake the past. We cannot safely divide the wealth equitably among all peoples so long as people reproduce at different rates. To do so would guarantee that our grandchildren and everyone else's grandchildren, would have only a ruined world to inhabit.

To be generous with one's own possessions is quite different from being generous with those of posterity. We should call this point to the attention of those who from a commendable love of justice and equality, would institute a system of the commons, either in the form of a world food bank, or of unrestricted immigration. We must convince them if we wish to save at least some parts of the world from environmental ruin.

Without a true world government to control reproduction and the use of available resources, the sharing ethic of the spaceship is impossible. For the foreseeable future, our survival demands that we govern our actions by the ethics of a lifeboat, harsh though they may be. Posterity will be satisfied with nothing less.

Guernica

PABLO PICASSO

On April 26, 1937, two years before the German Nazis rolled across Poland at the beginning of World War II, Hitler sent a contingent of airplanes on a practice run over the small market town of Guernica, a Basque village in northern Spain, to test their effectiveness at bombing a city into oblivion. Hitler had two goals: to support the right wing army of Generalissimo Francisco Franco in overthrowing the existing Spanish government and to perfect techniques of aerial bombardment needed in its planned blitzkrieg across Europe. The utter destruction of Guernica has come to symbolize the atrocity of modern warfare. Pablo Picasso, who had been commissioned by the Spanish Government to create a mural for Spain's exhibition building at the 1937 World's Fair in Paris, chose the horror of Guernica as his theme. Picasso's huge (11 feet by 26 feet), black and white, oil-on-canvas painting has become perhaps the world's most famous visual argument against war.

The Obligation to Endure

RACHEL CARSON

"The Obligation to Endure" is the second chapter of Rachel Carson's influential book The Silent Spring. *A marine biologist, meticulous researcher, and powerful writer, Carson is regarded as one of the world's most influential environmentalists.* The Silent Spring *(1962) exposed the subtle, insidious dangers of DDT, a pesticide that since its discovery in the 1940s had been hailed as a miracle substance that could wipe out mosquitoes and other disease-bearing or crop-destroying insects. According to the National Resource Defense Council, whose Web site contains an inspiring story about Carson's work,* The Silent Spring *"eloquently questioned humanity's faith in technological progress and helped set the stage for the environmental movement." In "The Obligation to Endure," which precedes the more technical portions of the book, Carson presents her causal argument showing how apparently beneficial chemicals can have disastrous unanticipated consequences. Her work was strenuously attacked by the chemical industry, which argued that if we followed Carson's recommendations we would return to the dark ages of insect-borne diseases and famine from failed agriculture. But Carson's carefully documented research defended her against the charges of the chemical industry. According to the National Resource Defense Council, the "threats Carson had outlined—the contamination of the food chain, cancer, genetic damage, the deaths of entire species—were too frightening to ignore. For the first time, the need to regulate industry in order to protect the environment became widely accepted, and environmentalism was born."*

The history of life on earth has been a history of interaction between living things and their surroundings. To a large extent, the physical form and the habits of the earth's vegetation and its animal life have been molded by the environment. Considering the whole span of earthly time, the opposite effect, in which life actually modifies its surroundings, has been relatively slight. Only within the moment of time represented by the present century has one species—man—acquired significant power to alter the nature of his world.

During the past quarter century this power has not only increased to one of disturbing magnitude but it has changed in character. The most alarming of all man's assaults upon the environment is the contamination of air, earth, rivers, and sea with dangerous and even lethal materials. This pollution is for the most part irrecoverable; the chain of evil it initiates not only in the world that must support life but in living tissues is for the most part irreversible. In this now universal contamination of the environment, chemicals are the sinister and little-recognized partners of radiation in changing the very nature of the world—the very nature of its life. Strontium 90, released through nuclear explosions into the air, comes to earth in rain or drifts down as fallout, lodges in soil, enters into the grass or corn or wheat grown there, and in time takes up its abode in the bones of a human being, there to remain until his death. Similarly, chemicals sprayed on croplands or forests or gardens lie long in soil, entering into living organisms, passing from one to another in a chain of poisoning and death. Or they pass mysteriously by underground streams until they emerge and, through the alchemy of air and sunlight, combine into new forms that kill vegetation, sicken cattle, and work unknown harm on those who drink from once pure wells. As Albert Schweitzer has said, "Man can hardly even recognize the devils of his own creation."

It took hundreds of millions of years to produce the life that now inhabits the earth—eons of time in which that developing and evolving and diversifying life reached a state of adjustment and balance with its surroundings. The environment, rigorously shaping and directing the life it supported, contained elements that were hostile as well as supporting. Certain rocks gave out dangerous radiation; even within the light of the sun, from which all life draws its energy, there were short-wave radiations with power to injure. Given time—time not in years but in millennia—life adjusts, and a balance has been reached. For time is the essential ingredient; but in the modern world there is no time.

The rapidity of change and the speed with which new situations are created follow the impetuous and heedless pace of man rather than the deliberate pace of nature. Radiation is no longer merely the background radiation of rocks, the bombardment of cosmic rays, the ultraviolet of the sun that have existed before there was any life on earth; radiation is now the unnatural creation of man's tampering with the atom. The chemicals to which life is asked to make its adjustment are no longer merely the calcium and silica and copper and all the rest of the minerals washed out of the rocks and carried in rivers to the sea; they are the synthetic creations of man's inventive mind, brewed in his laboratories, and having no counterparts in nature.

To adjust to these chemicals would require time on the scale that is nature's; it would require not merely the years of a man's life but the life of generations. And even this, were it by some miracle possible, would be futile, for the new chemicals come from our laboratories in an endless stream; almost five hundred annually find their way into actual use in the United States alone. The figure is staggering and its implications are not easily grasped—500 new chemicals to which the bodies of men and animals are required somehow to adapt each year, chemicals totally outside the limits of biologic experience.

Among them are many that are used in man's war against nature. Since the mid-1940's over 200 basic chemicals have been created for use in killing insects, weeds, rodents, and other organisms described in the modern vernacular as "pests"; and they are sold under several thousand different brand names.

These sprays, dusts, and aerosols are now applied almost universally to farms, gardens, forests, and homes—nonselective chemicals that have the power to kill every insect, the "good" and the "bad," to still the song of birds and the leaping of fish in the streams, to coat the leaves with a deadly film, and to linger on in soil—all this though the intended target may be only a few weeds or insects. Can anyone believe it is possible to lay down such a barrage of poisons on the surface of the earth without making it unfit for all life? They should not be called "insecticides," but "biocides."

The whole process of spraying seems caught up in an endless spiral. Since DDT was released for civilian use, a process of escalation has been going on in which ever more toxic materials must be found. This has happened because insects, in a triumphant vindication of Darwin's principle of the survival of the fittest, have evolved super races immune to the particular insecticide used, hence a deadlier one has always to be developed—and then a deadlier one than that. It has happened also because, for reasons to be described later, destructive insects often undergo a "flareback," or resurgence, after spraying, in numbers greater than before. Thus the chemical war is never won, and all life is caught in its violent crossfire.

Along with the possibility of the extinction of mankind by nuclear war, the central problem of our age has therefore become the contamination of man's total environment with such substances of incredible potential for harm—substances that accumulate in the tissues of plants and animals and even penetrate the germ cells to shatter or alter the very material of heredity upon which the shape of the future depends.

Some would-be architects of our future look toward a time when it will be possible to alter the human germ plasm by design. But we may easily be doing so now by inadvertence, for many chemicals, like radiation, bring about gene mutations. It is ironic to think that man might determine his own future by something so seemingly trivial as the choice of an insect spray.

All this has been risked—for what? Future historians may well be amazed by our distorted sense of proportion. How could intelligent beings seek to control a few unwanted species by a method that contaminated the entire environment and brought the threat of disease and death even to their own kind? Yet this is precisely what we have done. We have done it, moreover, for reasons that collapse the moment we examine them. We are told that the enormous and expanding use of pesticides is necessary to maintain farm production. Yet is our real problem not one of *overproduction*? Our farms, despite measures to remove acreages from production and to pay farmers *not* to produce, have yielded such a staggering excess of crops that the American taxpayer in 1962 is paying out more than one billion dollars a year as the total carrying cost of the surplus-food storage program. And is the situation helped when one branch of the Agriculture Department tries to reduce production while another states, as it did in 1958, "It is believed generally that reduction of crop acreages under provisions of the Soil Bank will stimulate interest in use of chemicals to obtain maximum production on the land retained in crops."

All this is not to say there is no insect problem and no need of control. I am saying, rather, that control must be geared to realities, not to mythical situations, and that the methods employed must be such that they do not destroy us along with the insects.

The problem whose attempted solution has brought such a train of disaster in its wake is an accompaniment of our modern way of life. Long before the age of man, insects inhabited the earth—a group of extraordinarily varied and adaptable beings. Over the course of time since man's advent, a small percentage of the more than half a million species of insects have come into conflict with human welfare in two principal ways: as competitors for the food supply and as carriers of human disease.

Disease-carrying insects become important where human beings are crowded together, especially under conditions where sanitation is poor, as in time of natural disaster or war or in situations of extreme poverty and deprivation. Then control of some sort becomes necessary. It is a sobering fact, however, as we shall presently see, that the method of massive chemical control has had only limited success, and also threatens to worsen the very conditions it is intended to curb.

Under primitive agricultural conditions the farmer had few insect problems. These arose with the intensification of agriculture—the devotion of immense acreages to a single crop. Such a system set the stage for explosive increases in specific insect populations. Single-crop farming does not take advantage of the principles by which nature works; it is agriculture as an engineer might conceive it to be. Nature has introduced great variety into the landscape, but man has displayed a passion for simplifying it. Thus he undoes the built-in checks and balances by which nature holds the species within bounds. One important natural check is a limit on the amount of suitable habitat for each species. Obviously then, an insect that lives on wheat can build up its population to much higher levels on a farm devoted to wheat than on one in which wheat is intermingled with other crops to which the insect is not adapted.

The same thing happens in other situations. A generation or more ago, the towns of large areas of the United States lined their streets with the noble elm tree. Now the beauty they hopefully created is threatened with complete destruction as disease sweeps through the elms, carried by a beetle that would have only limited chance to build up large populations and to spread from tree to tree if the elms were only occasional trees in a richly diversified planting.

Another factor in the modern insect problem is one that must be viewed against a background of geologic and human history: the spreading of thousands of different kinds of organisms from their native homes to invade new territories. This worldwide migration has been studied and graphically described by the British ecologist Charles Elton in his recent book *The Ecology of Invasions.* During the Cretaceous Period, some hundred million years ago, flooding seas cut many land bridges between continents and living things found themselves confined in what Elton calls "colossal separate nature reserves." There, isolated from others of their kind, they developed many new species. When some of the land masses were joined again, about 15 million years ago, these species began to move out into new territories—a movement that is not only still in progress but is now receiving considerable assistance from man.

The importation of plants is the primary agent in the modern spread of species, for animals have almost invariably gone along with the plants, quarantine being a comparatively recent and not completely effective innovation. The United States Office of Plant Introduction alone has introduced almost 200,000 species and varieties of plants from all over the world. Nearly half of the 180 or so major insect enemies of plants in the United States are accidental imports from abroad, and most of them have come as hitchhikers on plants.

In new territory, out of reach of the restraining hand of the natural enemies that kept down its numbers in its native land, an invading plant or animal is able to become enormously abundant. Thus it is no accident that our most troublesome insects are introduced species.

These invasions, both the naturally occurring and those dependent on human assistance, are likely to continue indefinitely. Quarantine and massive chemical campaigns are only extremely expensive ways of buying time. We are faced, according to Dr. Elton, "with a life-and-death need not just to find new technological means of suppressing this plant or that animal"; instead we need the basic knowledge of animal populations and their relations to their surroundings that will "promote an even balance and damp down the explosive power of outbreaks and new invasions."

Much of the necessary knowledge is now available but we do not use it. We train ecologists in our universities and even employ them in our governmental agencies but we seldom take their advice. We allow the chemical death rain to fall as though there were no alternative, whereas in fact there are many, and our ingenuity could soon discover many more if given opportunity.

Have we fallen into a mesmerized state that makes us accept as inevitable that which is inferior or detrimental, as though having lost the will or the vision to demand that which is good? Such thinking, in the words of the ecologist Paul Shepard, "idealizes life with only its head out of water, inches above the limits of toleration of the corruption of its own environ-ment...Why should we tolerate a diet of weak poisons, a home in insipid surroundings, a cir-cle of acquaintances who are not quite our enemies, the noise of motors with just enough re-lief to prevent insanity? Who would want to live in a world which is just not quite fatal?"

Yet such a world is pressed upon us. The crusade to create a chemically sterile, insect-free world seems to have engendered a fanatic zeal on the part of many specialists and most of the so-called control agericies. On every hand there is evidence that those engaged in spraying op-erations exercise a ruthless power. "The regulatory entomologists...function as prosecutor, judge and jury, tax assessor and collector and sheriff to enforce their own orders," said Connecticut entomologist Neely Turner. The most flagrant abuses go unchecked in both state and federal agencies.

It is not my contention that chemical insecticides must never be used. I do contend that we have put poisonous and biologically potent chemicals indiscriminately into the hands of persons largely or wholly ignorant of their potentials for harm. We have subjected enormous numbers of people to contact with these poisons, without their consent and often without their knowledge. If the Bill of Rights contains no guarantee that a citizen shall be secure against lethal poisons distributed either by private individuals or by public officials, it is surely only because our fore-fathers, despite their considerable wisdom and foresight, could conceive of no such problem.

I contend, furthermore, that we have allowed these chemicals to be used with little or no advance investigation of their effect on soil, water, wildlife, and man himself. Future gen-erations are unlikely to condone our lack of prudent concern for the integrity of the natural world that supports all life.

There is still very limited awareness of the nature of the threat. This is an era of specialists, each of whom sees his own problem and is unaware of or intolerant of the larger frame into which it fits. It is also an era dominated by industry, in which the right to make a dollar at whatever cost is seldom challenged. When the public protests, confronted with some obvious evidence of damaging results of pesticide applications, it is fed little tranquilizing pills of half truth. We urgently need an end to these false assurances, to the sugar coating of unpalatable facts. It is the public that is being asked to assume the risks that the insect controllers calcu-late. The public must decide whether it wishes to continue on the present road, and it can do so only when in full possession of the facts. In the words of Jean Rostand, "The obligation to en-dure gives us the right to know."

The Perils of Obedience

STANLEY MILGRAM

Yale psychologist Stanley Milgram published "The Perils of Obedience" in Harper's *in December 1963. The article reports experiments he began two years earlier at a time when Nazi war criminal Adolph Eichmann went to trial in Israel for his role in exterminating Jews in the Holocaust. Eichmann's defense was that he was a mid-level functionary who was simply "following orders." The utter ordinariness of Eichmann (as opposed to his be-ing a psychopathic anti-Semite) led philosopher Hannah Arendt to write* The Banality of

Evil, a book about Eichmann's trial that discredits our comfortable belief that ordinary people, unlike Eichmann, would resist following orders that harmed others. It was within this atmosphere that Stanley Milgram developed an experiment to study the average person's resistance to authority. As he explains in the article that follows, "I must conclude that Arendt's conception of the banality of evil comes closer to the truth than one might dare imagine.... This is, perhaps, the most fundamental lesson of our study: Ordinary people, simply doing their jobs, and without any particular hostility, can become agents in a terrible destructive process" (655). Milgram's experiment, along with later studies by other psychologists, particularly the Stanford Prison Experiment, revealed the dark heart of the ordinary person.

Obedience is as basic an element in the structure of social life as one can point to. Some system of authority is a requirement of all communal living, and it is only the person dwelling in isolation who is not forced to respond, with defiance or submission, to the commands of others. For many people, obedience is a deeply ingrained behavior tendency, indeed a potent impulse overriding training in ethics, sympathy, and moral conduct.

The dilemma inherent in submission to authority is ancient, as old as the story of Abraham, and the question of whether one should obey when commands conflict with conscience has been argued by Plato, dramatized in Antigone, and treated to philosophic analysis in almost every historical epoch. Conservative philosophers argue that the very fabric of society is threatened by disobedience, while humanists stress the primacy of the individual conscience.

The legal and philosophic aspects of obedience are of enormous import, but they say very little about how most people behave in concrete situations. I set up a simple experiment at Yale University to test how much pain an ordinary citizen would inflict on another person simply because he was ordered to by an experimental scientist. Stark authority was pitted against the subjects' strongest moral imperatives against hurting others, and, with the subjects' ears ringing with the screams of the victims, authority won more often than not. The extreme willingness of adults to go to almost any lengths on the command of an authority constitutes the chief finding of the study and the fact most urgently demanding explanation.

In the basic experimental designs two people come to a psychology laboratory to take part in a study of memory and learning. One of them is designated a "teacher" and the other a "learner." The experimenter explains that the study is concerned with the effects of punishment on learning. The learner is conducted into a room, seated in a kind of miniature electric chair, his arms are strapped to prevent excessive movement, and an electrode is attached to his wrist. He is told that he will be read lists of simple word pairs, and that he will then be tested on his ability to remember the second word of a pair when he hears the first one again. Whenever he makes an error, he will receive electric shocks of increasing intensity.[1]

The real focus of the experiment is the teacher. After watching the learner being strapped into place, he is seated before an impressive shock generator. The instrument panel consists of thirty lever

---

[1]The ethical problems of carrying out an experiment of this sort are too complex to be dealt with here, but they receive extended treatment in the book from which this article is taken.

switches set in a horizontal line. Each switch is clearly labeled with a voltage designation ranging from 14 to 450 volts.

The following designations are clearly indicated for groups of four switches, going from left to right: Slight Shock, Moderate Shock, Strong Shock, Very Strong Shock, Intense Shock, Extreme Intensity Shock, Danger: Severe Shock. (Two switches after this last designation are simply marked XXX.)

When a switch is depressed, a pilot light corresponding to each switch is illuminated in bright red; an electric buzzing is heard; a blue light, labeled "voltage energizer," flashes; the dial on the voltage meter swings to the right; and various relay clicks sound off.

The upper left hand corner of the generator is labeled SHOCK GENERATOR, TYPE ZLB. DYSON INSTRUMENT COMPANY, WALTHAM, MASS., OUTPUT 15 VOLTS – 450 VOLTS.

Each subject is given a sample 45 volt shock from the generator before his run as teacher, and the jolt strengthens his belief in the authenticity of the machine.

The teacher is a genuinely naive subject who has come to the laboratory for the experiment. The learner, or victim, is actually an actor who receives no shock at all. The point of the experiment is to see how far a person will proceed in a concrete and measurable situation in which he is ordered to inflict increasing pain on a protesting victim.

Conflict arises when the man receiving the shock begins to show that he is experiencing discomfort. At 75 volts, he grunts; at 120 volts, he complains loudly; at 150, he demands to be released from the experiment. As the voltage increases, his protests become more vehement and emotional. At 285 volts, his response can be described only as an agonized scream. Soon thereafter, he makes no sound at all.

For the teacher, the situation quickly becomes one of gripping tension. It is not a game for him: conflict is intense and obvious. The manifest suffering of the learner presses him to quit: but each time he hesitates to administer a shock, the experimenter orders him to continue. To extricate himself from this plight, the subject must make a clear break with authority.

The subject, Gretchen Brantt,[2] is an attractive thirty-one year old medical technician who works at the Yale Medical School. She had emigrated from Germany five years before.

On several occasions when the learner complains, she turns to the experimenter coolly and inquires, "Shall I continue?" She promptly returns to her task when the experimenter asks her to do so. At the administration of 210 volts she turns to the experimenter, remarking firmly, "Well, I'm sorry, I don't think we should continue."

EXPERIMENTER: The experiment requires that you go on until he has learned all the word pairs correctly.

BRANDT: He has a heart condition, I'm sorry. He told you that before.

EXPERIMENTER: The shocks may be painful but they're not dangerous.

BRANDT: Well, I'm sorry. I think when shocks continue like this they are dangerous. You ask him if he wants to get out. It's his free will.

EXPERIMENTER: It is absolutely essential that we continue....

BRANDT: I'd like you to ask him. We came here of our free will. If he wants to continue I'll go ahead. He told you he had a heart condition. I'm sorry. I don't want to be responsible for anything happening to him. I wouldn't like it for me either.

EXPERIMENTER: You have no other choice.

BRANDT: I think we are here on our own free will. I don't want to be responsible if anything happens to him. Please understand that.

---

[2]Names of subjects described in this piece have been changed.

She refuses to go further and the experiment is terminated.

The woman is firm and resolute throughout. She indicates in the interview that she was in no way tense or nervous, and this corresponds to her controlled appearance during the experiment. She feels that the last shock she administered to the learner was extremely painful and reiterates that she "did not want to be responsible for any harm to him."

The woman's straightforward, courteous behavior in the experiment, lack of tension, and total control of her own action seem to make disobedience a simple and rational deed. Her behavior is the very embodiment of what I envisioned would be true for almost all subjects.

An Unexpected Outcome

Before the experiments, I sought predictions about the outcome from various kinds of people—psychiatrists, college sophomores, middle-class adults, graduate students and faculty in the behavioral sciences. With remarkable similarity, they predicted that virtually all the subjects would refuse to obey the experimenter. The psychiatrist, specifically, predicted that most subjects would not go beyond 150 volts, when the victim makes his first explicit demand to be freed. They expected that only 4 percent would reach 300 volts, and that only a pathological fringe of about one in a thousand would administer the highest shock on the board.

These predictions were unequivocally wrong. Of the forty subjects in the first experiment, twenty-five obeyed the orders of the experimenter to the end, punishing the victim until they reached the most potent shock available on the generator. After 450 volts were administered three times, the experimenter called a halt to the session. Many obedient subjects then heaved sighs of relief, mopped their brows, rubbed their fingers over their eyes, or nervously fumbled cigarettes. Others displayed only minimal signs of tension from beginning to end.

When the very first experiments were carried out, Yale undergraduates were used as subjects, and about 60 percent of them were fully obedient. A colleague of mine immediately dismissed these findings as having no relevance to "ordinary" people, asserting that Yale undergraduates are a highly aggressive, competitive bunch who step on each other's necks on the slightest provocation. He assured me that when "ordinary" people were tested, the results would be quite different. As we moved from the pilot studies to the regular experimental series, people drawn from every stratum of New Haven life came to be employed in the experiment—professionals, white collar workers, unemployed persons, and industrial workers. The experimental outcome was the same as we had observed among the students.

Moreover, when the experiments were repeated in Princeton, Munich, Rome, South Africa, and Australia, the level of obedience was invariably somewhat higher than found in the investigation reported in this article. Thus one scientist in Munich found 85 percent of his subjects obedient.

Fred Prozi's reactions, if more dramatic than most, illuminate the conflicts experienced by others in less visible form. About fifty years old and unemployed at the time of the experiment, he has a good-natured, if slightly dissolute, appearance, and he strikes people as a rather ordinary fellow. He begins the session calmly but becomes tense as it proceeds. After delivering the 180-volt shock, he pivots around in the chair and, shaking his head, addresses the experimenter in agitated tones:

PROZI: I can't stand it I'm not going to kill that man in there. You hear him hollering?

EXPERIMENTER: As I told you before, the shocks may be painful, but…

PROZI: But he's hollering. He can't stand it. What's going to happen to him?

EXPERIMENTER (his voice is patient, matter-of fact):   The experiment requires that you continue, Teacher.

PROZI: Aah, but, unh, I'm not going to get that man sick in there—know what I mean?

EXPERIMENTER: Whether the learner likes it or not, we must go on, through all the word pairs.

PROZI: I refuse to take the responsibility. He's in there hollering.

EXPERIMENTER: It's absolutely essential that you continue, Prozi.

PROZI: (indicating the unused questions): There's too many left here, I mean, Jeez, if he gets them wrong, there's too many of them left. I mean, who's going to take the responsibility if anything happens to that gentleman?

EXPERIMENTER: I'm responsible for anything that happens to him. Continue, please.

PROZI: All right. (Consults list of words.) The next one's "Slow—walk, truck, dance, music." Answer please. (A buzzing sound indicates the learner has signaled his answer.) Wrong. A hundred and ninety-five volts. "Dance." (Zzumph!)

LEARNER (yelling):   Let me out of here! My heart's bothering me. (Teacher looks at experimenter.)

EXPERIMENTER: Continue, please.

LEARNER (screaming):   Let me out of here! You have no right to keep me here! Let me out of here, my heart's bothering me, let me out!

PROZI (shakes head, pats the table nervously):   You see he's hollering. Hear that? Gee, I don't know.

EXPERIMENTER: The experiment requires…

PROZI (interrupting):   I know it does sir, but I mean—hunh! He don't know what he's getting in for. He's up to 195 volts! (Experiment continues, through 210 volts, 225 volts, 240 volts, 255 volts, 270 volts, at which point Prozi, with evident relief, runs out of word-pair questions.)

EXPERIMENTER: You'll have to go back to the beginning of that page and go through them again until he's learned them all correctly.

PROZI: Aw, no. I'm not going to kill that man. You mean I've got to keep going up with the scale? No sir. He's hollering in there. I'm not going to give him 450 volts.

EXPERIMENTER: The experiment requires that you go on.

LEARNER: Ohh. I absolutely refuse to answer anymore. (Shouting urgently now.) Let me out of here! You can't hold me here! Get me out! Get-me-out-of-here!

EXPERIMENTER: Continue. The next word is "green," please.

PROZI: "Green—grass, hat, ink, apple." (Nothing happens. No answering buzz. Just gloomy silence.)

PROZI: I don't think he is going to answer.

EXPERIMENTER: If the learner doesn't answer in a reasonable time, about four or five seconds, consider the answer wrong. And follow the same procedures you have been doing for wrong answers. Say, "Wrong," tell him the number of volts, give him the punishment, read him the correct answer. Continue, please.

PROZI: "Green—grass, hat, ink, apple." Answer, please. (More silence. Subject just sits there.)

EXPERIMENTER: Go on with the procedure, please.

PROZI: Three hundred and fifteen volts. The answer is "ink." (Zzumph!)

LEARNER: Ohh. Ooohh!

PROZI: (relieved to hear response). Next one…

LEARNER: I absolutely refuse to answer.

PROZI: You got to. You get a shock if you don't answer. (Experiment continues with learner refusing to answer, and, finally failing even to grunt or groan. At 375 volts, the subject stands up.)

PROZI: I think something's happened to that fellow in there. I don't get no answer. He was hollering at less voltage. Can't you check in and see if he's all right, please?

EXPERIMENTER: (with same detached calm): Not once we've started. Please continue, Teacher.

PROZI (sits down, sighs deeply): "Cool—day, shade, water, paint." Answer please. Are you all right in there? Are you all right?

EXPERIMENTER: Please continue, Teacher. Continue, please. (Subject pushes lever. Zzumph!)

PROZI (swiveling around in his chair): Something's happened to that man in there. (Swiveling back.) Next one. "Low—dollar, necklace, moon, paint." (Turning around again.) Something's happened to that man in there. You better check in on him, sir. He won't answer or nothing.

EXPERIMENTER: Continue. Go on, please.

PROZI: You accept all responsibility?

EXPERIMENTER: The responsibility is mine. Correct. Please go on. (Subject returns to his list, starts running through words as rapidly as he can read them, works through to 450 volts.)

PROZI: That's that.

EXPERIMENTER: Continue using the 450 switch for each wrong answer. Continue, please.

PROZI: But I don't get anything!

EXPERIMENTER: Please continue. The next word is "white."

PROZI: Don't you think you should look in on him, please?

EXPERIMENTER: Not once we've started the experiment.

PROZI: What if he's dead in there? (Gestures toward the room with the electric chair.) I mean, he told me he can't stand the shock, sir. I don't mean to be rude, but I think you should look in on him. All you have to do is look in on him. All you have to do is look in the door. I don't get no answer, no noise. Something might have happened to the gentleman in there, sir.

EXPERIMENTER: We must continue. Go on, please.

PROZI: You mean keep giving that? Four-hundred-fifty volts, what he's got now?

EXPERIMENTER: That's correct. Continue. The next word is "white."

PROZI (now at a furious pace): "White—cloud, horse, rock, house." Answer, please. The answer is "horse." Four hundred and fifty volts. (Zzumph!) Next words, "Bag—paint, music. clown, girl." The next answer is "paint." Four hundred and fifty volts. (Zzumph!) Next word is "Short—sentence, movie..."

EXPERIMENTER: Excuse me, Teacher. We'll have to discontinue the experiment.

Peculiar Reactions

Morris Braverman, another subject, is a thirty-nine-year-old social worker. He looks older than his years because of his bald head and serious demeanor. His brow is furrowed, as if all the world's burdens were carried on his face. He appears intelligent and concerned.

When the learner refuses to answer and the experimenter instructs Braverman to treat the absence of an answer as equivalent to a wrong answer, he takes his instruction to heart. Before administering 300 volts he asserts officiously to the victim, "Mr. Wallace, your silence has to be considered as a wrong answer." Then he administers the shock. He offers halfheartedly to change places with the learner, then asks the experimenter, "Do I have to follow these instructions literally?" He is satisfied with the experimenter's answer that he does. His very refined and authoritative manner of speaking is increasingly broken up by wheezing laughter.

The experimenter's notes on Mr. Braverman at the last few shocks are:

Almost breaking up now each time gives shock. Rubbing face to hide laughter.
Squinting, trying to hide face with hand, still laughing.
Cannot control his laughter at this point no matter what he does.
Clenching fist, pushing it onto table.

In an interview after the session, Mr. Braverman summarizes the experiment with impressive fluency and intelligence. He feels the experiment may have been designed also to "test the effects on the teacher of being in an essentially sadistic role, as well as the reactions of a student to a learning situation that was authoritative and punitive."

When asked how painful the last few shocks administered to the learner were, he indicates that the most extreme category on the scale is not adequate (it read EXTREMELY PAINFUL) and places his mark at the edge of the scale with an arrow carrying it beyond the scale.

It is almost impossible to convey the greatly relaxed, sedate quality of his conversation in the interview. In the most relaxed terms, he speaks about his severe inner tension.

EXPERIMENTER: At what point were you most tense or nervous?

MR. BRAVERMAN: Well, when he first began to cry out in pain, and I realized this was hurting him. This got worse when he just blocked and refused to answer. There was I. I'm a nice person, I think, hurting somebody, and caught up in what seemed a mad situation…and in the interest of science, one goes through with it.

When the interviewer pursues the general question of tension, Mr. Braverman spontaneously mentions his laughter.

"My reactions were awfully peculiar. I don't know if you were watching me, but my reactions were giggly, and trying to stifle laughter. This isn't the way I usually am. This was a sheer reaction to a totally impossible situation. And my reaction was to the situation of having to hurt somebody. And being totally helpless and caught up in a set of circumstances where I just couldn't deviate and I couldn't try to help. This is what got me."

Mr. Braverman, like all subjects, was told the actual nature and purpose of the experiment, and a year later he affirmed in a questionnaire that he had learned something of personal importance: "What appalled me was that I could possess this capacity for obedience and compliance to a central idea, i.e., the adherence to this value was at the expense of violation of another value, i.e., don't hurt someone who is helpless and not hurting you. As my wife said, 'You can call yourself Eichmann.' I hope I deal more effectively with any future conflicts of values I encounter."

The Etiquette of Submission

One theoretical interpretation of this behavior holds that all people harbor deeply aggressive instincts continually pressing for expression, and that the experiment provides institutional justification for the release of these impulses. According to this view, if a person is placed in a situation in which he has complete power over another individual, whom he may punish as much as he likes, all that is sadistic and bestial in man comes to the fore. The impulse to shock the victim is seen to flow from the potent aggressive tendencies, which are part of the motivational life of the individual, and the experiment, because it provides social legitimacy, simply opens the door to their expression.

It becomes vital, therefore, to compare the subject's performance when he is under orders and when he is allowed to choose the shock level.

The procedure was identical to our standard experiment, except that the teacher was told that he was free to select any shock level of any on the trials. (The experimenter took pains to point out that the teacher could use the highest levels on the generator, the lowest, any in between, or any combination of levels.) Each subject proceeded for thirty critical trials. The learner's protests were coordinated to standard shock levels, his first grunt coming at 75 volts, his first vehement protest at 150 volts.

The average shock used during the thirty critical trials was less than 60 volts—lower than the point at which the victim showed the first signs of discomfort. Three of the forty subjects did not go beyond the very lowest level on the board, twenty-eight went no higher than 75 volts, and thirty-eight did not go beyond the first loud protest at 150 volts. Two subjects provided the exception, administering up to 325 and 450 volts, but the overall result was that the great majority of people delivered very low, usually painless, shocks when the choice was explicitly up to them.

The condition of the experiment undermines another commonly offered explanation of the subjects' behavior—that those who shocked the victim at the most severe levels came only from the sadistic fringe of society. If one considers that almost two-thirds of the participants fall into the category of "obedient" subjects, and that they represented ordinary people drawn from working, managerial, and professional classes, the argument becomes very shaky. Indeed, it is highly reminiscent of the issue that arose in connection with Hannah Arendt's 1963 book, *Eichmann in Jerusalem.* Arendt contended that the prosecution's effort to depict Eichmann as a sadistic monster was fundamentally wrong, that he came closer to being an uninspired bureaucrat who simply sat at his desk and did his job. For asserting her views, Arendt became the object of considerable scorn, even calumny. Somehow, it was felt that the monstrous deeds carried out by Eichmann required a brutal, twisted personality, evil incarnate. After witnessing hundreds of ordinary persons submit to the authority in our own experiments, I must conclude that Arendt's conception of the banality of evil comes closer to the truth than one might dare imagine. The ordinary person who shocked the victim did so out of a sense of obligation—an impression of his duties as a subject—and not from any peculiarly aggressive tendencies.

This is, perhaps, the most fundamental lesson of our study: ordinary people, simply doing their jobs, and without any particular hostility on their part, can become agents in a terrible destructive process. Moreover, even when the destructive effects of their work become patently clear, and they are asked to carry out actions incompatible with fundamental standards of morality, relatively few people have the resources needed to resist authority.

Many of the people were in some sense against what they did to the learner, and many protested even while they obeyed. Some were totally convinced of the wrongness of their actions but could not bring themselves to make an open break with authority. They often derived satisfaction from their thoughts and felt that—within themselves, at least—they had been on the side of the angels. They tried to reduce strain by obeying the experimenter but "only slightly," encouraging the learner, touching the generator switches gingerly. When interviewed, such a subject would stress that he "asserted my humanity" by administering the briefest shock possible. Handling the conflict in this manner was easier than defiance.

The situation is constructed so that there is no way the subject can stop shocking the learner without violating the experimenter's definitions of his own competence. The subject fears that he will appear arrogant, untoward, and rude if he breaks off. Although these inhibiting emotions appear small in scope alongside the violence being done to the learner, they suffuse the mind and feelings of the subject, who is miserable at the prospect of having to repudiate the authority to his face. (When the experiment was altered so that the experimenter gave his instructions by telephone instead of in person, only a third as many people were fully obedient through 450 volts.) It is a curious thing that a measure of compassion on the part of the subject—an unwillingness to "hurt" the experimenter's feelings—is part of those binding forces inhibiting his disobedience. The withdrawal of such deference may be as painful to the subject as to the authority he defies.

Duty Without Conflict

The subjects do not derive satisfaction from inflicting pain, but they often like the feeling they get from pleasing the experimenter. They are proud of doing a good job, obeying the experimenter under difficult circumstances. While the subjects administered only mild shocks on their own initiative, one experimental variation showed that, under orders, 30 percent of them were willing to deliver 450 volts even when they had to forcibly push the learner's hand down on the electrode.

Bruno Batta is a thirty-seven-year-old welder who took part in the variation requiring the use of force. He was born in New Haven, his parents in Italy. He has a rough-hewn face that conveys a conspicuous lack of altertness. He has some difficulty in mastering the experimental procedure and needs to be corrected by the experimenter several times. He shows appreciation for the help and willingness to do what is required. After the 150 volt level, Batta has to force the learner's hand down on the shock plate, since the learner himself refuses to touch it.

When the learner first complains, Mr. Batta pays no attention to him. His face remains impassive, as if to dissociate himself from the learner's disruptive behavior. When the experimenter instructs him to force the learner's hand down, he adopts a rigid, mechanical procedure. He tests the generator switch. When it fails to function, he immediately forces the learner's hand onto the shock plate. All the while he maintains the same rigid mask. The learner, seated alongside him, begs him to stop, but with robotic impassivity he continues the procedure.

What is extraordinary is his apparent total indifference to the learner; he hardly takes cognizance of him as a human being. Meanwhile, he relates to the experimenter in a submissive and courteous fashion.

At the 330 volt level, the learner refuses not only to touch the shock plate but also to provide any answers. Annoyed, Batta turns to him, and chastises him: "You better answer and get it over with. We can't stay here all night." These are the only words he directs to the learner in the course of an hour. Never again does he speak to him. The scene is brutal and depressing, his hard, impassive face showing total indifference as he subdues the screaming learner and gives him shocks. He seems to derive no pleasure from the act itself, only quiet satisfaction at doing his job properly.

When he administers 450 volts, he turns to the experimenter and asks, "Where do we go from here, Professor?" His tone is deferential and expresses his willingness to be a cooperative subject, in contrast to the learner's obstinacy.

At the end of the session he tells the experimenter how honored he has been to help him, and in a moment of contrition, remarks, "Sir, sorry it couldn't have been a full experiment."

He has done his honest best. It is only the deficient behavior of the learner that has denied the experimenter full satisfaction.

The essence of obedience is that a person comes to view himself as the instrument for carrying out another person's wishes, and he therefore no longer regards himself as responsible for his actions. Once this critical shift of viewpoint has occurred, all of the essential features of obedience follow. The most far-reaching consequence is that the person feels responsible to the authority directing him but feels no responsibility for the content of the actions that the authority prescribes. Morality does not disappear—it acquires a radically different focus: the subordinate person feels shame or pride depending on how adequately he has performed the actions called for by authority.

Language provides numerous terms to pinpoint this type of morality: loyalty, duty, discipline are all terms heavily saturated with moral meaning and refer to the degree to which a person fulfills his obligations to authority. They refer not to the "goodness" of the person per se but to the adequacy with which a subordinate fulfills his socially defined role. The most frequent defense of the individual who has performed a heinous act under command of authority is that he has simply done his duty. In asserting this defense, the individual is not introducing an alibi concocted for the moment but is reporting honestly on the psychological attitude induced by submission to authority.

For a person to feel responsible for his actions, he must sense that the behavior has flowed from "the self." In the situation we have studied, subjects have precisely the opposite view of their actions—namely, they see them as originating in the motives of some other person. Subjects in the experiment frequently said, "if it were up to me, I would not have administered shocks to the learner."

Once authority has been isolated as the cause of the subject's behavior, it is legitimate to inquire into the necessary elements of authority and how it must be perceived in order to gain his compliance. We conducted some investigations into the kinds of changes that would cause the experimenter to lose his power and to be disobeyed by the subject. Some of the variations revealed that:

The experimenter's physical presence has a marked impact on his authority—As cited earlier, obedience dropped off sharply when orders were given by telephone. The experimenter could often induce a disobedient subject to go on by returning to the laboratory.

Conflicting authority severely paralyzes actions—When two experimenters of equal status, both seated at the command desk, gave incompatible orders, no shocks were delivered past the point of their disagreement.

The rebellious action of others severely undermines authority—In one variation, three teachers (two actors and a real subject) administered a test and shocks. When the two actors disobeyed the experimenter and refused to go beyond a certain shock level, thirty-six of forty subjects joined their disobedient peers and refused as well.

Although the experimenter's authority was fragile in some respects, it is also true that he had almost none of the tools used in ordinary command structures. For example, the experimenter did not threaten the subjects with punishment—such as loss of income, community ostracism, or jail—for failure to obey. Neither could he offer incentives.

Indeed, we should expect the experimenter's authority to be much less than that of someone like a general, since the experimenter has no power to enforce his imperatives, and since participation in a psychological experiment scarcely evokes the sense of urgency and dedication found in warfare. Despite these limitations, he still managed to command a dismaying degree of obedience.

I will cite one final variation of the experiment that depicts a dilemma that is more common in everyday life. The subject was not ordered to pull the lever that shocked the victim, but merely to perform a subsidiary task (administering the word-pair test) while another person administered the shock. In this situation, thirty-seven of forty adults continued to the highest level of the shock generator. Predictably, they excused their behavior by saying that the responsibility belonged to the man who actually pulled the switch. This may illustrate a dangerously typical arrangement in a complex society: it is easy to ignore responsibility when one is only an intermediate link in a chain of actions.

The problem of obedience is not wholly psychological. The form and shape of society and the way it is developing have much to do with it. There was a time, perhaps, when people were able to give a fully human response to any situation because they were fully absorbed in it as human beings. But as soon as there was a division of labor things changed. Beyond a certain point, the breaking up of society into people carrying out narrow and very special jobs takes away from the human quality of work and life. A person does not get to see the whole situation but only a small part of it, and is thus unable to act without some kind of overall direction. He yields to authority but in doing so is alienated from his own actions.

Even Eichmann was sickened when he toured the concentration camps, but he had only to sit at a desk and shuffle papers. At the same time the man in the camp who actually dropped Cyclon-b into the gas chambers was able to justify his behavior on the ground that he was only following orders from above. Thus there is a fragmentation of the total human act; no one is confronted with the consequences of his decision to carry out the evil act. The person who assumes responsibility has evaporated. Perhaps this is the most common characteristic of socially organized evil in modern society.

■ ■ ■ **FOR CLASS DISCUSSION**   **Argument Classics**

1. Each of the arguments in this unit is trying to persuade its audience toward the writer's (or the artist's) position or angle of vision on a major problem. Working in small groups or as a whole class, explore your answers to the following questions for one of the arguments selected by your instructor:
   a. What is the question or problem addressed by the writer (artist)?
   b. What is the writer's (artist's) position or angle of vision?
   c. What positions or views is the writer (artist) pushing against or opposing?
   d. What is at stake?
2. Working in small groups or as a whole class, choose an argument and analyze the rhetorical strategies used by the writer (or artist) to persuade his or her audience. Then evaluate the effectiveness of these strategies. To generate ideas for this discussion, use the "Questions for Rhetorical Analysis" in Chapter 8, pages 149–150 and List 2, pages 426–427.   ■ ■ ■

WRITING ASSIGNMENT   Rhetorical Analysis

Write a thesis-driven rhetorical analysis of one of the classic arguments chosen by your professor. Follow the instructions and guidelines for a rhetorical analysis essay as explained in Chapter 8, pages 158–160. ■

> For additional writing, reading, and research resources, go to
> www.mycomplab.com

Credits

Text

Page 6. Dr. Louis Sullivan, "Let the Facts Decide, Not Fear…Veto AB1108." Copyright © Louis Sullivan. Reprinted with permission.

Page 17. Brent Schotenboer, "College Athletes Caught in Tangled Web." *San Diego Union Tribune*, May 24, 2006. Copyright © 2006. Used with permission.

Page 17. Excerpt from "Homeless Hit the Streets to Protest Proposed Ban." Reprinted by permission of the Associated Press.

Page 19. Gordon F. Adams, "Petition to Waive the University Math Requirement." Reprinted with the permission of the author.

Pages 29-31. Michael Banks, student writing. Reprinted with the permission of the author.

Page 39. John F. Kavanaugh, "Amnesty?" *America*, March 10, 2008. Copyright © 2008. All rights reserved. Reprinted by permission of America Press.

Page 43. Michael Banks, student writing. Reprinted with the permission of the author.

Page 47. Fred Reed, "Why Blame Mexico?" *The American Conservative*, March 10, 2008. Copyright © 2008. Reprinted by permission.

Page 52. Michael Banks, "Should the United States Grant Legal Status to Undocumented Immigrant Workers?" Reprinted with the permission of the author.

Pages 71, 87. Carmen Tieu, student writing. Reprinted with the permission of the author.

Page 106. Carmen Tieu, "Why Violent Video Games Are Good for Girls." Reprinted with the permission of the author.

Page 112. Bobbi Buchanan, from "Don't Hang Up, That's My Mom Calling," *The New York Times,* December 8, 2003, p. A31.

Page 130. John Tierney, "Recycling Is Garbage," *New York Times Magazine,* June 30, 1996, p. 28. Copyright © 1996 John Tierney. Used with permission.

Page 133. Marybeth Hamilton, from "First Place: A Healing School for Homeless Children." Reprinted with the permission of the author.

Page 136. Ellen Goodman, "Minneapolis Pornography Ordinance." *The Boston Globe.* Copyright © 1985 The Washington Post Writers Group. Reprinted with permission.

Page 141. David Langley, "'Half-Criminals' or Urban Athletes? A Plea for Fair Treatment of Skateboarders." Reprinted with the permission of the author.

Page 157. Rebekah Taylor, "A Letter to Jim." Reprinted with the permission of the author.

Page 151. Kathryn Jean Lopez, "Eggheads." *National Review*, September 1, 1998. Copyright © 1998 by National Review, Inc., 215 Lexington Ave., New York, NY 10016. Reprinted by permission.

Page 160. Ellen Goodman, "Womb for Rent, for a Price." *The Washington Post*, February 11, 2008. Copyright © 2008 Washington Post Writers Group. Used with permission.

Page 162. Zachary Stumps, "A Rhetorical Analysis of Ellen Goodman's 'Womb for Rent, for a Price.'" Reprinted with the permission of the author.

Page 188. Athletes Against Steroids web page. © 2008 Athletes Against Steroids. Used with permission.

Page 208. Aaron Friedman, "All that Noise for Nothing," *The New York Times,* December 11, 2003. Copyright © 2003 New York Times Company, Inc. Used with permission.

Page 229. Jenefer Domingo, "Protecting Our Homes Can Lead to Animal Cruelty." Reprinted with the permission of the author.

Page 436. John Seigenthaler, Sr., "A False Wikipedia Biography," *USA Today*, November 29, 2005. Copyright © 2005 John Seigenthaler. Used with permission.

Page 438. Alice Mathias, "The Fakebook Generation," *The New York Times*, October 6, 2007.

Page 440. Dana L. Fleming, "Youthful Indiscretions; Should colleges protect social network users form themselves and others?" *The New England Journal of Higher Education*, Winter 2008, pp. 27-29. Copyright 2008. Used with permission.

Page 443. Adam Sternbergh, "Hey There, Lonelygirl," *New York Magazine*, August 20, 2006. Copyright © 2006 New York Magazine. Reprinted with permission.

Page 445. "A Message from the Creators." Copyright © 2008. Used with permission. www.lg15.com.

Page 449. Craig Anderson & Douglas Gentile, "ISU psychologists publish studies on violent video game effects on youths." Copyright © 2007. Reprinted by permission of the authors and Iowa State News Service.

Page 450. Henry Jenkins, "Reality Bytes. Eight Myths about Video Games Debunked." Copyright © Henry Jenkins. Used with permission.

Page 454. Malcolm Gladwell, "Brain Candy." *The New Yorker*, May 16, 2005. Copyright © 2005 Malcolm Gladwell. Reprinted by permission.

Page 457. www.icedgame.com. © breakthrough, 2010. www.breakthroughtv.com

Page 458. Michael Humphrey, "For a virtual dose of reality, a different kind of video game," *National Catholic Reporter,* March 7, 2008. Copyright © 2008 Michael Humphrey. Reprinted by permission of the author.

Page 460. William Lugo, "Violent Video Games Recruit American Youth." Reproduced with permission of the journal, *Reclaiming Children and Youth,* Web site: http://www.reclaiming.com. First published in 15:1, Spring 2006, pp. 11–14.

Page 467. William Powers, "The Massless Media." *Atlantic Monthly* January/February 2005. Copyright © 2005 William Powers. Used with permission.

Page 473. Dan Kennedy, "Plugged in, tuned out: Young Americans are embracing new media but failing to develop an appetite for news." *Commonwealth* Fall 2007. Copyright © 2007 Dan Kennedy. Reprinted by permission.

Page 479. Chris Shaw, "Should killers be given air time?" *The Guardian* April 19, 2007. Copyright Guardian News & Media Ltd. 2007.

Page 480. "Those Terrible Virginia Tech Cartoons." © Daryl Cagle and CaglePost.com.

Page 482. Sydney Schanberg, "Not a Pretty Picture." *Village Voice* May 17, 2005. Copyright © 2005 Sydney Schanberg. Reprinted by permission.

Page 486. Francisco X. Gaytan et al., "Understanding and responding to the needs of newcomer immigrant youth and families." *The Prevention Researcher* No. 14, Vol. 4, Nov. 2007, pp. 10-13. Copyright © 2007 Integrated Research Services. Used with permission.

Page 493. Mitali Perkins, "A Note to Immigrants," *Teaching Tolerance Magazine* 28, Fall 2005. Copyright © 2005 Teaching Tolerance. www.tolerance.org

Page 494. Maileen Hamto, "Being American." *The Asian Reporter* January 15, 2008. Copyright © 2008 The Asian Reporter Newspaper. Used with permission.

Page 496. "Miss or Diss?" http://scarfacewearingheadscarfinamerica.blogspot.com. Copyright © 2008 Umma Ali. Used with permission.

Page 498. Fatemeh Fakhraie, "Scarfing it Down." *Bitch: Feminist Response to Pop Culture*, Vol. 39, Spring 2008, pp. 15–16. Copyright © 2008 Fatehem Fakhraie. Used with permission.

Page 500. Jay Nordlinger, "Bassackwards: Construction Spanish and other signs of the times," *National Review*, January 29, 2007. Copyright © 2007 by National Review, Inc., 215 Lexington Ave., NY NY 10016. Reprinted by permission.

Page 507. Linda Chavez, "Harvard's Prez's Admission: Men and Women are Different," *Jewish World*, January 19, 2005. Copyright © 2005 Linda Chavez. Reprinted by permission of Creators Syndicate.

Index